Lecture Notes in Artificial Intelligence   12412

Subseries of Lecture Notes in Computer Science

Sergei O. Kuznetsov · Aleksandr I. Panov ·
Konstantin S. Yakovlev (Eds.)

Artificial Intelligence

18th Russian Conference, RCAI 2020
Moscow, Russia, October 10–16, 2020
Proceedings

 Springer

Editors
Sergei O. Kuznetsov
National Research University Higher School
Moscow, Russia

Aleksandr I. Panov 🆔
Moscow Institute of Physics and Technology
Dolgoprudny, Russia

Konstantin S. Yakovlev 🆔
Federal Research Center Computer Science
and Control
Moscow, Russia

ISSN 0302-9743   ISSN 1611-3349 (electronic)
Lecture Notes in Artificial Intelligence
ISBN 978-3-030-59534-0   ISBN 978-3-030-59535-7 (eBook)
https://doi.org/10.1007/978-3-030-59535-7

LNCS Sublibrary: SL7 – Artificial Intelligence

This Springer imprint is published by the registered company Springer Nature Switzerland AG
The registered company address is: Gewerbestrasse 11, 6330 Cham, Switzerland

Preface

Welcome to the proceedings of the 18th Russian Conference on Artificial Intelligence (RCAI 2020), held in Moscow, Russia. The conference was organized by the Russian Association for Artificial Intelligence, Federal Research Center Computer Science and Control of the Russian Academy of Science, Moscow Institute for Physics and Technology, and the National Research Nuclear University (MEPhI). Being a long-standing member of the European Association for Artificial Intelligence (EurAI, formely – ECCAI), the Russian Association for Artificial Intelligence has a great deal of experience in running important international AI events.

The first Soviet (Russian, from 1992) Conference on AI was held in Pereslavl-Zalessky in 1988. Since then, it was held every other year, until 2018, and then became an annual event. The conference gathers the leading specialists from Russia and other countries, in the field of AI. The participants were mainly members from the research institutes of the Russian Academy of Sciences and universities all over Russia. Topics of the conference included data mining and knowledge discovery, text mining, reasoning, decision making, natural language processing, vision, intelligent robotics, multi-agent systems, machine learning, AI in applied systems, ontology engineering, etc. Each submitted paper was reviewed by three reviewers, experts in the field of AI, to whom we would like to express our gratitude. The conference received 140 submissions in total, and 35 of them were selected by the International Program Committee for publication in this volume. The editors of the volume would like to express their special thanks to Prof. Oleg P. Kuznetsov, co-chair of RCAI 2020, for his support in producing the volume. We hope that the appearance of this volume will stimulate the further research in various domains of AI.

This year, our community was struck by sudden death of our colleagues Dr. Sci. Prof. Dmitry A. Pospelov and Dr. Sci. Prof. Gennady S. Osipov.

Dmitry Pospelov was a famous scientist and AI enthusiast, as well as the author of more than 20 books and 300 papers on various aspects of AI, including knowledge representation, applied semiotics, and situational control. His support of AI research in Russia cannot be overestimated. In 1988 he started the National Conference on Artificial Intelligence (RCAI) and in 1989 he founded the Soviet (Russian, since 1992) Association for Artificial Intelligence (RAAI). He was the first president of RAAI during 1989–1996.

Gennady Osipov, an EurAI Fellow, was a well-known specialist in AI and his interests spanned across a wide range of topics, including cognitive modeling, semantic analysis, knowledge management, intelligent dynamic systems, etc. He supervised a plethora of qualified researchers, now doctors and/or full professors, calling themselves the descendants of the Osipov's school of AI. He was a talented organizer and the second president of the RAAI (1996–2020). Gennady was one of the originators of the RCAI and we are immensely grateful to him for the contribution he made to the advancement of AI in Russia and in the world.

We would like to dedicate this volume to our teachers, colleagues, and friends, Dmitry A. Pospelov and Gennady S. Osipov.

July 2020

Sergei O. Kuznetsov
Aleksandr I. Panov
Konstantin S. Yakovlev

Organization

General Chair

Igor A. Sokolov — Federal Research Center Computer Science and Control, RAS, Russia

General Co-chair

Gennady S. Osipov — Artificial Intelligence Research Institute, Federal Research Center Computer Science and Control, RAS, Russia

Organizing Committee Chair

Oleg P. Kuznetsov — V.A. Trapeznikov Institute of Control Sciences, RAS, Russia

International Program Committee Chair

Sergei O. Kuznetsov — National Research University Higher School of Economics, Russia

International Program Committee Co-chairs

Aleksandr I. Panov — Artificial Intelligence Research Institute, Federal Research Center Computer Science and Control, RAS, Russia

Konstantin Yakovlev — Artificial Intelligence Research Institute, Federal Research Center Computer Science and Control, RAS, Russia

International Program Committee Members

Ilya Afanasyev — Innopolis University, Russia
Jaume Baixeries — Universitat Politècnica de Catalunya, Spain
Ildar Batyrshin — Instituto Politecnico Nacional, Mexico
Nikolay Bazenkov — V.A. Trapeznikov Institute of Control Sciences, RAS, Russia
Aimene Belfodil — INSA Lyon, France
Alexander Buyval — Innopolis University, Russia
Yves Demazeau — French National Center for Scientific Research, Grenoble Computer Science Laboratory, France

Contents

Intelligent Systems and Applications

Automated Reasoning and Data Mining

Axiomatization of Classes of Domain Cases Based on FCA

Dmitry E. Palchunov[1,2]([⊠])

[1] Sobolev Institute of Mathematics, Novosibirsk, Russian Federation
palch@math.nsc.ru
[2] Novosibirsk State University, Novosibirsk, Russian Federation

Abstract. The article is devoted to the application of Formal Concept Analysis to the development of domain semantic models. The paper deals with the problem of axiomatization of classes of cases from various domains.

The research is based on the model theoretical approach to the formalization of domains and on Formal Concept Analysis. We consider the four-level semantic model that conceptually describes the given domain. The third level of the semantic model is the set of domain cases. To describe sets of domain cases we use formal contexts; the objects of these formal contexts are models formalizing domain cases. We represent classes of domain cases as classes of models having different signatures. Theories of classes of domain cases and axiomatizable classes of domain cases are investigated. They are defined as intents and extents of formal concepts of the corresponding formal contexts. It is shown that the introduced notion of theory of class of cases, i.e., theory of class containing models with different signatures, is a generalization of the notion of theory of a class of models in the classical sense.

Keywords: FCA · Subject domain · Domain case · Domain theory · Theory of class · Axiomatizable class · Ontological model

1 Introduction

In the paper we consider the problem of axiomatization of case classes for various subject domains. The studies are based on the model-theoretical approach to formalizing subject domains and on Formal Concept Analysis (FCA) [1, 2].

Formal Concept Analysis is a very successful tool for the representation and processing of knowledge [3–7]. We combine FCA with a model-theoretic approach to formalizing knowledge about subject domains [8, 9].

The article is devoted to the problem of formalization of knowledge about subject domains. In particular, it is necessary to formalize knowledge about cases of subject domains. In the framework of the model-theoretic approach to the formalization of subject domains, we consider the formal representation of a case of a subject domain in the form of an algebraic system (or model – in this paper, the terms "model" and "algebraic system" are synonyms). Thus, a subject domain can be formally represented as a class of algebraic systems formalizing the cases of this subject domain.

© Springer Nature Switzerland AG 2020
S. O. Kuznetsov et al. (Eds.): RCAI 2020, LNAI 12412, pp. 3–14, 2020.
https://doi.org/10.1007/978-3-030-59535-7_1

The problem is that domain cases may be described using different sets of concepts. Therefore, in this case, the subject domain will be formalized by a class of algebraic systems having different signatures. Such situations often occur in medical research [10–17], in the development of formal enterprise models for automating business processes [18] and user support systems [19], as well as in other business applications, in particular in the development of smart contracts [18, 20].

We continue our research started in [21–23]. Theories of classes of cases of subject domains and axiomatizable classes of cases are investigated. They are defined as intents and extents of formal concepts of respective formal contexts.

We solve the problem of axiomatization of classes of algebraic systems that contain models with different signatures. To do this, it is necessary to define the theory of such classes of algebraic systems, as well as introduce the notion of axiomatizable class of algebraic systems having different signatures.

The definition of the theory of a class of algebraic systems containing systems having different signatures is introduced. It is shown that the proposed notion of a theory of a class of models having different signatures is a generalization of the notion of the classical theory of a class of models.

The definition of axiomatizable class of models with different signatures is proposed. The problems of decidability of theories of such classes of models are investigated. It is shown that for the case of classes of models having the same signature, the introduced generalized definition of axiomatizable class coincides with the classical one.

2 Preliminaries

2.1 Domain Cases

In our previous research [19, 22, 23] we developed methods for identifying payment plans and services which would be optimal for a given mobile network subscriber. Such knowledge allows mobile operator to make really useful recommendations for subscribers.

The ontological model [15] of the domain "Mobile Networks" was constructed by integration of data extracted from depersonalized subscriber profiles. The signature of this ontological model contains predicates which describe subscriber's behavior and features of payment plans and services [19] (see Fig. 1).

Firstly, we constructed Case Model based on the known information about behavior patterns of mobile network subscribers. We represented the Case Model as a relatively axiomatizable class of models. On the base of this Case Model we defined a formal context.

To generate meaningful recommendation of alternative services and payment plans, we consider formal contexts where objects are subscriber models, and attributes are formulas of first-order predicate logic. We investigate concept lattices and association rules of these formal contexts to get high-quality recommendation.

2.2 Formal Contexts of Axiomatizable Classes

Let us introduce some necessary definitions.

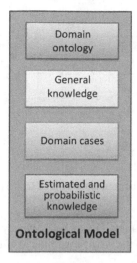

Fig. 1. Four levels of knowledge representation.

Algebraic system (a model) is a tuple
$\mathfrak{A} = \langle A; P_1, ..., P_n, f_1, ..., f_m, c_1, ..., c_k \rangle$, where the set $|\mathfrak{A}| = A$ is called universe,
$P_1, ..., P_n$ are predicates defined on the set A, $f_1, ..., f_m$ are functions defined on the set
A and $c_1, ..., c_k$ are constants.

The tuple $\sigma = \langle P_1, ..., P_n, f_1, ..., f_m, c_1, ..., c_k \rangle$ is called signature of the algebraic
system $\mathfrak{A}$. Sentence is a formula without free variables. We denote:

$$F(\sigma) \leftrightharpoons \{\varphi \mid \varphi \text{ is a formula of the signature } \sigma\},$$

$$S(\sigma) \leftrightharpoons \{\varphi \mid \varphi \text{ is a sentence of the signature } \sigma\},$$

$$K(\sigma) \leftrightharpoons \{\mathfrak{A} \mid \mathfrak{A} \text{ is a model of the signature } \sigma\}.$$

First let us consider the notion of axiomatizable class [24].

Definition 1. Let $K \subseteq K(\sigma)$. We say that K is *axiomatizable class* if there exists a set
$\Gamma \subseteq S(\sigma)$ such that $K = \{\mathfrak{A} \in K(\sigma) \mid \mathfrak{A} \vDash \Gamma\}$.

The set of sentences Γ is called a set of axioms of the class K.

In [21], we investigated the relationship between axiomatizable classes and lattices
of formal concepts.

For each class $K \subseteq K(\sigma)$ and a set $\Delta \subseteq S(\sigma)$ we consider the formal context
$(K, \Delta, \vDash)$ (see Fig. 2).

For a formal context (G, M, I) by $\underline{\mathfrak{B}}$(G, M, I) we denote the lattice of formal concepts
of the formal context (G, M, I).

2.3 Relatively Axiomatizable Classes

A generalization of the notion of axiomatizable class is the notion of relatively
axiomatizable class [21].

K_σ	\multicolumn{8}{c}{$S(\sigma)$}

K_σ	φ_1	φ_2	φ_3	...	φ_k	φ_{k+1}	φ_{k+2}	...
$\mathfrak{A}_1$	+		+			+		
$\mathfrak{A}_2$		+			+	+		
...			+					+
$\mathfrak{A}_k$		+			+	+		
...			+		+			+
$\mathfrak{A}_n$	+					+		

Fig. 2. The formal context $(K(\sigma), S(\sigma), \vDash)$.

Definition 2. Let $K, K_1 \subseteq K(\sigma)$ and $\Delta \subseteq F(\sigma)$. We say that the class K_1 is axiomatizable in the class K relatively to the set of formulas Δ if there exists a set $\Gamma \subseteq \Delta$ such that

$$K_1 = \{\mathfrak{A} \in K | \mathfrak{A} \vDash \Gamma\}.$$

Definition 3. For $K \subseteq K(\sigma)$ and $\Delta \subseteq F(\sigma)$ we denote.

$$\mathbb{B}(K, \Delta) \leftrightharpoons \{K_1 | K_1 \ is \ axiomatizable \ in \ K \ relatively \ to \ the \ set \ of \ formulas \ \Delta\}$$

and

$$T_\Delta(K) \leftrightharpoons \{\varphi \in \Delta | K \vDash \varphi\}.$$

So instead of the formal context $(K(\sigma), S(\sigma), \vDash)$ we consider the formal context $(K, \Delta, \vDash)$ which is a subcontext of the formal context $(K(\sigma), S(\sigma), \vDash)$ (see Fig. 3).

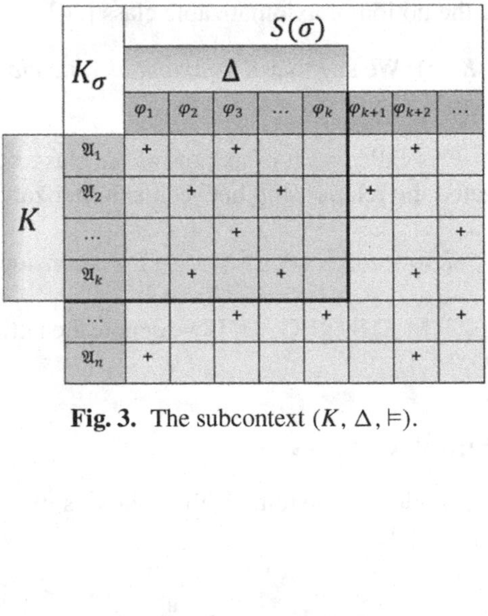

K_σ / K	φ_1	φ_2	φ_3	...	φ_k	φ_{k+1}	φ_{k+2}	...
$\mathfrak{A}_1$	+		+			+		
$\mathfrak{A}_2$		+			+	+		
...			+					+
$\mathfrak{A}_k$		+			+	+		
...			+		+			+
$\mathfrak{A}_n$	+					+		

($S(\sigma)$, with Δ spanning columns $\varphi_1 \ldots \varphi_{k+1}$)

Fig. 3. The subcontext $(K, \Delta, \vDash)$.

Lattice isomorphism

Proposition 1 [21]. Let $K \subseteq K(\sigma)$, $\Delta \subseteq F(\sigma)$, $A \subseteq K$ and $B \subseteq \Delta$. Then $(A, B) \in \mathfrak{B}(K, \Delta, \vDash)$ if and only if A is axiomatizable in the class K relatively to the set of formulas Δ and $B = T_\Delta(A)$.

We consider $\mathbb{B}(K, \Delta)$ as a set ordered by inclusion $\subseteq$. So $\mathbb{B}(K, \Delta)$ is a lattice.

Proposition 2 [21]. The lattices $\mathfrak{B}(K, \Delta, \vDash)$ and $\mathbb{B}(K, \Delta)$ are isomorphic, i.e., $\mathfrak{B}(K, \Delta, \vDash) \cong \mathbb{B}(K, \Delta)$, for any $K \subseteq K(\sigma)$ and $\Delta \subseteq F(\sigma)$.

3 Axiomatization of Classes of Domain Cases

3.1 Sentences Permissible for Models

It is necessary to point out a fundamentally important circumstance: in the above definitions of axiomatizable class and relatively axiomatizable class, classes of models of the same pre-fixed signature are considered. The same situation takes place when in the model theory relations of isomorphism and elementary equivalence of algebraic systems, as well as homomorphisms, epimorphisms and elementary embeddings are considered.

However, to investigate domain cases for different subject domains [10–20, 22, 23] we need to find out what regularities holds for each case. It is necessary when we process knowledge presented on second and third levels of the ontological model [15]: general knowledge (2) and statements which are true for domain cases (3) (see Fig. 1). Note that description of different cases from the given subject domain may contain different sets of concepts. So, models which represent domain cases may have different signatures.

So our goal is to generalize the notion of axiomatizable class and the notion of theory of a class of algebraic systems to the case of classes of systems of different signatures.

To do this, in particular, we need to replace in the formal context $(K(\sigma), S(\sigma), \vDash)$ the relation of the truth of a sentence on a model $\vDash$ to another incidence relation.

Indeed, let $\mathfrak{A}_1 \in K(\sigma_1)$, $\mathfrak{A}_2 \in K(\sigma_2)$, $\varphi \in \mathrm{Th}(\mathfrak{A}_2)$, and $\varphi \notin S(\sigma_1)$. Then the statement $\mathfrak{A}_1 \vDash \varphi$ is neither true nor false, but is meaningless; so we can not talk about the truth of the theory of model $\mathfrak{A}_2$ on model $\mathfrak{A}_1$. However it is uninteresting to limit oneself to considering sentences of a signature $\sigma = \sigma_1 \cap \sigma_2$, because then we will again consider a theory of a class of models of the same signature – a class of reducts of the considered models to the signature of σ.

Consider a model $\mathfrak{A} \in K(\sigma_1)$ and a sentence $\varphi \in S(\sigma_2)$. Instead of the truth of the sentence φ on the model $\mathfrak{A}$, we consider another condition: the truth on $\mathfrak{A}$ of all meaningful (on the model $\mathfrak{A}$) consequences of the sentence φ.

Definition 4. The signature $\sigma(\varphi)$ of a sentence φ is the set of all signature symbols included in the sentence φ.

The signature $\sigma(\Gamma)$ of a set of sentences Γ is the set of all signature symbols included in the set of sentences Γ.

By $\mathrm{Th}(\varphi) = \{\psi \in S(\sigma(\varphi)) | \varphi \vdash \psi\}$ we denote the theory axiomatized by a sentence φ, and $\mathrm{Th}(\Gamma) = \{\psi \in S(\sigma(\Gamma)) | \Gamma \vdash \psi\}$ is a theory axiomatized by the set of sentences Γ (i.e., $\mathrm{Th}(\Gamma)$ is the deductive closure of the set of sentences Γ).

Definition 5. Let $\mathfrak{A} \in K(\sigma)$ and $\varphi \in S(\sigma_1)$. We denote $\mathfrak{A} \| \varphi$ if $\mathfrak{A} \vDash (\text{Th}(\varphi) \cap S(\sigma))$. We say that the sentence φ is permissible for the model $\mathfrak{A}$.

Similarly, we can define the relation $\|$ for a set of sentences.

Definition 6. Let $\mathfrak{A} \in K(\sigma)$ and $\Gamma \subseteq S(\sigma_1)$. We denote $\mathfrak{A} \| \Gamma$ if

$$\mathfrak{A} \vDash (\text{Th}(\Gamma) \cap S(\sigma)).$$

We say that the set of sentences Γ is permissible for the model $\mathfrak{A}$.

These definitions are generalizations of the definitions of $\mathfrak{A} \vDash \varphi$ and $\mathfrak{A} \vDash \Gamma$ for the case when $\sigma(\varphi) \subseteq \sigma(\mathfrak{A})$ (respectively, when $\sigma(\Gamma) \subseteq \sigma(\mathfrak{A})$).

Remark 1. Let $\mathfrak{A} \in K(\sigma)$, $\sigma(\varphi) \subseteq \sigma$, and $\sigma(\Gamma) \subseteq \sigma$. Then

a) $\mathfrak{A} \vDash \varphi$ if and only if $\mathfrak{A} \vDash (\text{Th}(\varphi) \cap S(\sigma))$.
b) $\mathfrak{A} \vDash \Gamma$ if and only if $\mathfrak{A} \vDash (\text{Th}(\Gamma) \cap S(\sigma))$.

Instead of the relation $\|$ between a model and a sentence (a set of sentences), we can consider other relation between sets of sentences.

Proposition 3. a) $\mathfrak{A} \| \varphi$ if and only if $\text{Th}(\mathfrak{A}) \cup \{\varphi\} \nvdash$.

b) $\mathfrak{A} \| \Gamma$ if and only if $\text{Th}(\mathfrak{A}) \cup \Gamma \nvdash$.

This statement is also true for the relations $\mathfrak{A} \vDash \varphi$ and $\mathfrak{A} \vDash \Gamma$ in the case when $\sigma(\varphi) \subseteq \sigma(\mathfrak{A})$ (respectively, when $\sigma(\Gamma) \subseteq \sigma(\mathfrak{A})$).

Remark 2. Let $\mathfrak{A} \in K(\sigma)$, $\sigma(\varphi) \subseteq \sigma$, and $\sigma(\Gamma) \subseteq \sigma$. Then

a) $\mathfrak{A} \vDash \varphi$ if and only if $\text{Th}(\mathfrak{A}) \cup \{\varphi\} \nvdash$
b) $\mathfrak{A} \vDash \Gamma$ if and only if $\text{Th}(\mathfrak{A}) \cup \Gamma \nvdash$.

3.2 Theories of Classes of Models Having Different Signatures

Recall that our purpose is to define the notions of *theory of a class of models* and *axiomatizable class* for classes of models having different signatures.

By analogy with the way we acted for axiomatizable classes and theories in the classical theory of models, we may consider the formal context $(KS(\sigma), S(\sigma), \|)$, where $KS(\sigma)$ is the class of all models whose signature is contained in σ. Namely, $KS(\sigma) = \{\mathfrak{A} \mid \sigma(\mathfrak{A}) \subseteq \sigma\}$, that is,

$$KS(\sigma) = \bigcup_{\sigma' \subseteq \sigma} K(\sigma').$$

However, we face a serious problem.

Let a pair (A, B) be a formal concept of the formal context $(KS(\sigma), S(\sigma), \|)$. This, in particular, means that

$$B = \{\varphi \in S(\sigma) \mid \mathfrak{A} \| \varphi \text{ for any model } \mathfrak{A} \in A\}.$$

The problem is that in this case the set of sentences B, firstly, may be not a theory, and secondly, B may be contradictory. Moreover, as the following two statements show, this may be true even for the case of a singleton set of models A.

Proposition 4. Let $\mathfrak{A}$ be a finite Boolean algebra considered in the standard signature of Boolean algebras $\sigma_B = \{\cap, \cup, ^-, 0, 1\}$, let I be a symbol of unary predicate. We consider two sentences $\varphi, \psi \in S(\sigma_B \cup \{I\})$:

the sentence φ says that I is a maximal ideal, and
the sentence ψ implies that I is not a principal ideal generated by the complement of an atom. Namely,

$$\varphi = ((I-\text{is an ideal})\&(1 \notin I)\&(\forall x((x \notin I \rightarrow \bar{x} \in I)))),$$
$$\psi = x(((x \in I)\&\forall y((y \in I) \rightarrow y \leq x))(\bar{x} - \text{ is not an atom})).$$

Then
a) We have $\mathfrak{A}\|\varphi$ and $\mathfrak{A}\|\psi$, but it is not true that $\mathfrak{A}\|\{\varphi, \psi\}$.
b) The set of sentences $\{\mathfrak{A}\}' = \{\xi \in S(\sigma_B \cup \{I\})|\mathfrak{A}\|\xi\}$ is contradictory.

Proposition 5. Let $\mathfrak{A}$ be the countable atomless Boolean algebra considered in the signature $\sigma_B = \{\cap, \cup, ^-, 0, 1\}$, let I be a symbol of unary predicate. Let us consider two sentences $\varphi, \psi \in S(\sigma_B \cup \{I\})$:

$$\varphi = x((x \in I)(x \text{ is atomic})),$$

$$\psi = x((x \in I)\&(x0)).$$

Then

a) We have $\mathfrak{A}\|\varphi$ and $\mathfrak{A}\|\psi$, but it is not true that $\mathfrak{A}\|\{\varphi, \psi\}$.
b) The set of sentences $\{\mathfrak{A}\}' = \{\xi \in S(\sigma_B \cup \{I\})|\mathfrak{A}\|\xi\}$ is contradictory.

Thus, when axiomatizing classes of algebraic systems of different signatures, we cannot directly use the approach that we used for the classical model-theoretic notion of axiomatizable class.

We denote by $\wp(S(\sigma))$ the set of all subsets of the set $S(\sigma)$ of sentences of a signature σ. Instead of the formal context $(KS(\sigma), S(\sigma),\|)$ let us consider the formal context $(KS(\sigma), \wp(S(\sigma)), \|)$. In this formal context, instead of sentences $\varphi \in S(\sigma)$ we deal with sets of sentences $\Gamma \subseteq S(\sigma)$ (see Fig. 4).

Next we will study formal concepts of the formal context $(KS(\sigma), \wp(S(\sigma)),\|)$, and with their help we will introduce the notions of theory of class and axiomatizable class for the case of classes of models of different signatures.

Namely, the extents A of formal concepts (A, B) will be considered as generalization of axiomatizable classes, and the intents B of the formal concepts (A, B) will be considered as generalization of theories of classes.

Definition 7. Let $K \subseteq KS(\sigma)$ and $\Gamma \subseteq S(\sigma_1)$. We denote $K\|\Gamma$ if for any

$KS(\sigma)$	$\wp\big(S(\sigma)\big)$							
	Γ_1	Γ_2	Γ_3	...	Γ_k	Γ_{k+1}	Γ_{k+2}	...
$\mathfrak{A}_1$	+		+				+	
$\mathfrak{A}_2$		+		+		+		
...			+					+
$\mathfrak{A}_k$		+		+			+	
...			+		+			+
$\mathfrak{A}_n$	+						+	

Fig. 4. Formal context $(KS(\sigma), \wp(S(\sigma)), \|)$.

system $\mathfrak{A} \in K$ we have $\mathrm{Th}(\mathfrak{A}) \cup \Gamma \nvdash$.

Remark 3. Let $K \subseteq KS(\sigma)$ and $\Gamma \subseteq S(\sigma)$.
For the formal context $(KS(\sigma), \wp(S(\sigma)), \|)$, the following conditions are equivalent:

a) $K \| \Gamma$;
b) $K \subseteq \Gamma'$;
c) $\Gamma \subseteq K'$.

Remark 4. Suppose that $\Gamma_1 \subseteq \Gamma_2$. Then:

a) If $\mathfrak{A} \| \Gamma_2$, then $\mathfrak{A} \| \Gamma_1$.
a) If $K \| \Gamma_2$, then $K \| \Gamma_1$.

Definition 8. Consider the formal context $(KS(\sigma), \wp(S(\sigma)), \|)$, let $K \subseteq KS(\sigma)$. The set $QT(K) = K' = \{\Gamma \subseteq S(\sigma) | K \| \Gamma\}$ is called *quasi-theory* of the class K.

Note that for classes of models of the same signature, quasitheories are quite simple.

Remark 5. Consider a class $K \subseteq K(\sigma)$.

a) The quasi-theory $QT(K) = \{\Gamma | \Gamma \subseteq \mathrm{Th}(K)\} = \wp(\mathrm{Th}(K))$ is the set of all subsets of the theory $\mathrm{Th}(K)$ of the class K.
b) The theory $\mathrm{Th}(K)$ of the class K is the largest element of the poset

$$\langle QT(K), \subseteq \rangle.$$

Thus, for the class $K \subseteq K(\sigma)$, the theory $\mathrm{Th}(K)$ is the unique maximal element in $\langle QT(K), \subseteq \rangle$. Further, our goal is to investigate the maximal elements of the partially ordered set $\langle QT(K), \subseteq \rangle$ for arbitrary class $K \subseteq KS(\sigma)$.

Proposition 6. Let $K \subseteq KS(\sigma)$ and Γ be a maximal element of the poset $\langle QT(K), \subseteq \rangle$. Then Γ is a theory.

Proposition 7. Let $K \subseteq KS(\sigma)$ and $\Gamma \in QT(K)$. Then there is a theory $T \supseteq \Gamma$ such that T is a maximal element of the poset $\langle QT(K), \subseteq \rangle$.

Denote $= \{\mathbb{T} \subseteq S(\sigma) | T$ is a theory of the signature $\sigma\}$. Then we have $\mathbb{T} \subseteq \wp(S(\sigma))$. Thus instead of the formal context $(KS(\sigma), \wp(S(\sigma)), \parallel)$ we may consider its subcontext – the formal context $(KS(\sigma), \mathbb{T}, \parallel)$ (see Fig. 5).

$KS(\sigma)$	$\mathbb{T} \subseteq \wp(S(\sigma))$							
	T_1	T_2	T_3	...	T_k	T_{k+1}	T_{k+2}	...
$\mathfrak{A}_1$	+		+				+	
$\mathfrak{A}_2$		+		+		+		
...			+					+
$\mathfrak{A}_k$		+		+			+	
...			+		+			+
$\mathfrak{A}_n$	+						+	

Fig. 5. Formal context $(KS(\sigma), \mathbb{T}, \parallel)$.

Now we can formulate a definition generalizing the definition of the theory of class of models of the same signature.

Definition 9. Let $K \subseteq KS(\sigma)$. We call the set

$$ST(K) = \{\Gamma \subseteq S(\sigma) \mid \Gamma \text{ is maximal with the property } \mathrm{Th}(\mathfrak{A}) \cup \Gamma \nvdash$$
$$\text{for any } \mathfrak{A} \in K\}$$

a super-theory of the class K.

Note that this definition depends on the choice of the embracing signature σ. This can be avoided by setting $\sigma = \sigma(K)$.

Corollary 1. If $T \in ST(K)$, then T is a theory, that is, a deductively closed set of sentences.

Corollary 2. Suppose that $K \subseteq K(\sigma)$. Then $ST(K) = \{\mathrm{Th}(K)\}$.

Summing up, we can formulate the following statement.

Theorem 1. Consider the formal context $(KS(\sigma), \wp(S(\sigma)), \parallel)$.

a) Let (A, B) be a formal concept of this formal context. Then

$$B = \{\Gamma \mid \Gamma \subseteq T \text{ for some } T \in ST(A)\}.$$

b) Suppose that $K \subseteq KS(\sigma)$. Then $K' = \{\Gamma \mid \Gamma \subseteq T \text{ for some } T \in ST(K)\}$.

3.3 Axiomatizable Classes and Decidability of Theories

In this section we introduce a definition of axiomatizable class of models having different signatures. We investigate the problems of decidability of theories of such classes of models.

Definition 10. The class $K_0 \subseteq KS(\sigma)$ is said to be a *signature class* if $K(\sigma(\mathfrak{A})) \subseteq K_0$ holds for any $\mathfrak{A} \in K_0$, that is, K_0 is the class of all models of some given collection of signatures.

Definition 11. Let a class $K_0 \subseteq KS(\sigma)$ be a signature class. A class $K \subseteq K_0$ is said to be *axiomatizable* if the pair $(K, QT(K))$ is a formal concept of the formal context $(K_0, \wp(S(\sigma)), \parallel)$.

Next, we consider the class of Boolean algebras with an arbitrary finite set of distinguished ideals (for different algebras included in the class, the number of distinguished ideals can be different), as well as the class that is the union of the class of Boolean algebras with one distinguished ideal (an arbitrary finite set of distinguished ideals) and the class of Boolean algebras with one distinguished subalgebra.

Proposition 8. a) The class of Boolean algebras with a finite number of distinguished ideals is *axiomatizable*. Its super-theory is a *one-element* set.

b) The class of Boolean algebras with one distinguished ideal or one distinguished subalgebra is axiomatizable. Its super-theory is a *one-element* set.
c) The class of Boolean algebras with a finite number of distinguished ideals or with one distinguished subalgebra is *axiomatizable*. Its super-theory is a *one-element* set.

Theorem 2. A super-theory of the class of Boolean algebras with a finite number of distinguished ideals is *decidable*.

Theorem 3. a) A super-theory of the class of Boolean algebras with one distinguished ideal or one distinguished subalgebra is *undecidable*.

b) A super-theory of the class of Boolean algebras with a finite number of distinguished ideals or with one distinguished subalgebra is *undecidable*.

4 Conclusion

In the paper we considered the problem of axiomatization of classes of domain cases. We examined a situation where cases of the same subject domain are described by different sets of concepts. Therefore, models of cases of the same subject domain may have different signatures. To solve the problem of axiomatization of subject domains in this case, it is necessary to work with the notion of theory of class of models having different signatures and with the notion of axiomatizable class of models having different signatures.

In the article we introduced the notion of theory of class of models having different signatures and the notion of axiomatizable class of models having different signatures. It is shown that these notions are generalizations of the classical notions of the theory of class of models and of axiomatizable class of models for the case of classes of models of the same signature. In particular, if we consider the classes of models of the same signature, then the introduced generalized notions coincide with the classical ones.

As an example, the axiomatizability of some classes of algebraic systems and the decidability of their generalized theories are investigated.

The theoretical results obtained in the paper may be used as a methodological basis for modeling business processes and business domains. Formalized descriptions of divisions of an enterprise in the form of algebraic systems may have different signatures. However, they must comply with all general laws and regulations. They must be fulfilled even if the signatures of the sentences of predicate logic, which are formal representations of these laws and regulations, are not subsets of the signatures of algebraic systems formalizing the divisions of the enterprise.

References

1. Ganter, B., Wille, R.: Formal Concept Analysis. Springer, Heidelberg (1999). https://doi.org/10.1007/978-3-642-59830-2
2. Ganter, B., Stumme, G., Wille, R. (eds.): Formal Concept Analysis. LNCS (LNAI), vol. 3626. Springer, Heidelberg (2005). https://doi.org/10.1007/978-3-540-31881-1
3. Kuznetsov, S.O., Poelmans, J.: Knowledge representation and processing with formal concept analysis. Wiley Interdisc. Rev.: Data Mining Knowl. Disc. 3(3), 200–215 (2013)
4. Poelmans, J., Kuznetsov, S.O., Ignatov, D.I., Dedene, G.: Formal concept analysis in knowledge processing: a survey on models and techniques. Source Doc. Exp. Syst. Appl. 40(16), 6601–6623 (2013)
5. Buzmakov, A., Kuznetsov, Sergei O., Napoli, A.: Fast generation of best interval patterns for nonmonotonic constraints. In: Appice, A., Rodrigues, P.P., Santos Costa, V., Gama, J., Jorge, A., Soares, C. (eds.) ECML PKDD 2015. LNCS (LNAI), vol. 9285, pp. 157–172. Springer, Cham (2015). https://doi.org/10.1007/978-3-319-23525-7_10
6. Kuznetsov, S.O., Makhalova, T.: On interestingness measures of formal concepts. Inf. Sci. 442, 202–219 (2018)
7. Makhalova, T., Kuznetsov, S.O., Napoli, A.: MDL for FCA: is there a place for background knowledge? In: CEUR, pp. 45–56 (2018)
8. Palchunov, D.E.: The solution of the problem of information retrieval based on ontologies. Bisnes-informatika 1(3), 3–13 (2008)
9. Palchunov, D.E.: Virtual catalog: the ontology-based technology for information retrieval. In: Wolff, K.E., Palchunov, D.E., Zagoruiko, N.G., Andelfinger, U. (eds.) KONT/KPP -2007. LNCS (LNAI), vol. 6581, pp. 164–183. Springer, Heidelberg (2011). https://doi.org/10.1007/978-3-642-22140-8_11
10. Shi, W., Barnden, J.A.: Using inductive rules in medical case-based reasoning system. In: Gelbukh, A., de Albornoz, Á., Terashima-Marín, H. (eds.) MICAI 2005. LNCS (LNAI), vol. 3789, pp. 900–909. Springer, Heidelberg (2005). https://doi.org/10.1007/11579427_92
11. Baxter, D., Shepard, D., Siegel, N., Gottesman, B., Schneider, D. Interactive natural language explanations of Cyc inferences. In: AAAI 2005 International Symposium on Explanation-aware Computing (2005)

12. Lin, R.H., Chuang, C.L.: A hybrid diagnosis model for determining the types of the liver disease. Comput. Biol. Med. **7**(40), 665–670 (2010)
13. Wang, Y., Rudd, A.G., Wolfe, C.D.A.: Age and ethnic disparities in incidence of stroke over time. Stroke **44**, 3298–3304 (2013)
14. Sharaf-El-Deen, D.A., Moawad, I.F., Khalifa, M.E.: A new hybrid case-based reasoning approach for medical diagnosis systems. J. Med. Syst. **2**(38), 1–11 (2014)
15. Naydanov, C., Palchunov, D.E., Sazonova, P.: Development of automated methods for the critical condition risk prevention, based on the analysis of the knowledge obtained from patient medical records. In: Proceedings of the International Conference on Biomedical Engineering and Computational Technologies (SIBIRCON/SibMedInfo—2015), pp. 33–38. IEEE Press (2015)
16. Palchunov, D.E., Yakhyaeva, G., Yasinskaya, O.: Software system for the diagnosis of the spine diseases using case-based reasoning. Siberian Sci. Med. J. **1**(36), 97–104 (2016)
17. Palchunov, D.E., Tishkovsky, D.E., Tishkovskaya, S.V., Yakhyaeva, G.E.: Combining logical and statistical rule reasoning and verification for medical applications. In: Proceedings of the International Multi-Conference on Engineering, Computer and Information Sciences, (SIBIRCON), pp. 309–313. IEEE Press (2017)
18. Gumirov V.S., Matyukov P.Y., Palchunov D.E.: Semantic domain-specific languages. In: 2019 International Multi-Conference on Engineering, Computer and Information Sciences (SIBIRCON), pp. 0955–0960. IEEE Press (2019)
19. Palchunov D., Yakhyaeva G., Dolgusheva E.: Conceptual methods for identifying needs of mobile network subscribers. In: Proceedings of the Thirteenth International Conference on Concept Lattices and their Applications, CEUR, CEUR Workshop Proceedings, vol. 1624, pp. 147–160. (2016)
20. Galieva A.G., Palchunov D.E.: Logical methods for smart contract development. In: 2019 International Multi-CONFERENCE on Engineering, Computer and Information Sciences (SIBIRCON), pp. 0881–0885. IEEE Press (2019)
21. Pal'chunov, D.E.: Lattices of relatively axiomatizable classes. In: Kuznetsov, S.O., Schmidt, S. (eds.) ICFCA 2007. LNCS (LNAI), vol. 4390, pp. 221–239. Springer, Heidelberg (2007). https://doi.org/10.1007/978-3-540-70901-5_15
22. Palchunov D., Yakhyaeva G.: Application of boolean-valued models and FCA for the development of ontological models. In: Proceedings of the 2nd International Workshop on Formal Concept Analysis for Knowledge Discovery (FCA4KD), CEUR, CEUR Workshop Proceedings, vol. 1921, pp. 77–87 (2017)
23. Palchunov D.E., Yakhyaeva G.E.: Integration of fuzzy model theory and FCA for big data mining. In: 2019 International Multi-conference on Engineering, Computer and Information Sciences (SIBIRCON), pp. 0961–0966. IEEE Press (2019)
24. Chang, C.C., Keisler, H.J.: Model Theory, 3rd edn. Elsevier Science Pub. Co., North-Holland (1990)

The Combined Method of Automated Knowledge Acquisition from Various Sources: The Features of Development and Experimental Research of the Temporal Version

Galina V. Rybina[✉], Alexandr A. Slinkov, and Dmitriy R. Buyanov

National Research Nuclear University «MEPhI», Moscow, Russia
gvrybina@yandex.ru

Abstract. The experience in the development and evolutionary development of technology of knowledge acquisition from various sources on the basis of the original combined method of knowledge acquisition, which is an important part of the problem-oriented methodology for building integrated expert systems for static and dynamic problem domains, are analyzed. Particular emphasis is placed on experimental software modeling of the processes of temporal knowledge acquiring from experts, NL texts and temporal databases and analysis of the results (using the example of medical diagnostics).

Keywords: Artificial intelligence · Problem-oriented methodology · Integrated expert systems · AT-TECHNOLOGY workbench · Combined method of knowledge acquisition · Integration · Temporal knowledge · Temporal database · NL-texts

1 Introduction

An important place among the priority areas defined by the Decree of the President of the Russian Federation (No. 490 dated 10.10.2019) in the National Strategy for the Development of Artificial Intelligence for the period until 2030 is given to the development of software that uses basic technologies of artificial intelligence (AI) like technology of knowledge acquisition from various sources and the intellectual analysis of big data; forecasting and decision support technologies; technologies of planning and multi-agent management of targeted behavior in unstructured environments; natural language (NL) processing technologies, etc.

Nowadays the typology of knowledge sources is no longer limited only to experts, since significant amounts of expert knowledge are accumulated in NL-texts, various applied ontologies, and also in the database of modern information business systems. Therefore, automated technologies are actively developing in knowledge acquisition from NL-texts (Text Mining), and various technologies of knowledge acquisition from databases (Data Mining, Deep Data Mining, Knowledge Discovery in Databases, etc.).

© Springer Nature Switzerland AG 2020
S. O. Kuznetsov et al. (Eds.): RCAI 2020, LNAI 12412, pp. 15–25, 2020.
https://doi.org/10.1007/978-3-030-59535-7_2

However, as a rule, all technologies of knowledge acquisition from various sources appeared and developed independently, therefore today such autonomy and distribution do not allow for the effective development, maintenance and monitoring of such significant information resources as knowledge bases, ontologies and databases that possess intelligent systems, in particular integrated expert systems (IES) [1–5], used to solve a wide class of non-formalized and formalized tasks of various practical significance and complexity. The problems of integrating Text Mining and Data Mining methods and technologies, as well as research in the field of creating tools and technologies for distributed knowledge acquisition, are most relevant today, as evidenced by a number of works, for example [6–11], etc.

The experience in the development of applied IES, including dynamic IES [2, 3, 5], on the basis of a problem-oriented methodology [1] and the AT-TECHNOLOGY tool kit supporting it, it has shown the effectiveness of the joint use of three sources of knowledge - experts, NL texts and databases. For example, the analysis of experimental data obtained during the creation of the KB of several applied IES using the combined method of knowledge acquisition (CMKA) [1–5, 12, 13], which is an integral part of this methodology, indicates that the local use of the database as an additional source of knowledge can replenish the volume of developed knowledge bases by 10–20%, depending on the specifics of the problem domain (PD).

The current stage in the development of technology of knowledge acquisition from various sources, in particular, the creation of a dynamic version of CMKA and means of its support, functioning as part of a new generation of WorkBench tools - the AT-TECHNOLOGY complex, is associated with the automation of the processes of acquiring, presenting and processing temporal knowledge for constructing knowledge bases in dynamic IES. The relevance of the study is due to the fact that at present, despite the existence of a significant number of approaches to the presentation of temporal dependencies, the issues of acquiring temporal knowledge from NL-texts and temporal databases for constructing temporal knowledge bases in dynamic intelligent systems are practically not considered, in particular, in dynamic IES [5].

The aim of this work is to present new results in the field of integration of Text Mining and Data Mining technologies, which were obtained on the basis of experimental software modeling of temporal knowledge acquisition processes for the automated construction of knowledge bases in dynamic IES (using the example of medical diagnostics).

2   The Evolution of the Combined Method of Knowledge Acquisition and Means of Its Implementation

The basic version of CMKA [1, 2, 12] and its support tools are constantly being developed and successfully used to automate the development of knowledge bases in static software, and today a distributed version of computer knowledge acquisition is supported [12, 13], which provides, within the framework of the client-server architecture, the integration of three types of knowledge sources (experts, NL-texts, databases), taking into account their geographical distribution. Based on the context of this work, we focus only on those features of the CMKA that are most important for the automated construction of temporal knowledge bases in dynamic IES.

The general organization of the process of direct knowledge acquiring from experts by means of computer interviewing at all stages of the life cycle of the construction of the IES is based on the author's approach of "focusing on a model for solving a typical problem" [1], according to which managerial knowledge of strategies (methods) solutions of specific classes of problems that can be solved in a similar way, are made out in the form of some heuristic model of a typical problem [1] (diagnostics, design, planning, etc.). Therefore, the processes of knowledge acquisition are controlled using sets of models for solving typical tasks, for which a number of techniques and approaches have been developed and are constantly being developed that allow you to create scripts of dialogs with experts, reflecting as a thematic dialogue structure (i.e., a scheme for solving a typical problem [1, 2]), as well as the local structure of the dialogue (dialogue steps [1, 2]), i.e. a set of specific actions and reactions between the expert and the system.

The processes of knowledge acquisition from experts and NL-texts are computer simulations that allow, on the basis of the method of simulation of consultation, to build an action-reaction scheme of partners, to build all the components of the model for solving a typical problem and to form knowledge fields as fragments [1, 2] (an intermediate representation of structured knowledge used to verify information obtained from various sources), and the corresponding fragments of the knowledge base.

The general structure of the basic means of the CMKA and the technology of using KMPZ at various stages of the life cycle of the construction of the IES are presented in Fig. 1 [1]. All expert interviewing processes are supported by the dialog script interpreter, and each script corresponds to a specific type of problem being solved, including screen forms for entering unreliable knowledge [1] (uncertainty, inaccuracy, fuzziness) and connecting means that implement the adaptive method of repertory lattices [1] (for differentiating diagnoses in the case of activating a script for a medical diagnosis). In the software for supporting the basic and distributed CMKA (see Fig. 1), an important place is occupied by a specialized linguistic processor and a set of dynamically updated dictionaries (the linguistic aspects of CMKA are described in detail in [1, 2, 12]).

Thus, CMKA is a concrete example of the integration of interconnected computer interviewing processes of experts with methods for processing NL-texts introduced during the interviewing session and after completion in the form of interview protocols, as well as with methods of knowledge acquisition from the temporal databases [14, 15] based on the modified Random Forest algorithm [16].

The essence of the modification of the well-known Random Forest algorithm was the use of a multidimensional feature space, one of which is a timestamp. The ensemble of decision trees is constructed in accordance with Random Forest; however, the calculation of the partition criterion value has undergone changes due to the use of the multidimensional feature space (the arithmetic mean of the calculated information entropy values will be the partition criterion). In addition, unlike decision trees built on the basis of temporal ID3 [17, 18] or the CART and C4.5 algorithms used in the basic version of CMKA [12, 13], here the tree is constructed until all the subsampling elements have been processed, and without the use of branch clipping procedures. The algorithm for constructing decision trees is performed as many times as necessary in order to minimize the classification error of objects from the test sample (objects are classified by voting by analogy with the basic version of Random Forest [16]).

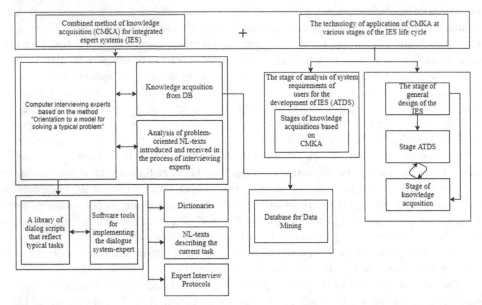

Fig. 1. The general organization of processes for the automated knowledge acquisition from various sources.

As for the issues related to comparing and combining the elements of the knowledge field obtained as a result of conducting interviews with experts and acquiring knowledge from the database (objects and rules), here, taking into account the "temporal" component, algorithms and software are used designed for basic and distributed CMKA. A detailed description of the proposed approach is contained in [12, 13] and is a topic for separate consideration. Here, we briefly note that in CMKA an approach to solving the problem of combining objects, based on the theory of multisets [19] was developed: The objects are grouped into multisets according to names and synonyms of names, or by calculating the distance between multisets using the metric, similar measure of Hamming's similarity.

In the basic version of CMKA to merge sets of rules, extended decision tables (EDT) are used [12, 13], which are a set of rows and columns where 2 cells are located at their intersection, in which information about the premise and conclusion of a particular rule is stored. As we consider the rules that make up the knowledge field, the EDT is replenished with new lines that are uniquely identified by the pair "object - attribute of the object". Rules are presented in EDT by its columns. In each EDT cell, the "type" of the premise/conclusion is recorded, which takes the following values: 0 - the premise/conclusion is absent in the rule; 1 - the premise/conclusion is present in the rule. Based on the analysis of EDT, a table of measures of similarity of rules is constructed by counting the matching attributes involved in the rules. At the intersection of each column and row of the table of similarity measures, there are two cells designed to store the similarity measures of parcels and the conclusions of the rules, on the basis of which a decision is subsequently made to combine them.

In the temporal version of CMKA, to solve the task of temporal knowledge merging, a new stage is added - combining temporal objects (events and intervals). To merge events and intervals, an algorithm similar to the algorithm for combining rules is used. The difference consists in constructing a table of similarity measures: for events at the intersection of each column, there is one cell designed to store similarity measures of a pair of events; for the intervals at the intersection of each column, there are two cells designed to store measures of similarity of the start conditions and the end conditions of a pair of intervals.

In addition, to combine the rules containing temporal entities, the basic algorithm has undergone changes, since the rules in the premise can use not a pair of «attribute - attribute value» , but a combination of two intervals or events and a temporal connective. The difference is as follows: EDT lines are mapped not only to the pair «attribute - attribute value» , but also to the triple «interval (event), interval (event), temporal connective» ; at the stage of constructing the table of similarity measures, not only pairs «attribute - attribute value» are also used, but also triples «interval (event), interval (event), temporal connective».

Thus, the urgent problem of the current stage of research is the further evolution of CMKA, with the aim of developing methods and tools for the automated construction of temporal knowledge bases in dynamic IES. To date, models, methods and software for representing and processing temporal knowledge have already been developed and tested when creating several prototypes of dynamic IESs [2–5]. The following is a description of the current results of the experimental software modeling of the temporal version of the CMKA.

3 Features of the Organization of Software Experiments Based on the Temporal Version of CMKA

3.1 General Organization of the «Language Experiment»

To model the processes of knowledge acquisition from experts and NL-texts (a sub-language of business prose [1]), a typical task was used - medical diagnostics, and a complex diagnosis of breast diseases and diagnosis of knee joint injuries was considered as an PD. Model dialogues were conducted in the form of a "language experiment" [2, 4, 5] related to the search for temporal information, i.e., temporal relations, both within each NL-proposal coming from an expert (taking into account the current state of the local dialogue structure), and with the search for relations indicating the time of creation of the text.

For these purposes, we used the dictionary of temporal tokens developed on the basis of [20, 21], a specialized linguistic processor, and interviewing support tools that operate as part of the AT-TECHNOLOGY complex. Within the framework of the "language experiment", about 50 sessions of interviewing were conducted with the participation of students who introduced lexemes (temporary prepositions, target prepositions, causal prepositions, particles, adverbs of time, and so on) on the basis of the "doctor to himself" principle in the appropriate screen forms for building fragments of the knowledge field.

Based on the experiments, we obtained a set of modified scenarios that describe the thematic and local structure of the dialogue in solving the typical problem of medical diagnostics, which allowed us to implement the elements of the "through" technology for direct acquisition and presentation (in terms of an expanded language of knowledge representation [2]).

In Fig. 2 we present examples of pie charts showing the quantitative result of the above experiments, for which scenarios were developed that included: adding new events and intervals to model dialogs, due to which the dictionary of temporal tokens was replenished; the inclusion in the field of knowledge of events and intervals without references and/or with incorrect values to test the reaction of means of supporting verification of the field of knowledge to anomalies (negative check); the use of synonymous events and intervals for subsequent experimental research of means for combining elements of the knowledge field obtained from sources of various typologies.

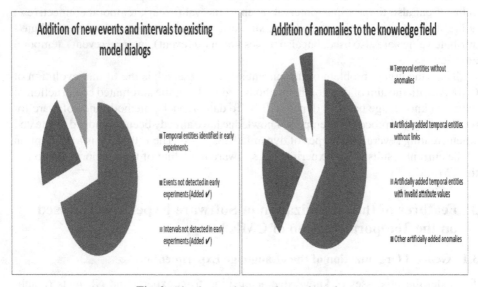

Fig. 2. Pie charts with experimental results

Thus, the use of a set of model dialogs allowed us to experimentally determine which temporal entities (markers) [4] can be identified on the basis of the algorithms and software of the temporal version of CMKA, significantly replenish the current dictionary of temporal tokens, and modify individual software components.

3.2 General Organization of Experiments with Temporal Database

Another set of experiments was carried out with a modified Random Forest algorithm and its implementation tools used to acquire knowledge from a medical temporal database containing data in a specific format, and a set of medical data was exported to a database under the control of a SqLite 3 DBMS, and then to a separate table with identifiers with assigned classes (i.e., a table is formed with objects that contains their attributes at each moment of time, and a table with classes). According to this temporal database, the Random Forest algorithm constructs an ensemble of trees, where each committee tree assigns a classified object to one of the classes, i.e. votes, and the class for which the largest number of trees voted wins.

In the context of this work, the main task is to implement the process of constructing elements of the knowledge field after completion of the Random Forest algorithm. Here, on the ensemble of trees, a special algorithm is applied, on the basis of which the decision trees are converted into knowledge field elements (objects and rules), using some additional information from the temporal database. The resulting fragment is suitable for further verification and integration [1, 2, 12, 13] with fragments of the knowledge field obtained as a result of expert interviewing sessions.

The scenario of experiments with a temporal database included (Fig. 3): registration of a temporal database in the dynamic version of the AT-TECHNOLOGY complex (registration means adding a file containing a temporal database to the directory where the executable file is located); opening the database and reading data stored in the database, namely: identifiers of objects, classes and timestamps; creation of files with serialization of the ensemble of trees, a description of the knowledge field in the extended language of knowledge representation, as well as a description of the knowledge field in the internal representation.

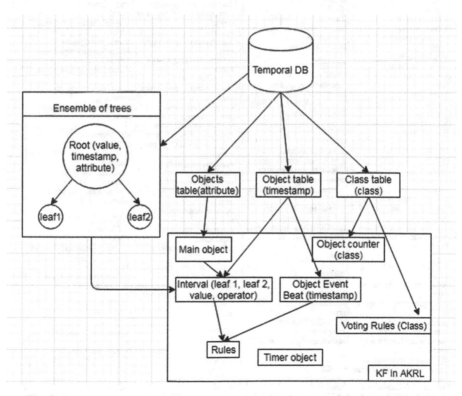

Fig. 3. The mapping of the temporal database to the elements of the knowledge field

It should be noted that the Random Forest algorithm was tested on several temporal databases that have the same structure, but a different number of objects, classes, timestamps, as well as with different formats of timestamps. In addition, during testing, ensembles of 100 trees were built.

3.3 Merging of Knowledge Field's Elements

The experiment was conducted on a "cross-cutting" example of the task of medical diagnostics, namely the diagnosis of breast cancer, for which sessions of interviewing experts in this field were conducted, and a model database containing temporal information was also used. Figure 4 shows 2 knowledge field fragments for this PD obtained from various sources, including 12 rules, 14 intervals, 5 events.

Фрагмент поля знаний, полученный от эксперта	Фрагмент поля знаний, полученный из темпоральной БД	контур	образования анэхогенная в течение 10 минут"
ТИП ТИП1 ЧИСЛО ОТ 0 ДО 100000 КОММЕНТАРИЙ number	ТИП ТИП1 ЧИСЛО ОТ 0 ДО 100000 КОММЕНТАРИЙ number	образования дольчатый со второй по десятую минуту исследования и в образовании давно имеется переферийное обывествление" "длина образования больше чем ширина, контур	КОММЕНТАРИЙ перечислите ультразвуковые признаки об исследуемом образовании в молочной железе.
ТИП ТИП3 СИМВОЛ "2 дня назад" "большой период времени" "в конце исследования" "в момент исследования" "всегда" "во время исследования" "в течение долгого времени" "в течение 10 минут" "давно" "по десятую минуту" "постоянно" "со второй" "с прошлого года" КОММЕНТАРИЙ Время	ТИП ТИП3 СИМВОЛ "08:32:25" "2 дня назад" "во время исследования" "в течение 10 минут" КОММЕНТАРИЙ Время	образование имеет вид экстратиреоидного распространения с прошлого года и в образовании микрокальцинаты большой период времени" "длина образования больше чем ширина, контур образования ровный и в образовании включений нет постоянно" "длина образования больше чем ширина, контур	ИМЯ "Пациент" ГРУППА "Объект" АТРИБУТЫ Атрибут1: Диагноз Атрибут2: Время Атрибут3: Перечислите предварительные жалобы пациента и уровень кровотока Атрибут4: Перечислите ультразвуковые признаки об исследуемом образовании в молочной железе Атрибут5: Перечислите параметры и включения исследуемого образования в молочной железе
ТИП ТИП2 СИМВОЛ "Образование без подозрений на злокачественное." "Образование вероятно является доброкачественным изменением" "Образование имеет высокий риск злокачественности." "Образование точно доброкачественное." "Образование является подозрительным" КОММЕНТАРИЙ Диагноз	ТИП ТИП3 СИМВОЛ "Образование без подозрений на злокачественное." "Образование точно не доброкачественное." КОММЕНТАРИЙ Диагноз	образования ровный и в образовании имеются макрокальцинаты постоянно" "длина образования больше чем ширина в конце исследования, контур образования имеет вид экстратиреоидного распространения и в образовании имеется переферийное обывествление в момент исследования" "ширина образования больше чем длина, контур	ИМЯ "Интервал1" ГРУППА "Интервал" АТРИБУТЫ Длительность: Пациент.Атрибут2=во исследования Количество возникновений: числовой Активность: числовой
ТИП ТИП6 СИМВОЛ "длина (высота) образования больше чем ширина, контур образования невозможно определить и в образовании имеется переферийное обывествление большой период времени" "длина образования больше чем ширина контур образование имеет вид экстратиреоидного распространения постоянно и в образовании имеются макрокальцинаты" "длина образования больше чем ширина,	ТИП ТИП6 СИМВОЛ "ширина образования больше чем длина, контур образования невозможно определить во время исследования и в образовании имеются макрокальцинаты" "ширина образования МЕНЬШЕ чем длина, контур образования невозможно определить и в образовании включений нет: 08:32:25" КОММЕНТАРИЙ перечислите параметры и включения исследуемого образования в молочной железе	образования всегда неровный и в образовании имеются микрокальцинаты" "ширина образования больше чем длина, контур образования невозможно определить во время исследования и в образовании имеются макрокальцинаты" "ширина образования больше чем длина, контур образования невозможно определить и в образовании включений нет" КОММЕНТАРИЙ перечислите параметры и включения исследуемого образования в молочной железе	ИМЯ "Интервал2" ГРУППА "Интервал" АТРИБУТЫ Длительность: Пациент.Атрибут2=в течение 10 минут Количество возникновений: числовой Активность: числовой
	ТИП ТИП4 СИМВОЛ "у пациентки 2 дня назад на месте образования были травмы" КОММЕНТАРИЙ перечислите предварительные жалобы пациента и уровень кровотока	ТИП ТИП4 СИМВОЛ "у пациентки 2 дня назад на месте образования были травмы" КОММЕНТАРИЙ перечислите предварительные	ИМЯ "Правило1" ТИП "Обычное" ЕСЛИ (Пациент.Атрибут3=у пациентки 2 дня назад на месте образования были травмы) & (Пациент.Атрибут4=эхоструктура образования кистозная и эхогенность образования анэхогенная в
	ТИП ТИП5 СИМВОЛ "эхоструктура образования кистозная и эхогенность		

Fig. 4. Fragments of knowledge field obtained from various sources

Figure 5 shows a fragment of the constructed EDT and a table of adjacency measures for events.

Fig. 5. EDT and the table of similarity measures for events merging

The volume of the final knowledge field obtained for the task of medical diagnostics was 65 rules, 35 intervals and 19 events. After combining all fragments of the knowledge field, the number of intervals decreased by approximately 15%, and the number of events by 30% without loss of quality.

4 Conclusion

The conducted experimental studies showed the efficiency of the developed methods, algorithms and technologies for acquiring temporal knowledge from various sources (experts, NL texts, databases), which is especially important for medical PD, where significant amounts of temporal information are accumulated even about one patient, including all his previous conditions and diseases in a wide time range.

Acknowledgement. This work was supported by RFBR (project No. 18-01-00457).

References

1. Rybina, G.V.: Teoriya i tekhnologiya postroeniya integrirovannyh ekspertnyh si-stem. Monografiya. Nauchtekhlitizdat, Moscow (2008). 482 p.
2. Rybina, G.V.: Intellektual'nye sistemy: ot A do YA. Seriya monografij v 3 knigah. Kniga 2. Intellektual'nye dialogovye sistemy. Dinamicheskie in-tellektual'nye sistemy. Nauchtekhlitizdat, Moscow (2015). 160 p.
3. Rybina, G.V.: Sovremennye arhitektury dinamicheskih intellektual'nyh si-stem: problemy integracii i sovremennye tendencii. Pribory i sistemy. Upravlenie, Kontrol', Diagnostika (2), 1–12 (2017)
4. Rybina, G.V., Danyakin, I.D.: Combined method of automated temporal information acqui-sition for development of knowledge bases of intelligent systems. In: Proceedings of the 2017 2nd International Conference on Knowledge Engineering and Applications, London, pp. 117–123. IEEE (2017)
5. Rybina, G.V.: Dinamicheskie integrirovannye ekspertnye sistemy: tekhnologiya avtoma-tizirovannogo polucheniya, predstavleniya i obrabotki temporal'nyh znanij. Informacionnye izmeritel'nye i upravlyayushchie sistemy **1 6**(7), 20–31 (2018)
6. Aggarwal, C.C., Zhai, C.: Mining Text Data. Springer, Boston (2012). 535 p.
7. Pan, E.: Learning Temporal Information from Text. Encyclopedia of Data Ware-Housing and Mining, 2nd edn. Montclair State University, USA, pp. 1146–1149 (2009)
8. Efimenko, I.V., Khoroshevsky, V.F.: Identification of promising high-tech solutions in big text data with semantic technologies: energy, pharma, and many others (Chapter 16. advanced methods). In: Daim, T., Pilkington, A. (eds.) Innovation Discovery. Network Analysis of Research and Invention Activity for Technology Management (2018)
9. Khovrichev, M., Elkhovskaya, L., Fonin, V., Balakhontceva, M.: Intelligent approach for het-erogeneous data integration: information processes analysis engine in clinical remote mon-itoring systems. In: 8th International Young Scientists Conference, vol. 156, pp. 134–141 (2019)
10. Aljawarneh, S., Anguera, A., Atwood, J.W., Lara, J.A., Lizcano, D.: Particularities of data mining in medicine: lessons learned from patient medical time series data analysis. Eurasip J. Wirel. Commun. Netw. **2019**(1). Article 260 (2019)
11. Cvetkova, L.A., CHerchenko, O.V.: Vnedrenie tekhnologij Big Data v zdravoohrane-nie: ocenka tekhnologicheskih i kommercheskih perspektiv. Ekonomika nauki **2**(2), 139–150 (2016)
12. Rybina, G.V.: Kombinirovannyj metod priobreteniya znanij dlya postroeniya baz znanij inte-grirovannyh ekspertnyh sistem. Pribory i sistemy. Uprav-lenie, kontrol', diagnostika **8**, 19–41 (2011)

13. Rybina G.V., Dejneko A.O., Raspredelennoe priobretenie znanij dlya avtoma-tizirovannogo postroeniya integrirovannyh ekspertnyh sistem. Iskusstven-nyj intellekt i prinyatie reshenij (4), 55–62 (2010)

14. Kaufmann, M., et al.: Timeline index: a undefied data structure for processing queries on temporal data in SAP HANA. In: Proceedings of the 2013 ACM SIGMOD International Conference of Management of Data, pp. 1173–1184. ACM, New York (2013)

15. Ishak, W., et al.: Mining temporal reservoir data using sliding window technique. CiiT Int. J. Data Min. Knowl. Eng. **3**(8), 473–478 (2011)

16. Tzacheva, A.A., Bagavathi, A., Ganesan, P.D.: MR – Random forest algorithm for distributed action rules discovery. Int. J. Data Min. Knowl. Manage. Process **6**(5), 15–30 (2016)

17. Vagin, V., Fomina, M., Morosin, O., Antipov, S.: Temporal decision trees in diagnostic systems. In: 2018 International Conference on Advances in Big Data, Computing and Data Communication Systems, ICABCD 2018 (2018)

18. Antipov, S.G., Fomina, M.V.: Metod formirovaniya obobshchennyh ponyatij s ispol'zovaniem temporal'nyh derev'ev reshenij. Iskusstvennyj intellekt i prinyatie reshenij (2), pp. 64–76 (2010)

19. Petrovskij, A.B.: Teoriya izmerimyh mnozhestv i mul'timnozhestv. Nauka, Moskva (2018). 359 s

20. Efimenko, I.V.: Semantika vremeni: modeli, metody i algoritmy identifika-cii v sistemah avtomaticheskoj obrabotki estestvennogo yazyka. Vestnik Moskovskogo gosudarstvennogo oblastnogo universiteta Seriya «Lingvisti-ka» . № 2, MGU, Izdatel'stvo, Moscow (2007)

21. Arutyunva, N.D., Yanko, T.E.: Logicheskij analiz yazyka: YAzyk i vremya. Otv.red. Indrik, Moscow (1997)

Multi-agent Systems, Intelligent Robots and Behavior Planning

Multi-agent Path Finding with Kinematic Constraints via Conflict Based Search

Anton Andreychuk[1,2](✉) [iD]

[1] Federal Research Center "Computer Science and Control" of Russian Academy
of Sciences, Moscow, Russia
`andreychuk@mail.com`
[2] Peoples' Friendship University of Russia (RUDN University), Moscow, Russia

Abstract. The paper considers a problem of planning a set of collision-free trajectories for a group of mobile agents operating in the shared environment, i.e. multi-agent path-finding (MAPF). A modification of the Continuous Conflict Based Search (CCBS) algorithm is proposed that takes kinematic constraints into account. The resultant planner explicitly supports rotation actions as well as agents of different sizes and moving speeds. Thus, it is more suitable for a range of practical applications involving real robots subject to kinematic constraints. An extensive empirical evaluation is conducted in which the suggested algorithm is compared to the state-of-the-art MAPF planners. The results of this evaluation provide a clear evidence that the proposed method is as efficient as predecessor that is limited to translation only action model.

Keywords: Path-planning · Heuristic search · Grid · Conflict based search · Multi-agent systems · CBS · MAPF

1 Introduction

Multi-agent navigation is one of the most challenging problems in AI and robotics. It appears when multiple agents operate in a shared environment and have to reach their own goals avoiding other agents or dynamic obstacles. Its solutions are aimed at increasing the degree of autonomy of modern robotic systems. A striking example of such systems are autonomous warehouse systems, similar to Amazon Warehouses [4], where groups of robots transport goods inside warehouses.

Nowadays, there are a number of algorithms that can solve different sorts of multi-agent navigation problems and have their certain pros and cons. All of them can be divided into two groups - reactive and deliberative. Algorithms using a reactive approach, such as ORCA [13] or ALAN [6], uses special techniques to avoid collisions during the local agent interactions. Each agent, observing the nearest neighbors and their current direction of movement, chooses its own movement direction in such a way to be able to avoid a collision. The advantages of this approach are high computational efficiency and the ability to scale up to hundreds and even thousands of agents, because each agent makes its decisions

S. O. Kuznetsov et al. (Eds.): RCAI 2020, LNAI 12412, pp. 29–45, 2020.
https://doi.org/10.1007/978-3-030-59535-7_3

independently and a centralised planning process is not carried out. The disadvantages of this approach are the lack of optimality, i.e. the guarantee of finding the best solution, as well as the lack of completeness, i.e. in general case, it is not guaranteed that a solution will be found even if it exists.

In contrast, algorithms based on the deliberative approach create a coordinated plan before the agents are actually start to move. In case if all agents follow the plan precisely, there will be no collisions. The problem of finding a set of collision-free paths is called multi-agent path finding problem or MAPF and in this work we are mainly focused on it.

Finding an optimal solution for MAPF problem is NP-hard. However, there are a bunch of algorithms that can solve it with some assumptions. Most of them are based on heuristic search approach. In this case the search space is modeled by a graph, where the vertices represent possible positions of the agents and the edges represent the actions that transfer the agent from one position to another. During the planning process these algorithms take into account possible collisions between the agents and considers all viable alternatives of their elimination. State-of-the-art algorithms of such kind are CBS [11], ICTS [12], M* [16]. They possess the properties of completeness and optimality. However, they cannot scale well to the problems with large numbers of agents as the complexity grows exponentially.

There are a bunch of algorithms that can solve the MAPF problem non-optimally, but scales much better. Most of them use prioritized approach [5], when agents' trajectories are planned one by one according to the assigned priorities and all previously planned trajectories are considered as dynamic obstacles and have to be avoided to eliminate collisions. Examples of such kind of algorithms are AA-SIPP(m) [20] or MAPP [18]. It's worth to note that this type of algorithms is complete only in cases if the problem fits the conditions of well-formed infrastructure [3].

There is also an approach when MAPF problem is transformed into another problem, such as satisfiability problem (SAT) [15] or pebble-motion problem [19]. Both of the mentioned algorithms are complete, while SAT-based solver is also able to find optimal solutions.

The main drawbacks of most of the state-of-the-start algorithms are the assumptions they make. Many of them considers timeline as a sequence of discrete time steps, i.e. at each time step each agent can perform a move or a wait action. That means that all actions have uniform duration. To meet this assumption as a model of the search space a 4-connected grid is usually used. That means that possible movement actions are limited to only 4 cardinal directions. Moreover, the agents shapes are usually ignored considering only that each agent at each time moment occupies some grid cell. These assumptions allows to simplify some procedures of the algorithms such as collision detection process as well as to reduce the size of the search space.

There are some works that partially solve the indicated cons of state-of-the-art MAPF solvers. For example, AA-SIPP(m) algorithm [20], takes into account agents' shapes, their headings and handle actions with arbitrary duration. Nevertheless, it is based on prioritized approach, which drawback is lack of optimality and completeness in general case. A modification of CBS algorithm that takes into account agents shapes was proposed in [9]. The disadvantage of a discretized timeline was eliminated in modifications of CBS and ICTS algorithms, namely, Continuous CBS [1] and Extended ICTS [17]. They consider a continuous timeline, that also forces them to take into account agents' shapes. However, the considered agent's action model in these algorithms doesn't take into account kinematic constraints of real robotic systems associated with the direction of movement and time required for its change.

In this work we introduce a modification of CCBS algorithm, called CCBS-kc (kinematic constraints), that not only takes into account agents' geometric shapes and handles actions with arbitrary duration, but also takes into account agents' headings and time required for rotations, while still saving the conditions of completeness and optimality. Moreover, the proposed algorithm allows agents to be heterogeneous, i.e. agents may have different sizes, movement speed or rotation speed. To the best of our knowledge, it's the first algorithm of such kind. Model experimental studies demonstrate the differences in the performance of the original CCBS method and the proposed modification.

2 Problem Statement

The workspace is modeled by a grid. Each of its cells corresponds to a certain area of the workspace and can be either passable or blocked. The cell is blocked if the corresponding area contains an obstacle. The edges of the grid are elementary transitions between the centers of two vertices. In this work we assume that each vertex is connected with 2^k neighbours as shown in Fig. 1.

An agent is modeled by an open disk of radius r and can perform the following three types of actions: 1) translation with a constant speed v ; 2) rotation in place with a constant speed ω; 3) waiting in place. The timeline is continuous so all the actions have arbitrary duration. Agents can perform turn and wait actions only at the centers of the grid cells. Moreover, it is assumed that agents can have different values of r, v, and ω.

Each trajectory π contains a sequence of actions associated with the time-moments: $\pi = (a_1, t_1), ..., (a_k, t_k)$, where (a_i, t_i) is an action a_i that starts at time-moment t_i. Each action is defined by the initial configuration, end configuration and duration of the action. Each configuration contains the agent's location (a graph vertex in which the agent is located) and its heading (current direction of movement). In case of wait-action initial and end configuration are equal. In case of rotating actions configurations differ only in headings. In case of move action configurations differ only in locations.

Trajectory π_i is called feasible if agent i that follows this trajectory never intersects any of the blocked cells w.r.t. its radius r. Two trajectories are considered to be collision-free if at any moment of time the distance between the centers of the agents is greater or equal than the sum of their radii: $\forall t : dist(\pi_i(t), \pi_j(t)) \geq r_i + r_j$, where $\pi_i(t)$ is the position of agent i at the moment t.

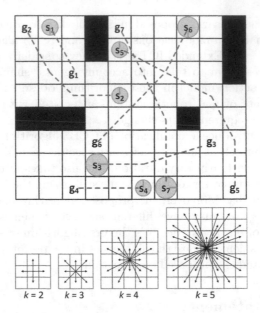

Fig. 1. Above: an example of grid-graph. s_i are the vertices corresponding to the starting locations of the agents, g_i are the goal ones. The lines inside the circles show the initial headings of the agents. The dashed lines show the planned trajectories of the agents, taking into account the possibility of transitions in 32 directions (2^5-connected grid). Below: Possible moves according to the grid's connectedness.

MAPF problem is formulated as follows. Let n disk-shaped agents operating in a two-dimensional space discretized into a grid, be given. For each agent i, radius r_i, translation speed v_i, and rotation speed ω_i are specified as well as start s_i and goal g_i configurations. For the goal state heading can be arbitrary. The problem is to find a set of collision-free trajectories for all agents $\pi_1, ..., \pi_n$ from their start states to the goal ones. As a criterion for assessing the quality of the solution found, the sum of the times required for the execution of the trajectories (flowtime) is used, i.e. $cost(solution) = \sum duration(\pi_i), 1 \leq i \leq n$, where $duration(\pi_i)$ is the sum of durations of actions contained in π. In this work we are focused on finding optimal solutions.

3   Suggested Approach

To solve the considered MAPF problem, it is proposed to modify Continuous CBS algorithm [1], which in turn is a modification of CBS algorithm [11]. Thus, before the explaining of made modifications, we will start from a brief overview of these methods.

3.1   Conflict Based Search Algorithm

Conflict based search is a two-level algorithm. On the top level it operates with the so-called constraint tree where each node contains a partial solution. The root of this tree is the initial solution containing a set of trajectories of all agents that were planned independently. At each step, the algorithm extracts a partial solution with minimal cost from this tree and validates it, i.e. checks it for collisions. The algorithm identifies two types of collisions: 1) two agents i and j at time-moment t occupy the same vertex u; 2) agent i at the time-moment t moves along the edge e from the vertex u_k to the vertex u_m, while agent a_j at the same time-moment t makes the same transition, but in the opposite direction. If there are no collisions in the selected partial solution, then the desired solution is found. If it contains at least one collision, then two new solutions are created where the found collision is eliminated by imposing constraint on one of the two agents participating in the conflict. The constraint is represented as a tuple $\langle i, u, t \rangle$ or $\langle a_i, e, t \rangle$ depending on the type of collision CBS forbids the agent i to either occupy the vertex u or to make the transition along the edge e at time-moment t. An example from [11] is shown in Fig. 2.

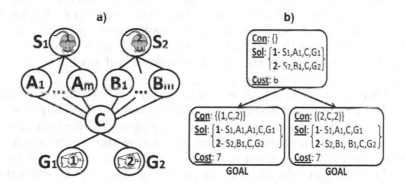

Fig. 2. From [11] a) MAPF example b) Corresponding constraint tree. Initial solution contains a collision as both agents tries to occupy vertex C at the same time-moment. CBS splits it into two new solutions, where either agent 1 or 2 is prohibited to occupy vertex C at time-moment 2. To satisfy the constraint the corresponding agent has to perform a wait action in the previous vertex. Resulting solutions are both collision-free and have cost 7.

Imposed constraints are considered during the planning of individual trajectories at the lower level. In the original CBS algorithm, a variant of A* algorithm [8] with discrete time dimension support is used as a low-level planner. However, any other path-planning algorithm with the completeness and optimality properties and capable of taking into account the constraints imposed is allowed.

Thus, at each step, the algorithm selects the current best partial solution, validates it and splits it into two new partial solutions in case if collision is found. The process continues until a collision-free solution is found. Due to the fact that the algorithm considers all available partial solutions and does this in order of increasing cost, it has the properties of completeness and optimality. The formal proofs of these properties are considered in [11].

3.2 Continuous Conflict Based Search Algorithm

Unlike the original method, CCBS supports continuous timeline, allows agents to perform actions of arbitrary duration and directly takes into account the agents' shapes. These features are primarily achieved by modifying the low-level planner as well as the principle of collision-detection mechanism and the type of constraints that must be imposed on agents to resolve the conflicts.

The ability to work with continuous time has a Safe Interval Path Planning algorithm (SIPP) [10]. Unlike the A* algorithm, where each state is characterized by one time-moment, in SIPP, each state contains a safe interval - the contiguous period of time during which the agent can occupy the vertex without any collisions with other agents. SIPP, as well as A*, has all the necessary properties, including completeness and optimality. The principle of operation of SIPP will be described in more detail later in Sect. 4.1.

Since agents movements are not limited to uniform durations, there is a variety of new types of collisions between them that can occur even when they move along different edges of the graph. Moreover, agents perform actions at arbitrary time-moments. In this regard, a collision in CCBS is defined as a tuple $\langle a_i, t_i, a_j, t_j \rangle$, where a_i, a_j are the actions of agents i and j, while t_i, t_j are the moments when these actions began.

To resolve the conflict, it is necessary to impose a constraint on one of the agents. Moreover, it is not enough to impose a constraint on only one time-moment, since if, for example, it is forbidden for agent i to perform an action a_i at time-moment t_i, then it can perform action a_i at time $t_i + \epsilon$, which again leads to a conflict. It is required to impose a constraint on the time interval during which the agent cannot perform an action. That is, the restriction is represented in the form of a tuple $\langle i, a_i, [t_{begin}, t_{end}) \rangle$, which prohibits agent i from performing the action a_i during the interval $[t_{begin}, t_{end})$.

Thus, using another algorithm for planning individual trajectories, as well as modifying the representation of conflicts, the method for identifying and resolving them, the Continuous CBS algorithm was obtained that supports continuous time, actions of arbitrary duration and takes into account agents' geometric shapes. Moreover, the algorithm has the properties of completeness and optimality, as well as the original method.

However, CCBS algorithm does not take into account the kinematic constraints imposed by real robotic systems associated with the inability to instantly change the movement direction. To fix this issue we need to modify the low-level planner further to take the headings into account and time required for rotations.

3.3   Safe Interval Path Planning with Rotations

Safe Interval Path Planning (SIPP) is a heuristic search algorithm that works on the same principle as A*. The algorithm operates with two lists - *open* and *closed*. The *open* list contains states - candidates for expansion, ordered in increasing order of f-value, which is equal to the sum of g and h-values, where g is the time required to reach the considered state from the starting state, while h is a heuristic estimate of the cost of the remaining path, i.e. the time required to reach the goal from the current state. At each step, the algorithm extracts the state with the lowest f-value from the *open* list and expands it. After that, the state is sent to *closed* - a list of all states that have already been expanded. Expansion is a successor generating process, i.e. consideration of all adjacent vertices and calculation of the time required to achieve them, taking into account the constraints.

Each state in the search space consists of a pair $\langle cfg, [t, t'] \rangle$, where cfg is the configuration; $[t, t']$ - safe interval, i.e. the period of time during which the agent can occupy the corresponding vertex. Thus, one vertex of the graph corresponds to many different states, which can differ in safe intervals and headings. Initially, each vertex contains only one safe interval $[0; +\infty)$. When constraints appear that limit the ability of the agent to occupy some vertex, a collision interval occurs and the safe interval is divided into two new ones. That is, if constraint $\langle i, a_i, [t_{begin}, t_{end}) \rangle$ is specified and it prohibits agent i to occupy some vertex v during the interval $[t_{begin}, t_{end})$, then the interval $[0; +\infty)$ for this vertex is replaced by two disjoint sub-intervals - $[0; t_{begin})$ and $[t_{end}; +\infty)$. Thus, the number of safe intervals is finite and directly proportional to the number of constraints imposed.

The amount of possible directions of movement is also limited and depends on the connectedness of the graph as the heading depends on the vertex from which the current state was reached, i.e. vertex of the parent state. In case of 4-connected grid, when only cardinal movements are allowed, the number of different headings is limited to 4. If we consider a 2^k-connected grid, then the number of possible headings is limited to 2^k. In general case, the number of possible headings does not exceed the value $n - 1$, where n is the number of vertices in the graph.

As one can see, due to considering of different headings, the size of the search space can dramatically increase. However, there is no need to generate, store and expand states with all possible headings. We can use an approach for decreasing the amount of considered states with different headings introduced in [21]. Since agents can rotate in place at a certain speed ω, the direction of motion required to generate the successor can be obtained by rotation. Moreover, some states can be discarded due to their dominance by other states. Let two states $s_1 = \langle cfg_1, [t, t'] \rangle$ and $s_2 = \langle cfg_2, [t, t'] \rangle$ be given, where cfg_1 and cfg_2 correspond to the same vertex of the graph, but differ in headings. If $g(s_1) + rotate\_cost(cfg_1, cfg_2) \leq g(s_2)$, where $rotate\_cost$ is a function that calculates the time required to change direction from cfg_1 to cfg_2 with respect to speed ω, then state s_1 dominates state s_2. Obviously, all successors generated via s_2 can be generated via s_1 with a smaller or equivalent g-value. Thus the expansion of the state s_2 is not needed. If neither state dominates the other one, then both of them should be added to the *open* list. The latter case is shown in Fig. 3.

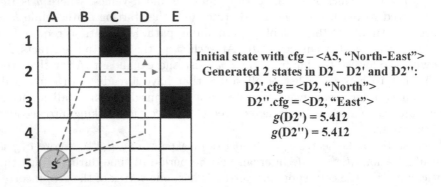

Fig. 3. An example where two states were generated, but none of them dominates the other one. If only one of these states is expanded, then either D1 or E2 will be reached in a non-optimal way

The original SIPP algorithm was developed to plan individual trajectories in the environments with dynamic obstacles. In the case under consideration, there are no dynamic obstacles, but there are constraints imposed by the high-level of CCBS that must be taken into account during the planning of the individual trajectories. If the constraint prohibits the agent to occupy some vertex, then it is converted to a collision interval and can lead to a split of one safe interval into two new sub-intervals. If constraint is imposed on a translation from one vertex to another one and the time-moment when the action begins belongs to the collision interval, then to satisfy this constraint the beginning of the action is shifted to the end of the interval, i.e. in fact, the wait action is added before the move action. Moreover, if the moment when the action begins is beyond the safe interval of the current state, then this action cannot be performed from it. A similar check is carried out for a safe interval of the state that corresponds to the end configuration. From the point of view of imposed constraints, the rotation action is actually equivalent to the waiting action, because there are no differences in identifying collisions between them, at least with the considered agent shape, which is an open disk of an arbitrary radius.

The pseudo-code of SIPP with the proposed state dominance logic, as well as adapted to work with CCBS constraints, is shown in Fig. 4.

3.4   Implementation Details

Collision Detection. In the original CBS algorithm, where all the actions have one timestep duration and only two types of conflicts are considered, the procedures for identifying conflicts and calculating restrictions are quite trivial. To identify conflicts, collision avoidance table is used. It contains all the positions of all agents at each timestep. If two or more agents are written in the same cell in the table, then a conflict occurs when the agents try to occupy the same vertex at the same timestep. By comparing adjacent cells, the one can determine the conflict when agents try to simultaneously go along one edge in different directions. At the same time, restrictions are not required to be calculated. It is enough to forbid one of the agents to occupy the vertex or cross the edge at a particular timestep.

In the case when the actions of agents can have an arbitrary duration, it is impossible to apply this method. To solve this problem, CCBS algorithm uses an approach based on the collision detection method described in [7]. It allows to calculate the minimum distance between a pair of agents, having initial positions of the agents and their velocities, i.e. movement directions. If the distance is less than the sum of agents' radii while they both perform the considered actions then there is a collision between them.

Computing Constraints. In order to compute the constraints imposed on agents to resolve conflicts, it is necessary to calculate the time interval during which the agent cannot perform the corresponding action. Let a conflict $\langle a_i, t_i, a_j, t_j \rangle$ be found and it is necessary to calculate the constraint for agent i, i.e. calculate the time interval $[t_{begin}, t_{end})$ during which it cannot perform the action a_i, otherwise it will lead to a collision with the action a_j of another agent. The beginning of this interval is essentially already known and corresponds to the moment t_i, since performing an action a_i at this moment, the conflict already occurs. It is necessary to calculate the end of the collision interval. For this purpose, it is proposed to use the binary search method. By definition of collision, it exists between a pair of actions, i.e. as long as both agents perform them. If agent j completes the action a_j, then there can no longer be a collision between the considered pair of actions. Therefore, using collision-detection formula, a conflict is checked at time $t = t_j + duration(a_j)$, where $duration(a_j)$ corresponds to the amount of time required to perform the action a_j. In fact, a situation is simulated in which a delay $wait = t - t_i$ is added to the agent. If at this moment in time the distance between the agents is less than the sum of their radii, then the end of the collision interval t_{end} is found, because at this moment, the action of the second agent ends. If at this moment there is no collision between the agents, then the delay $wait = wait - \delta$ decreases. The initial value of δ equals $wait/2$ and at each iteration it decreases by half: $\delta = \delta/2$. Depending on whether there is a collision between the agents, the delay value either increases or decreases by δ. Thus, for a finite number of checks, the one can determine the end of the collision interval with any required accuracy.

Algorithm 1: SIPP-based Low-Level Planner ($agent, constraints$)

1 $g(agent.s_{start}) = 0; OPEN = \oslash; CLOSED = \oslash;$
2 insert $agent.s_{start}$ into $OPEN$ with $f(agent.s_{start}) = h(agent.s_{start});$
3 **while** $agent.s_{goal}$ is not expanded **do**
4   **if** $OPEN = \oslash$ **then**
5   **return** path not found;
6     $s :=$ state with the smallest f-value in $OPEN$;
7   move s from $OPEN$ to $CLOSED$;
8   **for** each cfg in $NEIGHBORS(s.cfg)$ **do**
9        $successors :=$ getSuccessors(cfg, s);
10   **for** each state s' in $successors$ **do**
11   add_to_OPEN := true;
12   **for** each visited state s'' such that $s''.cfg.vertex = s'.cfg.vertex$ and $s''.interval = s'.interval$ **do**
13   **if** $g(s') \geq g(s'') + rotate\_cost(s'.cfg, s''.cfg)$ **then**
14   add_to_OPEN := false;
15   **else if** $g(s'') > g(s') + rotate\_cost(s'.cfg, s''.cfg)$ and $s'' \in OPEN$ **then**
16   remove s'' from $OPEN$;
17   **if** add_to_OPEN = true **then**
18   insert s' into $OPEN$ with $f(s') := g(s') + h(s');$

19 **return** $path$ reconstructed form $agent.s_{goal};$

Algorithm 2: Function getSuccessors(cfg, s)

1 $successors := \oslash;$
2 $duration := distance(s.cfg, cfg)/agent.v_t + rotate\_cost(s.cfg, cfg);$
3 $t_{min} := g(s) + duration;$
4 $t_{max} := endTime(s.interval) + duration;$
5 $intervals :=$ get all safe intervals for cfg;
6 **for** each safe interval i in $intervals$ **do**
7   **if** $startTime(i) > t_{max}$ or $endTime(i) < t_{min}$ **then**
8   continue;
9     $start\_t := max(g(s), startTime(i) - duration);$
10    $a :=< s.cfg, cfg, start\_t, duration >;$
11   **if** action a collides with $constraints$ **then**
12       $t :=$ earliest arrival time from s to cfg during interval i with no collisions;
13   **else**
14       $t = start\_t + duration;$
15   **if** t exists **then**
16       $s' :=$ state of configuration cfg with interval i;
17       $g(s') := t;$
18   insert s' into $successors$;

19 **return** $successors$;

Fig. 4. Pseudo-code of the main loop and the successor generation function of the adapted SIPP algorithm used as the low-level planner

Heuristic Function. The problem of any CBS-based algorithm is the requirement of performing planning of individual trajectories hundreds or even thousands of times during the search process. To make the low-level planner as efficient as possible the most accurate heuristic function is required, since its performance significantly affects the overall efficiency. For this purpose CBS-based algorithms use a pre-calculated heuristic function. Although heuristic function cannot take into account the trajectories of other agents, because they are still unknown, but at least it can consider static obstacles on the map. For this purpose CBS-based algorithms launch the Dijkstra algorithm from the goal locations of the agents, that actually calculates the shortest paths to all vertices in the graph, taking into account static obstacles. Due to the fact that all edges in grids are non-oriented, the heuristic function preserves the admissibility properties, i.e. it doesn't overestimate the actual minimal possible cost of the path.

Using a heuristic function that does not take into account the time required to change the direction of movement, in the case when it is actually required, is possible, because the properties of monotony and admissibility are not violated. However, the results of the experimental evaluation has shown that the use of such heuristic can significantly affect the efficiency of the algorithm. To increase the accuracy of the heuristic function, a similar logic of state dominance was implemented, and during the calculation of the paths, the time required for agents to change the movement direction was taken into account. Due to the fact that in general case the number of possible directions of movement can be significant, for each vertex for one agent, just one value was stored - the best one.

4   Experimental Evaluation

During the experimental evaluation, there were performed 3 series of experiments. First of all we compared the efficiency of CCBS and CCBS-kc algorithms. Secondly we compared CCBS-kc with AA-SIPP(m) algorithm [20], that can also handle agents' headings, geometric shapes and non-uniform duration actions, but uses a prioritized approach. In the last series of experiments we have shown an impact of the modified heuristic function for the low-level planner on the overall efficiency of the algorithm.

Tests were carried out on two maps - a 16×16 map without static obstacles and warehouse-10-20-10-2-2-2 map, taken from a benchmark widely used to test MAPF algorithms [14]. This map has a size of 170×84 cells and simulates storage facilities (see Fig. 5). The connectedness of the grids in all the experiments was set to k = 3, i.e. 8-connected grids were used.

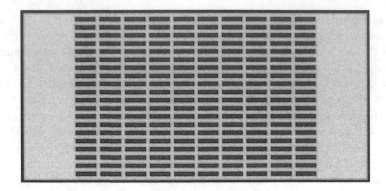

Fig. 5. Graphical representation of a warehouse-10-20-10-2-2 map. Dark areas of the map correspond to untraversable areas, i.e. static obstacles

There were generated 100 scenarios for both of these maps. Each scenario contains starting and goal locations for 120 agents. In the case of an empty map, the starting and goal locations were randomly generated with the only restriction - they must be unique for each agent. However, one vertex can be simultaneously the starting location for one agent and the goal one for another agent. In the case of warehouse map, the starting and goal locations were randomly selected from the two lateral rows of the map. At the same time, tasks were generated in such a way that if the starting location of the agent is on the left side, then the goal location is selected from the extreme row on the right and vice versa. Thus, all agents must go through the entire map in order to reach their goals. Moreover, due to this arrangement of starting and goal locations, these scenarios possess the properties of a well-formed infrastructure, i.e. algorithms based on a prioritized approach are guaranteed to find a solution using any sequence of priorities.

Although CCBS and CCBS-kc algorithms guarantee to find solution if it exists, it can take a huge amount of time to find it. Therefore, if the algorithm did not fit into the allotted timelimit (30 s), then the operation of the algorithm was interrupted and the task was considered as failed. The difficulty of the tasks increased gradually. Initially, the task contained only one agent from the scenario. If the algorithm was able to solve it, then another agent from the script file was added to the task. Gradually, the number of agents in the tasks increased until the algorithm could solve it. If the algorithm did not cope with the task containing n agents, then it was believed that the algorithm could not solve all subsequent more complex tasks of the same scenario with the number of agents exceeding n.

4.1　CCBS vs CCBS-kc

In the first series of experiments the performance of CCBS and CCBS-kc algorithms was compared. It does not make sense to evaluate the difference in terms of the solution cost, because both algorithms guarantee to find an optimal solution according to the flowtime criterion. At the same time, it is obvious that the cost of the solutions found by CCBS-kc can be higher, since it takes into account the time required for agents to change the direction of movement. All agents have identical properties - radius $r = 0.5$, which is equivalent to the radius of a circle inscribed at the grid cell; transition speed $v = 1.0$, i.e. the time spent on the transition between two arbitrary vertices is equivalent to the Euclidean distance between them; rotation speed $\omega = 0.5$, which is equivalent to 90 degrees per 1 unit of time. Initial heading for all agents in all scenarios was set to 0 ("East"), while the goal heading was enabled to be arbitrary.

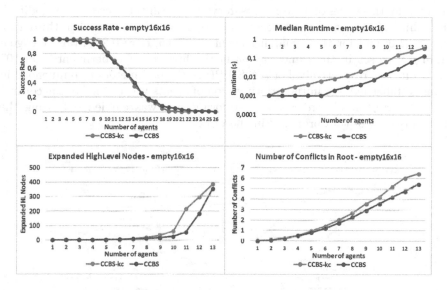

Fig. 6. The results of the first series of experiments. Analysis and comparison of the performance of the CCBS and CCBS-kc algorithms on $empty16 \times 16$ map

The results of the first series of experiments are presented in Fig. 6. To evaluate the efficiency of the algorithm, we measured such indicators as the percentage of successfully solved tasks (Success Rate), the total runtime of the algorithm (Runtime), as well as the number of expanded nodes at the high-level of the algorithm (Expanded HighLevel Nodes) and the number of conflicts that contains the initial solution (Root Conflicts). During the calculation of the average values, only those tasks were taken into account that were successfully solved by both algorithms, and the values are given only for those numbers of agents where the number of tasks solved by both algorithms is at least 40% of the total number of tested scenarios.

The results have shown that though CCBS-kc needs more time to find a solution, this does not affect the percentage of successfully solved tasks. The increase in the average runtime is also can be explained by the increased time required to calculate the heuristic function. Minor discrepancies in the plots are explained by the fact that the algorithms build different trajectories that lead to different conflicts. In general, accounting the kinematic constraints, with an increase in the number of agents, leads to more conflicts. This fact leads to an increased number of high-level nodes, which the algorithm has to expand in order to find a collision-free solution.

4.2   AA-SIPP(m) vs CCBS-kc

In the second series of experiments, CCBS-kc and AA-SIPP(m) algorithms were tested. Empty 16×16 and warehouse-10-20-10-2-2 maps and the same scenarios were used for this series of experiments, however, the agent speeds were modified. For a third of the agents were set $v = 1.0$, $\omega = 0.5$; for another third $v = 2.0$, $\omega = 1.0$; and for the remaining agents $v = 0.5$, $\omega = 0.25$. Start and goal headings were set in the same way as in the first set of experiments, i.e. "0" and "arbitrary" respectively. For AA-SIPP(m), the parameters recommended in [2] were established, i.e. initial prioritization of agents was carried out according to the "shortest first" order, and re-prioritization was carried out using the deterministic algorithm proposed in the work.

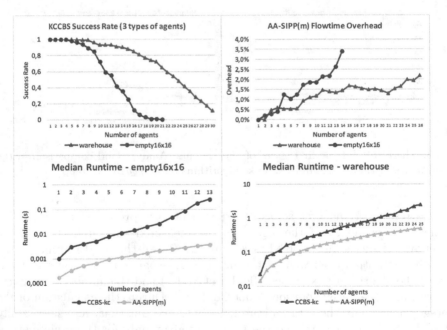

Fig. 7. The results of the second series of experiments. Comparison of the performance of CCBS-kc and AA-SIPP(m) algorithms

The results of the second series of experiments are presented in Fig. 7. The plot of successfully completed tasks (Success Rate) contains only data according to CCBS-kc, since AA-SIPP(m) was able to solve all the tasks in the range of the number of agents, where CCBS-kc has a nonzero percentage of successfully solved tasks. Moreover, the solutions found by AA-SIPP(m) are not optimal. To assess their quality, the cost ratio of the optimal solutions and the solutions found by AA-SIPP(m) (Flowtime Overhead) was calculated. As it was expected the quality of the solutions found by the prioritized algorithm worsens with an increase in the number of agents. This is explained by the fact that with an increase in the number of agents, the number of conflicts also grows, which the prioritized algorithm eliminates in an non-optimal way. In terms of runtime, CCBS-kc is significantly inferior to AA-SIPP(m), as it has to perform multiple replannings for optimal conflict resolution and finding the best solution.

4.3 Comparison of Heuristic Functions

It's worth to note that during the tests of CCBS-kc in the first two series of experiments, a modified heuristic function was used that takes into account the time that agents need to spend to change the direction of movement. To assess the impact of this modification on overall performance, CCBS-kc was tested on a warehouse-10-20-10-2-2 map using both versions of heuristic. In this test the same values of agents' radii, transition and rotation speeds as in the first series of experiments were used. A modified version is marked as "with_headings", while "no_headings" is the version of CCBS-kc with regular heuristic function that does not take into account agents' headings and time required for rotations.

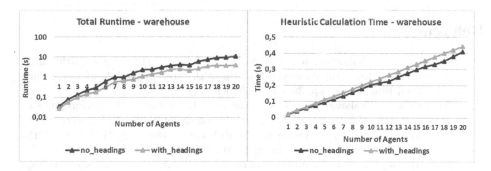

Fig. 8. Comparison of the efficiency of CCBS-kc algorithm depending on the heuristic function used. Left plot shows the total runtime of the algorithm, while right one - time spent on the preliminary calculation of the heuristic function

The results of comparing the efficiency of CCBS-kc depending on the heuristic function used are presented in Fig. 8. The complexity of calculating the heuristic function linearly depends on the number of agents, and the difference in time required to calculate the modified and unmodified heuristic functions is about 15–20%. In this case, the total operating time of the algorithm when using a modified heuristic is reduced by approximately half. Such a significant difference is due to the fact that the low-level planner with unmodified heuristic function expands an average 63.8% more states - 1510 versus 921. This naturally leads to a general increase in the runtime of the algorithm. Moreover, in some cases, an increase in the runtime of the low-level planner led to the fact that CCBS-kc could not meet the allotted timelimit (30 s). The total number of solved tasks on the warehouse map for the modified and unmodified heuristic functions is 1517 and 1473, respectively.

5   Conclusion

In this paper, a modification of the Continuous Conflict Based Search - CCBS-kc algorithm was proposed, which, unlike the original method, takes into account the kinematic limitations of real robotic systems associated with the need to spend a certain amount of time to change movement direction. The proposed modification is also able to plan sets of collision-free trajectories for groups of heterogeneous agents, i.e. take into account the individual characteristics of each agent, such as size, movement speed and rotation speed. The experimental evaluation has shown that taking into account additional properties and limitations by the CCBS-kc algorithm does not affect its efficiency compared to the original method.

Acknowledgment. This work was supported by RSF project #16-11-00048 (developing of the algorithm and its experimental evaluation) and by RUDN University Program "5-100" (data preparation).

References

1. Andreychuk, A., Yakovlev, K., Atzmon, D., Stern, R.: Multi-agent pathfinding with continuous time. In: Proceedings of the 28th International Joint Conference on Artificial Intelligence, pp. 39–45. AAAI Press (2019)
2. Andreychuk, A., Yakovlev, K.: Two techniques that enhance the performance of multi-robot prioritized path planning. In: Proceedings of the 17th International Conference on Autonomous Agents and MultiAgent Systems, pp. 2177–2179 (2018)
3. Čáp, M., Novák, P., Kleiner, A., Selecký, M.: Prioritized planning algorithms for trajectory coordination of multiple mobile robots. IEEE Trans. Autom. Sci. Eng. **12**(3), 835–849 (2015)
4. D'Andrea, R.: Guest editorial: a revolution in the warehouse: a retrospective on Kiva Systems and the grand challenges ahead. IEEE Trans. Autom. Sci. Eng. **9**(4), 638–639 (2012)
5. Erdmann, M., Lozano-Perez, T.: On multiple moving objects. Algorithmica **2**, 1419–1424 (1987)
6. Godoy, J., Chen, T., Guy, S.J., Karamouzas, I., Gini, M.: ALAN: adaptive learning for multi-agent navigation. Auton. Rob. **42**(8), 1543–1562 (2018). https://doi.org/10.1007/s10514-018-9719-4
7. Guy, S.J., Karamouzas, I.: Guide to anticipatory collision avoidance. In: Game AI Pro 2: Collected Wisdom of Game AI Professional, pp. 195–207. AK Peters/CRC Press (2015)

8. Hart, P.E., Nilsson, N.J., Raphael, B.: A formal basis for the heuristic determination of minimum cost paths. IEEE Trans. Syst. Sci. Cybern. **4**(2), 100–107 (1968)
9. Li, J., Surynek, P., Felner, A., Ma, H., Kumar, T.S., Koenig, S.: Multi-agent path finding for large agents. In: Proceedings of the AAAI Conference on Artificial Intelligence, vol. 33, pp. 7627–7634 (2019)
10. Phillips, M., Likhachev, M.: SIPP: safe interval path planning for dynamic environments. In: 2011 IEEE International Conference on Robotics and Automation, pp. 5628–5635. IEEE (2011)
11. Sharon, G., Stern, R., Felner, A., Sturtevant, N.R.: Conflict-based search for optimal multi-agent pathfinding. Artif. Intell. **219**, 40–66 (2015)
12. Sharon, G., Stern, R., Goldenberg, M., Felner, A.: The increasing cost tree search for optimal multi-agent pathfinding. Artif. Intell. **195**, 470–495 (2013)
13. Snape, J., Van Den Berg, J., Guy, S.J., Manocha, D.: The hybrid reciprocal velocity obstacle. IEEE Trans. Robot. **27**(4), 696–706 (2011)
14. Sturtevant, N.R.: Benchmarks for grid-based pathfinding. IEEE Trans. Comput. Intell. AI Games **4**(2), 144–148 (2012)
15. Surynek, P.: Multi-agent path finding with continuous time and geometric agents viewed through satisfiability modulo theories (SMT). In: Twelfth Annual Symposium on Combinatorial Search (2019)
16. Wagner, G., Choset, H.: M*: a complete multirobot path planning algorithm with performance bounds. In: 2011 IEEE/RSJ International Conference on Intelligent Robots and Systems, pp. 3260–3267. IEEE (2011)
17. Walker, T.T., Sturtevant, N.R., Felner, A.: Extended increasing cost tree search for non-unit cost domains. In: Proceedings of the 27th International Joint Conference on Artificial Intelligence, pp. 534–540 (2018)
18. Wang, K.H.C., Botea, A.: MAPP: a scalable multi-agent path planning algorithm with tractability and completeness guarantees. J. Artif. Intell. Res. **42**, 55–90 (2011)
19. de Wilde, B., ter Mors, A.W., Witteveen, C.: Push and rotate: cooperative multi-agent path planning. In: Proceedings of The 2013 International Conference on Autonomous Agents and Multi-Agent Systems, pp. 87–94 (2013)
20. Yakovlev, K., Andreychuk, A., Vorobyev, V.: Prioritized multi-agent path finding for differential drive robots. In: Proceedings of The 2019 European Conference on Mobile Robots (ECMR), pp. 1–6. IEEE (2019)
21. Yakovlev, K., Andreychuk, A., Belinskaya, J., Makarov, D.: Combining safe interval path planning and constrained path following control: preliminary results. In: Ronzhin, A., Rigoll, G., Meshcheryakov, R. (eds.) ICR 2019. LNCS (LNAI), vol. 11659, pp. 310–319. Springer, Cham (2019). https://doi.org/10.1007/978-3-030-26118-4_30

Map-Merging Algorithms for Visual SLAM: Feasibility Study and Empirical Evaluation

Andrey Bokovoy[1,2]([✉]) [iD], Kirill Muraviev[1,3] [iD], and Konstantin Yakovlev[1,3,4] [iD]

[1] Artificial Intelligence Research Institute, Federal Research Center for Computer Science and Control of Russian Academy of Sciences, Moscow, Russia
{bokovoy,yakovlev}@isa.ru, kirill.mouraviev@yandex.ru
[2] Peoples' Friendship University of Russia (RUDN University), Moscow, Russia
[3] Moscow Institute of Physics and Technology, Dolgoprudny, Russia
[4] National Research University Higher School of Economics, Moscow, Russia

Abstract. Simultaneous localization and mapping, especially the one relying solely on video data (vSLAM), is a challenging problem that has been extensively studied in robotics and computer vision. State-of-the-art vSLAM algorithms are capable of constructing accurate-enough maps that enable a mobile robot to autonomously navigate an unknown environment. In this work, we are interested in an important problem related to vSLAM, i.e. map merging, that might appear in various practically important scenarios, e.g. in a multi-robot coverage scenario. This problem asks whether different vSLAM maps can be merged into a consistent single representation. We examine the existing 2D and 3D map-merging algorithms and conduct an extensive empirical evaluation in realistic simulated environment (Habitat). Both qualitative and quantitative comparison is carried out and the obtained results are reported and analyzed.

Keywords: Map-merging · Vision-based simultaneous localization and mapping · Autonomous navigation · Robotics

1 Introduction

Simultaneous localization and mapping (SLAM) is one of the major problem in mobile robotics as the ability to construct a map and localize itself on this map is vital for autonomous navigation in a wide range of scenarios. Different perception capabilities require different SLAM techniques. For example, different approaches exist for LiDAR [1,13], RGB-D cameras [11,14], sonars [28] and other sensors.

One of the most challenging SLAM formulation is monocular vision-based SLAM (vSLAM) when only the data from a single camera is available. This problem is of particular importance when it comes down to compact mobile robots that could not be equipped with wide array of sensors due to low payload

© Springer Nature Switzerland AG 2020
S. O. Kuznetsov et al. (Eds.): RCAI 2020, LNAI 12412, pp. 46–60, 2020.
https://doi.org/10.1007/978-3-030-59535-7_4

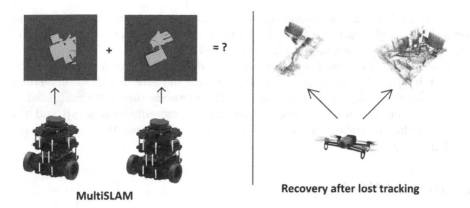

Fig. 1. Different scenarios in which the need for map-merging arises. Left: two robots navigate the same environment via different trajectories. Right: a single robot has to recover after the tracking has lost.

and battery limitations. Often a single camera is the only sensor that a robotic system is equipped with. Indeed this brings its own challenges and issues [24, 26] that need to be taken into account, when designing vSLAM methods.

One of the common problems that is addressed in more advanced applications of vSLAM algorithms, is the problem of combining several local maps into a single global map. This is the case for at least two different scenarios (see Fig. 1):

1. A single robot moves through an unknown environment. The localization and mapping get lost several times (e.g. in low structured visual environment) causing the algorithm to reinitialize each time and build a new local map without taking into account the previously built ones;
2. Multiple robots operate in an unknown environment. Each robot builds its own local map without knowing other robots' maps and positions.

To construct a consistent global map in both scenarios one needs to find overlaps between the local maps, adjust the robot(s)' position(s) appropriately (translate from local coordinate frame to a global one) and construct a single joint map. This problem is known as **map-merging** [6, 21, 25]. Noteworthy that within a visual SLAM framework, both 2D and 3D maps can be merged.

Indeed there exist methods and algorithms that address map-merging problem. However, most of these algorithms are typically validated on an exact single/multi robot system, whilst quantitative and qualitative comparison with the other approaches is left out of the scope due to the complexity of the experimental evaluation. To this end, we focus on analyzing different map-merging methods (both 2D and 3D) by running a wide set of reproducible experiments in a realistic simulated environment. The contribution of the paper is twofold. First, we create a dataset that enables the evaluation of map-merging algorithms by using a photorealistic simulated environment Habitat [32] (and make this dataset available to the community). Second, we conduct a thorough empirical evaluation and comparison of 3 different map-merging algorithms paired with 2 different vSLAM methods on the created dataset. Both qualitative and qualitative comparison are carried out and reported.

This paper is organized as follows: Sect. 2 describes the current state of the research in general vSLAM area and map-merging in particular. Section 3 states the problem formally. Section 4 describes the methods that were evaluated as well as the metrics used. Section 5 presents the experimental setup and the results of the empirical evaluation as well as our interpretation and analysis. Section 6 concludes.

2   Related Work

2.1   vSLAM Algorithms

Vision-based simultaneous localization and mapping algorithms vary depending on the vision-sensor which is used to gather the data, differentiating between the monocular, stereo and RGB-D settings. In each case an input for a map-merging algorithm is different, thus the vSLAM pipeline is different as well.

vSLAM methods that rely on a videoflow from a single camera (monocular vSLAM) can be divided into two major groups: feature-based and dense. Feature based methods, e.g. [18,22], are fast and accurate enough in terms of localization. However the resultant maps are sparse and lack details. On the other hand, dense methods, like [8,9], provide highly detailed maps, at the cost of higher runtimes. Thus their application for real-time on-board processing is limited when it comes to compact robotic systems that are not equipped with powerful computers.

In stereo-based SLAM [10,12] a disparity map from a pair of images is obtained and further used for computing a depth map. This map is then used for localization and mapping purposes. Naturally, processing two video streams instead of one adds additional computation costs.

The RGB-D cameras [17,35] construct depth maps on-the-fly and provide them to a vSLAM algorithm along with a single RGB video stream. As a result, RGB-D vSLAM methods [16,33] are accurate in terms of localization, provide detailed maps and do not incur extra computational costs. However, RGB-D sensors are notably larger and heavier than RGB cameras and consume more power, which limits their usage onboard of compact mobile robots.

Overall, when it comes to hard constraints imposed on robot's size, weight and power the most reasonable choice is i) equipping it with a single compact and light-weight RGB sensor, i.e. a video-camera; ii) relying on monocular vSLAM algorithms. One of the way to enhance the performance of the latter is to augment them with modern depth reconstruction algorithms that are fast enough to be executed on-board in real time. Such algorithms, indeed, exists – see [3,34] and they typically rely on using convolutional neural networks (CNN). Within this approach an image from monocular camera is combined with a CNN reconstructed depth map, which turns monocular camera into an RGB-D sensor. This provides a reasonable trade-off between the localization/map accuracy, map density and processing speed. In this work we chose this approach as a baseline for further evaluation of map-merging algorithms.

2.2   Map-Merging Algorithms

Generally the input of a map-merging algorithm is a set of maps constructed by a vSLAM method(s). These maps are typically represented as 3D point-clouds [30]. Meanwhile, in most cases, map-merging algorithms operate with occupancy grids [19], which are obtained by selecting a plane, e.g. a ground plane in case of a wheeled robot, slicing the point cloud and, finally, forming a grid representation of the slice. Each element of such grid corresponds to a probability for particular cell being an obstacle, free space or unknown environment. This grid is usually represented as an image and computer vision techniques are used in order to analyse its structure.

In [2] the problem of multi-robot mapping is considered when the integration of different maps obtained by different robots into a joint one is needed. The authors propose a method to estimate map similarity as well as a stochastic search algorithm (Carpin's Adaptive Random Walk) for merging. This algorithm finds the maximum overlap between the input maps and calculates the transform between them in order to combine the robots' poses and maps into a single representation model. The method is evaluated on 6 real robots. The algorithm is computationally expensive and its success rate was low when some of the input parameters (threshold for random walk) was set inappropriately.

In [31] the occupancy maps are considered as images and each map is processed through 3 major steps: preprocessing (edge detection, edge smoothing), finding overlaps (segmentation, segment verification, cross validation) and relative pose finding. The edge detection is done with Canny edge detector. Detected edges are then segmented into blocks, which are compared across the maps in order to find the overlaps. If an overlap is found, the relative pose is calculated using the translation and rotation of one of the maps. The algorithm is fast but not robust as it relies on Canny detector which is known to perform poorly in un-structured environments.

The robust overlap estimation is addressed in [15]. The map comparison is done with the ORB feature detector [29] and the RANSAC algorithm is used in order to find transformation, merge the maps and find the pose transformation. The code of this method is open-sourced.

The robustness of the overlap procedure can be increased by considering 3D maps, which contain much more features compared to their 2D slices. Indeed, this comes at a cost of higher runtimes. In [4] the pointcloud maps are represented as pose graphs and the overlaps are found by per-node comparison of two maps, where each node contains local sub-maps. When the match is found 2 maps are merged into a single graph and the global optimization is carried out. Both these operations are computationally expensive, thus the overall algorithm may not be suitable for real-time onboard usage.

3   Problem Statement

We are motivated by the following scenario. Two mobile robots are moving through the indoor environment. Each robot is equipped with an RGB camera and a modern onboard GPU (e.g. NVidia Jetson) which are used for vision-based simultaneous localization and mapping. Each robot is performing vSLAM independently and at each time step outputs its pose and a 3D map of the environment. The task is to merge two individual maps into a single (global) map either at each time step or at the end of a mission.

Formally the problem can be defined as follows. Let K be the current time step. At this time step two maps are given as the pointclouds:

$$M^1 = \{m_i^1\}, M^2 = \{m_j^2\}, i, j \in N, m_i^1, m_j^2 \in R^3 \tag{1}$$

Similarly two poses are given:

$$P_k^1 = (p_k^1, q_k^1), P_k^2 = (p_k^2, q_k^2), k = 1, 2, ..., K \tag{2}$$

where $p_k^i = (x^i, y^i, z^i)_k$ represents a position of robot i at time step k, and $q_k^i = (q_x^i, q_y^i, q_z^i, q_w^i)_k$ – an orientation of the camera[1]. These poses, represented as sequences correspond to trajectories of the robots: $T_1 = \{P_k^1 \mid k = 1, ..., K\}$ and $T_2 = \{P_k^2 \mid k = 1, ..., K\}$

Map and trajectory merging are, formally, the functions:

$$f_{mm} : 2^{R^3} \times 2^{R^3} \to 2^{R^3}, f_{tm} : 2^{R^7} \times 2^{R^7} \to 2^{R^7}, \tag{3}$$

where $M_e = f_{mm}(M^1, M^2)$ – is the merged map and $T_e = f_{tm}(T^1, T^2)$ – is the merged trajectory.

In practice, these functions are often represented as $M_e = M_1 \cup A(M_2)$ (or $M_e = A(M_1) \cup M_2$), $T_e = T^1 \cup B(T^2)$ (or $T_e = B(T^1) \cup T^2$), where $A : R^3 \to R^3$ is usually represented (but no limited to) as affine transformation, and $B : R^7 \to R^7$ is an arbitrary transformation.

To measure the quality of the merged map/trajectory we assume that the ground truth map/trajectory is given, M_{gt}, T_{gt}, as well as the error functions, $L_M(M_e, M_{gt})$, $L_T(T_e, T_{gt})$, that measure the error w.r.t. ground truth.

The merging problem can now be represented as a tuple $\langle M^1, M^2, M_{gt}, T^1, T^1, T_{gt}, L_M, L_T \rangle$ and stated as:

$$\text{Find } M_e, T_e$$
$$\text{s.t.} \tag{4}$$
$$L_M(M_e, M_{gt}) \to min$$
$$L_T(T_e, T_{gt}) \to min$$

In this work we are interested mainly in map merging problem, thus we will omit the estimation of T_e and the computation of L_T.

---

[1] We assume camera to be fixed firmly to the body of a robot.

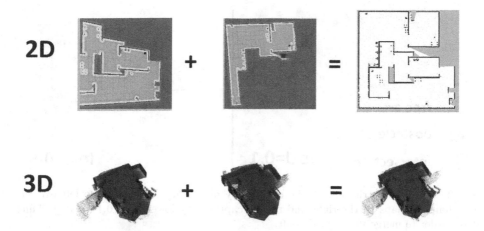

Fig. 2. Map-merging in 2D and 3D.

4 Methods and Metrics Overview

In this work we are interested both in 2D and 3D map-merging methods (see Fig. 2). In order for the former to be applied to the maps constructed by a monocular vSLAM algorithm, these (pointcloud) maps should be first converted to 2D. We use grid representation of 2D maps:

$$M^p = f_{pr}(M), M^p \in \{0, 1, -1\}^{A \times B} \tag{5}$$

where, $f_{pr} : R^3 \rightarrow R^2$ is a projection or slicing operation that results in a 2D grid composed of the $A \times B$ cells, each being either free – 0, occupied – 1, or unknown – -1.

To measure how difficult the merging task is we compute an intersection over union ($IoU \in (0; 1]$) between the two individual maps:

$$IoU = \frac{|M_{gt}^1 \cap M_{gt}^2|}{|M_{gt}^1 \cup M_{gt}^2|} \tag{6}$$

Here, M_{gt}^i stands for the ground-truth map (either 2D or 3D) for a robot i. The closer IoU is to 0 the less two map overlap. Thus it's harder to find correspondences between 2 maps, thus it is harder to merge the maps. On the contrary, if $IoU = 1$ no computations are needed to merge as maps are equivalent. Figure 3 illustrates this concept.

To measure the error of merging we use the following error function:

$$L_M = \frac{1}{G} \sum_{l=1}^{G} \rho(m_e^l, m_{gt}^l) \tag{7}$$

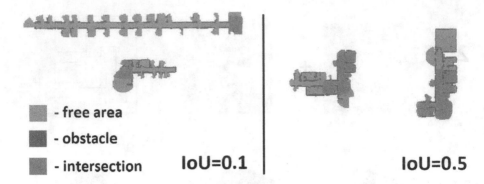

Fig. 3. The IoU metric reflects the complexity of merging. Maps on the left overlap less than the maps on the right and that is captured by lower IoU (0.1 vs. 0.5). Thus it is harder to merge maps on the left.

where ρ is the proximity measure for an element of the merged map, m_e, and the corresponding element of the ground-truth map, m_{gt}, and G is the number of elements (points) that compose the merged map. Intuitively this metric represent a proximity between two maps. In our experiments we used an implementation of this error-function which is a part of the CloudCompare software package[2]. It relies on the Euclidean distance as the proximity measure. To estimate the correspondence between m_e and m_{gt} it searches across all elements of M_{gt} to find the one which is the closest to m_e. We will refer to this exact error-function as L_{cc} further on.

We would also like to take into account the difficulty of merging when computing an error of the merge. This can be done by multiplying Lcc by a scalar representing how difficult the merge is. In our case this measure of difficulty is IoU, so the scaled metrics is $wL_{CC} = IoU * L_{cc}$.

Moreover we are also interested to assess the map merging outcome not only quantitatively but qualitatively as well. To this end we introduce the success metric. I.e. a human expert analyzes the merged map and reports whether the resultant map is a successful merge of the input or not.

Algorithms. We chose 3 map-merging algorithms for our evaluation based on the following criteria: they have to be open-sourced and targeted for the application on real robots. First, the we chose map_merge_2d[3] and map_merging[4] algorithms (noted as **MM1** and **MM3** accordingly). These 2D algorithms require the occupancy grids as the input (so 3D pointclouds, obtained by vSLAM, need to be projected first as described above) and treat these grids as images to extract features from them which are further used to estimate the correspondences and merge the maps. The main difference between **MM1** and **MM3** is in feature detector method (SIFT for **MM1**, SURF for **MM3**).

---

[2] http://www.cloudcompare.org/.

[3] https://github.com/hrnr/m-explore.

[4] https://github.com/emersonboyd/MultiSLAM.

Second, the map_merge_3d[5] (**MM2**) was chosen for 3D map-merging. This algorithm pre-processes the maps first to get the outliers removed with nearest neighbour outliter removal algorithm (if a point doesn't have neighbours in a certain area, it gets removed). Then, a 3D feature extraction algorithm detects the SIFT points or Harris corners on each map with corresponding descriptors. After this step, the features are compared to find the correspondences and transformation. If the match was successful the maps are merged.

5 Experimental Evaluation and Results

5.1 Setup

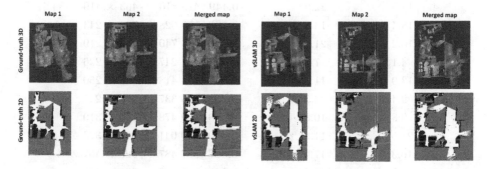

Fig. 4. Part of the dataset used for the evaluation. On the left – two separate maps, obtained by relying on ground-truth from the simulator, and a merged one. On the right – the maps of the same environment constructed by a monocular vSLAM that did not have an access to ground-truth depths.

We used Robot Operating System [27] as the main framework. It provides a set of ready-to-use algorithms for many robotics applications and also has tools for data visualization, recording, analysis etc. For modeling the navigation of robots through the indoor environments we chose Habitat simulator[6]. In this simulator we selected 6 scenes of Matterport 3D dataset [5], that were built using motion capture systems. Habitat allows to simulate the movement of a robot (camera) through the environment and at each moment of time one is able to acquire the robot's pose in the world coordinate system, ground-truth depth image and an RGB image. Using this data we are able to reconstruct a map of the environment by direct re-projecting, i.e. without the need to run a SLAM algorithm. Such maps will be referred to as ground-truth ones (Fig. 4).

Individual Trajectories. Overall we conducted 40 separate runs of a virtual robot through the simulated environment that were grouped into 20 overlapping pairs (see Table 1). During each run the set of RGB-images and depth

---

[5] https://github.com/hrnr/map-merge.
[6] https://github.com/facebookresearch/habitat-sim.

maps as well as camera positions were recorded for further ground-truth map reconstruction. The dataset with corresponding rosbags is available at: https:// github.com/CnnDepth/matterport_overlapping_maps.

Table 1. Trajectories and maps used in experimental evaluation.

Pair	Trajectory 1 length in m	Trajectory 2 length in m	IoU	Points 3D	Resolution 2D
1	21.7	20.3	0.480	405 288	399 × 403
2	32.9	20.8	0.295	493 070	448 × 509
3	13.7	15.9	0.619	130 162	234 × 399
4	19.0	22.9	0.449	415 810	463 × 419
5	18.4	13.8	0.437	175 628	383 × 243
6	16.2	21.2	0.402	193 740	444 × 219
7	4.1	7.8	0.479	121 247	239 × 236
8	13.9	11.0	0.457	163 418	329 × 250
9	9.4	4.3	0.302	88 337	211 × 245
10	9.8	10.0	0.399	189 478	250 × 310
11	21.5	11.2	0.399	240 041	330 × 379
12	16.3	17.4	0.327	397 487	528 × 407
13	22.2	21.0	0.535	266 472	329 × 425
14	13.9	15.8	0.420	214 593	327 × 484
15	12.6	21.1	0.202	277 755	397 × 314
16	21.6	17.8	0.266	267 133	400 × 284
17	10.8	6.5	0.388	164 773	349 × 238
18	13.7	12.3	0.512	156 416	255 × 326
19	15.6	14.1	0.417	183 705	228 × 319
20	18.9	19.9	0.283	251 173	293 × 465

The lengths of the obtained trajectories varied from 4.1 m to 32.9 m. The intersection was between 20% and 62%. When constructing the pointclouds we used 5cm as a resolution. With this resolution the number of points that constitute the maps varied from 88 337 to 493 070. The corresponding 2D projections (grids) varied in sized as shown in the last column of Table 1.

The experimental hardware/software setup was as follows:

– CPU - Intel Core i5, 6-core
– GPU - GeForce RTX 2060
– RAM - 32 GB
– OS: Ubuntu 18.04
– ROS version: Melodic

5.2   Results

Reconstructing Individual Maps. Besides ground-truth maps from the simulator we also used the following SLAM-constructed maps. First, we ran two RGB-D SLAM algorithms on the data from the simulator to construct the individual maps for further merging. These algorithms are: RTAB-Map[7] [20] and RGBDSLAM_v2[8] [7]. Next, we constructed individual maps by relying only on RGB video, i.e. we infer depth data from RGB by a convolutional neural network [23][9] and used this data in RTAB-Map and RGBDSLAM_v2 to construct the final maps.

Table 2 shows the accuracy of the maps constructed by RTAB-Map and RGBDSLAM_v2 relying on RGB-D data from simulator, i.e. images and ground-truth depths for each pixel on that images. As one can see RGBDSLAM_v2 maps are less accurate thus it is expected that these maps should be harder to merge compared to the ones produces by RTAB-Map.

Table 2. Accuracy of the RTAB-MAP and RGBDSLAM_v2 maps that were constructed using the ground-truth depths from the simulator.

Pair	RTAB-Map + gt-depth		RGBDSLAM_v2 + gt-depth	
	Map1 L_{CC}	Map2 L_{CC}	Map1 L_{CC}	Map2 L_{CC}
1	0.142	0.081	0.277	0.090
2	0.377	0.137	0.242	0.249
3	0.032	0.155	0.080	1.188
4	0.310	0.081	1.115	0.123
5	0.054	0.122	0.138	0.040
6	0.170	0.120	0.289	0.564
7	0.071	0.048	0.052	0.049
8	0.105	0.078	0.119	0.284
9	0.048	0.095	0.053	0.030
10	0.062	0.080	0.040	0.258
11	0.238	0.052	0.291	0.053
12	0.068	0.111	0.954	0.373
13	0.061	0.097	8.425	0.285
14	0.071	0.089	0.408	0.370
15	0.112	0.074	0.201	0.312
16	0.246	0.086	0.380	1.042
17	0.035	0.050	0.226	0.116
18	0.044	0.117	0.097	0.307
19	0.091	0.179	0.094	0.267
20	0.086	0.088	0.424	0.615

[7] https://github.com/introlab/rtabmap.
[8] https://github.com/felixendres/rgbdslam_v2.
[9] https://github.com/CnnDepth/tx2_fcnn_node.

Table 3. Accuracy of the maps constructed by RTAB-MAP using CNN inferred depths.

Pair	Map1 L_{CC}	Map2 L_{CC}	Map1 L_{CC} (scaled)	Map2 L_{CC} (scaled)
1	0.588	0.483	0.253	0.321
2	2.598	0.490	1.448	0.180
3	1.677	1.067	0.196	0.217
4	0.453	0.385	0.313	0.385
5	1.696	1.272	0.263	0.242
6	1.389	2.047	0.359	0.227
7	0.694	0.653	0.415	0.256
8	1.399	1.263	0.225	0.359
9	0.818	0.848	0.336	0.153
10	0.420	0.746	0.391	0.356
11	1.078	0.428	0.233	0.333
12	0.315	0.429	0.268	0.358
13	0.468	0.454	0.304	0.309
14	0.336	0.300	0.278	0.233
15	0.409	1.123	0.305	0.228
16	0.615	1.294	0.300	0.211
17	1.102	0.546	0.192	0.214
18	1.361	1.399	0.205	0.213
19	2.164	1.951	0.217	0.168
20	2.510	1.798	0.182	0.407

Table 3 shows the accuracy of the maps produced by RTAB-Map algorithm relying on CNN reconstructed depths. In this case, we found that FCNN algorithm reconstructs the depth with constant scale error for each map[10]. Thus we automatically adjusted this scale factor for each map in order to minimize the mismatch from the ground-truth. Unfortunately RGBDSLAM_v2 algorithm was not able to construct a single individual map relying on CNN-inferred depths, thus Table 3 does not contain information on RGBDSLAM_v2 + CNN.

Map-Merging The results of running different map-merging algorithms on the individual maps constructed by RTAB-Map provided with ground-truth depths are shown in Table 4. To estimate L_{CC} error of merged 2D maps, we used projection provided by RTAB-Map (in */proj_map* topic). Successful merges are denoted with + sign. Accuracy metric, L_{cc}, is shown as well[11].

---

[10] We believe the main reason for this was that the training of CNN had been conducted on a different dataset.

[11] Please note, that in case of **MM1** we have to find a transform between the merged map and the ground-truth map manually in order to compute L_{cc}, as the algorithm does not provide this transform. We used the transform that minimized L_{cc}.

Table 4. Merging results for RTAB-MAP + ground truth depths.

Pair	MM1	MM2	MM3	MM1 L_{CC}	MM2 L_{CC}	MM3 L_{CC}	MM1 wL_{CC}	MM2 wL_{CC}	MM3 wL_{CC}
3	+	+	+	0.080	0.168	0.155	0.050	0.104	0.096
5	+	+	+	0.464	0.127	0.139	0.203	0.055	0.061
6	−	+	+	x	0.104	0.108	x	0.042	0.043
7	+	+	+	0.063	0.086	0.076	0.030	0.041	0.036
9	−	+	−	x	0.127	x	x	0.038	x
10	+	−	−	0.124	x	x	0.049	x	x
11	+	−	−	0.159	x	x	0.063	x	x
12	−	+	−	x	0.110	x	x	0.036	x
13	+	+	+	0.148	0.119	0.078	0.079	0.064	0.042
14	+	+	+	0.069	0.118	0.229	0.029	0.050	0.096
16	−	+	+	x	0.096	0.065	x	0.026	0.017
18	−	+	+	x	0.117	0.103	x	0.060	0.053
19	−	+	−	x	0.149	x	x	0.062	x
20	+	−	+	0.080	x	0.261	0.023	x	0.074

MM2 algorithm was able to merge 11 pairs of maps, compared to 8 for MM1 and 9 for MM3. The lowest error, L_{cc}, was obtained with MM2 algorithm on pair 14, however, the close results were obtained with MM1. None of the algorithms were able to merge the (pair 15 with IoU = 0.202), however the MM2 algorithm was able to merge pair 16 with IoU = 0.266 and achieved $wL_{CC} = 0.026$.

The results of running map-merging methods on the individual maps constructed by RGBDSLAM_v2 provided with ground-truth depths are shown in Table 5. Recall, that for RGBDSLAM_v2 the L_{CC} of the individual maps was poor thus only 6 pairs of maps were successfully merged and L_{CC} of the merged maps varied from 0.106 to 0.448 (this is 2–5 times worse compared to RTAB-Map + ground truth). We got 4 successful merges from MM1 algorithm, 5 merges be the MM2 and 1 successful merge from MM3 algorithm.

Table 5. Merging results for RGBDSLAM_V2 algorithm + ground-truth depths.

Pair	MM1	MM2	MM3	MM1 L_{CC}	MM2 L_{CC}	MM3 L_{CC}	MM1 wL_{CC}	MM2 wL_{CC}	MM3 wL_{CC}
5	+	−	+	0.072	x	0.147	0.028	x	0.057
7	+	+	−	0.056	0.106	x	0.016	0.031	x
9	+	+	−	0.393	0.248	x	0.097	0.061	x
11	+	+	−	0.255	0.448	x	0.054	0.095	x
17	−	+	−	x	0.303	x	x	0.117	x
18	−	+	−	x	0.203	x	x	0.097	x

We also tried to merge maps constructed by RTAB-Map relying on CNN-estimated depths. Each of MM1, MM2 and MM3 algorithms was able to merge only 2 pairs of maps. Merging results are shown in Table 6. The lowest L_{CC} error was 0.369, the highest L_{CC} error was 2.209. The error of maps merged by MM1

Table 6. Merging results with RTABMAP + CNN-inferred depths.

Pair	MM1	MM2	MM3	MM1 L_{CC}	MM2 L_{CC}	MM3 L_{CC}	MM1 wL_{CC}	MM2 wL_{CC}	MM3 wL_{CC}
3	+	−	+	0.821	0.982	x	0.508	0.608	x
4	+	−	−	0.369	x	x	0.166	x	x
6	−	+	+	x	1.611	2.209	x	0.648	0.888
16	−	+	−	x	x	1.391	x	x	0.370

and MM2 algorithms was less than the error of corresponding individual maps, and the error of maps merged by MM3 was more than error of individual maps. However MM3 was able to merge challenging pair 16 (IoU = 0.266), whereas MM1 and MM2 merged only pairs with IoU more than 0.4.

Overall, the obtained results show that map merging is a hard-to-accomplish task even for maps that were constructed by vSLAM algorithms that have access to ground-truth depths. In case depth data is not available during SLAM but rather has to be inferred with CNN the quality of the individual maps degrade to the extent that map-merging becomes extremely hard.

6   Conclusion

In this paper, we have considered a map-merging problem when the source maps come from visual-based SLAM algorithms. Metric that reflects the hardness of merging task as well as the one reflecting the quality of the merge was described. To evaluate different map-merging approaches a large dataset was created via the Habitat simulator environment. Using this simulator allowed us to get access to ground-truth map models that are very hard to construct in real-world experiments. Relying on this ground-truth data we evaluated several map-merging algorithms (both 2D and 3D) paired with two different vSLAM algorithms. The results of empirical evaluation provide a clear evidence that map-merging of vSLAM-constructed maps is a non-trivial problem that is lacking general solution yet, i.e. numerous problem instances remain unsolved by state-of-the-art merging algorithms. This clearly provides avenues for future research, especially for 3D map-merging.

Acknowledgements. This work was supported by Russian Science Foundation project #16-11-0048 (CNN-based depth reconstruction, RTAB-MAP + FCNN implementation, experimental evaluation of map-merging algorithms) and by the "RUDN University Program 5-100" (data preparation).

References

1. Alismail, H., Baker, L.D., Browning, B.: Continuous trajectory estimation for 3D SLAM from actuated lidar. In: 2014 IEEE International Conference on Robotics and Automation (ICRA), pp. 6096–6101. IEEE (2014)
2. Birk, A., Carpin, S.: Merging occupancy grid maps from multiple robots. Proc. IEEE **94**(7), 1384–1397 (2006)

3. Bokovoy, A., Muravyev, K., Yakovlev, K.: Real-time vision-based depth recon-struction with Nvidia Jetson. In: 2019 European Conference on Mobile Robots (ECMR), pp. 1–6. IEEE (2019)
4. Bonanni, T., Della Corte, B., Grisetti, G.: 3D map merging on pose graphs. IEEE Robot. Autom. Lett. **PP**, 1–1 (2017). https://doi.org/10.1109/LRA.2017.2655139
5. Chang, A., et al.: Matterport3D: learning from RGB-D data in indoor environ-ments. arXiv preprint arXiv:1709.06158 (2017)
6. Dinnissen, P., Givigi, S.N., Schwartz, H.M.: Map merging of multi-robot slam using reinforcement learning. In: 2012 IEEE International Conference on Systems, Man, and Cybernetics (SMC), pp. 53–60. IEEE (2012)
7. Endres, F., Hess, J., Sturm, J., Cremers, D., Burgard, W.: 3-D mapping with an RGB-D camera. IEEE Trans. Robot. **30**(1), 177–187 (2013)
8. Engel, J., Koltun, V., Cremers, D.: Direct sparse odometry. IEEE Trans. Pattern Anal. Mach. Intell. **40**(3), 611–625 (2017)
9. Engel, J., Schöps, T., Cremers, D.: LSD-SLAM: large-scale direct monocular SLAM. In: Fleet, D., Pajdla, T., Schiele, B., Tuytelaars, T. (eds.) ECCV 2014. LNCS, vol. 8690, pp. 834–849. Springer, Cham (2014). https://doi.org/10.1007/978-3-319-10605-2_54
10. Engel, J., Stückler, J., Cremers, D.: Large-scale direct SLAM with stereo cameras. In: 2015 IEEE/RSJ International Conference on Intelligent Robots and Systems (IROS), pp. 1935–1942. IEEE (2015)
11. Engelhard, N., Endres, F., Hess, J., Sturm, J., Burgard, W.: Real-time 3D visual SLAM with a hand-held RGB-D camera. In: Proceedings of the RGB-D Workshop on 3D Perception in Robotics at the European Robotics Forum, Vasteras, Sweden, vol. 180, pp. 1–15 (2011)
12. Gomez-Ojeda, R., Moreno, F.A., Zuñiga-Noël, D., Scaramuzza, D., Gonzalez-Jimenez, J.: PL-SLAM: a stereo SLAM system through the combination of points and line segments. IEEE Trans. Robot. **35**(3), 734–746 (2019)
13. Hess, W., Kohler, D., Rapp, H., Andor, D.: Real-time loop closure in 2D LIDAR SLAM. In: 2016 IEEE International Conference on Robotics and Automation (ICRA), pp. 1271–1278. IEEE (2016)
14. Hu, G., Huang, S., Zhao, L., Alempijevic, A., Dissanayake, G.: A robust RGB-D SLAM algorithm. In: 2012 IEEE/RSJ International Conference on Intelligent Robots and Systems, pp. 1714–1719. IEEE (2012)
15. Hörner, J.: Map-merging for multi-robot system. Prague (2016). https://is.cuni.cz/webapps/zzp/detail/174125/
16. Kerl, C., Stueckler, J., Cremers, D.: Dense continuous-time tracking and mapping with rolling shutter RGB-D cameras. Santiago, Chile (2015)
17. Keselman, L., Iselin Woodfill, J., Grunnet-Jepsen, A., Bhowmik, A.: Intel RealSense stereoscopic depth cameras. In: Proceedings of the IEEE Conference on Computer Vision and Pattern Recognition Workshops, pp. 1–10 (2017)
18. Klein, G., Murray, D.: Parallel tracking and mapping for small AR workspaces. In: 2007 6th IEEE and ACM International Symposium on Mixed and Augmented Reality, pp. 225–234. IEEE (2007)
19. Konolige, K.: Improved occupancy grids for map building. Auton. Robot. **4**(4), 351–367 (1997)
20. Labbé, M., Michaud, F.: RTAB-Map as an open-source lidar and visual simultane-ous localization and mapping library for large-scale and long-term online operation. J. Field Robot. **36**(2), 416–446 (2019)
21. Lee, H.C., Lee, S.H., Choi, M.H., Lee, B.H.: Probabilistic map merging for multi-robot RBPF-SLAM with unknown initial poses. Robotica **30**(2), 205–220 (2012)

22. Mur-Artal, R., Tardós, J.D.: ORB-SLAM2: an open-source slam system for monocular, stereo, and RGB-D cameras. IEEE Trans. Robot. **33**(5), 1255–1262 (2017)
23. Muravyev, K.F., Bokovoy, A., Yakovlev, K.S.: The evaluation on vision-based simultaneous localization and mapping algorithm in simulated environment, pp. 129–135, January 2020. https://doi.org/10.31799/978-5-8088-1446-2-2020-15-129-135
24. Namdev, R.K., Krishna, K.M., Jawahar, C.: Multibody vSLAM with relative scale solution for curvilinear motion reconstruction. In: 2013 IEEE International Conference on Robotics and Automation, pp. 5732–5739. IEEE (2013)
25. Özkucur, N.E., Akın, H.L.: Cooperative multi-robot map merging using fast-SLAM. In: Baltes, J., Lagoudakis, M.G., Naruse, T., Ghidary, S.S. (eds.) RoboCup 2009. LNCS (LNAI), vol. 5949, pp. 449–460. Springer, Heidelberg (2010). https://doi.org/10.1007/978-3-642-11876-0_39
26. Pirchheim, C., Schmalstieg, D., Reitmayr, G.: Handling pure camera rotation in keyframe-based SLAM. In: 2013 IEEE International Symposium on Mixed and Augmented Reality (ISMAR), pp. 229–238. IEEE (2013)
27. Quigley, M., et al.: ROS: an open-source robot operating system. In: ICRA Workshop on Open Source Software, Kobe, Japan, vol. 3, p. 5 (2009)
28. Ribas, D., Ridao, P., Neira, J., Tardos, J.D.: SLAM using an imaging sonar for partially structured underwater environments. In: 2006 IEEE/RSJ International Conference on Intelligent Robots and Systems, pp. 5040–5045. IEEE (2006)
29. Rublee, E., Rabaud, V., Konolige, K., Bradski, G.: ORB: an efficient alternative to SIFT or SURF. In: 2011 International Conference on Computer Vision, pp. 2564–2571. IEEE (2011)
30. Rusu, R.B., Cousins, S.: 3D is here: point cloud library (PCL). In: 2011 IEEE International Conference on Robotics and Automation, pp. 1–4. IEEE (2011)
31. Saeedi, S., Paull, L., Trentini, M., Li, H.: Occupancy grid map merging for multiple robot simultaneous localization and mapping. Int. J. Robot. Autom. **30**(2), 149–157 (2015)
32. Savva, M., et al.: Habitat: a platform for embodied AI research. In: Proceedings of the IEEE/CVF International Conference on Computer Vision (ICCV) (2019)
33. Whelan, T., Kaess, M., Johannsson, H., Fallon, M., Leonard, J.J., McDonald, J.: Real-time large-scale dense RGB-D SLAM with volumetric fusion. Int. J. Robot. Res. **34**(4–5), 598–626 (2015)
34. Wofk, D., Ma, F., Yang, T.J., Karaman, S., Sze, V.: FastDepth: fast monocular depth estimation on embedded systems. In: 2019 International Conference on Robotics and Automation (ICRA), pp. 6101–6108. IEEE (2019)
35. Zhang, Z.: Microsoft Kinect sensor and its effect. IEEE Multimedia **19**(2), 4–10 (2012)

Can a Robot Be a Moral Agent?

Valery E. Karpov[1,2](✉)

[1] National Research Centre "Kurchatov Institute", 1 Ac. Kurchatov Sq., Moscow 123182,
Russian Federation
karpov.ve@gmail.com
[2] Moscow Institute of Physics and Technology (State University), MIPT, Institutskiy per. 9,
141701 Dolgoprudny, Moscow Region, Russian Federation

Abstract. Issues of the ethically aligned design of intelligent/autonomous systems have now moved into the fields of normative and technical regulation. If a system must make ethically determined decisions, then it must be recognized as a moral agent. This paper provides a list of the properties of a moral agent and shows not only that an artificial agent can have such properties, but also that they are technically determined as manifestations of adaptive mechanisms. In particular, it is shown that mechanisms such as the presence of the "I" component in the sign-oriented picture of the agent's world, the presence of an emotional-needs architecture, and the mechanism for comparing the observed conspecific with the "I" make it possible to realize the phenomena of social learning and a property such as empathy.

Keywords: Moral agent · Emotional-needs architecture · Empathy · Social learning · Imitative behavior · Ethically aligned design

1 Introduction

The ethical issues of artificial intelligence have long been an actively discussed topic, and, in recent years, these issues have moved from the category of humanitarian considerations into the field of technical regulation. For example, the IEEE has launched a global initiative for research in the field of the ethics of AI. The results of such studies should be technical regulations governing the development and implementation of AI systems, with requirements for their ethical behavior. The title of the document is noteworthy: "Ethically Aligned Design". Another illustrative example is UNESCO's report on ethics of robots, entitled "Report of COMEST on Robotics Ethics" (authored by COMEST—the World Commission on the Ethics of Scientific Knowledge and Technology) [1].

Most discussions about the ethics of intelligent/autonomous systems (I/AS) concern various kinds of threat, the social and economic consequences of their use, the ethics of the developers themselves, etc. In this work, we are interested in a different aspect of the ethics of I/AS: we are interested in systems that autonomously make decisions critically important for humans. The method of application of ethical mechanisms in decision making is not significant. For example, ethical considerations may apply to evaluating a

S. O. Kuznetsov et al. (Eds.): RCAI 2020, LNAI 12412, pp. 61–70, 2020.
https://doi.org/10.1007/978-3-030-59535-7_5

particular decision or action. Evaluation of an action D can be determined by technical, legal, and moral considerations:

$$Eval(D) = technical\_evaluation(D) + legal\_evaluation(D) + moral\_evaluation(D)$$
(1)

Variations of the notorious trolley problem can be used as an illustration of such reasoning. and moral considerations can be presented as a kind of filter. The task of the latter is to make a choice among many alternatives. If the decision cannot be determined on the basis of technical and legal requirements, then some additional heuristics should be applied. These heuristics are ethical rules, which comprise the ethical behavior of I/AS. Conventionally, this can be represented as follows (Fig. 1):

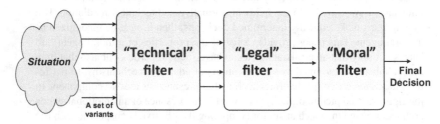

Fig. 1. Moral choice as a way to resolve ambiguity

Suppose that we can formalize the provisions of moral philosophy so that they can be represented by a certain system of rules (although this is a difficult task that requires a separate discussion). The problem then inevitably arises that, if the decision is based on moral principles (it is subjective, poorly verified, vague, etc.), then there is only one way to increase confidence in it: acceptance that the decision was made by a so-called moral agent, i.e., some entity to which we have delegated the right to apply ethical considerations. The question is then raised of whether there are prerequisites for I/AS to become a moral agent.

2   A Moral Agent

The basic definitions of the essence of a moral agent are usually anthropocentric and concise; as Parthemore and Whitby write, "by 'moral agent', we mean any agent that is appropriately held responsible for its actions" [2]. The reasoning is usually added that a moral agent acts in accordance with its role (see Mayo's work [3]), which speaks to freedom and is regarded as a necessary condition of a man being a moral agent, knowing that certain things are "right" or "wrong". Parthemore and Whitby state that a moral agent is necessarily a conceptual agent, i.e., an agent that possesses and employs concepts (units of structured thought), including the concept of "self".

We do not undertake to discuss the full list of properties that a moral agent should have, which is a purely philosophical problem that is compounded by the lack of consistent, constructive definitions of the basic concepts of ethics. Instead, we are interested in the purely applied aspect of creating I/AS, and the behavior (decision-making) of the created I/AS should correspond to our general ideas about the behavior of a moral agent. In this case, we will rely on the assumption that a moral agent can be not only a person, but any entity, including an artificial agent. A human monopoly on moral issues has long been questioned (see, for example, de Waal [4]), and we take the next step, moving away from biological chauvinism altogether.

We postulate that the many manifestations of the properties of a moral agent are determined by three basic mechanisms. These are (1) the agent's possession of a world model in which there is an "I" component (cognizing subject), (2) a mechanism for comparing the observed other agent (conspecific) with the "I", and (3) the presence of an emotional-needs architecture of the lower-level control system. At the same time, we will try to show that all these components have a very practical, real embodiment in technical systems, and we will further consider how these mechanisms allow the realization of a number of behavioral phenomena inherent in a moral agent.

3 Phenomena and Mechanisms

3.1 Emotions and Needs

Let us start with the lower level of the organization of agents. The role of emotions in the formation of ethical norms—and how emotions determine the ethics of human behavior—is being actively explored by both philosophers and sociologists [5–7], and Marvin Minsky [8] suggests treating emotions as another way of thinking.

There is every reason to believe that emotions (on the physiological level) and temperament (on the psychic level) can be inherent in a technical system as purely pragmatic mechanisms that affect the success of an artificial agent in complex nondeterministic environments, see Karpov [9, 10]. In these works, emotions are viewed as a property of the control system that facilitates the realization of functions known in psychology as contrasting perception, behavior stabilization, state indicating, working in conditions of incompleteness of information, and so on [11–13].

We note here that, in the architecture of the control system, the reactions of the system—defined as emotional—are determined by positive feedback loops. These connections are responsible for estimating the situation and determining the magnitude of the emotional state according to Simonov's Information Theory of Emotions [11]:

$$E = f(N, \ p(I_{need}, \ I_{has})) \tag{2}$$

where E is emotion, its magnitude, and sign (quality); N is the strength and quality of the current need; $p(I_{need}, I_{has})$ is the assessment of the ability to satisfy a need on the basis of innate and acquired life experience; I_{need} is information on how to satisfy needs; and I_{has} is information on the means (resources) available to the agent that are required to satisfy actual needs. It is important here that the behavior of the agent (robot) is determined by its needs and emotional state.

Figure 2 illustrates an example of the basic architecture of the emotional-needs control system. An "emotional" agent is equipped with a set of simple sensors and solved a standard behavioral task, using some simple rules such as: "IF (hungry) THEN (find food)", "IF (detect obstacle) THEN (run away)" etc. The influence of emotions on agent's behavior is realized as a positive form of feedback between the output signals (current actions or procedure) and behavior rules.

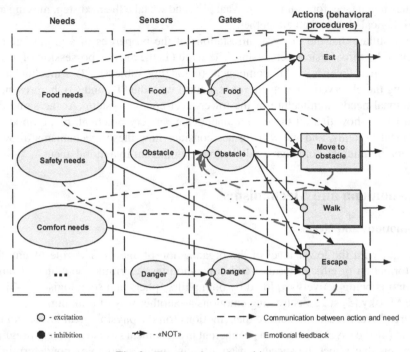

Fig. 2. Emotional-needs architecture.

An "Actions" block is a set of behavioral procedures. Every procedure is activated by signals from a "Needs" block and signals from special "Gate" elements. The "Gate" is an element that accepts direct signals from sensors and feedback signals from output elements. Every output procedure has its own emotional "weight". This signal is an input value for the gate element. It means that the positive emotion, associated with action a_i, ("Eat", "Walk", ...) will cause an increase in the activity of this action (manifestation of the positive feedback loop). We emphasize that emotional-needs architecture is the physiological, basic, or reflex level of a control system. Here the main function of emotions is to stabilize behavior.

3.2 Model of the World, "I"

An important attribute of the management system of an intelligent agent is the availability of knowledge about the world around it. If a component called "I" (the subject of activity) is added to this model of the world, then we get what is called a picture of the world (PW) (see Osipov [14]). In a certain sense, PW can be considered as some kind of superstructure over the basic stimulus-reactive level. From an architectural point of view, this is the component that implements the impact on the sensory system, determines the significance of certain needs, and, thus, changes the nature of the system's behavior, its goal-setting, etc. One of the most effective models for representing knowledge in PW is the symbolic or semiotic model, in which the main essence—the sign—is represented by four of its components: name n, percept p (image, form of expression), value m (method of use), and personal meaning a (goals, motives, personal meaning). In the model, homogeneous components each form a network, i.e., here we are dealing with four networks.

The following assumptions are important. We assume that the elements of the control system are equipped with one more confirming input—in addition to the exciting or initiating input—which is the input for the signal from the top of the "I". Thus, the action will not be activated if there is no confirmation signal from the "I", interpreted as the "belonging" of this action to the agent. In a certain sense, it is a feeling (sensation) of the self, i.e., identification or perception of an object as one's own. Without such a sensation, a mismatch of activity occurs in nature, such as the complex neuropsychiatric disorder called "alien hand syndrome", of which one clinical symptom is the presence of subjective sensations of the foreignness of a limb. From the point of view of semiotics, this means that these actions are the *meaning* of the sign "I", i.e., the question of conditionality is resolved in the most natural way.

The second assumption is that the activation of a component of a sign entails the activation of its other components, and associative connections arise between simultaneously active network nodes.

3.3 Imitative Behavior

This model quite naturally implements such phenomena as imitative behavior and social learning (learning by observing others). For example, let the agent know that the objects α_1 and α_2 are edible, i.e., belonging to the category of stimulus S (food) for action R (eat). Let the agent further observe that someone (conspecific) eats the object x, which was not previously considered by the agent as edible. Then, as a result of this observation, the agent will also classify this object as edible. A diagram for this is shown in Fig. 3.

In Fig. 3a, S_m is the component of the meaning of the "edible object" sign; R_m and R_p are the components of the meaning and perception of the sign "eating", respectively; and $Self_m$ and $Self_p$ are the values and percept of the sign "I", respectively.

$Obs(A')$ and $Obs(R_{A'})$ are the results of observation: the agent sees that conspecific A' performs action R. Performing action R_m activates some motor function act (actually eating), and the execution of the procedure is accompanied by the issuance of some signal (*Signal*).

So, the animat sees that the agent A' performs some action R with respect to the object X. Moreover, X was not previously considered by the subject as a determining factor for the stimulus S (the X-S connection was not part of the subject's personal experience). Observation of the conspecific's actions leads to activation of the R_p sign percept. The presence of the percept-value relationship means the activation of the value element R_m: $Obs(R_{A'}) \rightarrow R_p \rightarrow R_m$. At the same time, the observed conspecific is compared with "I": the $Self_p$ percept is activated, which leads to the activity of $Self_m$: $Obs(A') \rightarrow Self_p \rightarrow Self_m$.

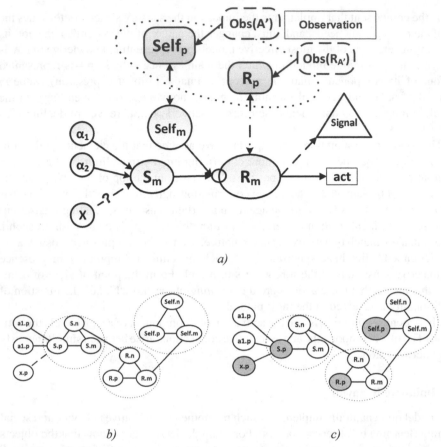

Fig. 3. The schema of imitative behavior. a) The conceptual scheme: solid lines are the relationships between value elements. The dashed-dotted lines are the connections between the components of the sign—the percept-value. b) The initial state of the system: all vertices are inactive, and there are a priori connections between the signs and the components of the sign. Communication S.p-x.p is optional (dotted line). c) The situation of monitoring the actions of the other agent.

This is the result of matching the conspecific with "I". Thus, all components of the circuit are in an excited state—R, S, and the actual object of observation, X. An associative connection is formed between X and S; that is, during observation, object X is included in the animat's behavioral experience, and this is done on the basis of observing the conspecific's behavior. This is imitative behavior; adding an evaluation element to this scheme then allows us to describe another phenomenon—the formation of reflex reactions, which are also formed on the basis of observation.

In this scheme, the most important point is the comparison of the subject with the conspecific ("I" and the other), determining the degree of their proximity. In nature, this identification is probably similar to what is called kin selection, when behavior determined by the degree of kinship of interacting individuals becomes evolutionarily beneficial (see, for example, Wilson [15]).

3.4 Empathy

This term refers to the ability to respond to the emotional states of surrounding individuals of varying degrees of proximity. Empathy is believed to determine the emotional propensity for collaboration and the manifestation of altruism. Of course, an individual's predisposition to empathy is a necessary, but not sufficient, property for the morality of the individual. Moreover, empathy is not a purely human property; in ethology, one of the mandatory mechanisms for the formation of the social interaction of individuals is the so-called sympathetic induction, the definition of which is identical to the definition of empathy. We are interested in two aspects of empathy: the mechanism of its implementation and the object of the empathy.

The realization of the empathy mechanism is possible on the same principle of identification (or determination of the degree of proximity) of the observed agent with the "I". The "formula" for empathy is quite simple and is determined by the components of the I/AS control system:

$$Empathy = \{Emotions + Identification\ of\ the\ conspecific + Imitative\ behavior\} \quad (3)$$

With the object of empathy, the situation is somewhat more complicated. In a certain sense, emotions are, first of all, a way of integrally assessing an individual's state (see [11]). Moreover, we assume that there is an external manifestation of the emotional state of agents, and it is significant here that empathy is the basis for a higher level of management related to goal-setting and planning. In terms of moral philosophy, this means the action of the golden rule: either implement a plan of action in which the other will feel good (increase the level of emotional state—a positive wording of the rule: "act in such a way…") or form a plan that does not lead to the appearance of negative conspecific emotions (negative wording: "do no harm"). In any case, the conspecific's emotional state influences the formation of the agent's behavior motive and goal. This is the main role of empathy from a technical point of view.

3.5 Characteristic Properties of Moral Agents

Next, we summarize some characteristic properties attributed to moral agents.

Language. Morality cannot exist without a symbolic language. The animal world does well without language; what is sometimes called a language is signal communication, i.e., the external manifestation of the internal state of the animal (see, for example, the work of Panov [16]). The role of signaling communication is certainly great, and many mechanisms of social behavior and interaction are built on this, including empathy, as discussed above.

Motive. The issues of motivating the behavior of a moral agent are considered so diverse in moral philosophy that we can find any convenient point of view (as, incidentally, on almost all other issues). For example, the view of John Locke is very convenient: personal interest is the only reasonable motive (cited in [17]).

Feelings. If, by feelings, we understand a certain process that reflects a subjective evaluative attitude to some objects, then those processes that occur in an emotional-needs architecture can rightfully be called feelings. A robot can really feel. If it is implied that a moral agent must possess "moral sentiment" (see, for example, [18]), then the task is simplified. So, we can completely abandon the consideration of this property and, at the same time, refer to Kant, who removed feelings from the realm of morality, considering their participation in the motivation of acts to be a prerequisite for the moral inferiority of the latter [19].

Alternatively, consider that, according to Hutcheson, moral feeling cannot directly motivate but is a response to a motive (cited in [17]). This also speaks to David Hume's assertion that moral feeling is the result of the action of simpler psychological principles—sympathy and the association of ideas. Any motives leading to human happiness are approved, and good consequences are indirectly experienced through sympathy, leading to a positive feeling about such motives.

Sympathy. This phenomenon is also the result of a comparison of the observed other agent (not even necessarily conspecific) with the "I". Naturally, the strength of sympathy depends on the degree of proximity of the observed agent. It should be noted that this can be considered as a direct consequence of the organization of a sign-oriented picture of the world. Excitation of some components of the sign (percept, value or personal meaning) leads to the excitation of its other components, including the name "I".

Responsibility. The moral agent is held responsible for its actions. Here, everything can turn out to be very simple. According to Parthemore and Whitby, a moral agent must possess certain key concepts and have the ability, over an extended period of interactions between the agent and its social and physical environment, to deploy those concepts appropriately [2]. This view of responsibility does not help either: "Thus, to be morally responsible for something, say an action, is to be worthy of a particular kind of reaction — praise, blame, or something akin to these — for having performed it", see M. Talbert [20].

Sometimes, the requirement for the independence of decisions expressed in judgments and actions is added to a personal responsibility for the consequences of decisions, where independence means that the subject should not act in accordance with a program laid down by someone else. However, this kind of reasoning usually—and quickly—becomes speculative. It is interesting that such a statement of the question of the boundary between what is laid down by nature and what is free will and independence is very rarely posed in a technical interpretation. There is usually a clear understanding that, on the one hand, there is some fixed, a priori specified part of the control system, and, on the other, that there are dynamically changing components. Consider the animat architecture; it clearly distinguishes the lower physiological, fixed, reflex level (on which, by the way, the emotional part of the control system works) and a superstructure thereof—the cognitive level, which is represented, for example, by a semiotic system.

So, we can at least state that many of the properties of a moral subject can be inherent in an artificial agent—and here, we are not talking about simulating mental or cognitive processes, properties of consciousness, and so on, but about dealing with purely technical solutions that are designed to increase the adaptive capabilities of a technical device. These decisions (models and mechanisms) can also be interpreted in humanitarian terms.

We have carefully avoided issues of moral philosophy; discussions about utilitarianism, evolutionary ethics, and even pragmatism are not within our competence. We have only tried to ask the question: if there is a certain list of properties that a moral agent should possess, are there reasons why we cannot recognize such an artificial agent—a robot?

4 Conclusion

The mankind comes to the idea that we are delegating intelligent/autonomous systems making independent decisions that are critical for people. If, in a situation of choice, both technical and legal arguments are exhausted, then moral criteria remain, and trust in such an "ethical" decision is possible only when the decision-making entity is a moral agent.

We emphasize once again that all the mechanisms described above were introduced exclusively for reasons of technical expediency, in order to solve the problem of creating effective adaptive mechanisms in three stages, by solving three classes of problems. At the first stage, these mechanisms should allow the technical device to act expediently in a complex, nondeterministic, dynamic environment. At the second stage, the task of organizing interaction within a group of agents was solved until the appearance of forms of social organization, and the formation of agent societies was also considered as an adaptation mechanism. The third stage is the task of purposefully managing social behavior, and, again, additional adaptation mechanisms were needed here, allowing society to maintain its stability. One of the most important factors of stabilization is the existence of mechanisms for resolving conflicts within society, and this is the main task and essence of morality.

These questions are not new to moral philosophy. For example, according to Drobnitsky, the essence of normative regulation is that "the action of social laws passes into the actions of individual agents" and thus "the social whole reproduces itself through individual mass behavior," and morality is a special case of this process [21, 19].

Today, there is intensive and fairly successful development of cognitive and social abilities of intelligent autonomous systems. However, in the field of ethics of I/AS behavior, promotion is fraught with a number of difficulties, and the main problem is the lack of constructive models that researchers expect from moral philosophy. Their absence often leads to models and methods remaining at the level of amateur understanding of moral problems.

Acknowledgments. This work was partially supported by the RFBR grant 17-29-07083-ofi_m.

References

1. UNESCO, "Report of COMEST on Robotics Ethics." UNESCO, COMEST, Paris, p. 64 (2017)
2. Parthemore, J., Whitby, B.: What makes any agent a moral agent? Reflections on machine consciousness and moral agency. Int. J. Mach. Conscious. **05**(2), 105–129 (2013)

3. Mayo, B.: The moral agent, in Royal Institute of Philosophy Lectures, pp. 47–63 (1968)
4. de Waal, F.: The Bonobo and the Atheist: In Search of Humanism Among the Primates. W W Norton & Co, New York (2013)
5. Neu, J.: An Ethics of Emotion? Oxford University Press, Oxford (2009)
6. Callahan, S.: The role of emotion in ethical decision making. Hastings Cent. Rep. **18**(3), 9 (1988)
7. Connelly, J.E.: Emotions and the process of ethical decision-making. J. South Carolina Med. Assoc. **86**(12), 621–623 (1990)
8. Minsky, M.: The Emotion Machine: Commonsense Thinking, Artificial Intelligence, and The Future of the Human Mind. Simon & Schuster, New York City (2006)
9. Karpov, V.E.: Emotions and temperament of Robots: Behavioral Aspects, Journal of Computer and Systems Sciences International, ISSN 1064-2307, Original Russian Text © V.E. Karpov, 2014, published in Izvestiya Akademii Nauk. Teoriya i Sistemy Upravleniya, 2014, No. 5, pp. 126–145., vol. 53, no. 5. Pleiades Publishing, Ltd., pp. 743–760, 2014
10. Karpov, V.: Robot's temperament. Biol. Inspired Cogn. Archit. **7**, 76–86 (2014)
11. Simonov, V.P.: Thwarted action and need – informational theories of emotions. Int. J. Comp. Psychol. **5**(2), 103–107 (1991)
12. Ilyin, E.P.: Emotions and Feelings. Piter, Saint-Petersburg (2001). (in Russian)
13. Rai, M., Yadav, R.K., Husain, A.A., Maity, T., Yadav, D.K.: Extraction of facial features for detection of human emotions under noisy condition, no. September, pp. 49–62 (2018)
14. Osipov, G.S., Panov, A.I., Chudova, N.V., Kuznecova, J.M.: Znakovaja kartina mira sub'ekta povedenija (Semiotic view of world for behavior subject). Fizmatlit, Moscow (2018)
15. Wilson, E.O.: Genesis: The Deep Origin of Societies (2019)
16. Panov, E.: Evolution of dialogue. Communication in development: From microorganisms to humans. Moscow (2014). (in Russian)
17. Darwall, S.: The foundations of morality: virtue, law, and obligation. In: Rutherford, D. (ed.) The Cambridge Companion to Early Modern Philosophy, pp. 221–249. Cambridge University Press, Cambridge (2007)
18. Smith, A.A.: The Theory of Moral Santiments, 6th ed. MetaLibri (2006)
19. Apresyan, R.G., Artemyeva, O.V., Prokofiev, A.V.: The phenomenon of moral imperative. Critical essays. Institute of Philosophy, RAS, Moscow (2018). (in Russian)
20. Drobnitsky, O.: The concept of morality. Historical and critical essay. Science, Moscow (2007). (in Russisn)

Navigating Autonomous Vehicle at the Road Intersection Simulator with Reinforcement Learning

Michael Martinson[1], Alexey Skrynnik[2], and Aleksandr I. Panov[1,2]([✉])

[1] Moscow Institute of Physics and Technology, Moscow, Russia
panov.ai@mipt.ru
[2] Artificial Intelligence Research Institute, Federal Research Center "Computer Science and Control" of the Russian Academy of Sciences, Moscow, Russia

Abstract. In this paper, we consider the problem of controlling an agent that simulates the behavior of an self-driving car when passing a road intersection together with other vehicles. We consider the case of using smart city systems, which allow the agent to get full information about what is happening at the intersection in the form of video frames from surveillance cameras. The paper proposes the implementation of a control system based on a trainable behavior generation module. The agent's model is implemented using reinforcement learning (RL) methods. In our work, we analyze various RL methods (PPO, Rainbow, TD3), and variants of the computer vision subsystem of the agent. Also, we present our results of the best implementation of the agent when driving together with other participants in compliance with traffic rules.

Keywords: Reinforcement learning · Self-driving car · Road intersection · Computer vision · Policy gradient · Off-policy methods

1 Introduction

Control architectures for mobile robotic systems and self-driving vehicles currently allow us to solve basic tasks for planning and self-driving in complex urban environments. Often the applied methods are based on pre-defined scenarios and rules of behavior, which significantly reduces the degree of autonomy of such systems. One of the promising areas for the increasing degree of autonomy is the use of machine learning methods. These methods are using for automatically generating generalized object recognition procedures, including dynamic ones, in the external environment. A significant disadvantage of such approaches is the need for pre-training on pre-generated data, which often requires handcrafted markup. However, there are currently a large number of data sets and simulators that can be used for pre-training without significant manual configuration or markup.

In this paper, we consider the task of learning an agent that simulates a self-driving car that performs the task of passing through the road intersection.

© Springer Nature Switzerland AG 2020
S. O. Kuznetsov et al. (Eds.): RCAI 2020, LNAI 12412, pp. 71–84, 2020.
https://doi.org/10.1007/978-3-030-59535-7_6

As a basic statement of the problem, we consider a realistic scenario of using data from the sensors of the agent (images from cameras within the field of view, lidars, etc.), data coming from video surveillance cameras located in complex and loaded transport areas, in particular at road intersections. The considering scenario for agent behavior looks followed. The agent drives up to the intersection and connects to the surveillance cameras located above the intersection to receive an online video stream. The agent switches to driving mode for a dangerous area and uses a pre-trained model that uses data from the agent's camera and sensors to follow traffic rules and pass the intersection in the shortest possible time. In this paper, we describe the simulator which we developed for this case. Also, we investigate methods based on reinforcement learning approaches to generate such agent.

We analyzed the effectiveness of using computer vision methods to generate an agent's environment description and conducted a series of experiments with various reinforcement learning methods, including policy gradient (PPO) and off-policy methods (Rainbow).

We did not link our research to any specific robot or self-driving architecture. At the same time, we consider that a real robot will have some simple sensors (speed, coordinate estimation, etc.) and basic control operations (wheel rotation, acceleration, braking).

Also, we understand that the use of such systems for ordinary crossroads with people is unlikely to become legally possible soon. Therefore, we propose to consider the task in the context of a "robotic" intersection without any pedestrians. Note that this assumption does not make the problem less relevant since it is fully applicable to delivery robots.

The presentation is structured as follows. Section 2 provides a brief overview of reinforcement learning methods, simulators, and approaches for modeling intersections. Section 3 presents the RL methods used in this paper. In Sect. 4, we describe the environment and the main parameters of the simulator. Section 5 presents the main results of the experiments.

2   Related Works

The direct launch of learning methods on robotic platforms and self-driving vehicles in the real world is expensive and very slow. In this regard, various simulators are widely used, which would reflect the interaction of the agent with the environment as realistically as possible. Such works include Carla [4] and simulator Nvidia Drive which used in work [2]. These 3D simulators have a huge number of settings and can generate data from many different sensors - cameras, lidars, accelerometers, etc. The disadvantage of this is the large computing power required only for the operation in these environments.

A representative of a slightly different class of simulators is SUMO [13]. This simulator permits to simulate large urban road networks with traffic lights and control individual cars.

The task of managing the self-driving car can be divided into several subtasks, which are more or less covered and automated in modern works. For example, the paper [9] investigates an agent driving a car in a TORCS [12] environment based on a racing simulator. The works [1,15,21,22] investigate the ability of an agent to change lanes, and [21] continue this study in cooperative setup. The work [16] explores the mechanism of keeping the car on the track. Paper [23] the authors provide a comparison of various computer vision methods, which include car detection and methods for evaluating the angles of car rotation. It is also necessary to mention a large recent work [8], which reviewed many traffic simulators and agents.

Despite the abundance of existing methods and solutions for sub-tasks of managing self-driving agents, we believe that the multi-agent formulation of the problem of moving agents at the intersection is quite popular.

3 Background

The Markov decision process [19] (MDP) is used to formalize our approach for learning agents. MDP is defined as a tuple $\langle S, A, R, T, \gamma \rangle$, which consists of a set of states S, a set of actions A, a reward function $R(s_t, a_t)$, a transition function $T(s_t, a_t, s_{t+1}) = P(s_{t+1}|s_t, a_t)$ and the discount coefficient γ. In each state of the environment $s_t \in S$, the agent performs the action $a_t \in A$, after which it receives a reward according to R and moves to the new state s_{t+1}, according to T Agent policy π determines which action the agent will choose for a specific state. The agent's task is to find a π that maximizes the expected discounted reward during interaction with the environment. In our work, we will consider episodic environments – MDP in which the agent's interaction with the environment is limited to a certain number of steps.

There are many algorithms to find the optimal policy π. In this paper, we consider modern approaches based on the Value function (Value-Based Methods) and approaches based on the policy gradient (Policy Gradient Methods).

The Q-function $Q^\pi(s, a)$, for the state-action pair, estimates the expected discounted reward that will be received in the future if the agent chooses the action a, in the state s and will continue its interaction with the environment, according to the policy π. The optimal Q-function $Q^*(s, a)$, can be obtained by solving the Bellman equation:

$$Q^*(s_t, a_t) = \mathbb{E}\left[R(s_t, a_t) + \gamma \sum_{s'} P(s_{t+1}|s_t, a_t) \max_{a_{t+1}} Q^*(s_{t+1}, a_{t+1})\right].$$

The optimal policy is $\pi(s_t) = argmax_{a_t \in A} Q^*(s_{t+1}, a_{t+1})$. In modern works for approximating the Q-function $Q(s_t, a_t)$ uses Deep Q-network (DQN) [14]. To evaluate $Q(s_t, a_t)$ the neural network receives the input state s_t and predicts the utility for each action $Q_\theta(s_t, a_t)$, where θ are the parameters of the neural network. We consider classic algorithms, such as Rainbow [7], which is applicable for discrete action space and Twin Delayed Deep Deterministic Policy Gradients (TD3) [6], which allows to use a continuous set of actions.

Rainbow [7] – is an improvement on the classic DQNalgorithm. The loss function for the DQN algorithm has the form:

$$L_{DQN} = \left[Q(s_t, a_t) - (R_t + \gamma \cdot max_{a'} Q_{target}(s_{t+1}, a')) \right]^2,$$

The learning process consists of interacting with the environment and saving all tuples (s_t, a_t, R_t, s_{t+1}) in memory of replays. where R_t – reward at time t, Q_{target} – copy of Q(S,A), delayed for episodes. Q-function optimization is performed using batches that are uniformly sampled from the replay buffer. The authors of Rainbow consider 6 improvements to the DQN algorithm, a combination of which significantly accelerate its convergence:

1. Double DQN is designed to solve the problem of overestimation that exists in DQN due to the maximization step. To solve this problem, two Q networks are used: Q_θ and $Q_{\bar{\theta}}$. When performing the maximization step, the best action is selected based on the current network, and its value is calculated based on the other one:

$$L_{double} = \left[Q_\theta(s_t, a_t) - (R_t + \gamma \cdot Q_{\bar{\theta}}(s_{t+1}, \arg\max_{a'} Q_\theta(s_{t+1}, a'))) \right]^2.$$

   The network, for which the loss function will be applied at the current update step is selected by random.
2. Prioritized Experience Replay improves the standard replay buffer of the DQN algorithm. Prioritized replay buffer samples more often transitions, with a larger TD error. The probability of sampling a single transition is defined as:

$$p_t \propto \left| R_{t+1} + \gamma_{t+1} \max_{a'} Q_{\bar{\theta}}(s_{t+1}, a') - Q_\theta(s_t, s_t) \right|^\omega,$$

   where ω is a hyperparameter that defines the distribution form. New data entering the prioritized buffer gets the maximum sampling probability.
3. Dueling Network Architecture – the approach is to make two calculation streams, the value stream V and the advantage stream a_ψ. They use a common convolutional encoder and are combined by a special aggregator, which corresponds to the following factorization of the Q-function:

$$Q_\theta(s, a) = V_\eta(f_\xi(s)) + a_\psi(f_\xi(s), a) - \frac{\sum_{a'} a_\psi(f_\xi(s), a')}{N_{\text{actions}}},$$

   where ξ, η, and ψ are common encoder parameters f_ξ, v_η value function flow, a_ψ advantage function flow, and $\theta = \{\xi, \eta, \psi\}$ their concatenation.
4. N-step return – uses N-step evaluation, which is defined as:

$$R_t^{(n)} \equiv \sum_{k=0}^{n-1} \gamma_t^{(k)} R_{t+k+1}.$$

So the new loss function:

$$L_{\text{N-step}} = \left[m(s_t, a_t) - (R_t^{(p)} + \gamma_t^{(p)} \max_{a'} Q_{goal}(s_{T+N}, a')) \right]^2.$$

5. Distributional RL – a distribution-based approach – the algorithm does not predict the Q-function itself, but its distribution. In this case, the C51 algorithm was used.
6. Noisy nets – this approach adds the layer to the neural network that is responsible for exploring the environment. The Noisy Nets approach offers a linear network layer that combines deterministic input and noise input:

$$\mathbf{y} = (\mathbf{b} + \mathbf{Wx}) + (\mathbf{b}_{noisy} \odot \epsilon^b + (\mathbf{W}_{noisy} \odot \epsilon^w)\mathbf{x}),$$

where ϵ^b and ϵ^w are sampled from standard normal distribution, and $\odot$ means elementwise multiplication. This transformation can be used instead of the standard linear transformation $\mathbf{y} = \mathbf{b} + \mathbf{Wx}$. The idea is that over time, the network learns to ignore the flow of noise, but the adjustment to noise occurs in different ways for different parts of the state space.

The second method we use is Proximal Policy Optimization (PPO) [17]. This is an on-policy method that belongs to the Actor-Critic (AC) class. The critic predicts the Value-function V and the loss function for it is MSE:

$$L_{critic} = [V(s) - R_t - \gamma \cdot V_{target}(s_{t+1})]^2$$

The actor loss function for PPO is similar to the improvement of AC - Advantage Actor-Critic (A2C) [20] and uses the advantage function, but with additional modifications.. As one of the main modifications is a clipping of possible deviation from the old policy. So if the standard A2C actor loss function has the form:

$$L_{policy} = \mathbb{E}\left[\pi(s_t, a_t) \cdot A(s_t, a_t)\right],$$

then for PPO:

$$L_{policy} = \mathbb{E}\left[clip(\frac{\pi(s_t, a_t)}{\pi_{old}(s_t, a_t)}, 1 - \varepsilon, 1 + \varepsilon) \cdot A(s_t, a_t)\right],$$

where P is the actor's policy, $clip(a, b, c) = \min(\max(a, b), c)$. Our implementation also used some PPO improvements from [5], such as clipping not only the actor policy but also the Value-function.

The third method, which was applied, is already introduced TD3 [6] - an off-policy algorithm that makes several stabilizing and convergence-accelerating improvements to the Deep Deterministic Policy Gradient (DDPG) [11]. Both methods belong to the Actor-Critic class. And correspondingly for DDPG Critic train by minimizing the almost standard loss function:

$$L_{critic} = [Q(s_t, , a_t) - R_r - \gamma \cdot Q_{target}(s_{t+1}, \pi(s_{t+1}))]^2,$$

where the only difference is the presence of $P(s_{t+1})$ - prediction by the policy of the action actor from the state s_{t+1}. For the actor itself DDPG use:

$$L_{policy} = -Q(s_t, \pi(s_t))$$

from which the gradient for policy parameters is taken.

TD3 introduces 3 more major changes. First is adding white noise to policy predictions at the stage of L_{policy} calculation. The second is a delayed update of the actor - namely one policy update for $n \in \mathbb{N}$ of the critic updates. And the last one is the usage of two independent estimations for the Q-function and using the minimum of them in calculations, as the authors of TD3 claim this helps to reduce the impact of bias overestimation.

4   Environment Description

Our environment - CarInersect is based on the simulator [18], physical engine Box2D and the OpenAI gym framework [3]. Technical details and bot behavior are described in the Sect. 4.1. The environment simulates the behavior of cars at a road intersection. The agent's goal is to manage one of these cars and drive it along the specified track. Although a human can easily complete such tacks, this is difficult for an artificial agent. In particular, when testing the environment, we found that a reward system different from a dense line of check-points with positive reward hardly leads to agent convergence.

4.1   Technical Details

The pybox2d physics engine is used for physical simulation of collisions, accelerations, deceleration, and drift of cars. So after a long selection of constants to control the car, we still could not achieve ordinary behavior, so we used the code for calculating the forces acting on the car from the OpenAI gym CarRacing.

The environment has the same functionality as the OpenAI gym framework environments. Every environment settings are passed through the configuration file. This file consists of three parts: the first part describes the reward function; the second part describes the behavior of the environment - the number of bots, their tracks, the agent's track, the type of observation; and the third part describing the background image, its markup, and sets of images of bots and the agent. The tracks description is the usual CVAT XML markup of the background image.

Bots ride along their tracks. These tracks selected uniformly from the list of available ones in a moment of bot creating. When moving, the bot goes to the next checkpoint of its track. To decide, where to steer, it takes into account the next two checkpoints. When bot leaves the road or collides with other vehicles, it disappears. If the agent encounters a bot, the agent receives a fine (reward -1), and the episode ends prematurely. Bots give priority to the car approaching from the right.

4.2   Actions

Each action is represented by a tuple $a_t = (st_t, g_t, b_t)$, where:

- $st_t \in [-1, 1]$ - steering
- $g_t \in [0, 1]$ - gas, has impact to acceleration
- $b_t \in [0, 1]$ - brake, stopping the car (not immediately)

Fig. 1. Types of tracks: small rotation, medium rotation, line, rotation (or full rotation); the control points are marked in red; if reaching them give 0.5 reward each

4.3   State

As a state, the environment returns an image and the agent's car feature vector. A feature vector is formed using the computer vision subsystem of the agent [23]. All vector features are concatenated. All coordinates are normalized to $[0-1]$; all angles are set by 3 numbers: their value in radians, sin and cos; the car points are the center of the hull and the centers of 4 wheels. Possible vector features (Fig. 1):

- hull_position – two numbers, x and y coordinates of the center of the car
- hull_angle – the angle of rotation of the car
- car_speed – two numbers, speeds on x and y coordinates normalized to 1000
- wheels_positions – 8 numbers - 4 pairs of x and y coordinates of the car wheels
- track_sensor – 1 if all car points are inside the track polygon, 0 otherwise
- road_sensor – 1 if all car points are inside the polygon of the road, 0 otherwise
- finish_sensor – 1 if at least one car point is close to the last point of the track
- cross_road_sensor – 1 if at least one car point is inside the area marked as an intersection area
- collide_sensor – 1 if the car is currently colliding with another car, otherwise 0
- car_radar_$\{N = 1, 2, 3\}$ – each of the N radar vectors is 6 numbers describing a single car:
  1. 0 or 1 is there data, if 0, then the other 5 numbers are 0
  2. normalized distance to the object
  3. sin and cos of the relative angle
  4. sin and cos of the angle between the velocity vectors
- time – 3 numbers, sin of time and sin of doubled and tripled time, where time itself is an integer number of steps since the creation of the car (this time encoding is done by analogy with the position encoding in Natural Language Processing [10]).

4.4   Reward Function

The reward system for the environment is defined in the configuration file. We used the same reward system for all agents: 0.5 for reaching checkpoints, which are uniformly spaced along the track; 2 for reaching the final point; −1 for leaving the track and crash. The episode ends when the agent reaches the finish line, leaves the track, or after 500 steps.

4.5   Environment Performance

To measure performance, the environment was run for 100,000 steps on a computer with an Intel ® Core^{TM} i5-8250U CPU @ 1.60 GHz 8, 15.6 GB RAM. Table 1 shows the average number of frames per second for various environment configurations. A slight slowdown occurs when images are used as the state. A significant slowdown occurs when bots are added.

Table 1. Simulator performance – mean number of frames per second (FPS) for state as vector, image and combined (vector and image).

Bots	Vector FPS	Image FPS	Combined FPS
No	1065	798	747
Yes	302	268	268

5   Experiments

The experiments were performed using 3 algorithms: PPO, TD3, and Rainbow. PPO and TD3 operate in a continuous action space, which is preferable for transferring an agent to the real world. Rainbow works in discrete action space, as shown in the Table 2. The source code for the environment and algorithms is available via the following link[1].

5.1   Results for Tracks Without Bots and States Represented as Vector

The results of experiments for tracks without bots and vectors as state-space are shown in Fig. 2. The following set of vector features was used for the experiment: hull_position, hull_angle car_speed, checkpoint_sensor, finish_sensor.

   As can be seen from the charts on all types of track, agents based on the PPO method show a stable but slow convergence. We suppose that such happens due to the lack of replay memory. Because there are control points that are difficult to

---

[1] Source code: github.com/MartinsonMichael/CarRacing_agents.

Table 2. Action discretization for Rainbow

Action	Steer st	Gas g	Break b	Description
A_1	0.0	0.0	0.0	Noop action
A_2	−0.6	0.0	0.0	Left steer
A_3	0.6	0.0	0.0	Right steer
A_4	0.0	0.9	0.0	Gas
A_5	0.0	0.0	1.0	Break

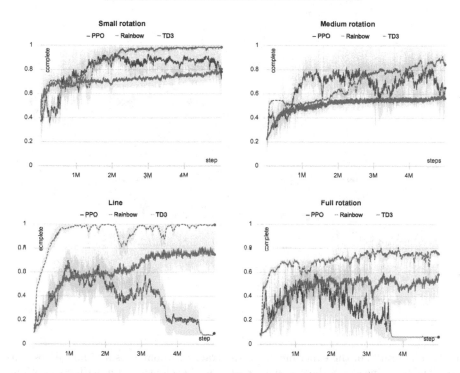

Fig. 2. The results of the experiments on the tracks without bots and vector observations. The bold line shows the average for 10 runs of each algorithm, with a smoothing of 0.6. The transparent line shows the standard deviation. For each of the algorithms, a preliminary search was performed for the best hyperparameters.

reach, such as around a bend. And in one update, PPO uses too little examples with positive point-reaching, so it takes longer to converge.

For tracks Line and Full Rotation, Rainbow also learns significantly faster than the other methods, most likely due to the design of the tracks themselves. Since they contain long straight sections for which many groups of state-space points have the same optimal policy.

5.2 Results for Tracks Without Bots and States Represented as Image

The next series of experiments was conducted using the image as the main feature. The architecture proposed in this paper [14] was used for image processing. The image is resized to 84×84 pixels, as the compression method used bilinear interpolation. The results shown in Fig. 3

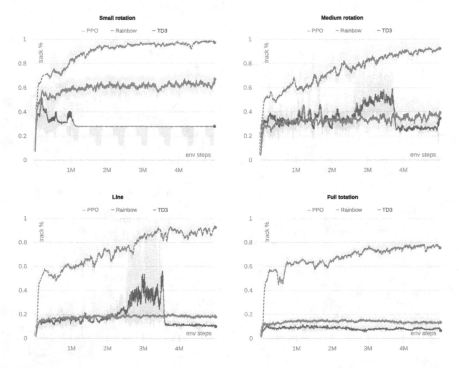

Fig. 3. The results of the experiments on the tracks without bots and image observations. The bold line shows the average for 10 runs of each algorithm, with a smoothing of 0.6. The transparent line shows the standard deviation.

As it can be observed from charts, it is more difficult for all methods to control the car using a pure image rather than a vector. We also faced the difficulty of configuring TD3 hyperparameters, as you can see in the first and last charts, this method gets stuck in suboptimal policies, namely, it starts to stand still or rotate on start point.

5.3 Influence of Different Sets of Vectors Features on the Convergence of the Algorithms

At this point, we investigated the effect of a set of vector features on the convergence of the algorithm. The key feature sets are shown in the Table 3.

As can be seen from the table, the results of the algorithms can differ greatly for the same sets of features. If on a Full rotation track PPO using only `hull_position` and `wheels_position` can only reach 20%, then Rainbow on both features reaches 60%, which corresponds to the end of the straight section before the turn itself. Adding an angle to both coordinate features – `hull_angle` greatly increases the performance (+17% for PPO and +30% for Rainbow). The combination of both coordinate attributes with an angle gives the best results for Rainbow and PPO.

You can also see that for PPO and Rainbow, the track sensor – `track_sensor` greatly increases the track % and the finish %. We believe that the sensor allows the agent to determine the closeness to the border of the route in advance. In contrast to the case when the agent distinguishes traveling outside the boundaries only by reward.

5.4   Results for Tracks with Bots

In this section, the environment state was represented as a combination of vector and image. Image processing was performed in a same way as in Sect. 5.2. To join image and vector we concatenate them along the channel dimension (copy of duplicated vector was used $h \times w$ times). So from image with shape $h \times w \times c$, and vector with shape v, we make observation matrix with shape $h \times w \times (c+v)$ shape.

The experimental results for the state of the environment consisting of the image and `hull_position`, `hull_angle` presented in Fig. 4. The best result was shown by the Rainbow algorithm, which learned to pass the intersection completely and without collisions. The PPO algorithm also converges, but much more slowly.

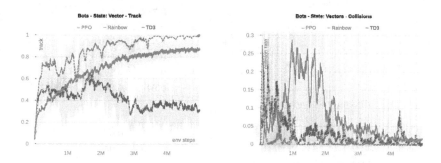

Fig. 4. Results of experiments on tracks with bots and vectors as the state of the environment. The percentage of the completed track, and the average number of collisions.

The experimental results for the state of the environment consisting of the image and `hull_position`, `hull_angle`, `car_radar_2`, `collide_sensor` presented in Fig. 5. In this case, TD3 and PPO algorithms learned to pass only a small part of the road.

Table 3. Key feature sets in increasing order by % track. Notation: T - time - time, V - car_speed, C_s - checkpoint_sensor, XY_w - wheels_position, T_s - track_sensor, F_s - finish_sensor, xy_h - hull_position, α - hull_angle; % track - the average percentage of the track passed by the agent by the end of training; % finish - the average number of episodes ended at finish point.

C_s	T_s	F_s	V	Img	T	α	XY_w	XY_h	% track	% finish
PPO on line track										
			+			+		+	0.074	0.000
				+					0.166	0.000
								+	0.228	0.000
+		+	+			+		+	0.675	0.578
+						+		+	0.949	0.900
					+	+		+	0.957	0.750
PPO on full rotation track										
				+					0.122	0.000
							+		0.188	0.000
						+		+	0.375	0.000
+		+	+			+		+	0.497	0.000
	+					+		+	0.524	0.000
						+	+		0.567	0.000
					+	+		+	0.663	0.000
						+	+	+	0.672	0.000
Rainbow on line track										
	+					+		+	0.916	0.950
				+					0.921	0.639
						+	+	+	0.942	0.750
Rainbow on full rotation track										
								+	0.600	0.000
							+		0.616	0.000
			+			+		+	0.712	0.000
+		+	+			+		+	0.770	0.115
						+	+		0.936	0.250
	+					+		+	0.936	0.550
						+	+	+	0.941	0.800
						+		+	0.947	0.300
TD3 on line track										
			+						0.117	0.000
+		+	+			+		+	0.217	0.083
+						+		+	0.939	0.950
TD3 on full rotation track										
+		+	+			+		+	0.063	0.000
				+					0.098	0.000
C_s	T_s	F_s	V	Img	T	α	XY_w	XY_h	% track	% finish

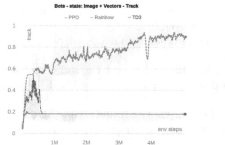
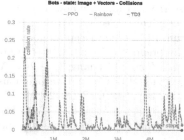

Fig. 5. Results of experiments on trajectories with bots and images as the state of the environment.

6 Conclusion

In this paper, we have described a developed environment, which allows to simulate driving through an intersection with realistic dynamics and the ability to train various reinforcement learning algorithms.

We have developed and described an effective learning method based on off-policy method Rainbow. We presented the results of a large series of experiments comparing our approach with other implementations that use a different combination of basic features used in describing the state.

Future plans of our research include improvements to the environment for simulating more complex interactions (priorilized roads, traffic lights, etc.). We also plan to integrate computer vision and reinforcement learning methods more closely to simulate the real environment in a more complete way.

Acknowledgements. The reported study was supported by RFBR, research Project No. 17-29-07079.

References

1. An, H., Jung, J.I.: Decision-making system for lane change using deep reinforcement learning in connected and automated driving. Electronics **8**, 543 (2019)
2. Bojarski, M., et al.: End to end learning for self-driving cars. arXiv preprint arXiv:1604.07316 (2016)
3. Brockman, G., et al.: Openai gym (2016). http://arxiv.org/abs/1606.01540, cite arxiv:1606.01540
4. Dosovitskiy, A., Ros, G., Codevilla, F., Lopez, A., Koltun, V.: CARLA: an open urban driving simulator. In: Proceedings of the 1st Annual Conference on Robot Learning, pp. 1–16 (2017)
5. Engstrom, L., et al.: Implementation matters in deep RL: A case study on PPO and TRPO. In: International Conference on Learning Representations (2019)
6. Fujimoto, S., van Hoof, H., Meger, D.: Addressing function approximation error in actor-critic methods. In: Proceedings of Machine Learning Research, vol. 80, pp. 1587–1596 (2018)

7. Hessel, M., et al.: Rainbow: combining improvements in deep reinforcement learning. In: Thirty-Second AAAI Conference on Artificial Intelligence (2018)
8. Kiran, B.R., et al.: Deep reinforcement learning for autonomous driving: a survey. arXiv preprint arXiv:2002.00444 (2020)
9. Li, D., Zhao, D., Zhang, Q., Chen, Y.: Reinforcement learning and deep learning based lateral control for autonomous driving [application notes]. IEEE Comput. Intell. Mag. **14**(2), 83–98 (2019)
10. Li, H., Wang, A.Y., Liu, Y., Tang, D., Lei, Z., Li, W.: An augmented transformer architecture for natural language generation tasks. arXiv preprint arXiv:1910.13634 (2019)
11. Lillicrap, T.P., et al.: Continuous control with deep reinforcement learning. CoRR abs/1509.02971 (2015)
12. Loiacono, D., Cardamone, L., Lanzi, P.L.: Simulated car racing championship: Competition software manual. CoRR abs/1304.1672 (2013). http://arxiv.org/abs/1304.1672
13. Lopez, P.A., et al.: Microscopic traffic simulation using sumo. In: The 21st IEEE International Conference on Intelligent Transportation Systems. IEEE (2018). https://elib.dlr.de/124092/
14. Mnih, V., et al.: Playing atari with deep reinforcement learning. arXiv preprint arXiv:1312.5602 (2013)
15. Mukadam, M., Cosgun, A., Nakhaei, A., Fujimura, K.: Tactical decision making for lane changing with deep reinforcement learning, December 2017
16. Oh, S.Y., Lee, J.H., Doo Hyun, C.: A new reinforcement learning vehicle control architecture for vision-based road following. IEEE Trans. Veh. Technol. **49**, 997–1005 (2000)
17. Schulman, J., Wolski, F., Dhariwal, P., Radford, A., Klimov, O.: Proximal policy optimization algorithms. CoRR abs/1707.06347 (2017). http://arxiv.org/abs/1707.06347
18. Shikunov, M., Panov, A.I.: Hierarchical reinforcement learning approach for the road intersection task. In: Samsonovich, A.V. (ed.) BICA 2019. AISC, vol. 948, pp. 495–506. Springer, Cham (2020). https://doi.org/10.1007/978-3-030-25719-4_64
19. Sutton, R.S., Barto, A.G., et al.: Introduction to Reinforcement Learning, vol. 135. MIT press Cambridge, Cambridge (1998)
20. Sutton, R.S., McAllester, D.A., Singh, S.P., Mansour, Y.: Policy gradient methods for reinforcement learning with function approximation. In: Solla, S.A., Leen, T.K., Müller, K. (eds.) Advances in Neural Information Processing Systems, vol. 12, pp. 1057–1063. MIT Press (2000). http://papers.nips.cc/paper/1713-policy-gradient-methods-for-reinforcement-learning-with-function-approximation.pdf
21. Wang, G., Hu, J., Li, Z., Li, L.: Cooperative lane changing via deep reinforcement learning. arXiv preprint arXiv:1906.08662 (2019)
22. Wang, P., Chan, C., de La Fortelle, A.: A reinforcement learning based approach for automated lane change maneuvers. CoRR abs/1804.07871 (2018). http://arxiv.org/abs/1804.07871
23. Yudin, D.A., Skrynnik, A., Krishtopik, A., Belkin, I., Panov, A.I.: Object detection with deep neural networks for reinforcement learning in the task of autonomous vehicles Path Planning at the Intersection. Opt. Memory Neural Netw. **28**(4), 283–295 (2019). https://doi.org/10.3103/S1060992X19040118

Logic-Based Multi-agent Path Finding with Continuous Movements and the Sum of Costs Objective

Pavel Surynek$^{(\boxtimes)}$ (iD)

Faculty of Information Technology, Czech Technical University in Prague,
Thákurova 9, 160 00 Praha 6, Czechia
`pavel.surynek@fit.cvut.cz`

Abstract. Multi-agent path finding with continuous movements and time (denoted MAPF$^{\mathcal{R}}$) is addressed. The task is to navigate agents that move smoothly between predefined positions to their individual goals so that they do not collide. Recently a novel solving approach for obtaining makespan optimal solutions called SMT-CBS$^{\mathcal{R}}$ based on *satisfiability modulo theories* (SMT) has been introduced. We extend the approach further towards the sum-of-costs objective which is a more challenging case in the yes/no SMT environment due to more complex calculation of the objective. The new algorithm combines collision resolution known from conflict-based search (CBS) with previous generation of incomplete propositional encodings on top of a novel scheme for selecting decision variables in a potentially uncountable search space. We experimentally compare SMT-CBS$^{\mathcal{R}}$ and previous CCBS algorithm for MAPF$^{\mathcal{R}}$.

Keywords: Path finding · Multiple agents · Robotic agents · Logic reasoning · Satisfiability modulo theory · Sum-of-costs optimality

1 Introduction

In *multi-agent path finding* (MAPF) [6, 15, 24–27, 30, 37] the task is to navigate agents from given starting positions to given individual goals. The problem takes place in undirected graph $G = (V, E)$ where agents from set $A = \{a_1, a_2, ..., a_k\}$ are placed in vertices with at most one agent per vertex. The navigation task can be then expressed formally as transforming an initial configuration of agents $\alpha_0 : A \to V$ to a goal configuration $\alpha_+ : A \to V$ using instantaneous movements across edges assuming no collision occurs.

To reflect various aspects of real-life applications, variants of MAPF have been introduced such as those considering *kinematic constraints* [9], *large agents* [17], *generalized costs* of actions [36], or *deadlines* [19] - see [18,28] for more variants. Particularly in this work we are dealing with an extension of MAPF introduced only recently [1,33] that considers continuous movements and time (MAPF$^{\mathcal{R}}$). Agents move smoothly along predefined curves interconnecting predefined positions placed arbitrarily in some continuous space. It is natural in MAPF$^{\mathcal{R}}$ to assume geometric agents of various shapes that occupy certain volume in the space - circles in the 2D space, polygons, spheres in the 3D space etc. In contrast to MAPF, where the collision is defined as

© Springer Nature Switzerland AG 2020
S. O. Kuznetsov et al. (Eds.): RCAI 2020, LNAI 12412, pp. 85–99, 2020.
https://doi.org/10.1007/978-3-030-59535-7_7

the simultaneous occupation of a vertex or an edge by two agents, collisions are defined as any spatial overlap of agents' bodies in MAPF$^\mathcal{R}$.

The motivation behind introducing MAPF$^\mathcal{R}$ is the need to construct more realistic paths in many applications such as controlling fleets of robots or aerial drones [7, 10] where continuous reasoning is closer to the reality than the standard MAPF.

The contribution of this paper consists in generalizing the previous makespan optimal approach for MAPF$^\mathcal{R}$ [31, 33] that uses satisfiability modulo theory (SMT) reasoning [5, 20] for the sum-of-costs objective. The SMT paradigm constructs decision procedures for various complex logic theories by decomposing the decision problem into the propositional part having arbitrary Boolean structure and the complex theory part that is restricted on the conjunctive fragment. Our SMT-based algorithm called SMT-CBS$^\mathcal{R}$ combines the Conflict-based Search (CBS) algorithm [8, 25] with previous algorithms for solving the standard MAPF using incomplete encodings [32] and continuous reasoning.

1.1 Previous Work

Using reductions of planning problems to propositional satisfiability has been coined in the SATPlan algorithm and its variants [11–14]. Here we are trying to apply similar idea in the context of MAPF$^\mathcal{R}$. So far MAPF$^\mathcal{R}$ has been solved by a modified version of CBS that tries to solve MAPF lazily by adding collision avoidance constraints on demand. The adaptation of CBS for MAPF$^\mathcal{R}$ consists in implementing continuous collision detection while the high-level framework of the algorithm remains the same as demonstrated in the CCBS algorithm [1].

We follow the idea of CBS too but instead of searching the tree of possible collision eliminations at the high-level we encode the requirement of having collision free paths as a propositional formula [4] and leave it to the SAT solver as done in [34]. We construct the formula *lazily* by adding collision elimination refinements following [32] where the lazy construction of incomplete encodings has been suggested for the standard MAPF within the algorithm called SMT-CBS. SMT-CBS works with propositional variables indexed by *agent a*, *vertex v*, and *time step t* with the meaning that if the variable is *TRUE a* in *v* at time step *t*. In MAPF$^\mathcal{R}$ we however face major technical difficulty that we do not know necessary decision (propositional) variables in advance and due to continuous time we cannot enumerate them all. Hence we need to select from a potentially uncountable space those variables that are sufficient for finding the solution.

The previous application of SMT in MAPF$^\mathcal{R}$ [33] focused on the makespan optimal solutions where the shortest duration of the plan is required. The **sum-of-costs** is another important objective used in the context of MAPF [26, 36]. Calculated as the summation over all agents of times they spend moving before arriving to the goal. Due to its more complex calculation, the sum-of-costs objective is more challenging to be integrated in the SMT-based solving framework.

1.2 MAPF with Continuous Movements and Time

We use the definition of MAPF with continuous movements and time denoted $\text{MAPF}^{\mathcal{R}}$ from [1]. $\text{MAPF}^{\mathcal{R}}$ shares components with the standard MAPF: undirected graph $G = (V,E)$, set of agents $A = \{a_1, a_2, ..., a_k\}$, and the initial and goal configuration of agents: $\alpha_0 : A \to V$ and $\alpha_+ : A \to V$. A simple 2D variant of $\text{MAPF}^{\mathcal{R}}$ is as follows:

Definition 1. *($\text{MAPF}^{\mathcal{R}}$) Multi-agent path finding with continuous time and space is a 5-tuple $\Sigma^{\mathcal{R}} = (G = (V,E), A, \alpha_0, \alpha_+, \rho)$ where G, A, α_0, α_+ are from the standard MAPF and ρ determines continuous extensions:*

- *$\rho.x(v), \rho.y(v)$ for $v \in V$ represent the position of vertex v in the 2D plane*
- *$\rho.speed(a)$ for $a \in A$ determines constant speed of agent a*
- *$\rho.radius(a)$ for $a \in A$ determines the radius of agent a; we assume that agents are circular discs with omni-directional ability of movements*

For simplicity we assume circular agents with constant speed and instant acceleration. The major difference from the standard MAPF where agents move instantly between vertices (disappears in the source and appears in the target instantly) is that smooth continuous movement between a pair of vertices (positions) along the straight line interconnecting them takes place in $\text{MAPF}^{\mathcal{R}}$. Hence we need to be aware of the presence of agents at some point in the 2D plane at any time.

Collisions may occur between agents in $\text{MAPF}^{\mathcal{R}}$ due to their volume; that is, they collide whenever their bodies **overlap**. In contrast to MAPF, collisions in $\text{MAPF}^{\mathcal{R}}$ may occur not only in a single vertex or edge being shared by colliding agents but also on pairs of edges (lines interconnecting vertices) that are too close to each other and simultaneously traversed by large agents.

We can further extend the continuous properties by introducing the direction of agents and the need to rotate agents towards the target vertex before they start to move. Also agents can be of various shapes not only circular discs [17] and can move along various fixed curves. For simplicity we elaborate our implementations for the above simple 2D continuous extension with circular agents. We however note that all developed concepts can be adapted for MAPF with more continuous extensions.

A solution to given $\text{MAPF}^{\mathcal{R}}$ $\Sigma^{\mathcal{R}}$ is a collection of temporal plans for individual agents $\pi = [\pi(a_1), \pi(a_2), ..., \pi(a_k)]$ that are **mutually collision-free**. A temporal plan for agent $a \in A$ is a sequence $\pi(a) = [((\alpha_0(a), \alpha_1(a)), [t_0(a), t_1(a))); ((\alpha_1(a), \alpha_2(a)), [t_1(a), t_2(a))); ...; ((\alpha_{m(a)-1}(a), \alpha_{m(a)}(a)), [t_{m(a)-1}(a), t_{m(a)}(a)))]$ where re $m(a)$ is the length of individual temporal plan and $t_{m(a)}$ is its duration. Each pair $(\alpha_i(a), \alpha_{i+1}(a))$, $[t_i(a), t_{i+1}(a)))$ corresponds to traversal event between a pair of vertices $\alpha_i(a)$ and $\alpha_{i+1}(a)$ starting at time $t_i(a)$ and finished at $t_{i+1}(a)$.

It holds that $t_i(a) < t_{i+1}(a)$ for $i = 0, 1, ..., m(a) - 1$. Moreover consecutive events in the individual temporal plan must correspond to edge traversals or waiting actions, that is: $\{\alpha_i(a), \alpha_{i+1}(a)\} \in E$ or $\alpha_i(a) = \alpha_{i+1}(a)$; and times must reflect the speed of agents for non-wait actions.

The duration of individual temporal plan $\pi(a)$ is called an *individual makespan*; denoted $\mu(\pi(a)) = t_{m(a)}$. The overall *makespan* of π is defined as $\max_{i=1}^{k}\{\mu(\pi(a_i))\}$. The individual makespan is sometimes called an *individual cost*. A *sum-of-cost* for

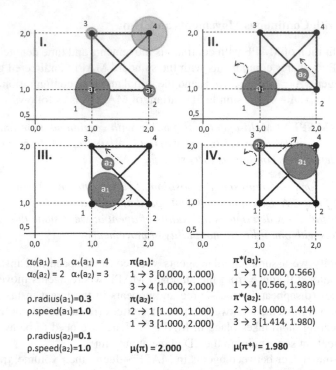

$\alpha_0(a_1) = 1$ $\alpha_+(a_1) = 4$ $\pi(a_1)$:

$\alpha_0(a_2) = 2$ $\alpha_+(a_2) = 3$ $1 \to 3$ [0.000, 1.000)

                                 $3 \to 4$ [1.000, 2.000)

p.radius(a_1)=0.3 $\pi(a_2)$:

p.speed(a_1)=1.0 $2 \to 1$ [1.000, 1.000)

                                 $1 \to 3$ [1.000, 2.000)

p.radius(a_2)=0.1

p.speed(a_2)=1.0 $\mu(\pi) = 2.000$

$\pi^*(a_1)$:

$1 \to 1$ [0.000, 0.566)

$1 \to 4$ [0.566, 1.980)

$\pi^*(a_2)$:

$2 \to 3$ [0.000, 1.414)

$3 \to 3$ [1.414, 1.980)

$\mu(\pi^*) = 1.980$

Fig. 1. An example of MAPF$^{\mathcal{R}}$ instance with two agents. A feasible makespan/sum-of-costs sub-optimal solution π (makespan $\mu(\pi) = 2.0$) and makespan/sum-of-costs optimal solution $\pi*$ (makespan $\mu(\pi*) = 1.980$) are shown.

given temporal plan $\pi(a)$ is defined as $\sum_{i=1}^{k} \mu(\pi(a_i))$ An example of MAPF$^{\mathcal{R}}$ and makespan/sum-of-costs optimal solution is shown in Fig. 1.

Through straightforward reduction of MAPF to MAPF$^{\mathcal{R}}$ it can be observed that finding a makespan or sum-of-costs optimal solution with continuous time is an NP-hard problem [22,38].

2   Solving MAPF with Continuous Time

Let us recall CCBS [1], a variant of CBS [25] modified for MAPF$^{\mathcal{R}}$. The idea of CBS algorithms is to resolve conflicts lazily.

2.1   Conflict-Based Search

CCBS for finding the sum-of-costs optimal solution is shown in Algorithm 1. The high-level of CCBS searches a *constraint tree* (CT) using a priority queue ordered according to the sum-of-costs in the breadth first manner. CT is a binary tree where each node N contains a set of collision avoidance constraints $N.cons$ - a set of triples $(a_i, (u, v), [\tau_0, \tau_+))$ forbidding agent a_i to start smooth traversal of edge $\{u, v\}$ (line) at any time between $[\tau_0, \tau_+)$, a solution $N.\pi$ - a set of k individual temporal plans, and the sum-of-costs $N.\xi$ of $N.\pi$.

Algorithm 1: CCBS algorithm for solving MAPF$^{\mathcal{R}}$ for the sum-of-costs objective.

---

1 **CBS$^{\mathcal{R}}$** $(\Sigma^{\mathcal{R}} = (G = (V,E), A, \alpha_0, \alpha_+, \rho))$
2 $\quad R.cons \leftarrow \emptyset$
3 $\quad R.\pi \leftarrow \{$shortest temporal plan from $\alpha_0(a_i)$ to $\alpha_+(a_i) \mid i = 1, 2, ..., k\}$
4 $\quad R.\xi \leftarrow \sum_{i=1}^{k} \mu(N.\pi(a_i))$
5 $\quad$ OPEN $\leftarrow \emptyset$
6 $\quad$ insert R into OPEN
7 $\quad$ **while** OPEN $\neq \emptyset$ **do**
8 $\quad\quad$ $N \leftarrow \min_{\xi}($OPEN$)$
9 $\quad\quad$ remove-Min$_{\xi}($OPEN$)$
10 $\quad\quad$ *collisions* $\leftarrow$ validate-Plans$(N.\pi)$
11 $\quad\quad$ **if** *collisions* $= \emptyset$ **then**
12 $\quad\quad\quad$ **return** $N.\pi$
13 $\quad\quad$ **let** $(m_i \times m_j) \in$ *collisions* where $m_i = (a_i, (u_i, v_i), [t_i^0, t_i^+))$ and $m_j = (a_j, (u_j, v_j), [t_j^0, t_j^+))$
14 $\quad\quad$ $([\tau_i^0, \tau_i^+); [\tau_j^0, \tau_j^+)) \leftarrow$ resolve-Collision(m_i, m_j)
15 $\quad\quad$ **for** *each* $m \in \{(m_i, [\tau_i^0, \tau_i^+)), (m_j, [\tau_j^0, \tau_j^+))\}$ **do**
16 $\quad\quad\quad$ **let** $((a, (u, v), [t_0, t_+)), [\tau_0, \tau_+)) = m$
17 $\quad\quad\quad$ $N'.cons \leftarrow N.cons \cup \{(a, (u, v), [\tau_0, \tau_+))\}$
18 $\quad\quad\quad$ $N'.\pi \leftarrow N.\pi$
19 $\quad\quad\quad$ update$(a, N'.\pi, N'.cons)$
20 $\quad\quad\quad$ $N'.\xi \leftarrow \sum_{i=1}^{k} \mu(N'.\pi(a_i))$
21 $\quad\quad\quad$ insert N' into OPEN

The low-level in CCBS associated with node N searches for individual temporal plan with respect to set of constraints $N.cons$. For given agent a_i, this is the standard single source shortest path search from $\alpha_0(a_i)$ to $\alpha_+(a_i)$ that at time t cannot start to traverse any $\{(u, v) \in E \mid (a_i, (u, v), [\tau_0, \tau_+)) \in N.cons \wedge t \in [\tau_0, \tau_+)\}$. Various intelligent single source shortest path algorithms such as SIPP [21] can be used here.

CCBS stores nodes of CT into priority queue OPEN sorted according to the ascending sum-of-costs. At each step CBS takes node N with the lowest makespan from OPEN and checks if $N.\pi$ represents non-colliding temporal plans. If there is no collision, the algorithms returns valid solution $N.\pi$. Otherwise the search branches by creating a new pair of nodes in CT - successors of N. Assume that a collision occurred between a_i traversing (u_i, v_i) during $[t_i^0, t_i^+)$ and a_j traversing (u_j, v_j) during $[t_j^0, t_j^+)$. This collision can be avoided if either agent a_i or agent a_j waits after the other agent passes. We can calculate for a_i so called maximum *unsafe interval* $[\tau_i^0, \tau_i^+)$ such that whenever a_i starts to traverse (u_i, v_i) at some time $t \in [\tau_i^0, \tau_i^+)$ it ends up colliding with a_j assuming a_j did not try to avoid the collision. Hence a_i should wait until τ_i^+ to tightly avoid the collision with a_j. Similarly we can calculate maximum unsafe interval for a_j: $[\tau_j^0, \tau_j^+)$. These two options correspond to new successor nodes of N: N_1 and N_2 that inherit set of constraints from N as follows: $N_1.cons = N.cons \cup \{(a_i, (u_i, v_i), [\tau_i^0, \tau_i^+))\}$ and $N_2.cons = N.cons \cup \{(a_j, (u_j, v_j), [\tau_j^0, \tau_j^+))\}$. $N_1.\pi$ and $N_1.\pi$ inherits plans from $N.\pi$ except those for agents a_i and a_j respectively that are recalculated with respect to the constraints. After this N_1 and N_2 are inserted into OPEN.

2.2 A Satisfiability Modulo Theory Approach

A recent algorithm called SMT-CBS$^{\mathcal{R}}$ [33] rephrases CCBS as problem solving in *satisfiability modulo theories* (SMT) [5,35]. The basic use of SMT divides the satis-fiability problem in some complex theory T into a propositional part that keeps the Boolean structure of the problem and a simplified procedure $DECIDE_T$ that decides fragment of T restricted on *conjunctive formulae*. A general T-formula Γ being decided for satisfiability is transformed to a *propositional skeleton* by replacing its atoms with propositional variables. The standard SAT solver then decides what variables should be assigned *TRUE* in order to satisfy the skeleton - these variables tells what atoms hold in Γ. $DECIDE_T$ then checks if the conjunction of atoms assigned *TRUE* is valid with respect to axioms of T. If so then satisfying assignment is returned. Otherwise a conflict from $DECIDE_T$ (often called a *lemma*) is reported back to the SAT solver and the skeleton is extended with new constraints resolving the conflict. More generally not only new constraints are added to resolve the conflict but also new atoms can be added to Γ.

T will be represented by a theory with axioms describing movement rules of MAPF$^{\mathcal{R}}$; a theory we will denote $T_{MAPF^{\mathcal{R}}}$. $DECIDE_{MAPF^{\mathcal{R}}}$ can be naturally represented by the plan validation procedure from CCBS (validate-Plans).

2.3 RDD: Real Decision Diagram

The key question in the propositional logic-based approach is what will be the decision variables. In the standard MAPF, time expansion of G for every time step can be done resulting in a multi-value decision diagram (MDD) [34] representing possible positions of agents at any time step. Since MAPF$^{\mathcal{R}}$ is no longer discrete we cannot afford to use a decision variable for every time moment. We show how to restrict the decision variables on finitely many important moments only without compromising soundness nor optimality of the approach.

Analogously to MDD, we introduce *real decision diagram* (RDD). RDD$_i$ defines for agent a_i its space-time positions and possible movements. Formally, RDD_i is a directed graph (X^i, E^i) where X_i consists of pairs (u, t) with $u \in V$ and $t \in \mathbb{R}_0^+$ is time and E_i consists of directed edges of the form $((u, t_u); (v, t_v))$. Edge $((u, t_u); (v, t_v))$ correspond to agent's movement from u to v started at t_u and finished at t_v. Waiting in u is possible by introducing edge $((u, t_u); (u, t_u'))$. Pair $(\alpha_0(a_i), 0) \in X_i$ indicates start and $(\alpha_+(a_i), t)$ for some t corresponds to reaching the goal position.

RDDs for individual agents are constructed with respect to collision avoidance con-straints. If there is no collision avoidance constraint then RDD$_i$ simply corresponds to a shortest temporal plan for agent a_i. But if a collision avoidance constraint is present, say $(a_i, (u,v), [\tau_0, \tau_+))$, and we are considering movement starting in u at t that interferes with the constraint, then we need to generate a node into RDD_i that allows agent to wait until the unsafe interval passes by, that is node (u, τ^+) and edge $((u, \tau^0); (u, \tau^+))$ are added.

Similarly for wait constraints $(a_i, (u,u), [\tau_0, \tau_+))$ that forbid waiting in u during $[\tau_0, \tau_+)$. In such a case, we need to anticipate the constraint before entering u, that is we can wait until $\tau_+ - t_x$ in the source vertex before entering u where t_x is the time needed to traverse the edge towards u.

The process of building RDDs is described in details in [33]. An example of RDDs is shown in Fig. 2.

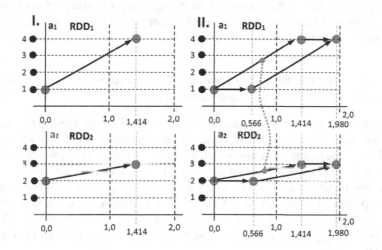

Fig. 2. Real decision diagrams (RDDs) for agents a_1 and a_2 from MAPF$^{\mathcal{R}}$ from Fig. 1. Decisions corresponding to shortest paths for agents a_1 and a_2 moving diagonally towards their goals are shown: $a_1 : 1 \rightarrow 4$, $a_2 : 2 \rightarrow 3$ (left). This however results in a collision whose resolution is either waiting for agent a_1 in vertex 1 from 0.000 until 0.566 or waiting for agent a_2 in vertex 2 from 0.000 until 0.566; reflected in the next RDDs (right). Mutex is depicted using dotted line connecting arcs form RDD_1 and RDD_2.

2.4   SAT Encoding from RDD

We introduce a decision variable for each node and edge $[RDD_1, ..., RDD_k]$; $RDD_i = (X^i, E^i)$: we have variable $\mathcal{X}_u^t(a_i)$ for each $(u,t) \in X^i$ and $\mathcal{E}_{u,v}^{t_u,t_v}(a_i)$ for each directed edge $((u,t_u); (v,t_v)) \in E^i$. The meaning of variables is that $\mathcal{X}_u^t(a_i)$ is *TRUE* if and only if agent a_i appears in u at time t and similarly for edges: $\mathcal{E}_{u,v}^{t_u,t_v}(a_i)$ is *TRUE* if and only if a_i moves from u to v starting at time t_u and finishing at t_v.

MAPF$^{\mathcal{R}}$ rules are encoded on top of these variables so that eventually we want to obtain formula $\mathcal{F}(\mu)$ that encodes existence of a solution of makespan μ to given MAPF$^{\mathcal{R}}$. We need to encode that agents do not skip but move along edges, do not disappear or appear from nowhere etc. We show below constraints stating that if agent a_i appears in vertex u at time step t_u then it has to leave through exactly one edge connected to u (constraint (2) although Pseudo-Boolean can be encoded using purely propositional means):

$$\mathcal{X}_u^{t_u}(a_i) \Rightarrow \bigvee_{(v,t_v) \mid ((u,t_u),(v,t_v)) \in E^i} \mathcal{E}_{u,v}^{t_u,t_v}(a_i), \tag{1}$$

$$\sum_{(v,t_v) \mid ((u,t_u),(v,t_v)) \in E^i} \mathcal{E}_{u,v}^{t_u,t_v}(a_i) \le 1 \tag{2}$$

$$\mathcal{E}_{u,v}^{t_u,t_v}(a_i) \Rightarrow \mathcal{X}_v^{t_v}(a_i) \tag{3}$$

Analogously to (2) we have constraint allowing a vertex to accept at most one agent through incoming edges; plus we need to enforce agents starting in α_0 and finishing in α_+. Let us summarize soundness of the encoding in the following proposition (proof omitted).

Proposition 1. *Any satisfying assignment of $\mathcal{F}(\mu)$ correspond to valid individual temporal plans for $\Sigma^{\mathcal{R}}$ whose makespans are at most μ.*

We a-priori do not add constraints for eliminating collisions; these are added lazily after assignment/solution validation. Hence, $\mathcal{F}(\mu)$ constitutes an *incomplete model* for $\Sigma^{\mathcal{R}}$: $\Sigma^{\mathcal{R}}$ is solvable within makespan μ then $\mathcal{F}(\mu)$ is satisfiable. The opposite implication does not hold since satisfying assignment of $\mathcal{F}(\mu)$ may lead to a collision.

From the perspective of SMT, the propositional level does not understand geometric properties of agents so cannot know what simultaneous variable assignments are invalid. This information is only available at the level of theory $T = \text{MAPF}^{\mathcal{R}}$ through $DECIDE_{MAPF^{\mathcal{R}}}$. We also leave the bounding of the sum-of-costs at the level of $DECIDE_{MAPF^{\mathcal{R}}}$.

2.5 Lazy Encoding of Mutex Refinements and Sum-of-Costs Bounds

The SMT-based algorithm itself is divided into two procedures: SMT-CBS$^{\mathcal{R}}$ representing the main loop (Algorithm 2) and SMT-CBS-Fixed$^{\mathcal{R}}$ solving the input MAPF$^{\mathcal{R}}$ for a fixed maximum makespan μ and sum-of-costs ξ (Algorithm 3).

Procedures *encode-Basic* and *augment-Basic* in Algorithm 3 build formula $\mathcal{F}(\mu)$ according to given RDDs and the set of collected collision avoidance constraints. New collisions are resolved **lazily** by adding *mutexes* (disjunctive constraints). A collision is avoided in the same way as in CCBS; that is, one of the colliding agent waits. Collision eliminations are tried until a valid solution is obtained or until a failure for current μ and ξ which means to try bigger makespan and sum-of-costs.

For resolving a collision we need to: **(1)** eliminate simultaneous execution of colliding movements and **(2)** augment the formula to enable avoidance (waiting). Assume a collision between agents a_i traversing (u_i, v_i) during $[t_i^0, t_i^+)$ and a_j traversing (u_j, v_j) during $[t_j^0, t_j^+)$ which corresponds to variables $\mathcal{E}_{u_i,v_i}^{t_i^0,t_i^+}(a_i)$ and $\mathcal{E}_{u_j,v_j}^{t_j^0,t_j^+}(a_j)$. The collision can be eliminated by adding the following **mutex** (disjunction) to the formula:

$\neg \mathcal{E}_{u_i,v_i}^{t_i^0,t_i^+}(a_i) \vee \neg \mathcal{E}_{u_j,v_j}^{t_j^0,t_j^+}(a_j)$. Satisfying assignments of the next $\mathcal{F}(\mu)$ can no longer lead to this collision. Next, the formula is augmented according to new RDDs that reflect the collision - decision variables and respective constraints are added.

After resolving all collisions we check whether the sum-of-costs bound is satisfied by plan π. This can be done easily by checking if $\mathcal{X}_u^t(a_i)$ variables across all agents together yield higher cost than ξ or not. If cost bound ξ is exceeded then corresponding *nogood* is recorded and added to $\mathcal{F}(\mu)$ and the algorithm continues by searching for a new satisfying assignment to $\mathcal{F}(\mu)$ now taking all recorded *nogoods* into account. The nogood says that $\mathcal{X}_u^t(a_i)$ variables that jointly exceed ξ cannot be simultaneously set to *TRUE*.

Formally, the nogood constraint can be represented as a set of variables $\{\mathcal{X}_{u_1}^{t_1}(a_1), \mathcal{X}_{u_2}^{t_2}(a_2), ... \mathcal{X}_{u_k}^{t_k}(a_k)\}$. We say the nogood to be *dominated* by another nogood $\{\mathcal{X}_{u_1}^{t_1'}(a_1), \mathcal{X}_{u_2}^{t_2'}(a_2), ... \mathcal{X}_{u_k}^{t_k'}(a_k)\}$ if and only if $t_i' \leq t_i$ for $i = 1, 2, ... k$ and $\exists i \in \{1, 2, ..., k\}$ such that $t_i' < t_i$. To make the nogood reasoning more efficient we do not need to store nogoods that are dominated by some previously discovered nogood. In such case however, the single nogood does not forbid one particular assignment but all assignments that could lead to dominated nogoods.

Algorithm 2: High-level of SMT-CBS$^{\mathcal{R}}$ for the sum-of-costs objective.

1 **SMT-CBS$^{\mathcal{R}}$** $(\Sigma^{\mathcal{R}} = (G = (V,E), A, \alpha_0, \alpha_+, \rho))$
2   *constraints* $\leftarrow \emptyset$
3      $\pi \leftarrow \{\pi^*(a_i)$ a shortest temporal plan from $\alpha_0(a_i)$ to $\alpha_+(a_i) \mid i = 1, 2, ..., k\}$
4      $\mu \leftarrow \max_{i=1}^k \mu(\pi(a_i))$; $\xi \leftarrow \Sigma_{i=1}^k \mu(\pi(a_i))$
5   **while** *TRUE* **do**
6        $(\pi, constraints, \mu_{next}, \xi_{next}) \leftarrow$ SMT-CBS-Fixed$^{\mathcal{R}}(\Sigma^{\mathcal{R}}, constraints, \mu, \xi)$
7   **if** $\pi \neq UNSAT$ **then**
8          $\lfloor$ **return** π
9        $\mu \leftarrow \mu_{next}$; $\xi \leftarrow \xi_{next}$

The set of pairs of collision avoidance constraints is propagated across entire execution of the algorithm. Constraints originating from a single collision are grouped in pairs so that it is possible to introduce mutexes for colliding movements discovered in previous steps.

Algorithm 2 shows the main loop of SMT-CBS$^{\mathcal{R}}$. The algorithm checks if there is a solution for $\Sigma^{\mathcal{R}}$ of makespan μ and sum-of-costs ξ. It starts at the lower bound for μ and ξ obtained as the duration of the longest from shortest individual temporal plans ignoring other agents and the sum of these lengths respectively.

Then μ and ξ are iteratively increased in the main loop following the style of SATPlan [14]. The algorithm relies on the fact that the solvability of MAPF$^{\mathcal{R}}$ w.r.t. cumulative objective like the sum-of-costs or makespan behaves as a non decreasing function. Hence trying increasing makespan and sum-of-costs eventually leads to finding the optimum provided we do not skip any relevant value.

We need to ensure important property in the makespan/sum-of-costs increasing scheme: any solution of sum-of-costs ξ has the makespan of at most μ. The next sum-of-costs to try is be obtained by taking the current sum-of-costs plus the smallest duration of the continuing movement (lines 17–27 of Algorithm 3).

The following proposition is a direct consequence of soundness of CCBS and soundness of the encoding (Proposition 1) and soundness of the makespan/sum-of-costs increasing scheme (proof omitted).

Proposition 2. *The SMT-CBS$^{\mathcal{R}}$ algorithm returns sum-of-costs optimal solution for any solvable MAPF$^{\mathcal{R}}$ instance $\Sigma^{\mathcal{R}}$.*

Algorithm 3: Low-level of SMT-CBS$^{\mathcal{R}}$

---

1 **SMT-CBS-Fixed**$^{\mathcal{R}}(\Sigma^{\mathcal{R}}, cons, \mu, \xi)$

2 $\quad$ RDD $\leftarrow$ build-RDDs($\Sigma^{\mathcal{R}}, cons, \mu$)

3 $\quad$ $\mathcal{F}(\mu) \leftarrow$ encode-Basic(RDD, $\Sigma^{\mathcal{R}}, cons, \mu$)

4 $\quad$ **while** *TRUE* **do**

5 $\quad\quad$ $assignment \leftarrow$ consult-SAT-Solver($\mathcal{F}(\mu)$)

6 $\quad\quad$ **if** $assignment \neq UNSAT$ **then**

7 $\quad\quad\quad$ $\pi \leftarrow$ extract-Solution($assignment$)

8 $\quad\quad\quad$ $collisions \leftarrow$ validate-Plans(π)

9 $\quad\quad\quad$ **if** $collisions = \emptyset$ **then**

10 $\quad\quad\quad\quad$ **while** *TRUE* **do**

11 $\quad\quad\quad\quad\quad$ $nogoods \leftarrow$ validate-Cost(π, ξ)

12 $\quad\quad\quad\quad\quad$ **if** $nogoods = \emptyset$ **then**

13 $\quad\quad\quad\quad\quad\quad$ **return** $(\pi, \emptyset, UNDEF, UNDEF)$

14 $\quad\quad\quad\quad\quad$ $\mathcal{F}(\mu) \leftarrow \mathcal{F}(\mu) \cup nogoods$

15 $\quad\quad\quad\quad\quad$ $assignment \leftarrow$ consult-SAT-Solver($\mathcal{F}(\mu)$)

16 $\quad\quad\quad\quad\quad$ **if** $assignment = UNSAT$ **then**

17 $\quad\quad\quad\quad\quad\quad$ $(\mu_{next}, \xi_{next}) \leftarrow$ calc-Next-Bounds($\mu, \xi, cons$, RDD)

18 $\quad\quad\quad\quad\quad\quad$ **return** $(UNSAT, cons, \mu_{next}, \xi_{next})$

19 $\quad\quad\quad\quad\quad$ $\pi \leftarrow$ extract-Solution($assignment$)

20 $\quad\quad\quad$ **else**

21 $\quad\quad\quad\quad$ **for** *each* $(m_i \times m_j) \in collisions$ *where* $m_i = (a_i, (u_i, v_i), [t_i^0, t_i^+))$ *and* $m_j = (a_j, (u_j, v_j), [t_j^0, t_j^+))$ **do**

22 $\quad\quad\quad\quad\quad$ $\mathcal{F}(\mu) \leftarrow \mathcal{F}(\mu) \wedge (\neg \mathcal{E}_{u_i, v_i}^{t_i^0, t_i^+}(a_i) \vee \neg \mathcal{E}_{u_j, v_j}^{t_j^0, t_j^+}(a_j))$

23 $\quad\quad\quad\quad\quad$ $([\tau_i^0, \tau_i^+); [\tau_j^0, \tau_j^+)) \leftarrow$ resolve-Collision(m_i, m_j)

24 $\quad\quad\quad\quad\quad$ $cons \leftarrow cons \cup \{[(a_i, (u_i, v_i), [\tau_i^0, \tau_i^+)); (a_j, (u_j, v_j), [\tau_j^0, \tau_j^+))]\}$

25 $\quad\quad\quad$ RDD $\leftarrow$ build-RDDs($\Sigma^{\mathcal{R}}, cons, \mu$)

26 $\quad\quad\quad$ $\mathcal{F}(\mu) \leftarrow$ augment-Basic(RDD, $\Sigma^{\mathcal{R}}, cons$)

27 $\quad$ $(\mu_{next}, \xi_{next}) \leftarrow$ calc-Next-Bounds($\mu, \xi, cons$, RDD)

28 $\quad$ **return** $(UNSAT, cons, \mu_{next}, \xi_{next})$

---

3   Experimental Evaluation

We implemented SMT-CBS$^{\mathcal{R}}$ in C++ to evaluate its performance and compared it with CCBS [1].

SMT-CBS$^{\mathcal{R}}$ was implemented on top of Glucose 4 SAT solver [2] which ranks among the best SAT solvers according to recent SAT solver competitions [3]. The solver is consulted in the incremental mode if the formula is extended with new clauses. In case of CCBS, we used the existing C++ implementation [1].

3.1   Benchmarks and Setup

SMT-CBS$^{\mathcal{R}}$ and CCBS were tested on benchmarks from the movinai.com collection [29]. We tested algorithms on three categories of benchmarks:

 (i) **small** empty grids (presented representative benchmark empty-16-16),
 (ii) **medium** sized grids with regular obstacles (presented maze-32-32-4),
 (iii) **large** game maps (presented ost003d, a map from Dragon Age game).

In each benchmark, we interconnected cells using the 2^K-neighborhood [23] for $K = 3, 4, 5$ - the same style of generating benchmarks as used in [1] ($K = 2$ corresponds to MAPF hence not omitted). Instances consisting of k agents were generated by taking first k agents from random scenario files accompanying each benchmark on movinai.com. Having 25 scenarios for each benchmarks this yields to 25 instances per number of agents.

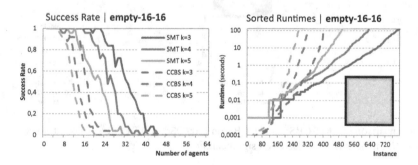

Fig. 3. Comparison of SMT-CBS$^{\mathcal{R}}$ and CCBS on empty-16-16. **Left:** Success rate (the ratio of solved instances out of 25 under 120 s), the higher plot is better. **Right:** and sorted runtimes where the lower plot is better are shown.

Part of the results obtained in our experimentation is presented in this section[2]. For each presented benchmark we show *success rate* as a function of the number of

---

[1] To enable reproducibility of presented results we will provide complete source code of our solvers on the author's website: http://users.fit.cvut.cz/surynpav/research/rcai2020.

[2] All experiments were run on a system with Ryzen 7 3.0 GHz, 16 GB RAM, under Ubuntu Linux 18.

agents. That is, we calculate the ratio out of 25 instances per number of agents where the tested algorithm finished under the timeout of 120 s. In addition to this, we also show concrete runtimes sorted in the ascending order. Results for one selected representative benchmark from each category are shown in Figs. 3, 4, and 5.

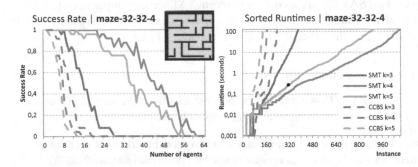

Fig. 4. Comparison of SMT-CBS$^{\mathcal{R}}$ and CCBS on maze-32-32-4. Surprisingly the best performance with SMT-CBS$^{\mathcal{R}}$ highly connected neighborhoods ($K = 4, 5$ is easier than $K = 3$).

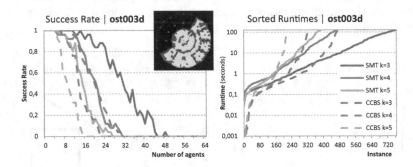

Fig. 5. Comparison of SMT-CBS$^{\mathcal{R}}$ and CCBS on ost003d. SMT-CBS$^{\mathcal{R}}$ is fastest for $K = 3$ but for higher K the performance decreases significantly.

The observable trend is that the difficulty of the problem increases with increasing size of the $K-$neighborhood with notable exception of maze-32-32-4 for $K = 4$ and $K = 5$ which turned out to be easier than $K = 3$ for SMT-CBS$^{\mathcal{R}}$.

Throughout all benchmarks SMT-CBS$^{\mathcal{R}}$ tends to outperform CCBS. The dominance of SMT-CBS$^{\mathcal{R}}$ is most visible in medium sized benchmarks. CCBS is, on the other hand, faster in instances containing few agents. The gap between SMT-CBS$^{\mathcal{R}}$ and CCBS is smallest in large maps where SMT-CBS$^{\mathcal{R}}$ struggles with relatively big overhead caused by the big size of the map (the encoding is proportionally big). Here SMT-CBS$^{\mathcal{R}}$ wins only in hard cases.

4   Discussion and Conclusion

We extended the approach based on *satisfiability modulo theories* (SMT) for solving MAPF$^{\mathcal{R}}$ from the makespan objective towards the sum-of-costs objective. Our approach builds on the idea of treating constraints lazily as suggested in the CBS algorithm but instead of branching the search after encountering a conflict we refine the propositional model with the conflict elimination disjunctive constraint as it has been done in previous application of SMT in the standard MAPF. Bounding the sum-of-costs is done in similar lazy way through introducing nogoods incrementally. If it is detected that a conflict free solution exceeds given cost bound then decisions that jointly induce cost greater than given bound are forbidden via a nogood (that is, at least one of these decisions must not be taken).

We compared SMT-CBS$^{\mathcal{R}}$ with CCBS [1], currently the only alternative algorithm for MAPF$^{\mathcal{R}}$ that modifies the standard CBS algorithm, on a number of benchmarks. The outcome of our comparison is that SMT-CBS$^{\mathcal{R}}$ performs well against CCBS. The best results SMT-CBS$^{\mathcal{R}}$ are observable on medium sized benchmarks with regular obstacles. We attribute the better runtime results of SMT-CBS$^{\mathcal{R}}$ to more efficient handling of disjunctive conflicts in the underlying SAT solver through *propagation, clause learning,* and other mechanisms. On the other hand SMT-CBS$^{\mathcal{R}}$ is less efficient on large instances with few agents.

The important restriction which our concept rely on is that agents cannot move completely freely in the continuous space. We strongly assume that agents only move on the fixed embedding of finite graph $G = (V, E)$ into some continuous space where vertices are assigned points and edges are assigned curves on which the definition of smooth movement is possible. Hence for example using curves other than straight lines for interconnecting vertices does not change the high-level SMT-CBS$^{\mathcal{R}}$.

We plan to extend the RDD generation scheme to directional agents where we need to add the third dimension in addition to space (vertices) and time: *direction* (angle). The work on MAPF$^{\mathcal{R}}$ could be further developed into multi-robot motion planning in continuous configuration spaces [16].

Acknowledgements. This research has been supported by GAČR - the Czech Science Foundation, grant registration number 19-17966S. We would like to thank anonymous reviewers for their valuable comments.

References

1. Andreychuk, A., Yakovlev, K.S., Atzmon, D., Stern, R.: Multi-agent pathfinding with continuous time. In: Proceedings IJCAI 2019, pp. 39–45 (2019)
2. Audemard, G., Simon, L.: Predicting learnt clauses quality in modern SAT solvers. In: IJCAI, pp. 399–404 (2009)
3. Balyo, T., Heule, M.J.H., Järvisalo, M.: SAT competition 2016: recent developments. In: AAAI 2017, pp. 5061–5063 (2017)
4. Biere, A., Biere, A., Heule, M., van Maaren, H., Walsh, T.: Handbook of Satisfiability. IOS Press, Amsterdam (2009)
5. Bofill, M., Palahí, M., Suy, J., Villaret, M.: Solving constraint satisfaction problems with SAT modulo theories. Constraints **17**(3), 273–303 (2012)

6. Botea, A., Surynek, P.: Multi-agent path finding on strongly biconnected digraphs. In: AAAI, pp. 2024–2030 (2015)
7. Cáp, M., Novák, P., Vokrínek, J., Pechoucek, M.: Multi-agent RRT: sampling-based cooperative pathfinding. In: Proceedings AAMAS 2013, pp. 1263–1264 (2013)
8. Felner, A., Li, J., Boyarski, E., Ma, H., Cohen, Kumar, L., Satish Kumar, T.K., Koenig, S.: Adding heuristics to conflict-based search for multi-agent path finding. In: Proceedings of ICAPS 2018, pp. 83–87 (2018)
9. Hönig, W., et al.: Summary: multi-agent path finding with kinematic constraints. In: Proceedings IJCAI 2017, pp. 4869–4873 (2017)
10. Janovsky, P., Cáp, M., Vokrínek, J.: Finding coordinated paths for multiple holonomic agents in 2-d polygonal environment. In: Proceedings of AAMAS 2014, pp. 1117–1124 (2014)
11. Kautz, H.A.: Deconstructing planning as satisfiability. In: Proceedings, The Twenty-First National Conference on Artificial Intelligence and the Eighteenth Innovative Applications of Artificial Intelligence Conference, 2006, pp. 1524–1526. AAAI Press (2006)
12. Kautz, H.A., Selman, B.: Planning as satisfiability. In: Proceedings ECAI 1992, pp. 359–363 (1992)
13. Kautz, H.A., Selman, B.: Pushing the envelope: planning, propositional logic and stochastic search. In: Proceedings of AAAI 1996, pp. 1194–1201 (1996)
14. Kautz, H.A., Selman, B.: Unifying sat-based and graph-based planning. In: Proceedings of IJCAI 1999, pp. 318–325 (1999)
15. Kornhauser, D., Miller, G.L., Spirakis, P.G.: Coordinating pebble motion on graphs, the diameter of permutation groups, and applications. In: FOCS 1984, 241–250 (1984)
16. LaValle, S.M.: Planning Algorithms. Cambridge University Press, Cambridge (2006)
17. Li, J., Surynek, P., Felner, A., Ma, H., Koenig, S.: Multi-agent path finding for large agents. In: Proceedings of AAAI 2019. AAAI Press (2019)
18. Ma, H., et al.: Overview: generalizations of multi-agent path finding to real-world scenarios. CoRR abs/1702.05515 (2017), http://arxiv.org/abs/1702.05515
19. Ma, H., Wagner, G., Felner, A., Li, J., Kumar, T.K.S., Koenig, S.: Multi-agent path finding with deadlines. In: Proceedings of IJCAI 2018, pp. 417–423 (2018)
20. Nieuwenhuis, R.: SAT modulo theories: getting the best of SAT and global constraint filtering. In: Proceedings of CP 2010, pp. 1–2 (2010)
21. Phillips, M., Likhachev, M.: SIPP: safe interval path planning for dynamic environments. In: Proceedings of ICRA 2011, pp. 5628–5635 (2011)
22. Ratner, D., Warmuth, M.K.: NXN puzzle and related relocation problem. J. Symb. Comput. 10(2), 111–138 (1990)
23. Rivera, N., Hernández, C., Baier, J.A.: Grid pathfinding on the 2k neighborhoods. In: Proceedings of AAAI 2017, pp. 891–897 (2017)
24. Ryan, M.R.K.: Exploiting subgraph structure in multi-robot path planning. J. Artif. Intell. Res. (JAIR) 31, 497–542 (2008)
25. Sharon, G., Stern, R., Felner, A., Sturtevant, N.: Conflict-based search for optimal multi-agent pathfinding. Artif. Intell. 219, 40–66 (2015)
26. Sharon, G., Stern, R., Goldenberg, M., Felner, A.: The increasing cost tree search for optimal multi-agent pathfinding. Artif. Intell. 195, 470–495 (2013)
27. Silver, D.: Cooperative pathfinding. In: AIIDE, pp. 117–122 (2005)
28. Stern, R.: Multi-agent path finding – an Overview. In: Osipov, G.S., Panov, A.I., Yakovlev, K.S. (eds.) Artificial Intelligence. LNCS (LNAI), vol. 11866, pp. 96–115. Springer, Cham (2019). https://doi.org/10.1007/978-3-030-33274-7_6
29. Sturtevant, N.R.: Benchmarks for grid-based pathfinding. Comput. Intell. AI Games 4(2), 144–148 (2012)
30. Surynek, P.: A novel approach to path planning for multiple robots in bi-connected graphs. In: ICRA 2009, pp. 3613–3619 (2009)

31. Surynek, P.: Multi-agent path finding with continuous time and geometric agents viewed through satisfiability modulo theories (SMT). In: Surynek, P., Yeoh, W. (eds.) Proceedings of the Twelfth International Symposium on Combinatorial Search, SOCS 2019, pp. 200–201. AAAI Press (2019)

32. Surynek, P.: Unifying search-based and compilation-based approaches to multi-agent path finding through satisfiability modulo theories. In: Proceedings of IJCAI, 2019, pp. 1177–1183 (2019)

33. Surynek, P.: On satisfisfiability modulo theories in continuous multi-agent path finding: compilation-based and search-based approaches compared. In: Rocha, A.P., Steels, L., van den Herik, H.J. (eds.) Proceedings of the 12th International Conference on Agents and Artificial Intelligence, ICAART 2020, vol. 2, pp. 182–193. SCITEPRESS (2020)

34. Surynek, P., Felner, A., Stern, R., Boyarski, E.: Efficient SAT approach to multi-agent path finding under the sum of costs objective. In: ECAI, pp. 810–818 (2016)

35. Tinelli, C.: Foundations of satisfiability modulo theories. In: Dawar, A., de Queiroz, R. (eds.) WoLLIC 2010. LNCS (LNAI), vol. 6188, p. 58. Springer, Heidelberg (2010). https://doi.org/10.1007/978-3-642-13824-9_6

36. Walker, T.T., Sturtevant, N.R., Felner, A.: Extended increasing cost tree search for non-unit cost domains. In: Proceedings of IJCAI 2018, pp. 534–540 (2018)

37. Wang, K., Botea, A.: MAPP: a scalable multi-agent path planning algorithm with tractability and completeness guarantees. JAIR **42**, 55 90 (2011)

38. Yu, J., LaValle, S.M.: Optimal multi-robot path planning on graphs: structure and computational complexity. CoRR abs/1507.03289 (2015)

Small Networks of MIMO Agents with Two Activity Types

Liudmila Yu. Zhilyakova$^{(\boxtimes)}$ (ID)

V. A. Trapeznikov Institute of Control Sciences of Russian Academy of Sciences,
65, Profsoyuznaya Street, Moscow 117997, Russia
zhilyakova.ludmila@gmail.com

Abstract. We study a formal model describing network interaction of heterogeneous agents with many inputs and many outputs (MIMO agents). The paper
presents a continuation of the research. The introduced model has a large number of
parameters, which complicates its analytical study. The simulation demonstrated
that by varying the values of agent parameters, it is possible to achieve fundamentally different dynamics of nodes activity in a network. For different parameters, it
is possible to obtain the predominance of one activity type in the whole network,
the periodic change of different types, attenuation, and the involvement of the
entire network, or its parts, in the stationary activity of one or different types. This
research is devoted to the analytical study of the reduced model to determine the
key properties for generating various kinds of behavior. The model itself has also
undergone some significant changes. We consider small networks of agents and
describe the conditions under which they can generate stable activity patterns. We
introduce the concepts of ensemble and rhythmic activity generator for several
activity types.

Keywords: Networks of complex agents · Threshold models · MIMO agents ·
Network activity

1 Introduction

Activity propagation in networks of various nature have been studied for decades. However, the diversity of subject areas and differences both in the structural elements of
networks and in the distribution processes themselves entail the development of new
models or a fresh look at existing models and their unexpected applications. So, in the
present research, the concept of a MIMO agent is transferred from the field of the synchronization and consensus study of linear and nonlinear MIMO agents in multi-channel
networks [1, 2]. Agents in these networks are usually represented by symmetric systems
[3].

On the other hand, the formalism proposed in this paper inherits the properties of
many models of information influence and the activity spreading in social networks

This work was partially supported by the Russian Foundation for Basic Research, projects no.
20-07-00190A, 18-29-22042мк, 19-07-00525A.

© Springer Nature Switzerland AG 2020
S. O. Kuznetsov et al. (Eds.): RCAI 2020, LNAI 12412, pp. 100–114, 2020.
https://doi.org/10.1007/978-3-030-59535-7_8

[4–6]. Heterogeneity is added to these networks using mechanisms similar to the multi-transmitter interaction of neurons in biological neural networks [7–9].

This paper is a continuation of the study described in [10, 11]. The first of these two articles presents a formal model for the interaction of complex MIMO agents that represent users of a social network who, when choosing an action, take into account the state of their environment at the moment and for a certain time interval. Moreover, the choice of action is not binary: to be activated or not – an agent must also choose the type of activity. The choice of type depends on the agent preferences and the type by which his neighbors are active. In [11], a simulation model and a number of its results are described.

In general terms, the proposed model is too complicated for analytical research. Considerable arbitrariness in the choice of parameters makes it difficult to interpret the results. A wide range of behavior repertoires can be implemented in the model; however, the dependence of behavior changes on parameter changes is not always evident. Therefore, in this work, we will minimize the model similarly to [12], where the richer model proposed in [7–9] was reduced to a small number of principal parameters and investigated analytically.

Besides, based on the results of simulation modeling, we were able to correct the formalism; therefore, here we consider not only a reduced but also an improved model.

Our results have many intersections with the results obtained for homogeneous stationary ensembles [13].

2   Model Description

We define the formal model of heterogeneous network interactions of complex agents as a system S = <N, G, C> .

N = $\{1,\ldots, N\}$ is a set of *agents* with an internal structure.

G = (N, E) is a directed graph of influence. Its nodes are agents belonging to the set N. Each edge e_{ij} denotes the effect of agent i on agent j.

In general, the graph is weighted, the weights of the arcs are given by the matrix $R \in \mathbb{R}^{N \times N}$. If $r_{ij} > 0$, then agent i affects agent j with the power r_{ij}.

By *activity*, we mean some abstract resource that is transmitted from node to node, and by the *type of activity*, we mean the color of this resource. In this sense, the network is multi-product.

The system operates in discrete time t.

We assume that an agent can receive resources of all types, i.e. has many inputs and that he can generate information of various kinds. That is, each node in the network represents a MIMO agent.

Simulation models based on this formal apparatus are investigated in [11].

This paper is aimed at an analytical study of the model. Here we restrict ourselves to two types of propagated activity: $\{c_1, c_2\}$.

2.1   Agent Characteristics

Each agent i is assigned a stochastic vector of length 2, consisting of weight coefficients: $p_i = (p_{i1}, p_{i2}), p_{i1} + p_{i2} = 1$. The values $p_{ik}, k = 1, 2$, characterize the "attitude" of agent

i to types $c_{1,2}$. When the agent becomes active, he chooses the activity type depending on his vector p_i and the structure of the activity in his environment.

Remark 2.1. Below, for the agent i, we will call the type of activity that has the largest value p_{ik} *the own type*. If both coordinates of vector p are the same, we will assume that this agent has no preferences.

The second characteristic of an agent is his activation threshold. The threshold characterizes the resistance of the agent to external influences. The lower it is, the less external excitation is required for the agent to be activated.

2.2 Two Factors of Influence on the Agent

Each agent can be affected by the set of his neighbors. If agent j affects agent i, in the graph of influence G, there exists an edge $e_{ji} = (j, i)$. Under the influence, we understand the following. If agent j is active at time step t, then agent i, when calculating his state at time step $t + 1$, takes into account the activity of agent j. Moreover, the agent i calculates the influence value taking into account two weighting factors: *constant* and *variable*.

The *constant*, or *structural*, component is the weight of the edge r_{ji}. It characterizes the degree of trust of agent i to agent j. The weights r_{ji} are given by the structural matrix R.

The *dynamic*, or *functional*, component of the influence of agent j on agent i depends on the type by which agent j is active and on the distribution of the weight coefficients of agent i: $p_i = (p_{i1}, p_{i2})$.

This means that the trust of the agent in his environment is combined with the trust in the activity type at a given time step.

The influence of the type of activity is described by the corresponding component of the vector p – the larger it is, the stronger the effect. Then, if agent j is active at time t by type c_k, its impact on agent i is calculated according to the formula:

$$e_{jik}(t) = p_{ik}(t|j) \cdot r_{ji}, k \in \{1, 2\},$$

where $p_{ik}(t|j)$ is a component of vector p corresponding to activity type of agent j at timestep t.

Then it is possible to derive formulas for calculating the effect on the time step t on agent i for each type separately $e_{ik}(t)$ and the total effect on him $E_i(t)$ (formulas (1), (2), respectively):

$$e_{ik}(t) = p_{ik} \sum\nolimits_{j=1}^{N} r_{ji} y_{jk}(t-1), \quad k = 1, 2, \tag{1}$$

$$E_i(t) = p_{i1} \sum\nolimits_{j=1}^{N} r_{ji} y_{j1}(t-1) + p_{i2} \sum\nolimits_{j=1}^{N} r_{ji} y_{j2}(t-1), \tag{2}$$

where $y_{jk}(t) \in \{0, 1\}$ is the activity of agent j at time t (formula (5) below).

2.3 Activity of Agents

At each time step, the agent undergoes an external effect described by formulas (1)–(2). Besides, the agent remembers the previous network conditions and takes them into account when determining the total effect.

Agent activity at timestep t is specified by the vector $y_i(t)$ of length 2, in which all components, except possibly one, are zero. If the agent at timestep t is active by type c_k, then $y_{ik}(t) = 1$.

Agent Memory. Each agent in a network has a memory of depth Θ. To calculate the total excitation of an agent at time step t, the effects from all his neighbors active at one or more steps in the interval $[t - \Theta + 1, t]$, are summed with the corresponding discount factors.

The potential of agent for activation can be calculated both for each type separately, and for both types together.

$$a_{ik}(t) = \sum_{\theta=1}^{\Theta} \mu_\theta e_{ik}(t - \theta) = \sum_{\theta=1}^{\Theta} \mu_\theta p_{ik} \sum_{j=1}^{N} \sum r_{ji} y_{jk}(t - \theta), k = 1, 2 \quad (3)$$

$$A_i(t) = \sum_{\theta=0}^{\Theta-1} \mu_{i\theta} E_i(t - \theta) =$$

$$= \sum_{\theta=0}^{\Theta-1} \mu_{i\theta} \left(p_{i1} \sum_{j=1}^{N} r_{ji} y_{j1}(t - \theta) + p_{i2} \sum_{j=1}^{N} r_{ji} y_{j2}(t - \theta) \right), \quad (4)$$

where μ_θ are non-negative discount factors satisfying the relation:

$$1 = \mu_1 > \mu_2 \geq \ldots \geq \mu \geq 0.$$

For some agents with a short memory, tails may be equal to zero.

Agent i is active at time step t if the value $A_i(t)$ has exceeded the *threshold value* (see the next paragraph).

If the agent activates at time t, his memory resets. The memory accumulation occurs while the agent is not active. In this case, formulas (3) and (4) need to be adjusted. It will be done in formulas (6)–(7) after all the necessary values are determined.

Activation Threshold. The threshold value of agent Th_i characterizes his readiness for activation.

- If the agent himself starts an activity, his threshold is 0.
- If the agent responds to each external activity, he has a threshold value satisfying inequality

$$Th_i < \min_{k=1,2} p_{ik} \cdot \min_{j=\overline{1,N}} r_{ji}.$$

- The agent, which is practically unaffected by the environment, has a threshold close to the value

$$Th_i \sim \max_{k=1,2} p_{ik} \cdot \sum_{j=1}^{N} r_{ji}.$$

Even though agents perceive the activity of both types, each agent has one threshold.

If the threshold Th_i is exceeded, the agent activates according to one of the types defined by the components of the vector $a_i(t)$ (Eq. (3)).

Activation Type. Agent i activates by the type c_k if k satisfies the condition:

$$k = \arg\max_l a_{il}(t).$$

That is, the agent chooses the type from which he experiences the strongest impact. Then,

$$y_{ik}(t) = \begin{cases} 1, & \text{if } A_i(t) \geq Th_i \ \& \ k = \arg\max_{l=1,2} a_{il}(t)); \\ 0 & \text{otherwise.} \end{cases} \tag{5}$$

There may be a situation in which the maximum impact is achieved, not on one, but on both types, that is, the agent experiences two identical influences, taking into account his preferences. Then to select the activation type, he needs to take several additional steps.

1. If the agent was active at the previous time step by one of these types, he saves this type.
2. If the agent was not active, he chooses the type according to his preferences: he selects the type as $\arg\max_{l=1,2} p_{il}$.
3. If vector components p_{il} are equal, and therefore the effects are the same, then he chooses one of the types randomly with a probability of 0.5.

Let's write out the formulas of the agent's accumulating memory, taking into account the zeroing of memory upon activation.

$$a_{ik}(t) = \sum_{\theta=0}^{\Theta-1} \left(\prod_{l=0}^{\theta} (1 - y_{i1}(t-l) - y_{i2}(t-l)) \right) \mu_{i\theta} e_{ik}(t-\theta), \quad k = 1, 2, \tag{6}$$

$$A_i(t) = a_{i1}(t) + a_{i2}(t). \tag{7}$$

Network States. At each time step, each agent is in one of the three states (passive or active by the first or by the second type). Then the dynamics of the network as a whole can be considered as a change of some subset of 3^N states $S(t)$ defined by the tuples $(\alpha_1, ..., \alpha_N)$, where $\alpha_i \in \{0, c_1, c_2\}$.

$$\alpha_i = \begin{cases} 0, & \text{if } y_{ij}(t) = 0, \quad j = 1, 2; \\ c_1, & \text{if } y_{i1}(t) = 1 \text{ and } y_{i2}(t) = 0; \\ c_2, & \text{if } y_{i2}(t) = 1 \text{ and } y_{i1}(t) = 0. \end{cases}$$

Definition 2.1. States $S(t) = (\alpha_1, ..., \alpha_N)$ will be called the *external states* of the network.

We number all the external states of the network in lexicographic order from $s_0 = (0, ..., 0)$ to $s_{3^N-1} = (c_2, ..., c_2)$.

Definition 2.2. *Internal states* are characterized by the values $A_i(t)$, and, generally speaking, their set is infinite.

Each external state is uniquely determined by the internal state. The arbitrary state $S(t) = (c_{j_1}, \dots, c_{j_N})$ can be determined by the following system:

$$\begin{cases} j_1 = H(A_1(t) - Th_1) \cdot \arg\max_{l=1,2} a_{1l}(t); \\ \qquad \dots \\ j_N = H(A_1(t) - Th_N) \cdot \arg\max_{l=1,2} a_{Nl}(t). \end{cases} \tag{8}$$

Here $H(\bullet)$ is the Heaviside function.

2.4 Analysis of Model Parameters

Consider a network of N agents with two types of activity. The network graph is defined by a non-negative matrix $R = (r_{ij})_{N \times N}$. Each agent is characterized by the vector $p_i = (p_{i1}, p_{i2})$, the threshold value Th_i, and the coefficients $\mu_{i\theta}$, $\theta = \overline{1, \Theta}, i = \overline{1, N}$. Thus, the entire system can be described by the number of parameters equal to $N^2 + 2N + N + \Theta N = N^2 + (3 + \Theta) N$.

Not all of these parameters are independent. Thus, the elements of the matrix R and the thresholds Th_i directly depend on each other: when these values change in the same proportion, the model remains the same. Indeed, let $R_1 = \alpha R$, $Th_{i1} = \alpha Th_i$. Since all the dependencies in the system are linear, we get that formula (5) will be transformed as follows

$$y_{ik}(t) = \begin{cases} 1, \text{если } \alpha A_i(t) \geq \alpha Th_i \ \& \ k = \arg\max_{l=1,2} \alpha a_{il}(t)) \\ 0, \text{otherwise} \end{cases}. \tag{9}$$

Formulas (5) and (9) are equivalent, and, accordingly, the system of equalities (8) will also not change.

In this study, we will consider a particular case of the model for which it is possible to obtain clear and interpretable analytical results. Let's assume that the matrix R is a binary (0, 1)-matrix, where one means the presence of influence, and zero means its absence. Then the agent thresholds will be distributed within the interval $[0, N - 1]$.

3 Types of Activity Dynamics in Small Networks

Consider the different types of activity distribution in the proposed model. For the same set of agents and the constant matrix R, one can obtain different network behavior by varying the parameters. This statement is obvious: by changing the thresholds of agents, we can get a network with undamped activity (zero thresholds) and a network without any activity (high thresholds). We will be interested in intermediate options: the appearance and attenuation of activity, the change in the type of activity of agents, the appearance of patterns of rhythmic activity in the network, the allocation of active subnets. Let us define several concepts that we will use further.

Definition 3.1. The external state the network $S(t) = s_k$ will be called stable if $\forall\, h = \overline{1,\Theta}\; S(t+h) = s_k$.

This definition means that a steady state does not change after any number of time steps. In a network without memory, for stability, it is enough that the equality $S(t) = S(t+1)$ is fulfilled. This condition is not sufficient for a network with memory. In this case, agents can accumulate potential for some time, leaving the network state stable, and then activate. However, if the state does not change in Θ steps, this means that all passive agents could not accumulate the potential for activation, and then their memory will not increase – according to formulas (6)–(7), it stabilizes at some subthreshold values.

In a network with memory, you can judge stability by two consecutive steps only for those states in which all agents are either active or passive at the same time.

Remark 3.1. The state $s_0 = (0, \ldots, 0)$, in which all agents are passive, is stable for any network with nonzero agent thresholds. We will call it a trivial state. In the future, we will consider only nontrivial stable states.

Definition 3.2. By a *subnet* $G_{i_1,\ldots,i_q}$ we mean the selected connected set of agents $i_1, \ldots, i_q$ and all the connections between them.

Definition 3.3. By a *homogeneous stationary q-ensemble* $A_{i_1,\ldots,i_q}$ of type c_k, we mean the maximum inclusion subnet of q agents, capable of generating stable activity of type c_k at certain initial states, regardless of the states of other agents in the network.

Remark 3.2. The property of *maximum inclusion* means that the ensemble $A_{i_1,\ldots,i_q}$ is not contained entirely in any other ensemble. It follows from this that sub-ensembles themselves are not ensembles.

Definition 3.4. By a *universal stationary q-ensemble* $U_{i_1,\ldots,i_q}$, i.e., an ensemble without specifying the type of activity, we mean the maximum inclusion subnet of q agents, capable of generating stable activity by any type, common to all agents inside a subnetwork, regardless of the states of other agents in the network.

Definition 3.5. By a *heterogeneous stationary q-ensemble* $H_{i_1,\ldots,i_q}$ of type c_1-c_2, we mean an ensemble of q agents capable of generating such stable activity under certain initial conditions that there are two subsets of agents active by different types (c_1 and c_2, respectively).

Remark 3.3. A heterogeneous ensemble in the general case is not a combination of two ensembles of different types since, in some cases, many agents active on different types can support joint activity, but each subset of agents of the same type individually does not form an ensemble.

Definition 3.6. A *d-phase generator of rhythmic activity* $Gd_{i_1,\ldots,i_q}$ is a subnetwork of q agents capable of generating rhythmic (cyclic) activity with a period $d > 1$ at certain initial states starting from a certain finite time step t_0: $\forall\, t > t_0\; S(t+d) = S(t)$. Moreover, each agent is active at least at one time step, i.e., the subnet does not contain agents that are silent all the time. At $d = 1$, the generator turns into an ensemble.

As in the case of ensembles, a generator can support different types of activities: a rhythm of only one specific type, rhythms of both "pure" types (depending on the initial state), or a heterogeneous rhythm, that is, containing two types at the same time.

In a network of agents whose thresholds are nonzero, none of them can start an activity. Therefore, when setting the initial state, we will assume that some nodes have a point activating control effect. Control actions can also be applied to agents in the course of network operation.

Definition 3.7. The *control action* $u_{ik}(t)$ on agent i of type c_k at time step t is the change in effect from his neighbors of this type. For agents without memory, there are two types of effects: *activating* and *deactivating*. An activating effect is a positive term to sum for $E_i(t)$ (formula (2)), which makes the total value above the threshold; a deactivating effect reduces the value of $E_i(t)$ if it is nonzero, and makes the total effect below the threshold. For an agent with memory, a change in the influence of neighbors can affect activity not only directly on a given time step, but indirectly through a change in memory, in this case, the control action can have an *excitatory* and an *inhibitory* effect.

Remark 3.4. A control action of type c_k on agent i makes sense only if $p_{ik} > 0$. If the corresponding coordinate of the vector p is zero, then the agent is not sensitive to this type of activity, and accordingly, to control actions of this type.

Note a critical property of ensembles, both homogeneous and heterogeneous. If the ensemble is active, it does not matter if the agents have memory because, after activation, the memory resets. Using this property, we investigate the stable activation of agents as if they don't have memory.

4 Ensembles in Networks with Two Types of Activity

4.1 Homogeneous Ensembles

Consider connected subnetwork $G_{i_1,\ldots,i_q}$, consisting of q agents. They form a *homogeneous ensemble* $A_{i_1,\ldots,i_q}$, if these agents can be permanently active according to the type c_k, regardless of the activity of agents outside the subnetwork. To satisfy this condition, the following inequality must be fulfilled:

$$d_A^-(i) \cdot p_{ik} \geq Th_i, \quad i = \overline{i_1, i_q} \tag{10}$$

Here $d_A^-(i)$ is the indegree of the vertex i inside the subnetwork $G_{i_1,\ldots,i_q}$. Edges incoming from the outside are not taken into account in this formula. Thus, the left side of inequality (10) contains only the amount of activity c_k that came to the agent from all his neighbors in the ensemble.

Theorem 4.1. Connected subnetwork $G_{i_1,\ldots,i_q}$ is a stationary ensemble $A_{i_1,\ldots,i_q}$ of type c_k iff inequality (10) holds for all vertices $i_1, \ldots, i_q$, and there is no such set of vertices $G^* = \{i_{w_1}, \ldots, i_{w_v}\}$, $G^* \geq 1$, located in the same connected component with $G_{i_1,\ldots,i_q}$, that for all vertices of subnetwork $G_{i_1,\ldots,i_q} \cup G^*$ inequality (10) also holds.

Proof.

1. If at a certain time step t all agents from $G_{i_1,...,i_q}$ are active by type c_k, then they will be active by the same type at all subsequent steps under inequality (10). The second condition of the theorem means that the subnetwork $G_{i_1,...,i_q}$ is maximum inclusion. And this, in turn, means that $G_{i_1,...,i_q}$ is an ensemble of type c_k.
2. Prove sufficiency by contradiction. Suppose there is an ensemble $A_{i_1,...,i_q}$ and there exists an agent i_r for which (10) does not hold. If at a certain time step t all the agents from $G_{i_1,...,i_q}$ are active by type c_k, then for the agent i_r to be active at the next time step, there is not enough activity coming from the agents forming the ensemble. In this situation, two cases are possible:

    *   Agent i_r becomes passive at time step $t + 1$. In this case the subnetwork $G_{i_1,...,i_q}$ is not an ensemble.
    *   Agent i_r remains active at time step $t + 1$. Then this activity is supported by other active agents outside $G_{i_1,...,i_q}$. Since t and $t + 1$ are two arbitrary sequential time steps, we find that in addition to agents $i_1, \dots, i_q$, other agents are active all the time outside of $G_{i_1,...,i_q}$ in the same connection component. Then $G_{i_1,...,i_q}$ is an integral part of the ensemble, but not an independent ensemble.

Let us construct examples of homogeneous ensembles.

Consider a network consisting of three connected agents (Fig. 1). Sectors of circles correspond to the coordinates of the vectors p. The weights of all arcs, as stated in the previous section, are 1. The matrix R has units everywhere except the main diagonal.

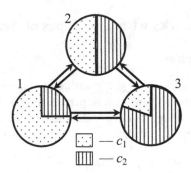

Fig. 1. The network of three agents. Sectors of circles correspond to the coordinates of the vectors p_i

For a network of three elements with two types of activity, there are 27 states s_j defined by triples $(\alpha_1, \alpha_2, \alpha_3)$, where $\alpha_i \in \{0, c_1, c_2\}$.

$$\alpha_i(t) = \begin{cases} 0, & \text{if } H(A_i(t) - Th_i) = 0; \\ c_1, & \text{if } H(A_i(t) - Th_i) \cdot \arg\max_{l=1,2} a_{il}(t) = 1; \\ c_2, & \text{if } H(A_i(t) - Th_i) \cdot \arg\max_{l=1,2} a_{il}(t) = 2. \end{cases}$$

We number the states s_j from $s_0 = (0, 0, 0)$ to $s_{26} = (c_2, c_2, c_2)$.

Consider all types of dynamics of such a network for the agents without memory: $\Theta = 1$. For such agents, the equalities hold: $a_i(t) = e_i(t)$; $A_i(t) = E_i(t)$.

Example 4.1. We construct various ensembles in the network from Fig. 1, fixing the parameters of agents.

Agent vectors are $p_1 = (0.75, 0.25)$, $p_2 = (0.5, 0.5)$, $p_3 = (0.2, 0.8)$.

Let the agent thresholds be the same and equal to 0.45.

1) *2-ensemble of type c_1*

Let's activate the first and second agents by type c_1. We get the following dynamics.

$t = 0$: $S(0) = (c_1, c_1, 0) = s_{12}$.

Calculate the network state at the next time step.

The first agent is affected by the second agent by type c_1 with a power of 0.75; he activates by the same type.

The second agent is affected by the first with a power of 0.5. This value is also above the threshold; the second agent activates by type c_1.

Agents 1 and 2 have a combined effect on the third agent with a power of $0.2 + 0.2 = 0.4$, which is below the threshold. The third agent remains inactive, and upon switching to step 1, the state of the network will not change:

$t = 1$: $S(1) = (c_1, c_1, 0) = s_{12}$.

Since we consider a network of agents without memory, this state will be stable.

This steady activation means that nodes 1 and 2 form a 2-ensemble of type c_1. These nodes cannot form an ensemble of the c_2 type.

2) *3-ensemble of type c_2*

Let's activate the first and second agents by type c_1.

$t = 0$: $S(0) = (0, c_2, c_2) = s_8$.

Find the network state at the next time step.

The second and third agents affect the first agent by type c_2 with a power of 2.0.25 = 0.5; this value is above the threshold. So, the first agent activates by the same type.

The second agent is affected by the third with type c_2 and a power of 0.5; he also activates by type c_2.

The second agent affects on the third with a power of 0.75, and he also activates at the next step:

$t = 1$: $S(1) = (c_2, c_2, c_2) = s_{26}$.

Further, all three agents remain active, supporting each other's activity.

Thus, the examples show that a network of agents with the same parameters can generate different ensembles for different types of activity, and these ensembles may intersect.

4.2 Universal Ensembles

Theorem 4.2. Connected subnetwork $G_{i_1,\dots,i_q}$ is a universal ensemble $U_{i_1,\dots,i_q}$ of type c_k iff it is an ensemble of both types.

The statement of this theorem is quite obvious. However, it should be emphasized that it suggests that not every intersection of homogeneous ensembles is a universal ensemble. This intersection will be an ensemble if and only if the symmetric difference of the corresponding subnets is empty.

Example 4.2. The universal ensemble is easy to obtain by changing the activation threshold of the third agent in the network in Fig. 1.

Agent preference vectors will remain the same: $p_1 = (0.75, 0.25)$, $p_2 = (0.5, 0.5)$, $p_1 = (0.2, 0.8)$.

The thresholds of the first and second agents are the same, and equal to 0.45, the threshold of the third agent is 0.3. Having performed calculations similar to those shown in Example 4.1, we find that upon activation of any pair of agents by any type, the whole network is activated in the next time step.

4.3 Heterogeneous Ensembles

First, we formulate two simple statements.

Statement 4.1. A subnetwork of two nodes $G_{i_1 i_2}$ cannot be a heterogeneous ensemble. In other words, heterogeneous 2-ensembles do not exist.

The proof follows directly from formula (5). An agent can be activated only by the type from which it experiences excitation. Thus, the agent, under the influence of only one type, cannot be activated by another type.

Statement 4.2. A subnetwork of three nodes $G_{i_1 i_2 i_3}$ cannot be a heterogeneous ensemble. Heterogeneous 3-ensembles also do not exist.

The proof is similar to the previous one. Of the three agents in a heterogeneous ensemble, one must be active in one type and two in another. But then the first agent is affected only by the second type of activity, and is forced to activate by this type, or to remain passive.

In general, for m types of activity, for the existence of a heterogeneous ensemble that includes all types, at least $2m$ agents will be needed so that at least two agents are active for each type.

The same statements apply to agents with memory.

Let us construct an example of a heterogeneous 4-ensemble.

Example 4.3. Consider the subnet in Fig. 2. Agent preference vectors are distributed in pairs: $p_1 = p_3 = (0.25, 0.75)$, $p_2 = p_4 = (0.75, 0.25)$. The thresholds of agents are the same and equal to 0.5.

In the initial state, let us activate the first agent by type c_1, the second agent bt type c_2. We get the following dynamics.

$t = 0$: $S(0) = (c_1, c_2, 0, 0)$.

At the next time step, the first agent will receive an impact value 0.75 by type c_2, the second agent will receive an impact of the same value by type c_1. Both agents activate according to their respective types.

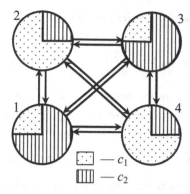

Fig. 2. A network of four agents. Complete graph

The third and fourth agents receive an impact of both types. For the third agent, the effect specified by the vector $(1, 1)$ will be corrected by the coefficients of the vector p as $(0.25, 0.75)$, for the fourth: $(0.75, 0.25)$. Accordingly, each of them activates by his *own* type (see Remark 2.1 in Sect. 2.1):

$t = 1$: $S(1) = (c_2, c_1, c_2, c_1)$.

From this step, the network state is stabilized, and a heterogeneous ensemble arises.

The effect on each agent is 3 (indegree), and it is distributed in the following proportions: for the first and third agents: $(2, 1)$, for the second and fourth ones $(1, 2)$, that is, for each agent, the external activity of the "not his own" type is stronger. However, the effect is corrected by the components of the vector p. For the first and third agents, type c_1 has an impact value $2.0.25 = 0.5$, type c_2 (*own* type): $1.0.75 = 0.75$. Thus, the impact of *own* type outweighs. For the second pair of agents, the situation will be symmetrical. Thus, the state $S(1) = (c_2, c_1, c_2, c_1)$ is stable.

Remark 4.1. The considered example is trivial, in the sense that for the initial states $S(0) = (c_2, 0, c_2, 0)$ and $S(0) = (0, c_1, 0, c_1)$, we obtain two homogeneous 2-ensembles: A_{13} of type c_2 and A_{24} of type c_1. However, by changing the threshold values, it is possible to achieve that a heterogeneous 4-ensemble will not be decomposed into two pairs.

For example, let the thresholds of the third and fourth agents be equal to 1. Then these agents can be activated only via the combined effect of at least two neighbors, and 2-ensembles in such a network are impossible.

The subnetwork in Fig. 2, with the parameters from Example 4.3, can also be a universal ensemble. This can be easily verified by setting in the initial state the activity of any two agents of the same common type.

We formulate a necessary and sufficient condition for a subnetwork to form a heterogeneous ensemble.

Consider the subnetwork $G_{i_1, \ldots, i_q}$, consisting of q agents. For these agents to constitute a heterogeneous ensemble $H_{i_1, \ldots, i_q}$, a condition similar to (10), but more complicated, must be fulfilled. There must be a partition of these agents into two subsets $G_{i_{1_1}, \ldots, i_{q_1}}$ and $G_{i_{1_2}, \ldots, i_{q_2}}$ of power q_1 and q_2, respectively, $q_1, q_2 > 1$, $q_1 + q_2 = q$, such that if agents from the first subset are active by the first type, and agents in the second subset are active by the second type, then each of them experiences an effect that exceeds the threshold value.

$$d_{G_{q_1}}^-(i) \cdot p_{i1} + d_{G_{q_2}}^-(i) \cdot p_{i2} \geq Th_i, i = \overline{i_1, i_q}. \tag{11}$$

Here $d_{G_{q_1}}^-(i)$ and $d_{G_{q_2}}^-(i)$ are the numbers of incoming edges, giving in total the indegree of vertex i inside the subnetwork $G_{i_1,\ldots,i_q}$. Edges entering a vertex from the outside, as in (10), are not taken into account in this formula.

Statement 4.3. The subnets $G_{i_{1_1},\ldots,i_{q_1}}$ and $G_{i_{1_2},\ldots,i_{q_2}}$ do not have isolated vertices.

Proof. Without loss of generality, assume that in the subnetwork $G_{i_{1_1},\ldots,i_{q_1}}$ there is an isolated vertex k. Then all its incoming edges lead from the vertices of the subnet $G_{i_{1_2},\ldots,i_{q_2}}$, and it cannot become active by type c_1.

Remark 4.2. In general, the subnets $G_{i_{1_1},\ldots,i_{q_1}}$ and $G_{i_{1_2},\ldots,i_{q_2}}$ can be nonconnected.

Theorem 4.3. Connected subnetwork $G_{i_1,\ldots,i_q}$ is a heterogeneous ensemble $H_{i_1,\ldots,i_q}$ iff there exists a partition for the set of its vertices $i_1, \ldots, i_q$ for which inequality (11) holds and there is no such set of vertices $G^* = \{i_{w_1}, \ldots, i_{w_v}\}$, $\|G^*\| \geq 1$, located in the same connected component with $G_{i_1,\ldots,i_q}$, that for all vertices of subnetwork $G_{i_1,\ldots,i_q} \cup G^*$ inequality (11) also holds.

The proof of this theorem coincides with the proof of Theorem 4.1.

Remark 4.3. There are networks (for example, with agents that have vectors $(0.5, 0.5)$) in which the partition from Theorem 4.3 can be constructed in more than one way. This theorem is an existence theorem and does not provide a constructive algorithm for constructing a heterogeneous ensemble.

Remark 4.4. The property of a subnet to be heterogeneous, or some other ensemble, does not contradict the fact that this subnet can generate activity of a completely different kind under other initial conditions. Note that if in Example 4.3 we change the types of activation of agents at the initial moment, we will get a two-phase generator.

If $S(0) = (c_2, c_1, 0, 0)$, agents 1 and 2 activate agents 3 and 4, but cannot activate each other. Then the state at the step $t = 1$ will be $S(1) = (0, 0, c_2, c_1)$. Further, since the subnetwork is symmetric with respect to the pairs $(1, 2)$, $(3, 4)$, the activity will be repeated: $S(2) = (c_2, c_1, 0, 0)$, etc.

Thus, G_{1234} from Example 4.3 is at the same time a universal ensemble, a heterogeneous ensemble, and a two-phase generator. Its different behaviors depend on the initial control actions.

5   Generators of Rhythmic Activity

As shown in Remark 4.4 to Theorem 4.3, the ability of a subnetwork to generate rhythmic activity does not contradict the fact that the same subnetwork can become a stationary ensemble. This means that it is impossible to single out a universal criterion for "being a generator" for a subnetwork. However, this does not mean that it is impossible to formulate any meaningful statements regarding generators. A significant difference between these statements is that they will contain restrictions imposed not only and not so much on the graph structure as on the initial conditions.

Any generator can be made a stationary ensemble by activating all the vertices in the initial state at the same time. Thus, the set of network generators is a subset of the set of ensembles.

The presence of activation thresholds for agents makes the model significantly different from the diffusion models on the graph. If the activity was transmitted regardless of how strong the activating effect on the agent is, then only ergodic cyclic networks could produce rhythmic activity [14], that is, networks in which the greatest common divisor (GCD) of all cycle lengths is greater than 1. Regular networks (networks in which GCD = 1) could create only stationary ensembles. Threshold activation makes the model richer, and its behavior more diverse.

6 Conclusion

The paper describes the study of activity in small networks consisting of MIMO agents. Agents can generate and support two types of activity. Each agent is characterized by a stochastic vector of dimension 2, defining its relation to these types. The larger the component of the vector, the more preferable the corresponding type for this agent. In addition to the vector, an important characteristic of agents is the threshold value. The lower it is, the easier the agent is activated under external influences. Choosing the type of activation, the agent takes into account both personal preferences (components of the stochastic vector) and the prevailing activity of his environment. Following [13], we introduce the concept of an ensemble as the maximum subnetwork capable of supporting stationary activity. Since there can be two types of activity in the network, we distinguish four types of ensembles: by the first type, by the second type, by both types (universal ensemble) and by the mixed type (heterogeneous ensemble).

In the model, agents have memory. However, upon activation, the agent's memory is zeroed; therefore, when considering ensembles, agents with and without memory behave identically. When considering other types of activity, such as, for example, the generation of simple rhythms or more complex patterns, the presence of memory agents will be crucial. One example of the operation of a small network with memory was considered in [10, 11]. A systematic analysis of the patterns of rhythmic activity of small networks will be made in future studies.

References

1. Sharf, M., Zelazo, D. Analysis and synthesis of mimo multi-agent systems using network optimization. arXiv:1711.04287v3. (2018)
2. Zhu, L., Chen, X., Chen, Z., Hill, D.J.: Output synchronization of linear mimo heterogeneous multi-agent systems via output communication/ IFAC PapersOnLine **50–1**, 1748–1753 (2017)

3. Hanada, K., Wada, T., Masubuchi, I., Asai, T., Fujisaki, Y.: Stochastic consensus over multi-channel networks of MIMO linear symmetric agents/transactions of the institute of systems. Control Inf. Eng. **32**(2), 55–62 (2019)
4. Kempe, D., Kleinberg, J., Tardos, E.: Maximizing the spread of influence through a social network. In: Proceedings of the 9-th ACM SIGKDD International Conference on Knowledge Discovery and Data Mining, pp. 137–146 (2003)
5. Breer, Vladimir V., Novikov, Dmitry A., Rogatkin, Andrey D.: Mob Control: Models of Threshold Collective Behavior. SSDC, vol. 85. Springer, Cham (2017). https://doi.org/10.1007/978-3-319-51865-7
6. Chkhartishvili, Alexander G., Gubanov, Dmitry A., Novikov, Dmitry A.: Social Networks: Models of Information Influence, Control and Confrontation. SSDC, vol. 189. Springer, Cham (2019). https://doi.org/10.1007/978-3-030-05429-8
7. Bazenkov, N., et al.: Discrete modeling of neuronal interactions in multi-transmitter networks. Sci. Tech. Inf. Process. **45**(5), 283–296 (2018). https://doi.org/10.3103/S0147688218050015
8. Bazenkov, N.I., Boldyshev, B.A., Dyakonova, V., Kuznetsov, O.P.: Simulating small neural circuits with a discrete computational model. Biol. Cybern. **114**(3), 349–362 (2020). https://doi.org/10.1007/s00422-020-00826-w
9. Kuznetsov, O.P., Bazenkov, N.I., Boldyshev, B.A., Zhilyakova, LYu., Kulivets, S.G., Chistopolsky, I.A.: An asynchronous discrete model of chemical interactions in simple neuronal systems. Sci. Tech. Inf. Process. **45**(6), 375–389 (2018). https://doi.org/10.3103/S0147688218060072
10. Zhilyakova, LYu.: Modeling the structure of MIMO-agents and their interactions. In: Kuznetsov, S.O., Panov, A.I. (eds.) RCAI 2019. CCIS, vol. 1093, pp. 3–16. Springer, Cham (2019). https://doi.org/10.1007/978-3-030-30763-9_1
11. Zhilyakova, L., Petrov, I.: Study of activity patterns in interaction of MIMO-agents in heterogeneous networks. In: Proceedings of MLSD'2019, Moscow: ICS RAS, pp. 1213–1215 (2019). (in Russian)
12. Kuznetsov, O.P.: Asynchronous threshold networks with multisorted signals/Doklady Mathematics, vol. 100, no. 1, pp. 392–395. Pleiades Publishing, Ltd. (2019). https://doi.org/10.31857/S0869-5652487111-14
13. Kuznetsov, O.P.: Stationary ensembles in threshold networks. Automat. Remote Control **78**(3), 475–489 (2017). https://doi.org/10.1134/S0005117917030080
14. Kemeny, J.G., Snell, J.L.: Finite Markov Chains, 2nd edn, vol. XII, p. 226. Springer, New York (1976). https://www.springer.com/gp/book/9780387901923

Fuzzy Models and Soft Computing

Designing a Neural Network Primitive for Conditional Structural Transformations

Alexander Demidovskij and Eduard Babkin[✉]

Higher School of Economics, Bolshaya Pecherskaya Street 25/12,
Nizhny Novgorod 603005, Russia
{ademidovskij,eababkin}@hse.ru

Abstract. Among the problems of neural network design the challenge of explicit representing conditional structural manipulations on a sub-symbolic level plays a critical role. In response to that challenge the article proposes a computationally adequate method for design of a neural network capable of performing an important group of symbolic operations on a sub-symbolic level without initial learning: extraction of elements of a given structure, conditional branching and construction of a new structure. The neural network primitive infers on distributed representations of symbolic structures and represents a proof of concept for the viability of implementation of symbolic rules in a neural pipeline for various tasks like language analysis or aggregation of linguistic assess-ments during the decision making process. The proposed method was practically implemented and evaluated within the Keras framework. The network designed was tested for a particular case of transforming active-passive sentences represented in parsed grammatical structures.

Keywords: Tensor product representations · Artificial neural networks · Linguistic decision making · Natural language processing

1 Introduction

Despite existing advances in mathematical models and technologies of deep learning, neural-inspired computational architectures researchers outline a considerable gap between connectionist sub-symbolic and logic-based symbolic approaches to representation and higher level reasoning [2,3,15]. From the symbolic perspective, it seems quite apparent that human cognition operates with complex symbolic data structures: graphs, trees, shapes, grammars etc., performs symbolic manipulations with means of symbolic logic. However the processing of these structures in mind is performed on the neural level. At the same time, existing attempts to build artificial neural systems lose in terms of representational compositionality [14]. In the framework of neural-symbolic computation, there is the proved *in principle* equivalence between dynamical systems with distributed representations and symbolic systems in terms of representational or problem-solving capabilities [19]. At the same time there are no exact rules of

S. O. Kuznetsov et al. (Eds.): RCAI 2020, LNAI 12412, pp. 117–133, 2020.
https://doi.org/10.1007/978-3-030-59535-7_9

obtaining a sub-symbolic counterpart to symbolic models and vice versa. In practice, little attention was given to development of practically achievable software implementations of such sub-symbolic models.

In the neural-symbolic paradigm Artificial Neural Networks (ANN) are the means of parallel distributed computation and robust learning. In this field there is an important scientific task of constructing neural networks that perform significant intellectual tasks without preliminary training stage [25] in massively parallel computation environments like multi-agent systems or Internet Of Things (IoT). Each component of such systems plays a role of a single neuron or a small sub-network [33]. These distributed computational platforms should be not only distributed, but also robust to unit failures, self-improving in time and avoid central control. The first step towards solving that task would be design of ANN capable of producing an exact solution for a selected motivating problem, which combines different intellectual operations on complex symbolic structures.

The task of multi-criteria linguistic based decision making can be selected as an example of appropriate motivating problem [10,32]. Creation of monolithic neural-symbolic systems for various expert and decision support systems is an actual task [16,25]. Linguistic assessments aggregation is a key element of fuzzy decision making models [5] and it seems to be a hard requirement for any neural-symbolic decision support system.

In order to put step forward on the way of obtaining a practical sub-symbolic solution a bottom-up approach is proposed. According to that approach separate neural networks which perform critical sub-tasks of manipulation without training (called *primitives*) should be designed and combined within a single meta-network capable of producing a final solution of the multi-criteria choice problem. The term 'network' is widely used in different contexts, so we use attribution 'neural' in our own method to clearly specify that our approach is based on combination of existing modules that implement the functionality of neurons. The application of existing implementations of such modules enables actual software design of our proposals. Following the approach proposed a certain schema of combination of required primitives was designed, see Fig. 1.

There are several recent advances in the field that allow building such sub-symbolic solutions and prove viability of the proposed approach. Usually the integrated symbolic and sub-symbolic flow consists of following steps:

1. encoding the symbolic structure as a distributed representation with a neural network. In [8] a new encoder design was proposed for the simple structure that has only one nesting level.
2. flattening the distributed representation to a vector format with a neural network [12].
3. performing domain specific analysis of the structure on the neural level. For example, aggregation of linguistic assessments during decision making or voice identification of a sentence during linguistic analysis.
4. structural manipulations on the neural level, for example, joining of two trees in one [12].
5. decoding the new structure from a distributed representation to symbolic level [8].

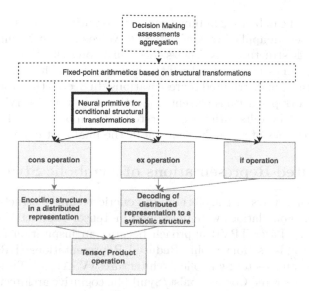

Fig. 1. Evolution of sub-symbolic methods required for expression of linguistic assessments aggregation during decision making process. Grayed cells refer to the existing research, thick-bordered cell represents current research direction, dashed-bordered cells stand for directions of further research.

Aforementioned papers use the idea of compiling neural networks, therefore, training step is not required [23]. Such compiled networks produce results equivalent to those produced by the symbolic algorithm, while other, and more popular nowadays, examples of trainable neural-symbolic systems perform reasoning probabilistically [22].

This paper offers a novel design of a neural network which is capable of performing conditional transformations of arbitrary structures expressed in terms of Tensor Product Variable Binding. Such neural network can be embedded to more complex networks for different computational tasks, thus we call it a neural network primitive. In particular, the proposed neural network primitive consists of a cascade of three small neural networks: the first one extracts the marker from an input structure for a conditional module, the second network performs conditional extraction of specific structural elements and the final model constructs a new structure from elements of the input one. We present design and evaluation results of the network capable of logical branching. This primitive is based on the analysis of arbitrary symbolic structures and can be considered as a sub-symbolic equivalent of IF logical operator in traditional programming languages. Careful engineering of the network provides better comprehensibility and maintenance, as well as potential reuse for solving other symbolic operations translation to the sub-symbolic level. The network inference result is a symbolic structure encoded in a form of distributed representation. This method of generating neural networks that are capable of encoding and manipulating structures on the tensor level can be used in broad range of cognitive systems. The designed network addresses an applied task of detecting voice of English language.

The article is structured as follows. Section 2 presents the context of the research and outlines the most relevant achievements in the field of encoding symbolic structures in distributed representations. In Sect. 3 the proposed design of a neural network primitive is presented. Section 4 contains overview and analysis of experimental results with the elaborated sub-symbolic model. Conclusions and further directions of research are given in the final part of the paper.

2   Distributed Representations of Symbolic Structures

There are multiple ways of transforming a generic recursive structure in a distributed format. Foundations were developed in Tensor Product Variable Binding (TPVB) [27]. Later TPVB approach became an inspiration for such representation methods as Holographic Reduced Representations (HRRs), Binary Spater Codes [4] and Vector Symbolic Architectures (VSA) [15]. These ideas were generalized as Integrated Connectionist/Symbolic cognitive architecture [29] and later resulted in Gradient Symbolic Computation (GSC) framework [6,28]. Huge investments are made in research of Knowledge Base (KB) translation to a form of First-Order Logics (FOLs) with strictly defined rules and further encoding of such expressions [26,31]. FOL expressions can be represented as a labelled directed graph which may be translated to distributed representation with one of existing conjunctive non-temporal binding mechanism proposed in [24].

We consider TPVB as a relevant approach in our research due to its generic nature and continuing extensions of the original ideas. For example, recent works demonstrate applicability of TPVB for such tasks as image captioning [17] or question answering [21]. Also, TPVB can be used as the mechanism of structure recovery from a distributed representation to analyse the neural network ability to generalize and include structural properties of objects embeddings for which it learns to create [30]. Recent advances in deep learning architectures allowed several research groups to investigate an idea of learning structural embeddings so that a neural network decides how to encode the structure [20].

From the encoding strategy perspective, TPVB is a set of predefined rules for constructing a distributed representation of an arbitrary symbolic structure with no information loss and corresponding symbolic operations in the weights of the network so that the resulting structure emerges as a network output. Tensor Product Variable binding allows to build recursively such distributed representations on top of atomic elements: fillers and roles.

Definition 1. *Fillers and roles [27]. Let S be a set of symbolic structures. A role decomposition F/R for S is a pair of sets (F, R), the sets of fillers and roles, their Cartesian product $F \times R$ respectively and a mapping:*

$$\mu_{F/R} : F \times R \mapsto Pred(S); (f, r) \mapsto f/r. \tag{1}$$

For any pair $f \in F, r \in R$, the predicate on S $\mu_{F/R}(f, r) = f/r$ is expressed: f fills role r.

Definition 2. *Let s be a symbolic structure that consists of pairs $\{f_i, r_i\}$, where f_i represent a filler and r_i represents a role. Tensor product ψ is calculated in the following way:*

$$\psi = \sum_i f_i \bigotimes r_i \tag{2}$$

Given notation of roles and fillers, there are two primitive operations defined: *cons* and *ex*. The $cons(p, q)$ operation takes two trees as arguments and creates another tree that has tree p as a left child, or in terms of TPRs gets the role r_0, and q as a right child, or in terms of TPRs gets the role r_1. The important requirement is to select roles vectors so that they are linearly independent. The same requirement applies for the set of fillers vectors. As it was proved in [29] the *cons* operation can be expressed as a matrix-vector multiplication.

Definition 3. *Let r_0, r_1 denote role vectors, p, q - symbolic structures. Then, joining operation cons is defined:*

$$cons(p, q) = p \bigotimes r_0 + q \bigotimes r_1$$
$$= W_{cons_0} p + W_{cons_1} q \tag{3}$$

Definition 4. *Let r_0 denote a role vector, A is a length of any filler vector. Then joining matrix W_{cons_0} is calculated in the following way:*

$$W_{cons_0} = I \bigotimes 1_A \bigotimes r_0, \tag{4}$$

where I is the identity matrix on the total role vector space, 1_A is the identity matrix $A \times A$. W_{cons_1} matrices are defined in the manner similar to the W_{cons_0} matrices that join two sub-trees in one structure [29]. Extraction operation *ex* is defined in analogous way, however, it is used to extract an element stored in the tree by the given role, for example $ex_0(p)$ extracts the child of tree p that is placed under role r_0. The only difference in formulation of W_{ex_0} matrix is that dual role vectors are used instead of direct roles: r_0 or r_1. This operation is used in both extraction branches that are described in Sect. 3.

Definition 5. *Let r_0 denote a role vector, $s = cons(p, q)$ - a symbolic structure. Then, extraction operation ex_0 is defined:*

$$ex_0(s) = ex_0(cons(p, q)) = p, \tag{5}$$

Definition 6. *Let u_0 denote an extraction (or so-called unbinding [29]) vector, which belongs to the basis dual to the basis which includes r_0, A is a length of any filler vector. Then extraction matrix W_{ex_0} is calculated in the following way:*

$$W_{ex_0} = I \bigotimes 1_A \bigotimes u_0, \tag{6}$$

Aforementioned operations *cons*, ex_0, ex_1 are equivalent to operations over lists in software general-purpose functional programming languages like Lisp:

cons, *car*, *cdr*. These are universal operators that allow implementation of huge set of algorithms. Considering support of conditional operator, the representational power of these operators is even bigger. Therefore implementation of these operations, or equivalent *cons*, ex_0, ex_1, on the neural level opens the horizon for neural-symbolic computation of symbolic algorithms built on top of *cons*, *car* and *cdr*. Indeed, the matrices W_{ex_0} and W_{cons_0} determine the weights of a neural network, capable performing corresponding symbolic operations. In [29] a formal specification of their combination is given to produce a neural network equivalent for an arbitrary list manipulation operation.

Many models are already known for representation of linguistic intelligence capabilities in terms of sub-symbolic neural computations, like [4,6,28] or pre-trained deep bidirectional representations from unlabeled text like [13]. Among different approaches we distinguish Active-Passive Network (APNet) proposed by P. Smolensky [18]. This network performs two tasks: classification of a voice of a sentence and semantic analysis that allows to extract nominal subject and direct object dependencies in a form of a structure. Further analysis of this architecture through lenses of neural-symbolic computation identifies that the network relies on existence of three actions: extraction of specific elements of a structure, conditional branching, and construction of new structure from elements of input structures. Therefore, elaboration of a software design for this theoretical architecture allows further development of the field and construction of neural-symbolic means of performing linguistic assessments aggregation.

This network was designed to work over semantic parse trees, estimate the voice of a sentence and construct a predicate-calculus expression that contains information about verb V and relationship between agent A and patient P parts of such trees (Fig. 3a, Fig. 3b). It was proposed to use existence of *Aux* filler at a role r_{001} as a universal marker of Passive voice (Fig. 3a). Such a notation of roles should be read as left child (0) of the left child (0) of the right child (1) of the root of the given structure. Aforementioned primitive *ex* can be used to extract passive voice marker from a given sentence (7).

$$PassiveMarkerF(s) = ex_0(ex_0(ex_1(s))) \tag{7}$$

Once the voice of the input sentence is defined, it is possible to construct a desired predicate-calculus expression. In order to do that, each filler that is a part of such target structure (Fig. 3c) should be extracted from the corresponding input structure. For the Passive voice case extraction rules (8) for each fillers are different compared to extraction rules of analogous fillers in Active voice case (9).

$$
\begin{aligned}
V = V_{passive} &= ex_1(ex_0(ex_1(s))) \\
A = A_{passive} &= ex_1(ex_1(ex_1(s))) \\
P = P_{passive} &= ex_0(s)
\end{aligned}
\tag{8}
$$

$$
\begin{aligned}
V = V_{active} &= ex_0(ex_1(s)) \\
A = A_{active} &= ex_0(s) \\
P = P_{active} &= ex_1(ex_1(s))
\end{aligned}
\tag{9}
$$

Finally, once the fillers are found, the *cons* operation is used to obtain the desired structure (Fig. 3c).

$$AP(s) = cons(V, cons(A, P)) \qquad (10)$$

The aim of this research is elaboration of the neural network primitive capable of preforming several symbolic operations: conditional branching and extraction of elements. The aim of Active-Passive Network is intellectual analysis of parsed grammatical structures that implies application of symbolic operations mentioned above. Therefore, the design of the neural primitive proposed in this paper reflects the applied task of Active-Passive Net while persisting generality of the solution for future re-use in building neural-symbolic decision support system. Proposed neural design is covered in the next section.

3 Proposed Neural Design of Network with Conditional Branching

3.1 Network Architecture

Current research is targeted to propose a novel design of neural network primitive that is capable of performing various tasks on a distributed representation of a symbolic structure: extraction of elements, condition branching and construction of a new structure. As a demonstration the Active-Passive Network was chosen. The proposed design is shown on Fig. 2a. In general the neural network consists of three important blocks: one classification and two processing branches. The classification branch is aimed at identification of whether the given sentence is in Passive or Active voice. At the same time, processing branches extract necessary elements of a symbolic structure from its distributed representation in order to construct a predicate-calculus expression. Each branch is considered separately below.

Classification Branch. According to the semantic parse trees that are obtained from raw sentences there is an obvious marker that can be used for identification of a voice in a sentence. As it was mentioned in [18], existence of *Aux* is a clear marker of a sentence in a Passive voice iff it is placed as a left-child-of-left-child-of-right-child-of-root. When TPRs notation is applied to such structures, marker is expressed as existence of *filler Aux* with a positional role r_{001}. The overall idea of the classification branch of the proposed Active-Passive network is to check this filler on the given position and output a binary value, where *1* represents that given sentence is in Passive voice and *0* means that it is in Active voice. The structure of this branch is shown on Fig. 2b.

Inputs. Classification branch has one variable input that is an one-order tensor representing the encoded symbolic structure of the semantic parse tree. In our approach construction of such parse tree on the basis of an initial text is

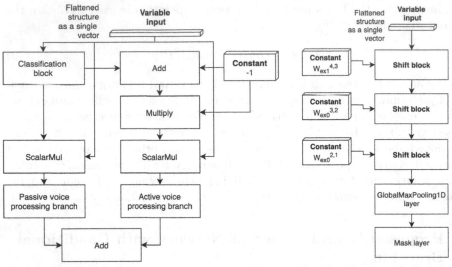

a. Overall design of a network.   b. Classification block design.

Fig. 2. Proposed architecture of a neural network primitive the performs: extraction of symbolic counterparts, conditional branching and construction of a new structure from input structure elements.

considered as an external task. The semantic parse tree can have an arbitrary structure, and algorithms from [12] can be used to encode it to the vector format. Apart from one variable input the network has three constant inputs that contain weights for the extraction operation. Those three inputs are by design matrices for operation ex: W_{ex_0} and W_{ex_1}. Matrices are generated in advance according to the recursive definition (4).

Shift Block. The classification branch of the Active/Passive Network contains three shift blocks. Each of them receives current tree representation and performs extraction of the particular child of this tree. More specifically, as the aim of the branch is to find the *Aux* filler, there is a sequence of three extraction or 'shift' blocks that perform retrieval of left child, left child and right child correspondingly. The output of each shift block is the distributed representation of the particular part of the input structure.

Outputs. As it was mentioned above the classification branch can be considered as a self-contained neural network capable of performing a basic task of classifying the voice of a sentence. The only output of a classification branch is binary and equals *1* when sentence is in Passive voice. From the engineering perspective, output is implemented as a Keras Mask layer[1].

---

[1] From now on network description contains terminology accepted in the Keras [7] and TensorFlow [1] software frameworks.

a. Input sentence in the Passive voice.   b. Input sentence in the Active voice.

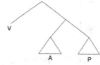

c. Output structure produced by a network.

Fig. 3. Types of symbolic structures used as inputs/output in a proposed neural network primitive.

Processing Branch. Processing branches play an important role in the Active-Passive Network and they perform construction of a new structure. It is impossible to exaggerate the importance of the fact that two most valuable structural operations, such as joining of two trees in a bigger one and extraction of the tree elements, can be performed on a sub-symbolic level. These two operations are key ones as a majority of other operations can be expressed with a help of just *cons* and *ex* primitives. There are two parallel processing branches due to the fact that sentences in Passive and Active voice have different architecture that is reflected in Fig. 3a and Fig. 3b respectively. As a result of each processing branch it is required to obtain a predicate-calculus expression that itself is a structure and consists of three elements: agent, patient and verb. Refer to Fig. 3c as a visual representation of the network output.

Inputs. Each of these branches accepts the one-order tensor that is used for further manipulations and construction of a new structure. This vector either contains the distributed representation of the input structure or is a placeholder filled with zeros. This completely depends on the type of the branch and results of the model classification.

When the sentence is in Passive voice then the input of the Passive voice processing branch is exactly the distributed representation of the input structure and Active voice processing branch receives a placeholder. In case a sentence is in Active voice, the first processing branch accepts a placeholder with zeros while the second branch receives the embedding of the structure. This behaviour is handled by the masking head before the Active voice processing branch. The idea behind such a switch implemented on the neural level is that in Active voice the sentence has a completely different structure and in order to extract particular filler, for example *V* (*Verb*), the completely different set and sequence of operations is needed.

The overall architecture of the processing branch is reflected in Fig. 4. In general, it consists of two parts: extraction and joining logic. Extraction part is

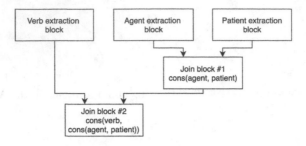

Fig. 4. Architecture of processing branch.

voice-specific and is different between sentences in Passive and Active voice. At the same time construction part is common and does not depend on the type of input sentence. Details about each type of processing branch elements are covered below.

Extraction Blocks. As it was stated above, extraction rules are fully defined by the type of the sentence. For example, in order to extract verb from the sentence in Passive voice it is required to perform operation $ex_1(ex_0(ex_1(s)))$ while for the Active voice sentence it is enough to execute $ex_1(ex_0(s))$ in order to extract V (*Verb*). Difference in operations results in different architecture of extraction branches. Figure 5a reflects extraction of V in Passive voice sentence and Fig. 5b shows extraction of the same filler in an Active voice sentence.

It is important to note that the idea of the extraction block is to extract a given filler from the input structure encoded in a form of a vector. This brings several limitations. The biggest one is that input sentences have to be encoded in a vector of the same size. This implies that Active voice sentence have to be encoded with an additional placeholder tensor in order to be on par with the Passive voice sentence. As a consequence, extraction of the left child of the root results not in the vector representing a filler A (*Agent*) but in a vector of bigger format. In order to satisfy the condition that any extraction branch results in the vector representing a filler, the additional cropping operation has to be introduced. In this task, it is specific for Active voice branch and is reflected on the Fig. 5b.

There are three extraction blocks in each extraction branch in the proposed design on the Active-Passive network due to the fact that the resulting structure (Fig. 3c) is constructed from three fillers.

Join Blocks. The next step after all the required fillers are extracted is to perform construction of the new structure that stands for the predicate-calculus expression (Fig. 3c). It is suggested to reuse existing mechanism of joining trees in one bigger tree with appropriate role assignment [8,12]. A scheme of such a join block is shown in Fig. 6. Each joining block accepts two variable inputs each representing the tree that would become a part of a resulting structure. Also, there are two constant inputs that represent the joining matrix (4) and

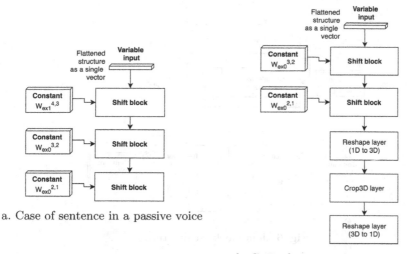

a. Case of sentence in a passive voice

b. Case of sentence in an active voice

Fig. 5. Example architecture of extraction branches

one is used as a utility constant when there is mismatch between the two variable inputs. A final operation of this branch is an addition operation that joins shifted sub-trees in a single distributed representation. The block shown in Fig. 6 represents the second join block in Fig. 4.

Outputs. The output of each processing branch is either a distributed representation of a new structure or a placeholder of the same dimension. According to the aforementioned condition, distributed representation of a new structure is presented as an output of the Passive branch if a sentence is in Passive voice and, in contrary, in case a sentence is in Active voice, distributed representation of a new structure appears as an output of an Active voice processing branch. The final sum of outputs of both branches is needed because there is no a-priori knowledge about input sentence voice. The output of the Active-Passive neural network is a distributed representation of a valid structure and it can be decoded with an existing methods of extracting fillers [18,27].

3.2   Network Analysis

The proposed architecture demonstrates practical feasibility of expressing symbolic operations in a distributed and robust manner that is a neural network. It is implemented with the Keras framework [7] and Tensorflow backend [1]. There is a clear separation of responsibilities in the network and selected parts can be considered as standalone neural networks that solve more specific task. Moreover, the proposed neural network combines both joining and extraction operations and also contains conditional branching for handling conditions on

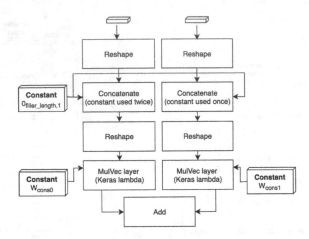

Fig. 6. Join block architecture

the sub-symbolic level. However, there are several important aspects that should be considered as directions of further research:

1. common sub-graphs sharing. More strict analysis of the proposed architecture would reveal that parallel processing branches as well as classification branch contain execution sub-graphs that are common by the operation they perform. At the same time, in the neural network this property is not re-used, although more smart construction rules would allow to decrease computational complexity of the solution. At the same time, there should be a certain trade-off because once those sub-graphs become common across all the branches the overall network cannot be expressed as a cascade of smaller neural networks that can be also executed separately on different instances of hardware. The maximum performance gain and various optimization options should be investigated in order to understand the best possible trade off between network architecture expressiveness and utility.
2. generation of the network that solves the task described by arbitrary combination of primitive operations like *cons* or *ex*. The overall goal of research in this field is building a bridge between symbolic and sub-symbolic computations. Therefore, elaboration of a flexible network generator would allow to make a step forward in this direction. However, this is a challenging task that requires thorough research and identification of minimum set of operations that should be supported by such generator in order to express arbitrary symbolic algorithm in a distributed manner.
3. comparison of semantic tree embeddings obtained with TPRs approaches and deep learning. Due to the fact that TPRs allow getting embeddings of a sentence it would be extremely interesting to analyse validity of using them in a generic text analysis task. However, in order to prove it, those embeddings have to be really representative and reflect the context of the usage.

This direction is the most open one and goes far beyond elaboration of neural architectures for expressing symbolic operations.

The proposed neural design considers generation of the network that is not trainable and produces results equivalent to those produced by the symbolic algorithm, compared to other examples of trainable neural-symbolic systems [22] that perform reasoning probabilistically. Network generation, or compilation, is not a novel topic in the field of neural architectures applied to neural-symbolic computation, for example networks compiled from logic formulas [23]. Such networks are characterised by thousands of neural units and connections between them. However, due to the fact that neural networks are by design distributed and parallel, it is a topic of another research to analyze large-scale gains of massive parallelism that would make such architectures computationally justified. The Active-Passive Network works on top of distributed Tensor Product Representations that provide compact and scalable binding capabilities for expressing symbolic structures and operations on them.

4   Evaluation of the Proposed Method

In order to explain application of the developed primitive for conditional structural transformations, we embedded it inside the APNet for active-passive voice recognition. In [9] detailed examples of actual text sentences are given those parsing trees correspond to symbolic structures from Fig. 3a and Fig. 3b. In order to encode each structure in a distributed form each filler and role are defined as linearly independent vectors, exact values are selected randomly as they do not play any role other than encoding a particular element.

$$A = \begin{bmatrix} 7\ 0\ 0\ 0\ 0 \end{bmatrix} V = \begin{bmatrix} 0\ 4\ 0\ 0\ 0 \end{bmatrix}$$
$$P = \begin{bmatrix} 0\ 0\ 2\ 0\ 0 \end{bmatrix} Aux = \begin{bmatrix} 0\ 0\ 0\ 5\ 0 \end{bmatrix} \quad (11)$$
$$by = \begin{bmatrix} 0\ 0\ 0\ 0\ 3 \end{bmatrix} r_0 = \begin{bmatrix} 10\ 0 \end{bmatrix} r_1 = \begin{bmatrix} 0\ 5 \end{bmatrix}$$

According to the rules defined in [27] and using the lightweight binding network proposed in [8,12], both sentences are translated to the distributed representation (12), (13).

$$S_{Passive} =$$

$$\begin{bmatrix} 0 \\ 0 \\ 0 \\ 0 \\ 0 \end{bmatrix}, \begin{bmatrix} [0,0] \\ [0,0] \\ [20,0] \\ [0,0] \\ [0,0] \end{bmatrix}, \begin{bmatrix} [[0,0],[0,0]] \\ [[0,0],[0,0]] \\ [[0,0],[0,0]] \\ [[0,0],[0,0]] \\ [[0,0],[0,0]] \end{bmatrix},$$

$$\begin{bmatrix} [[[0,0],[0,0]],[[0,0],[0,875]]] \\ [[[0,0],[0,0]],[[0,1000],[0,0]]] \\ [[[0,0],[0,0]],[[0,0],[0,0]]] \\ [[[0,2500],[0,0]],[[0,0],[0,0]]] \\ [[[0,0],[0,750]],[[0,0],[0,0]]] \end{bmatrix} \quad (12)$$

$$S_{Active} =$$

$$\begin{bmatrix} 0 \\ 0 \\ 0 \\ 0 \\ 0 \end{bmatrix}, \begin{bmatrix} [70,0] \\ [0,0] \\ [0,0] \\ [0,0] \\ [0,0] \end{bmatrix}, \begin{bmatrix} [[0,0],[0,0]] \\ [[0,200],[0,0]] \\ [[0,0],[0,50]] \\ [[0,0],[0,0]] \\ [[0,0],[0,0]] \end{bmatrix} \tag{13}$$

One of the requirements for correct inference of the classification branch is that representation of active and passive sentences should be of the same size. For that, the Active sentence representation is extended with an additional tensor filled with zeros. When classification branch is executed, the *Aux* filler is extracted. For the Passive voice sentence this filler is extracted without any loss, while for the Active voice sentence it is absent and application of the extraction rules results in the vector of the same size as any of fillers is but filled with all zeros. As a result, the branch outputs *1* for the first sentence and *0* for the second one.

Another important aspect is the output of the model. As it was described above, the output of the model is the distributed representation of the new structure that stands for the predicate-calculus expression. For this example, such representation would be the same for both sentences (14) as we encode fillers but not particular words of those sentences.

$$S_{Result} =$$

$$\begin{bmatrix} 0 \\ 0 \\ 0 \\ 0 \\ 0 \end{bmatrix}, \begin{bmatrix} [0,0] \\ [0,40] \\ [0,0] \\ [0,0] \\ [0,0] \end{bmatrix}, \begin{bmatrix} [[0,350],[0,0]] \\ [[0,0],[0,50]] \\ [[0,0],[0,00]] \\ [[0,0],[0,0]] \\ [[0,0],[0,0]] \end{bmatrix} \tag{14}$$

Finally, each filler can be extracted according to the rules defined in [27]. The proposed neural network solves the task of defining the voice of the sentence as well as allows constructing the new structure from the elements of input sentence in a scalable and robust manner. From the performance perspective, grammatical parse trees encoding takes approximately 1.3 ms, Active-Passive Network generation and inference take 5.5 and 1.4 ms respectively. Benchmarking was made with the following setup: Intel(R) Core(TM) i7-4770HQ CPU 2.20GHz (not fixed frequency). Implementation of the neural network primitive is available as an open-source project[2]. Experimentation results show that the developed neural network primitive enables conditional distributed computations as required.

The method proposed imposes limitations to the maximum depth of the processed symbolic structures. Thus a designer should know the maximum depth of the structures in advance and use it as a parameter for generating the corresponding primitive.

---

[2] https://github.com/demid5111/ldss-tensor-structures.

5   Conclusion

The results obtained in this paper contribute to the neural-symbolic paradigm by demonstrating execution of symbolic operations on the sub-symbolic level [2]: translation of symbolic knowledge into the network, executing the network or performing reasoning and knowledge extraction from the network output. Our method enables automatic design of Keras-based software implementation of a distributed computational structure for a generic primitive for conditional structural transformations. Authors consider that primitive as an important building element of a linguistic-based decision-making support system as it was depicted in Fig. 1. A recent work [11] demonstrates joint application of the developed primitive with other elements of that scheme for distributed implementation of arithmetic operations, which in own turn will be applied for distributed implementation of aggregation operators. The results of these works contribute to the support of the principal hypothesis, which states that linguistic information aggregation can be expressed in the form of structural manipulations and if it is true, then this aggregation step of multiple decision-making methods can be expressed in a distributed and robust manner of sub-symbolic, or connectionist, computation. The development of such models would allow for construction of fully-integrated monolithic neural-symbolic systems. At the same time, there is an important practical aspect of the selected binding mechanism (TPRs) that should be further analyzed: the size of the distributed representations and the dependence of this size on the size of the input structures that should be encoded.

Acknowledgements. Authors sincerely appreciate all valuable comments and suggestions given by the reviewers. The reported study was funded by RFBR, project number 19-37-90058.

References

1. Abadi, M., et al.: TensorFlow: large-scale machine learning on heterogeneous systems (2015). http://tensorflow.org/. Software available from tensorflow.org
2. Besold, T.R., et al.: Neural-symbolic learning and reasoning: a survey and interpretation. arXiv preprint arXiv:1711.03902 (2017)
3. Besold, T.R., Kühnberger, K.U.: Towards integrated neural-symbolic systems for human-level AI: two research programs helping to bridge the gaps. Biol. Inspired Cogn. Archit. **14**, 97–110 (2015)
4. Browne, A., Sun, R.: Connectionist inference models. Neural Netw. **14**(10), 1331–1355 (2001)
5. Cheng, P., Zhou, B., Chen, Z., Tan, J.: The topsis method for decision making with 2-tuple linguistic intuitionistic fuzzy sets. In: 2017 IEEE 2nd Advanced Information Technology, Electronic and Automation Control Conference (IAEAC), pp. 1603–1607. IEEE (2017)
6. Cho, P.W., Goldrick, M., Smolensky, P.: Incremental parsing in a continuous dynamical system: sentence processing in gradient symbolic computation. Linguistics Vanguard **3**(1), 1–10 (2017)
7. Chollet, F., et al.: Keras (2015). https://keras.io

8. Demidovskij, A.: Implementation aspects of tensor product variable binding in connectionist systems. In: Bi, Y., Bhatia, R., Kapoor, S. (eds.) IntelliSys 2019. AISC, vol. 1037, pp. 97–110. Springer, Cham (2020). https://doi.org/10.1007/978-3-030-29516-5_9

9. Demidovskij, A.: Automatic construction of tensor product variable binding neural networks for neural-symbolic intelligent systems. In: Proceedings of 2nd International Conference on Electrical, Communication and Computer Engineering, pp. not published, accepted. IEEE (2020)

10. Demidovskij, A., Babkin, E.: Developing a distributed linguistic decision making system. Business Informatics 13(1 (eng)) (2019)

11. Demidovskij, A., Babkin, E.: Towards designing linguistic assessments aggregation as a distributed neuroalgorithm. In: 2020 XXII International Conference on Soft Computing and Measurements (SCM)), pp. not published, accepted. IEEE (2020)

12. Demidovskij, A.V.: Towards automatic manipulation of arbitrary structures in connectivist paradigm with tensor product variable binding. In: Kryzhanovsky, B., Dunin-Barkowski, W., Redko, V., Tiumentsev, Y. (eds.) NEUROINFORMATICS 2019. SCI, vol. 856, pp. 375–383. Springer, Cham (2020). https://doi.org/10.1007/978-3-030-30425-6_44

13. Devlin, J., Chang, M.W., Lee, K., Toutanova, K.: Bert: pre-training of deep bidirectional transformers for language understanding. arXiv preprint arXiv:1810.04805 (2018)

14. Fodor, J.A., Pylyshyn, Z.W., et al.: Connectionism and cognitive architecture: a critical analysis. Cognition $28(1–2)$, 3–71 (1988)

15. Gallant, S.I., Okaywe, T.W.: Representing objects, relations, and sequences. Neural Comput. $25(8)$, 2038–2078 (2013)

16. Golmohammadi, D.: Neural network application for fuzzy multi-criteria decision making problems. Int. J. Prod. Econ. $131(2)$, 490–504 (2011)

17. Huang, Q., Smolensky, P., He, X., Deng, L., Wu, D.: Tensor product generation networks for deep NLP modeling. In: Proceedings of the 2018 Conference of the North American Chapter of the Association for Computational Linguistics: Human Language Technologies, vol. 1 (Long Papers), pp. 1263–1273. Association for Computational Linguistics, New Orleans (2018). https://doi.org/10.18653/v1/N18-1114. https://www.aclweb.org/anthology/N18-1114

18. Legendre, G., Miyata, Y., Smolensky, P.: Distributed recursive structure processing. In: Advances in Neural Information Processing Systems, pp. 591–597 (1991)

19. Leitgeb, H.: Interpreted dynamical systems and qualitative laws: from neural networks to evolutionary systems. Synthese $146(1–2)$, 189–202 (2005)

20. McCoy, R.T., Linzen, T., Dunbar, E., Smolensky, P.: RNNS implicitly implement tensor product representations. arXiv preprint arXiv:1812.08718 (2018)

21. Palangi, H., Smolensky, P., He, X., Deng, L.: Question-answering with grammatically-interpretable representations. In: Thirty-Second AAAI Conference on Artificial Intelligence (2018)

22. de Penning, H.L.H., Garcez, A.S.d., Lamb, L.C., Meyer, J.J.C.: A neural-symbolic cognitive agent for online learning and reasoning. In: Twenty-Second International Joint Conference on Artificial Intelligence (2011)

23. Pinkas, G.: Reasoning, nonmonotonicity and learning in connectionist networks that capture propositional knowledge. Artif. Intell. $77(2)$, 203–247 (1995)

24. Pinkas, G., Lima, P., Cohen, S.: A dynamic binding mechanism for retrieving and unifying complex predicate-logic knowledge. In: Villa, A.E.P., Duch, W., Érdi, P., Masulli, F., Palm, G. (eds.) ICANN 2012. LNCS, vol. 7552, pp. 482–490. Springer, Heidelberg (2012). https://doi.org/10.1007/978-3-642-33269-2_61

25. Pinkas, G., Lima, P., Cohen, S.: Representing, binding, retrieving and unifying relational knowledge using pools of neural binders. Biol. Inspired Cogn. Archit. **6**, 87–95 (2013)
26. Serafini, L., Garcez, A.d.: Logic tensor networks: deep learning and logical reasoning from data and knowledge. arXiv preprint arXiv:1606.04422 (2016)
27. Smolensky, P.: Tensor product variable binding and the representation of symbolic structures in connectionist systems. Artif. Intell. **46**(1–2), 159–216 (1990)
28. Smolensky, P., Goldrick, M., Mathis, D.: Optimization and quantization in gradient symbol systems: a framework for integrating the continuous and the discrete in cognition. Cogn. Sci. **38**(6), 1102–1138 (2014)
29. Smolensky, P., Legendre, G.: The Harmonic Mind: From Neural Computation to Optimality-theoretic Grammar (Cognitive Architecture), Vol. 1. MIT press, Cambridge (2006)
30. Soulos, P., McCoy, T., Linzen, T., Smolensky, P.: Discovering the compositional structure of vector representations with role learning networks. arXiv preprint arXiv:1910.09113 (2019)
31. Teso, S., Sebastiani, R., Passerini, A.: Structured learning modulo theories. Artif. Intell. **244**, 166–187 (2017)
32. Wei, C., Liao, H.: A multigranularity linguistic group decision-making method based on hesitant 2-tuple sets. Int. J. Intell. Syst. **31**(6), 612–634 (2016)
33. Yousefpour, A., et al.: Failout: achieving failure-resilient inference in distributed neural networks. arXiv preprint arXiv:2002.07386 (2020)

Incremental Structure-Evolving Intelligent Systems with Advanced Interpretational Properties

Sergey Kovalev[1] (ORCID), Anna Kolodenkova[2], and Andrey Sukhanov[1](✉) (ORCID)

[1] JSC "NIIAS" Rostov Branch, Lenina Street 44/13, Rostov-on-Don 344038, Russia
{ksm,a.suhanov}@rfniias.ru
[2] Samara State Technical University, Molodogvardeyskaya Street 244, Samara 443100, Russia
anna82_42@mail.ru

Abstract. The paper considers some problems related to interpretability of evolving intelligent systems and online design and optimization methods for such systems under streaming data control. In the proposed online approach, the main criteria are the modeling accuracy, which is based on mean squared error minimization, and the set of the interpretability criteria, some of which are the complexity and the consistency of the knowledge base from fuzzy system. The novel incremental algorithm of fuzzy model structure reformation based on incremental clustering procedure is presented. The possibility of development of the novel immunological approach to intelligent data processing based on proposed evolving systems is considered.

Keywords: Evolving fuzzy systems · Interpretability of fuzzy systems · Structure adaptation · Double plasticity

1 Introduction

In modern industrial and production systems, the tasks of online adaptation of system models to newly incoming data are becoming increasingly important. This is due to the growing complexity of the considered systems and the variability of external conditions, which, during the functioning of the system, can bring it to new modes that were not incorporated into the initial version of the model. Attempts to construct mathematical models that are able to fully describe the behavior of the system in all possible modes lead to unreasonably high costs associated with the attracting a large number of experts and performing additional research on preliminary analysis of available data, such as this is done with solving some classification problems in decision support systems [1].

To solve the above-mentioned problems, the so-called Evolving models based on the paradigms of incremental training and evolutionary modeling are actively developed [2]. Among them, Evolving Intelligent Systems (EIS) can be highlighted [3]. EIS based on the hybridization of fuzzy models like those, which are used in the modern ANFIS versions [4], with online machine learning methods, have the ability to extract and update knowledge from data streams taking into account changing conditions.

© Springer Nature Switzerland AG 2020
S. O. Kuznetsov et al. (Eds.): RCAI 2020, LNAI 12412, pp. 134–151, 2020.
https://doi.org/10.1007/978-3-030-59535-7_10

These systems have several advantages that provide them with wide practical application [5, 6].

Developers of EIS face to a number of problems, one of which is the search for a balance between the stability of the developed model, which ensures its optimality over a sufficiently long time interval, and plasticity, which ensures its ability to respond dynamically to input data [7]. Such a balance is called stability-plasticity dilemma [8]. The ability to strike a balance between the stability and plasticity of the EIS is their important distinguishing feature, which attracts new application areas. In particular, specific artificial immune systems [9] can be taken into account, where information is processed based on double plasticity principle. The key factor of such systems is the ability to implement a fundamentally new approach to information processing based on the analysis of structural and parametric changes occurring in the model, and not in the traditional input data analysis. To realize this possibility, it is fully necessary to give the EIS one more important property related to the transparency or interpretability of a fuzzy system. There is also a number of reasons to advance the interpretability of EIS [10–12]. A relatively new application field of EIS with advanced interpretational properties is the development of socio-economic models that can describe the reasons of the sharp change in housing prices depending on the changing socio-economic conditions in the region [13] or stock market indices fluctuations. In such tasks, the EIS should represent the main causal relationships in the modelled process via user-friendly linguistic descriptions [14].

A general idea of existing methods and systems with incremental training can be found in [15]. Particular approaches are ePL [16], eT2FIS [17], eTS [18], FLEXFIS [6], SAFIS [19], SONFIN [20], SOFNN [21]. There are a number of approaches based on optimal granulation of the input variable space, which ensures the exclusion of nonexistent or unlikely model states, as, for example, is implemented in systems SAFIS, SOFNN or SONFIN. A complete review on the subject under consideration is given in [22].

EIS are significantly different from many other incremental training models that rely on black box architectures such as neural networks or support vector machines, which in principle are not interpretable. However, automatically designed EISs under the control of streaming data may also not have or lose their interpretability. These losses can sometimes be compensated by introducing special interpretational restrictions into the training process [23] or using post-processing to increase the interpretative properties of the created model [24]. A complete analysis of these methods can be found in [25]. Nevertheless, up to now, in the field of designing an EIS, the main attention have been being paid not to interpretational criteria but to accuracy ones, which as a rule based on minimization of the mean square error of modeling.

The aim of this work is to develop a new approach to the design of interpreted EIS by integrating a number of interpretational criteria into incremental training schemes. The main attention is paid to the structural adaptation of the EIS with a focus on simultaneous structural changes that occur under the influence of continuous parametric model updates.

2 Streaming Data and Takagi-Sugeno Model

One of the main reasons for developing proposed EIS is the ever-increasing need for online streaming data processing. In general, a data stream is an endless sequence of vector-numerical values that cannot be processed in batch mode. It is characterized by the following properties [5]:

- Data samples are continuously obtained in the system;
- Data samples are ordered in time and the system cannot change this order;
- The data stream is not limited in size, and the data is available while information is collected by sensors and other input devices;
- After a sample or a piece of data is processed, it is excluded from the system and is not available in future.

Formally, data stream can be defined as endless sequence $\mathbf{z}(t) = [\mathbf{x}(t); \mathbf{y}(t)]$, ($t = 1$, 2,...), where $\mathbf{x}(t) = (x_1, ..., x_n)$ is the input data vector, $\mathbf{y}(t) = (y_1, ..., y_m)$ is the output data vector. Commonly, the main problem of EIS is the prediction of $\mathbf{y}(t)$ using $\mathbf{x}(t)$.

Data processing in stream data modelling requires the use of incremental algorithms based on the concept of incremental heuristic search [26]. Incremental algorithms must create and adapt the model step-by-step when obtaining every new data sample. Formally, incremental update of fuzzy model $M(t)$ is defined as follows:

$$M(t) = F_{inc}(M(t-1), \mathbf{z}(t)).$$

Therefore, increment update of fuzzy model is based on the current data values and the previously obtained model without use of the previously obtained data.

There are two update modes of EIS during incremental training. The first one is the parameters update (parametric adaptation), which changes all or the part of parameters of the initial model preserving the number of parameters. The second one is the structure update (structure adaptation), which exclude or include fuzzy rules, variables or operators into knowledge base (KB).

The most important aspect of incremental training is the so-called stability-plasticity dilemma [8], which is connected with the searching for compromise between flexible changes of parameters of a model and its structure convergence. On the one hand, intensive updating of the EIS is required in some cases. For example, it is required in conditions of a significant drift in the stream characteristics. On the other hand, it is desirable that the incremental algorithm does not respond to one-time "outliers" and converges to some optimal solution, for example, to the same as the hypothetical package solution obtained using all the data. The tool for processing streaming data is evolving fuzzy systems, among which the most popular are evolving fuzzy models such as Takagi-Sugeno (eTS models, or simply eTS). Structure of eTS is defined by the fuzzy rules, input variables, fuzzy sets, linguistic connections and output mechanism. Fuzzy rule of eTS can be defined as:

$$r_i : \ IF \ (x_1 = x_{i1}^*) \ AND, \ ..., \ AND \ (x_n = x_{in}^*) \ THEN \ y_i = a_{i0} + \sum_{j=1}^{n} a_{ij}x_j. \quad (1)$$

where $x_{ik}^* (k = 1,..,n)$ are the fuzzy terms of the antecedent; a_{i0} is the point parameter of the consequent; a_{ij} are the linear parameters of the consequent.

Consequents of fuzzy eTS rules are linear functions, while antecedents are usually described by Gaussian functions:

$$\mu_{ij}(x_j) = \exp\left(-\frac{(c_{ij} - x_j)^2}{2\sigma_{ij}^2}\right), \ i = 1, \ldots, R, \ j = 1, \ldots, n. \qquad (2)$$

Where $\mu_{ij}(x_j)$ is the membership function (MF) of the current input data point to jth variable in ith fuzzy rule, c_{ij} is the focal center of jth variable in ith rule; σ_{ij} is the deviation (width) of $\mu_{ij}(x_j)$ on axis of jth variable.

The activation degree of a fuzzy rule on $\mathbf{x}(t)$, which is also called as truth degree of fuzzy rule, defined as T-norm [27], which is often defined as production operator:

$$\tau^i(\mathbf{x}(t)) = T^j(\mu_{i1}(x_1), \ldots, \mu_{in}(x_n)) = \prod_{j=1}^{n} \mu_{ij}(x_j). \qquad (3)$$

where $\tau^i(\mathbf{x}(t))$ is the activation degree of ith fuzzy rule.

Each fuzzy rule of eTS approximates the output signal in a certain local area of the feature space centered at the focal point. In this case, the degree of activation of the rule depends on the distance from the focal point, and is represented in Gaussian form (2). Due to the fuzzy specification of antecedents, any nonlinear system can be an approximate set of fuzzy locally linear subsystems represented by fuzzy eTS rules [28]. The output signal of eTS with R rules is calculated by a linear combination of normalized outputs of individual fuzzy rules:

$$y = \sum_{i=1}^{R} \lambda_i(\mathbf{x}) \cdot y_i = \sum_{i=1}^{R} \left(\lambda_i(\mathbf{x}) \cdot \pi_i^{\mathrm{T}} \cdot \mathbf{x}_e\right), \ \mathbf{x}_e = [1; \mathbf{x}] \qquad (4)$$

where $\lambda_i(\mathbf{x})$ is the normalized activation degree of ith rule, y_i is the ith rule output, $\pi_i = (a_{i0}, \ldots, a_{in})$ is the vector of the linear parameters of ith rule's consequent, $\mathbf{x}_e$ is the extended input data vector, R is the total number of the fuzzy rules in eTS.

$\lambda_i(\mathbf{x})$ is defined as follows:

$$\lambda_i(\mathbf{x}) = \tau^i(\mathbf{x}) \left/ \sum_{j=1}^{R} \tau^j(\mathbf{x}) \right.$$

In practical applications in the consequent part of eTS, first-order functions, represented by point values a_{i0}, are often used. In this case, the output formula is simplified:

$$y = \sum_{i=1}^{R} \lambda_i(\mathbf{x}) a_{i0} \qquad (5)$$

3   Generalized Criterion Based Approach to ETS Design

Conventional training problem for eTS is divided into two tasks [29]: training the knowledge base by new rules creation and determining the parameters of the fuzzy terms (c_{ij} and σ_{ij}) from MF; training linear parameters from the consequents of the fuzzy rules.

Criterion of training, as a rule, is the mean squared error (MSE) minimization on the training set. The first task can be solved by clustering the input-output space represented by training dataset.

For given training set $\mathbf{z}(t)$ it is required to find the set of c_{ij}, σ_{ij}, a_{i0} for fuzzy rules, which minimize the target function:

$$J_{A_{cc}}(c_{ij},\ \sigma_{ij},\ a_{i0}) = \sum_t \left[y(t) - \sum_{i=1}^{R} \lambda_i(\mathbf{x}(t))a_{i0} \right]^2. \tag{6}$$

Formula (6) can be presented more compactly:

$$J_{A_{cc}}(c_{ij},\ \sigma_{ij},\ a_{i0}) = \sum_{t=1}^{L} \left[y(t) - \boldsymbol{\lambda}^{\mathrm{T}}(t) \cdot \mathbf{x}(t) \right]^2, \tag{7}$$

where $\boldsymbol{\lambda}(t) = (\lambda_1(\mathbf{x}(t)),\ldots, \lambda_R(\mathbf{x}(t)))$ is the vector of normalized activation degrees.

For fixed parameters of c_{ij}, σ_{ij}, the second task is to estimate the point parameters a_{i0} of the rules' conclusions. It can be solved using the recursive least squares method [30], or the local consequent optimization method supporting incremental mode [31]. Criterion (7) improves the accuracy of modeling. The easiest way to increase the interpretability properties of eTS is to introduce a "penalty" correction term in the accuracy criterion (7) that "punishs" decision options that poorly meet the requirements of interpretability. Let $\varsigma_1,\ldots, \varsigma_p$ denote particular criteria characterizing various interpretability indices, such as completeness and compactness of description, consistency of the rule base, etc. [15]. Note that the interpretability criteria depend on the same parameters of fuzzy rules as the main, precision criterion (7), i.e., $\varsigma_l = \varsigma_l(c_{ij}, \sigma_{ij}, a_{i0})$. To aggregate particular criteria into a single indicator, they are combined on the basis of geometric mean:

$$J_{Int}(c_{ij},\ \sigma_{ij},\ a_{i0}) = \sqrt[p]{\prod_{l=1}^{p} \varsigma_l(c_{ij},\ \sigma_{ij},\ a_{i0})},\ i = 1,\ldots,n,\ j = 1,\ldots,m_i, \tag{8}$$

where n is the number of variables, m is the number of fuzzy terms for ith variable, p is the number of particular criteria. Aggregated interpretational criterion $J_{Int}(c_{ij}, \sigma_{ij}, a_{i0})$ acts as a correctional penalty term, which forms a combined criterion by adding to the accuracy criterion (7):

$$I(c_{ij}, \sigma_{ij}, a_{i0}) = \alpha \cdot J_{Acc}(c_{ij}, \sigma_{ij}, a_{i0}) + (1 - \alpha) \cdot J_{Int}(c_{ij}, \sigma_{ij}, a_{i0}) \tag{9}$$

where α is the coefficient reflecting the significance of the main accuracy criterion (7) with respect to the aggregated interpretation criterion (8). Thus, the problem of the online design of interpreted eTS models is the development of an incremental approach and algorithms for the online adaptation of eTS, represented by expressions (1)–(5), under the control of stream data that minimize the combined criterion (9).

The criteria and methodology of eTS incremental adaptation is considered below. The methodology enables the optimization of criterion (9) based on the use of the incremental clustering procedure with a built-in mechanism for interpretational properties accounting.

4   Interpretational Criteria for Fuzzy Systems

Despite the fact that today a single interpretability index for fuzzy systems (FS) has not been developed, this criterion is most often associated with a property expressed in terms such as minimalism of KB, simplicity of description, compactness, transparency or readability [25]. This criterion (it is arbitrarily called as Simplicity) is important because it is directly related to a number of other interpretability criteria, such as distinguishability of fuzzy rules, consistency or redundancy of knowledge bases. In addition, some interpretability criteria indirectly affect simplicity, for example, the complexity of the rules' conclusion, the number of variables and operators in the rules' descriptions. In many problems, the simplicity of FS description acts, along with accuracy, as the main design criterion, for example, in the tasks of automatic knowledge extraction. A general definition of the simplicity of FS through the size of the KB is given in [15].

Definition 1.
Let F_1 be the FS formed using one of the accuracy criteria, for example, the minimum of MSE. Then the most simplified version of the FS satisfies the following criterion:

$$\min_{\|F\|}\{(\|F_1\| > \|F\|) \wedge (acc(F) \geq acc(F_1) - \varepsilon)\}, \tag{10}$$

where $\|F\|$ is the fuzzy rule number in maximally reduced FS, which is enough accurate, acc is the accuracy of the fuzzy system, ε is the possible accuracy loss. Formula (10) means that loss of accuracy ε defined by user is possible for the simplest FS.

Obviously, the simplicity of FS is directly related to the size of its KB or to the number of the included fuzzy rules. As a part of an incremental approach, it is proposed to determine a criterion of simplicity via the concept of instantaneous complexity of NS. The latter is characterized by the number of fuzzy rules $\|F(t)\|$ in the KB of the FS at current time t. The instant complexity of the FS is determined on the basis of the available statistics as follows:

$$Sim_t(F) = \frac{\|F(t)\|}{\|\overline{F}\| + \sigma_{KB}}, \tag{11}$$

where σ_{KB} is the mean squared error, $\|\overline{F}\|$ is the average number of rules in KB at time t, which is calculated as:

$$\|\overline{F}\| = \sum_{i=1}^{t} \|F_i\| \Big/ t.$$

Another important criterion of interpretability, which allows implementation within the framework of incremental design of FS, is the inconsistency of the knowledge base. Inconsistency of the knowledge base arises if there are conflicting or inconsistent fuzzy rules in it, that is, rules that are similar in the antecedent but not similar in the consequent.

Definition 2 [15].

Rule r_1 is inconsistent with rule r_2 if and only if
$S_{ante}(r_1, r_2) \geq S_{cons}(r_1, r_2)$ with $S_{ante}(r_1, r_2) \geq th$
where S_{ante} is the similarity degree for antecedent part, S_{cons} is the similarity degree for consequent part, th is the threshold selected by user.

As S_{ante}, aggregation of any previously considered similarity measure of fuzzy sets via T-conorm is suitable. As a measure of the similarity of consequents, one of the simplest is

$$S_{cons}(r_1, r_2) = \frac{1}{1 + (a_{10} - a_{20})^2},$$

where a_{10}, a_{20} are the point parameters of consequents.

In the further calculations, the measure of consequent difference is required. It is calculated as follows:

$$\overline{S}_{cons}(r_1, r_2) = 1 - S_{cons}(r_1, r_2) = \frac{(a_{10} - a_{20})^2}{1 + (a_{10} - a_{20})^2}$$

In [15], more complex way of consistency measurement for fuzzy rules is proposed:

$$Cons(r_1, r_2) = e^{-\left(\frac{S_{ante}(r_1, r_2)}{S_{cons}(r_1, r_2)} - 1\right)^2 / \left(\frac{1}{S_{ante}}\right)^7}. \tag{12}$$

The motivation for choosing the consistency criterion in the form of (12) is associated with a stronger influence on the consistency of fuzzy rules of low similarity of antecedents than high one. The consistency of the knowledge base is determined based on the consistency of all pairs of rules included in it as follows:

$$Cons_{all} = Agg_{i,j=1; i \neq j}^{C} Cons(r_i, r_j), \tag{13}$$

where Agg is the aggregation operator, which is presented in form of T-norm or S-norm

For incremental implementation, it is convenient to use the following, more formal definition of consistency.

Definition 3. Measures of consistency for r_i and r_j are the following:

$Cons(r_i, r_j) = S_{ante}(r_i, r_j) \rightarrow S_{cons}(r_i, r_j)$,
which can be transformed into the following form using fuzzy udentity rule:

$$Cons(r_i, r_j) = \overline{S}_{ante}(r_i, r_j) \vee S_{cons}(r_i, r_j) \tag{14}$$

It should be noted that the measure of consistency (14) supports incremental implementation with the following choice of similarity measures between antecedents and consequents.

$$\overline{S}_{ante}(r_i, \ r_j) = 1 - \frac{1}{1 + d(A_i, \ A_j)} = \frac{d(A_i, \ A_j)}{1 + d(A_i, \ A_j)},$$

$$S_{cons}(r_i, \ r_j) = \frac{1}{1 + d(a_{i0}, \ a_{j0})}, \tag{15}$$

where A_i is the vector of antecedents for ith rule, $d(x,y)$ is the distance between a and b. In such choice, the consistency for r_i and r_j is the following:

$$Cons(r_i, \ r_j) = S\left(\frac{d(A_i, \ A_j)}{1 + d(A_i, \ A_j)}, \ \frac{1}{1 + d(a_{i0}, \ a_{j0})} \right),$$

where $S(\bullet)$ is S-norm.

Particularly, in Lukasiewicz logic, this measure is the following:

$$Cons(r_i, \ r_j) = \frac{1 + 3d(A_i, \ A_j) + d(a_{i0}, \ a_{j0}) + 2d(A_i, \ A_j)d(a_{i0}, \ a_{j0})}{(1 + d(A_i, \ A_j))(1 + d(a_{i0}, \ a_{j0}))}$$

5   Increment Clustering Based Approach to eTS Design

The main objective of this study is to develop a new incremental approach to the design of interpreted eTS with an emphasis on structural updates of the fuzzy model. Structural updates of eTS are carried out by updating fuzzy rules based on clustering of the feature space in the online mode, which is called incremental clustering.

The idea of incremental clustering is based on a recursive assessment of the density of data represented by points in the feature input space, and dynamic modification of clusters when the density of points is changed. For clustering problems, several methods have been developed for estimating data density: the nuclear method [32], mountain functions [33], potential methods [34], etc. As a rule, Gauss functions are used for density estimation:

$$P(\mathbf{z}(t)) = \exp\left(-\sum_{i=1}^{t-1} \frac{||\mathbf{z}(t) - \mathbf{z}(i)||^2}{2\sigma^2} \right)$$

where $\mathbf{z}(t)$ is the input sample at t, $\mathbf{z}(i)$ is the current data at ith time, σ is the deviation parameter (width of a cluster). However, as part of the development of incremental clustering methods, it was proposed to use a more computationally efficient Cauchy function [35]:

$$P(\mathbf{z}(t)) = \frac{1}{1 + \frac{1}{t-1}\sum_{i=1}^{t-1} \frac{||\mathbf{z}(t) - \mathbf{z}(i)||^2}{2\sigma^2}} \tag{16}$$

The data density, which is also called as potential P and calculated on the basis of (16), is the criterion for choosing points as cluster centers in the fuzzy clustering problem. Obviously, points with a higher density are the best candidates for cluster centers, and, consequently, for antecedents' centers of fuzzy eTS rules. Incremental data density is estimated based on the recursive procedure proposed in [35]:

$$P(\mathbf{z}(t)) = \frac{t-1}{(t-1)(a(t)+1) + b(t) - 2c(t)}, \tag{17}$$

where $a(t)$ and $c(t)$ are the variables considering current data and $b(t)$ is the accumulative additional variable:

$$a(t) = \sum_{j=1}^{n+m} z_j^2(t),$$

$$b(t) = b(t-1) + a(t-1); \quad b(1) = 0,$$

$$c(t) = \sum_{j=1}^{n+m} z_j(t) d_j(t),$$

where n is the input vector size, m is the output vector size, $d_j(t)$ is the same variable as $b(t)$ calculated as follows:

$$d_j(t) = d_j(t-1) + z_j(t-1); \quad d_j(t) = 0.$$

The value of σ is updated for the potential functions based on the following:

$$\sigma_{ij}^2(t) = \alpha \sigma_{ij}^2(t-1) + (1-\alpha) \frac{1}{N_i(t)} \sum_{l=1}^{N_i(t)} \left(\|z_i(t) - z_l(t)\|^2 \right),$$

where α is the training speed; $N_i(k)$ is the number of values, which belong to ith cluster, σ_{ij} (1) is the initial value of width, which commonly equals to 0.5.

It should be noted that at each step of the algorithm, when a new data sample arrives, the potentials of all previously formed cluster centers should be updated. It is caused because every new data sample changes the potentials of all previously received points according to (16). Cluster center potentials $P(\mathbf{z}_i^C(t))$ is updated as follows:

$$P(\mathbf{z}_i^C(t)) = \frac{t-1}{t-1 + (t-2)\left(\frac{1}{P(\mathbf{z}_i^C(t-1))} - 1 \right) + \sum_j \left(x_{ij}^C - x_j(t) \right)^2} \tag{18}$$

where x_{ij}^C is the projection of ith fuzzy cluster on jth axis, $x_j(t)$ is the ith coordinated of the current input vector $\mathbf{x}(t)$

The described clustering procedure can be taken as the basis for an incremental approach to the formation and adaptation of the eTS database. Let it be based on the following principles, which also support the interpretational properties of FS together with accuracy:

1. Data with maximum potentials is chosen in order to increase the generalizing abilities of fuzzy rules and reduce the knowledge base. It should be done for the focal centers formation;
2. Newly arrived data sample $z(t)$ should be chosen as the focal center if the value of the generalized criterion $I(c_{ij}, \sigma_{ij}, a_{i0})$ is significantly reduced or the point $z(t)$ is far from the formed clusters (in order to ensure the completeness of the knowledge base);
3. To choose focal points, the utility of fuzzy rules should be taken into account in the context of their influence on the simulation result;
4. It is necessary to exclude less significant variables and rules with a slight effect on the simulation result in order to reduce the knowledge base;
5. Similar fuzzy rules in the KB should be combined to reduce the KB;
6. Non-relevant rules formed in the distant past and not used in the present should be excluded from the KB.

The above principles are basic in the development of an online methodology for the formation and adaptation of the eTS database under the control of streaming data. The implementation of these principles are considered in the online design of eTS.

6 Online Implementation of Principles of eTS Design Based on Interpretability Restrictions

Structural adaptation of eTS in the online mode is carried out under the control of input data. It is made via updating fuzzy rules of the knowledge base in accordance with the above mentioned principles and criteria. At the same time, it is proposed to integrate a number of criteria directly into the incremental clustering algorithm by additional correction of potential values. The correction procedure is considered using the example of the consistency criterion of the eTS knowledge base.

The formalization of the criteria and integration ways into incremental training procedures are presented below:

1. The first principle is directly implemented in the above-described incremental clustering procedure by choosing focal center points $z(t)$ with the most potential $P(z(t))$:

$$P(z(t)) > \max_{i=1,\ldots,R} P(z_i^C(t)),$$

where R is the total number of rules in KB of eTS at t.

2. The second principle provides the possibility of new clusters creation in a remote area of the input-output space:

$$P(z(t)) < \min_{i=1,\ldots,R} P(z_i^C(t)).$$

3. To implement the third principle, it is proposed to evaluate the utility of each data sample $\mathbf{z}(t)$ in the context of the influence of corresponding fuzzy rule $r(\mathbf{x}(t))$ on the eTS output. The more different the results of eTS output before and after including the corresponding rule in the knowledge base, the more useful the rule is, and vice versa. Let the input of *eTS* is the sample $\mathbf{z}(t)$ at current time t. Then the instantaneous utility $\theta_i(\mathbf{x}(t))$ of the corresponding fuzzy rule r_i when processing the input sample $\mathbf{x}(t)$ is determined through the relative difference of the results obtained before and after the inclusion of this rule in the eTS database. Omitting the output the final formula $\theta i\,(\mathbf{x}(t))$ calculation is the following:

$$\theta_i(\mathbf{x}(t)) = T^i(\mathbf{x}(t))a_{i0} \bigg/ \sum_{j=1}^{R} T^j(\mathbf{x}(t))a_{j0}, \qquad (19)$$

where $T^i(\mathbf{x}(t))$ is the T-norm for MF of fuzzy variables in antecedent of ith rule, R is the number of fuzzy rules in KB.

4. The length of the antecedent parts can be minimized by reducing the input variables based on the concept of variable utility. It is determined based on an assessment of the influence of variable x_j on the output of the eTS model. The more sensitive the output of the eTS model to the corresponding variable, the greater its utility. Omitting the output the formula for the instantaneous utility $Q_j(\mathbf{x}_t)$ of the input variable can be given:

$$Q_j(\mathbf{x}(t)) = \frac{\sum\limits_{i=1}^{R} (1 - \mu_{ij}(x_j))T^i(\mathbf{x}\backslash x_j)a_{i0}}{\max_i a_{i0} - \min_i a_{i0}}, \qquad (20)$$

where $\mu_{ij}(x_j)$ is the value of MF for jth variable at ith rule.

5. Fuzzy rule pair combination in the knowledge base according to the similarity criterion is based on the centers averaging weighted by support measures the rules:

$$c_j^{new} = \frac{c_j^{r_1}k_1 + c_j^{r_2}k_2}{k_1 + k_2}, \qquad (21)$$

where $c_j^{r_1}, c_j^{r_2}$ are the centers of rules r_1 and r_2 at jth variable, k_1, k_2 are the support measures (number of times, when a rule has the maximum activation degree (3)) for r_1 and r_2.

Width of MF for the newly formed fuzzy rule is the following [36]:

$$\sigma_j^{new} = \sqrt{\frac{k_1(\sigma_j^{r_1})^2}{k_1 + k_2} + (c_j^{r_1} - c_j^{new})^2 + \frac{(c_j^{new} - c_j^{r_2})^2}{k_1 + k_2} + \frac{k_2\sigma_j^{r_1}}{k_1 + k_2}}. \qquad (22)$$

6. To implement principles 6 and 7, the criterion of relevance of a fuzzy rule is introduced through the concept of relative age of ith rule [2]:

$$Age_i(t) = t - \frac{\sum_{l=1}^{t_{k_i}} t_l}{k_i}, \tag{23}$$

where t_l is the lth time, when the rule has the maximum activation degree (3). Relevance of ith fuzzy rule is defined using (23):

$$Rel_i(t) = 1 - \frac{Age_i(t)}{t}. \tag{24}$$

Let Imp_i be the integral criterion of importance of ith fuzzy rule, which is calculated as geometric mean between utility and relevance:

$$Imp_i = \sqrt{\theta_i(\mathbf{x}(t)) Rel_i(t)}. \tag{25}$$

Imp_l can be used as a threshold during optimization of KB.

7 Incremental Restructuring of the ETS Model Rule Base

With the aim of a deeper hybridization of accuracy and interpretational criteria, it is proposed that the eTS knowledge base is generated and optimized in two directions. The first one is related to the adjustment of the incremental clustering algorithm by clarifying the potentials of the focal centers taking into account the interpretation requirements. The second one is related with a direct change of the knowledge base by introducing additional conditions for the inclusion/exclusion of fuzzy rules in order to increase the interpretational properties and accuracy of eTS.

The incremental clustering procedure consists of two stages that are performed upon each new data sample $\mathbf{z}(t)$ is obtained: 1) calculation of the potential $P(\mathbf{z}(t))$ based on the recursive formula (17); 2) correction of potentials of existing cluster centers based on formula (18). In order to increase the interpretational properties of eTS, the fuzzy rules of which are formed on the basis of cluster centers, it is proposed to take into account the criteria for consistency of fuzzy rules at the stage of adjusting the potentials of cluster centers. This is achieved by including a dynamic parameter in Eq. (18) via the T-norm that characterizes the criterion of consistency of the rule base.

The consistency for rule $r(t)$, which is formed based on $\mathbf{z}(t)$, with the existing rules r_j $(j = 1,...,)$ $(\bigcup_{j=1}^{R} r_j = F)$ is calculated via the consistency measure (14) with each r_j. Let (14) be presented in conjunctive form as follows:

$$Cons(r(t), r_j) = \overline{\overline{S}_{ante}(r(t), r_j) \vee S_{cons}(r(t), r_j)} = S_{ante}(r(t), r_j) \wedge \overline{S}_{cons}(r(t), r_j). \tag{26}$$

Using (15) and choosing the production operator as a fuzzy conjunction, (26) can be rewritten as follows:

$$Cons(r(t),\ r_j) = \left(1 - \frac{1}{1 + d(\mathbf{x}(t),\ \mathbf{x}_j^C)} \frac{d(a_{i0},\ a_{j0})}{1 + d(a_{i0},\ a_{j0})}\right). \tag{27}$$

The consistency measure of $r(t)$ with set F is also calculated via the production T-norm:

$$Cons(r(t),\ F) = \prod_{j=1}^{R} Cons(r(t),\ r_j) \tag{28}$$

It should be noted as the new sample $\mathbf{z}(t)$ is obtained the value of $Cons(r(t),\ F)$ is decreased because each fuzzy rules introduces its "piece of Inconsistency" in the KB. Therefore, the more flexible mechanism of KB adaptation is performed by excluding potential candidates having low consistency with existing rules. It can be made if $Cons(r(t),\ F)$ is multiplied by $P(\mathbf{z}(t))$. Based on the above mentioned, the formula for cluster centers recalculation in the incremental clustering procedure using consistency criterion, takes the following form:

$$P^S(\mathbf{z}_i^C(t)) = \frac{t-1}{t-1+(t-2)\left(\frac{1}{P(\mathbf{z}_i^C(t-1))}-1\right)+||x_i^C - x(t)||} Cons(r(t),\ F). \tag{29}$$

This formula is used in the clustering algorithm of the input-output space for incremental formation and adaptation of the fuzzy rules base of eTS. The restructuring of the knowledge base is carried out by inclusion/exclusion of fuzzy rules from it. The restructuring is based on a comparison of the instantaneous values of the criteria for the interpretability of fuzzy rules with their limiting statistical estimates obtained at the current time. This approach avoids the use of excessive parameters in the algorithm in the form of the criteria threshold values.

The algorithm includes a set of comparative conditions that increase the interpretability of the current knowledge base. When this or that condition is triggered, corresponding change occurs in the knowledge base excluding, including or forming new fuzzy rules. The conditions for criteria triggering used in the eTS structural adjustment online algorithm are formalized as follows:

Condition $C1$: IF $P(z(t)) > \max\limits_{i=1,\ldots,R} P(\mathbf{z}_i^C)$ OR $J\left(c_{ij}, \sigma_{ij}, a_{i0}\right)(t) > J(t)$.

Condition $C2$: IF $P(\mathbf{z}(t)) < \min\limits_{i=1,\ldots,R} P(\mathbf{z}_i^C)$.

Condition $C3$: IF $\exists r_j \in F(t)\quad \theta_{rj}(t) < \theta_j + \sigma_{\theta_j}$.

Condition $C4$: IF $\exists r_j r_j \in F(t)\quad Cons(r(t), r_j) > Cons + \sigma_S$.

Condition $C5$: IF $\exists x_j \in \mathbf{x}(t)\quad Q_{x_j}(\mathbf{x}(t)) < Q_j + \sigma_{Q_j}$.

Condition $C6$: IF $\exists r_j \in F(t)\quad Imp_j < Imp_j + \sigma_{Imp_j}$.

where $\hat{x}$ is the statistical mean of criterion x and σ_x is its mean squared error.

Based on the above mentioned study, the incremental algorithm for KB online adaptation is the following:

1. $t = 1$

$$i = 1;\ d_j(t) = 0;\ j = [1, n];\ \sigma_j(t) = 0,5;\ b(t) = 0;\ \hat{\theta}_{r_j}(t) = 0;\ \sigma_{\theta_j} = 0,5;$$

$$\sigma_S = 0,5;\ \hat{Q}_{x_j}(t) = 0;\ \sigma_{Q_j} = 0,5;\ \widehat{Imp}_{r_j}(t) = 0;\ \widehat{Cons}(t) = 0;\ \sigma_{Imp_j} = 0,5.$$

Initial data input:
$\mathbf{z}(1) = [\mathbf{x}(1); y(1)]$
Initial rule base formation:

$$r_i:\ IF\ x_1 = x_1(1)\ AND,\ \ldots, AND\ x_n = x_n(1)\ \ THEN\ y = y(1),$$

$c_{ij} = x_j(t);\ a_{i0} = y(t).\ F(t) = \{r_i\};\ R = 1.$

2. $t = t + 1$
3. New data input:

$\mathbf{z}(1) = [\mathbf{x}(1), y(1)]$

4. Calculation of $P(\mathbf{z}(t))$ based on (17)
5. Potentials correction according to (29)
6. Verification of conditions $C1-C6$:

   a. If $C1$ or $C2$ then $i = i + 1$; $R = R + 1$; $\mathbf{z}_i^C(t) = \mathbf{z}(t)$; $r_i = r(\mathbf{z}(t))$; $F(t) = F(t) \cup r_i$; potential recalculation based on (18)
   b. If $C3$ or $C6$ then $F(t) = F(t)\backslash r_j$; $R = R - 1$
   c. If $C4$ then $F(t) = F(t)\backslash\{r_j, r_i\}$; $i = i + 1$; r_i formation based on (21) and (22); $R = R+1$
   d. If $C5$ then $\mathbf{x}(t) = \mathbf{x}(t)\backslash x_j$; $n = n - 1$.

7. Recalculation of mean and mean squared error. Return.

Presented above algorithm performs the continuous processing of data stream $\mathbf{z}(t)$. As a result, KB including R fuzzy rules is dynamically formed and adapted.

8 Computational Experiment

Nowadays, online design of EIS with interpretational properties is relatively novel and not enough studied area. Because of this, well-known benchmarking is not available for such kind of problems yet. This paper indirectly tries to approve utility of interpretational properties for system modeling. In this purpose, the interpretability impact calculation for one fuzzy model, which is called accessory model, on the efficiency of another fuzzy model, which is called main model, is shown below. The output of the accessory model is used as one of the main model inputs.

As the main model, prognostic Takagi-Sugeno model for velocity prediction of railway car cuts on hump yards is used. Velocity prediction for a railway cut depends on the set of parameters, one of which is the technical state of retarder regulating the velocity of cuts. The state of retarder is estimated based on accessory model, inputs of which are the initial raw data from the hump yard sensors.

The main model requires continuous adaptation of their structure because of dynamical and noisy character of data. The efficiency of adaptation is highly affected by the accessory model output and also by interpretability of this output. To objectively check how the interpretability of the accessory model effects on the output of the main model, two accessory models having different interpretational properties were constructed and computed with respect to accuracy.

The experiment was performed in two stages. The first one considers two adaptive diagnostic models for the retarder estimation:

Artificial neural network ("Black box", BB);

Fuzzy neural network having interpretational properties in form of linguistic rules ("White box", WB).

During the experiment, BB was used as the reference model and WB was used as the tested one. Both models had the same input data describing the sensors data and output one describing retarder state (working, fault, unknown). A difference in these models was presented in the way of output representation. In addition to the output data, the tested model infers descriptions in form of the interpreted fuzzy rules generating this data.

The second stage considers the main TS-model construction based on the outputs of one of the accessory models. TS-model process the received information in different manner due to the different form of their representation. In case of WB, "interpretational appendage" in form of fuzzy rules was used as the additional input. These rules are incorporated as the correction rules for TS-model for adjusting the model output, when the retarder state is changed. Computational results for both pairs of models are shown in Table 1.

Table 1. Prediction accuracy for the experimental couples of models

Model	No.		
	100% working states	99% working states	95% working states
BB-TS	93%	87%	85%
WB-TS	93%	92%	92%

Every experiment included 500 continuous samples. First experiment had only working samples, second one had 5 fault samples and the last had 25 fault samples. The accuracy was calculated based on the Root Mean-Squared Error:

$$Acc = 1 - \sqrt{\frac{\sum\limits_{i=1}^{500} (V_{real} - V_i)^2}{500}},$$

where V_{real} is the real velocity after retarding, V_i is the real one in the ith sample.

Based on the computational experiment, the following conclusion can be made:

Both accessory models together with main one obtain almost the same results on the set with working states.

When the fault is obtained in the set, BB-TS model shows worse result than WB-TS one. It can be described by the adjustment procedure in the TS model, which is based on analysis of the interpretational outputs from WB.

As the frequency of state changes is increased, as the accuracy of BB-TS is increased too because of more frequent use of adjustment procedure.

Therefore, the results of this experiment indirectly show the increase of efficiency of fuzzy models by increase their interpretability. This effect is achieved via more complete information about the system operations, which are included into interpreted fuzzy rules of TS-model.

9 Conclusions

The paper considers the well-known, as well as some new aspects and design concepts of evolving fuzzy systems of the Takagi-Sugeno type taking into account interpretation criteria. The design of eTS is carried out in incremental mode under the control of streaming data.

The main attention is paid to the issues of incremental adaptation of eTS, and the emphasis is placed on the structural adaptation related to updating the knowledge base. In the proposed approach, the restructuring of eTS is performed via one-time updates of the knowledge base by including or excluding fuzzy rules from it. At the same time, structural changes in the eTS knowledge base are expected to occur relatively rarely, only at the time of significant changes in the input data stream and are initiated by frequent parametric adjustments that continuously occur in the fuzzy model.

The structural adaptation of eTS is based on a unified principle of comparing the instantaneous values of criteria with their limiting statistical estimates accumulated at the current moment. In addition, some of the proposed criteria, in particular, consistency, allow natural integration directly into the basic clustering algorithm, which can significantly increase the efficiency of model adaptation.

The paper does not present empirical material and test results, partly due to the abstract nature of the presentation and the authors' desire to focus on new design principles of fuzzy systems, and partly due to insufficient accumulated statistics on the use of new incremental algorithms for structural learning and adaptation in solving specific tasks.

Acknowledgement. This work was supported by RFBR (Grants No. 19-07-00263, 19-07-00195, 19-08-00152, 20-07-00100).

References

1. Eitzinger, C., et al.: Assessment of the influence of adaptive components in trainable surface inspection systems. Mach. Vis. Appl. **21**(5), 613–626 (2010)
2. Angelov, P.: Evolving takagi-sugeno fuzzy systems from streaming data (eTS+). In: Evolving Intelligent Systems: Methodology and Applications, vol. 12, p. 21. Wiley Online Library (2010)
3. Kasabov, N., Filev, D.: Evolving intelligent systems: methods, learning, & applications. In: 2006 International symposium on evolving fuzzy systems, pp. 8–18. IEEE (2006)
4. Cortés-Antonio, P., et al.: Learning rules for Sugeno ANFIS with parametric conjunction operations. Appl. Soft Comput. **89**, 106095 (2020)
5. Gama, J.: Knowledge Discovery from Data Streams. CRC Press, Boca Raton (2010)
6. Lughofer, E.: Flexible evolving fuzzy inference systems from data streams (FLEXFIS++). In: Sayed-Mouchaweh, M., Lughofer, E. (eds.) Learning in Non-Stationary Environments, pp. 205–245. Springer, New York (2012). https://doi.org/10.1007/978-1-4419-8020-5_9
7. Shahparast, H., Jahromi, M.Z., Taheri, M., Hamzeloo, S.: A novel weight adjustment method for handling concept-drift in data stream classification. Arabian J. Sci. Eng. **39**(2), 799–807 (2014)
8. Abraham, W.C., Robins, A.: Memory retention–the synaptic stability versus plasticity dilemma. Trends Neurosci. **28**(2), 73–78 (2005)
9. Kovalev, S.M., Sukhanov, A.V., Sukhanova, M.V., Sokolov, S.V.: Adaptive approach for anomaly detection in temporal data based on immune double-plasticity principle. In: Abraham, A., Kovalev, S., Tarassov, V., Snasel, V., Vasileva, M., Sukhanov, A. (eds.) IITI 2017. AISC, vol. 679, pp. 234–243. Springer, Cham (2018). https://doi.org/10.1007/978-3-319-68321-8_24
10. Korbicz, J., Koscielny, J.M., Kowalczuk, Z., Cholewa, W.: Fault diagnosis: models, artificial intelligence, applications. Springer, Heidelberg (2012). https://doi.org/10.1007/978-3-642-18615-8
11. Lughofer, E., Eitzinger, C., Guardiola, C.: Online quality control with flexible evolving fuzzy systems. In: Sayed-Mouchaweh, M., Lughofer, E. (eds.) Learning in Non-Stationary Environments, pp. 375–406. Springer, New York (2012). https://doi.org/10.1007/978-1-4419-8020-5_14
12. Stylios, C.D., Georgopoulos, V.C., Malandraki, G.A., Chouliara, S.: Fuzzy cognitive map architectures for medical decision support systems. Appl. Soft Comput. **8**(3), 1243–1251 (2008)
13. Lughofer, E., Trawiński, B., Trawiński, K., Kempa, O., Lasota, T.: On employing fuzzy modeling algorithms for the valuation of residential premises. Inf. Sci. **181**(23), 5123–5142 (2011)
14. Leite, D., Costa, P., Gomide, F.: Interval approach for evolving granular system modeling. In: Sayed-Mouchaweh, M., Lughofer, E. (eds.) Learning in non-stationary environments, pp. 271–300. Springer (2012). https://doi.org/10.1007/978-1-4419-8020-5_11
15. Lughofer, E.: On-line assurance of interpretability criteria in evolving fuzzy systems–achievements, new concepts and open issues. Inf. Sci. **251**, 22–46 (2013)
16. Lima, E., Hell, M., Ballini, R., Gomide, F.: Evolving fuzzy modeling using participatory learning. Evolving intelligent systems: methodology and applications, pp. 67–86 (2010)
17. Tung, S.W., Quek, C., Guan, C.: An evolving type-2 neural fuzzy inference system. In: Zhang, B.-T., Orgun, Mehmet A. (eds.) PRICAI 2010. LNCS (LNAI), vol. 6230, pp. 535–546. Springer, Heidelberg (2010). https://doi.org/10.1007/978-3-642-15246-7_49
18. Angelov, P.P., Filev, D.P.: An approach to online identification of Takagi-Sugeno fuzzy models. IEEE Trans. Syst. Man Cybern. Part B (Cybern.) **34**(1), 484–498 (2004)

19. Rong, H.J., Sundararajan, N., Huang, G.B., Saratchandran, P.: Sequential adaptive fuzzy inference system (SAFIS) for nonlinear system identification and prediction. Fuzzy Sets Syst. **157**(9), 1260–1275 (2006)
20. Juang, C.F., Lin, C.T.: An online self-constructing neural fuzzy inference network and its applications. IEEE Trans. Fuzzy Syst. **6**(1), 12–32 (1998)
21. Leng, G., Zeng, X.J., Keane, J.A.: An improved approach of self-organising fuzzy neural network based on similarity measures. Evol. Syst. **3**(1), 19–30 (2012)
22. Leite, D., Škrjanc, I., Gomide, F.: An overview on evolving systems and learning from stream data. Evol. Syst. **11**, 181–198 (2020)
23. Fiordaliso, A.: A constrained Takagi-Sugeno fuzzy system that allows for better interpretation and analysis. Fuzzy Sets Syst. **118**(2), 307–318 (2001)
24. Setnes, M.: Simplification and reduction of fuzzy rules. In: Casillas, J., Cordón, O., Herrera, F., Magdalena, L. (eds.) Interpretability Issues in Fuzzy Modeling, vol 128, pp. 278–302. Springer, Heidelberg (2003). https://doi.org/10.1007/978-3-540-37057-4_12
25. Gacto, M.J., Alcala, R., Herrera, F.: Interpretability of linguistic fuzzy rule-based systems: an overview of interpretability measures. Inf. Sci. **181**(20), 4340–4360 (2011)
26. Koenig, S., Likhachev, M., Liu, Y., Furcy, D.: Incremental heuristic search in artificial intelligence. Artif. Intell. Mag. **25**(2), 99–112 (2004)
27. Filev, D., Yager, R.R.: Learning OWA operator weights from data. In: Proceedings of 1994 IEEE 3rd International Fuzzy Systems Conference, pp. 468–473. IEEE (1994)
28. Yager, R.R., Filev, D.P.: Approximate clustering via the mountain method. IEEE Trans. Syst. Man Cybern. **24**(8), 1279–1284 (1994)
29. Yager, R.R., Filev, D.P.: Essentials of fuzzy modeling and control, New York, vol. 388 (1994)
30. Lughofer, E.: Evolving Fuzzy Systems-Methodologies, Advanced Concepts and Applications, vol. 53. Springer, Heidelberg (2011). https://doi.org/10.1007/978-3-642-18087-3
31. Angelov, P., Lughofer, E., Zhou, X.: Evolving fuzzy classifiers using different model architectures. Fuzzy Sets Syst. **159**(23), 3160–3182 (2008)
32. Elgammal, A., Duraiswami, R., Harwood, D., Davis, L.S.: Background and foreground modeling using nonparametric kernel density estimation for visual surveillance. Proc. IEEE **90**(7), 1151–1163 (2002)
33. Yager, R.R., Filev, D.P.: Learning of fuzzy rules by mountain clustering. In: Applications of Fuzzy Logic Technology, vol. 2061, pp. 246–254. International Society for Optics and Photonics (1993)
34. Chiu, S.L.: Fuzzy model identification based on cluster estimation. J. Intell. Fuzzy Syst. **2**(3), 267–278 (1994)
35. Angelov, P.: An approach for fuzzy rule-base adaptation using on-line clustering. Int. J. Approximate Reasoning **35**(3), 275–289 (2004)
36. Lughofer, E., Bouchot, J.L., Shaker, A.: On-line elimination of local redundancies in evolving fuzzy systems. Evol. Syst. **2**(3), 165–187 (2011)

On Analytical Solutions to the Problems
of Maintaining Local Consistency

Anatolii G. Maksimov[1,2]([⊠]) [iD] and Arseniy D. Zavalishin[1,2] [iD]

[1] St. Petersburg Institute for Informatics and Automation of the Russian Academy
of Sciences, St. Petersburg, Russia
maksimov.20.43@gmail.com
[2] St. Petersburg State University, St. Petersburg, Russia

Abstract. One of the primary problems, arising in algebraic Bayesian networks, is the problem of checking and maintaining consistency of the knowledge pattern. It can be reduced to the linear programming problem, which methods of solving are well studied. However, acting as black box, this approach is ill-suited to solution of another important problem—research of the sensitivity of the probabilistic logical inference. In this work we prove the analytical representation of solutions of maintaining the local consistency problem for the knowledge pattern of small size and show the results of the experiment, comparing effectiveness of the solution using obtained formulae and simplex-method. The problem is being solved for the first time.

Keywords: Algebraic Bayesian networks · Maintaining consistency · Extremal problems · Linear programming · Systems of constraints

1 Introduction

Algebraic Bayesian networks (ABN) [21] belong to the class of probabilistic graphical models and are represented by an undirected graph, at the vertices of which there are knowledge patterns [21]. The ideal of the conjunct is the mathematical model of the knowledge pattern, each element of which is assigned a scalar or interval estimate of the probability of truth [21]. Interval estimates of truth are necessary, for example, in the transformation of expert estimates, data in natural language, as well as in cases of incomplete or imperfect data. The possibility of working with interval estimates of the probabilities of truth of elements is the key advantage of ABN over related probabilistic graphical models.

An extremely important task in such models is the task of evaluating their *sensitivity*, that is, determining how much the output will change when probabilistic logical inference is made, if the input is slightly changed. Currently, most of the questions of probabilistic logical inference in the theory of Bayesian algebraic networks can be reduced to a series of linear or hyperbolic programming problems. In particular, the problem of linear programming reduces the

© Springer Nature Switzerland AG 2020
S. O. Kuznetsov et al. (Eds.): RCAI 2020, LNAI 12412, pp. 152–163, 2020.
https://doi.org/10.1007/978-3-030-59535-7_11

problem of maintaining the consistency of [19]. There is a wide range of methods for solving the corresponding extreme problems: the simplex method [3], the interior-point method [8], the ellipsoid method [9] and others. However, for the problem of assessing sensitivity, these methods are not the best way, since they act as a black box. Thus, it seems relevant to solve the problem of obtaining an explicit form of solutions to emerging extreme problems.

The goal of this work is to first approach to obtaining an explicit form of solving linear programming problems while maintaining local consistency of the knowledge pattern by obtaining analytical formulas for small knowledge patterns, as well as to compare the speed of operation using the simplex method and the obtained formulas. As far as the authors know, the problem is being solved for the first time. The theoretical significance of the result lies in the fact that such formulas will make it possible to approach the problem of assessing sensitivity from a new perspective. The practical significance lies in the fact that the explicit form of solutions can significantly accelerate the operations of probabilistic logical inference.

2 Related Works

The basis of algebraic Bayesian networks [21], like any probabilistic graphical model [14], is the assumption about the possibility of *decomposition* of the subject area into knowledge patterns that reflect the connections between 2–3 entities. The ABN are represented by an undirected graph whose vertices are knowledge pattern [22]. The mathematical model of the knowledge pattern in the theory of ABN is the ideal of conjuncts, each element of which is assigned a scalar or interval estimate of the probability of its truth [19]. More formally, a knowledge pattern is a pair of $\langle C, P_C \rangle$, where C is the quotient set of finite chains of conjunctions over a certain set of variables by logical equality $\equiv$, and P_C is a vector of length $|C|$ containing the estimate of probability of the truth of each element of C. Figure 1 shows an example of a knowledge pattern. The probabilistic logical inference in the ABN is based on the probabilistic logic proposed by Nilsson [12] and developed by Fajin, Helpern and Mejiddo [4,5].

Over several years of research on algebraic Bayesian networks, serious results have been achieved. In particular, matrix-vector representations of the main tasks of probabilistic logical inference were formalized: maintaining local consistency, a priori and a posteriori inference in the knowledge pattern [17]. The work [18] showed a solution to the problem of global a posteriori inference in joint trees, while the work [6] showed a method for reducing an cyclic ABN to acyclic based on the structure theorem on cycles. The structural cycle theorem, in addition, allows us to predict the cyclic nature of the global ABN structure only by the set of knowledge pattern [7]. A significant result was obtained in [13]—it was proved that graphs of algebraic Bayesian networks are minimized in inclusion and minimized in the number of edges at the same time.

One of the alleged areas of application of Bayesian algebraic networks is the study of social engineering attacks [10,11,15].

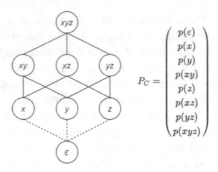

Fig. 1. Knowledge pattern example. ε is an empty conjunction

3   Maintaining Local Consistency

The task of maintaining local consistency is to check the adequacy of the estimates in the existing knowledge pattern, and also to clarify these estimates, if possible. As noted above, this problem can be reduced to a series of linear programming problems. Before proceeding with the description of these tasks, it is necessary to give three definitions.

Definition 1. *Kronecker product (or tensor product) [1]* $\mathbf{A} \otimes \mathbf{B}$ *if A is $n \times n$ matrix and B is $m \times m$ matrix is the block matrix* $\mathbf{C} = (a_{ij}\mathbf{B})_{1 \leqslant i,j \leqslant n}$, *where a_{ij}—corresponding element of matrix* $\mathbf{A}$.

Definition 2. *Tensor power [1] of matrix* $\mathbf{A}$ *is defined by the following recurrence formula:*
$$\mathbf{A}^{[1]} = \mathbf{A}; \mathbf{A}^{[n]} = \mathbf{A}^{[n-1]} \otimes \mathbf{A}, n \geqslant 2.$$

Definition 3. *Matrix family* $\mathbf{I}_n$ *[19] is defined by the following recurrence formula:*
$$\mathbf{I}_1 = \begin{bmatrix} 1 & -1 \\ 0 & 1 \end{bmatrix};$$
$$\mathbf{I}_n = \begin{bmatrix} \mathbf{I}_{n-1} & -\mathbf{I}_{n-1} \\ \mathbf{0} & \mathbf{I}_{n-1} \end{bmatrix} = \mathbf{I}_1^{[n]}.$$

Let the vector $\mathbf{P}_n$ be a vector of variables containing probabilities of the truth of the conjuncts. We arrange the variables in this vector as follows: the variable number j enters the conjunction number i if and only if the bit number j is equal to one in the binary representation of the number i (if you count it on the right). Such numbering is very useful since it allows us to state the following theorem.

Theorem 1. *Constraints of probability theory axioms can be obtained as the product* $\mathbf{I}_n \times \mathbf{P}_n$ *[20].*

Thanks to this theorem, it was shown in [21] that to solve the problem of maintaining local consistency, it is enough to solve a series of linear programming problems of the form:

$$p^-(f) = \min_{\mathcal{R}}\{p(f)\},$$

$$p^+(f) = \max_{\mathcal{R}}\{p(f)\},$$

where $\mathcal{R} = \mathcal{E} \cup \mathcal{D}$, $\mathcal{E}$ are constraints of probability theory axioms, $\mathcal{D}$ are domain constraints and $p^-(f)$ and $p^+(f)$ are the refined lower and upper bounds for the probability of the truth of the conjunction f. From Theorem 1 it is clear that the constraint system $\mathcal{R}$ is linear.

4   Analytical Solutions to LPP

In this section, we will assume that the domain constraints are adequate to probability theory, that is, the bounds on the estimates of conjunct probability of true in the interval $[0; 1]$. We also assume that the system of constraints is consistent.

4.1   Knowledge Pattern with One Variable

In the case of one variable in the knowledge pattern, the constraint system degenerates into a single requirement $p(x_1)^- \leqslant p(x_1) \leqslant p(x_1)^+$. Such a system of constraints always has a solution, and the minimum and maximum x_1 is exactly $p(x_1)^-$ and $p(x_1)^+$ respectively.

4.2   Knowledge Pattern with Two Variables

For two variables, we write in explicit form the constraints of the probability theory axioms:

$$\mathcal{E}^{(2)} = \left\{ \begin{array}{ll} p(x_1x_2) \geqslant 0, & (1) \\ p(x_1) - p(x_1x_2) \geqslant 0, & (2) \\ p(x_2) - p(x_1x_2) \geqslant 0, & (3) \\ 1 - p(x_1) - p(x_2) + p(x_1x_2) \geqslant 0 & (4) \end{array} \right\},$$

as well as domain constraints:

$$\mathcal{D}^{(2)} = \left\{ \begin{array}{l} p(x_1)^- \leqslant p(x_1) \leqslant p(x_1)^+, \\ p(x_2)^- \leqslant p(x_2) \leqslant p(x_2)^+, \\ p(x_1x_2)^- \leqslant p(x_1x_2) \leqslant p(x_1x_2)^+ \end{array} \right\}.$$

First of all, we solve the problem for a maximum of $p(x_1x_2)$, since this variable is bound by the greatest number of constraints.

$$\left\{ \begin{array}{ll} p(x_1x_2) \leqslant p(x_1x_2)^+ & \text{follows from the domain constraints,} \\ p(x_1x_2) \leqslant p(x_1)^+ & \text{follows from the second constraint of } \mathcal{E}, \Rightarrow \\ p(x_1x_2) \leqslant p(x_1)^+ & \text{follows from the third constraint of } \mathcal{E} \end{array} \right.$$

$$p(x_1x_2) \leqslant \min(p(x_1)^+, p(x_2)^+, p(x_1x_2)^+)$$

Theorem 2. *Maximum* $p(x_1 x_2)$ *is exactly*

$$\min(p(x_1)^+, p(x_2)^+, p(x_1 x_2)^+).$$

Proof. To prove this, it is necessary to find such values of $p(x_1)$ and $p(x_2)$, that, together with the chosen $p(x_1 x_2)$, satisfy all the constraints. We note immediately that the first constraint of $\mathcal{E}$ is satisfied regardless of our choice. Let us set $p(x_1) = \max(p(x_1)^-, p(x_1 x_2))$ and $p(x_2) = \max(p(x_2)^-, p(x_1 x_2))$. First, such a choice will ensure that the domain constraints are satisfied, since the expression for $p(x_1 x_2)$ is at most $p(x_1)^+, p(x_2)^+$, that is, $p(x_1), p(x_2)$ are at most their upper bounds. At the same time, because of max, they are no less than their lower bounds. If the value of $p(x_1 x_2)$ is outside the valid limits, then for one of the variables $p(x_1), p(x_2)$ the upper bound is less than the lower bound for $p(x_1 x_2)$, and in this case the system is inconsistent. Secondly, it guarantees the satisfied of the second and third constraints of the probability theory axioms. It remains to verify that $1 - p(x_1) - p(x_2) + p(x_1 x_2) \geqslant 0$. We rewrite it in a more convenient form:

$$p(x_1 x_2) + 1 \geqslant p(x_1) + p(x_2).$$

Let's analyze two cases:

1st case: $p(x_1 x_2) = p(x_1)^+$ or $p(x_1 x_2) = p(x_2)^+$.
In this case, in inequality 1, we can subtract $p(x_1 x_2)$ from the left side and $p(x_1)$ from the right side, since $p(x_1) \leqslant p(x_1)^+$. Then the one will remain on the left side, and a certain probability on the right side, that is, the inequality will be satisfied. Similarly for $p(x_2)^+$.
2nd case: $p(x_1 x_2) = p(x_1 x_2)^+$, that is, we need to check the inequality $p(x_1 x_2)^+ + 1 \geqslant p(x_1) + p(x_2)$. This case is divided into two subcases:

- The maximum in the expression for $p(x_1)$ or $p(x_2)$ is realized as $p(x_1 x_2)$
  Add to both sides minus $p(x_1 x_2)$, the remaining inequality is manifestly satisfied.
- Otherwise, the inequality takes the form $1 + p(x_1 x_2)^+ \geqslant p(x_1)^- + p(x_2)^-$.
  Note that the left side cannot become larger, and the right cannot become smaller. In other words, if such an inequality is not satisfied, then the system of constraints is inconsistent. $\square$

Before determining the minimum of $p(x_1 x_2)$, we first solve the problem of the minimum of $p(x_1)$ and $p(x_2)$. We hasten to add that all the constraints are symmetric with respect to $p(x_1)$ and $p(x_2)$, therefore it is enough to carry out the proof for only one of them.

Theorem 3

$$\min\{p(x_1)\} = \max(p(x_1)^-, p(x_1 x_2)^-),$$
$$\min\{p(x_2)\} = \max(p(x_2)^-, p(x_1 x_2)^-).$$

Proof. To begin with, we determine the lower bound for the desired quantity.

$$\begin{cases} p(x_1) \geqslant p(x_1)^- & \text{follows from the domain constraints,} \\ p(x_1) \geqslant \mu(x_1 x_2) & \text{follows from the second constraint of } \mathcal{E} \end{cases} \Rightarrow$$

$$p(x_1) \geqslant \max(p(x_1)^-, p(x_1 x_2)^-).$$

We show now that this estimate is exact. Let us set $p(x_1 x_2) = \min(p(x_1), p(x_2), p(x_1 x_2)^+)$. This ensures that the first three axioms of $\mathcal{E}$ are satisfied. We now verify the fourth one. Again, we analyze two cases:

1st case: the minimum in the expression $p(x_1 x_2)$ is realized as $p(x_1)$ (or $p(x_2)$)
    Subtract then the equality $p(x_1 x_2) = p(x_1)$ from inequality (4). The resulting inequality $1 \geqslant p(x_2)$ is always satisfied.
2nd case: the minimum in the expression for $p(x_1 x_2)$ is realized as $p(x_1 x_2)^+$
Then the left side of inequality (4) reached its maximum, and the right minimum. If the inequality is not satisfied, the system of constraints is inconsistent.   □

Theorem 4. $\min\{p(x_1 x_2)\} = \max(p(x_1 x_2)^-, p(x_1)^- + p(x_2)^- - 1).$

Proof. From the domain constraints $p(x_1 x_2) \geqslant p(x_1 x_2)^-$. From constraint (4) $p(x_1 x_2) \geqslant p(x_1) + p(x_2) - 1$, in particular $p(x_1 x_2) \geqslant p(x_1)^- + p(x_2)^- - 1$. Therefore, $p(x_1 x_2) \geqslant \max(p(x_1 x_2)^-, p(x_1)^- + p(x_2)^- - 1)$. Let us show that this estimate is exact. Again, we analyze two cases:

1st case: The indicated maximum is realized as $p(x_1)^- + p(x_2)^- - 1$.
In this case, let us set $p(x_1) = p(x_1)^-, p(x_2) = p(x_2)^-$. Then all the domain constraints are satisfied, constraint (1) is satisfied, and constraint (4) degenerates into equality. It remains to verify that constraints (2) and (3) are satisfied.
We rewrite (2) as $p(x_1)^- \geqslant p(x_1)^- + p(x_2)^- - 1$. Subtract $p(x_1)^-$ from both sides and transfer the one to the other side. The resulting inequality $1 \geqslant p(x_2)^-$ is always satisfied.
2nd case: The indicated maximum is realized as $p(x_1 x_2) = p(x_1 x_2)^-$.
Let us set $p(x_1) = \max(p(x_1 x_2)^-, p(x_1)^-)$ and $p(x_1 x_2) = \max(p(x_1 x_2)^-, p(x_2)^-)$. If, with such a set of values, the domain constraints are not satisfied, then $p(x_1 x_2)^- \geqslant p(x_1)^+$ (or the same for $p(x_2)^+$), that is, the system is inconsistent. Constraints (1), (2), and (3) are also satisfied, and it remains for us to check only (4), i.e. $p(x_1 x_2)^- + 1 \geqslant p(x_1)^- + p(x_2)^-$. Since the maximum in the expression for $p(x_1 x_2)$ is realized as $p(x_1 x_2)^-$, we know that $p(x_1 x_2)^- \geqslant p(x_1)^- + p(x_2)^- - 1$. We substitute this inequality into the previous one: $p(x_1)^- + p(x_2)^- - 1 + 1 \geqslant p(x_1)^- + p(x_2)^-$. This inequality is always satisfied.   □

Finally, we solve the problem for a maximum of $p(x_1)$ and $p(x_2)$. But before that, recall the following definition:

Definition 4. *Truncated subtraction [23] is a function of two variables defined by the ternary operator $x > y ? x - y : 0$. That is, the truncated difference coincides with the "classical" if the result is positive, and is equal to zero otherwise. We assume that the priority of the truncated subtraction is higher than the priority of the "classical" subtraction.*

Theorem 5.
$$\begin{cases} \max\{p(x_1)\} = \min(p(x_1)^+, 1 - p(x_2)^- \dot- p(x_1x_2)^+) \\ \max\{p(x_2)\} = \min(p(x_2)^+, 1 - p(x_1)^- \dot- p(x_1x_2)^+) \end{cases}$$

Proof. We carry out the proof for $p(x_1)$.

We analyze the cases of the relative position of the boundaries of probability estimates (Fig. 2).

Fig. 2. The first case. Solid borders correspond to $p(x_1x_2)$, dotted lines correspond to $p(x_2)$

In the first case, $p(x_2)^- \dot- p(x_1x_2)^+ = 0$. This means that in the expression for $p(x_1)$ the minimum is realized as $p(x_1)^+$, since $p(x_1)^+ \leqslant 1$. We choose $p(x_1x_2) = p(x_2) = p(x_1x_2)^-$. Then the constraints of the subject area are fulfilled, and also the constraints (1) and (3) are fulfilled. If constraint (2) is not satisfied, then the system is not compatible, since $p(x_1)$ cannot become larger, and $p(x_1x_2)$ cannot become smaller. Constraint (4) is satisfied since $p(x_2) = p(x_1x_2)$, that is, it is only necessary to check $p(x_1) \leqslant 1$, which is true (Fig. 3).

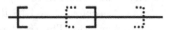

Fig. 3. The second case. Solid borders correspond to $p(x_1x_2)$, dotted lines correspond to $p(x_2)$

In the second case, the truncated difference $p(x_2)^- \dot- p(x_1x_2)^+$ is trivial again, and $p(x_1)$ is again equal to $p(x_1)^+$. We choose $p(x_2) = p(x_2)^-, p(x_1x_2) = \min(p(x_1)^+, p(x_2)^-)$.

It would be convenient for us to choose for $p(x_1x_2)$ the value $p(x_2)^-$, since then the second case would be completely analogous to the first. However, with this choice, inequality (2) is not satisfied. If it fails, reduce $p(x_1x_2)$ to $p(x_1)^+$. This cannot spoil the constraints (3), but also preserves the satisfaction for (4). If $p(x_1)^+ < p(x_1x_2)^-$, then the constraint system is inconsistent.

Note that $p(x_1)$ just cannot be greater than $p(x_1)^+$, therefore in these two cases the maximum problem is solved correctly.

Fig. 4. The third case. Solid borders correspond to $p(x_1x_2)$, dotted lines correspond to $p(x_2)$

Third case is the only possible case in which the truncated difference $p(x_2)^- \dot{-} p(x_1x_2)^+$ is nontrivial, since $p(x_2)^- > p(x_1x_2)^+$. Since we cannot definitive determine how the minimum in the expression for $p(x_1)$ is realized, we analyze two cases (Fig. 4):

1st case: $p(x_1) = 1 - p(x_2)^- + p(x_1x_2)^+$
Let us set $p(x_2) = p(x_2)^-, p(x_1x_2) = p(x_1x_2)^+$. Constraints (1) and (3) are fulfilled, as well as domain constraints. (2) is satisfied since $1 - p(x_2)^- \geqslant 0$, that is, $p(x_1)$ is equal to the sum of $p(x_1x_2)^+$ and a non-negative term. We verify the satisfaction of (4). The inequality $1 + p(x_1x_2)^+ \geqslant 1 - p(x_2)^- - + p(x_1x_2)^+ + p(x_2)^-$ is equivalent to the inequality $0 \geqslant 0$, which is true.
2nd case: $p(x_1) = p(x_1)^+$
Note that then $p(x_1)^+ \geqslant 1 - p(x_2)^- + p(x_1x_2)^+$. Let us set $p(x_2) = p(x_2)^-, p(x_1x_2) = \min(p(x_1x_2)^+, p(x_1)^+)$. If the domain constraints are not satisfied, then $p(x_1x_2)^- > p(x_1)^+$, that is, the system is inconsistent. Also, constraints (1), (2), and (3) are fulfilled. We verify inequality (4).
If the minimum in $p(x_1x_2)$ is realized as $p(x_1)^+$, then we simply subtract $p(x_1)^+$ from both sides of (4) and obtain the valid inequality $1 \geqslant p(x_2)^-$. Otherwise, $p(x_1x_2) = p(x_1x_2)^+$. Add to both sides of the inequality $p(x_2)^-$ noted above. Then the inequality persists and coincides with (4).

Finally, since $p(x_1) \leqslant p(x_1)^+$ from the domain constraints, as well as $p(x_1) \leqslant 1 - p(x_2) + p(x_1x_2)$, and in particular $p(x_1) \leqslant 1 - p(x_2)^- + p(x_1x_2)^+$, from the constraints of the probability theory axioms, $p(x_1)$ cannot exceed the minimum indicate in Theorem 5, that is, the maximum problem is solved correctly.   □

5   Experiment

To test the effectiveness of the explicit form of solutions against the simplex method, we conducted an experiment. We have done 100 iterations of the following loop:

- The cnt variable is set to 0. It will store the number of cases in which the system was consistent;
- 6 points are taken from the range $[0, 1]$;
- Iterates over all permutations of these points to take into account all possible relative arrangements of $p(x_1), p(x_2), p(x_1x_2)$;
- The first pair of points is assumed to be $p(x_1)$, the second pair is $p(x_2)$, the third pair is $p(x_1x_2)$;

- Start time is measured;
- The local consistency is maintained by the simplex method;
- The time of using the simplex method is recorded;
- If the system is consistent:
  - Start time is measured;
  - Consistency is maintained by explicit formulae;
  - The time for maintaining consistency by explicit formulae if recorded;
  - The cnt variable is incremented by one.

Figure 5 shows the resulting distribution of the average time for maintaining local consistency using the simplex method, and the Fig. 6, using the proposed explicit formulae. Also, the Fig. 7 shows a summary graph of average times.

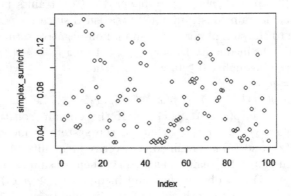

Fig. 5. The vertical axis is the average consistency maintaining time by the simplex method.

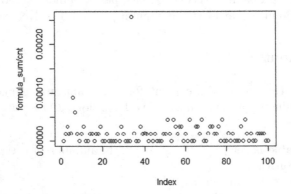

Fig. 6. The vertical axis is the average consistency maintaining time by the explicit formulae.

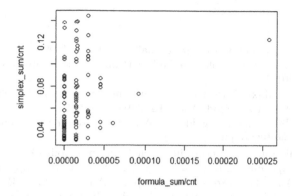

Fig. 7. Summary plot. The vertical axis is the average consistency maintaining time by the simplex method. The horizontal axis is the average time for maintaining consistency by explicit formulae.

It is easy to see that explicit formulae give significant time gains even for two variables. In fact, this result is in line with expectations. We know a nonasymptotic bound of the expected length of the effective path of the simplex method: $const \cdot d^3 n^{1/(d-1)}$. This result belongs to Borgwardt [2], where n is the number of variables, and d is the number of constraints. In other words, the expected time of the simplex method is proportional to the cube of the size of the constraint system. At the same time, the constraint systems arising in ABN problems over n atomic variables are $2^n + 2^n$ [16], that is, quite large. Another reason for the importance of obtaining the general form of the proposed formulas is that it will significantly accelerate the probabilistic logical inference in the ABN.

Note that the results when using an analytical solution are less exposed to problems associated with the accuracy of calculations than when using a simplex algorithm.

6 Conclusion

The paper presents and proves explicit solutions for the problem of maintaining local consistency in a knowledge pattern with a small number of variables, and also compares their effectiveness with the simplex method. The theoretical significance lies in the new possibilities for studying the sensitivity of algebraic Bayesian networks. The practical significance lies in the substantial acceleration of the maintaining of local consistency, as can be seen from the results of the experiment. In the future, the authors hope to generalize the results to knowledge pattern of arbitrary size and to study in detail the issues of sensitivity.

Acknowledgements. The research was carried out as part of the project according to the state task SPIIRAS No. 0073-2019-0003 as well as with particle financial support from the Russian Foundation for Basic Research, project No. 18-01-00626.

References

1. Bellman, R.: Introduction to Matrix Analysis. SIAM (1999)
2. Borgwardt, K.H.: The Simplex Method: A Probabilistic Analysis, vol. 1. Springer, Heidelberg (2012)
3. Dantzig, G.B.: Maximization of a linear function of variables subject to linear inequalities. Act. Anal. Prod. Alloc. **13**, 339–347 (1957)
4. Fagin, R., Halpern, J.Y., Megiddo, N.: A Logic for Reasoning about Probabilities. Report RJ 6190 (60900) 4/12/88 (1988)
5. Fagin, R., Halpern, J.Y.: Uncertainty, belief, and probability-2. In: Proceedings of the IEEE Symposium on Logic and Computer Science, vol. 7, pp. 160–173 (1991)
6. Filchenkov, A.A., Frolenkov, K.V., Tulupyev, A.L.: Algebraic Bayesian network secondary structure cycles elimination based on its quaternary structure analysis. SPIIRAS Proc. **2**(21), 143–156 (2012)
7. Filchenkov, A.A., Tulupyev, A.L.: The algebraic Bayesian network minimal join graphs cycles analysis. SPIIRAS Proc. **17**, 151–173 (2011)
8. Karmarkar, N.: A new polynomial-time algorithm for linear programming. In: Proceedings of the Sixteenth Annual ACM Symposium on Theory of Computing, pp. 302–311 (1984)
9. Khachiyan, L.G.: A polynomial algorithm in linear programming. Doklady Akademii Nauk Russ. Acad. Sci. **244**(5), 1093–1096 (1979)
10. Khlobystova, A., Abramov, M., Tulupyev, A.: An approach to estimating of criticality of social engineering attacks traces. In: Dolinina, O., Brovko, A., Pechenkin, V., Lvov, A., Zhmud, V., Kreinovich, V. (eds.) ICIT 2019. SSDC, vol. 199, pp. 446–456. Springer, Cham (2019). https://doi.org/10.1007/978-3-030-12072-6_36
11. Korepanova, A.A., Oliseenko, V.D., Abramov, M.V., Tulupyev, A.L.: Application of machine learning methods in the task of identifying user accounts in two social networks. Comput. Tools Educ. J. **3**, 29–43 (2019). https://doi.org/10.32603/2071-2340-2019-3-29-43
12. Nilsson, N.J.: Probabilistic logic. Artif. Intell. **28**, 7–87 (1986). Amsterdam: Elsevier Science Publishers B.V., vol. 47, pp. 71–87 (1986)
13. Oparin, V.V., Filchenkov, A.A., Sirotkin, A.V., Tulupyev, A.L.: Matroidal representation for the adjacency graphs family built on a set of knowledge patterns. Sci. Tech. J. Inf. Technol. Mech. Opt. **4**(68), 73–76 (2010)
14. Pearl, J.: Probabilistic Reasoning in Intelligent Systems: Networks of Plausible Inference. Elsevier, Amsterdam (2014)
15. Shindarev, N., Bagretsov, G., Abramov, M., Tulupyeva, T., Suvorova, A.: Approach to identifying of employees profiles in websites of social networks aimed to analyze social engineering vulnerabilities. Adv. Intell. Syst. Comput. **679**, 441–447 (2018). https://doi.org/10.1007/978-3-319-68321-8_45
16. Sirotkin, A.V.: Algebraic Bayesian networks reconciliation: computational complexity. SPIIRAS Proc. **4**(15), 162–192 (2010)
17. Sirotkin, A.V., Tulupyev, A.L.: Matrix-vector equations for local probabilistic logic inference in algebraic Bayesian network. SPIIRAS Proc. **6**, 131–139 (2008)
18. Tulupyev, A.L.: Algebraic Bayesian Networks: Global Probabilistic Logic Inference in Join Trees. SPb.: SPbSU; Publishing House Anatolia (2007)
19. Tulupyev, A.L.: Algebraic Bayesian Networks: Local Probabilistic Logic Inference. SPb.: SPbSU; Publishing House Anatolia (2007)
20. Tulupyev, A.L.: Join tree with conjunction ideals as an acyclic algebraic Bayesian network. SPIIRAS Proc. **3**(1), 198–227 (2006)

21. Tulupyev, A.L., Nikolenko, S.I., Sirotkin, A.V.: Bayesian Networks. A Probabilistic Logic Approach. SPb.: Science (2006)
22. Tulupyev, A.L., Stolyarov, D.M., Mentyukov, M.V.: A representation for local and global structures of an algebraic Bayesian network in Java applications. SPIIRAS Proc. **5**, 71–99 (2007)
23. Vereschchagin, N.K., Shen, A.: Computable functions. Translated by V. N. Dubrovskii. American Mathematical Society (2003)

Abduction with Estimates for Statements in Fuzzy Propositional Logic

Gerald S. Plesniewicz$^{(\boxtimes)}$

National Research University MPEI, Krasnokazarmennaya Street 14, Moscow, Russia
salve777@mail.ru

Abstract. *Estimates* are expressions of the form $\varphi \geq r$, $\varphi > r$, $\varphi \leq r$, $\varphi < r$, $\varphi \leq \psi$ or $\varphi < \psi$ where φ and ψ are propositional formulas and r is a real number from the unit interval $[0, 1]$. We consider the classic fuzzy interpretations of formulas φ, i.e., those based on the t-norm $\min\{x, y\}$ and negation $1 - x$. Such interpretations is naturally extended to estimates. *Logic of estimates* **LE** is the set of all Boolean compositions of estimates that are interpreted with the usual sense of the propositional connectives. We have developed, for the logic **LE,** a complete system of inference rules in the style of analytic tableaux. It is shown how to apply the rules for abduction in the logic **LE.**

Keywords: Logical inference · Fuzzy logics · Analytic tableaux · Estimates for fuzzy statements · Abductive inference

1 Introduction. Main Definitions

Abduction is a method of inference (reasoning) used in numerous application areas and tasks, in particular, in bioinformatics, medicine, automation of scientific research, robotics, automatic planning, engineering diagnostics, data engineering, ontological modeling, multi-agent systems, life cycle analysis in production, etc. (see, for example, [3, 4, 6–11]).

Abduction is a form of ampliative reasoning, i.e. such that allows for acquiring new knowledge that does not follow logically from a given knowledge [2]. In general, logical abduction is associated with the following scheme that includes:

- logical language **L** for representing knowledge;
- a set **Int** of *interpretations* of the language **L**;
- a set **Obs** $\subseteq$ **L** whose members are called *observations*;
- a set **Hyp** $\subseteq$ **L** whose members are called *hypotheses*;
- a *knowledge base Kb* which is a finite satisfied subset of **L**.

The purpose of abductive reasoning is, for a given observation $O \in$ **Obs** such that $Kb \not\models O$, to find a hypothesis $H \in$ **Hyp** with $Kb \cup \{H\} \models O$ (where $\models$ is the sign of logical consequence). Usually, some constraints of "parsimony" on the desired hypotheses are used.

Consider the simple scheme **S** of abduction where

© Springer Nature Switzerland AG 2020
S. O. Kuznetsov et al. (Eds.): RCAI 2020, LNAI 12412, pp. 164–176, 2020.
https://doi.org/10.1007/978-3-030-59535-7_12

- **L** is the propositional language with atoms $p_i, q_i (i = 1, 2, \ldots)$;
- **Int** is the set of usual interpretations with the standard sense of propositional connectives;
- **Obs** is the set of all conjunctions of literals p_i and $\sim p_j$ without contrarian pairs of literals (for example, $\sim p_1 \wedge p_3 \wedge \sim p_2 \in$ **Obs**);
- **Hyp** is the set of all conjunctions of literals q_i and $\sim q_j$ without contrarian pairs of literals.

Hereinafter, using medical terminology, we call p_i symptoms and q_j diseases. Thus, the observation $\sim p_1 \wedge p_3 \wedge \sim p_2$ is read as "there is the symptom p_3 and there are no symptoms p_1 and p_2", and the hypothesis $q_3 \wedge \sim q_1$ is read as "there is the disease q_3 and there is no the disease q_1". We also represent conjunctions of symptoms and conjunction of diseases by finite sets (for example, we write $\{\sim p_1, p_3, \sim p_2\}$ for $\sim p_1 \wedge p_3 \wedge \sim p_2$).

For a knowledge base Kb, we denote $P(Kb) = \{p_i, \sim p_i | p_i$ enters $Kb\}$ and $Q(Kb) = \{q_i, \sim q_i | p_i$ enters $Kb\}$. For any finite set of formulas F, we also denote by $F^\wedge$ the conjunction of all formulas from F, i.e., $F^\wedge = \wedge \{\varphi | \varphi \in F\}$.

Let us take a DNF $N = C_1 \vee C_2 \vee \ldots \vee C_t$ for the formula $Kb^\wedge$ (where C_i are conjuncts of the formula) and denote $C(Kb) = \{C_1, C_2, \ldots, C_t\}$. Let also denote $P(Kb) = \{p_1, \sim p_1, p_2, \sim p_2, \ldots, p_m, \sim p_m\}$ and $Q(Kb) = \{q_1, \sim q_1, q_2, \sim q_2, \ldots, p_n, \sim p_n\}$

With any knowledge base Kb and DNF N (for Kb), we associate some graph $\Gamma(Kb, N)$ which will be used for abduction over that knowledge base. The graph $\Gamma(Kb, N)$ have the following vertices and edges:

- $P(Kb) \cup C(Kb) \cup Q(Kb)$ is the set of $\Gamma(Kb, N)$ vertices. We say that a vertex of P (Kb), C (Kb) and Q (Kb) is left, central and right, respectively.
- The $\Gamma(Kb, N)$ edges are defined by the following rules:

(R1): (p_i, C_j) and $(\sim p_i, C_j)$ are edges if and only if C_j contains p_i and $\sim p_i$, respectively;
(R2): (C_j, q_k) and $(C_j, \sim q_k)$ are edges if and only if C_j contains $\sim q_i$ and q_i, respectively.

Remark. The graph $\Gamma(Kb, N)$ can be also used for deduction and query answering over the knowledge base Kb.

The main goal of the present article is to extend to so-called logic of estimates the abduction method based on the use of associated graphs.

By *estimates* we mean the expressions of the form $\varphi \geq r, \varphi > r, \varphi \leq r, \varphi < r, \varphi \leq \psi, \varphi < \psi$ where r is a real number from the unit interval $[0, 1]$ and φ, ψ are propositional formulas with fuzzy interpretations. More exactly, let **L** be the set of all formulas built from the atoms p_i and q_j using the propositional connectives $\sim, \wedge, \vee, \rightarrow$ (for example, $\sim q_1 \wedge p_1 \rightarrow \sim p_2$ is a formula from **L**, and $\sim q_1 \wedge p_1 \rightarrow \sim p_2 \geq 0.8$ is an estimate).

Set **Int** consists of fuzzy interpretations. An interpretation "•" $\in$ **Int** is determined by assigning the values "p_i", "q_i" $\in [0, 1]$. The assignment is extended to **L** formulas such that for any $\varphi, \psi \in$ **L**:

$$\text{``}\sim\varphi\text{''} = 1 - \text{``}\varphi\text{''}, \quad \text{``}\varphi \wedge \psi\text{''} = \min\{\text{``}\varphi\text{''}, \text{``}\psi\text{''}\}, \quad \text{``}\varphi \vee \psi\text{''} = \max\{\text{``}\varphi\text{''}, \text{``}\psi\text{''}\},$$
$$\text{``}\varphi \rightarrow \psi\text{''} = \max\{1 - \text{``}\varphi\text{''}, \text{``}\psi\text{''}\}.$$

Estimates are interpreted in natural way: every estimate is true or false in any interpretation "•" and

"$\varphi \geq r$" = 1 (truth) $\Leftrightarrow$ "φ" $\geq r$, "$\varphi > r$" = 1 $\Leftrightarrow$ "φ" $> r$, "$\varphi \leq r$" = 1 $\Leftrightarrow$ "φ" $\leq r$,
"$\varphi < r$" = 1 $\Leftrightarrow$ "φ" $< r$, and "$\varphi \leq \psi$" = 1 $\Leftrightarrow$ "φ" $\leq$ "ψ".

Consider by example how to calculate the value of an estimate in a given interpretation. Let "•" be an interpretation with "p_1" = 0.7, "p_2" = 0.3 and "q_1" = 0.5. Then for the estimate $\sim q_1 \wedge p_1 \to \sim p_2 \geq 0.8$ we have

"$\sim q_1 \wedge p_1 \to \sim p_2 \geq 0.8$" = 1 $\Leftrightarrow$ "$\sim q_1 \wedge p_1 \to \sim p_2$" $\geq 0.8 \Leftrightarrow$
$\max\{1- $"$\sim q_1 \wedge p_1$", "$\sim p_2$"$\} \geq 0.8 \Leftrightarrow \max\{1- \min\{$"$\sim q_1$", "$p_1$"$\}, 1-$"$p_2$"$\} \geq 0.8 \Leftrightarrow$

$\max\{1- \min\{1-$"q_1","p_1"$\}, 1-$"p_2"$\} \geq 0.8 \Leftrightarrow \max\{1-\min\{1- 0.5, 0.7\}, 1- 0.3\} \geq$
0.8
$\Leftrightarrow 0.7 \geq 0.8.$

Thus, "$\sim q_1 \wedge p_1 \to \sim p_2 \geq 0.8$" = 0, i.e., the estimate $\sim q_1 \wedge p_1 \to \sim p_2 \geq 0.8$ is false in the interpretation "•".

The language **LE** of *Logic of Estimates* consists of sentences that are compositions of estimates using the propositional connectives. Here is an example of **LE** sentence:

$$\alpha: \sim (\sim q_1 \wedge p_1 \to \sim p_2 \geq 0.8) \wedge (p_2 \leq p_1).$$

How to interpret **LE** sentences is clear from the following example. Let "•" be an interpretation with "p_1" = 0.7, "p_2" = 0.3 and "q_1" = 0.5. Then we have

"α"= $\min\{$"$\sim (\sim q_1 \wedge p_1 \to \sim p_2 \geq 0.8)$", "$p_2 \leq p_1$"$\}$ =
$\min\{1 - $"$(\sim q_1 \wedge p_1 \to \sim p_2 \geq 0.8)$", $0.3 \leq 0.7\} = \min\{1- 0, 1\} = 1.$

Thus, the sentence α is true in the interpretation "•".

The logic **LE** of estimates will be described at Sect. 2 in detail. In Sect. 3 we will show how to build graphs $\Gamma(Kb, N)$ for given knowledges Kb and DNF N.

2   Logic of Estimates

The logic of estimates **LE** has logical equivalences which are similar to ones that take place in classic propositional logic. The main equivalences are written in Lemma 1.

Lemma 1. Let φ and ψ be propositional formulas and $r \in [0, 1]$. Then the following equivalences are valid:

$$\sim\varphi \geq r \Leftrightarrow \varphi \leq 1-r, \tag{2.1}$$

$$\sim\varphi \geq r \Leftrightarrow \varphi \geq 1-r,$$

$$\varphi \wedge \psi \geq r \Leftrightarrow (\varphi \geq r) \wedge (\psi \geq r), \tag{2.2}$$

$$\varphi \wedge \psi \leq r \Leftrightarrow (\varphi \leq r) \vee (\psi \leq r),$$
$$\varphi \vee \psi \geq r \Leftrightarrow (\varphi \geq r) \vee (\psi \geq r),$$
$$\varphi \vee \psi \leq r \Leftrightarrow (\varphi \leq r) \wedge (\psi \leq r),$$
$$\sim(\varphi \leq r) \Leftrightarrow \varphi > r,$$
$$(\varphi \geq r) \wedge (\varphi \geq s) \Leftrightarrow \varphi \geq \max\{r, s\}, \qquad (2.3)$$

$$(\varphi \leq r) \wedge (\varphi \leq s) \Leftrightarrow \varphi \geq \min\{r, s\},$$
$$(\varphi \geq r) \vee (\varphi \geq s) \Leftrightarrow \varphi \geq \min\{r, s\},$$
$$(\varphi \leq r) \vee (\varphi \leq s) \Leftrightarrow \varphi \geq \max\{r, s\},$$

and also the same equivalences but with signs $>$ and $<$ instead of $\geq$ and $\geq$ (respectively). Here are the proofs of (2.1), (2.2) and (2.3):

- "$\sim\varphi \geq r$" = 1 $\Leftrightarrow$ "$\sim\varphi$" $\geq r \Leftrightarrow 1-$ "φ" $\geq r \Leftrightarrow$ "φ" $\leq 1-r \Leftrightarrow$ "$\varphi \leq 1-r$" = 1.

- "$\varphi \vee \psi \leq r$" = 1 $\Leftrightarrow$ "$\varphi \vee \psi$" $\leq r \Leftrightarrow \max\{$"$\varphi$","$\psi$"$\} \leq r \Leftrightarrow$ "φ" $\leq r$ и "ψ" $\leq r \Leftrightarrow$ "$\psi \leq r$" = 1 и "$\psi \leq r$" = 1 $\Leftrightarrow$ "$\varphi \leq r$" $\wedge$ "$\psi \leq r$" = 1 $\Leftrightarrow \min\{$"$\varphi \geq r$","$\psi \geq r$"$\} \Leftrightarrow$ "$(\varphi \geq r) \wedge (\psi \geq r)$" = 1.

- "$(\varphi \geq r) \wedge (\varphi \geq s)$" = 1 $\Leftrightarrow$ "$\varphi \geq r$" = 1 и "$\varphi \geq s$" = 1 $\Leftrightarrow$ "φ" $\geq r$ and "φ" $\geq s \Leftrightarrow$ "φ" $\geq \max\{r, s\} \Leftrightarrow$ "$\varphi \geq \max\{r, s\}$" = 1.

Like any logic, **LE** induces the relation $\models$ of logical consequence. Let Kb be a knowledge base in **LE** and $\varphi \in$ **LE**. Then $Kb \models \varphi$ if and only if there is no interpretation "$\bullet$" such that "φ" = 0 and "ψ" = 1 for all $\psi \in Kb$.

We offer the inference rules with which we can verify the relation $Kb \models \varphi$. These rules belong to analytical tableaux methods [1, 5]. The rules are presented in Table 1, Table 2 and Table 3.

Table 1. Inference rules for **LE** formulas with the signs "$>$" and "$<$".

Rule number	Antecedents	Consequent
1	$+ \sim \varphi$	$-\varphi$
2	$- \sim \varphi$	$+\varphi$
3	$+\varphi \wedge \psi$	$+\varphi$ and $+\psi$
4	$-\varphi \wedge \psi$	$-\varphi$ or $-\psi$
5	$+\varphi \vee \psi$	$+\varphi$ or $-\psi$
6	$-\varphi \vee \psi$	$-\varphi$ and $-\psi$
7	$+\varphi \rightarrow \psi$	$-\varphi$ or $+\psi$
8	$-\varphi \rightarrow \psi$	$+\varphi$ and $-\psi$

Table 2. Inference rules for estimates.

Rule number	Antecedents	Consequent
1	$\sim\varphi \geq r$	$\varphi \leq 1-r$
2	$\sim\varphi \leq r$	$\varphi \geq 1-r$
3	$\varphi \wedge \psi \geq r$	$\varphi \geq r$ and $\psi \geq r$
4	$\varphi \wedge \psi \geq r$	$\varphi \leq r$ or $\psi \leq r$
5	$\varphi \vee \psi \geq r$	$\varphi \geq r$ or $\psi \geq r$
6	$\varphi \vee \psi \geq r$	$\varphi \leq r$ and $\psi \leq r$
7	$\varphi \rightarrow \psi \geq r$	$\varphi \leq 1-r$ or $\psi \geq r$
8	$\varphi \rightarrow \psi \leq r$	$\varphi > 1-r$ and $\psi < r$
	and the same rules but with the signs $>$ and $<$ instead of $\geq$ and $\geq$	

Table 3. Binary inference rules.

Rule number	Antecedents	Consequent
1	$+\varphi, -\varphi$	X
2	$\varphi \leq r, \varphi \geq s, r < s$	X
3	$\varphi \leq \psi, \psi \leq \rho$	$\varphi \leq \rho$
4	$\varphi \leq r, \varphi \leq s$	$\varphi \geq \min\{r,s\}$
4	$\varphi \geq r, \varphi \geq s$	$\varphi \geq \max\{r,s\}$
	and the same rules but with other inequality signs	

When applying the method of analytic tableaux, inferences are presented in the form of trees such that their vertices are the sentences, and their edges are determined from the applied inference rules.

Consider Fig. 1 which shows some inference tree obtained by applying the rules from Table 1. Its vertices are the signed **LE** formulas with labels. For example, the tree has the vertex "1: $+p_1 \wedge p_2 \wedge \sim p_3$ [1–3] (7,3,1)" where the right labels [1–3] and (7,3,1) indicate that rule 3 from Table 1 in step 2 and the binary rule 1 from Table 3 in step 7 were applied to the formula $+p_1 \wedge p_2 \wedge \sim p_3$. The left label "1:"indicates that the formula $+p_1 \wedge p_2 \wedge \sim p_3$ was obtained in step 1 from the formula $+q_1 \rightarrow p_1 \wedge p_2 \wedge \sim p_3$ by applying the rule 3 from Table 1. The right label (7,3,1) was attached also to the formula $-p_1 \wedge p_2 \wedge \sim p_3$. Thus, the rule 1 from Table 3 was applied in step 7 to the formulas $+p_1 \wedge p_2 \wedge \sim p_3$ and $-p_1 \wedge p_2 \wedge \sim p_3$ as antecedents. These formulas gave a contradiction that was denoted by the symbol "X".

When constructing the inference tree, we use the standard tactics for sequencing of applicable rules [5]. In particular, we used the priority for non-alternative rules.

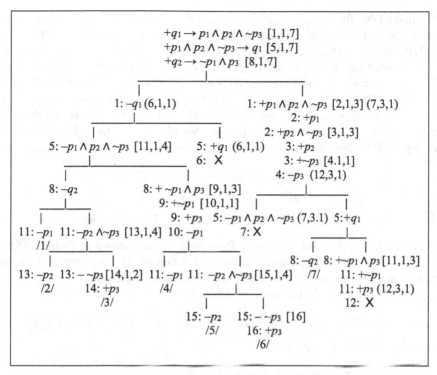

Fig 1. Inference tree for Kb from Example 1

3 Building Graphs $\Gamma(Kb, N)$ for Knowledge Bases in Propositional Logic

We consider, by example, how to build graphs $\Gamma(Kb, N)$ for knowledge bases written in the language of propositional logic.

Example 1. Consider the task of diagnosis in a situation where there are two diseases q_1, q_2 and three symptoms p_1, p_2, p_3. Suppose the following knowledge defines relations between these diseases and symptoms:

(a) the disease q_1 is completely characterized by the presence of the symptoms p_1, p_2 and the absence of the symptom p_3, i.e., q_1 occurs if and only if the symptoms of p_1 and p_2 appear, but there is no symptom p_3;

(b) if there is the disease q_2, then the symptom p_3 is observed, but the symptom p_1 is absent.

The knowledge (a) can be represented by the formula $q_1 \leftrightarrow p_1 \wedge p_2 \wedge \sim p_3$ or by two formulas $q_1 \rightarrow p_1 \wedge p_2 \wedge \sim p_3$ и $p_1 \wedge p_2 \wedge \sim p_3 \rightarrow q_1$. The knowledge (b) can be represented by the formula $q_2 \rightarrow \sim p_1 \wedge p_3$. Thus, we have the knowledge base

$$Kb = \{q_1 \rightarrow p_1 \wedge p_2 \wedge \sim p_3, p_1 \wedge p_2 \wedge \sim p_3 \rightarrow q_1, q_2 \rightarrow \sim p_1 \wedge p_3\}.$$

We find a DNF for the formula $Kb^\wedge$ (which is the conjunctions of the formulas from Kb) using the method of analytic tableaux by means of the rules from Table 1. The result of applying the rules is the tree shown in Fig. 1. In the tree there are three closed branches and seven open branches. (A branch is open if it contains a contrary pair of formulas).

Take, for example, the third (on the left) branch /3/ of the tree and write out all signed atoms entering the branch: $-q_1$, $-q_2$, $+p_3$. Then we define the conjunct $p_1 \wedge \sim q_1 \wedge \sim q_2$. Other conjuncts are similarly obtained. Note that the fourth branch /4/ and the sixth branch /6/ define the same conjunct C_4. Thus, we obtain from the inference tree the following DNF for the formula $Kb^\wedge$: $N = C_1 \vee C_2 \vee C_3 \vee C_4 \vee C_5 \vee C_6$ where

$$C_1 = \sim p_1 \wedge \sim q_1 \wedge \sim q_2, \, C_2 = \sim p_2 \wedge \sim q_1 \wedge \sim q_2, \, C_3 = p_3 \wedge \sim q_1 \wedge \sim q_2,$$
$$C_4 = \sim p_1 \wedge p_3 \wedge \sim q_1,$$
$$C_5 = \sim p_1 \wedge \sim p_2 \wedge p_3 \wedge \sim q_1, \, C_6 = p_1 \wedge p_2 \wedge \sim p_3 \wedge q_1 \wedge \sim q_2.$$

It is easy to see that, due the lemma from Sect. 2, this method of finding DNF is correct. We also can apply another method which consists in transforming formulas using logical identities. In the present example, we can do as follows.

At first, we represent the formula $Kb^\wedge$ in the form

$$\left[a \colon (1 \colon \sim q_1 \vee 2 \colon p_1 \wedge p_2 \wedge \sim p_3)\right] \wedge \left[b \colon (1 \colon \sim p_1 \vee 2 \colon \sim p_2 \vee 3 \colon p_3 \vee 4 \colon q_1)\right] \wedge$$
$$\left[c \colon (1 \colon \sim q_2 \vee 2 \colon \sim p_1 \wedge p_3)\right].$$

Then we perform the following transformations:

- $a \wedge b = 11 \colon \sim q_1 \wedge \sim p_1 \vee 12 \colon \sim q_1 \wedge \sim p_2 \vee 13 \colon \sim q_1 \wedge p_3 \vee 14 \colon \sim q_1 \wedge q_1 \vee$
  $21 \colon p_1 \wedge p_2 \wedge \sim p_3 \wedge \sim p_1 \vee 22 \colon p_1 \wedge p_2 \wedge \sim p_3 \wedge \sim p_2 \vee 23 \colon p_1 \wedge p_2 \wedge \sim p_3 \wedge p_3 \vee$
  $24 \colon p_1 \wedge p_2 \wedge \sim p_3 \wedge q_1.$
- $a \wedge b \wedge c = 111 \colon \sim q_1 \wedge \sim p_1 \wedge \sim q_2 \vee 121 \colon \sim q_1 \wedge \sim p_2 \wedge \sim q_2 \vee 131 \colon \sim q_1 \wedge \sim p_3 \wedge \sim q_2 \vee$
  $241 \colon p_1 \wedge p_2 \wedge \sim p_3 \wedge q_1 \wedge \sim q_2 \vee 112 \colon \sim q_1 \wedge \sim p_1 \wedge \sim p_1 \wedge p_3 \vee$
  $122 \colon \sim q_1 \wedge \sim p_2 \wedge \sim p_1 \wedge p_3 \vee 132 \colon \sim q_1 \wedge p_3 \wedge \sim p_1 \wedge p_3 \vee$
  $242 \colon p_1 \wedge p_2 \wedge \sim p_3 \wedge q_1 \wedge \sim p_1 \wedge p_3 = 11 \colon \sim q_1 \wedge \sim p_1 \wedge \sim q_2 \vee 121 \colon \sim q_1 \wedge \sim p_2 \wedge \sim q_2 \vee$
  $131 \colon \sim q_1 \wedge p_3 \wedge \sim q_2 \vee 241 \colon p_1 \wedge p_2 \wedge \sim p_3 \wedge q_1 \wedge \sim q_2 \vee 112 \colon \sim q_1 \wedge \sim p_1 \wedge p_3 \vee$
  $122 \colon \sim q_1 \wedge \sim p_2 \wedge \sim p_1 \wedge p_3 \vee 132 \colon \sim q_1 \wedge p_3 \wedge \sim p_1 =$
  $(\sim p_1 \wedge \sim q_1 \wedge \sim q_2) \vee (\sim p_2 \wedge \sim q_1 \wedge \sim q_2) \vee (p_3 \wedge \sim q_1 \wedge \sim q_2) \vee (\sim p_1 \wedge p_3 \wedge \sim q_1) \vee$
  $(\sim p_1 \wedge \sim p_2 \wedge p_3 \wedge \sim q_1) \vee (p_1 \wedge p_2 \wedge \sim p_3 \wedge q_1 \wedge \sim q_2).$

Thus, we obtained the same DNF as that was obtained before from the inference tree.

Remark. These two methods for building DNF for formulas of propositional logic have almost the same computational complexity. However, the tableaux method has more potential for generalization.

Figure 2 shows the graph $\Gamma(Kb, N)$ built from these knowledge base and DNF using the rules R1 and R2 (see Sect. 1).

Let $\omega(\bullet)$ be the *neighborhood* function in the graph:
$\omega(v) = \{u | (v, u) \text{ is an edge of the graph } \Gamma(Kb, N)\}.$

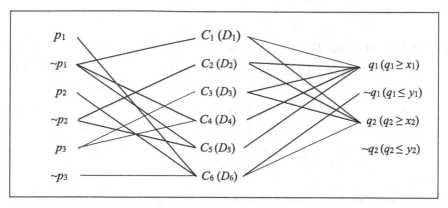

Fig. 2. Graphs $\Gamma(Kb,N)$ and $\Gamma(Kbe,M)$ from Example 1 and Example 4

In this case we have

$\omega(p_1) = \{C_6\}, \omega(\sim p_1) = \{C_1, C_4, C_5\}, \omega(p_2) = \{C_7\}, \omega(\sim p_2) = \{C_?, C_5\},$
$\omega(C_1) = \{\sim p_1, q_1, q_2\}, \omega(C_2) = \{\sim p_2, q_1, q_2\}, \omega(C_3) = \{p_3, q_1, q_2\},$
$\omega(C_4) = \{\sim p_1 p_3, q_1, q_2\}, \omega(C_5) = \{\sim p_1, \sim p_2, q_1\}, \omega(C_6) = \{\sim p_1, p_2, \sim p_3, \sim q_1\},$
$\omega(q_1) = \{C_1, C_2, C_3, C_4, C_5\}, \omega(\sim q_1) = \{C_6\}, \omega(q_2) = \{C_1, C_2, C_3\}, \omega(\sim q_2) = \{C_6\}.$

4 Examples of Abductive Inferences Over Knowledge Bases in Propositional logic

Consider two examples of abductive inferring over knowledge bases.

Example 2. It is clear that $Kb \cup \{H\}| = O \Leftrightarrow Kb \cup \{H\} \cup \{\sim O\}$ is inconsistent. In particular, let Kb is the knowledge base and N is the DNF for $Kb^{\wedge}$ from Example 1. Suppose that the observation $O = \{p_1\}$ takes place. Then we have

$$Kb \cup \{H\}| = O \Leftrightarrow N \wedge H \wedge \sim O = 0 \Leftrightarrow$$
$$(C_1 \vee C_2 \vee C_3 \vee C_4 \vee C_5 \vee C_6) \wedge \sim p_1 \wedge H = 0 \Leftrightarrow$$
$$(C_1 \vee C_2 \vee C_3 \vee C_4 \vee C_5 \vee C_6) \wedge H = 0.$$

The last equation has the least (by the number of literals) solution $H = q_1$.

Thus, if the symptom p_1 is detected, then the most plausible diagnosis is the disease q_1.

Example 3. Suppose the symptom p_3 is present, but the symptom p_1 is absent, i.e. we have the observation $O = \{\sim p_1, p_3\}$. Then, we have

$Kb \cup \{H\} \mid = O \Leftrightarrow N \wedge H \wedge \sim O = 0 \Leftrightarrow$

$$(C_1 \vee C_2 \vee C_3 \vee C_4 \vee C_5 \vee C_6) \wedge \sim (\sim p_1 \wedge p_3) \wedge H = 0 \Leftrightarrow$$
$$(C_1 \vee C_2 \vee C_3 \vee C_4 \vee C_5 \vee C_6) \wedge (p_1 \vee \sim p_3) = 0 \Leftrightarrow$$
$$(C_1 \vee C_2 \vee C_3 \vee C_4 \vee C_5 \vee C_6) \wedge p_1 \vee$$
$$(C_1 \vee C_2 \vee C_3 \vee C_4 \vee C_5 \vee C_6) \wedge \sim p_3 = 0 \Leftrightarrow$$
$$[(C_2 \vee C_3 \vee C_6) \vee (C_1 \overset{\vee}{} C_2 \vee C_6) \wedge H] = 0 \Leftrightarrow$$
$$(C_1 \vee C_2 \vee C_3 \vee C_6) \wedge H = 0.$$

The last equation has the least solution $H = \sim q_1 \wedge q_2$.

Thus, if the symptom p_3 is detected and there is no the symptom p_1 then the most plausible diagnosis is that there is the disease q_2 but there is no disease q_1.

Now, we describe, in graph terms, the abduction procedure which can be corresponded to Example 2 and Example 3.

Abduction procedure $\Pi 1$ (for propositional logic).

Step 0. Given are a knowledge base Kb (written in propositional logic) and an observation O.

Step 1. Find any DNF N for the formula $Kb^{\wedge}$ (by tableaux method).

Step 2. Build the graph $\Gamma(Kb, N)$.

Step 3. Find $B := \cup\{-\omega(v) \mid v \in O\}$. Here $\omega(\bullet)$ is the neighborhood function in the graph $\Gamma(Kb, N)$, and $-\omega(v)$ is the complement of $\omega(v)$ in the part $Q(\Gamma)$, i.e., $-\omega(v) = Q(\Gamma) \backslash \omega(v)$.

Step 4. Find (one of) the least covering A of the set B, i.e., $\omega(A) \supseteq B, A \subseteq Q(\Gamma)$ and if $\omega(X) \supseteq B, X \subseteq Q(\Gamma)$ then $|A| \leq |X|$.

Step 5. Return the hypothesis A.

5 Building Graphs $\Gamma(Kbe, M)$ for Knowledge Bases in Logic of Estimates

We consider two examples of building graphs for knowledge bases written in **LE**.

Example 4. Take again the knowledge base Kb from Example 1, and replace its propositional formulas with the following estimates:

$$Kbe = \{q_1 \rightarrow p_1 \wedge p_2 \wedge \sim p_3 \geq 0.6, p_1 \wedge p_2 \wedge \sim p_3 \rightarrow q_1 \geq 0.6, q_2 \rightarrow \sim p_1 \wedge p_3 \geq 0.3\}$$

Figure 3 shows the inference tree for the knowledge base Kbe. The tree was built using the rules from Table 2 and Table 3. The tree has 7 open branches from which we obtain the following conjuncts of the DNF $M = D_1 \vee D_2 \vee D_3 \vee D_4 \vee D_5 \vee D_6$:

$$D_1 = (p_1 \leq 0.4) \wedge (q_1 \leq 0.4) \wedge (q_2 \leq 0.7), D_2 = (p_2 \leq 0.4) \wedge (q_1 \leq 0.4) \wedge (q_2 \leq 0.7),$$
$$D_3 = (p_3 \geq 0.4) \wedge (q_1 \leq 0.4) \wedge (q_2 \leq 0.7), D_4 = (p_1 \leq 0.3) \wedge (p_3 \geq 0.4) \wedge (q_1 \leq 0.4),$$
$$D_5 = (p_1 \leq 0.3) \wedge (p_2 \leq 0.4) \wedge (q_1 \leq 0.4),$$
$$D_6 = (p_1 \geq 0.6) \wedge (p_2 \geq 0.6) \wedge (p_3 \leq 0.4) \wedge (q_1 \geq 0.6) \wedge (q_2 \leq 0.7).$$

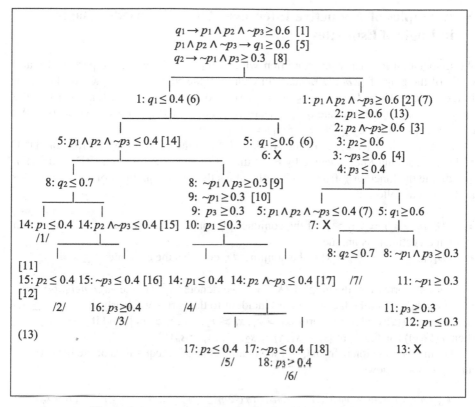

Fig. 3. Inference tree with estimates for *Kbe* from Example 4

Consider, for example, how the conjunct D_4 is obtained from the fourth branch /4/. We write out from /4/ the elementary estimates (i.e., the estimates for propositional variables): $q_1 \leq 0.4$, $p_3 \geq 0.3$, $p_1 \leq 0.3$, $p_1 \leq 0.4$. Then we define $D_4 = (p_1 \leq 0.3) \wedge (p_3 \geq 0.4) \wedge (q_1 \leq 0.4)$.

The graph $\Gamma(Kbe, M)$ has the following vertices: $P(\Gamma) = \{p_1, \sim p_1, p_1, \sim p_1, p_1, \sim p_1\}$,

$$C(\Gamma) = \{D_1, D_2, D_3, D_4, D_5, D_6\}, \quad Q(\Gamma) = \{q_1 \geq x_1, q_1 \leq y_1, q_2 \geq x_2, q_2 \leq y_2\}.$$

The edges of the graph $\Gamma(Kbe, M)$ are defined using the following rules that are similar the rules R1 and R2 from Sect. 1:

(R1*): (p_i, C_j) and $(\sim p_i, C_j)$ are edges if and only if C_j contains the literals p_i and $\sim p_i$, respectively;

(R2*): (C_j, q_k) and $(C_j, \sim q_k)$ are edges if and only if C_j contains the literals $\sim q_i$ and q_i, respectively

The Fig. 2 show the graph $\Gamma(Kbe, M)$. (There the vertices of $C(\Gamma)$ and $Q(\Gamma)$ are enclosed in brackets).

6 Examples of Abductive Inferences Over Knowledge Bases in Logic of Estimates

We associate a inconsistency condition with every edge between the parts $C(\Gamma)$ and $Q(\Gamma)$ of the graph $\Gamma(Kbe, M)$. Take, for example, the edge $(D_5, q_1 \geq x_1)$ of the graph in Example 4. There $D_5 = (p_1 \leq 0.3) \wedge (p_2 \leq 0.4) \wedge (q_1 \leq 0.4)$. It is clear that the conjunct D_5 and the estimate $q_1 \geq x_1$ are contradictory if and only if $x_1 > 0.4$. We denote this situation by $\chi(D_5, q_1 \geq x_1) = (x_1 > 0.4)$.

In general, let $\Gamma(Kbe, M)$ be the graph built for some knowledge base Kbe and DNF M for the formula $Kbe^\wedge$. Denote by $E(\Gamma)$ the set of all edges between $C(\Gamma)$ and $Q(\Gamma)$, and define the function χ from $E(\Gamma)$ with values that are inequalities of the form $x_i > r$ and $y_i < s$ as follows:

- $\chi(D_i, q_j \geq x_i) = (x_j > r)$ if the conjunct D_i contains the estimate $x_j \geq r$ (note that such an estimate is unique);
- $\chi(D_i, q_j \leq y_i) = (y_j < s)$ if the conjunct D_i contains the estimate $x_j \leq s$.

For any vertex v of the graph $\Gamma(Kb, M)$, we denote by $\Omega(v)$ the *edge-neighborhood* of v, i.e., the set of all edges which are incident to the vertex v. Clearly, if $v = (q_i \geq x_i)$ then the set $\chi(\Omega(v))$ has the form $\{x_i > r_1, x_i > r_2, \ldots, x_i > r_m\}$, and if $v = (q_i \leq y_i)$, then $\chi(\Omega(v))$ has the form $\{y_i < s_1, y_i < s_2, \ldots, y_i < s_n\}$.

Define the function μ from $Q(\Gamma)$ with values that are inequalities of the form $x_i > r$ and $y_i < s$ as follows:

- $\mu(q_i \geq x_i) = (q_i > \min\{r_1, r_2, \ldots, r_m\})$ if $\chi(\Omega(q_i \geq x_i)) = \{x_i > r_1, x_i > r_2, \ldots, x_i > r_m\}$;
- $\mu(q_i \geq y_i) = (q_i > \max\{r_1, r_2, \ldots, r_m\})$ if $\chi(\Omega(q_i \geq x_i)) = \{y_i < s_1, y_i > s_2, \ldots, y_i > s_n\}$.

For the graph $\Gamma(Kb, M)$ from Example 4 there are the following values of the function μ:

$$\mu(q_1 \geq x_1) = (q_1 > 0.4), \mu(q_1 \leq y_1) = (q_2 < 0.6), \mu(q_2 \geq x_2) = (q_2 > 0.7). \tag{6.1}$$

Indeed, we have for the last value:

$$\Omega(q_2 \geq x_2) = \{(D_1, q_2 \geq x_2), (D_2, q_2 \geq x_2), (D_3, q_2 \geq x_2), (D_6, q_2 \geq x_2)\},$$
$$\chi(\Omega(q_2 \geq x_2)) = \{\chi(D_1, q_2 \geq x_2), \chi(D_2, q_2 \geq x_2), \chi(D_3, q_2 \geq x_2), \chi(D_6, q_2 \geq x_2)\}$$
$$= \{x_2 > 0.4, x_2 > 0.4, x_2 > 0.4, x_2 > 0.7\},$$
$$\max\{0.4, 0.4, 0.4, 0.7\} = 0.7, \mu(q_2 \geq x_2) = (q_2 > 0.7).$$

The function μ is used in the abduction procedure $\Pi 2$ over knowledge bases written in the logic of estimates **LE**. The procedure $\Pi 2$ has 4 parts with the following functionalities: (1) finding, for a given observation O, the set B of those conjuncts D_j that should be deleted from M in order to obtain logical consequence $M' \models O$ where M' is the resulting DNF; (2) finding the least covering A of the set of vertices which are conjuncts entering DNF M'; (3) applying the function μ to the covering A.

Abduction procedure $\Pi 2$ (for the logic of estimates **LE**).

Step 0. Given are a knowledge base *Kbe* (written in the logic **LE**) and an observation *O*.
Step 1. Find any DNF *M* for the formula *Kbe*^ (using the rules from Table 1, Table 2, and Table 3 tableaux method).
Step 2. Build the graph $\Gamma(Kbe, M)$.
Step 3. Find $B := \cup\{-\omega(v)|v \in O\}$.
Step 4. Find (one of) the least covering *A* of the set *B*.
Step 5. Apply the function μ to *A*.
Step 6. Return the hypothesis $\mu(A)$ (written in **LE**).

Consider two examples of applying the procedure $\Pi 2$.

Example 5. Suppose the symptom p_1 is detected. Then we have:

0. $Kbe = \{q_1 \rightarrow p_1 \wedge p_2 \wedge \sim p_3 \geq 0.6, p_1 \wedge p_2 \wedge \sim p_3 \rightarrow q_1 \geq 0.6, q_2 \rightarrow \sim p_1 \wedge p_3 \geq 0.3\}$,
   $O = \{p_1\}$.
1. $M = \{D_1: (p_1 \leq 0.4) \wedge (q_1 \leq 0.4) \wedge (q_2 \leq 0.7),$
   $\qquad D_2: (p_2 \leq 0.4) \wedge (q_1 \leq 0.4) \wedge (q_2 \leq 0.7),$
   $\qquad D_3: (p_3 \geq 0.4) \wedge (q_1 < 0.4) \wedge (q_2 \leq 0.7),$
   $\qquad D_4: (p_1 \leq 0.3) \wedge (p_3 \geq 0.4) \wedge (q_1 \leq 0.4),$
   $\qquad D_5: (p_1 \leq 0.3) \wedge (p_2 \leq 0.4) \wedge (q_1 \leq 0.4),$
   $\qquad D_6: (p_1 \geq 0.6) \wedge (p_2 \geq 0.6) \wedge (p_3 \leq 0.4) \wedge (q_1 \geq 0.6) \wedge (q_2 \leq 0.7)\}.$
2. $\Gamma(Kbe, M)$.
3. $B = -m(U) = -\omega(p_1) = \{D_1, D_2, D_3, D_4, D_5\}.$
4. $A = \{q_1 \geq x_1\}.$
5. $\mu(A) = \mu(\{q_1 \geq x_1\}) = \mu(\{q_1 \geq x_1\}) = \{q_1 > 0.4\}$ (see ref. (6.1)).
6. $\{q_1 > 0.4\}.$

Example 6. Suppose the symptom p_3 is present, but the symptom p_1 is absent, i.e. we have the observation $O = \{\sim p_1, p_3\}$. Then, we have:

0. $Kbe = $ ref. 0 (Example 5), $O = \{\sim p_1, p_3\}.$
1. $M = $ ref. 1 (Example 5)
2. $\Gamma(Kbe, M)$.
3. $B = -\omega(O) = -\omega(\{\sim p_1, p_3\}) = -[\omega(\sim p_1) \cup \omega(p_3)] =$
   $-[\{D_1, D_4, D_5\} \cup \{D_3, D_4\}] = \{D_2, D_6\}$
4. $A = \{q_1 \geq x_1, q_2 \geq x_2\}.$
5. $\mu(A) = \mu(\{q_1 \geq x_1, q_2 \geq x_2\}) = \mu(\{q_1 \geq x_1\}) \cup \mu(\{q_2 \geq x_2\}) = \{q_1 > 0.4, q_2 > 0.7\}.$
6. $\{q_1 > 0.4, q_2 > 0.7\}.$

7 Conclusion

We introduced the Logic of Estimates **LE** which is a metalogic for classical fuzzy propositional logic. Its sentences have the forms $\varphi \geq r, \varphi > r, \varphi \leq r, \varphi < r, \varphi \leq \psi$ or $\varphi < \psi$ and Boolean compositions of such expressions. Here φ and ψ are propositional formulas, and r is a real number from the unit interval [0, 1]. We offered inference rules in the style of analytical tableaux. The system of these rules is valid and complete. We show how the system can be applied to abductive reasoning in the logic **LE**. Further research will be directed to studies of metalogics for more expressive fuzzy logics.

Acknowledgment. This work was supported by Russian Foundation for Basic Research (projects 17-07-01332 and 18-29-03088).

References

1. Agostino, M., Gabbay, D., Hahnle, R., Possega, J.: Handbook of Tableaux Methods. Springer, Dordrecht (2001)
2. Aliseda, A.: Abductive reasoning. Springer, Dordrecht (2006). https://doi.org/10.1007/1-4020-3907-7
3. Elsenbroich, C., Kutz, O., Sattler U.: A case for abductive reasoning over ontologies. In: Proceedings of the Third International Workshop OWL: Experiences and Directions. CEUR-WS.org (2011). http://ceur-ws.org/Vol-216/submission_25.pdf
4. Eshghi, K.: Abductive planning with event calculus. In: Proceedings of the Fifth International Conference on Logic Programming, pp. 562–579 (1988)
5. Fitting, M.: First-Order Logic and Automated Theorem Proving. Springer, New York (1996). https://doi.org/10.1007/978-1-4612-2360-3
6. Kovács, G., Spens, K.M.: Abductive reasoning in logistics research. Int. J. Phys. Distrib. Logist. Manag. **35**(2), 132–144 (2005)
7. Lopes, J.S., Alvarez-Napagao, S., Reis, S., Vazquez-Salceda, J.: Reasoning about abductive inferences in BDI agents. Techical report LSI-09-12-R, Univ. Politechnica de Catalunia, pp. 3–8 (2009)
8. Peraldi, S.E., Kaya, A., Möller, R.: Formalizing multimedia interpretation based on abduction over description logic ABoxes. In: Description Logics, vol. 477. CEUR Workshop Proceedings, pp. 281–290 (2009)
9. Shanahan, M.P.: An abductive event calculus planner. J. Log. Program. **44**(1–3), 207–240 (2000)
10. Vimla, L., Patel, J.F.: Arocha, J.Z: Thinking and reasoning in medicine. In: Holyoak, K.J., Robert, G., Morrison, R.G. (eds.) The Cambridge Handbook of Thinking and Reasoning. Cambridge University Press, Cambridge (2005)
11. Wiles, J.: Reasoning, robots, and navigation: dual roles for deductive and abductive reasoning. Behav. Brain Sci. **34**(2), 92–93 (2011)

Complex Graphs in the Modeling of Multi-agent Systems: From Goal-Resource Networks to Fuzzy Metagraphs

Valery B. Tarassov$^{(\boxtimes)}$ and Yuriy E. Gapanyuk

Bauman Moscow State Technical University, Moscow, Russia
vbulbov@yahoo.com, gapyu@bmstu.ru

Abstract. Two basic trends in specifying and studying complex graphs and networks to model multi-agent systems are discussed. The authors associate the complexity of graphs with such factors as heterogeneity, hierarchy, granularity, hybrid structure, emergence, capacity to cope with uncertainty or fuzziness. In this context some basic representations of fuzzy graphs and metagraphs are considered, models of nested and interval-valued fuzzy metagraphs are introduced. An example of heterogeneous network called goal-resource network is given on the basis of detailed agent architecture and their types classification. Some goal-resource networks with colored vertices to show the interactions between agents of different types are proposed. The metagraph interpretation of such a network is suggested too.

Keywords: Artificial Intelligence · Agent · Multi-agent system · Complex graphs · Heterogeneous networks · Metagraph · Metavertice · Nested vertices · Hypergraph · Hyperedge · Fuzzy graph · Interval-valued fuzzy graph · Bipolar fuzzy graph · Hypernetwork · Goal-resource network · Colored GRN vertices

1 Introduction

The objective of our investigation consists in analyzing existing graph models and synthesizing non-traditional heterogeneous and complex graph models to reveal the modes of interactions between agents in multiagent systems. To attain this objective, three basic problems ought to be solved: 1) investigation of basic modern trends in the field of graph theory and its applications, in particular, matching the properties of planar straight line graphs with the needs of applied areas; 2) study of the problem domain, including the consideration of intelligent agent architecture, specification of agent types and analysis of necessary conditions and strategies of their interactions; 3) development of appropriate network models, their validation and practical use.

The paper is organized as follows. In Sect. 2 the concept of network as a weighted graph is given, flow models of networks are presented – from classical transportation

The work is supported by Russian Foundation for Basic Research, projects № 20-07-00770, 19-07-01208.

S. O. Kuznetsov et al. (Eds.): RCAI 2020, LNAI 12412, pp. 177–198, 2020.
https://doi.org/10.1007/978-3-030-59535-7_13

network to resource network. The main attention is paid to discussing the concepts of «complex graph» and «complex network» and analyzing two basic approaches to graph complexity interpretation. In addition to usual concept of complex graphs related to enormous number of vertices and/or edges a system of structure complexity factors is introduced that includes hierarchy, heterogeneity, hybridity, granularity, uncertainty/fuzziness modeling, emergence, and so on. A short review of publications on complex graphs and networks is made.

In Sect. 3 the methodology of «apriori universal planar graphicism» (this term is coined by analogy with logicism) is criticized. The use of this methodology means: a) primarily taking a graph type with predefined geometry and properties; b) then considering problem to be solved. An alternative approach is proposed that supposes: 1) a detailed ontological analysis with taking into account main complexity factors to justify some basic requirements to graph definition, geometry and structure; 2) selection or generation of adequate graph model with taking singular or granular graph primitives – vertices and edges.

To illustrate this approach, we take the area of communications between agents and formation of multi-agent systems. The Subsect. 3.1 is devoted to specifying an «ontological skeleton» of agent, selection of the types of agents and modes of theirs interactions. On the basis of these results, in Subsect. 3.2 we perform an agent-based synthesis of an heterogeneous Goal-Resource Network with colored vertices to represent the types of interacting agents. Various situations of interactions between agents are visualized is Subsect. 4.1.

An example of heterogeneous goal-resource network based on detailed agent architecture and specification of agents types is considered in Sect. 3 in order to model various strategies of interactions between agents. Different specifications of fuzzy graphs and metagraphs are overviewed, developed and suggested in Sect. 4. Finally, in Sect. 5 a new metagraph-based solution for designing agents communication in MAS is proposed.

2   Motivation, Scope and Related Works

Our motivation consists in developing a granular approach to constructing complex graph and networks on the basis of nested vertices and hyperedges concepts, as well as in creating hybrid models of complex graphs and networks by integrating metagraphs and fuzzy graphs representations. We also introduce an instance of heterogeneous network called goal-resource network to specify the interactions of intelligent agents in multi-agent systems.

To explain the scope of our investigation, we draw an analogy between two important applied mathematical areas of Artificial Intelligence – modern Mathematical Logic and Graph Theory. For a long time mathematical logic was driven by the ideas of logicism. According to the logicism paradigm, formal logic has to deal with logical calculi. In fact, logicism imposed hard restrictions on reasoning approaches: only these reasoning methods were accepted that were representable in the form of logical calculi. Using a philosophical language, we can state that calculi are primary and reasoning techniques are secondary. Nowadays a need of applying logic in modern Artificial Intelligence, specifically, for the modeling of both common-sense knowledge and practical reasoning, brings about the logical pluralism and synthesis of various reasoning types. The pragmatic issues have transformed the logicism doctrine: the first we investigate descriptive models of synthetic reasoning, depending on ontological considerations, and the second we select or create the appropriate formal techniques. It means the synergy of both psychologism and logicism paradigms in the context of developing contemporary applied logics for artificial agents.

The same processes occur today in the field of graph theory and network applications. Here the canonical theory, a sort of «pure graphicism» , includes graph enumeration, graph invariants, isomorphisms, connectivity, cyclomatics, and so on. The graph visualization is usually fixed: it consists in representing vertices (nodes) as points on the plane and considering edges as line segments. A basic approach of classical graphicism is the following: first of all take a planar graph and give its matrix representation, study graph properties and develop basic algorithms on graphs, then reduce a faced practical problem to planar formulation. It means the ubiquitous use of planar graphs in spite of the problem domain. In other words, the structure of graphs as visulization and modeling tools is seen as independent with respect to problem domain ontology.

Nevertheless, in many applications the available information is too complex to be adequately modeled by classical graphs. In particular, the need in the modeling complex networks in AI, for example, related to multi-agent systems and artificial societies, requires non-standard graph models. For this reason some new graph formalisms have been introduced, such as *higraphs*, *compound digraphs*, *metagraphs*, *clustered graphs*, *hierarchical graphs* and so on (see [6]). Development of spatial graphs with non-Euclidean geometries, for example, spherical graphs or elliptic graphs, multiple representations of graph primitives seem to be promising areas of future graph theory. Such a pluralism of basic graph structures corresponds to a variety of real-world complex networks.

In our paper we try to outline some keystones of «graphical pluralism» by focusing on intrinsically granular concepts in graph, such as metavertice, hyperedge, non-standard generating set, and so on.

2.1 From Weighted Graphs to Resource Networks

In classical graph theory the word «network» means a graph or directed graph equipped with a function that makes in correspondence to each edge (arc) e a non-negative real number w [7]: $NET = \langle V, E, W \rangle$, where V is a set of vertices, E is the set of edges, and $W: E \to R^+$ is the set of weights (non-negative real numbers). In particular, weights may be restricted to rational numbers or integers.

A typical network example is a flow network (also known as a transportation network) – a directed graph without loops, where each arc has a capacity (or conductivity) w and each arc receives a flow. Here the amount of flow on an arc cannot exceed the capacity of this arc. Such a network can be used to model road traffic, fluids in pipes, currents in an electrical circuit, or anything similar in which something travels through a network of nodes. A classical network method is the Ford-Fulkerson algorithm which computes the maximum flow in a network [13].

Among non-classical networks for Artificial Intelligence (AI) Pospelov's deeds (action) frames are worth mentioning in the context of linking actions and communications between agents (with social evaluation of acts – see [30]). A flow graph [28] and an extended flow graph [23] can be employed for representing, analyzing and discovering knowledge in databases. They may be seen as a good graph framework for data mining and knowledge discovery based on information flow distribution. Flow graphs are used as a mathematical tool to analyze information flow in decision algorithms, in contrast to material flow optimization considered in classical flow network analysis. An overview of graph theoretic methods for multi-agent systems can be found in [25].

In 2009 O.P.Kuznetsov proposed a new network model called a Resource Network (RN) [21, 42]. The resource network is a flow model represented by oriented weighted graph, in which every two vertices are either not adjacent or connected by a pair of oppositely directed arcs. To differ from conventional transportation networks and Ford-Fulkerson model, where the resources flowing from source to sink vertices are located in the arcs, in RN all resources are assigned to the vertices, and the weights of arcs indicate their capacities. The vertices exchange resources, following the definite rules. At the time t the state of RN is specified by a vector of resource values in the vertices.

Multi-agent systems (MAS), in particular, the exchange of resources in MAS, are a natural application of RN. Here, the basic problem consists in analyzing the stabilization of exchange processes.

The resource network is homogeneous if all its capacities are equal. In [21] only homogeneous RN were considered. Generally, when the MAS includes agents of different types, the appropriate resource network is not homogeneous, because both resource amount and capacity values depend on the agent type.

Later on a classification of RN by network topology and arc capacity was constructed. The dynamics and asymptotics of states and flows for various classes of RN (both ergodic and non-ergodic, symmetric and asymmetric) were investigated. The properties of absorbing resource networks were studied, the comparison between RN and other dynamic network model was made [42].

2.2 Complex Graphs: Two Trends

Nowadays, the development of applied intelligent systems, from visualization of classical knowledge models up to agent-based communications in multi-agent systems, requires the construction and use of complex graphs and networks. Here the terms «complex graphs» and «complex networks» are often viewed as synonyms. Nevertheless, the phrase «complex network» is mainly employed in a practical sense to express a sophisticated structure of real-world system, whereas «complex graph» is ordinarily considered as a mathematical model of such a system.

There exist two basic trends in studying complex networks. The first one is related to considering planar graphs of enormous sizes (hundreds of thousands and millions of vertices having rich connections). The edges of such graphs can be either directed or undirected. Sometimes, multigraphs are taken, where any two vertices can be joined by several edges. Here some popular graph numbers are used to represent complexity factors, for instance, graph vertex degree, mean degree or graph diameter. Such graph techniques as specification of strongly connected subgraphs and maximal cliques are frequently used. The random graph theory for the study of complex networks is of special concern.

Among leading Russian researchers, sharing this vision and developing sophisticated graph-theoretic approaches to complex network modeling, first of all O.P.Kuznetsov [22] and I.A.Yevin [38] are worth mentioning.

The second, more recent trend consists in building new network concepts, e.g. synergetic networks with emergence, and forming non-standard graph structures to model complex graphs. In this paper we will associate the complexity of graph with such factors as its heterogeneity, hierarchy, granularity, hybrid structure, emergence, uncertainty or fuzziness of information. Such graphs are based on a sophisticated representation of vertices, edges and/or their location (hierarchy of vertices with metavertices, multiarity of edges and appearance of hyperedges, non-line, e.g. spherical graphs, nested graphs, etc.). It means the conceptual shift to the consideration and analysis of such basic models as heterogeneous graphs, hypergraphs, metagraphs, fuzzy graphs, hypernetworks, and formation of hybrid models like fuzzy metagraphs and fuzzy hypernetworks.

Let us briefly present these variants of complex graphs. Heterogeneous graphs possess vertices and/or edges of different types. A hypergraph [7] is a generalization of graph in which each edge can join any number of vertices. Such an edge, having many endpoints, is called hyperedge. A metagraph [6] is a hierarchical graph structure, where every node is a set having one or more elements. In a metagraph there is a set-to-set mapping instead of vertice-to-vertice as in a classical graph structure.

Let us compare hypergraphs and metagraphs. Though the hypergraph has hyper edges, the modeling of complex hierarchical dependences is not supported, because it is not a real network with an emergence. To differ from hypergraph, metagraph structure allows us to model complex hierarchical dependences in a natural way, being a sort of network with an emergence.

The hyperedges in hypergraph join only vertices, whereas the metanode in metagraph can include both vertices and metavertices and edges. The metanode enables the specification of metagraph fragment, making annotation of its additional properties. In essence, such fragments are similar to Koestler's holons (holonic structures are simultaneously viewed as a whole and a part of the whole – see [35]) and, hence, metagraphs generate holarchies – hierarchies of organic type.

Two hypernetwork models were proposed independently by V.K.Popkov [29] and J.Johnson [16]. In the latter model a hypernetwork intended to deal with complex systems generalizes the concept of a relation between two objects to relations between many objects. Here the notion of relational simplex extends the concept of network edge. Such relational simplices have multi-dimensional connectivity associated with hypergraphs and Galois lattice of maximally connected sets of elements.

Let us present in detail Popkov's *Abstract Hypernetwork*, possibly the first model of the network with an emergence. It is given by a sixtuple

$$AHN = (V, B, E, \alpha, \beta, \gamma), \tag{1}$$

where V is the set of vertices in a primary graph, B is the set of branches in a primary graph, E is the set of edges in a secondary graph, $\alpha: B \to 2^V$ is the mapping that puts in correspondence each element $b \in B$ to the subset $a(b) \subseteq V$; $\beta : E \to 2^B$ is the mapping

that puts in correspondence each element $e \in E$ to the subset $\beta(e) \subseteq B$ of its branches;
$\forall e \in E, \gamma : e \rightarrow 2^{\alpha(\beta(e))}$

The hypernetwork includes hypergraphs and mappings. Here the mapping α specifies the hypergraph $PN = (B, E, \alpha)$ called a primary network of the AHN and the mapping γ forms the hypergraph $SN = (V, E, \gamma)$ called a secondary network of the AHN. Such a hypernetwork provides a more adequate model of hierarchical complex networks than conventional graphs. It is depicted in Fig. 1.

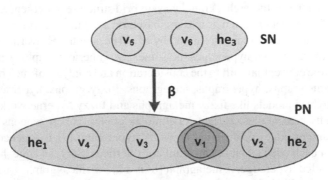

Fig. 1. Representation of Popkov's basic hypernetwork. Here $v_1, .., v_6$ stand for vertices, he_1, he_2, he_3 are hyperedges, PN stands for primary network and SN is a secondary network.

Below in Sect. 3 we will highlight the basic principle of graph theory as an «empirical science» for AI: firstly problem domain ontological specification and secondarily network structure generation, by taking an example of designing agents interactions to form multi-agent systems with homogeneous or heterogeneous agents. The developed model of Goal-Resource Network in an extension of Kuznetsov's Homogeneous Resource Network [21].

3   A Case of Heterogeneous Graphs: Goal-Resource Networks

Very important sub-classes of complex graphs are heterogeneous graphs, in particular, heterogeneous graph-based neural networks. To differ from homogeneous graphs with uniform vertices and edges, heterogeneous graphs, or shortly *heterographs*, contain various types of nodes and edges. Here some kinds $k \in K$ of vertices are connected with different types of edges. It brings about the consideration of different types of attributes selected to capture the characteristics of these kinds of vertices and types of edges. It is worth noticing that generally heterographs are much more adapted to solve specific domain problems, than homogeneous graphs.

We shall consider heterogeneous graphs be taking the example of Goal-Resource Networks (GRN). In order to synthesize adequate network structures for communicating agents we will give a classification of agent types, present some fundamentals of activity theory for autonomous agents and provide the reasons of their interaction.

3.1 Ontological Basis of Agent. Types of Agents and Conditions of Their Efficient Interactions

Let us specify an ontological basis of agent as the structure «Goal-Resources-Perception-Action» (Fig. 2). We begin with clarifying interrelations between these concepts. The reason for any agent's activity is the need viewed as a distance between desired and current agent's state. The relevant interpretation of this need is referred to as motivation; the role of motivation in Activity Theory (see [35]) is the same as the role of force in mechanics. The motive formation leads to a goal (target) appearance as a model of agent's wanted future.

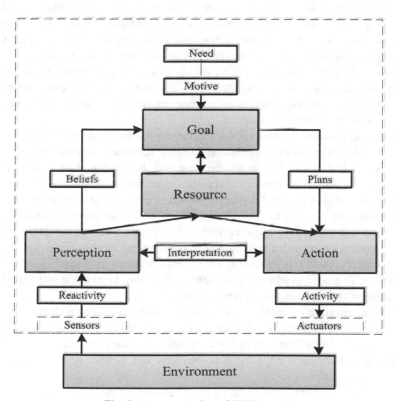

Fig. 2. Representation of GRPA model

Let us stress that goal-driven activity and autonomy are basic agent's features. Agent's autonomy is enabled by available resources, as well as by their periodic acquisition from the environment (including other agents). Often the pair «autonomy – intelligence» is viewed as agent's keynote characteristic [32, 37]. Here *intelligence* is mainly related to the synthesis of multi-sensor data, knowledge elicitation and reasoning, whereas *autonomy* is associated with decision-making, planning and acting, agent's resource allocation and re-allocation.

Various resources are required to achieve a goal. The term «resources» is viewed here in a wide sense as any means useful for achieving goals of agent or multi-agent

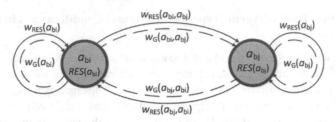

Fig. 3. Simple goal-resource network for the communication of two benevolent agents

system. For instance, the resources of manufacturing systems are workers, machines, raw materials, robots. We specify two main resource attributes: 1) resource amount that is its spatial measure, and 2) resource action that is its temporal measure. It is evident that the same amount of resources can bring about different resource actions.

The general agent architecture GRPA (Goal-Resources-Perception-Action) [11] is presented in Fig. 2. Here Goals and Resources are seen as keynote characteristics of agent's internal environment, whereas agent's perception and actions are basic processes of interaction with external environment.

Establishing communications between agents is the first step in building MAS; it results in forming bilateral and multilateral dynamic relations. According to synergetic methodology [17, 35], interactions are primary and the generated structures are secondary, i.e. communications are the sources of organizations. Multi-agent systems are polystructural by their nature and ensure the fusion of extensive and intensive structures. From the viewpoint of graph theory, the amplification of extensive structures supposes generation of new vertices to compare with initial graph, whereas the deployment of intensive structures is provided with adding multiple edges.

The necessary conditions for starting interactions between agents are: 1) *goal* sharing or imposition; 2) a need in additional *resources*, including knowledge and experience; 3) *commitments* and *agreements* between agents.

The communication of agents in MAS is ordinarily associated with resource allocation, exchange and shared use. Generally resources have two basic parameters: a) location; b) accessibility. The idea of resource agentification [12] consists in providing each resource with the knowledge about its own structure, location and state to facilitate resource employment.

The possibility and structure of interactions between agents depends on their types. Let us introduce basic agent's types by taking two criteria: a) capacity to generate individual goals and allocate the appropriate resources; b) capacity to form shared goals and organize the exchange of resources to achieve such collective goals. Then three basic agent types are straightforwardly specified (Table 1): 1) benevolent agent a_b; 2) self-interested or egoist agent a_e; 3) altruistic agent a_a.

So the total set of agents A is partitioned into three subsets of benevolent, egoist and altruistic agents: $A = A_b \cup A_e \cup A_a$, where, $A_b \cap A_e = \varnothing, A_b \cap A_a = \varnothing, A_e \cap A_a = \varnothing$.

Let us give a short goal-resource description of each agent type. The benevolent agent a_b has both individual goal and the capacity to form/take collective goal. He takes an active part in exchanging resources and saves some resources for proper needs. The egoist agent a_e strives to achieve only his goals and ignores the goals of other agents.

Table 1. Specification and visualization of agent type

Agent type	Individual goal	Collective goal	Colored agent denotation
Benevolent agenta_b	+	+	Green
Egoist agent a_e	+	–	Red
Altruistic agenta_a	–	+	Deep blue

He imposes his goal and initiates resource sharing only for his own benefit; in fact the resource exchange is substituted here by the flow of resources to the a_e. At last, the altruistic agent a_a takes anyone else's goal as his own goal and is ready to the resource exchange even if he loses from this.

The own agent's goal is a decisive factor for his self-preservation by keeping a needed part of resources, whereas the goal sharing is a necessary condition to obtain some coalition.

Such a specification of agent types opens the opportunity to build various multi-agent organizations or exclude some of them. For instance, multi-agent systems that include only egoist agents, as well as MAS formed of altruistic agents, cannot exist. In the first case we observe the inability of A_e to goal sharing and mutually beneficial exchange of resources. In the second case only altruistic agents cannot form individual goals (and spend the appropriate resources), as well as generate collective goals.

The availability of resources can influence the agent type. For example, a significant inflow of resources can turn the benevolent agent a_b into the egoist agent a_e. Inversely, the lack of resources can transform the benevolent agent a_b into the altruistic agenta_a. The necessary conditions for MAS formation can be formulated as follows: (1) $res(a_a(t)) \geq res_{min}$ (a living minimum for the altruistic agent); (2) $res(a_e(t)) < res_{max}$ (a social ability preservation by the egoist agent).

The above mentioned considerations show the need in introducing three kinds of vertices and two types of edges into the model presented below.

3.2 Specification of Goal-Resource Network as an Heterogeneous Weighted Graph

The analysis made in Subsect. 2.1 allows us to propose the following agent-grounded definition and visualization of Goal-Resource Network as an heterogeneous directed graph, where vertices (agents) have such attributes as type (marked by symbol or color) and amount of resources, and edges also have types (goal links and resource links) and capacity.

Definition 1. *A Goal-Resource Network(GRN)* for MAS is an heterogeneous *weighted* (twice) directed graph

$$GRN = \langle A, K, G, RES, R, W, t \rangle, \tag{2}$$

where a collection of vertices A is viewed as a set of agents a having such attributes as the type $k \in K$, $|K| = 3$, $K = \{$benevolent, egoist, altruistic$\}$and the resources *res*

$\in RES$; G is the set of (qualitative) goals $G = \{g(a_e)\}$ circulated in the network (this set can be reduced to a singleton, for instance $G = \{g(a_e)\}$; it includes both personal goals of agents $g(a_e)$, $g(a_b)$ and formed collective goals $G(A)$; R is a set of edges (arcs) that is partitioned into two non-overlapping subsets: a subset of goal arcs R_G and a subset of resource arcs R_{RES}: $R = R_G \cup R_{RES}$, $R_G \cap R_{RES} = \varnothing$. Each arc $r \in R$ has some conductivity value $w \in W$ and W is also partitioned into a subset of resource conductivities W_{RES} and a subset of goal conductivities W_G. Finally a discrete time set is given, $t = 0, 1, 2, \ldots, n$. Generally, the values of input and output conductivities can be different.

Let n be the total number of agents in A. In any discrete time t the state of MAS is given by the goal state vector $G_A(t) = (g(a_1), \ldots, g(a_m))$ and resource state vector $RES_A(t) = (res(a_1), \ldots, res(a_n))$, where m is the number of goal-generating agents, $m < n$. A state of MAS is called stable, if $G_A(t) = \text{const}$ and $RES_A(t) = \text{const}$. A state of MAS is called asymptotically reachable for an infinitesimal ξ, $\xi > 0$, if $\forall i = 1, \ldots, n$ the following inequality takes place $|res(a_i(t+1)) - res(a_i(t))| < \xi$.

Definition 2. AGRN is called colored, if it includes colored vertices corresponding to the types of agents. Below we will denote benevolent agents by green color, self-interested (egoist) agents–by red color, and altruistic agents–by deep blue color.

Let us consider main communication situations and behavior strategies for homogeneous (benevolent) and heterogeneous agents interactions. We begin with pairwise communication (simple goal-resource networks).

I. Communication of two benevolent agents a_b. Let us denote two benevolent agents by a_{bi} and a_{bj} (Fig. 4). Here an equitable information exchange leads to a formation of shared goal and resource exchange.

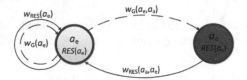 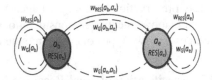

Fig. 4. Simple goal-resource network for the communication between egoist agent and altruistic agent

Fig. 5. Simple goal-resource network for the communication between egoist agent and benevolent agent

A multi-agent system that includes n benevolent agents seems to be the most effective architecture to implement «democratic» strategies of Decentralized AI, when a complete graph structure appears.

II. Communication of egoist agent a_e and altruistic agent a_a. Here an egoist agent a_e imposes his goal to an altruistic agent a_a and employs the a_a resources to achieve it (see Fig. 4). In fact, it is a transfer of resources from a_a to a_e that can lead to the death of the altruistic agent, if $res(a_a(t)) < res_{min}$. A basic star structure (1 egoist and n altruistic agents) degenerates with a time and becomes an isolated vertex – the resource monopoly.

III. Communication of egoist agent a_e and benevolent agent a_b. Such a communication can happen, only when the agent a_b accepts the goal of a_e (Fig. 5). In fact, an illusion of the resource exchange appears. The egoist agent a_e needs some resources for achieving his goal, but, in response, he tries not to give anything away. Usually, the benevolent agent a_b avoids such a communication and participates in it only in case of emergency. Here any communication between a_b and a_e stops, if $res(a_b(t))$ is close to res_{min} (the instinct of self-preservation in a_b).

The communication schemes B and C lead to the formation of «autocratic» strategies of distributed intelligence.

IV. Communication of benevolent agent a_e and altruistic agent a_a. Here effective resource exchanges take place, because a_a shares the goal of a_b (see Fig. 6) and the latter does not allow the situation of resource depletion in the former. In case of one benevolent agent a_b and n altruistic agents a_a a natural wheel or star structure of GRN is formed.

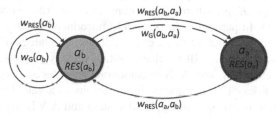

Fig. 6. Simple goal-resource network for the communication between benevolent agent and altruistic agent

In all the considered examples of GRN, some constant types of agents are analyzed that do not change in the process of communication. Besides, interesting situations of modifying agent type by changing the amount of available resources or goal settings are of special concern, for instance, a transmutation of benevolent agent a_b to egoist agent a_e or an acquisition of purposefulness by an altruistic agent a_a.

Generally the agent's type is not crisp, and we have to give a triple of membership functions $\mu_{ab}, \mu_{ae}, \mu_{aa}$ on the set $K = \{a_b, a_e, a_a\}$ (the degrees of benevolence, egoism and altruism respectively).

It is well-known from graph theory that the degree of the vertex is determined by the number of arcs incident to this vertex. For goal-resource networks we should take into consideration both the number of arcs and their total conductivity. Thus, the potential influence of agent in a multi-agent system is given by a quadruple

$$I(a_i(t)) = \langle res(a_i(t)), w_S(a_i(t)), m_I(a_i(t)), t \rangle,$$

where $res(a_i(t)$ stands for the amount of resources in the agent a_i at the time t, $w_S(a_i(t))$ is the sum number of conductivities related to a_i at the time t and $m_I(t)$ is the number of agents interacting with a_i at the time t. The main influence criterion is agent-to-resource relation. The more are the agent resources, the more he can influence other agents and the more is the amount of potentially reachable resources for him.

Let us note that the GRN defined by (1) is not able to tackle the issues of imprecision, uncertainty and fuzziness. To enable a well-founded specification of fuzzy GRN we discuss various definitions of fuzzy graphs. Furthermore, it provides a conventional vertice-to-vertice mapping, whereas in many cases we need polymorphic mappings, such as vertice-to-set mapping or set-to-set mapping. Thus, in the next section some definitions of metagraphs are given, followed by original and new specifications of fuzzy metagraphs.

4   Fuzzy Metagraph Models

4.1   Various Fuzzy Sets, Fuzzy Relations and Fuzzy Graphs

The basic definition of binary *fuzzy relation FR* was given by L.Zadeh [39] in the form $FR = \{(x, y) | \mu_R(x, y)\}$, $\forall(x, y) \in X \times X$, $\mu_R \in [0, 1]$ or, simply, by a membership function $\mu_R : X \times X \to [0, 1]$. In 1975 A.Rosenfeld [31] considered the concept of *fuzzy graph*, whose basic idea was proposed and depicted in 1973 by A.Kaufmann [19] as a triple $FG = \langle V, E, \rho \rangle$, where V is a non empty set of vertices, E is a set of edges, $\rho : E \to [0, 1]$. In particular, A. Rosenfeld introduced fuzzy relations on fuzzy sets and developed the structure of fuzzy graphs, obtaining analogs of several ordinary graph-theoretic concepts. Then P. Bhattacharya obtained fuzzy graphs results concerning their center and eccentricity, and A. Somasundaram introduced domination in fuzzy graphs. Later on L.Koczy [20] considered fuzzy graphs as a valuable tool to evaluate and optimize different networks. Finally, L.S.Berstein and A.V.Bozhenuk [8] specified fuzzy chromatic set, fuzzy internal stability and other invariants of fuzzy graphs, as well as developed fuzzy temporal graphs to model dynamic complex systems.

The notion of totally fuzzy set was suggested by D.Ponasse as a triple $\langle X, \mu, \sigma \rangle$, where $\mu : X \to [0, 1]$ is the membership function and $\alpha : X \times X \to [0, 1]$ is the indistinguishability function. Below we take the following basic formula.

Definition 3 [26]. A *fuzzy graph FG* is given by a triple

$$FG = \langle V, \mu, \rho \rangle, \tag{3}$$

where V is a non empty set of vertices equipped with a pair of functions: $\mu : V \to [0, 1]$ and $\rho : V \times V \to [0, 1]$ such that $\rho(v_i, v_j) \leq \mu(\mu_i) \wedge \mu(\mu_j)$, $\forall(v_i v_j) \in V \times V$.

Let us note that Zadeh's fuzzy set can be represented through decomposition theorem [27] in the following way: $\mu_A = \bigcup_{\alpha \in [0,1]} (\alpha \mu_{A\alpha})$, where $\mu_{A\alpha}(x) = 1$, if $\mu_A(x) \geq \alpha$, and 0 otherwise.

This decomposition underlies the second way of representing fuzziness, when it is specified by a *family* of *nested* crisp *sets*. So for n membership grades we give the so-called *n*-fuzzy (flou) set as follows: $FS = \langle M_1, \ldots, M_n \rangle$, where $M_i, \subseteq X$, $i = 1, .., n$, and $M_1 \subseteq \ldots \subseteq M_n$ (see [5]). More generally, we obtain the mapping $M : [0, 1] \to 2^X$.

The class of all these mappings $\Phi([0, 1]) = \{M | M : [0, 1] \to 2^X\}$, such that: a) $M(0) = X$; b) $\forall \alpha, \beta \in [0, 1]$, $\alpha \leq \beta \Rightarrow M(\alpha) \supseteq M(\beta)$, is isomorphic with respect to the set of all fuzzy subsets $[0, 1]^X = \{\mu | \mu : \to [0, 1]\}$. From this theorem we obtain the equivalent representation of fuzzy graph by a hierarchy of vertices in a graph. Similarly we can construct the mapping $N: [0, 1] \rightarrow 2^{X \times X}$ and specify the appropriate class of mappings for fuzzy relations.

Some other ways of specifying fuzzy graphs are also associated with various definitions of fuzzy sets and fuzzy relations. Here *fuzzy sets of type 2*, i.e. fuzzy sets with fuzzy membership values [39] are of primary concern. It means that we take a granular (in the sense of L.Zadeh [40]) membership ontology.

An interval in partially ordered set is a subset of elements x that meet the inequality $\{x | l \le x \le r\}$, where l and r stand for the left (lower) and right (upper) bounds of the interval. An important special case of granular membership functions is *an Interval-Valued Fuzzy Set (IVFS)* $A = \{(x, [\mu_A^l(x), \mu_A^r(x)])\}$, where μ_A^l and μ_A^r stand for the left and right bounds of the interval membership value $\mu_A(x)$ [19, 34]. It is defined by a membership function $\mu_A: X \rightarrow 2^{[0,1]}$. An interval-valued fuzzy relation is given by $\mu_R: X \times X \rightarrow 2^{[0,1]}$.

A useful counterpart of interval-valued fuzzy set is Hirota's *probabilistic set* with randomized membership function, where each membership value is characterized by an expected value and variance due to random noise.

The concept of *Interval-Valued Fuzzy Graph (IVFG)* was proposed in [2]. Below we give the following definition.

Definition 4. An interval-valued fuzzy graph is given by a triple

$$IVFG = \langle V, \mu_I, \rho_I \rangle, \tag{4}$$

where $\mu_I: V \rightarrow 2^{[0,1]}$, $\rho_I: V \times V \rightarrow 2^{[0,1]}$. Here $\mu_I = [\mu^l, \mu_A^r]$, $\rho_I = [\rho^l, \rho^r]$.

A membership ontology in Zadeh's fuzzy set is based on the assumption that membership $\mu_A(x)$ and non-membership $m_{A'}(x)$ values are complementary on a hard opposition scale: $\mu_A(x) + \mu_{A'}(x) = 1$, for any $x \in X$. For instance, if the membership value is 0.7, then the non-membership value is automatically taken as 0.3.

Another opportunity of specifying non-standard fuzzy graphs consists in weakening ties between membership and non-membership with considering the latter rather independently. For instance, an *Intuitionistic Fuzzy Set* [4] is defined by an ordered triple $A = \{(x, \mu_A(x), v_A(x)\}, \forall x \in X$, where $\mu_A(x)$ specifies the degree of membership, and $v_A(x)$ – the degree of non-membership of the element x to the set A that is the subset of X. Here $\mu_A: X \rightarrow [0, 1], v_A: X \rightarrow [0, 1]$, and for every element $x \in X 0 \le \mu_A(x) + v_A(x) \le 1$. Besides, $\pi_A(x) = 1 - \mu_A(x) - v_A(x)$ is called the hesitation margin of x in A.

The concept of *Intuitionistic Fuzzy Graph (IFG)* was introduced in [33] and discussed in detail in [18].

Definition 5. An intuitionistic fuzzy graph is given by a quintuple

$$IFG = \langle V, \mu, v, \rho, \psi \rangle, \tag{5}$$

where V is a non empty set of vertices, $\mu: V \rightarrow [0, 1], v: V \rightarrow [0, 1], \rho: V \times V \rightarrow [0, 1],$ $\psi: V \times V \rightarrow [0, 1]$. Here the triple (v_i, μ_i, v_i) characterizes the degree of membership and non-membership of the vertex $v_i \in V, 0 \leq \mu_i(v_i) + \nu_i(v_i) \leq 1$, whereas the triple (v_i, ρ_i, ψ_i) denotes the degree of membership and non-membership of edge relations $e_{ij} = (v_i, v_j)$ on V. Atanassov used five Cartesian products to define various IFG.

A rather close to *IFG* approach is based on bipolarity phenomena and *Bipolar Fuzzy Sets (BPFS)*. Various bipolar scales can be generated by using at least two criteria: 1) the strength of opposition between two poles; 2) the status or interpretation of neutral value. Thus, different kinds of fuzzy bipolarity may be introduced. The concept of BPFS was initiated by W.Zhang in 1994 [41] to deal with opposite properties, such as «strong-weak», «large-small», «tall –short», and so on. It supposes the interpretation of neutrality as irrelevance and rather loose relationships between the poles.

Bipolar fuzzy sets extend conventional fuzzy sets and take their values in the interval $[-1, +1]$. Here the membership degree 0 means that the element x is irrelevant to a considered property. The membership value $(0, +1]$ shows that the element x satisfies with some degree the positive property, and the membership degree $[-1, 0)$ indicates that x rather meets the negative property (counter-property). The status of property (positive or negative) depends on the problem domain: for instance, «tall» is a positive property for volleyball player, but it was a negative property in selecting the first cosmonauts.

Let X be a non-empty set. A *bipolar fuzzy set A* in X is written in the following way $A = \{(x, \mu_A^P(x), \mu_A^N(x)\}, \forall x \in X$, where $\mu_A^P : X \rightarrow [0, +1], \mu_A^N : X \rightarrow [-1, 0]$. Generally, we can consider 3 cases: 1) $v_A^P(x) \neq 0$, but $\mu_A^N(x) = 0$ (in this case x has only positive satisfaction); 2) inversely, $\mu_A^P(x) = 0$, but $\mu_A^N(x) \neq 0$ (it means that x satisfies only counter-property); 3) both $\mu_A^P(x) \neq 0$ and $\mu_A^N(x) \neq 0$ (it is a common case, when the membership function for positive property overlaps the membership function for a negative property).

A mapping $\rho_{BP} : V \times V \rightarrow [-1, +1]$ is called a bipolar fuzzy relation, such that $\rho^P(x, y) \in [0, +1]$ and $\rho^N(x, y) \in [-1, 0]$.

The concept of *bipolar fuzzy graph (BPFG)* appeared in [1, 24], where regular *BPFG* and bipolar fuzzy line graphs were specified too. Below we suggest the following definition.

Definition 6. A bipolar fuzzy graph is specified by a triple

$$BPFG = \langle V, \mu_{BP}, \rho_{BP} \rangle, \tag{6}$$

where $\mu_{BP} : V \rightarrow [-1, +1]$. $\rho_{BP} : V \times V \rightarrow [-1, +1]$. Here $\mu_{BP} = (\mu^P, \mu_A^N)$, $\rho_{BP} = [\rho^P, \rho^N]$. Furthermore, $\rho^P(x, y) \leq \min (\mu^P(x), \mu^P(y))$ and $\rho^N(x, y) \geq \max(\mu^N(x), \mu^N(y))$.

In the last section of this paper we will take the concept of heterogeneous fuzzy set by A.Kaufmann [19] to define an hierarchical heterogeneous fuzzy metagraph based on three different types of vertices.

4.2 An Original Basu-Blanning Metagraph Model

The concept of Metagraph was introduced by A. Basu and R.W. Blanning in 1994 as a graphical structure, in which edges represent directed relations between elements (see the monograph [6]).

Let E denote the set of edges. An edge e in a metagraph is an ordered pair $e = \langle V_e, W_e \rangle$ consisting of an invertex $V_e \subset X$ and an outvertex $W_e \subset X$; each of them may contain any number of elements. The different elements in the invertex (outvertex) are called *coinputs (cooutputs)* of each other.

Let $X = \{x_1, \ldots, x_m\}$ be the *generating set* of a metagraph.

Definition 7 [6]. A *metagraph* is an ordered pair

$$MG = \langle X, E \rangle, \tag{7}$$

specified by its generating set X and a set of edges E defined on the generating set.

Remark 1. The metagraphs extend both directed graphs (by allowing multiple elements in vertices) and hypergraphs (by including directions in edges). Nevertheless, in Definition 7 both the concepts of hierarchy of vertices and metavertices are not explicitly formulated.

A *simple path* $h(x, y)$ from an element x to an element y is a sequence of edges $e_1, e_2, \ldots, e_n$ such that: a) $x \in$ invertex (e_1); b) $y \in$ outvertex (e_n); c) for all e_i, i = $1, \ldots, n - 1$, outvertex $(e_i) \cap$ invertex $(e_{i+1}) \neq \varnothing$.

Remark 2. Simple paths do not describe all of the connectivity properties of metagraphs. The concept of metapath is introduced to solve this problem.

Given a metagraph $MG = \langle X, E \rangle$, a metapath $M(B, C)$ from a source $B \subset X$ to a target $C \subset X$ is a set of edges $E' \subset E$. such that: (1) $e' \in E'$ is on a simple path from some element in B to some element in C; (2) $\bigcup_{e'} V_{e'} \setminus \bigcup_{e'} W_{e'} \subseteq B$; (3) $C \subset \bigcup_{e'} W_{e'}$.

Remark 3. The emergence in the model of A.Bazu and R. Blanning is achieved through the use of edges. It can be noted that this version of the metagraph model is more suitable for modeling directed processes than for representing complex data/ knowledge structures.

It is clear that a general way of extending this model consists both in taking other primitives than points (for instance, intervals) in the generating set and in specifying non-standard subsets of the generating sets, such as rough sets, fuzzy sets, interval-based fuzzy sets and so on.

4.3 A Hierarchical Metagraph Model with Metavertices and Meta-Edges

A rich conceptual framework for metagraphs was proposed in a short, but important paper [3]. Both metavertices and meta-edges were introduced; besides, a valuable idea of hierarchy for metavertices was suggested.

Definition 8. A hierarchical metagraph with metavertices and meta-edges is defined by a quadruple

$$HMG = \langle V, MV, E, ME \rangle, \tag{8}$$

where V is a set of vertices (generating set), MV is a set of metavertices, E is s set of edges, ME is a set of meta-edges defined on the union of metavertices and vertices $V \cup MV$. So a meta-edge in this model can conncct a vertex with a meta-vertex or two metavertices.

A fundamental idea of the paper [3] consists in introducing the concept of a *nested metagraph*, where a nested set of vertices is viewed. It follows from the representation theorem for fuzzy sets that a nested sequence of vertices can be seen as a flou set.

Let us take again the example of MAS generation in the process of interaction between agents (Fig. 3, 4, 5 and 6) and draw an hierarchical metagraph (Fig. 7). Here we consider three types of vertices: ordinary vertices $v_1, v_2, \ldots, v_m$ (for instance, altruistic agents a_{a1}, a_{a2}, a_{a3}, benevolent agents a_{b1}, a_{b2}), metavertices of the first type $mv_1, mv_2, mv_3, mv_4, mv_5,$ including some ordinary vertices or vertices incident to metaedges (for example, $a_{e1}, a_{e2}, A_a, A_b, A_{bb}$, a metavertice of the second type mmv containing both vertices and metavertices of the first type.

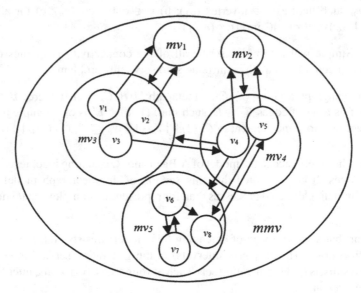

Fig. 7. Representaion of interactions between agents of various types by a nested metagraph

This metagraph with nested vertices can be viewed as a case of *n-flou* graph.

4.4 A Recursive Annotating Metagraph

The annotating metagraph model was proposed in [9] as an extension of the original Basu-Blanning model. Here the metagraph vertex is described by a set of attributes [14] such as type, degree, resources, etc. The metagraph edge is specified by the set of attributes, the source and destination vertices (or metavertices), the edge direction flag (*eo = true* – directed edge, *eo = false* – undirected edge)]. The main peculiarity of this model consists in introducing the concept of metagraph fragment-holon. Here the term «annotating» means highlighting or underlining key pieces of the model by using recursions [15].

Definition 9. The annotating metagraph is a quintuple

$$HMG = \langle V, MV, E, ME, MG_i \rangle, \tag{9}$$

where V is a set of metagraph vertices (generating set), MV is a set of metagraph metavertices, E is a set of metagraph edges, ME is a set of metagraph meta-edges, and MG_i is a metagraph fragment-holon, $MG_i = \{ev_j\}$, $ev_j \in (V \cup E \cup MV \cup ME)$.

Thus, metavertex, in addition to the attributes, includes a fragment of the metagraph. The presence of private attributes and connections for metavertex is a distinguishing feature of this metagraph. It makes the definition of metagraph holonic – metavertex may include a number of lower-level elements and, in its turn, may be included in a number of higher-level elements. The metagraph fragment MG_i may contain nested meta-edges that makes recursive the description of meta-edge.

As soon as a new concept is introduced as a metavertice, it obtains «all the rights» to have its own properties, connections and so on, because such a new concept possesses new quality and cannot be reduced to the subgraph of basic concepts. Hence this metagraph can be characterized as a «complex graph with emergence».

Let us depict an example of metagraph with both nested and intersecting metavertices. The metagraph (Fig. 8) contains three metavertices: mv_1, mv_2, and mv_3. Here the metavertex mv_1 contains vertices v_1, v_2, v_3 and connecting edges e_1, e_2, e_3. The metavertex mv_2 contains vertices v_4, v_5, and edge e_6. The edges e_4, e_5 are instances of edges connecting vertices v_2–v_4 and v_3–v_5 are contained in different metavertices mv_1 and mv_2. The edge e_7 is an instance of the edge connecting metavertices mv_1 and mv_2. The edge e_8 is an instance of the edge connecting the vertex v_2 and metavertex mv_2. The metavertex mv_3 contains the metavertex mv_2, the vertices v_2, v_3, and the edge e_2 from metavertex mv_1 and also edges e_4, e_5, e_8 showing the holonic nature of the metagraph structure.

Unlike the previously considered models, in this model a metavertex can include both vertices and edges. The vertices, edges, and metavertices are used for data description while the meta-edges are used for process description.

From Fig. 8 it is obvious that metavertices can be characterized by indices of inclusion and intersection. For instance, the index of intersection for metavertices mv_1 и mv_3 can be defined in the form of Jaccard similarity measure

$$S_J = |mv_1 \cap mv_3| / |mv_1 \cap mv_3|.$$

An example of a directed meta-edge is shown in Fig. 9. The directed meta-edge contains metavertices $mv_S, \ldots mv_i, \ldots mv_E$ and connecting them edges. The source metavertex contains a nested metagraph fragment. During the transition to the destination metavertex, the nested metagraph fragment became more complex, new vertices,

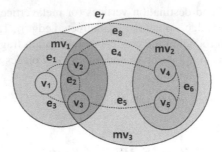

Fig. 8. An example of metagraph

edges, and metavertices are added. So a meta-edge allows binding the stages of nested metagraph fragment development to the steps of the process described by this meta-edge.

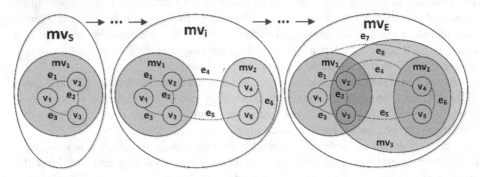

Fig. 9. An example of directed meta-edge

5 Two Definitions of Fuzzy Metagraphs

Since a generating set underlies the formal definition of metagraph, a direct way to fuzzy metagraph consists in selecting a fuzzy generating set [10].

A natural version of fuzzy extension of initial Basu-Blanning (see Definition 7) model was proposed in [36]. We give it in the following form.

Definition 10. *A fuzzy metagraph* is a quadruple

$$FMG = \langle X, E, \mu, FE \rangle, \tag{10}$$

where X is a generating set, E is a set of edges, $\mu: X \to [0, 1]$, $\rho: E \to [0, 1]$, $FE = [0, 1]^{E} = \{\rho | \rho : E \to [0, 1]\}$. Here FE is the set of fuzzy subsets-edges.

Below we proposed another definition of fuzzy metagraph that is based on the concept of *heterogeneous fuzzy set* by A.Kaufmann [19]. Fuzzy sets having been considered in Subsect. 4.1 are homogeneous in the sense that the same structure of membership function domain is taken for all the elements of the universal set X.

Let us consider the generating set X as the union $V \cup MV \cup MMV$, where V is a set of vertices, MV is a set of metavertices, and MMV is a set of meta-metavertices. We shall represent the appropriate fuzzy sets as $\mu_V: V \to [0, 1]$, $\mu_{MV}: MV \to 2^{[0,1]}$,, $\mu_{MMV}: | MMV \to [0, 1]^{[0,1]}$ respectively. In other words, the function μ_V defines a standard fuzzy set, a function μ_{MV} – an interval-valued fuzzy set, and μ_{MMV} – a fuzzy set of type 2. So metavertices and meta-metavertices are granular structures. Similarly the set of fuzzy subsets of edges is specified as $FE = [0, 1]^E = \{\rho_E | \rho_E : X \times X \to [0, 1]\}$ and the set of interval-valued fuzzy subsets of meta-edges $FME = 2^{[0,1]E} = \{\rho_{ME} | \rho_{ME} : X \times X \to 2^{[0,1]}\}$.

Definition 11. An heterogeneous fuzzy metagraph is an octuple

$$HFMG = \langle V, \mu_V, MV, \mu_{MV}, MMV, \mu_{MMV}, FE, FME \rangle, \tag{11}$$

where a generating set is a covering $X = V \cup MV \cup MMV$, μ_V is an ordinary fuzzy subset defined on a set of vertices V, $\mu_V: V \to [0, 1]$, is an interval-valued fuzzy subset defined on a set of metaverices MV: $\mu_{MV}: MV \to 2^{[0,1]}$, μ_{MMV} is a fuzzy set of type 2 defined on a set of meta-metaverices MV, $\mu_{MMV}: MMV \to [0, 1]^{[0,1]}$, FE is the set of fuzzy subsets of edges, $FE = [0, 1]^E = \{\rho_E | \rho_E: V \times V \to [0, 1]\}$ and FME is the set of interval-valued fuzzy subsets of meta-edges, $FME = 2^{[0,1]E} = \{\rho_{ME} | \rho_{ME}: V \times V \leftarrow 2^{[0,1]}\}$.

Remark 4. This definition of heterogeneous fuzzy metagraph corresponds to the earlier considered in Subsect. 4.4 Principle of Emergence that consists in generating new primitives, connections and properties in the hierarchy of holonic graph structures.

6 Conclusion

The following tasks have been performed, and some results have been obtained in the field of developing complex graphs and networks for the modeling MAS.

1. Two basic trends in modern complex networks investigations have been analyzed in the context of suitable MAS representation. The first trend is founded on canonical planar graphs with singular primitives, where the vertices are points and the edges are given by non-crossing line segments. The second, rather new trend, appeared in response to the need in modifying basic graphs primitives (both vertices and edges) in order to construct granular and hierarchically ordered primitives, including metavertices and hyperedges.
2. The system of structural factors of network complexity has been specified. Hence some ways of constructing non-standard graph models for MAS have been discussed with the emphasis on heterogeneous and fuzzy graphs, hypernetworks and metagraphs, as well as some hybrid graph models.

3. By analogy with the paradigm of «logicism» in classical logic the paradigm of «universal planar graphicism» has been described, where classical graph primitives – vertices as points and straight lines as edges, as well as planar graph structures are considered to be universal graphs characteristics not depending on applications.

The authors have suggested an alternative approach illustrated by the example of synthesizing heterogeneous goal-resource network as a model of agents interactions and MAS formation. A primary ontological analysis of agents with specification of agent types and conditions of their effective interactions have been induced a detailed concept and structure of applied heterogeneous network with three types of colored vertices, two types of edges and two types of loops.

4. To extend the possibilitie of graph models in synthesizing complex networks the analysis and systematization of fuzzy graphs has been performed with the emphasis on granular fuzzy graph primitives and loose relations between endpoints of underlying bipolar scale, as well as the consideration of the basic model metagraph and its generalizations. On the basis of Negoita-Ralescu theorem taken f both for fuzzy sets and fuzzy relations, the assertion of the equivalence between the representation of fuzzy graphs and nested metagraphs has been grounded. A unified representation of four situations of agent interactions by a metagraph with nested vertices has been introduced.
5. Two models of fuzzy metagraphs have been considered, including the model of heterogeneous fuzzy metagraphs proposed by the authors.

The nearest plans of our work are related to the further development of fuzzy metagraphs formalisms and investigation of their properties, the elaboration of ontological models based on nested vertices and development of hybrid structures of MAS on the basis fuzzy graphs, fuzzy hypergraphs and fuzzy metagraphs.

In our further work, we hope to simulate and compare various types of Fuzzy Complex Networks in the context of Industry 4.0 and develop an ontological system for mutual understanding and joint work of artificial agents in such networks.

The authors are grateful to Prof. Oleg P.Kuznetsov and Prof. Gerald S. Plesniewicz for initiating this work and giving some useful comments.

References

1. Akram, M.: Bipolar fuzzy graphs. Inf. Sci. **181**, 5548–5564 (2011)
2. Akram, M., Dudek, W.A.: Interval-valued fuzzy graphs. Comput. Math Appl. **61**, 289–299 (2011)
3. Astanin, S.V., Dragnish, N.V., Zhukovskaya, N.K.: Nested metagraphs as models of complex objects. InzhnerniyVestnik Dona **23**, 76–81 (2012). (in Russian)
4. Atanassov, K.: Intuitionistic fuzzy sets. Fuzzy Sets Syst. **20**(1), 87–96 (1986)
5. Averkin, A.N., Batyrshin, I.Z., Tarassov, V.B., et al.: Fuzzy Sets in the Models of Control and Artificial Intelligence. Nauka, Moscow (1986). (in Russian)
6. Basu, A., Blanning, R.W.: Metagraphs and Their Applications. Springer, New York (2007). https://doi.org/10.1007/978-0-387-37234-1

7. Berge, C.: Hypergraphs: Combinatorics of Finite Sets. Elsevier, Amsterdam (1989)
8. Berstein, L.S., Bozhenyuk, A.V.: Fuzzy graphs and fuzzy hypergraphs. In: Encyclopedia of Artificial Intelligence, vol. 3, pp. 704–709. IGI Global, Hershey PA (2009)
9. Chernenkiy, V.M., Terekhov, V.I., Gapanyuk, Yu.E.: Representation of complex networks on the basis of metagraphs. Neuroinformatics-2016. Proceedings of XVIII All-Russia Scientific-Technical Conference, pp. 172–178. MEPhIPublishers. Moscow (2016)
10. Dashore, P., Jain, S.: Fuzzy metagraph and hierarchical modeling. Int. J. Comput. Sci. Eng. 3(1), 435–449 (2011)
11. Dyundyukov, V.S., Tarassov, V.B.: Goal-resource networks and their application to agents communication and co-ordination in virtual enterprise. In: Proceedings of the 7th IFAC Conference on Manufacturing Modelling, Management and Control, MIM 20013, St. Petersburg, Russia, 19–21 June 2013. IFAC Proceedings Volumes 46(9), 347–352 (2013)
12. Emelyanov, V.V.: A multi-agent model of decentralized resource management. In: Proceedings of the International Conference on Intelligent Control – New Intelligent Technologies in Control Problems, ICIT 1999, Pereslavl-Zalesski, Yaroslavl Region, Russia, 6–9, December 1999, pp. 121–126. PhysMathLit, Moscow (1999). (in Russian)
13. Ford Jr., L.R., Fulkerson, D.R.: Flows in Networks. Princeton University Press, Princeton (2010)
14. Gapanyuk, Yu.E.: The semantic complex event processing based on metagraph approach. In: Samsonovich, Alexei V. (ed.) BICA 2019. AISC, vol. 948, pp. 99–104. Springer, Cham (2020). https://doi.org/10.1007/978-3-030-25719-4_13
15. Gapanyuk, Yu., Kaganov, Yu., Revunkov, G.I.: The implementation of graphodynamic paradigm using the metagraph approach. Open Semant. Technol. Intell. Syst. 2, 147–152 (2018)
16. Johnson, J.: Hypernetworks in the Science of Complex Systems. Imperial College Press, London (2013)
17. Karpov, Valery E., Tarassov, Valery B.: Synergetic artificial intelligence and social robotics. In: Abraham, A., Kovalev, S., Tarassov, V., Snasel, V., Vasileva, M., Sukhanov, A. (eds.) IITI 2017. AISC, vol. 679, pp. 3–15. Springer, Cham (2018). https://doi.org/10.1007/978-3-319-68321-8_1
18. Karunambigai, M.G, Parvathi, R, Kalaivani, O.K.: A study of Atanassov's intuitionistic fuzzy graphs. In: Proceedings of 2011 IEEE International Conference on Fuzzy Systems (FUZZ-IEEE 2011), pp. 649–655 (2011)
19. Kaufmann, A.: Introduction a la théorie des sous-ensembles flous, vol. 1, 2. Masson, Paris (1972–1973)
20. Koczy, L.: Fuzzy graphs in the evaluation and optimization of networks. Fuzzy Sets Syst. 46, 307–319 (1992)
21. Kuznetsov, O.P.: Homogeneous resource networks. 1. Complete graphs. Autom. Remote Control 11, 136–147 (2009). (in Russian)
22. Kuznetsov, O.P.: Complex networks and activity spreading. Autom. Remote Control 76, 2091–2109 (2015)
23. Liu, H., Sun, J., Zhang, H., Liu, L.: Extended Pawlak's flow graphs and information theory. In: Gavrilova, M.L., Tan, C.J.K., Wang, Y., Chan, K.C.C. (eds.) Transactions on Computational Science V. LNCS, vol. 5540, pp. 220–236. Springer, Heidelberg (2009). https://doi.org/10.1007/978-3-642-02097-1_12
24. Mathew, S., Mordeson, John N., Malik, Davender S.: Fuzzy Graph Theory. SFSC, vol. 363. Springer, Cham (2018). https://doi.org/10.1007/978-3-319-71407-3
25. Mesbahi, M., Egerstedt, M.: Graph Theoretic Methods in Multiagent Networks. Princeton University Press, Princeton (2010)
26. Mordeson, J.N., Nair, S.: Fuzzy Graphs and Fuzzy Hypergraphs. Physica-Verlag, New York (2000)

27. Negoita, C.V., Ralescu, D.A.: Representation Theorems for Fuzzy Concepts. Kybernetes **4**, 169–174 (1975)
28. Pawlak, Z.: Flow graphs and data mining. In: Peters, James F., Skowron, A. (eds.) Transactions on Rough Sets III. LNCS, vol. 3400, pp. 1–36. Springer, Heidelberg (2005). https://doi.org/10.1007/11427834_1
29. Popkov. V.K.: Mathematical Models of Connectivity. ICM MG SB RAS Publishers, Novosibirsk (2006). (in Russian)
30. Pospelov, D.A.: Modeling of deeds in artificial intelligence systems. Appl. Artif. Intell. **7**(1), 15–27 (1993)
31. Rosenfeld, A.: Fuzzy graphs. In: Zadeh, L., Fu, K.S., Shimura, M. (eds.) Fuzzy Sets and Their Applications, pp. 77–95. Academic Press, New York (1975)
32. Russell, S.J., Norvig, P.: Artificial Intelligence: A Modern Approach, 3rd edn. Prentice Hall, Upper Saddle River (2009)
33. Shannon, A., Atanassov, K.: A first step to the theory of intuitionistic fuzzy graphs. In: Lakov, D. (ed.) Proceedings of the First Workshop on Fuzzy-Based Expert Systems, Sofia, 28–30 September, pp. 59–61 (1994)
34. Tarassov, V.B.: P-fuzzy sets in expert estimations. In: Proceedings of the IV-th Workshop on the Control under Fuzzy Categories, pp. 31–34. Ilim Publishers, Frunze, September 1981
35. Tarassov, V.B.: From Multi-Agent Systems to Intelligent Organization. Editorial URSS, Moscow (2002). (in Russian)
36. Thirunavukarasu, A., Maheswari, S.: Fuzzy metagraph and vague metagraph based techniques and their applications. Int. J. Comput. Appl. **56**(6), 157–166 (2012)
37. Wooldridge, M.: An Introduction to Multiagent Systems, 2nd edn. Wiley, Chichester (2010)
38. Yevin, I.A.: Introduction to the theory of complex networks. Comput. Stud. Model. **2**(2), 121–141 (2010). (in Russian)
39. Zadeh, L.A.: Fuzzy sets. Inf. Control **8**, 338–353 (1965)
40. Zadeh, L.A.: Toward a theory of fuzzy information granulation and its centrality in human reasoning and fuzzy logic. Fuzzy Sets Syst. **90**, 111–127 (1997)
41. Zhang, W.: Bipolar fuzzy sets. In: Proceedings of IEEE World Congress on Computational Science – Fuzz. IEEE, Anchorage, Alaska, May 1998
42. Zhilyakova, LYu., Kuznetsov, O.P.: Resource Network Theory. INFRA-M, Moscow (2017). (in Russian)

Natural Language Processing and Understanding of Texts

Automating Hierarchical Subject Index Construction for Scientific Documents

Elena I. Bolshakova[1]($\boxtimes$) and Kirill M. Ivanov[2]

[1] Lomonosov Moscow State University, Moscow, Russia
eibolshakova@gmail.com
[2] Yandex, Moscow, Russia
ivanov.kir.m@yandex.ru

Abstract. Subject, or back-of-the-book index consists of significant terms with relevant page numbers of the text document, thus providing an easy access to its content. The paper describes methods developed for automating main stages of subject indexing for specialized texts: namely, term extraction, selection of the most important ones, detecting their reference pages, as well as recognizing semantic relations among selected index terms in order to structure them into hierarchy. The developed methods are intended for processing scientific documents in Russian and are based both on formal linguistics rules and unsupervised machine learning. Experimental evaluation of the methods have shown their sufficient quality to be built into computer subject indexing system.

Keywords: Back-of-the-book indexing · Hierarchical subject index · Linguistic patterns and rules · Automatic term extraction · Recognition of term relations

1 Introduction

Subject, or back-of-the-book indexes are intended for reading large and medium-size text documents such as books, manuals, etc., especially in highly specialized domains. Typical subject index contains specific terms from the corresponding document, with reference pages, thereby facilitating navigation through the text and locating needed information. Such indexes are especially useful for readers of educational texts in difficult scientific and technical areas (textbooks, manuals, tutorials, etc.), since they represent key concepts of the text and also makes it easier to repeatedly read term definitions and other important fragments of texts.

To now, automatic back-of-the-book indexing is a little-researched area, although the first papers appeared long ago [17]. The main reasons are related with the complex nature of the problem and complexity of its subtasks. Nevertheless, the automation of these tasks is needed, because the high-laborious indexing work remains mainly manual, and useful subject indexes are absent in many modern textbooks and manuals, in particular, in texts of rapidly developing scientific and technical fields.

© Springer Nature Switzerland AG 2020
S. O. Kuznetsov et al. (Eds.): RCAI 2020, LNAI 12412, pp. 201–214, 2020.
https://doi.org/10.1007/978-3-030-59535-7_14

Among few works on automatic subject indexing, the most [7–9, 15] address extracting terms from a given text document, which is the central problem of index construction. The statistics-based and machine learning methods proposed in [7, 9, 18] showed low precision and recall for term extraction (about 27–28%). The works [9, 14, 20] are mainly based on linguistic rules for term extraction, but do not provide proper evaluation of developed methods.

The other tasks of subject index construction are less investigated, including selection of page numbers relevant for reference and revealing subordinate relations of terms to form hierarchical indexes. Certain decisions of these tasks are implemented in two subject indexing systems: InDoc [20] and commercial system TExtract[1], which are oriented to English or French texts.

It should be pointed out that any subject indexing system will inevitably be semi-automatic, since there are no standards on structure and content of indexes, and the work of human indexer may be highly subjective. Another reason is insufficient accuracy of applied techniques from artificial intelligence and natural language processing. Therefore, the resulting index needs to be validated and edited by author of the document or expert in problem domain.

The main objective of our work is to propose a combination of methods and to study their applicability for automating construction of subject indexes for scientific texts with their reach terminology. Our approach is characterized by the following.

- Subject indexing is considered as complex problem comprising term extraction, selection among them of the most important ones, recognition of their semantic relations, and also detecting their reference pages. According to specificity of each subtask, we apply rule-based or machine learning techniques.
- Since widely-used statistical measures developed for corpus-based terminology extraction [13, 19] perform poorly for individual documents [16], our term extraction techniques, as well as a method for recognition of subordinate term relations are mainly based on formalized linguistic patterns and rules similar to [12]. For the other indexing subtasks we propose unsupervised machine learning, namely, clustering extracted terms and their occurrences in text.
- Our subject indexing methods are aimed to processing scientific documents, mainly educational texts containing many specific terms with their definitions. They account for various terminological features of scientific texts including typical contexts of their usage, thereby achieving efficiency of the methods.
- In contrast to most works [7–9, 15, 18, 20] dealing with indexing English or French documents, we consider texts in Russian. The developed rule-based methods continue our previous researches [2, 3], they are close to those in [9, 20], but are performed for Russian scientific texts. As a result, a representative set of rules with lexico-syntactic patterns of terms and their contexts was created.
- In order to improve index term detection (comparing with [1, 7, 8]), we have elaborated a selection procedure accounting for various factors of terms importance.

---

[1] http://www.texyz.com/textract/.

The present paper develops our recent work [4] by refining the selection procedure and by proposing methods for the other subtasks of constructing subject index.

To implement the rule-based methods, we have exploited LSPL formal language [2] and its programming tools[2]. For evaluating the methods, we took several Russian medium-sized scientific texts, mainly on programming. For index term extraction and selection and for detecting reference pages, the developed methods were evaluated separately, since the methodology for evaluating the whole combination is unknown.

The experiments have showed rather good performance of them, in average 70–80% of precision and recall for index term extraction, which exceeds the results of early statistics-based and machine learning methods [7, 8] and also of the recent one [1]. Overall, our methods are suitable for computer-aided subject indexing system.

The paper starts with explanation of back-of-the-book index structure and description of main tasks (stages) of its construction, and along the way a short overview of corresponding methods developed in related works is given. In the next sections, the methods proposed for all the tasks are sequentially considered and described, with experimental evaluation for the most of them. Finally, the conclusions are drawn.

2 Problems and Stages of Back-of-the-Book Indexing

Fragments of typical back-of-the-book indexes are presented in Fig. 1. They contain index entries with specific terms from the text document (e.g., *graph*), proper names, and names of objects of the problem domain (such as *Lester Randolph Ford*). Index entries are associated with page numbers and page ranges that serve as pointers to important occurrences of the terms and names in the text.

– G –	– В –
graph, 39, 233, 467	высота
– directed acyclic, 93, 125	– бинарного дерева, 527-530
– H –	– красно-черного дерева, 309
height	– Г –
– of a binomial tree, 527-530	граф, 39, 233, 467
– of a black-red tree, 309	– ориентированный ациклический, 193
– L –	– Л –
Lester Randolph Ford, Jr., 432	Лестер Рэндольф Форд-младший, 432
– N –	– С –
network	сеть
– admissible, 749–750	– допустимая, 749–750
– flow (see *flow network*)	– потока (см. *сетевой поток*)

Fig. 1. Fragments of subject indexes

Many of subject indexes are hierarchical, as the examples in Fig. 1. Such indexes contain entries-headings representing generic concepts (e.g., *height*) and subheadings

---

[2] http://lspl.ru/.

(*height of a binomial tree*) that correspond to more specific concepts or particular objects. Such subordinate link between headings and subheadings often indicates generic-specific semantic relation of terms (hyperonym and hyponim term).

Subject indexes may include cross-references (e.g., *see flow network*), which present synonymy semantic relations between terms.

The process of automatic construction of subject index for a given text document generally comprises 4 stages (tasks) [9, 15, 20]: 1) extracting single-word and multi-word terms by applying linguistics and statistic criteria; 2) selecting the more appropriate ones among extracted terms; 3) detecting semantic relations of the selected terms and structuring them into hierarchy; 4) constructing pointers to important locations of index terms in the text (page numbers).

The first stage produces only a flat list of words and word combinations. The standard term extraction techniques [13, 19] based on linguistic features of terms (grammatical patterns) and statistical measures of word occurrences do not guarantee extracted units to be true terms (e.g., non-term phrases of general lexicon like *key idea*), so resulted units are considered as *term candidates* and needed to be filtered.

The filtering task is usually performed by evaluating and ranking the extracted term candidates with the aid of certain statistical measures (see [10, 13, 19]) and discarding the worst ones. The previous works on subject indexing based on such methods (even with machine learning) gave quite low precision and recall, about 27–28% [7]. Analogous techniques are applied for similar task of keywords extraction (terms denote concepts of problem domain, while keywords may be non-terms but represent main topics of the document) and also give low scores: the best reported in [11] are 35% of precision, 66% of recall, 45.7% of F-measure. The recent term extraction method [1] based on grammatical patterns of terms along with terms clustering shows 35–67% of F-measure (precision 21–51% and recall 90%) in experiments with software requirements documents, which is also not effective enough for our applied task.

Therefore, for reliable index term detection we propose to sequentially select index terms from term candidates pre-extracted by lexico-syntactic patterns, making use of various term importance factors and also C-value termhood measure [10] performing well for texts in highly technical domains [16].

To hierarchically structure the selected index terms, headings and corresponding subheadings (and cross-references) are to be identified, which can be done in various ways. The only work [20] that proposed the way to automatically recognize generic-specific relations applies structural linguistics patterns similar to those in [10], as well as lexical similarity of multi-word terms that have common words (e.g., *acyclic directed graph* and *directed graph*). Our method exploits lexico-syntactic patterns for detecting such subordinate and also synonymy links, as well term clustering based on certain similarity measures, in order to reveal additional index terms and their semantic relations. Similar clustering techniques proposed in the paper [1] was specifically used for construction glossaries and differs from ours by similarity measures.

The last stage of index construction implies identifying important term occurrences truly relevant for indexing. We should note that importance and relevance may be understand in different ways [5], thus giving various automatic methods. The work [9] proposes text segmentation and selection of the most frequent terms in all segments, but the method was not evaluated. Our decision of the problem accounts for density of term occurrences in the text by clustering page numbers, and we have evaluated the proposed method.

3   Term Candidates Extraction

For our tasks, the collection of LSPL rules from the work [3], which encode linguistic information on structure and typical contexts of terms in Russian scientific texts was revised and supplemented, in order to extract from texts a more wide set of term candidates. The resulted set of rules encompasses three groups with various lexico-syntactic patterns:

- rules that specifies typical grammatical patterns of one- and multi-word scientific terms, by indicating part of speech of words (POS) and their grammatical characteristics (case, gender, etc.);
- rules formalizing typical contexts of definitions for new terms (*author's terms*), which are often encountered in scientific and educational papers (so defined terms are certainly be included in subject index being constructed);
- rules specifying typical contexts for introducing terminological synonyms and abbreviations (including synonyms for author's terms).

The first group includes, in particular, rules with grammatical patterns $A\ N$ (e.g., *союзный список* – *linked list*) and $N1\ A\ N2{<}c{=}gen{>}$ (*высота бинарного дерева* – *height of a binomial tree*), where N, $N1$, $N2$ are nouns, A is an adjective, and $N2$ is specified in genitive case ($c{=}gen$). For the second pattern, the extraction rule is:

$$N1\ A\ N2{<}c{=}gen{>}\ {<}A{=}N1{>}\ (N1)\ {=>}\ A\ \#N1\ N2{<}c{=}gen{>}$$

where the adjective of the first noun are grammatically agreed ($A{=}N1$). Symbol $=>$ denotes extraction of the recognized phrase (text item), in accordance with the pattern in the right-hand side of the rule (the sign # denotes lemmatization of the first noun).

The second group covers most of typical Russian-language phrases-definitions of terms in scientific texts. The rules include both particular lexical units (e.g., verbs *понимать, определять* – *mean, define*) and auxiliary pattern *Term* denoting phrase with grammatical pattern specified by the first group of rules. For example, the definition phrase *...под термином изменение климата будем понимать...* (*...under the term climate change we will mean ...*) is detected by the following rule:

$$\textit{"под термином" Term{<}c{=}ins{>}\ "будем понимать" ={>}\ \#Term}$$

where *Term* should be in instrumental case ($c = ins$), but extracted in normal form.

Rules of the third group recognizes and extracts pairs of term synonyms (of valid grammatical pattern), in such contexts as *...разрядность, или просто длина слова"* (*...bitness, or simply the length of a word ...*). In the following rule recognition relies on comma and lexical markers (words *или просто*, the latter *просто* is optional):

$$\textit{Term1\ ","\ "или"\ ["просто"]\ Term2\ ={>}\ \#\ Term1\ "-"\ \#Term2}$$

Extraction by the described rules yields three sets of term candidates: S_{gramm}, S_{auth}, S_{syn}, respectively, and the sets are intersected, in particular, there are terms extracted by patterns of grammatical structure and also by patterns of term definition. Therefore, a procedure is necessary, for selecting unique and more significant term candidates for a subject index.

For this purpose, we have estimated precision of term extraction for each group of rules, taking several textbooks of medium size in computer science (each is about 20 thous. words), which contain back-of-the-book indexes constructed by their authors (the problem encountered while performing experiments is the lack of human-built indexes in many Russian textbooks). The experiments have expectedly shown high recall but low precision (about 8–12%) for the first rule group, but for the second group rules the results were opposite, with high precision (91–95%), due to lexical markers used in them. We have formed a subset of very-high precision (VHP) rules from the second group, since for them extracted terms are to be obligatory included into subject index. The third group of rules show a rather good precision: 63–67%, and we also include the extracted terms into index.

4 Selection of Terms

The developed heuristics procedure iteratively forms a collection of index terms from pre-extracted sets of term candidates S_{gramm}, S_{auth}, S_{syn}, aiming at reliable selection of the most important terms by accounting for the following factors.

- There are many non-terms among S_{gramm}, most of them can be filtered through applying lists of stopwords (auxiliary words and words of general lexicon);
- Terms extracted by very-high precision (VHP) extraction rules of term definitions should be selected first;
- According to Zipf's law, the most significant terms are units with an average frequency, so the most frequent and rare candidates must be discarded;
- Statistical measure C-value [10] estimating termhood (by accounting nesting of terms) and thus measuring term importance is useful for ranking selected terms;
- Terms occurred in content section (if any) of the text document or used in titles of its sections/subsections should be included in the index;
- Term candidates that are synonymous to already selected index terms can also be added to the subject index;
- Since index terms are often lexically similar (they refer to close concepts), a term candidate can be added into the index if it has common words (at least one) with any yet selected term (e.g., terms *second order predicate* and *logical predicate* are lexically similar).

The selection procedure encompasses three stages. The first stage involves filtering pre-extracted sets of term candidates with the aid of pre-compiled lists of stop words. The first list contains words that cannot themselves be terms (*план, начало – plan, start*, and so on), while the second list contains words that cannot be part of terms (e.g., *данный, низкий – given, low*). From all the sets S_{gramm}, S_{auth}, S_{syn}, their elements are excluded that: a) are encountered in the first list; b) contain words from the second list; c) consist of words from the first list. Thereby many collocations of common scientific lexicon such as *given plan* are discarded.

At the second stage, for all filtered term candidates, frequencies of their occurrences the text are calculated, and for frequencies of units from S_{gramm} the percentiles are calculated with the levels $p_1 = 0.4$ (rounding down) and $p_2 = 0.95$ (rounding up), respectively. Values p_i are exploited as thresholds for eliminating unlikely candidates (both rare and frequent).

Then, the resulting set R of subject index terms is incrementally formed by taking elements from the filtered S_i, through the following steps (initially R is empty):

1. Term candidates from the set S_{auth} obtained by VHP rules and with the frequency in the range $[p_1, p_2]$ are included in the set R.
2. Term candidates from the set S_{gramm}, with frequency in the range $[p_1, p_2]$ are added to R, provided that i) they are encountered in any title of sections/subsections in the text document (or list of content, if any) or ii) they have common words (at least one) with any term selected in Step 1.
3. Term candidates remaining in the set S_{auth} (i.e. unconsidered in Step 1) and having common words (at least one) with any element from current R are added to R.
4. Term candidates from the set S_{auth} or S_{syn}, which are synonymous to a term from R, are added to R.
5. All pairs of synonyms from the set S_{syn}, whose total frequency is in the range $[p_1, p_2]$ for percentiles calculated for total frequencies of all synonymous pairs, are added to R.
6. Term candidates from the set S_{gramm} with frequency in the range $[p_1, p_2]$, are added to R, provided they have common words with any element from current R.
7. Elements of R are ordered according their C-value and only the first N_{top} elements (considered as more significant) are remained in the resulted index list.

The thresholds for percentiles p_1, p_2 and the order of the described steps were chosen experimentally. The value of N_{top} is determined by the size of the source document, because the larger the text, the longer the list of candidate terms, and the less significant terms are located at its end. The value of N_{top} may be about 50–90.

To experimentally evaluate efficiency of the described selection procedure, seven medium-sized (about 70–100 pages) educational scientific texts with human-built subject indexes were taken, the indexes were regarded as etalon sets of terms. The processed texts are devoted to programming systems (PS), programming languages (PL), formal grammars (FG), artificial intelligence (AI), discrete mathematics (DM). The results measured in precision (P), recall (R), and F-measure (F) are shown in Table 1. While evaluating, we took into account the coincidence of the concepts designated by formally different terms (such as *условная конструкция – условие, conditional construction – condition*), and N_{top} contains all the selected terms.

One can notice that our methods of term extraction and selection demonstrates quite good performance: its recall (in average 0.78) is sufficient, and precision (in average 0.71) is acceptable, as well as F-measure, 0.74), they exceed the rates of the above-considered methods of term extraction for subject indexes [1, 6, 7]. For comparison,

Table 1. Recall and precision of selection procedure

Text	Size (words)	Selected index terms		P	R	F
		#	Examples			
PS	11,699	67	функциональное тестирование (functional testing)	0.70	0.81	0.75
PL-1	21,060	140	ветвь условного выражения (branch of conditional expression)	0.74	**0.84**	0.79
PL-2	29,301	208	левое согласование (left matching)	0.56	0.82	0.67
PL-3	21,376	77	предикат второго порядка (second order predicate)	0.77	0.72	0.75
FG	15,890	73	нетерминальный символ (nonterminal symbol)	**0.79**	0.83	**0.81**
AI	19,471	98	алгоритм слепого перебора (blind search algorithm)	0.71	0.74	0.73
DM	20,786	222	компонента связности (component of connectivity)	0.73	0.71	0.72
Mean	19,940	126		**0.71**	**0.78**	**0.74**

we also have processed and evaluated the manual devoted to academic writing (11,699 words), it can hardly be attributed to scientific or technical text. The precision proved to be 72% and recall 55% (F-measure, 62%). The low recall may be partially explained by lack of explicit definitions of certain important but rare terms.

It should be noted that some extracted terms absent in the etalon subject indexes (such as term *proof tree* from the textbook on Prolog) are terms relevant for subject index, they may be omitted by human indexer because of subjectivity or intent to get a more short index. Thus, for subject index construction, recall is more crucial than precision: it is easier for human editor of the constructed index to discard some terms than to add new ones. Besides, to increase recall, the editor can change values p_1, p_2.

5   Identifying Subordinate Relations of Terms

To form hierarchical structure of subject index, subordinate links among pairs of selected terms are to be recognized, and corresponding headings and subheadings are to be formed. Our method of revealing subordinate relations makes use of information about structure of multi-word terms.

Admittedly, hyponym terms often originate from hyperonym terms by complementing them with qualifying words [6], e.g., *свертка* (*convolution*) – *левая свертка* (*left convolution*), *протокол передачи* (*transfer protocol*) – *протокол передачи почты* (*mail transfer protocol*). Accordingly, we determine potential hyperonyms (headings) based on grammatical patterns of compound terms, and particular LSPL rules with lexico-syntatic patterns are created for this purpose. Three examples of grammatical patterns and the corresponding grammatical patterns of potential heading are presented in Table 2.

Table 2. Grammatical patterns of heading and subheading

Patterns of terms	Examples of terms	Grammatical patterns, examples of heading terms	
A N	*Числовой атом – Numeric atom*	*N*	*Атом – Atom*
N1 N2<c=gen>	*Ветвь функции – Function branch*	*N1*	*Ветвь – Branch*
		N2	*Функция – Function*
A1 A2 N	*Ациклический ориентированный граф – Acyclic directed graph*	*N*	*Граф – Graph*
		A1 N	*Ациклический граф – Acyclic graph*
		A2 N	*Ориентированный граф – Directed graph*

In addition to grammatical patterns of headings, which were determined for all permissible multi-word terms, frequencies of terms in the document being processed are used, according to idea that any heading term should be more frequent than its subheadings.

Specifically, to form headings and subheadings, the following procedure is performed, for each compound term T of subject index. First, all words and phrases $\{T_p\}$, which can potentially become headings, are extracted from T. Then, occurrence frequencies both for T and for each element from $\{T_p\}$ are calculated. Finally, the following rule is applied: the word or phrase T_{p_i} with the highest frequency among $\{T_p\}$ is chosen as heading, provided that its frequency exceeds the frequency of the term T. If there are several such elements, then the first one is selected, according to alphabetical order of the terms. In the case when the frequencies of all $\{T_p\}$ do not exceed the frequency of T, T itself becomes the heading (without subheadings).

For example, for term *Ациклический ориентированный граф* (*Acyclic directed graph*), potential headings are: *граф* (*Graph*), *Ориентированный граф* (*Directed graph*), *Ациклический граф* (*Acyclic graph*). If term *Ориентированный граф* has the highest frequency, it becomes heading, and *Ациклический ориентированный граф* will be the corresponding subheading.

After selection of headings, a hierarchical structure for subject index terms is formed. From each subheading, its constituent part identical to the heading is deleted, and the rest is placed on the low level of the hierarchy. Resulting structure for the considered example is shown below:

Rus.: *Ориентированный граф*   **Eng.**: *Directed graph*
    – ациклический   *– acyclic*

6 Revealing Additional Index Terms and Semantic Relations

To increase recall of index term selection, we propose to additionally use clustering of terms candidates from S_{gramm}, since such clustering can reveal groups of semantically related units, which together with already selected terms include significant terms that were missed at the stage of term selection.

Term clustering is almost not investigated, the paper [1] applies clustering merely for term extraction, with the purpose to construct glossaries for documents. Resulted clusters contain semantically related groups of terms, but their semantic links are not identified and not represented in constructed glossaries. Since for processing individual texts, automatic identification and classification of semantic links is a really difficult task, we believe that within a back-of-the-book indexing system it is reasonable to leave such classification work to human editor of the index being constructed, and the system only reveals groups of semantically related terms.

It should be noted that in our work, synonymy relations needed for establishing cross-references in subject index, are mainly identified at the stage of term extraction: pairs of synonyms introduced by the author of the text are recognized by lexico-syntactic patterns of the third group. Besides such obvious synonyms, term variants [6], such as *пролог-интерпретатор* and *интерпретатор Пролога* (*Prolog interpreter* and *interpreter of Prolog*) are often encountered in scientific texts. As our experiments showed, such variants as well as another semantically related pairs are effectively detected by clustering.

In the experiments we applied Kmeans and DBSCAN clustering algorithms with context similarity measure that compares context words of two terms, from a window of size 4 (context is regarded as bag of words). Context similarity is evaluated with Jaccard index (the proportion of common context words in the set of all context words for the compared terms). Additionally we considered analogous measure with context words represented as vectors in distributional vector space, but we had to abandon it, since many words included in specific terms are absent in the known vector models RusVectores.[3]

Results of Kmeans algorithm were better than for DBSCAN, and its hyperparameter, i.e. the number of clusters was experimentally selected so that the average cluster size was 5–10. Below we present three examples of clusters yielded by Kmeans with the context similarity measure:

1) *регулярная грамматика, формальная грамматика, конечный автомат, автомат – regular grammar, formal grammar, finite state automaton, automaton*;

---

[3] https://rusvectores.org/ru/.

2) *шлюз, маршрутизатор, коммутатор, коммуникационное оборудование* – gateway, router, commutator, communication equipment;

3) *простая   рекурсия,   хвостовая   рекурсия,   косвенная рекурсия, характеристика** – simple recursion, tail recursion, indirect recursion, characteristic*.

One can notice that in these groups there are pairs of terms with subordinate relation that can not be detected by our build-in lexico-syntactic patterns for this relation (*regular grammar* and *formal grammar*), as well as co-hyponims (*simple recursion* and *indirect recursion*), terms with certain association semantic relation (*regular grammar* and *finite state automaton*; *commutator* and *communication equipment*). Such pairs can be useful for enriching subject index. At the same time clusters may include elements semantically unrelated with the others (in the above example, such elements are marked with *), therefore a human should analyze them.

The experiments showed that most clusters contain semantically related terms. To enrich the set of index terms, only those clusters that include at least one yet selected index term are automatically detected and then are presented to the human editor to identify additional relevant terms among the elements of each cluster.

7 Determining Reference Pages

Every term of subject index should be associated with page numbers or/and page ranges (for example: 5, 81–83) that indicate occurrences of the term in the text document. Some terms may be quite often used in the text, and it is not reasonable to include references to all pages with their occurrences. Usually, only significant places of term usage are detected and correspondent pages are placed into the subject index.

Evidently, pages with detected definitions of terms is significant, so we necessarily include them to a subject index being constructed. We determine significance of other pages, depending on occurrences frequency of the given term on these pages, which may be regarded as "density" of term usage.

To evaluate the density of occurrences for a particular term in the text, we propose to cluster the multi-set of page numbers for pages with occurrences of the term (a page number is repeated if the term is encountered several times in it) and then to form page ranges for each resulted cluster. In general case, each resulted cluster contains neighboring pages, which are concatenated into page range, but with the following reasonable restriction. The maximum permissible distance between two neighboring pages in page range is equal to M ($M = 1 or 2$), otherwise, the range may include more than M pages without occurrences of the term, and this is unacceptable for reader of the text. The number K ($K = 2, 3, 4, 5$) delimiting the number of page references (it also should be reasonable) is additional parameter of our method for determining page references.

For a given term, the steps of our method are as follows.

1. All occurrences of the term in the document are recognized (disregarding the exact form they take), and multi-set S_{page} of page numbers for term occurrences is formed: if the term is used several times on a page, then its number

is added to S_{page} as many times as term is encountered, for example: $S_{page} = \{12, 23, 23, 25, 28, 29, 29, 30, 31, 31, 31, 33, 50, 51, 70, 90\}$.

2. S_{page} is divided into clusters, with the DBSCAN density-based clustering algorithm and the parameter M; in our example $M = 1$ and six clusters are formed: $\{12\}\{23, 23, 25\}\{28, 29, 29, 30, 31, 31, 31, 33\}\{50, 51\}\{70\}\{90\}$.

3. Clusters are ordered by cardinality of multi-sets, in our example: $\{28, 29, 29, 30, 31, 31, 31, 33\}\{23, 23, 25\}\{50, 51\}\{12\}\{70\}\{90\}$; and then the first K ($K = 2$) clusters are taken: $\{28, 29, 29, 30, 31, 31, 31, 33\}, \{23, 23, 25\}$.

4. In each such cluster, the repeated elements (page numbers) are deleted, and the remaining ones are sorted in ascending order: $\{28, 29, 30, 31, 33\}\{23, 25\}$.

5. In the case when the page with definition of the given term (if any) is absent in these clusters (for example, 12), corresponding one-element cluster is added: $\{28, 29, 30, 31, 33\}\{23, 25\}\{12\}$.

6. The clusters are sorted by ascending order of their first element numbers: $\{12\}\{23, 25\}\{28, 29, 30, 31, 33\}$.

7. Each cluster with more than one element is converted to a page range while one-element clusters give separate pages: 12, 23–25, 28–33.

Since ways for estimating the quality of selecting reference pages were not proposed in the related works, we experimentally evaluated recall of our method, i.e. the degree of coverage of the pages indicated in the author's subject indexes with clusters of pages yielded by our method. For evaluation, texts of the same scientific textbooks were taken. The obtained coverage rates are from 84.4% to 94.3% (depending on particular text), which is quite good quality.

8 Conclusion and Future Work

In this paper we have proposed the methods for automating all the stages and tasks of constructing back-of-the-book index for an individual text document, including term extracting and filtering, detecting semantic relations of terms and important occurrences of index terms in the document. The methods were implemented and evaluated within a prototype subject indexing system with open code for Russian text documents. At all stages of subject index construction, the user of the system can set and change necessary parameters of the methods, can indicate a text fragment to be processed and then verify and edit the results.

The evaluation of the proposed methods have shown their quite good performance, in particular, our technique of term extraction and selection gives considerable increase of precision and recall in comparison with the previous related works. In our opinion, it is mainly due to built-in knowledge about terms in scientific and educational texts, which was formalized as the set of rules with lexico-syntactic patterns and used in combination with the heuristics about term importance.

On the way towards high-quality indexing tools, further experiments and improvements for our methods are needed, below we indicate some of them:

- To test and refine the heuristic selecting procedure for documents from another problem domains;

- To create procedures for extraction of named entities significant in text of certain problem domains (for example, in texts on programming these are names of built-in program function);
- To develop additional methods to automatically recognize semantic relations of terms based on models of distributional semantics.

References

1. Arora, C., Sabetzadeh, M., Briand, L., Zimmer, F.: Automated extraction and clustering of requirements glossary terms. IEEE Trans. Softw. Eng. **43**(10), 918–945 (2016)
2. Bolshakova, E., Efremova, N., Noskov, A.: LSPL-patterns as a tool for information extraction from natural language texts. In: New Trends in Classification and Data Mining, pp. 110–118. ITHEA, Sofia (2010)
3. Bolshakova, E.I., Efremova, N.E.: A heuristic strategy for extracting terms from scientific texts. In: Khachay, M.Yu., Konstantinova, N., Panchenko, A., Ignatov, D.I., Labunets, V.G. (eds.) AIST 2015. CCIS, vol. 542, pp. 297–307. Springer, Cham (2015). https://doi.org/10.1007/978-3-319-26123-2_29
4. Bolshakova, E., Ivanov, K.: Term extraction for constructing subject index of educational scientific text. In: Computational Linguistics and Intellectual Technologies: Papers from the Annual International Conference "Dialogue", Moscow, vo. 17, no. 24, pp. 143–152 (2018)
5. Christina, S., Oktaviani, E.: Identifying the relevant page numbers that referred by the back-of-book index using syntactic similarity and semantic similarity. In: Proceedings of 2017 Second International Conference on Informatics and Computing (ICIC), pp. 1–6 (2017)
6. Cram, D., Daille, B.: TermSuite: terminology extraction with term variant detection. In: Proceedings of the 54th Annual Meeting of the Association for Computational Linguistics—System Demonstrations, Berlin, pp. 13–18. ACL (2016)
7. Csomai, A., Mihalcea, R.: Investigations in unsupervised back-of-the-book indexing. In: Proceedings of the Florida Artificial Intelligence Research Society Conference, pp. 211–216 (2007)
8. Csomai, A., Mihalcea, R.: Linguistically motivated features for enhanced back-of-the book indexing. In: Proceedings of the Annual Conference of the Association for Computational Linguistics, ACL/HLT, vol. 8, pp. 932–940 (2008)
9. Da Sylva, L.: Integrating knowledge from different sources for automatic back-of-the-book indexing. In: Proceedings of the Annual Conference of CAIS/Actes du congrès annuel de l'ACSI (2013)
10. Frantzi, K., Ananiadou, S., Mima, H.: Automatic recognition of multi-word terms: the C-value/NC-value method. In: Nikolau, C., et al. (eds.) International Journal on Digital Libraries, vol. 3, no. 2, pp. 115–130 (2000)
11. Hasan, K.S., Ng, V.: Automatic keyphrase extraction: a survey of the state of the art. In: Proceedings of the 52th Annual Meeting of the ACL, pp. 1262–1273 (2014)
12. Hearst, M.A.: Automated discovery of WordNet relations. In: FellBaum, C. (ed.) WordNet: An Electronic Lexical Database, pp. 131–151. MIT Press, Cambridge (1998)
13. Korkontzelos, I., Ananiadou, S.: Term extraction. In: Oxford Handbook of Computational Linguistics, 2nd edn. Oxford University Press, Oxford (2014)
14. El Mekki, T., Nazarenko, A.: An application-oriented terminology evaluation: the case of back-of-the book indexes. In: Proceedings of the Workshop on Terminology Design: Quality Criteria and Evaluation Methods (LREC-TermEval), Genoa, Italy, pp. 18–21 (2006)

15. Reinholt, K., Lukon, S., Juola, P.: A machine-aided back-of-the-book indexer. In: Proceedings of DHCS 2010, Chicago, Illinois (2010)
16. Sajatovic, A., Buljan, M., Snajder, J., Basic, B.D.: Evaluating automatic term extraction methods on individual documents. In: Proceedings of the Joint Workshop on Multiword Expressions and WordNet (MWE-WN 2019), Florence, Italy, pp. 149–154 (2019)
17. Salton, G.: Syntactic approaches to automatic book indexing. In: Proceedings of the 26th Annual Meeting of the ACL, Morristown, NJ, USA, pp. 204–210 (1988)
18. Wu, Z., et al.: Can Back-of-the-Book Indexes be Automatically Created? In: Proceedings of the 22nd ACM International Conference on Information & Knowledge Management. ACM (2013)
19. Zhang, Z., Iria, J., Brewster, C., Ciravegna, F.: A comparative evaluation of term recognition algorithms. In: Proceedings of the Sixth International Conference on Language Resources and Evaluation (LREC08), Marrakech, Morocco, pp. 2108–2113 (2008)
20. Zargayouna, H., El Mekki, T., Audibert, L., Nazarenko, A.: IndDoc: an aid for the back-of-the-book indexer. Indexer 25(2), 122–125 (2006)

Automatic Labelling of Genre-Specific Collections for Word Sense Disambiguation in Russian

Angelina Bolshina$^{(\boxtimes)}$ and Natalia Loukachevitch

Lomonosov Moscow State University, Moscow, Russia
angelina_ku@mail.ru, louk_nat@mail.ru

Abstract. Supervised word sense disambiguation (WSD) models suffer from the knowledge acquisition bottleneck: the semantic annotation of large text collections is very time-consuming and requires much effort from experts. In this article we address the issue of the lack of sense-annotated data for the WSD task in Russian. We present an approach that is able to automatically generate text collections and annotate them with word senses. This method is based on the substitution and exploits monosemous relatives (related unambiguous entries) that can be located at relatively long distances from a target ambiguous word. Moreover, we present a similarity-based ranking procedure that enables to sort and filter monosemous relatives. Our experiments with WSD models, that rely on contextualized embeddings ELMo and BERT, have proven that our method can boost the overall performance. The proposed approach is knowledge-based and relies on the Russian thesaurus RuWordNet.

Keywords: Word sense disambiguation · Russian dataset · Monosemous relatives

1 Introduction

The word sense disambiguation (WSD) systems are intended to predict the correct sense of a polysemous word in a context given a particular sense inventory. WSD is widely used in many semantic-oriented applications such as semantic text analysis, knowledge graph construction, machine translation, question answering, etc. The key prerequisite for any supervised WSD model is the availability of a sense-annotated dataset. The creation of such resources is a very challenging and expensive task that requires much time and effort. There exist several large hand-crafted corpora for English with the sense annotation [1, 2]. However, it is extremely unlikely that such resources will be available for many other languages in the foreseeable future. This also holds true for the Russian language.

One of the possible alternatives to manual annotation is an automatic acquisition of training samples. In our research we investigate the method to automatically generate and label training collections with the help of monosemous relatives, that is a set of unambiguous words (or phrases) related to particular senses of a polysemous word.

© Springer Nature Switzerland AG 2020
S. O. Kuznetsov et al. (Eds.): RCAI 2020, LNAI 12412, pp. 215–227, 2020.
https://doi.org/10.1007/978-3-030-59535-7_15

However, as it was noted in [3], some senses of target words do not have monosemous relatives, and the noise can be introduced by some distant relatives. In our research we tried to address these issues.

The main contribution of this study is that we have expanded a set of monosemous relatives under consideration via various semantic relations and distances: in comparison with earlier approaches, now monosemous relatives can be situated at greater distance from a target ambiguous word in a graph. Moreover, we have introduced a numerical estimation of a similarity between a monosemous relative and a particular sense of a target word which is further used in the development of the training collection. In order to evaluate the created training collections, we utilized contextualized word representations – ELMo [4] and BERT [5][1].

The paper is organized as follows. In section two we review the related work. Section three is devoted to the data description. The fourth section describes the method applied to automatically generate and annotate training collections. The procedure of creating the collections is explained in the fifth section. In the sixth section, we describe a supervised word sense disambiguation algorithm trained on our collected material and demonstrate the results obtained by four different models. In this section we also present a comparative analysis of the models trained on different kinds of train collections. Concluding remarks are provided in the seventh section.

2   Related Work

To overcome the limitations, that are caused by the lack of annotated data, several methods of generating and harvesting large train sets have been developed. There exist many techniques based on different kinds of replacements, which do not require human resources for tagging. The most popular method is that of monosemous relatives [6]. Usually, WordNet [7] is used as a source for such relatives. WordNet is a lexical-semantic resource for the English language that contains a description of nouns, verbs, adjectives, and adverbs in the form of semantic graphs. All words in those networks are grouped into sets of synonyms that are called synsets.

Monosemous relatives are those words or collocations that are related to the target ambiguous word through some connection in WordNet, but they have only one sense, i.e. belong only to one synset. Usually, synonyms are selected as relatives but in some works hypernyms and hyponyms are chosen [8]. Some researchers replace the target word with named entities [9], some researchers substitute it with meronyms and holonyms [10]. In the work [3] distant relatives (including distant hypernyms and hyponyms) were used; the procedure of training contexts selection was based on the distance to a target word and the type of the relation connecting the target sense and a monosemous relative.

In the article [11] a special algorithm was created in order to select the best replacement out of all words contained within synsets of the target word and neighboring synsets. The algorithm described in [12] to construct an annotated training set is a combination of different approaches: monosemous relatives, glosses, and bootstrapping. Monosemous relatives can be also used in other tasks, for example, for finding the most frequent word

---

[1] The source code of our algorithm and experiments is publicly available at: https://github.com/ loenmac/russian_wsd_data.

senses in Russian [13]. Other methods of automatic generation of training collections for WSD exploit parallel corpora [2], Wikipedia and Wiktionary [14], topic signatures [15]. [16] created large training corpora exploiting a graph-based method that took an unannotated corpus and a semantic network as an input.

Various supervised methods including kNN, Naive Bayes, SVM, neural networks were applied to word sense disambiguation [17]. Recent studies have shown the effectiveness of contextualized word representations for the WSD task [18, 19]. The most widely used deep contextualized embeddings are ELMo [4] and BERT [5].

In ELMo (Embeddings from language models) [4] context vectors are computed in an unsupervised way by two layers of bidirectional LSTM, that take character embeddings from convolutional layer as an input. Character-based token representations help to tackle the problems with out-of-vocabulary words and rich morphology. BERT (Bidirectional Encoder Representations from Transformers) [5] has a different type of architecture, namely multi-layer bidirectional Transformer encoder. During the pre-training procedure, the model is "jointly conditioning on both left and right context in all layers" [5]. Moreover, BERT uses WordPiece tokens, that is subword units of words, which also helps to avoid the problem of out-of-vocabulary words. Since these contextualized word embeddings imply capturing polysemy better than any other representations, we employ them in our investigation.

3 Data

In our research as an underlying semantic network, we exploit Russian thesaurus RuWordNet [20]. It is a semantic network for Russian that has a WordNet-like structure. In total it contains 111.5 thousand of words and word combinations for the Russian language. RuWordNet was used to extract semantic relations (e.g. synonymy, hyponymy etc.) between a target sense of a polysemous word and all the words (or phrases) connected to it, including those linked via distant paths. The sense inventory was also taken from this resource. RuWordNet contains 29297 synsets for nouns, 63014 monosemous and 5892 polysemous nouns. In this research we consider only ambiguous nouns. Table 1 presents a summary of the number of senses per noun:

Table 1. Quantitative characteristics of polysemous words in RuWordNet.

Number of senses of a polysemous word	Number of words in RuWordNet
2 senses	4271
3 senses	997
4 senses	399
5 senses	149
>5 senses	76
Total number of senses	14 357

We utilized two corpora in the research. A news corpus consists of news articles harvested from various news sources. The texts have been cleaned from html-elements or any markup. Another corpus is Proza.ru, a segment of Taiga corpus [21], which is compiled of works of prose fiction. We exploit these two corpora in order to compare the performance of the WSD models trained on the collections obtained with these resources.

For evaluation of our algorithm of training data generation, we used three distinct RUSSE'18 datasets for Russian [22]. These datasets were created for the shared task on word sense induction for the Russian language. The first dataset is compiled from the contexts of the Russian National Corpus. The second dataset consists of the contexts from Wikipedia articles. And the last dataset is based on the Active Dictionary of the Russian Language [23] and contains contexts taken from the examples and illustration sections from this dictionary. All the polysemous words are nouns. From the RUSSE dataset, we excluded some polysemous words, and in Table 2 we overview the common reasons why it was done.

Table 2. Cases when a word from the RUSSE'18 dataset was not included in the final test set.

Explanation	Number of words	Example
A word has only one meaning in RuWordNet	34	The word *двойник* 'doppelganger' has only one meaning in RuWordNet whereas in RUSSE'18 it has 4
A word is missing in the RuWordNet vocabulary	9	The word *гипербола* 'hyperbole'
The senses from RuWordNet and RUSSE'18 dataset have only one sense in common	4	The word *мандарин* has two senses described in RUSSE'18: its sense 'tangerine' is included in the thesaurus, whereas its meaning 'mandarin, bureaucrat' is absent
Controversial cases of sense mapping	29	The word *демократ* 'democrat' has 2 senses: 'supporter of democracy' and 'a member of the Democratic Party'. But there's another one in RUSSE'18: 'a person of a democratic way of life, views'
Not enough examples for senses in the corpora	2	Words *карьер* 'quarry/a very fast gallop' and *шах* 'shah/check'
Words with morphological homonymy	1	The word *суда* 'court (Gen, Sg)/ship (Nom, Pl)'. Those words have distinct lemmas

The final list of the target ambiguous words contains 30 words in total, each having two different senses. We will call the resulting test dataset RUSSE-RuWordNet because it is a projection of RUSSE'18 sense inventory on the RuWordNet data.

We also created a small training dataset, that consists of the word sense definitions and examples of uses from Ozhegov dictionary [24] for every target polysemous word. This training data is utilized as a baseline for the WSD task. In this set each sense of ambiguous word has one definition and between 1 and 3 usage examples.

Table 3 demonstrates quantitative characteristics of all of the above-mentioned corpora.

Table 3. Quantitative characteristics of the corpora and datasets used in the experiments.

	Taiga-Proza.ru	News corpus	RUSSE-RuWordNet	Dictionary corpus (baseline)
Number of sentences	32,8 million	24,2 million	2 103	144
Number of lemmas	246,8 million	288,1 million	39 311	657
Number of unique lemmas	2,1 million	1,4 million	12 110	475

4 Candidate Selection and Ranking Algorithm

The central idea of our method is based on our assumption that a training collection can be built not only with the direct relations like synonymy, hypernymy and hyponymy but also with far more distant words, such as co-hyponyms. For example, most contexts for the word *крона* in the meaning 'krona, currency' match the contexts of the other words denoting currency like *английский фунт* 'pound sterling' as they have common hypernym *валюта* 'currency'.

The principal features of our approach are as follows:

1. We take into consideration not only the closest relatives to a target word sense, as it was done in previous works, but also more distant relatives.
2. We utilize similarity scores between a candidate monosemous relative and synsets close to a sense of a target polysemous word in order to evaluate how well this candidate can represent the sense of an ambiguous word.
3. We introduce the notion of *a nest* which is used to assess the potential of candidate's usage contexts for displaying target sense of a polysemous word. In order to measure the relevance and suitability of a monosemous candidate, we exploit a thesaurus set of words similar to a target sense. The group of synonyms to a target sense and all the words from directly related synsets within 2 steps from a target word comprise *the nest* for a target sense.
4. We check similarity scores to the nest for both closest and further located monosemous relatives because a word described as monosemous in the thesaurus can actually have polysemous usage in a corpus. For example, Russian word *ириска* 'toffee'

can also denote a nickname of Everton Football Club (The Toffees) [25]. Thus, all candidate monosemous relatives should be further checked on the source corpus.

5. We propose two distinct methods of compiling a training collection based on the monosemous relatives rating.

A target word sense is a sense of a polysemous word that we want to disambiguate. Candidate monosemous relatives are unambiguous words and phrases, that can be located in up to four-step relation paths to a polysemous word and include co-hyponyms, two step (or more) hyponyms and hypernyms. We consider only those words or word combinations, that have more than 50 occurrences in the corpus.

A fragment of the nest for the word *такса* 'dachshund' is given below:

(1) *"охотничий пёс, охотничья собака, пёсик, четвероногий друг, псина, собака, терьер, собачонка, борзая собака..."/*'hunting dog, hunting dog, doggie, four-legged friend, dog, dog, terrier, dog, greyhound dog...'

Our method of extracting monosemous relatives is based on comparison of distributional and thesaurus similarities. Embedding models are utilized to select the most appropriate monosemous relatives whose context serve as a good representation of a target word sense. In this work we utilized word2vec embedding models [26] based on neural network architecture CBOW. They are used to extract the most similar words to each monosemous word from the candidates list. In that way we collected the words that represent a distributional set of close words with the respective cosine similarities measures. Our selection and ranking method, thus, consists of the following steps:

1. We extract all the candidate monosemous relatives within 4 steps from a target polysemous word sense s_j.
2. We compile the nest ns_j which consists of synonyms to a target sense and all the words from the synsets within 2 steps from a target word s_j. The nest ns_j consists of N_k synsets.
3. For each candidate monosemous relative r_j, we find the most similar words according to the word2vec model trained on a reference corpus.
4. We intersect this list of similar words with the words included in the nest ns_j of the target sense s_j.
5. For each word in the intersection, we take its cosine similarity weight calculated with the word2vec model and assign it to the synset it belongs to. The final weight of the synset in the nest ns_j is determined by the maximum weight among the words $w_{k_1}^j, \ldots, w_{k_i}^j$ representing this synset in the intersection.
6. The total score of the monosemous candidate r_j is the sum of the weights of all synsets from the nest ns_j. In such a way more scores are assigned to those candidates, that resemble a greater number of synsets from the nest close the target sense of the ambiguous target word. Thus, the final weight of the candidate can be defined as follows:

$$Weight_{r_j} = \sum_{k=1}^{N_k} \max\left[cos\left(r_j, w_{k_1}^j\right), \ldots, cos\left(r_j, w_{k_i}^j\right)\right] \qquad (1)$$

The following fragment of list of monosemous relatives with similarity scores (given in brackets) was obtained for the noun *гвоздика* 'clove':

(2) *чёрный перец* 'black pepper' (7.5), *кардамон* 'cardamom' (6.8), *корица* 'cinnamon' (6.5), *имбирь* 'ginger' (6.4), *мускатный орех* 'nutmeg' (6) ... etc.

The pair of words *марля* and *байка* is an example where a monosemous word is connected to a sense of a target word but got zero similarity weight. The word *марля* 'gauze' is a cohyponym to the word *байка* in the meaning 'thick flannelette', but it was not included in the monosemous relatives list because its distributional set of close words did not have any intersection with the nest.

As a result of this procedure, all monosemous relatives are sorted by the weight they obtained. The higher-rated monosemous relatives are supposed to be better candidates to represent the sense of the target word and, consequently, their contexts of use are best suited as the training examples in the WSD task. The candidate ranking algorithm identifies which monosemous relatives are most similar to the target ambiguous word's sense. Once we have detected the monosemous candidates, we can extract from the corpus the contexts in which they occur. Then we substitute the monosemous relatives with the target ambiguous word in these texts and add them to a training collection.

In order to verify the applicability of our method to the RuWordNet material, we found candidate monosemous relatives for the ambiguous words in the thesaurus using our algorithm but without word2vec filter. Only two words out of 5895 do not have monosemous relatives within the four-step relation path in the RuWordNet graph. The quantitative characteristics of the candidate monosemous relatives are presented in Table 4. As it was mentioned in [2], 500 samples per sense is enough for training data. Table 5 demonstrates how many target senses have at least 500 samples of their monosemous relatives in a reference corpus. We also take into consideration the case when word2vec filter was applied to the candidate monosemous relatives. These tables show that by applying our approach to the RuWordNet data we would be able to find monosemous relatives to almost all the polysemous words in the thesaurus and create a training collection for a WSD system.

Table 4. Quantitative characteristics of candidate monosemous relatives for RuWordNet target senses.

Distance to a candidate monosemous relative	Number of target senses, that have at least one relative at this distance
0 (synset)	9 818
1	13 095
2	14 129
3	14 021
4	13 768

Table 5. Target senses with more than 500 occurrences of monosemous relatives in the corpora.

	Number of target senses when word2vec filter was not applied	Number of target senses when word2vec filter was applied
Taiga-Proza.ru	13 738	12 797
News corpus	14 017	13 099

5   Generating Training Data Using Monosemous Relatives

For comparison, we decided to create two separate training collections compiled from the news and Proza.ru corpora, and we also exploited two distinct approaches to a collection generation. In Table 6 we present the quantitative characteristics of the two collections, such as the relations connecting the target senses and their monosemous relatives, distances between them, and a proportion of monosemous relatives expressed as a phrase.

Table 6. Quantitative characteristics of monosemous relatives included in the balanced training collection.

Distance to a target sense	Proportion of occurrences in the news collection	Proportion of occurrences in Proza.ru collection
0 (synset)	2%	4%
1	13%	9%
2	38%	37%
3	31%	34%
4	16%	16%
Relation between a target sense and a monosemous relative		
Synonyms	2%	4%
Hyponyms	13%	8%
Hypernyms	11%	9%
Cohyponyms	28%	28%
Cohyponyms situated at three-step path	24%	28%
Cohyponyms situated at four-step path	19%	22%
Other	3%	1%
Word combinations	48%	29%

According to the first method, we compiled the collection only with a monosemous relative from the top of the candidate rating. We wanted to obtain 1000 examples for each of the target words, but sometimes it was not possible to extract so many contexts with one particular candidate. That is why in some cases we also took examples with words next on the candidates' list. For simplicity, we call this collection Corpus-1000 because we obtained exactly 1000 examples for each sense.

The second approach enables to harvest more representative collection with regard to the variety of contexts. The training examples for the target ambiguous words were collected with the help of all respective unambiguous relatives with non-zero weight. The number of extracted contexts per a monosemous candidate is in direct proportion to its weight. We name this collection a balanced one because the selection of training examples was not restricted to the contexts which have only one particular monosemous relative.

Two word2vec embedding models that we used in our experiments were trained separately on the news and Proza.ru corpora with the window size of 3. As a preprocessing step, we split the corpora into separate sentences, tokenized them, removed all the stop words, and lemmatized the words with pymorphy2 tool [27]. For each candidate monosemous relative with the help of these models, we extracted 100 most similar words, that are used to find an intersection with a synset nest. The words obtained from the word2vec models were filtered out – we removed the ones not included in the thesaurus.

6 Experiments

We conducted several experiments to determine whether our text collection can be used as a training dataset for a WSD model. Following [18], in our research we used an easily interpretable classification algorithm – non-parametric nearest neighbor classification (kNN) based on the contextualized word embeddings ELMo and BERT.

In our experiments we exploited two distinct ELMo models – the one trained by DeepPavlov on Russian WMT News and the other is RusVectōrēs [28] lemmatized ELMo model trained on Taiga Corpus [21]. The difference between these two models is that from the first model we extracted a vector for a whole sentence with a target word, whereas from the second model we extracted a single vector for a target ambiguous word. We also used two BERT models: BERT-base-multilingual-cased released by Google Research and RuBERT, which was trained on the Russian part of Wikipedia and news data by DeepPavlov [29]. To extract BERT contextual representations, we followed the method described by [5] and [18] and concatenated "the token representations from the top four hidden layers of the pre-trained Transformer" [5].

Tables 7 and 8 demonstrate the results obtained by different types of contextualized word embeddings, the training collections, and model parameters. As it can clearly be seen, all the systems surpassed the quality level of the baseline solution trained on the dataset of the dictionary definitions and usage examples. This means that we have managed not only to collect training data sufficient to train the WSD model but also to show a good performance on the RUSSE-RuWordNet dataset.

The algorithm based on the ELMo pre-trained embeddings by RusVectōrēs outperformed all other models achieving 0.857 F1 score. The second-best model in the WSD

Table 7. F1 scores for ELMo- and BERT-based WSD models, corpus-1000 collections.

Model	ELMo RusVectōrēs (target word)		ELMo DeepPavlov (whole sentence)		RuBERT DeepPavlov		Multilingual BERT	
k	Proza.ru	News collection	Proza.ru	News collection	Proza.ru	News collection	Proza.ru	News collection
1	0.809	0.794	0.765	**0.752**	0.751	0.735	0.668	0.67
3	0.826	0.811	**0.773**	0.749	0.781	0.756	0.684	0.673
5	0.834	**0.819**	0.77	0.748	0.793	0.771	0.694	0.667
7	**0.841**	**0.819**	0.767	0.746	**0.804**	**0.774**	0.699	0.673
9	0.84	0.816	0.762	0.747	0.802	0.769	**0.7**	**0.677**
Baseline	0.772		0.716		0.667		0.672	

Table 8. F1 scores for ELMo- and BERT-based WSD models, balanced collections.

Model	ELMo RusVectōrēs (target word)		ELMo DeepPavlov (whole sentence)		RuBERT DeepPavlov		Multilingual BERT	
k	Proza.ru	News collection	Proza.ru	News collection	Proza.ru	News collection	Proza.ru	News collection
1	0.812	0.797	0.745	0.758	0.746	0.75	0.669	0.662
3	0.833	0.81	0.775	0.753	0.778	0.755	0.707	0.681
5	0.845	0.81	0.776	0.756	0.792	0.769	0.717	0.682
7	**0.857**	0.815	**0.793**	**0.759**	0.802	0.768	0.723	0.683
9	0.856	**0.821**	0.791	0.753	**0.812**	**0.774**	**0.729**	**0.688**
Baseline	0.772		0.716		0.667		0.672	

task is RuBERT by DeepPavlov, followed by ELMo model by DeepPavlov. The lowest F1 score belongs to Multilingual BERT.

As for the difference in F1 scores between the Corpus-1000 and the balanced collection, we can observe the performance drop for the Corpus-1000 for all the models, which means that the approach used to generate the balanced collection is better suited for the task. Corpus-1000 does not include all possible monosemous relatives, so the collection lacks contextual diversity, the balanced collection, on the contrary, is more representative with regard to the variety of contexts.

The Proza.ru model achieves better results and outperforms the news model. The qualitative analysis of the classification errors caused by the model trained on the news collection showed that the main cause of mistakes were lexical and structural differences between training and test sets. The examples from the test dataset were from the Russian National Corpus and Wikipedia, whereas the training collections were composed of news articles. On the contrary, Proza.ru collection consists of various works of fiction, so, the training samples have more similar representations to the test ones.

In order to validate our assumption that a genre of training and test collections has an impact on the resulting performance, we evaluated the WSD model on a news dataset. This time, we took a test dataset that consist of the news articles from the paper Komsomolskaya Pravda, which is another segment of Taiga corpus [21]. We manually annotated 390 samples with 27 target ambiguous words (there were no contexts in this test dataset with the words *бор* 'pine forest/boron', *лук* 'onion/bow' and *гвоздика* 'clove/carnation'). In this evaluation experiment we used RusVectōrēs ELMo model. The best result on this test dataset was obtained by the model trained on the news collection and amounted to 0.784 F1; the model trained on the Proza.ru collections got 0.743 F1 score. Thus, this finding confirms our assumption, that the better performance in the WSD task is achieved when the genre of the training and test collections match.

In the last experiment we compared the WSD model performance trained on the automatically and manually labelled data. In this case we also used RusVectōrēs ELMo contextualized embeddings. We took the RUSSE-RuWordNet dataset; for each target sense we generated 5 random divisions of its samples into train and test sets in the ratio 2:1. Then we used this data to train and test 5 different WSD models. Among all the results obtained by each classifier, we took the maximum value, and the final performance score was the average of these 5 F1 values. The F1 in this setup amounted to 0.917.

Then we computed F1 score on these 5 test sets using our model trained on the news corpus. We obtained F1 score equal to 0.84. And, finally, we combined our news training collection with each train set described above, and measured the performance on the corresponding test sets. The F1 score was 0.94.

Despite the fact that manually annotated data gives better WSD performance, we can still count on the automatically labelled data as it also gives good results comparable with the results obtained with the hand-labelled data. Also, we see that our proposed algorithm provided a very good basis for future work and, certainly, can be further improved. Moreover, our results show that manually labelled data combined with the generated one can enhance the overall performance.

7 Conclusion

The issue that we addressed in this article is the lack of sense-annotated training data for supervised WSD systems in Russian. In this paper we have described our algorithm of automatic collection and annotation of training data for the Russian language. The main contribution of the paper is that we have utilized in the selection algorithm not only close monosemous relatives but also more distant ones. Moreover, we implemented the procedure of ranking monosemous relatives' candidates. Our training collections consist of the texts extracted from the news and Proza.ru corpora. The candidate scores were obtained from two word2vec models trained separately on each corpus.

In order to evaluate the training collections, we applied kNN classifier to the contextualized word embeddings extracted for target polysemous words and measured its performance on the RUSSE-RuWordNet test dataset. We have investigated the capability of different deep contextualized word representations to model polysemy. The best result on the generated text collections was obtained with the Proza.ru training collection and RusVectōrēs ELMo model and amounted to 0.857 F1 score. The combination of automatically and manually labelled training data gives the highest F1 score among all other WSD models under consideration. We also found out that the genre of the training collection has an impact on the performance on the test dataset of the same genre.

Acknowledgments. The work is partially supported by the RFBR foundation (project N 18-00-01226 (18-00-01240)).

References

1. Miller, G.A., Leacock, C., Tengi, R., Bunker, R.T.: A semantic concordance. In: Proceedings of the workshop on Human Language Technology, pp. 303–308. Association for Computational Linguistics (1993)
2. Taghipour, K., Ng, H.T.: One million sense-tagged instances for word sense disambiguation and induction. In: Proceedings of the Nineteenth Conference on Computational Natural Language Learning, pp. 338–344 (2015)
3. Martinez, D., Agirre, E., Wang, X.: Word relatives in context for word sense disambiguation. In: Proceedings of the Australasian Language Technology Workshop 2006, pp. 42–50 (2006)
4. Peters, M., et al.: Deep contextualized word representations. In: Proceedings of the 2018 Conference of the North American Chapter of the Association for Computational Linguistics: Human Language Technologies, pp. 2227–2237 (2018)
5. Devlin, J., Chang, M.-W., Lee, K., Toutanova, K. BERT: pre-training of deep bidirectional transformers for language understanding. In: Proceedings of the 2019 Conference of the North American Chapter of the Association for Computational Linguistics: Human Language Technologies, pp. 4171–4186 (2019)
6. Leacock, C., Miller, G.A., Chodorow, M.: Using corpus statistics and WordNet relations for sense identification. Comput. Linguist. **24**(1), 147–165 (1998)
7. Miller, G.: WordNet: a lexical database for English. Commun. ACM **38**(11), 39–41 (1995)
8. Przybyła, P.: How big is big enough? Unsupervised word sense disambiguation using a very large corpus. arXiv preprint arXiv:1710.07960 (2017)
9. Mihalcea, R., Moldovan, D.I.: An iterative approach to word sense disambiguation. In: FLAIRS Conference, pp. 219–223 (2000)
10. Seo, H.C., Chung, H., Rim, H.C., Myaeng, S.H., Kim, S.H.: Unsupervised word sense disambiguation using WordNet relatives. Comput. Speech Lang. **18**(3), 253–273 (2004)
11. Yuret, D.: KU: word sense disambiguation by substitution. In: Proceedings of the 4th International Workshop on Semantic Evaluations, pp. 207–213. Association for Computational Linguistics (2007)
12. Mihalcea, R.: Bootstrapping large sense tagged corpora. In: Proceedings of the Third International Conference on Language Resources and Evaluation (LREC-2002), Las Palmas, Canary Islands, Spain, vol. 1999 (2002)
13. Loukachevitch, N., Chetviorkin, I.: Determining the most frequent senses using Russian linguistic ontology RuThes. In: Proceedings of the Workshop on Semantic Resources and Semantic Annotation for Natural Language Processing and the Digital Humanities at NODALIDA 2015, pp. 21–27 (2015)
14. Henrich, V., Hinrichs, E., Vodolazova, T.: WebCAGe: a web-harvested corpus annotated with GermaNet senses. In: Proceedings of the 13th Conference of the European Chapter of the Association for Computational Linguistics, pp. 387–396. Association for Computational Linguistics (2012)

15. Agirre, E., De Lacalle, O.L.: Publicly available topic signatures for all WordNet nominal senses. In: LREC (2004)
16. Pasini, T., Navigli, R.: Train-O-Matic: large-scale supervised word sense disambiguation in multiple languages without manual training data. In: Proceedings of the 2017 Conference on Empirical Methods in Natural Language Processing, pp. 78–88 (2017)
17. Navigli, R.: Word sense disambiguation: a survey. ACM Comput. Surv. (CSUR) **41**(2), 10 (2009)
18. Wiedemann, G., Remus, S., Chawla, A., Biemann, C.: Does BERT make any sense? Interpretable word sense disambiguation with contextualized embeddings. arXiv preprint arXiv: 1909.10430 (2019)
19. Kutuzov, A., Kuzmenko, E.: To lemmatize or not to lemmatize: how word normalisation affects ELMo performance in word sense disambiguation. In: Proceedings of the First NLPL Workshop on Deep Learning for Natural Language Processing, pp. 22–28 (2019)
20. Loukachevitch, N.V., Lashevich, G., Gerasimova, A.A., Ivanov, V.V., Dobrov, B.V.: Creating Russian WordNet by conversion. In: Proceedings of Conference on Computational linguistics and Intellectual technologies Dialog-2016, pp. 405–415 (2016)
21. Shavrina, T., Shapovalova, O.: To the methodology of corpus construction for machine learning: «Taiga» syntax tree corpus and parser. In: Proceedings of "CORPORA2017", International Conference, Saint-Petersbourg (2017)
22. Panchenko, A., et al.: RUSSE'2018: a shared task on word sense induction for the Russian language. In: Computational Linguistics and Intellectual Technologies: Papers from the Annual International Conference "Dialogue", Moscow, Russia. RSUH, pp. 547–564 (2018)
23. Lopukhina, A.A., et al.: Active Dictionary of the Russian Language [Aktivnyj slovar' russkogo yazyka], vol. 3. Publishing House Nestor-Istoria, Moscow (2017)
24. Ozhegov, S.I.: Explanatory Dictionary of the Russian Language. Ed. by Skvortsova S.I., 8, p. 1376 (2014)
25. Loukachevitch, N.: Corpus-based check-up for thesaurus. In: Proceedings of the 57th Annual Meeting of the Association for Computational Linguistics, pp. 5773–5779 (2019)
26. Mikolov, T., Chen, K., Corrado G., Dean, J. Efficient estimation of word representations in vector space. In: Proceedings of Workshop at ICLR (2013)
27. Korobov, M.: Morphological analyzer and generator for Russian and Ukrainian languages. In: Analysis of Images, Social Networks and Texts, pp. 320–332 (2015)
28. Kutuzov, A., Kuzmenko, E.: WebVectors: a toolkit for building web interfaces for vector semantic models. In: Ignatov, Dmitry I., et al. (eds.) AIST 2016. CCIS, vol. 661, pp. 155–161. Springer, Cham (2017). https://doi.org/10.1007/978-3-319-52920-2_15
29. Kuratov, Y., Arkhipov, M.: Adaptation of deep bidirectional multilingual transformers for Russian language. arXiv preprint arXiv:1905.07213 (2019)

Revealing Implicit Relations in Russian Legal Texts

Dmitry Devyatkin[1]([✉])[iD], Anna Sofronova[2][iD], and Vasily Yadrintsev[1][iD]

[1] Federal Research Centre «Computer Science and Control» RAS, Moscow, Russia
{devyatkin,yadrintsev}@isa.ru
[2] «Technologies for Systems Analysis» LLC, Moscow, Russia
sofronova@tesyan.ru

Abstract. In this paper, new methods for detecting implicit links between legal documents are proposed. Those methods are based on approaches for building vector representations of words, such as Word2Vec, FastText, as well as vector representations of texts and sentences: BERT and Doc2Vec. In addition, as part of this study, we propose an approach to create a dataset for the detection of implicit links and provide such a dataset. The dataset contains more than 36K Russian legal documents. The experiments on that dataset show applicability of the proposed methods. Namely, BERT-based fine-tuned models show the best performance; however, they have the highest demand for memory and computational resources.

Keywords: Legal information extraction · Detection of implicit relationships · Word and document embeddings · Fine-tuning

1 Introduction

Every day, large amounts of data are created and analyzed in the field of normative activity. Despite such large amounts of information, automation in this area is still poorly developed. Existing digital systems that work with this type of information do not deeply analyze the received data, and their functions are limited only to the systematization of legislation in the form of electronic resources and reference books. At the same time, machine learning-based methods of extracting information from information search are hardly used [1, 2].

The main distinguishing feature of legal texts compared to other ones is a large number of explicit and implicit links to other documents. They also contain paraphrased or identical text fragments of other documents. Therefore, it would be helpful to create the method of automated identification of explicit and implicit links between documents. That may later lead to a change in the approach to the creation and adoption of legal acts, as well as to a significant increase in the efficiency of systematization and analysis of lawmaking activity. However, the main problem of such linking is that most of the

The paper is supported by Russian Foundation for Basic Research (grant № 18-29-16022 mk, grant № 18-29-16172 mk).

S. O. Kuznetsov et al. (Eds.): RCAI 2020, LNAI 12412, pp. 228–239, 2020.
https://doi.org/10.1007/978-3-030-59535-7_16

legal texts are fragmented. That means if one fragment links to a text, it really refers to a tiny part of that text only (and in case of implicit linking one does not know where that part is), whereas all other parts of the text are irrelevant.

In this paper, we propose new methods for identifying implicit links between legal documents. Those methods are based on embedding algorithms such as BERT [3], Doc2Vec [4], Word2Vec [5], and FastText [6], which allow us to evaluate the proximity of texts, with not only the pure lexis but also to consider latent relations between implicit high-level features. Besides, those methods presume fragment-wise comparison of the analyzed documents, which should mitigate the mentioned issue. Such methods would have the following applications.

- Assessment of coherence of some legal corpora. It might help reveal contradicting pairs of legal acts or state-level acts that are not supported well by acts of local communities and vice-versa local acts that outlaw the state-level ones.
- Automated linking of texts in legal corpora, including quality assessment of manual linking. This might gain the performance of the current legal information retrieval systems and systematization tools as well as significantly reduce the time required for their support.

However, the lack of datasets suitable for training such methods remains an issue. In this study, we collected a dataset of more than 450K legal documents containing regulatory documents from various areas of this activity to train the mentioned embedding models in an unsupervised manner. Besides, 36K documents from that dataset were extracted, automatically linked, and stored as a separate corpus, which we have employed to train and validate the proposed methods.

On the whole, the main contributions of the paper are the following.

1. Unlabeled corpus of various legal documents in Russian.
2. Doc2Vec, Word2Vec, and FastText embedding models pre-trained on the unlabeled corpus.
3. Russian legal text corpus with tagged relations between documents.
4. Multilayer neural network architectures for predicting implicit relations between legal texts in Russian.

The rest of the paper is organized as follows. Section 2 provides a brief review of the state-of-the-art approaches related to revealing the relation between legal texts. Section 3 contains a description of the approach to building labeled datasets for relation extraction as well as provides a description of such a dataset. Section 4 and 5 describe the proposed methods and presents the results of their experimental validation.

2 Related Work

Legal text processing is a prominent research topic for the last decades; however, the lack of labeled corpora leads to the condition when the most solutions for the legal text linking are still rule-based or consider shallow features only. For example, in [7], researchers propose a text similarity method for precedence retrieval. The method retrieves older cases which are similar to given ones from a set of legal documents. They consider lexical features, which are extracted from all the legal documents and apply cosine similarity scores to evaluate the similarity between each current case document and all the previous case ones. Then the list of prior case documents is ranked based on the similarity scores for each current case document. The similar approach is presented in [8]. The key idea here is to apply rule-based information extraction methodologies by identifying distinct expressions in a legal text to extract the references to other documents. In [9], researchers compared the performance of the rule-based approach with the SVM and HMM-based methods for revealing a structure of legal documents in Chinese. The results show that the rule-based approach outperforms the statistics based ones.

However, there are several studies devoted to the automated creation of datasets for legal text processing. Namely, the paper [10] presents an approach to developing a corpus of administrative regulations, related to domain name disputes. That approach requires a small amount of manual labeled data and rules to extend feature labels to the entire corpus automatically. Another way to infer rich features from legal texts can lie in unsupervised training of embeddings, language models or Transformer-based networks [11]. For example, in [12], the researchers propose an approach to train semantic feature representations over large corpora, comprised of legislations from the UK, EU, Canada, Australia, USA, and Japan. Besides, they have trained and qualitatively tested word2vec and FastText embedding models. The obtained results show that word2vec provides better interpretable results than FastText, which is because missing words is not an issue in most legal-related problems.

Those works make it possible to consider more complex NLP and legal-originated features and models. It is worth to note the paper [13], which presents a hybrid approach for evaluating the similarity between legal documents. The approach considers text features as well as exhaustive structural features to deal with a peculiar structure of legal documents. That approach outperforms the classical ones, such as LDA (Latent Dirichlet Allocation) [14] and Doc2Vec.

Language models are also widely used for legal information retrieval and extraction, for example, the paper [15] proposes the method, which combines text summarizing and a generalized language model in order to assess pairwise relevance of legal documents. Namely, at first, the TextRank [16] tool is applied to build a summarization of the texts, and then the BERT model predicts the score. Thus the researchers do not tackle the fragmenting problem in that work. Similarly, the paper [17] deals with a legal information retrieval problem. It suggests combining deep neural BERT model with BM25 scoring to tackle the problem. As a result, such an approach shows better retrieval precision than either BERT or BM25.

Some types of legal documents have a lot of abbreviations, especially in the links to other texts, therefore it is crucial to treat them properly. Paper [18] presents character-level language models for revealing cross-references to structural units in legal texts. The provided evaluation results show the proposed method is well applicable for that problem.

Another method for revealing links between legal texts has been presented in [19]. The method utilizes reinforcement learning; namely, it reinforces the cases when a link is correctly detected. A multi-layer neural network with Extractor-Rewarder architecture lies in the base of the method. However, the method shows only slightly better results in comparison to the baseline GRU-based network with attention.

It is worth to note the paper [20], which combines different-level vector representations to deal with the fragmenting issue. Namely, BERT is used to build token-level embeddings for each fragment, whilst LSTM aggregates them and generates the summary output. The BERT allows considering NLP as well as context features implicitly, while LSTM catches long-range dependencies between fragments. The experiments on a labeled dataset show the method outperforms a rule-based approach as well as an SVM-based classifier. It is worth noting that although LSTM mitigates the gradient vanishing problem, its applicability for analyzing large sequences is still significantly limited; thus, that method is more useful for short texts.

Paper [21] proposes to deal with the fragmenting issue in another way. First of all, they apply the topic search to filter the documents, which are totally dissimilar to the target. After that, they split the remaining documents onto passages, and check each passage with LSTM-based network with attention [22]. The provided evaluation on the MaRisk corpus [23] shows that the proposed approach outperforms the others in terms of precision and recall. A completely different approach is proposed in [24]. That approach consists of applying hierarchical clusterization for revealing fragments and links between them; therefore, it does not require any labeled corpora for training. However, there are some drawbacks, namely the approach relies on lexical features only, and it is quite hard to fine-tune it.

An alternative approach to deal with the linking problem is to build high-level representations for each fragment and then to utilize information retrieval (IR) algorithms. The motivation behind such an approach is that IR algorithms have high performance; therefore, they allow analyzing large legal corpora. For example, Tran with colleagues proposed a method for solving the problem via summarizing documents with the neural network-based phrase scoring framework [25]. They explored the benefits of merging lexical features and latent features generated with neural networks. The experiments show that lexical features and sophisticated hidden features created with neural networks complement each other to improve the retrieval system performance.

Having those works considered, we should conclude that there are two main obstacles in the legal text processing: the lack of labeled corpora and negligence to the structural and context features of legal documents. Hence we propose an automated approach to generating large legal text corpora with tagged relations between documents. Moreover, we applied the approach to create such a corpus for Russian legal texts. Besides, we propose several models which utilize word and paragraph-level embeddings as well as Transformer-based networks for linking legal documents.

3 Legal Text Data Set

The unlabeled dataset contains about 450K legal documents and almost 812M tokens, which have been crawled from several Russian legal resources [26]. The size of the texts varies significantly from short notes to whole codes. We used that dataset to train two embedding models for Russian legal text with FastText and Doc2Vec frameworks.

Gensim library was used to train and infer both models [27], and we relied mostly on the default hyper-parameters threshold, provided by that library. The only except is that due to the small size of the corpus, the dimensionality of the embeddings is quite small too. Namely, it is 60 and 20 for FastText and the Doc2Vec, respectively.

The labeled corpus has more than 36K legal documents on Russian, selected randomly from the unlabeled dataset. We processed all those documents in the following way (Fig. 1). First of all, we indexed all the unlabeled corpora with the TextAppliance informational retrieval system [28]. Then we split the selected documents into fixed-size fragments. The length of each fragment is 30 tokens. This was due to technical reasons; namely, as we are going to use BERT, it supports text length up to 512 tokens. However, we iteratively compare pairs of fragments, besides BERT has its own tokenizer, which splits long tokens into several parts. Therefore, we limited that size to such a small number, so as to have a room for each fragment. After that, we extracted explicit links with a simple rule-based approach and sought linked documents for each fragment with the TextAppliance. If the existing corpus lacked some referenced document, then we downloaded and added it. Finally, the explicit links were removed from the fragments.

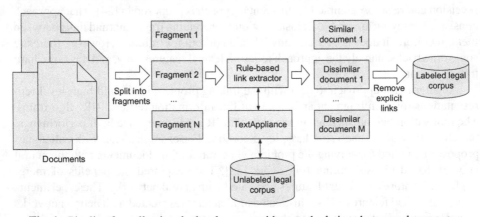

Fig. 1. Pipeline for collecting the legal corpus with tagged relations between documents

The obtained corpus contains more than 2 billion tokens and about 160K *<fragment, text, label>* tuples, where the label is set to "1" if there is a relation between the fragment and the text and to "0" otherwise.

4 Models for Predicting Implicit Relations

As we noted, the key issue of legal text linking is that the most legal documents are actually fragmented. That means if a paragraph has a link to some text, it usually refers to some very small passage of that text, and one often does not know where exactly that passage is, whereas all remaining parts are non-relevant in fact. Therefore common approaches, which summarize whole documents, are not well-suited for solving the problem. We propose several architectures which work on text fragment level and apply self-attention to tackle the mentioned issue. Namely, we propose a model for word embedding inputs (FastText or Word2Vec), a model for passage-level embedding inputs (Doc2Vec), and a model that incorporates the BERT network.

The Doc2Vec-based and Word-embeddings-based models both have similar architecture. They have two inputs: the first one is for a paragraph (we refer to it as "Targeted fragment") and the second one is for a text (separated on fragments as well, so we call them "Text fragments"). The only difference is that we added embedding summation for each fragment to the Word-embeddings-based model (Fig. 2). The latter model uses pre-summation for all word-level embeddings for each fragment. It is less efficient than generalization with recurrent layers; however, it leads to less memory consumption That is worth it because legal texts can be quite large, but at the same time, we want to ensure it works with limited hardware resources. Therefore, the size of the performance gap of the Word-embeddings-based models with the recurrent layer remains an open question and requires future research.

Both the models return probability score of the presence of a link between the paragraph and the text. All fragment-level embeddings are connected to attention layer, which gets "Target fragment" as a key and list of text fragments as a value and gains weights for the most important text fragments. Finally, the models obtain common flatten representation of the "Target Fragment" and the "Text Fragments" with pooling and concatenation. After that, there can be two types of the output layers.

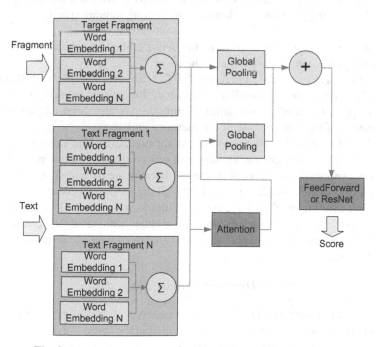

Fig. 2. Network architecture for Word2Vec and FastText inputs

1. A feedforward network with a softmax activation in the last layer processes the representations and outputs the score.
2. A residual network with a softmax activation in the last layer, which can help reducing gradient vanishing and increasing training speed.

As we used the softmax in the last layer, the obtained score varies from "0" for the definite absence of the link between the text and the target fragment to "1" in the opposite case.

We have implemented those models with TensorFlow-Keras library [29].

The architecture of the BERT-based model is presented in Fig. 3. At first, BERT layer builds representations for the "Target fragment" and "Text Fragments". We borrowed pre-trained BERT from Slavic BERT NER project [30] because it can process texts in Russian. The BERT model has not been trained on the legal dataset from scratch, just fine-tuned because we considered the existing datasets to be too small. After that, first token representations (CLS tokens) for each fragment are gathered from the BERT layer and put into the self-attention layer to gain the most important fragments. Finally, we consider using two types of summarization.

1. A global pooling layer and softmax activation to flatten the fragment representation and obtain the output score.
2. A Transformer-like residual network with a softmax activation in the last layer, which can help reducing gradient vanishing and increasing training speed.

Here we again used softmax like in the word embeddings-based model, so the interpretation of the output score remains the same.

We had to apply Pytorch [31] and AllenNLP [32] libraries to implement BERT-based networks, because of Tensorflow-caused memory limitations, related to a TimeDistributed wrapper. Gradient accumulation technique has also been employed for the training instead of batches, because of the memory limitations.

For all of the networks, we used dropout for regularization. Value of dropout as well as the size of inner layers was chosen with cross-validation. The type of the global pooling is not specified here (Max or Average), because we have obtained only slightly different results for them on all the models. As all the proposed networks have a single output, which varies from "0" to "1", we used binary cross-entropy loss to train them.

Besides, as a baseline we propose a simple algorithm, which evaluates cosine distance between the target and all fragments of the analyzed document and returns the minimal obtained distance:

$$dist(f, D) = \min_{d \in D}(\cos\_dist(f, d)), \tag{1}$$

where f – target fragment, and $D = \{d\}$ – document (set of fragments). Then we trained a simple metric classifier on those distances to predict the links.

a)

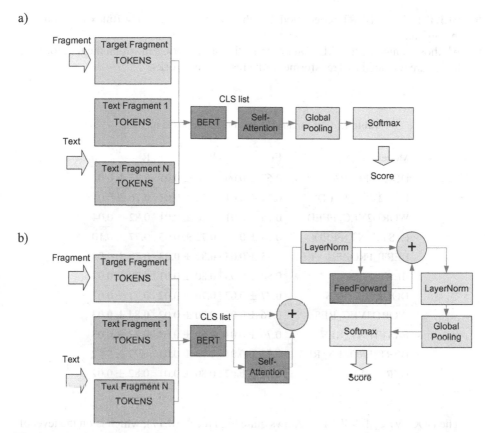

b)

Fig. 3. BERT-based networks: global pooling (a); transformer-like block and global pooling (b)

5 Experiment Results

We applied 5-fold cross-validation and commonly recognized scores (binary F_1, precision and recall) to assess the performance of the proposed models. The samples, for which the relationship exists, was chosen as the target ones [33]. Table 1 shows the obtained scores and their standard deviations. We use the following abbreviations on the table.

1. DOC2VEC_BASELINE – Baseline model, based on evaluating cosine similarity between Doc2Vec vectors.
2. DOC2VEC_FEED – Model with Doc2Vec inputs, global pooling and feedforward layers.
3. WORD2VEC_FEED, FASTTEXT_FEED – Model with Word2Vec or FastText inputs, global pooling and feedforward layers.
4. BERT_FROZEN_FEED – BERT-based model with global pooling and softmax activation in the output, on which layers of the BERT are fixed, they do not change during the training.

5. BERT_FEED – BERT-based model with global pooling and softmax activation in the output.
6. All those names with "_RES" at the end – the same models in which the feedforward layers are replaced to Transformers-like residual networks.

Table 1. Performance scores of the proposed models.

Model	F_1	P	R
DOC2VEC_BASELINE	0.67 ± 0.09	0.60 ± 0.01	0.77 ± 0.01
DOC2VEC_FEED	0.74 ± 0.01	0.72 ± 0.01	0.76 ± 0.01
WORD2VEC_FEED	0.75 ± 0.01	0.70 ± 0.01	0.82 ± 0.04
FASTTEXT_FEED	0.74 ± 0.03	0.72 ± 0.05	0.77 ± 0.10
BERT_FROZEN_FEED	0.75 ± 0.05	$\mathbf{0.81 \pm 0.03}$	0.70 ± 0.08
BERT_FEED	0.80 ± 0.03	0.80 ± 0.01	0.79 ± 0.03
DOC2VEC_RES	0.77 ± 0.02	0.76 ± 0.02	0.77 ± 0.02
WORD2VEC_RES	0.76 ± 0.01	0.70 ± 0.02	$\mathbf{0.84 \pm 0.03}$
FASTTEXT_RES	0.76 ± 0.01	0.69 ± 0.03	0.83 ± 0.03
BERT_FROZEN_RES	0.75 ± 0.01	0.73 ± 0.01	0.77 ± 0.02
BERT_RES	$\mathbf{0.81 \pm 0.02}$	0.80 ± 0.01	0.82 ± 0.02

The DOC2VEC_BASELINE shows quite high recall (0.77), which is on the level of the others; however, precision is low. That means cosine similarities between fragments do not always keep enough information to reveal relations accurately.

Notice, that BERT with frozen weights outperforms neither doc2vec-based nor word-level-based models; therefore, it seems that such an applying of BERT for that problem is not useful. However, BERT with enabled fine-tune (BERT_FEED, BERT_RES) out-performs the other models significantly, which makes the BERT-based models the most promising solution for the problem.

Another unexpected outcome is that Doc2Vec-based models only slightly outperform the word-level based ones. The reason for that seems to be in the quite small size of the fragments (30 tokens). Realizing that it is just a technical limitation of BERT, it would be promising to test Doc2Vec with other sizes of the fragments. It is also worth to note that exchanging feedforward layers to residual ones leads to increasing of F_1-score on about 1–2% and to more robust results for almost all of the models.

6   Conclusion and Future Work

In this study, we have implemented and evaluated several models for identifying implicit links between legal documents. Those models are based either on embedding algorithms such as Doc2Vec, Word2Vec, and FastText or Transformers (BERT). In contrast to baseline approaches, they allow evaluating the similarity of documents considering latent relations between implicit high-level features. Besides, they can deal with the fragmented structure of the analyzed documents. The experiment shows that the fine-tuned BERT-based model provides the highest accuracy of implicit relation revealing. However, it is also the most demanding in terms of memory consumption. Therefore, we are going to employ different lightweight implementations of BERT, such as RoBERTa [34] and Distill-BERT [35].

We are also going to test recurrent network-based language models such as ELMO [36] and ELMo Sentence Representation Convolutional (ESRC) [37] because they are lighter, but still keeping the fine-tuning ability. It is also would be useful to evaluate the proposed Doc2Vec-based model with different fragment sizes, because that network does not have any technical limits on the fragment size, so the better results could be obtained if we found some subject area-motivated threshold.

Another promising direction of developing for the current research would be testing cross-language embeddings, for example, LASER [38]. This way one could assess the conformity between state and international law.

References

1. Sannier, N., Adedjouma, M., Sabetzadeh, M., Briand, L.: Automated classification of legal cross references based on semantic intent. In: Daneva, M., Pastor, O. (eds.) REFSQ 2016. LNCS, vol. 9619, pp. 119–134. Springer, Cham (2016). https://doi.org/10.1007/978-3-319-30282-9_8
2. Kevin, D.: Automatically Extracting Meaning From Legal Texts: Opportunities and Challenges (2019)
3. Devlin, J., et al.: BERT: pre-training of deep bidirectional transformers for language understanding. arXiv preprint arXiv:1810.04805 (2018)
4. Le, Q., Mikolov, T.: Distributed representations of sentences and documents. In: International Conference on Machine Learning, pp. 1188–1196 (2014)
5. Mikolov, T., et al.: Distributed representations of words and phrases and their compositionality. In: Advances In Neural Information Processing Systems, pp. 3111–3119 (2013)
6. Mikolov, T., et al.: Advances in pre-training distributed word representations. In: Proceedings of the Eleventh International Conference on Language Resources and Evaluation (LREC 2018) (2018)
7. Thenmozhi, D., Kannan, K., Aravindan, C.: A text similarity approach for precedence retrieval from legal documents. In: FIRE (Working Notes), pp. 90–91 (2017)
8. Sakhaee, N., Wilson, M.C.: Information extraction framework to build legislation network. Artif. Intell. Law., 1–24 (2020)
9. Sun, B.: Information structure parsing for chinese legal texts: a discourse analysis perspective. Int. J. Technol. Hum. Interact. (IJTHI) 15(1), 46–64 (2019)
10. Ferro, L., et al.: Scalable methods for annotating legal-decision corpora. In: Proceedings of the Natural Legal Language Processing Workshop 2019, pp. 12–20 (2019)
11. Vaswani, A., et al.: Attention is all you need. In: Advances in Neural Information Processing Systems, pp. 5998–6008 (2017)
12. Chalkidis, I., Kampas, D.: Deep learning in law: early adaptation and legal word embeddings trained on large corpora. Artif. Intell. Law 27(2), 171–198 (2018). https://doi.org/10.1007/s10506-018-9238-9

13. Li, S., Guo, B., Cai, Y., Ye, L., Zhang, H., Fang, B.: Legal case inspection: an analogy-based approach to judgment evaluation. In: Sun, X., Pan, Z., Bertino, E. (eds.) ICAIS 2019. LNCS, vol. 11632, pp. 148–158. Springer, Cham (2019). https://doi.org/10.1007/978-3-030-24274-9_13

14. Blei, D.M., Ng, A.Y., Jordan, M.I.: Latent dirichlet allocation. J. Mach. Learn. Res. **3**, 993–1022 (2003)

15. Rossi, J., Kanoulas, E.: Legal information retrieval with generalized language models. In: Proceedings of the 6th Competition on Legal Information Extraction/Entailment. COLIEE (2019)

16. Mihalcea, R., Tarau, P.: TextRank: bringing order into text. In: Proceedings of the 2004 Conference on Empirical Methods in Natural Language Processing, pp. 404–411 (2004)

17. Gain, B., et al.: IITP in COLIEE@ ICAIL 2019: legal information retrieval using BM25 and BERT (2019)

18. Smywinski-Pohl, A., et al.: Application of character-level language models in the domain of polish statutory law. In: JURIX, pp. 217–222 (2019)

19. Jiang, X., Ye, H., Luo, Z., Chao, W., Ma, W.: Interpretable rationale augmented charge prediction system. In: Proceedings of the 27th International Conference on Computational Linguistics: System Demonstrations, pp. 146–151 (2018)

20. Shaffer, R., Mayhew, S.: Legal linking: citation resolution and suggestion in constitutional law. In: Proceedings of the Natural Legal Language Processing Workshop 2019, pp. 39–44 (2019)

21. Collarana, D., et al.: A question answering system on regulatory documents. In: JURIX, pp. 41–50 (2018)

22. Hochreiter, S., Schmidhuber, J.: Long short-term memory. Neural Comput. **9**(8), 1735–1780 (1997)

23. MaRisk corpus. https://www.bafin.de/SharedDocs/Veroeffentlichungen/EN/Meldung/2014/meldung_140815_marisk_uebersetzung_en.html. Accessed 29 Apr 2020

24. Wehnert, S., et al.: Concept hierarchy extraction from legal literature. In: Proceedings of the ACM CIKM (2018)

25. Tran, V., et al.: Encoded summarization: summarizing documents into continuous vector space for legal case retrieval. Artif. Intell. Law, 1–27 (2020)

26. Russian Legal Implicit Link Dataset and Embeddings. http://nlp.isa.ru/Jurist/. Accessed 29 Apr 2020

27. Rehurek, R., Sojka, P.: Software framework for topic modelling with large corpora. In: Proceedings of the LREC 2010 Workshop on New Challenges for NLP Frameworks (2010)

28. Osipov, G., Smirnov, I., Tikhomirov, I., Sochenkov, I., Shelmanov, A.: Exactus expert—search and analytical engine for research and development support. In: Hadjiski, M., Kasabov, N., Filev, D., Jotsov, V. (eds.) Novel Applications of Intelligent Systems. SCI, vol. 586, pp. 269–285. Springer, Cham (2016). https://doi.org/10.1007/978-3-319-14194-7_14

29. Abadi, M., et al.: TensorFlow: a system for large-scale machine learning. In: 12th USENIX Symposium on Operating Systems Design and Implementation (OSDI 2016), pp. 265–283 (2016)

30. Arkhipov, M., et al.: Tuning multilingual transformers for language-specific named entity recognition. In: Proceedings of the 7th Workshop on Balto-Slavic Natural Language Processing, pp. 89–93 (2019)

31. Paszke, A., et al.: PyTorch: an imperative style, high-performance deep learning library. In: Advances in Neural Information Processing Systems, pp. 8024–8035 (2019)

32. Gardner, M., et al. AllenNLP: a deep semantic natural language processing platform. In: Proceedings of Workshop for NLP Open Source Software (NLP-OSS), pp. 1–6 (2018)

33. Flach, P.: Machine Learning: The Art and Science of Algorithms that Make Sense of Data. Cambridge University Press, Cambridge (2012)

34. Liu, Y., et al.: RoBERTa: a robustly optimized bert pretraining approach. arXiv preprint arXiv: 1907.11692 (2019)
35. Sanh, V., et al.: DistilBERT, a distilled version of BERT: smaller, faster, cheaper and lighter. arXiv preprint arXiv:1910.01108 (2019)
36. Peters, M.E., et al.: Deep contextualized word representations. arXiv preprint arXiv:1802. 05365 (2018)
37. Jiang, Y., et al.: Team bertha von suttner at SemEval-2019 task 4: hyperpartisan news detection using ELMo sentence representation convolutional network. In: Proceedings of the 13th International Workshop on Semantic Evaluation, pp. 840–844 (2019)
38. Mikel, A., Schwenk, H.: Margin-based parallel corpus mining with multilingual sentence embeddings. arXiv preprint arXiv:1811.01136 (2018)

Detection of Social Media Users Who Lead a Healthy Lifestyle

Karim Khalil[1]([✉]), Maksim Stankevich[2], Ivan Smirnov[1,2], and Maria Danina[3]

[1] Peoples' Friendship University of Russia (RUDN University), Moscow, Russia
code.karim@gmail.com
[2] Federal Research Center Computer Science and Control of RAS, Moscow, Russia
{stankevich,ivs}@isa.ru
[3] Psychological Institute of Russian Academy of Education, Moscow, Russia
mdanina@yandex.ru

Abstract. Public healthcare is a big priority for society. The ability to diagnose and monitor various aspects of public health through social networks is one of the new problems that are of interest to researchers. In this paper, we consider the task of automatically classifying people who lead a healthy lifestyle and users who do not lead a healthy lifestyle by processing text messages and other profile information from the Russian-speaking social network VKontakte. We describe the process of extracting relevant data from user profiles for our dataset. We evaluate several machine learning methods and report experimental results. The best performance in our experiments was achieved by the model that was trained on a combination of N-gram features retrieved from user original posts and reposts.

Keywords: Healthy lifestyle · Social networks · Classification

1 Introduction

The protection of public health is a priority for the state. Much attention is paid to the prevention of various diseases in order to reduce the costs of treatment. The effectiveness of the healthcare system depends on how accurately and systematically the population complies with recommendations on health-related protective behavior. When developing and implementing programs to protect public health and prevent socially significant diseases, it is necessary to take the properties of a targeted audience into account in order to increase the effectiveness of implementation. These properties include behaviors, beliefs, attitudes towards health, and many other variables. Big data analysis on Internet user behavior, which allows us to identify these parameters indirectly, is a perspective research approach.

In particular, it seems important to identify people who do not follow the medical recommendations of preventive programs and do not lead a healthy

The reported study was funded by RFBR according to the research project 18-29-22041.

lifestyle. This allows us to form an idea of people at risk who need enhanced measures to involve them in health-related behavior. On the other side, identifying people leading a healthy lifestyle is a means of measuring the effectiveness of preventive programs. It is assumed that the transition of a person from a group of users leading an unhealthy lifestyle to a group of users leading a healthy lifestyle is a reliable criterion for behavioral changes. These changes can also be appreciated in the long run. Since health-related behavior is associated with social learning, studies on the spread of these behaviors within social networks are promising.

We assume that the parameters described above have objective markers in the activity of social network users. The machine learning approach can help to identify these users without conducting special surveys and focus groups, while gaining access to extensive data, immediately, on the entire population of social network users.

To sum up, identifying people with high and low levels of involvement in health-related behavior through questionnaires is expensive, time consuming and inefficient. Users can misrepresent information about themselves if this may affect their benefits. Automatic detection of people with low levels of involvement in a healthy lifestyle will help us obtain objective data in a way that is rapid, economical and scalable. It is possible to use this data in several ways. Firstly, it is essential information that can help plan targeted preventive interventions for certain communities. Secondly, it helps us to evaluate the impact of different agents on particular social networks on related users. Thirdly, changes in the number of such people in a given community are a reliable indicator of the effectiveness of interventions. It allows us to build large-scale data-driven strategies and make better decisions.

Individuals with a high level of involvement in a healthy lifestyle are agents of change for the entire community. Data on such users behavior, on the one hand, provides opportunities for studying factors that influence the healthy lifestyle motivation. On the other hand, we can use targeted strategies, involving healthy users in the process of restructuring and changing the behavior of people who do not lead a healthy lifestyle, thus maximizing the benefits and effectiveness of prevention programs.

For this study, we collected information on people's attitudes towards healthy lifestyles from 2686 users of the popular Russian-language social network VKontakte. Using this data, we distinguished 2 groups of subjects: users leading a healthy lifestyle and users not leading a healthy lifestyle. We processed the data that these users post on the social network and formed feature sets that were used to train different classification models.

2 Related Work

Finding ways in which a social media user's behavior online is related to their behavior in the real world is a growing field of interest. Methods of computational linguistics and other methods of data analysis yield tangible results in predicting an individual's interests or lifestyle preferences.

Information that can help categorize which lifestyle category an Instagram post falls into exists in the post's hashtags [1]. Word embeddings were used to classify hashtags like "training" and "fitness" under the "Sports and Health" category. It was found that these methods can classify posts based on the set of their hashtags.

The combination and frequency of use of different social media platforms can be used as an indicator of health risk and behavior in young adults [2]. A model using different classes such as Low Users, High Users, Professional Users, Creative Users, and Mainstream Users were used to categorize young adults based on their alcohol, tobacco, and other drugs (ATOD) use; and symptoms of depression and anxiety. It was found that the different classes differed significantly in their ATOD use and depression and anxiety levels.

M. Furini and G. Menegoni [3] classified user messages into different psychological and linguistic categories: affective (e.g. anger and anxiety), social (e.g. family and entity), medical (e.g. disease and vaccine related), and biological (e.g. body and health-related language). The results showed that anti vaccination users use language that is difficult to refute (e.g. not anxious, not focused on specific health issues) whereas pro vaccination users use language that shows more anxiety and specificity (e.g. family cases, specific diseases, or vaccines).

Eichstaedt et al. [4] predicted depression in Facebook users, using psycholinguistic markers. They were able to predict depression in users with an accuracy that was on par with traditional depression screening methods. Patterns emerged showing that depressed users tended to use negative words and first-person singular pronouns more often than non-depressed users.

3 Dataset

3.1 Survey Data

The idea of identifying people leading healthy and unhealthy lifestyles comes from collateral information that we collected to study intrinsic and extrinsic motivations of individuals to lead healthy lifestyles [5,6]. In order to perform our experiment, we asked people with VKontakte profiles to rate their attitude towards 18 different behavioral patterns on a scale of 1 to 5 and to indicate any intrinsic or extrinsic motivation to stick to that behavior. The list of behavioral patterns that we asked people to rate their attitude towards are (1) fast-food, (2) foods high in sugar content, (3) fruits and vegetables, (4) red meat, (5) alcohol, (6) smoking, (7) vitamins and dietary supplements, (8) regular diet, (9) regular hobbies, (10) proper rest from work and study, (11) regular room/workplace ventilation, (12) taking a walk regularly, (13) engagement in physical activity and active sports, (14) morning exercises, (15) limitation of laptop and smartphone use, (16) using dark and night screen modes during the evening, (17) reading literature about healthy lifestyles, (18) regular medical examinations. For this study, we did not take the volunteers' intrinsic and extrinsic motivations into account. We used the user ratings of the 18 behavioral patterns to define a kind of healthy lifestyle score. For each volunteer, we calculated the sum of how many

Table 1. Results of the survey. The table indicates how many people follow certain behavior patterns

Behaviour pattern	#users	Females	Males	Mean age
(1) limiting consumption of fast food	1208	80%	20%	23,88
(2) limiting intake of foods high in sugar	577	79%	21%	25,77
(3) eating fruits and vegetables	1552	84%	16%	22,54
(4) limiting consumption of red meat	1004	86%	14%	21,96
(5) limiting consumption of alcohol	1844	82%	18%	21,6
(6) limiting use of cigarettes	1916	83%	17%	21,99
(7) taking vitamins and dietary supplements	354	83%	17%	24,67
(8) maintaining a regular diet	1343	81%	19%	23,15
(9) maintaining regular hobbies	1440	82%	18%	22,06
(10) getting proper rest from work and study	998	83%	17%	21,94
(11) getting regular room/workplace ventilation	1679	83%	17%	22,62
(12) taking a walk regularly	1327	81%	19%	23,07
(13) partaking in physical activity and active sports	847	73%	27%	22,82
(14) doing morning exercises	420	75%	25%	23,61
(15) limiting laptop and smartphone use	217	77%	23%	26,78
(16) using dark and night screen modes	1022	85%	15%	21,3
(17) consuming health literature	716	80%	20%	24,39
(18) having regular medical examinations	565	86%	14%	23,78

answers were corresponded to healthy behavior. Thus, for each user, we calculated the survey scores that range from 0 to 18. We surveyed users and gathered data from their VKontakte pages during the months of April 2019 and November 2019, this yielded 2686 profile pages and survey results. We understand that we can observe our proposed "healthcare" score only as a generalization. These behavior patterns are not equal and some of them are more common than others (see Table 1). However, we assume that these limitations are not significant enough for the purpose of our study.

Figure 1 shows the distribution of the 2686 survey scores, the scores have a normal distribution with a mean score of 8.55 and a standard deviation of 3.08. To define the classification task, users with a score of 6 to 11 were removed from observation. We considered people with a score of lower than 6 to be our "unhealthy" users and users with a score of greater than 11 to be our "healthy" users. This balanced our dataset, giving us 919 users with 449, 470 users in the unhealthy and healthy groups respectively.

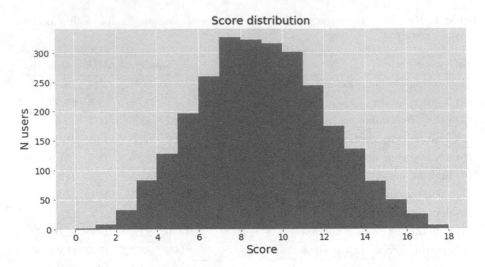

Fig. 1. Score distribution.

3.2 Social Media Data

Data that was of interest to us was the text that the users posted and the content that they were consuming (in the form of reposts and subscriptions to groups). Text that users post that was available to us via the VKontakte API consisted of original posts and reposts. These posts are often full of noise (hyperlinks, emojis, etc.) and we cleaned them before applying any analysis. There is also a significant number of users that do not have an adequate amount of posts for analysis, so we did not use these users when building our text classification models. We performed several actions to improve the quality of the data:

1. Removed all characters which are not in the alphabet or in the set of standard punctuation symbols from texts using regular expressions;
2. Removed all posts with more than 4500 characters or less than 2 characters;
3. Removed all users with less than 500 characters provided;
4. Considered only the most recent posts for each user up to a maximum of 60000 characters.

A significant amount of content that users post on their walls comes from other accounts and pages in the form of reposts. The assumption is that it is possible to find cues that determine behavior not only in text messages authored by a person but also in content retranslated by this person. We collected reposts that each user reposted from the time that they took our survey to one year in the past. We distinguish these reposts from the original posts that users' author and considered them as separate samples. We removed repost samples with overall less than 500 characters provided similar to the way that we did with original post samples.

To sum it up, we formed 3 sets of VKontakte data. We processed 919 profiles overall and retrieved general profile information and information about subscriptions from them. Among these profiles, we identified a subsample in which there was a sufficient amount of original posts and a subsample of profiles with a sufficient amount of repost data. Prior to generating our feature sets, we combined the text from each user's original post into one, combined body of text. A similar procedure was performed with reposts. We applied MyStem (https://yandex.ru/dev/mystem/) for tokenization, lemmatization, and part-of-speech tagging, and Udpipe [7] for syntax parsing. General statistics on this dataset are presented in Table 2. The mean age in the data is 23. The gender partition is strongly unbalanced: 723 (79%) females and 196 males (21%).

Table 2. General statistics on data

	"Healthy"	"Unhealthy"	Total
Total # Users	470	449	919
Mean age	29.00 ± 12.55	24.19 ± 8.19	23.26 ± 9.69
Males	110 (23%)	86 (19%)	196 (21%)
Females	360 (77%)	363 (81%)	723 (79%)
# Users with original posts	233	199	432
# Original posts	18721	11590	30311
# Users with reposts	240	226	466
# Reposts	18620	14919	33539
Average score	13.22 ± 1.27	4.04 ± 1.07	8.74 ± 4.74

4 Features and Methods

4.1 Profile Information, Psycholinguistic Markers, and Dictionaries

Considering the features that we can retrieve from VKontakte data, we want to outline some features that we adopted from our previous studies: profile information, psycholinguistic markers, and dictionaries. These features were used to address the task of predicting depression and the big five personality traits of social media users [8,9].

First of all, it is profile information (PI) features that indicate some quantitative and binary attributes of user profiles (e.g. number of friends, number of groups, number of posts, the average number of likes on posts, the post/repost ratio, availability of affiliate information) Considering our task, we extended this set with time features, which indicate how many posts or reposts were made by a user during morning (6:00 am–10:59 am) and night hours (00:00 am–05:59 am).

Another adopted feature set is psycholinguistic markers. Psycholinguistic markers (PM) are linguistic features of text that represent the psychological characteristics of the author and may signal their psychological disorders. For example, people in stress more frequently use the pronoun "we" [10]. Psycholinguistic markers are calculated on morphological and syntactic information and in a manner corresponding to the writing style of the author. Even though our current task is more dissociated from psychology topics like depression and personality traits, we were interested in how these features would perform on the data. We use more than 30 markers: (# unique words)/(# words), (# verbs)/(# adjectives), (# singular first-person pronouns)/(# pronouns), (# conjunctions + # prepositions)/(# sentences), (# infinitives)/(# verbs), etc. We extend these psycholinguistic markers with features based on the Linis-Crowd sentiment dictionaries and with the following features that are specific to social networks: uppercase characters ratio, number of exclamation marks, number of "sad" and "happy" emoticons.

To calculate dictionary features, we utilized 21 dictionaries which can be split into two groups: topic-based (e.g. terms related to healthcare, terms related to ecology, terms related to politics), and sentiment/mood-based (e.g. motivation lexicon, anxiety lexicon, invectives, negative and positive words). The dictionaries and psycholinguistic marker sets were formed for both original posts and reposts.

4.2   N-grams

Two n-gram sets were formed: unigrams and bigrams. N-grams that appeared less than in 6 texts or more than in 80% of texts were removed from the feature sets. Overall, the lexicon contains 20198, 56052, 22459, and 55744 items for original post unigrams, original post bigrams, repost unigrams, and repost bigrams respectively. We generated tf-idf values using these n-gram models for each user.

4.3   Subscription Matrix

We formed another feature set out of the groups, communities, pages, and popular accounts that people follow on VKontakte. We aggregated the IDs of all these groups and formed a 12543-dimensional vector. We generated one of these vectors for each user that contained binary values of zero and one for each of the IDs in that list. If a specific user was subscribed to a source in that list, they had a "1" value in the position of that source, and if they were not subscribed, they had a "0" value in that position.

4.4   Repost Matrix

The repost matrix was formed similarly to the way that we formed our subscription matrix. We aggregated a list of IDs for all the accounts and pages that users in our dataset reposted content from. This formed a 5340-dimensional vector. We built a vector for each user, containing the number of times that the user reposted content from each source.

Table 3. Feature sets and annotations

Feature set	Annotation	Data
Unigrams Original Posts	UGO	Original posts (432 users)
Bigrams Original Posts	BGO	
Dictionaries Original Posts	DO	
PM Original Posts	PMO	
Unigrams Reposts	UGR	Reposts (466 users)
Bigrams Reposts	BGR	
Dictionaries Reposts	DR	
PM Reposts	PMR	
Profile Information	PI	Full set (919 users)
Subscription Matrix	SM	
Repost Matrix	RM	

4.5 Evaluation Setup

We defined a binary classification task using our "healthy" and "unhealthy" demarcations, and the features we retrieved from the data. It is important to note that we trained our models with different features according to the data samples available for each set. Profile information, the subscription matrix, and the repost matrix were evaluated using our full set of 919 users. Text-based features were evaluated according to the number of samples available for original post and repost subsamples of the data. The short annotation for each of our feature groups is listed in Table 3.

To evaluate our feature sets, we used the average scores of 5 repetitions of a 5-fold cross-validation. We used scikit-learn [11] and xgboost [12] packages in order to perform our classifications. The following machine learning methods were evaluated:

- Support Vector Machine (SVM)
- Gradient Boosting Classifier (GBC)
- Random Forest (RF)
- Logistic Regression (LR)
- Naive Bayes (NB)
- Adaptive Boosting (ABC)
- XGBoost (XGB)

We normalized and scaled our feature sets before training machine learning models. Repost matrix, subscription matrix, and N-gram based feature sets were transformed by PCA to reduce dimensionality. A number of components for the PCA transformation was considered as a hyperparameter for a model tuning process.

5 Results

We used the ROC AUC score as the main evaluation metric. The average F1-score was also included in the classification report. In Table 4 we outline the best performing classifiers that were achieved on each feature set.

Table 4. Classification results of different feature sets

Feature set	Classifier	ROC AUC score	F1-score
UGO	ABC	0.63 ± 0.048	0.64 ± 0.054
BGO	GBC	0.62 ± 0.029	0.64 ± 0.033
DO	XGB	0.61 ± 0.060	0.62 ± 0.070
PMO	RF	0.60 ± 0.039	0.59 ± 0.048
UGR	ABC	0.67 ± 0.043	0.66 ± 0.053
BGR	GBC	0.68 ± 0.047	0.69 ± 0.012
DR	XGB	0.64 ± 0.026	0.66 ± 0.030
PMR	XGB	0.65 ± 0.026	0.63 ± 0.029
PI	GBC	0.60 ± 0.034	0.59 ± 0.035
SM	GBC	0.65 ± 0.025	0.63 ± 0.009
RM	GBC	0.60 ± 0.032	0.60 ± 0.027

The best result in Table 4 was yielded with a gradient boosting classifier on bigrams generated from reposts (0.68 ROC AUC score and 0.69 F1-score) and the second-best result was yielded by an adaptive boosting classifier on unigrams generated from reposts (0.67 ROC AUC score and 0.66 F1-score). The repost based dictionaries, repost psycholinguistic markers, and subscription matrix feature set followed closely behind. Surprisingly, all of the text based sets demonstrated better results with text from reposts compared to the same features coming from original posts. The subscription matrix performed well among other non-text based features sets with 0.65 ROC AUC score. As was expected, the psycholinguistic markers and dictionaries feature sets yielded lesser results compared to the N-gram based feature sets.

We also trained our classifiers using different combinations of feature sets. We reduced the dimensionality of our feature sets and then performed a grid-search in order to find the best combination of parameters and reduction in dimensionality. The best performing combinations of feature sets and classifiers are outlined in Table 5.

Combining the feature sets provided a noticeable increase in scores. A combination of the repost matrix, subscription matrix, unigram, and bigram feature sets classified by a random forest classifier performed best on our data (ROC AUC score of 0.75 and F1-score of 0.67).

Table 5. Classification results of combined, reduced dimensionality feature sets

Feature set	Classifier	AUC	F1-score	# of PCA components
UGO and BGO	XGB	0.67 ± 0.063	0.64 ± 0.038	UGO: 32 BGO: 32
UGO and UGR	XGB	0.72 ± 0.045	0.60 ± 0.123	UGO: 64 UGR: 64
UGR and BGR	ABC	0.67 ± 0.053	0.59 ± 0.041	UGR: 128 BGR: 8
UGO BGO UGR BGR	RF	0.75 ± 0.039	0.67 ± 0.102	UGO: 16 BGO: 64 UGR: 32 BGR: 64
RM SM UGO BGO	ABC	0.72 ± 0.045	0.70 ± 0.067	SM: 8 RM: 32 UGO: 16 BGO: 4
RM SM UGO BGO UGR BGR	XGB	0.74 ± 0.057	0.70 ± 0.079	UGO: 32 BGO: 16 UGR: 16 BGR: 32 SM: 16 RM: 16

6 Conclusion

In this study, we considered the task of identifying attitudes towards a healthy lifestyle among users of the Russian-speaking social network VKontakte. To address the task we used results of the survey to distinguish 2 groups of social media users: persons who lead healthy lifestyles and persons who not. We processed their posts, the content they are subscribed to, and the content that they are reposting and sharing. We formed text based feature sets including psycholinguistic markers, dictionaries, and n-grams using both texts from original posts authored by users and text from reposts they retranslate in their profiles. Information about user subscriptions and repost sources were utilized to form subscription and repost matrices.

The performed experiments revealed that text based features formed from repost texts yielding better classification results compared to the same features retrieved from original posts. The highest result with non-text based features was reached by the model that was trained on the subscription matrix. The best result in our experiments is a .75 ROC AUC score (.67 average F1-score) achieved by the model that was trained on a combination of the N-gram features computed over both reposts and original posts with a PCA dimensionality reduction. We consider the outcome of our experimental evaluation as a positive result that indicates the possibility of analyzing human attitudes towards healthy behavior by processing social media data. We also consider current classification performance as a preliminary result, since the proposed task was not evaluated before on a user-level within social media.

Thus, the analysis of social media profile data is a promising area that can possibly make the diagnosis and treatment of public health more broadly available. In future work, we plan to observe all of the 18 behavior patterns separately and address the task using a neural network model to retrieve features from reposts and original users' messages.

References

1. Khodorchenko, M., Butakov, N.: Developing an approach for lifestyle identification based on explicit and implicit features from social media. Procedia Comput. Sci. **136**, 236–245 (2018)
2. Ilakkuvan, V., Johnson, A., Villanti, A.C., Evans, W.D., Turner, M.: Patterns of social media use and their relationship to health risks among young adults. J. Adolesc. Health **64**(2), 158–164 (2019)
3. Furini, M., Menegoni, G.: Public health and social media: language analysis of vaccine conversations. In: 2018 International Workshop on Social Sensing (SocialSens), Orlando, FL, pp. 50–55 (2018)
4. Eichstaedt, J.C., et al.: Facebook language predicts depression in medical records. In: Proceedings of the National Academy of Sciences, October 2018, vol. 115, no. 44, pp. 11203–11208 (2018). https://doi.org/10.1073/pnas.1802331115
5. Ryan, R.M., Deci, E.L.: Intrinsic and extrinsic motivations: classic definitions and new directions. Contemp. Educ. Psychol. **25**(1), 54–67 (2000)
6. McLachlan, S., Hagger, M.S.: Do people differentiate between intrinsic and extrinsic goals for physical activity? J. Sport Exerc. Psychol. **33**(2), 273–288 (2011)
7. Straka, M., Straková, J.: Tokenizing, POS tagging, lemmatizing and parsing UD 2.0 with UDPipe. In: Proceedings of the CoNLL 2017 Shared Task: Multilingual Parsing from Raw Text to Universal Dependencies, pp. 88–99 (2017)
8. Stankevich, M., Latyshev, A., Kuminskaya, E., Smirnov, I., Grigoriev, O.: Depression detection from social media texts (2019)
9. Stankevich, M., Latyshev, A., Kiselnikova, N., Smirnov, I.: Predicting personality traits from social network profiles. In: Kuznetsov, S.O., Panov, A.I. (eds.) RCAI 2019. CCIS, vol. 1093, pp. 177–188. Springer, Cham (2019). https://doi.org/10.1007/978-3-030-30763-9_15
10. Pennebaker, J.W.: The secret life of pronouns. New Sci. **211**(2828), 42–45 (2011)
11. Pedregosa, F., et al.: Scikit-learn: machine learning in Python. J. Mach. Learn. Res. **12**(Oct), 2825–2830 (2011)
12. Chen, T., Guestrin, C.: XGBoost: a scalable tree boosting system. In: Proceedings of the 22nd ACM SIGKDD International Conference on Knowledge Discovery and Data Mining, pp. 785–794, August 2016

The Influence of Different Methods on the Quality of the Russian-Tatar Neural Machine Translation

Aidar Khusainov$^{(\boxtimes)}$![ORCID], Djavdet Suleymanov ![ORCID], and Rinat Gilmullin

Institute of Applied Semiotics of the Tatarstan Academy of Sciences, Kazan, Russia
khusainov.aidar@gmail.com, dvdt.slt@gmail.com,
rinatgilmullin@gmail.com

Abstract. This article presents the results of experiments on the use of various methods and algorithms in creating the Russian-Tatar machine translation system. As a basic algorithm, we used a neural network approach based on the Transformer architecture as well as various algorithms to increase the amount of parallel data using monolingual corpora (back-translation). For the first time experiments were conducted for the Russian-Tatar language pair on the use of transfer learning (based on Kazakh-Russian parallel corpus). As the main training data, we created and used the parallel corpus with a total volume of about 1 million Russian-Tatar sentence pairs. Experiments show that the created system is superior in quality to the currently existing Russian-Tatar translators. The best quality for the Russian-Tatar translation direction was achieved by our basic model (BLEU 35.4), and for the Tatar-Russian direction – by the model for which the back-translation algorithm was used (BLEU 39.2).

Keywords: Neural machine translation · The Tatar language · Low-resourced language

1 Introduction

The task of building high-quality machine translation systems remains relevant both for the largest world languages and for low-resource and small languages. In the first case, this is largely explained by economic factors, while for small languages the presence of modern text analysis systems, including machine translation systems, can ease the task of learning a language and contribute to the active use of languages in everyday life (including communication on the Internet).

The relevance of the development of the machine translation system for the Russian-Tatar language pair can be proved by the state status of these languages in the Republic of Tatarstan, as well as by a request for this tool from pupils, students, workers, state, and other institutions.

In this work, two problems are simultaneously solved: the construction of the most accurate Russian-Tatar machine translation system, as well as an analysis of the degree of

© Springer Nature Switzerland AG 2020
S. O. Kuznetsov et al. (Eds.): RCAI 2020, LNAI 12412, pp. 251–261, 2020.
https://doi.org/10.1007/978-3-030-59535-7_18

influence that modern methods and algorithms have on the final quality of the translation system.

In the "Datasets" section, we describe the created parallel corpus with 983 thousand pairs of Russian-Tatar sentences, containing news, literature, translations of laws and regulations. It also provides a description of the Russian and Tatar monolingual corpora used to improve translation quality.

The "Experiments" section presents the results of creating machine translation systems for the Russian-Tatar language pair. A neural network approach based on the Transformer network architecture is used, as well as various algorithms for increasing the volume of training data and the use of monolingual data. For the Russian-Tatar language pair, transfer learning experiments were conducted for the first time with the use of parallel data for other languages (the Kazakh-Russian parallel corpus). For all variants of the system, the values of the BLEU metric are calculated on a test subcorpus that was not used in the process of training the model.

2   Related Work

The first versions of machine translation systems for Turkic languages and the Russian language used a rule-based approach. So, for example, a Kazakh-Russian translator based on the Apertium system was created and described in [1]. However, the construction of the necessary rules is complicated because of significant differences in the structure of these languages, and the quality of the work of such systems is insufficient for successful use in practical applications.

At the Institute of Applied Semiotics, a statistical approach was initially chosen to solve the problem of machine translation between the Tatar and Russian languages. This choice determined the need for the creation of a Russian-Tatar parallel corpus, necessary for training statistical models.

The first practical result was achieved in the form of a statistical Russian-Tatar translation system based on phrases (phrase-based MT) and created jointly with Yandex in 2015 [2]. The first version of the Yandex.Translator for this language pair was trained using a morphoanalyzer and a parallel corpus developed by the Institute of Applied Semiotics.

In February 2018, we created the first neural network version of the Russian-Tatar machine translation system [3]. The encoder-decoder-attention network architecture was chosen; training was carried out using the Nematus toolkit [4, 5]. Taking into account the rich Tatar morphology, we used subword basic units for translation; the selection of these units was carried out based on the BPE (byte-pair encoding) algorithm [6, 7]. The model of dividing words into constituent parts was applied to the joint Russian-Tatar corpus.

The task of machine translation is solved using the so-called sequence-to-sequence models built, for example, on recurrent or convolutional neural networks, including elements of the encoder and decoder (encoder/decoder architecture). Models showing the best quality of work also include the implementation of the attention mechanism.

The role of the encoder is to build a continuous space describing the original sentence; the decoder is a neural network language model with an established dependence on the output values of the encoder. The parameters of both parts of the model are trained together maximizing the likelihood of receiving a target sentence based on a training parallel corpus. At the inference stage, an already trained neural network generates the translation using, for example, a beam search algorithm. There are various neural network architectures designed to speed up the training process and increase the quality of translation: recurrent neural networks [8], convolutional neural networks [9], Transformer [10] and Evolved Transformer models. Different types of attention mechanism were also proposed: multi-hop attention [9], self-attention [11] and multi-head attention [10].

The choice of technology for creating a machine translation system depends on the availability and amount of initial training data. In the absence of parallel and monolingual data in one of the languages, the "zero-shot learning" approach [12] can be used, in which neural network translation models trained on parallel data for certain pairs of languages can be used for the language pair for which no training data was provided.

The presence of large mono corpus for the source and target languages allows to use unsupervised approaches. The main idea of this approach is to build a single vector space of words/phrases for both languages. Currently, there are options for implementing this approach based on the statistical, neural network, and hybrid approaches.

Various options were also proposed for using monolingual corpora to improve the quality of translation in training with partial involvement of a teacher (semi-supervised approach) [13].

Another way to use monolingual data is to supplement the decoder with a language model [14]. This approach was used in the very early work of IBM, it was later shown that an additional language model for the target translation language allows systems based on a statistical approach to improve the naturalness and correctness of the translation. In addition to using LM during decoding, neural network language and translation models can be successfully integrated internally by combining latent states of models [15]. In addition, the neural network architecture allows the use of multi-task learning and parameter sharing [16].

And, finally, there is an approach to add an auxiliary autoencoding task for monolingual data, which generates the source sentence as a result of the sequential translation of the initial sentence in both directions [17, 18].

The approach proposed in [19] suggests a very effective way to automatically increase data for training (data augmentation). The method is called back-translation (BT): first, an auxiliary system is trained on available parallel data to translate from the target language to the source language, and then this system is used to translate the monolingual corpus of the target language, thereby increasing the volume of the parallel corpus. The resulting parallel corpus is used as training data for the machine translation system. BT is easy to use, as it does not require a change in the training algorithms of the machine translator. In addition to the main task of increasing the amount of training data for low-resource language pairs, it can also be used to use a monolingual corpus for the task of adapting the system to a specific domain.

One of the ideas for improving BT is to stop using beam search or greedy search. Both of these algorithms allow searching for the posterior maximum (MAP) to find a sentence with a maximum probability according to the model. However, the use of MAP can lead to a less diverse subcorpus of translations, since in cases of ambiguity the algorithm will always choose the most likely option. As an alternative, it is recommended to use the random sampling method [20]. This allows saving the lexical diversity of the generated sentence pairs.

3 Datasets

Despite the wide variety of proposed training methods and algorithms, a key aspect that affects the quality of a machine translation system is the availability of a large amount of training data. It is worth noting that modern commercial systems are trained on parallel corpora, the total volume of which is tens and hundreds of millions of pairs of sentences. Such representative corpora give a possibility to provide users with the quality translations of texts of various domains and styles.

For the Russian-Tatar language pair, we created a parallel corpus, that includes 983 thousand pairs of sentences. The corpus was created on the basis of two main sources of information: bilingual printed documents and from the Internet (news, literature, regulatory documents) and manual translations.

Creating the parallel corpus took place in several stages. The first stage involved collecting available data.

As one of the main sources is literary works, we signed an agreement between out Tatarstan Academy of Sciences and Tatar book publishing house on the transfer of rights to use some of their books. Books were scanned using professional scanning equipment (Elar PlanScan).

We also obtained data for our corpus from the Internet. There are two main web-sources for Tatar-Russian parallel documents: regional media companies and ministries/state departments. There is a law that obliges such organizations to provide all the official documents, news, legislative acts, etc. simultaneously in Russian and Tatar languages.

To download data from web sources we first manually prepared a list of domains that have parallel texts, then we developed a program that allows us to configure specific rules for downloading and parsing documents. Another task was to automatically determine the correspondence between the Russian and the Tatar pages, which was done based on manual rules for URL patterns, translation links on the source page, and using automatic algorithms for document aligning.

Data from the Internet and scanned documents were aligned using ABBYY Aligner 2.0 tool [21] and then filtered according to several criteria:

- both the source and the target sentences should contain at least 1 word;
- both the source and the target sentences should contain at most 80 words;
- duplicate sentences were removed.

We also manually corrected the results of the automatic alignment of several books: literary translations led to the situation where pairs of sentences were very different from each other. A group of 2 people completed this work in two months.

The second stage of creating the parallel corpus included manual translation work. We organized the work of a group of translators of 30 people using the ABBYY Smart-CAT tool [22]. The important aspect is that we decided to speed up the translation process by pre-translating sentences using intermediate NMT models. Our translators used these automatic translations as the basis, so the task changed to correct the translation. We understand the disadvantages of this approach, for instance, a decrease in lexical diversity, so we tried to minimize this effect by using several different NMT systems to produce 'basic' transcription.

The main characteristics of the resulting parallel corpus are presented in Table 1.

Table 1. The main characteristics of the Russian-Tatar parallel corpus.

Parameter	Value
# Parallel sentences	983 319
# Words in Russian sentences	15 032 363
The average length of Russian sentences	15,3 words per sentence
# Words in Tatar sentences	14 649 484
The average length of Tatar sentences	14,9 words per sentence
# sentences in train/test/valid parts	977539/2499/2499

Another linguistic resource that is potentially capable of improving the quality of translation is monolingual corpora. There are several options for using data from these corpora:

- use mono corpora via back-translation, dual learning algorithms, etc.;
- use corpora for building statistical language models for the purpose of further rescoring of the probabilities of translation hypotheses, which helps to find grammatically correct translations;
- as a parallel corpus: sentences from a mono corpus are used both as a source and a target sentences;
- use for building statistical language models that are directly included in the architecture of the neural network machine translation (LM deep fusion).

To test methods, monolingual corpora for the Russian and Tatar languages were used. Corpora from the collection of the University of Leipzig [23] were used as a data source. For the Russian language, the subcorpus of news (news_2010), Internet texts (web_2015) and the Wikipedia subcorpus (wiki-2016) were combined; for Tatar language - Internet (web-2018), news (news_2015), and mixed subcorpora (mix-2015).

Each of the listed subcorpora has a volume of 1 million sentences. Duplicates have been removed from the joint collection. The total volume of the Russian mono corpus is 2,999,489 sentences, of the Tatar – 2,355,738 sentences.

4 Experiments

For an objective assessment of the quality of machine translation, we used the BLEU metric [24]. The use of BLEU has well-known shortcomings [25] but remains the world standard in the field of evaluating the quality of machine translation systems.

4.1 Model Size and Training Duration

The first experiment was to assess the influence of the size of the neural network (the number of layers and neurons in the layers) and the number of training iterations on the quality of translation. Two standard neural network architectures were chosen:

- Base: batch size - 2048, the model dimension in the hidden layers is 512, inner layer dimension in the feedforward network (filter size) is 2048, number of heads to use in multi-headed attention 8, the maximum number of tokens per example - 256, number of layers in the encoder and decoder stacks - 6, the dropout value is 0.1, the learning rate is 2.0, and the beam size is 4;
- Big (only values of parameters that are different from the Base model are given): the batch size is 4096, the model dimension in the hidden layers is 1024, the filter size is 4096, number of heads is 16.

The training was carried out during 40 iterations for Base and 10 for Big models (Table 2).

Table 2. BLEU metric values for machine translation systems as part of the first experiment.

Neural net size	Training iterations	Translation direction	BLEU (uncased)
Base	10	RU-TT	33.57
		TT-RU	35.95
Base	20	RU-TT	34.82
		TT-RU	37.71
Base	30	RU-TT	35.27
		TT-RU	38.41
Base	40	RU-TT	**35.39**
		TT-RU	**38.42**
Big	10	RU-TT	34.08
		TT-RU	37.07

We chose the maximum number of training epochs for Base models (40–45 epochs) motivated first of all by our will to make it as high as possible, and secondly analyzing how the loss changed throughout the training. An example of the loss function for the training of the Russian-Tatar Base model presented in Fig. 1.

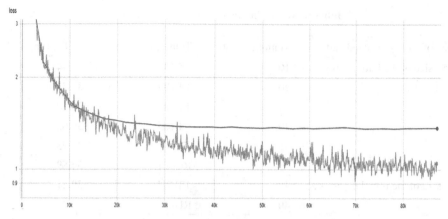

Fig. 1. RU-TT base model loss

For Big models, there was some possibility to improve their results by longer training procedure (see Fig. 2), but we stopped them earlier to save computational time for other experiments when it became clear that these models cannot outperform best Base models.

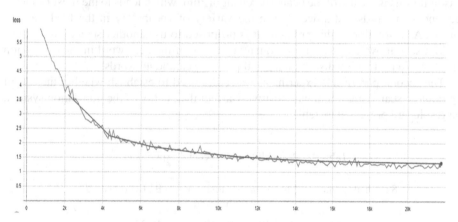

Fig. 2. TT-RU big model loss

4.2 Back-Translation

As part of the second experiment, we changed the size of the synthetic part of the parallel corpus, which was formed by back-translation of a monolingual corpus using Base-40 models, trained in the first experiment.

The results are presented in Table 3.

In contrast to the well-known published results of similar experiments, we do not observe a significant improvement in the quality of translation while increasing the volume of the back-translated part of the training corpus. For the Russian-Tatar directions,

Table 3. MT quality in the second experiment.

Size of back-translated part	Training iterations	Translation direction	BLEU (uncased)
0.5x size of the initial corpus size	10	TT-RU	36.84
	20	TT-RU	37.73
	30	TT-RU	38.50
	40	TT-RU	38.63
	45	TT-RU	38.93
	45	RU-TT	**34.89**
1x size of the initial corpus size	40	TT-RU	**39.21**
	40	RU-TT	34.42

the value of BLEU 34.89 turned out to be less than for Base-40-35.39; the growth of BLEU for the Tatar-Russian direction is 0.79 (growth from 38.42 to 39.21).

There is a hypothesis that the use of standard algorithms for a search of the most probable translation can adversely affect the process of synthetic corpus creation. The reason for this is the use of the beam search algorithm, which leads to the most probable sequences of words and a decrease in the variety of vocabulary in the final training corpus. As a solution to this problem, it is proposed to use another search algorithm - random search, which performs a sequential search of the next word in the translation based on the probability distribution of all possible candidate words.

The second part of this experiment was conducted to establish whether the use of the random search algorithm will positively affect the quality of the translation system; the results are presented in Table 4.

Table 4. MT quality in the second experiment.

Search algorithm	Model	Translation direction	BLEU (uncased)
Random search	Base-10	RU-TT	18.27
Random search	Base-10	TT-RU	19.13

4.3 Transfer Learning

The transfer training approach is aimed at using the knowledge gained by the neural network in solving one problem, to solve the target problem. There are various implementations of this approach; in this work, we tested the basic version of its application to the machine translation problem: we used neural network (pre-trained on a corpus for a related language pair) as the starting point.

Kazakh was chosen as a related language, as the closest related language, for which there is a sufficient amount of parallel data with the Russian language. During the WMT-2019 competition, a parallel Kazakh-Russian corpus consisting of 5 million pairs of sentences was published.

For the experiment, a joint BPE dictionary was built for the Russian, Tatar, and Kazakh languages. Further, models of the Russian-Kazakh and Kazakh-Russian machine translation were trained. The obtained weights were then used as the initial values of the network when training the Russian-Tatar language pair MT system.

The results of this experiment are presented in Table 5.

Table 5. MT quality in the third experiment.

Translation direction	Training iterations	BLEU (uncased)
RU-KK	10	50.01
RU-[KK]-TT	+10 iterations	34.41
KK-RU	10	61.47
TT-[KK]-RU	+10 iterations	36.08

The results indicate the need for additional experiments with both the size of the neural network and the duration of the training, and with the freezing of the parameters of certain layers in the process of retraining the neural network.

4.4 Comparison with Other Systems

We also conducted an experiment to compare the proposed translation model with already existing Russian-Tatar translation systems. At the time of writing the paper, there are three machine translation systems available that support Tatar-Russian language pair: ours (called Tatsoft) [26], Google Translate [27], and Yandex.Translate [2]. For test data, we used the same 2499 parallel sentences as for previous experiments. But taking into account the fact that the data used for training Yandex and Google MT systems are not open, we cannot guarantee that our test sentences were not used during the training stage.

Table 6. MT quality in the fourth experiment.

MT system	Translation direction	BLEU (uncased)
Tatsoft	RU-TT	35.39
Yandex.Translate	RU-TT	15.59
Google.Translate	RU-TT	17.00
Tatsoft	TT-RU	39.21
Yandex.Translate	TT-RU	18.16
Google.Translate	TT-RU	22.64

The results of this experiment are presented in Table 6.

5 Conclusions and Future Work

In this article, we presented the results of experiments on the development of a Russian-Tatar machine translation system based on the Transformer neural network algorithm. The parallel training corpus was prepared and modern methods of machine learning were applied.

As a continuation of this study, we plan to conduct a set of experiments, the purpose of which will be to show a complete picture of the influence of various combinations of methods, parameter values, and volumes of used cases on the quality of the final translation system. The results will allow one to make more informed decisions about the selection of priority areas of work on translators for other low-resource language pairs.

Acknowledgments. The reported study was funded by RFBR, project number 20-07-00823.

References

1. Forcada, M.L., Ginestí-Rosell, M., Nordfalk, J., et al.: Apertium: a free/open-source platform for rule-based machine translation. Mach. Trans. **25**, 127–144 (2011). https://doi.org/10.1007/s10590-011-9090-0
2. Yandex translate. https://translate.yandex.com/. Accessed 14 Mar 2019
3. Khusainov, A., Suleymanov, D., Gilmullin, R., Gatiatullin, A.: Building the Tatar-Russian NMT system based on re-translation of multilingual data. In: Sojka, P., Horák, A., Kopeček, I., Pala, K. (eds.) TSD 2018. LNCS (LNAI), vol. 11107, pp. 163–170. Springer, Cham (2018). https://doi.org/10.1007/978-3-030-00794-2_17
4. Open-source neural machine translation in Theano. https://github.com/rsennrich/nematus. Accessed 21 Nov 2019
5. Sennrich, R., et al.: The University of Edinburgh's neural Mt systems for WMT17. In: Proceedings of the Second Conference on Machine Translation, vol. 2: Shared Task Papers, Stroudsburg, PA, USA (2017)
6. Gage, P.: A new algorithm for data compression. C Users J. **12**(2), 23–38 (1994)
7. Sennrich, R., Haddow, B., Birch, A.: Neural machine translation of rare words with subword units. In: Proceedings of the 54th Annual Meeting of the Association for Computational Linguistics (ACL 2016), Berlin, Germany (2016)
8. Sutskever, I., Vinyals, O., Le, Q.V.: Sequence to sequence learning with neural networks. In: Advances in Neural Information Processing Systems, pp. 3104–3112 (2014)
9. Gehring, J., Auli, M., Grangier, D., Yarats, D., Dauphin, Y.N.: Convolutional sequence to sequence learning. In: International Conference of Machine Learning (ICML) (2017)
10. Vaswani, A., et al.: Attention is all you need. In: Conference on Advances in Neural Information Processing Systems (NIPS) (2017)
11. Paulus, R., Xiong, C., Socher, R.: A deep reinforced model for abstractive summarization. In: International Conference on Learning Representations (ICLR) (2018)
12. Johnson, M.: Google's multilingual neural machine translation system: enabling zero-shot translation. Trans. Assoc. Comput. Linguist. **5**, 339–351 (2017)
13. Irvine, A., Callison-Burch, C.: End-to-end statistical machine translation with zero or small parallel texts. Nat. Lang. Eng. **1**(1), 517 (2015)
14. Gulcehre, C., et al.: On using monolingual corpora in neural machine translation. arXiv:1503.03535 (2015)

15. Gulcehre, C., Firat, O., Xu, K., Cho, K., Bengio, Y.: On integrating a language model into neural machine translation. Comput. Speech Lang. **45**, 137–148 (2017)
16. Domhan, T., Hieber, F.: Using target-side monolingual data for neural machine translation through multi-task learning. In: Conference on Empirical Methods in Natural Language Processing (EMNLP) (2017)
17. Cheng, Y., et al.: Semi-supervised learning for neural machine translation. arXiv:1606.04596 (2016)
18. He, D., et al.: Dual learning for machine translation. In: Advances in Neural Information Processing Systems, pp. 820–828 (2016)
19. Sennrich, R., Haddow, B., Birch, A.: Improving neural machine translation models with monolingual data. arXiv preprint. arXiv:1511.06709 (2015)
20. Imamura, K., Fujita, A., Sumita, E.: Enhancement of encoder and attention using target monolingual corpora in neural machine translation. In: Proceedings of the 2nd Workshop on Neural Machine Translation and Generation, pp. 55–63 (2018)
21. Abbyy aligner 2.0. https://www.abbyy.com/ru-ru/aligner. Accessed 10 May 2019
22. Abbyy smartcat tool for professional translators. https://smartcat.ai/workspace. Accessed 02 Apr 2019
23. Corpora Collection Leipzig University. https://corpora.uni-leipzig.de/en. Accessed 10 Apr 2020
24. Papineni, K., Roukos, S., Ward, T., Zhu, W.: BLEU: a method for automatic evaluation of machine translation. In: Proceedings of the 40th Annual Meeting on Association for Computational Linguistics, pp. 311–318 (2002)
25. Baisa, V.: Problems of machine translation evaluation. In: Proceedings of Recent Advances in Slavonic Natural Language Processing, Brno (2009)
26. Tatsoft translate. https://translate.tatar/. Accessed 10 Jun 2020
27. Google translate. https://translate.google.ru/. Accessed 12 Apr 2020

Ontology-Controlled Geometric Solver

Sergey S. Kurbatov[1] ⓘ, Igor B. Fominykh[2], and Aleksandr B. Vorobyev[2](✉)

[1] Research Centre of Electronic Computing, 117587 Moscow, Russia
curbatow.serg@yandex.ru
[2] National Research University "MPEI", 111250 Moscow, Russia
igborfomin@mail.ru, abvorobyev@bk.ru

Abstract. The paper describes an ontology-controlled geometric solver. The solver functions as a part of an integrated problem-solving system with a natural language interface. It is implemented in a prototype version of the system for the "school geometry" subject area. We described the solver interaction with the system linguistic processor, ontology, and the graphic component. We provided examples demonstrating automated solving non-trivial geometric problems formulated in a natural language. We suggested using cognitive structures in the dialogue for an effective linguistic analysis and building up a correct drawing.

Keywords: Integrated system · Solver · Ontology · Natural language · Heuristic structures · Interactive visualization · Planimetry

1 Introduction

The issue of automatically solving problems and proving theorems has attracted researchers' attention virtually from the emergence of Artificial Intelligence (AI). Having initially a fairly narrow application area (simple propositional logic theorems, etc.), at the present stage, this direction achieved important scientific and practical results. Several complex mathematical theorems have been automatically solved (a good example is the four-color problem); automatic solving methods are successfully used to validate computer software and hardware. Currently, many automatic solvers have been developed, both intended to prove non-trivial mathematical theorems (provers) and essentially based on semantics (semantic reasoner). Among the most famous solutions, we shall mention Coq [1], HOL [2], Isabell [3], Wolfram [4], modifications of Cyc [5], Podkolzin [6, 7]. Automatic solving uses a logical apparatus, usually based on first-order predicate calculus and its computer support, e.g., using the widely known OWL and SPARQL languages Brief description of a number of solvers is provided below in "Related Works".

In general, all these systems are focused on the solution itself; they propose data input in a formal language, having a limited functionality to explain and to use interactive graphics. In modern automatic solver systems little attention is paid to translation from wording in a natural language to a formal representation; how the system comes to a solution, and what plausible reasoning is used therein; how to visualize the solving process, and how to generalize them.

S. O. Kuznetsov et al. (Eds.): RCAI 2020, LNAI 12412, pp. 262–273, 2020.
https://doi.org/10.1007/978-3-030-59535-7_19

The purpose of this paper is developing and studying an ontologically-oriented solver featuring a linguistic solution support, an essential use of the subject area ontology to explain the results, and an interactive visualization of the solving process. The solver software is implemented in a prototype version for the "school geometry" subject area and is based on the methodology of a famous scientist and educator G. Pólya [8]. The difficulty of creating such a solver naturally required narrowing the subject areas.

2 Materials and Methods

The solver that meets our objective was developed as a part of an integrated system. Figure 1 shows the general layout of the system and comments to the components interaction. The paper describes mainly the solver functioning; the operation details of the linguistic processor and the graphic component are not considered. Nevertheless, due to the integrated nature of the system, the solver can access other components to clarify the problem semantic structure and to build up a correct drawing.

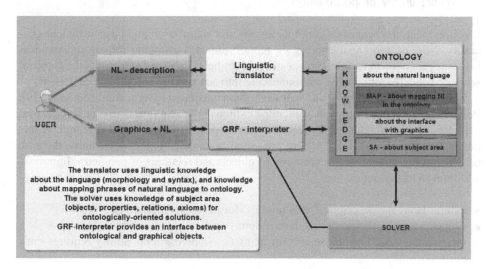

Fig. 1. General layout of the system

The graph structures (syntactic and semantic) described below, as well as logical and heuristic rules are provided in the computer by means of the original ontology. Ontology is implemented in the Progress DBMS environment in the main version; VBA Excel is used for the implementation in the simplified version (for applied purposes). The ontology contains the knowledge of:

- a domain specific language (geometry);
- a method of translation of the natural language descriptions into semantic structures;
- heuristic and logical rules for obtaining a solution;
- a method of graphical display of the result (solution graphs and drawing).

Logical rules are based on the axiomatics of subject area (geometry) and provide the deductive capabilities of the system; they fundamentally guarantee the truth of the consequence under the truth of the premises. Logical rules do not depend directly on the spectrum of knowledge in ontology. However, the choice of a logical rule by means of heuristic rules depends substantially on this knowledge. The connection between deductive and plausible reasoning is ensured by close interaction of the mechanisms of heuristic choice and logic output.

Examples of heuristics (for mathematics) actually used in the solver are as follows:

- casting off the parts of condition and analysis of sets intersection (a method of loci in geometry);
- reducing problem to an algebraic formulation (heuristic was used in the problem for construction of a right-angled triangle on a hypotenuse and a right-angle bisector);
- searching for a related problem (generalization or concretization of conditions using ontology);
- using a model for empirical guesses (equality of angles, segments, parallelism or perpendicularity, proportionality).

It is important that heuristics admit an algorithmic description and have sufficient generality. When developing the solver, the authors aimed at using the domain-independent heuristics common to various subject areas. Many heuristics are described in the classical work of Pólya [8], obviously, without taking into account the computer realizationt.

The issues of algorithmic and software of the integrated system are discussed in [9]. Pólya heuristic methodology was intended to humans (teachers and students); however, elements of its computer implementation were repeatedly used for AI research. In this paper, Pólya's recommendations are presented as knowledge base structures, the core of which is the semantic representation of objects and relations of geometry. Important additions to this structure are:

- natural-language description of heuristics (for the basic operation);
- syntactic representation of this description;
- meta data to speed up the search for heuristics (indices, applicability requirements, etc.);
- weighting factors for calculating the prospects of using heuristics.

In such an interpretation, the heuristics that is presented in the knowledge base should be considered as a cognitive structure. The activation of such a structure and its inclusion in the solution context can be initiated by the results of linguistic processing, empirical drawing data, and, surely, information about the current solution. That is why the solver should be referred to as ontologically-controlled one.

From the technical point of view, the solver algorithm can be considered as an informed heuristic search that uses the knowledge of a particular subject area (namely, about the area rather than the problem). More precisely, it is an algorithm exploring a graph by expanding the most promising nodes using heuristic rules according to the knowledge of the relevant subject area.

The specifics of the suggested solver are as follows:

- the graph nodes correspond to the semantic network fragments (the initial fragment corresponds to the problem condition) with objects to find (marked with a question mark "?");
- terminal nodes are defined as corresponding to fragments with found objects (the mark "?" is removed);
- the graph is interactive and focused on the dialogue with users at a high conceptual level;
- an interactive visualization allows to follow step by step the solving process on the drawing and on the semantic graph;
- settings allow to get several solutions;
- the expected effective branching coefficient is close to 1.

Let us describe the solution search algorithm scheme.

The initial semantic structure of the problem is input to the solver, where question marks indicate objects to be found (built).

Step 0. Create the current node referencing the original semantic structure of the problem.
Step 1. If resources are exhausted (time or the number of nodes), exit with failure.
Step 2. For the current node, create pairs (operation, prospects).
Step 3. For the current problem-solving graph, select the most promising pair.
Step 4. Perform the operation for this pair to generate a new node in the solution graph. Consider this node as the current one.
Step 5. If a solution is found (all nodes with a question mark are highlighted), then exit (solution presentation)
Step 6. Recalculate the prospects for all nodes of the current branch (from the initial to the current node). Go to Step 1.

Solution presentation means selecting a subtree that corresponds to such solution, and generating a program to build the drawing. Subtree selection is related to the availability of the XOR-type relations in the graph, which correspond, in terms of contents, to mutually exclusive solutions (e.g., lines intersect/are parallel/coincide; the point is on/off the line, etc.)

Let us describe the pair generation algorithm (operation, prospects). For the current semantic structure (that corresponds to the current node), we find the applicable operations by searching through the same. For each applicable operation, find heuristics that, taking into account the structure objects (given, output, highlighted with a question mark, etc.), generate digital values. Summing up these values determines the prospects of a pair.

Current branch recalculation function (see Step 6) in the current implementation:

$$P\_new(N) = P\_old(N) - D^{Nmax - N} \tag{1}$$

where $P\_new(N)$ is the new values of prospects, $P\_old(N)$ is the old value of prospects, $D < 1$, N is the distance between the node and the tree root.

This operation is performed on the semantic structure (SEMS). For example, an operation with an NL-description "Draw a segment with given points" generates a fragment (three nodes and two relations) to be visualized in SEMS, as shown in Fig. 2.

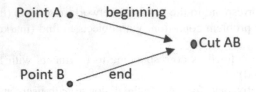

Fig. 2. Visualization result of an operation on SEMS.

$$point\,A - beginning \;\rightarrow\; cut\,AB \;\leftarrow\; end - point\,B \tag{2}$$

In the relational database, these triplets are presented in the same way as in Table 1:

Table 1. Table fragment for representing semantic triplets.

Type	Name	Relation	Type	Name	Stat-1	Stat-2	Stat-3
point	A	start	segment	AB	giv	true	giv

The table shows only the main fields; a real row includes several additional fields, particularly, determining structural features (e.g., a reference to the operation). The "type" field describes the general properties of the object; the "status" fields indicate that the objects are given (the field value = "giv"), and the relation shall have the "true" value.

The same operation for the drawing is interpreted using the JSXGraph [10] tools and generated the call of the function crt_segment ("AB", "A", "B", step number, argumentation). It is important that, at every solution step, the interactive visualization allows for rendering the solution graph, the semantic structure graph, and the drawing with relevant comments. This significantly increases the clarity, persuasiveness, and reliability of the decision result.

Execution of this operation on the semantic structure corresponds to the *deductive* step; the latter guarantees the result. The heuristic *choice* of the operation does not guarantee the need for the step, but plausible considerations for choice can dramatically reduce the search space. Such choice corresponds to the *inductive* step. It is this interaction of deduction and plausible reasoning that Pólya methodology is based on.

3 Results

The solver is tested in two modes:

- an autonomous mode (obtaining a complete solution and viewing its protocol);
- an interactive mode (solution control at every step).

Both modes are supported by interactive visualization. For testing, we selected several problems that are the most interesting in terms of demonstrating the solver and interactive visualization features. An example of the basic problem text, the graph of its solution, fragments of the semantic structure, and the drawing are shown below in Figs. 3, 4, and 5.

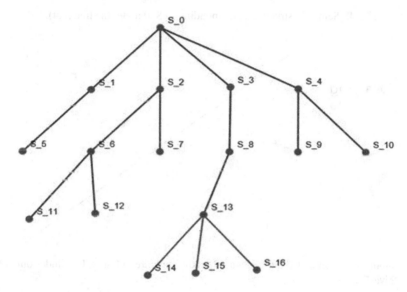

Fig. 3. Subtree (S_0, S_3, S_8, S_13, (S_14, S_15, S_16)) corresponds to the 1st found solution. (Color figure online)

Problem text: "Draw a circle passing through two given points and having a center on a given line". Based on this text, the linguistic processor generates semantic structure triplets, see Fig. 2. The drawing corresponding to this structure is shown in Fig. 5. The semantic structure is sent to the solver input; in Fig. 3, it is denoted as S_0 and corresponding to this node graph is shown in Fig. 4. In accordance with the algorithm of the previous section, pairs are created for S_0 (operation, prospects), the most promising pair is selected, and a new node is generated.

In terms of the contents, operations are the following constructions: "perpendicular from a point to a line", "segment drawn with two points", "perpendicular from a point on a line", etc. As a result of the operation, the semantic structure is supplemented with new elements. Figure 3 shows a fragment of the solution graph, the nodes of

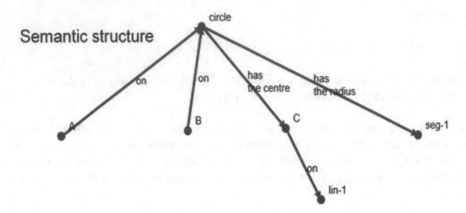

Fig. 4. Semantic structure corresponding to S_0 node (the tree root).

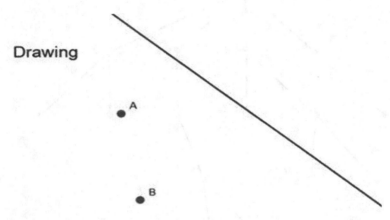

Fig. 5. Automatically generated drawing based on the structure in Fig. 4. It includes only object with the "given" status.

which correspond to semantic structures obtained after executing the chosen operation. Naturally, the drawing is also modified in this case, which is highlighted with green in Fig. 3.

Relations of the XOR type are highlighted: options that are mutually exclusive, but correspond to one solution subtree. In this graph, these are options "lines intersect/are parallel/coincide".

It is important that the graphs and the drawing are automatically generated, whereas the user is provided with the interactive visualization support for each of them. This allows not only to visualize the solving process, but also to get a natural-language description of the step (operation) and its argumentation. For this problem, the operation "draw segment AB" has the following argumentation: "point A is given, point B is given, segment AB is the circle chord, and the circle shall be drawn".

Subtree (S_0, S_3, S_8, S_13, (S_14, S_15, S_16)) is the 1st found solution to the problem. A back swing from nodes S_14, S_15, S_16 creates branches to the tree root S_0. The branches, each having a separate drawing, demonstrate all three solution options: a unique solution, no solution, infinitely many solutions.

The solver settings allow to continue searching for a solution, and for blocking some operations. This made it possible to obtain several solutions for a problem that is being widely discussed on the Internet; three solutions are shown in Figs. 6, 7, 8. The problem text: "In triangle ABC, angle A = 20°, angle C = 80°. On AC leg of the triangle, point D is selected so that AD = BC. Find angle BDC." A key step in the automatically found solution (Fig. 6) is selecting point E like the vertices of an equilateral triangle.

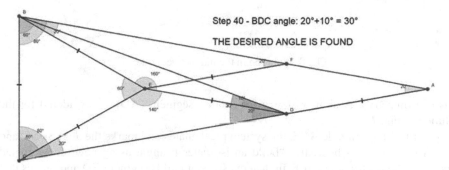

Fig. 6. Automatically obtained solution.

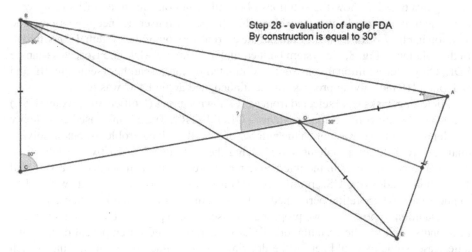

Fig. 7. Solution obtained in the semi-automatic mode.

The choice is justified by heuristics "build an equilateral triangle" with the following argumentation: "difference, sum, or product of given angles = 60°". The choice of leg (BC) on which the triangle is built is justified by heuristics "prefer a point on the object

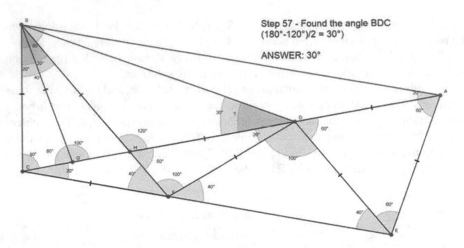

Fig. 8. Solution in the interactive mode.

axis of symmetry". A similar choice for another segment (AD) is considered for the solution in Fig. 7.

After building triangle BCE, the system recalculates and marks the angles (20° and 60°). Then, based on heuristics "build an isosceles triangle using newly constructed objects", it builds triangles BEF. In the next steps, it builds segment ED and proves that DEFA is a parallelogram. We emphasize that point F is to be built, whereas point D is given. Finally, recalculating the obtained angles allows to find the desired angle BDC.

Figures 6 and 7 show the solutions obtained in interactive mode of working with the system. In this mode, it is possible to directly perform user-defined operations. The solution in Fig. 7 is the most elegant, but the current version of the system did not find it. In the solution in Fig. 8, the system built equilateral triangle ADE and isosceles triangle FDE. Only after additional constructions initiated by the researcher (segments BF and BG, point H), the solving process was continued, and angle BDC was found.

For testing, tasks were selected from well-known sources (Unified State Exam (USE) 2020, 3,000 math competition problems – GEOMETRY, Trigg – increased complexity problems). The focus was not on the number of trivially solved problems, but on solving qualitatively different problems and studying the features of interactive visualization. To solve some problems in the interactive mode, we involved students of the 10th and 11th school grades (the USE profile level). During the discussion, students were asked to guess the next operation performed by the system and to substantiate their guess.

In addition to problems, we proposed for discussion a proof of the theorem (Euler's line) and search for the formulation of Ceva theorem based on empirical data. In the latter case, students could set on the drawing integer values of segments, into which the Cevians divide the two legs of a triangle. The segment ratios on the third leg were calculated by the system. Table 2 presents data of one experiment. An empirical formula was proposed by students after the first 4 rows of the table. The splitting of AC and AB sides was set by students, and the splitting of BC was determined by the system.

Table 2. Ratios of triangle leg segments as divided by Cevians.

1st side AC	2nd side AB	3rd side BC
½	2/1	4
1/3	3/1	9.02
½	3/1	6.01
1/3	4/1	12
1/5	5/1	25

Let the points X, Y, and Z lie on the sides BC, AC, and AB of the triangle ABC, and the segments AX, BY, and CZ intersect at the same point. Then, by theorem of Giovanni Ceva,

$$(AZ/BZ) * (BX/CX) * (CY/BY) = 1 \qquad (3)$$

4 Discussion

Out results showed that the problem-solving process features high clarity, naturalness, and reliability. This is important for the user to understand both the solution itself and the steps to find it. For a knowledge engineer, the solution graph visualization allows to quickly identify inaccuracies in ontology. The interactive graph demonstrated not only the premises for the output and its result, but also the associated environment (proofs, alternatives, etc.).

Messages at a high conceptual level that were requested in the dialogue (by clicking on an object or a relation), provided an informative description of emergency situations at some solving step (e.g., lack or wrong choice of alternative). In fact, the interactive graph acted as an intelligent log file, which is used in large information system in the analysis of controversial situations.

The significance and novelty of the results is in the fact that an integrated use of the ontologically-oriented solver and interactive visualization opens up new prospects for solving problems in the style of their human solution, as well as new opportunities for knowledge engineers who adapt and support ontology knowledge bases.

5 Related Work

Coq is a mathematician's assistant to check and search for proof of theorems. Coq requires some mathematical culture (knowledge of functional programming languages, data standardization specifics, recursive descriptions, tactics of proving). Coq allows one to work in the interactive mode, but on a high mathematical level; it does imply neither NL communication, nor developed graphic tools. Among the most well-known systems that compete with Coq, we can mention HOL [2] and Isabelle [3]. Slightly different are systems Wolfram [4] and modifications of Cyc [5].

Wolfram system [4] has an interpreter operator that allows for entering the problem text in a restricted NL. However, the interpreter features are rather limited (the authors worked with version 11.3 where input in Russian is not yet implemented). The ambitious project of the Cyc [5] system provides for creating a very extensive ontology knowledge base (containing hundreds of thousands of expressions and millions of statements), that is used for solving complex problems with the help of a semantic reasoning mechanism (a rule engine) involving common sense. The system drawbacks are largely related to its ambitiousness, as the common sense formalization problem is far from being completely resolved; in addition, the system is difficult to learn and even more difficult to add data manually.

Currently, the Russian system that has been developed at the Moscow State University [6, 7] includes over 40,000 solving techniques. The system authors suppose that the developed methods for computer simulation of logical processes will be successfully applied to natural language processing.

None of the above systems provides such holistic approach to the problem of automatic problem solving, especially related to the natural language interface and explanatory capabilities. Explanation at a high conceptual level means that a comment of this kind is not satisfactory: "two Horn clauses at resolving make up an empty clause"; a more meaningful description such as "lines *fall together* and lines are *different* means a contradiction" is required. It is the meaning of the predicates "coincide" and "be different" that not only makes the content of the decision step clear, but also allows substituting "direct" with any (not only the geometric) objects. A detailed comparative analysis of the solvers requires special consideration and is beyond the scope of this article.

Our ontologically-driven solver of geometric problems is significantly inferior to the above systems in terms of the scale and problem coverage, but it features linguistic support tools, a significant focus on the substantive-conceptual aspect of problems when solving and explaining the results, as well as interactive visualization based on dynamic geometry tools.

Some issues of the interaction between linguistic translation and a solver, as well as an anthropocentric approach to proving geometric theorems, are considered in [11–15]. The first of these works focuses on the problems of pedagogy, but using dynamic geometric environments. The last three ones are close on the ideological side to our research, but the use of another language and the lack of information about the organization of the ontology make it difficult to compare them correctly.

6   Conclusions

There is a significant increase in the user's confidence in the results obtained by the system. At the level of basic research, the study allows one to get better understanding of human cognitive mechanisms that are initiated when solving problems in the following range: passing from the natural-language formulation of the problem to formalization – searching for a solution using formal methods – graphic presentation of results – solution analysis and summarization.

In the school geometry, the assumption that the developed ontology-controlled solver tools allow one to significantly reduce the search space when solving non-trivial problems, has been confirmed to a certain extent. For more significant confirmation, we plan to study the solver on a much larger number and variety of problems.

However, already for the current version of the solver, it seems promising to create qualitatively new training systems on its basis that implement Pólya methodology in computers.

Acknowledgment. This study was supported by the Russian Foundation for Basic Research (projects ## 18-07-00098, 18-29-03088, 18-07-00213). The authors are grateful to A.P. Lobzin and T.N. Asmayan for their assistance in testing the system.

References

1. The Coq proof assistant (2019). https://coq.inria.fr/news/coq-890-is-out.html
2. HOL interactive theorem prover (2018). https://hol-theorem-prover.org/
3. Isabelle is a generic proof assistant. http://isabelle.in.tum.de/fff
4. Wolfram release 11.3. http://blog.stephenwolfram.com/2018/03/roaring-into-2018-with-another-big-release-launching-version-11-3-of-the-wolfram-language
5. Cyc is a long-living artificial intelligence project. https://www.cyc.com/
6. Podkolzin, A.S.: The study of logical processes by computer simulation. J. Intell. Syst. Theory Appl. **20**, 164–168 (2016). (in Russian)
7. Podkolzin, A.S.: Computer Simulation of Logical Processes. Architecture and Problem Solver Languages, p. 1024. Fizmatlit, Moscow (2008). (in Russian)
8. Polya, G.: Mathematical Discovery: On Understanding, Learning and Teaching Problem Solving, p. 432. Wiley, Hoboken (1981)
9. Kurbatov, S.S., Fominykh, I.B., Vorobyev, A.B.: Algorithmic and software cognitive agent based on the methodology. In: Poya, D. (ed.) Software Products and Systems/Software & Systems, vol. 32, no. 1, pp. 012–019 (2019). (in Russian)
10. JSXGraph. Dynamic mathematics with JavaScript, JSXGraph is a cross-browser JavaScript library for interactive geometry, function plotting, charting, and data visualization in the web browser. http://jsxgraph.uni-bayreuth.de/wp/index.html
11. Sergeeva, T.F., Shabanova, M.V., Grozdev, S.I.: Fundamentals of Dynamic Geometry, p. 152. Publishing house ASOU, Russia (2016). (in Russian)
12. Gan, W., Yu, X.: Automatic understanding and formalization of natural language geometry problems using syntax-semantics models. Int. J. Innovative Comput. Inf. Control ICIC **14**(1), 83–98 (2018)
13. Seo, M., Hajishirz, H., Farhadi, A., Etzioni, O., Malcolm, C.: Solving geometry problems: combining text and diagram interpretation. http://geometry.allenai.org/assets/emnlp2015.pdf
14. Wang, K., Su, Z.: Automated geometry theorem proving for human-readable proofs. In: Proceedings of the Twenty-Fourth International Joint Conference on Artificial Intelligence, Buenos Aires, Argentina, 25–31 July (2015)
15. Krötzsch, M.: Ontologies for knowledge graphs? In: Proceedings of the 30th International Workshop on Description Logics, Montpellier, France, 18–21 July (2017). http://ceur-ws.org/Vol-1879/invited2.pdf

Application of the BERT Language Model for Sentiment Analysis of Social Network Posts

Vadim Moshkin$^{(\boxtimes)}$ (ID), Andrey Konstantinov (ID), and Nadezhda Yarushkina (ID)

Ulyanovsk State Technical University, Severny Venetz Street, 32, 432027 Ulyanovsk, Russia
{v.moshkin,a.konstantinov,jng}@ulstu.ru

Abstract. The paper proposes a new algorithm for formation of training datasets for a neural network that provides sentiment analysis of social network posts. This article also describes the use of a neural network to determine the sentiment values of a social network posts using the word2vec and BERT algorithms. Also conducted experiments confirming the effectiveness of the proposed approaches.

Keywords: Sentiment analysis · BERT · Word2vec · Neural network · Social network

1 Introduction

The study of social networks every year is becoming increasingly important because of the need to ensure the safety of the population and the monitoring of public sentiment. Post analysis can help to assess changes in the mood of many users and find application in political and social studies including consumer preference research.

The results of the sentiment analysis of the user posts would allow us to conclude:

- emotional evaluation of users of various events and objects;
- individual user preferences;
- some features of the users' nature [1].

Sentiment text analysis is a classification task. At present, the best results of text classification by several criteria are shown by machine learning algorithms. This makes formation of training datasets when using neural network approaches.

In this paper, we consider the use of the word2vec and "BERT" language models for sentiment analysis of social network posts, preprocessing text data, and generating training datasets.

2 The Use of Machine Learning Algorithms in Sentiment Analysis of Social Network Data

Currently, researchers suggest the use of neural networks of various architectures, such as convolutional and recurrent neural networks [7, 8], to determine the sentiment values of

© Springer Nature Switzerland AG 2020
S. O. Kuznetsov et al. (Eds.): RCAI 2020, LNAI 12412, pp. 274–283, 2020.
https://doi.org/10.1007/978-3-030-59535-7_20

texts. Other favorite tools include support vector machines (SVM) [2], Bayesian models [3], various kinds of regressions [4], Word2Vec, Doc2Vec [5], CRF [6]. Analysis of social network texts require much resources for preprocessing, including formation of the training set.

Paper [9] describes a sentiment analysis model for posts from Twitter. Initially, a set of smiles was created for marking up the text and assigning the text to a specific emotion. Then the texts were presented in vector form using the "bag of words" approach.

Three classifiers were chosen to construct the classification model: logistic regression, decision tree, multilayer perceptron. The accuracy of determining the sentiment values of the posts was about 75–76% for each model.

In [10], two models of neural networks were selected to determine sentiment values of text messages: a neural network with two recurrent layers and a neural network with recurrent and convolutional layers.

The authors used two sets of hand-labeled texts for training a neural network. Texts are short messages up to 140 characters long. The classification accuracy was 69% using a network with two recurrent layers. The accuracy is slightly higher, 71% using a network with recurrent and convolutional layers.

Paper [11] presents the results of the development of an automatic classifier of Russian-language Internet texts. This classifier distributes texts into 8 classes in accordance with 8 basic emotions.

The classifier was based on the SVM. The input values for the classifier are various linguistic parameters, e.g., the frequency of use of punctuation marks and amplification adverbs. The accuracy of determining the emotional coloring of emotions "anger" and "fear" was 48%, "anguish" 40%, "disgust" 6%, and "joy" 7%.

As can be seen from the results of the above studies, the task of developing an approach to effectively assessing sentiment values of social networks texts is relevant.

3 An Approach to Sentiment Analysis of Social Network Data Using the "Word2vec" and "BERT" Models

We developed a new approach for sentiment analysis of the text data from social networks. This approach includes the following steps:

1. The formation of training and test sets.
2. Text vectorization using the word2vec and BERT models.
3. Training and classification using the neural network approach.

3.1 The Algorithm for the Formation of the Training Set

The formation of training and test sets requires pre-processing of textual information and the marking of the sentiment values of individual text posts.

Formally, the process of selecting posts can be represented by the scheme shown in Fig. 1. Each stage of the selection shown in the figure includes the process of selecting posts for each specific emotion.

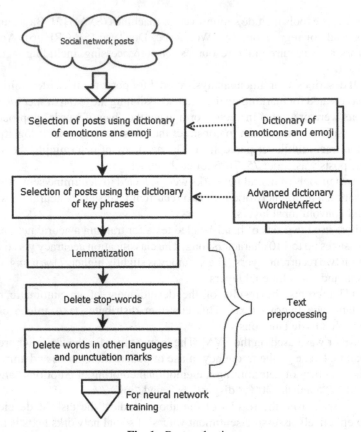

Fig. 1. Posts selection.

1. At the first stage, posts are selected based on expert dictionaries of emotion expression symbols (the so-called "emoticons" and "emoji"). If a post contains an author's symbol for expressing emotions, then it belongs to a specific class and is added to the corresponding list.
2. The second stage is the selection of posts based on dictionaries of key phrases. An extended Russian-language semantic thesaurus WordNetAffect [12] was used as a basic dictionary.

The developed dictionaries with symbols of expression of emotions and key phrases consist of objects of 7 classes:

$$D^E = \{D^E_{joy}, D^E_{sad}, D^E_{surp}, D^E_{anger}, D^E_{disg}, D^E_{cont}, D^E_{fear}\}$$

where D^E_{joy} is a class of objects with emotion "joy", D^E_{sad} is a class of objects with emotion "sadness", D^E_{surp} is a class of objects with emotion "surprise", D^E_{anger} is a class of objects with emotion "anger", D^E_{disg} is a class of objects with emotion "disgust", D^E_{cont}

is a class of objects with emotion "contempt", D_{fear}^{E} is a class of objects with emotion "fear".

In addition, at this stage, the lemmatization of each word of the post is performed. Then the post is checked for the content of each word from the dictionary. If a post contains a phrase, then it belongs to a specific class of emotional coloring.

3. At the stage of preprocessing posts, all characters are excluded except for Cyrillic characters and spaces, and all words are reduced to lower case.

3.2 Text Vectorization Algorithms

Two methods were used to represent words in a vector space: word2vec and "BERT" in the framework of this study.

The model of the BERT algorithm can be represented as a function, the input of which is text, and the output is a vector. In this algorithm, each syllable is converted to a number. Initially, a model trained for a particular language is loaded, according to which the sequence is divided into syllables. A detailed description of the algorithm is given in [13] and [14].

The loaded model of the BERT algorithm can be represented as:

$$\theta = \begin{bmatrix} w_1 \\ w_2 \\ \cdot \\ \cdot \\ w_n \end{bmatrix},$$

where θ is a vector that contains words included in the dictionary of words of the loaded model. The algorithm converts a word into a set of syllables or vectors, each syllable is obtained from a set of common words.

Let w_1, w_2 ... w_n be the set of words in the dictionary and s_{m1}, s_{m2} ... s_{mn} the set of syllables in the word w_n, then the function $(s_m) = f(w_{11}, w_{12}...w_{1n})$ allows you to get many syllables for a sequence of words. Then we get a vector representation of the sequence of words by the resulting syllables.

The word2vec algorithm was also used for comparison. The word2vec algorithm converts words to vectors. A detailed description of the algorithm is given in [15].

The Mathematical Model of the word2vec Algorithm. Initially, a dictionary of all the words that make up the dataset is compiled. Formally, all word vectors are:

$$\theta = \begin{bmatrix} V_{w1} \\ V_{w2} \\ \cdot \\ V_{wn} \\ U_{w1} \\ U_{w2} \\ \cdot \\ U_{wn} \end{bmatrix},$$

where θ is a long vector that contains vectors v and u of length d for all words.

The algorithm predicts the probability of a word in its context. Vector vectors are obtained; each word is assigned a probability value that is close to the probability value of meeting a word in this environment in real text.

$$P(w_o|w_c) = \frac{e^{s(w_o,w_c)}}{\sum w_i \in V e^{s(w_o,w_c)}}$$

where w_o is the vector of the target word, w_c is some context vector calculated (for example, by averaging) from the vectors surrounding other words of the desired word, $s(w_1,w_2)$ is a function that maps one number to two vectors.

Word probabilities are predicted and optimized in the standard model discussed above. The function for optimization is the Kullback–Leibler divergence:

$$KL(p||q) = \int p(x) \log \frac{p(x)}{q(x)} dx$$

where $p(x)$ is the probability distribution of words that is taken from the dataset, $q(x)$ is the distribution that is generated by the model. Divergence shows how much a distribution is different from another one.

3.3 Neural Network Model for Sentiment Analysis of Text Fragments

A neural network model can be represented in the form of layers used in its architecture. A neural network consists of seven layers and is shown in Fig. 2.

Mathematically, the only output of a neuron is determined by its inputs and a weight matrix as follows:

$$y = f(u), where u = \sum_{i=1}^{n} w_i x_i + w_0 x_0$$

where x_i and w_i are the signals at the inputs of the neuron and the weights of the inputs, respectively. The function u is called the induced local field, and $f(u)$ is called the transfer function. Input signals take values in the interval [0, 1]. Input x_0 and the corresponding weight w_0 are used to initialize the neuron. Initialization refers to a shift in the activation function of a neuron along the horizontal axis.

Each neuron is associated with the concept of an activation function, which can be given as:

$$f(x) = tx$$

where t is the factor responsible for the distribution of the activation function. The proposed neural network architecture has the following set of layers:

- The Embedding layer is the input layer of the neural network:

Embedding   ConvlD   MaxPooling1D   LSTM   LSTM   Dropout   Dense

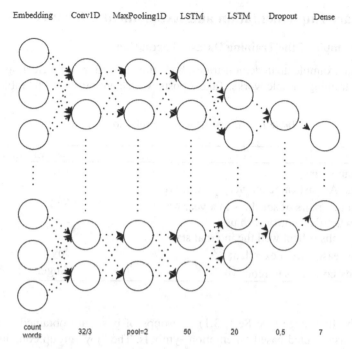

count words   32/3   pool=2   50   20   0.5   7

Fig. 2. The architecture of the developed neural network.

$$Emb = \{Size(D), Size(S_{vec}), L_{Sec}\},$$

where $Size(D)$ is the size of the dictionary in the text data, $Size(S_{vec})$ is the size of the vector space into which the words will be inserted, $Size(S_{vec}) = 32$, L_{Sec} is the length of the input sequences equal to the maximum size of the vector formed during word processing.

- The Conv1D layer is a convolutional layer, necessary for deep learning. With this layer, the accuracy of the classification of posts is increased by 5–7%. The number of filters is 32, each filter has length 3. The activation function is "ReLU".
- Layer MaxPooling1D is a layer responsible for storing temporary data. The maximum pool is 2.
- The LSTM layer is a recurrent neural network layer. The model uses 2 LSTM layers, one consists of 50 neurons, the second consists of 20 neurons.
- The Dropout layer is needed to avoid retraining the neural network. A value of 0.5 is given as a parameter, which means that a neural network can exclude up to half of inactive neurons.
- The Dense layer is an output layer of seven neurons. Each neuron is responsible for a specific emotion.

4 Software Implementation and Experimental Results

4.1 An Example of the Training Dataset Formation

Consider an example that demonstrates how the algorithm for selecting posts for obtaining a training sample works. Take 7 posts, which are presented in Table 1.

Table 1. The first stage of the selection of posts.

Text	Emotion
i love summer	Joy
July and August came out very productive -	-
I killed two pairs of sneakers in a year 😟	Sad
that's why it's so dirty with us	-
photographs reflect well the internal state	-
closing season went excellent ☺	Joy
my body continues to rebel 😡	Anger

After the first stage (see Sect. 3.1), 7 groups of posts are obtained. Each group contains posts selected based on emotion symbols. The "joy" group contains 2 posts, since they contain copyright symbols of emotions from the "joy" group in the example. The "sadness" and "anger" groups contain 1 post each, since they contain symbols of emotions from the corresponding groups. The remaining groups do not contain posts, since posts containing the author's emotion symbols for these groups did not meet.

At the second stage, the selection is based on key phrases. Each emotional group is specified based on a dictionary of key phrases. The selection result is presented in Table 2.

Table 2. The second stage of the post selection.

Text	Emotion
i love summer	Joy
I killed two pairs of sneakers in a year 😟	Sad
closing season went excellent ☺	Joy
my body continues to rebel 😡	Anger

The output consists of posts that contain keywords from the dictionary. For a group, "joy" is the words "love" and "excellent". For other posts, keywords for this emotional group were not found.

The number of posts after each selection stage is shown in Table 3. 2.5 million posts are sent to the entrance. The number of posts in each group is reduced on average by 2–3 times after each stage of selection. It should be noted that the generated set contains posts of various lengths.

Table 3. Formation of the training set.

Emotion	The number of posts after stage 1	The number of posts after stage 2
Joy	237837	74309
Sadness	7274	2629
Surprise	2739	1535
Fear	4640	2436
Anger	1363	512
Contempt	9960	5613
Disgust	5011	1206

4.2 The Algorithm for the Formation of a Training Dataset

A software system of sentiment analysis of social network posts was implemented to evaluate the effectiveness of the proposed models and algorithms.

The neural network was implemented in Python using the TensorFlow and Keras frameworks intended for machine learning. Python was chosen as the programming language.

Input data is 2.5 million posts from the social network VKontakte. Posts were automatically downloaded from open social network groups via the VKontakte API, and contain only textual information [16].

The neural network, consisting of seven layers, was trained at a different number of posts, from 500 to 1000 and more. The number of learning eras is 100. The set was divided into training and test datasets, 90% and 10% of the whole dataset, respectively.

Posts with lengths in a certain interval (40–50 words or 290–310 characters) were selected for experiments 4–7. For short posts the neural network cannot be trained.

During the experiments, the following hypothesis was verified: the training set, formed on the basis of the author's emoticons and key phrases, is better than:

- a set formed only on the basis of key phrases.
- a set formed only on the basis of emoticons.

3 training sets for experiments were formed:

- based on emoticons and key phrases (includes the first and second stages of selecting posts);
- based on only emoticons (includes only the first stage of the selection of posts, the second stage of selection is excluded);
- based on only key phrases (includes only the second stage of selection of posts, the first stage of selection is excluded).

The results of the experiments are shown in Table 4.

Table 4. The results of the experiments.

№	Algorithm	Number of posts	Selection training set by	The dataset is balanced	Class weights	Post length	Accuracy in the training set	Accuracy on test dataset
1	word2vec	1042	emoticons and keywords	No	No	40–50 words	0,98	0,77
2	word2vec	1042	emoticons and keywords	No	Yes	40–50 words	0,97	0,79
3	BERT	556	emoticons and keywords	No	No	290–310 characters	0,95	0,86
4	BERT	556	emoticons and keywords	No	Yes	290–310 characters	0,95	0,87
5	BERT	726	emoticons	No	Yes	290–310 characters	0,94	0,8
6	BERT	726	emoticons	No	No	290–310 characters	0,91	0,82
7	BERT	2100	Keywords	Yes	No	290–310 characters	0,87	0,83
8	BERT	513	emoticons and keywords, no stop-words	No	Yes	290–310 characters	0,95	0,82

Experiments № 4–6 show that a sample formed on the basis of copyright symbols of emotions and key phrases is better than a sample only on the basis of copyright symbols of expression of emotions or only based on key phrases.

Experiment №8 shows that a neural network trained on a sample with stop words has higher accuracy than that trained on a sample without stop words.

5   Conclusion

In this work the neural network LSTM architecture was used to determine the emotional coloring of posts in a social network. The best result was when using the BERT algorithm for text processing. During the study, accuracy rate 87% in determining the emotional coloring of the posts was achieved.

In future studies, we plan to improve the algorithm for the formation of training samples, including approaches based on expanding the dictionaries.

Acknowledgement. This study was supported by the Russian Foundation for Basic Research (Grants No. 18-47-732007, 18-47-730035 and 19-07-00999).

References

1. Vlasov, D., et al.: Description of the information image of a user of a social network taking into account its psychological characteristics. Int. J. Open Inf. Technol. **6**(4) (2018)
2. Sabuj, M.S., Afrin, Z., Hasan, K.M.Azharul: Opinion mining using support vector machine with web based diverse data. In: Shankar, B.U., Ghosh, K., Mandal, D.P., Ray, S.S., Zhang, D., Pal, Sankar K. (eds.) PReMI 2017. LNCS, vol. 10597, pp. 673–678. Springer, Cham (2017). https://doi.org/10.1007/978-3-319-69900-4_85
3. Dinu, L.P., Iuga, I.: The best feature of the set. In: Gelbukh, A. (ed.) Computational Linguistics and Intelligent Text Processing. CICLing 2012. Lecture Notes in Computer Science, vol. 718, pp. 556–567. Springer, Heidelberg (2012). https://doi.org/10.1007/978-3-642-19400-9_5
4. Chetviorkin, I.I., Loukachevitch, N.V.: Sentiment analysis track at ROMIP-2012. In: Computational Linguistics and Intellectual Technologies. Computer Linguistics and Intelligent Technologies: Dialogue 2013. Sat Scientific Articles, vol. 2, pp. 40–50 (2012)
5. Qufei, C., Sokolova, M.: Word2Vec and Doc2Vec in unsupervised sentiment analysis of clinical discharge summaries. CoRR abs/1805.00352 (2018)
6. Antonova, A., Soloviev, A.: Using the conditional random field method for processing texts in Russian. In: Computer Linguistics and Intelligent Technologies: Dialogue 2013. Sat Scientific Articles, vol. 12, no. 19, pp. 27–44. Publishing House of the Russian State Humanitarian University (2013)
7. Maas, A.L., Daly, R.E., Pham, P.T., Huang, D., Ng, A.Y., Potts, C.: Learning word vectors for sentiment analysis. In: The International Language Technologies-Volume 1 International Association for Computational Linguistics, pp. 142–150 (2011)
8. Moshkin, V., Yarushkina, N., Andreev, I.: The Sentiment Analysis of unstructured social network data using the extended ontology SentiWordNet. In: IEEE, 12th International Conference on Developments in eSystems Engineering (DeSE), Kazan, Russia, pp. 576–580 (2019). https://doi.org/10.1109/dese.2019.00110
9. Bogdanov, A.L., Dulya, I.S.: Sentiment analysis of short Russian-language texts in social media. Bull. Tomsk State Univ. Econ. **47**, 159–168 (2019)
10. Smirnova, O.S., Shishkov, V.V.: The choice of neural network topology and their application for the classification of short texts. Int. J. Open Inf. Technol. **4**(8), 50–54 (2016)
11. Kolmogorova, A.V., Vdovina, L.A.: Lexico-grammatical markers of emotions as parameters for sentiment analysis of Russian-language Internet texts. Bull. Perm Univ. Russ. Foreign Philol. **3**, 38–46 (2019)
12. WordNetAffect. http://wndomains.fbk.eu/wnaffect.html. Accessed 21 Apr 2020
13. Devlin, J., et al.: BERT: pre-training of deep bidirectional transformers for language understanding. arXiv preprint arXiv:1810.04805 (2018)
14. Horev, R.: BERT explained: state of the art language model for NLP. https://towardsdatascience.com/bert-explained-state-of-the-art-language-model-for-nlp-f8b21a9b6270. Accessed 21 Apr 2020
15. Algorithm Word2Vec. https://neurohive.io/ru/. Accessed 21 Apr 2020
16. Filippov, A., Moshkin, V., Yarushkina, N.: Development of a software for the semantic analysis of social media content. In: Dolinina, O., Brovko, A., Pechenkin, V., Lvov, A., Zhmud, V., Kreinovich, V. (eds.) ICIT 2019. SSDC, vol. 199, pp. 421–432. Springer, Cham (2019). https://doi.org/10.1007/978-3-030-12072-6_34

Keyword Extraction Approach Based on Probabilistic-Entropy, Graph, and Neural Network Methods

Anton A. Selivanov$^{(\boxtimes)}$ [ID], Ivan A. Moloshnikov [ID], Roman B. Rybka [ID], and Alexandr G. Sboev [ID]

NRC "Kurchatov Institute", Moscow, Russia
aaselivanov.10.03@gmail.com

Abstract. Nowadays, methods of automatic keyword extraction are developed based on statistical and graph features of texts. The transfer of learning approaches allows one to use additional word features obtained from deep neural network models fitted to solve different tasks. The paper proposes an integrated approach to keyword extraction based on a classification model that aggregates results of probabilistic-entropy, graph methods, and word features extracted from a neural network for text title generation. To validate the method, a dataset of news texts was gathered, with keywords manually selected through crowdsourcing. For the proposed approach F1-measure weighted by classes accuracy of keyword extraction is 72%, which is approximately 5% better in comparison with the existing methods.

Keywords: Machine learning · Natural language processing · Automatic keyword extraction

1 Introduction

The volume of unstructured text information grows fast, which leads to difficulties in its analysis. Thus, solutions are needed to help in navigation through huge amounts of text data. An example of such solutions is automatic text summarization, including keyword extraction methods.

Algorithms applied to this task are usually validated on a data, where keywords are chosen by authors, e.g. news articles, scientific papers abstracts. Such keywords often serve for purposes other than information extraction (like interaction with search engines, or categorization of a text on specific web-resource). Also, there is a probability of strong personal opinion influence.

A possible solution is to collect dataset with relevant keywords based on an aggregation of survey data from several independent respondents for each text. The difficulty is in the lack of an objective measure: how much a word characterizes a text. Any choice of words is subjective due to the personal text understanding of different people. Therefore, it is advisable to use a large number of keyword estimations.

© Springer Nature Switzerland AG 2020
S. O. Kuznetsov et al. (Eds.): RCAI 2020, LNAI 12412, pp. 284–295, 2020.
https://doi.org/10.1007/978-3-030-59535-7_21

The research goal is to develop an automatic keyword extraction method based on various features, and validate it on a special dataset collected on a crowdsourcing platform.

Automatic keyword extraction task is well studied in modern literature. There are several approaches: statistical-based and graph-based. In the course of research we propose two extensions of the existing instruments: knowledge-transferring method from a neural network trained to generate text title on a big text dataset, and classifier to aggregate estimations of different method to single word-ranking mechanism. Automatic keyword extraction methods are described in Sect. 2 (Related Works). The classifier is described in Sect. 3.1 (Developed Approach Based on a Machine Learning), and training data in Sect. 3.2 (Data Description). Computational experiments are presented in Sect. 4 (Experiments). Experimental results and their interpretation are presented in Sect. 5 (Results).

2 Related Works

2.1 Statistical Methods of Automatic Keyword Extraction

Term Frequency (TF) – number of word occurrences divided by overall number of words in particular document. Therefore, this method gives keywords which are occurring most frequently.

Rapid Automatic Keyword Extraction (RAKE) [1] – the first step is to choose keyphrase candidates: text is split into spans by a list of stop words and punctuation marks, then frequency threshold is set to exclude candidates with low frequency. The second step is to build co-occurrence matrix. The matrix contains number of co-occurrence for every word with other words in spans (this number called"word degree"), and a number of word occurrence in the whole text (word frequency). The rank of a word is word degree divided by word frequency.

KPMiner [2] – keyphrase candidates are chose the same way as in RAKE, but the final list of candidates includes only the ones that occurred three times minimum, and at least once before 400th character. Word rank based on term frequency. Also the word rank includes empiric coefficient, it addresses to the fact that phrases usually occurs less than separate words, but could be better in text characterization.

YAKE [3] – uses a set of features to calculate word's rank: acronym tags, frequency of word spelling with capital letter, word position in text, number of unique co-occurred words in window of 5 words. Ranked phrases are estimated by Levenstein distance to mark phrases as duplicates if the distance is small.

SBE [4] – text preprocessing includes splitting text on separate sentences and words, and stop words excluding. Word rank is based on the following features: informational entropy, that shows how uniform is word distribution over documents, weights calculated with Bernoulli distribution [5], indicator of general-use words (IDF analogue, calculated with word frequency from National Corpus of

Russian Language). In case of keyword extraction from the single text (without related text collection), informational entropy has less influence on a rank due to uniform word distribution over collection.

2.2   Graph Methods of Automatic Keyword Extraction

TextRank [6] – text is represented as a graph, where nodes are words (nouns or adjectives), and edges are words co-occurrence in windows of size between 2 and 10. Each edge weight calculation based on iterative stochastic algorithm PageRank [7].

SingleRank [8] – the method is TextRank analogue, but edges based on a wider window (from 2 to 20 words), and edge weight is scaled with co-occurence frequency.

TopicRank [9] – the main concept of the method is an extraction of keywords from the most important text topics, which are sets of similar keyphrase candidates. The candidates are continuous sequences of adjectives and nouns. Similar phrases are united in topics. Similarity metric is length of the most common part of two phrases after lemmatization: if compared phrases have more than 25% in common, they're ranked as the same topic. The automated process of topic extraction is based on an agglomerative hierarchical clustering. The topics are used as graph nodes. The edges weights are distances within the text between words of compared topics (i.e. a sum of pairwise distance calculation for words from different topics). Nodes are ranked the same way as TextRank. Resulting keyphrases from the topics are the ones that occurred in the text first.

PositionRank [10] – it's ranking takes on account words position on base of position-biased PageRank. Text graph includes nouns and adjectives only. Edges are based on co-occurence in window of size from 2 to 20. PageRank is modified with position parameter, which is sum of inverted positions of a word occurrences in text, normalized by a sum of estimations of all words. Therefore, rank of node v_i in position-based PageRank is the following:

$$S(v_i) = (1 - a) * p_i + a * \sum_{j=1}^{n_i} \frac{S(v_j) * w_{ji}}{O(v_j)},$$

where
   a – a "damping coefficient" of PageRank, a value, that defines algorithm's probability to switch a node i.
   w_{ji} – edge weight between nodes j and i;
   n_i – the number of nodes connected to a node i;
   $O(v_j) = sum(w_{jk})$.
   This algorithm generates phrases on base of sequences of length 3 from chosen words. Separate words ranks used to estimate phrases.

MultipartiteRank [11] – algorithm improves TopicRank approach. As in TopicRank, text is filtered and used to make topics. Topics are used to build multipartite graph, where keyphrase candidates are nodes, and parts of graph are topics. Edges weights are a sums of inverted distances between the occurrences of keyphrases. This approach let us to consider separate words with taking into account topics structure. Another difference is that graph in this method is directed: edges weights are rised if the edge is directed to word that occurred in the text earlier. TextRank algorithm is used to calculate final rank of the nodes.

3   Materials and Methods

3.1   Developed Approach Based on a Machine Learning

The hypothesis is that keyword extraction efficiency could be improved through fitting machine learning algorithm using the following word features: activities of the neural network for text title generation, and word ranking from statistics- and graph-based methods.

Neural network for text title generation [12] has Transformer [13,14] topology, which includes encoder and decoder, each of them is a sequence of six Multihead Attention layers.

Multihead Attention is a set of parallel topology parts called "heads" with the same structure. The structure is described in [13].

Input text is splitted to tokens – word parts represented as vectors inside encoder. Token dictionary is a result of model training. A word could be represented as a set of tokens, if dictionary doesn't contain it (for example word "kittycat" would be splitted into tokens "kitty" and "cat"). In prediction stage neural network activities are extracted from the multihead attention decoder layer for every input token, they form a matrix A with size of $m * n * k$, where m is number of the "heads", n is number of input tokens, k is a number of words in generated text title.

Average activities of heads is matrix A' of $n * k$. It's used for word features calculation. Each input word is matched with tokens and activities from the model. We use 5 first tokens for each word (the most of the words are represented as a set of tokens of the size from 1 to 5). Only 20 first values are taken from activities vector (so, k is equal to 20, all values after 20th are dropped). Thus, for each word there is activities matrix T of $n' * k'$, where n' – number of word tokens is 5, and k' – activity vector size for each token, is 20.

We used two variants of activities representation as word features:

1. token vectors are concatenated resulted in vector of 100 values, this feature called "NN activities" in the paper;
2. average value for each word token, that concatenated to vector of 5 values, this feature called "aggregated NN activities" in the paper.

Word position feature is inverted word number value (according to hypothesis, partly confirmed by effect of KPMiner and PositionRank, that takes into account word position).

Conceptual scheme of the keyword extraction algorithm based on a complex of probabilistic entropy, graph, and neural network methods with use of machine learning presented on Fig. 1.

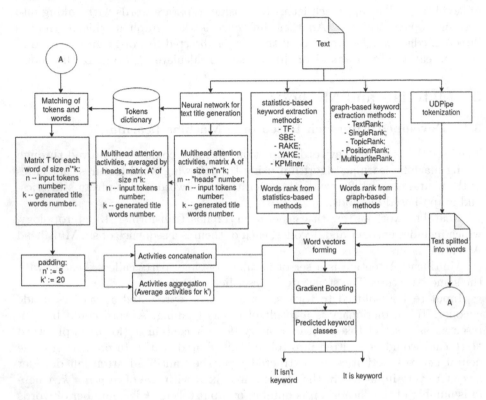

Fig. 1. Conceptual scheme of the keyword extraction algorithm based on a complex of probabilistic entropy, graph, and neural network methods with use of machine learning

Algorithm includes the following steps:

1. text segmentation;
2. word ranks calculation with various conventional methods:
   - statistical methods;
   - graph methods;
3. knowledge extraction from neural network model of text title generation:
   (a) input text tokenization with tokenizer of neural network model for text title generation (in this case it was multilingual BERT preliminary fitted on the entire Wikipedia dump for top-100 languages[1]);
   (b) matching BERT tokens with input text words obtained in step 1;

---

[1] Pre-fitted model could be found here: https://github.com/google-research/bert.

(c) title prediction for the input text to obtain activities for each input token. Model is preliminary trained and tested on the ria news dataset[2]. Resulting matrix is A, $m * n * k$, where m is multihead attention "heads" number, n is input tokens number, k is generated title length in words;

(d) calculation of average activities for each token (by "heads" of multihead attention), resulting matrix is A', $n * k$;

(e) calculation activities for each word, resulting matrix is T, $n' * k$;

(f) padding and cutting of T matrix, transform it ti the size $5 * 20$;

(g) calculation of "NN activities" and "aggregated NN activities" features described in the text before;

4. features concatenation in a single vector. We obtain vector for each word that was estimated on crowdsourcing platform, thus every word in resulting dataset could be classified as "keyword" or "not a keyword" (word estimation procedure described in Sect. 3.2);

5. training Gradient Boosting model on 75% of the texts (train set);

6. prediction of word classes for remaining 25% of the texts (test set).

We used normalized ranks of RAKE, YAKE, TF, SBE, KPMiner and position as statictical features, normalized ranks of TextRank, SingleRank, TopicRank, PositionRank, MultipartiteRank as graph features. Gradient boosting [15] was used as machine learning method, sklearn library [16] implementation. We used UDPipe [17] for text tokenization.

3.2 Data Description

Usually keyword extraction algorithms are validated with data, where authors defined keywords, for example news articles or science papers abstracts.

Disadvantage of the approach is that author's keywords could have goals different from text information representation (e.g., searching engine interaction or text categorization), and strong influence of personal opinion.

The difficulty of the task is lack of an objective measure: how much a word characterizes a text, any choice of words is subjective due to the text understanding is different for people. Therefore, it is advisable to use a large number of keyword estimates.

Possible solution is to collect dataset with relevant keywords based on an aggregation of survey data from independent respondents.

In the research we collected validation dataset with labeled keywords on a crowdsourcing platform[3]. Also we took into account necessity to distinguish conscientious annotators' responds from "random" and "incorrect".

We selected 200 articles in russian language from "RIA news" dataset. The same dataset were used to train title generation model. To be sure in correct experiment setup, texts were randomly chosen from the part of dataset used for model testing, so, the texts weren't the part of a neural network model fitting process.

---

[2] https://github.com/RossiyaSegodnya/ria_news_dataset.

[3] You could get an access to dataset through contacts available at https://sagteam.ru.

Average text length: 1862 characters, 301 words. Set of keyword candidates was obtained for every text with the statistical methods (SBE, RAKE) to let respondents estimate them on the following scale:

1. the word is complete nonsense or isn't related to text;
2. generally the word characterizes particular text part, but doesn't represent specificity/is to generic;
3. the word represents specific, distinctive details of the text.

To track bad-quality labeling, we included incorrect words in keyword candidates set: stop-words, and repeating words (three repeats of two words). Estimation of these words were used to calculate respondent error. Annotations of respondents with high error rate were excluded from the research.

Every validation text had 10 estimates from different respondents. Ground truth keywords are the ones, that has average estimation equal or higher than 2.5 (empirically chosen threshold, it means that respondents majority estimated the word with the maximum estimation – 3).

Therefore, each validation text has a set of keywords based on various subjective estimations. Collected dataset was used to evaluate methods of automatic keywords extraction.

4   Experiments

Initial validation sample splits into train sample (150 texts) and test sample (50 texts). The task formulated as binary classification: 0 class for non-keywords, 1st class for keywords. We used only words from estimated set (thus, every considered word has ground truth estimation based on a survey). Each word is represented as the vector matched with the first occurrence of the word in text – it's important for position feature and neural network activities. Test sample contains 730 words of class 0, and 578 words of class 1(keywords).

Weighted f1-score was used as an accuracy metric, formulas described further. Designations:

- $words$ – a set of text words, that were candidates for estimation on a crowd-sourcing platform;
- kw_{valid} – keywords, that respondents estimated as a keywords (words with average estimation equal or higher than 2.5 on the 1–3 scale on base of 10 estimations);
- kw_{non_valid} – words estimated as non-keywords (with estimation lower than 2.5).

$$kw_{non\_valid} = words \setminus kw_{valid}.$$

- kw_{method} – words that was ranked as keywords based on keyword extraction method, i.e. which rank is higher than 75% quantile. In case if method ranks phrases, we split them on separate words, each of them has phrase rank;
- kw_{non_method} – words ranked lower than 75% quantile.

$$kw_{non\_method} = words \backslash kw_{method}.$$

- tp – number of true positives;
- fp – number of false positives;
- fn – number of false negatives;
- i – number of the text.

For the class 0:

$$tp_0 = |\sum_{i=1}^{n_0} kw_{non\_method}^i \bigcap kw_{non\_valid}^i|;$$

$$fp_0 = |\sum_{i=1}^{n_0} kw_{non\_method}^i \bigcap kw_{valid}^i|;$$

$$fn_0 = |\sum_{i=1}^{n_0} kw_{method}^i \bigcap kw_{non\_valid}^i|;$$

$$n_0 = |kw_{non\_valid}|.$$

For the class 1:

$$tp_1 = |\sum_{i=1}^{n_1} kw_{method}^i \bigcap kw_{valid}^i|;$$

$$fp_1 = |\sum_{i=1}^{n_1} kw_{method}^i \bigcap kw_{non\_valid}^i|;$$

$$fn_1 = |\sum_{i=1}^{n_1} kw_{non\_method}^i \bigcap kw_{valid}^i|;$$

$$n_1 = |kw_{valid}|.$$

The following metrics are calculated for each class k:

$$precision_k = \frac{tp_k}{tp_k + fp_k};$$

$$recall_k = \frac{tp_k}{tp_k + fn_k};$$

$$f1_k = \frac{2 * precision_k * recall_k}{precision_k + recall_k};$$

$$weight_k = \frac{n_k}{\sum_{j=1}^{|k|} n_j};$$

$$f1_{weighted} = \frac{\sum_{j=1}^{|k|} weight_k * f1_k}{|k|}.$$

The following experiment task formulations were considered to obtain information about features contribution to accuracy of keyword extraction:

- word representation based on statistics methods (including word positions),
- word representation based on statistics methods (including word positions), and NN activities (including aggregated),
- word representation based on graph methods,
- word representation based on graph methods, and NN activities (including aggregated),
- word representation based on statistics methods (including word positions), and graph methods,
- word representation based on statistics methods (including word positions), and graph methods, and NN activities (including aggregated).

In case of NN activities usage, different configurations were considered: usage only aggregated activities, only unaggregated activities, or both, usage activities from different layers of Transformer: ([6], [5, 6], [4, 5, 6], [3, 4, 5, 6], [2, 3, 4, 5, 6], [1, 2, 3, 4, 5, 6]).

In result, it's possible to define, what neural network features bring in keyword extraction task resolved with machine learning algorithm.

5   Results

Different feature sets usage results are presented in Table 1.

Table 1. Results of the experiments over including different features into feature space

#	Features	Precision	Recall	F1-score
1	Statistics	0.69	0.69	0.69
2	Statistics and aggregated NN (layers: 2–6)	0.71	0.71	0.71
3	Graph	0.68	0.67	0.67
4	Graph and aggregated NN (layers: 5, 6)	0.69	0.68	0.68
5	Graph and statistics	0.69	0.68	0.69
6	**Statistics, graph, and NN (6th layer)**	**0.72**	**0.72**	**0.72**

According to results presented in the table, adding neural network features into feature space makes possible to achieve higher accuracy after fitting the model. Adding NN features to statistical features, accuracy increase is 2%, to graph features is 1%, and to set of statistical and graph features is 3.

Table 2. Comparison of automatic keyword extraction methods

#	Method type	Method	Precision	Recall	F1-score
1	**Combined**	**Gradient boosting**	**0.72**	**0.72**	**0.72**
2	Graph	PositionRank	0.68	0.68	0.67
3	Graph	MultipartiteRank	0.66	0.67	0.66
4	Graph	TopicRank	0.66	0.66	0.66
5	Graph	TextRank	0.66	0.66	0.66
6	Graph	SingleRank	0.65	0.65	0.64
7	Statistics	KPMiner	0.70	0.63	0.56
8	Statistics	NN-based	0.56	0.67	0.55
9	Statistics	Term Frequency	0.66	0.56	0.52
10	Statistics	RAKE	0.51	0.52	0.51
11	Statistics	SBE	0.70	0.55	0.49
12	Statistics	YAKE	0.49	0.53	0.47

Comparison of methods from Sects. 2.1 and 2.2 with the method based on additional model training presented in Table 2.

It should be noted that additional machine learning model even without NN features improves results of keyword extraction based on statistical features on 13% (first row of Table 1, see seventh row of Table 2).

6 Conclusion

The paper presents an improvement in solving the keyword extraction problem. The proposed approach is based on a gradient boosting model that aggregates scores obtained by statistics-based and graph-based methods, activation values from the decoding layer of a Transformer neural network for text title generation, and the position of the word. The proposed solution outperforms existing statistics-based and graph-based methods, demonstrating the f1-weighted score of 0.72 on the specially created labeled dataset of 200 news articles collected from the RIA news agency.

The results obtained lead to the following conclusions:

- the keyword extraction task in the considered formulation does not come down to achieving high accuracy with any single feature, but every feature makes a contribution to the result;
- adding machine learning method to statistical method of keyword extraction increases the weighted f1-score by 13%;
- adding neural network activities into feature space increases f1-score by 2% in case of statistical features, 1% in case of graph features, and 3% in case of using both types of features;

- adding machine learning method into keyword extraction process increases f1-score by 5%, in comparison with other keyword extraction methods.

   The following options could be considered as further development of the research:

- validation of the developed method on different open datasets (SemEval, Wikipedia);
- expansion of the feature space with features used in other keyword extraction methods, for example PageRank, frequency of words written in capital case, context- and sentence-related features, etc.;
- consideration of another machine learning algorithms including neural networks;
- adaptation of the developed method for keyphrase extraction.

Acknowledgements.. The reported study was funded by RFBR (project 18-29-10084). This work has been carried out using computing resources of the federal collective user center Complex for Simulation and Data Processing for Mega-science Facilities at NRC "Kurchatov Institute", http://ckp.nrcki.ru/.

References

1. Rose, S., Engel, D., Cramer, N., Cowley, W.: Automatic keyword extraction from individual documents. Text Min. Appl. Theory **1**, 1–20 (2010)
2. El-Beltagy, S.R., Rafea, A.: KP-miner: participation in SemEval-2. In: Proceedings of the 5th International Workshop on Semantic Evaluation, pp. 190–193 (2010)
3. Campos, R., Mangaravite, V., Pasquali, A., Jorge, A., Nunes, C., Jatowt, A.: YAKE! keyword extraction from single documents using multiple local features. Inf. Sci. **509**, 257–89 (2020)
4. Gydovskikh, D.V., Moloshnikov, I.A., Naumov, A.V., Rybka, R.B., Sboev, A.G., Selivanov, A.A.: A probabilistically entropic mechanism of topical clusterisation along with thematic annotation for evolution analysis of meaningful social information of internet sources. Lobachevskii J. Math. **38**(5), 910–913 (2017). https://doi.org/10.1134/S1995080217050134
5. Gianni, A., Rijsbergen, V.: Cornelis Joost probabilistic models of information retrieval based on measuring the divergence from randomness. ACM Trans. Inf. Syst. (TOIS) **20**(4), 357–389 (2002)
6. Mihalcea R., Tarau P. Textrank: Bringing order into text. In: Proceedings of the 2004 Conference on Empirical Methods in Natural Language Processing, pp. 404–411 (2004)
7. Page, L., Brin, S., Motwani, R., Winograd, T.: The pagerank citation ranking: Bringing order to the web. Stanford InfoLab, 11 November 1999
8. Wan, X., Xiao, J.: CollabRank: towards a collaborative approach to single-document keyphrase extraction. In: Proceedings of the 22nd International Conference on Computational Linguistics (Coling 2008), pp. 969–976 (2008)
9. Bougouin, A., Boudin, F.: TopicRank: topic ranking for automatic keyphrase extraction, no. 55. pp. 45–69 (2014)

10. Florescu, C., Caragea, C.: PositionRank: an unsupervised approach to keyphrase extraction from scholarly documents. In: Proceedings of the 55th Annual Meeting of the Association for Computational Linguistics, vol. 1, pp. 1105–1115 (2017)
11. Boudin, F.: Unsupervised keyphrase extraction with multipartite graphs. arXiv preprint arXiv:1803.08721 (2018)
12. Moloshnikov, I.A., Gryaznov, A.V., Vlasov, D.S., Sboev, A.G.: Vibor effectivnogo neirosetevovo metoda formirovaniya zagolovkov. In: NRNC MePhI. VI International Conference "Lasernie i plasmennie tehnologii i issledovaniya, LaPlaz-2020" proceedings, vol. 1., pp. 80–81 (2020)
13. Vaswani, A., et al.: Attention is all you need. In: Advances in Neural Information Processing Systems, pp. 5998–6008 (2017)
14. Sokolov, A.M.: Phrase-based attentional transformer dlya generacii zagolovkov. Kompyuternaya lingvistika i intellektualnie technologii (po materialam ezhegodnoi konferencii "Dialog"), no. 18 (2019). Additional tome
15. Friedman, J.: Greedy function approximation: a gradient boosting machine. Ann. Stat. **29**(5), 1189–1232 (2001)
16. Pedregosa, F.: Scikit-learn: machine learning in Python. J. Mach. Learn. Res. **12**(Oct), 2825–2830 (2011)
17. Straka, M., Straková, J.: Tokenizing, POS Tagging, lemmatizing and parsing UD 2.0 with UDPipe. In: Proceedings of the CoNLL 2017 Shared Task: Multilingual Parsing from Raw Text to Universal Dependencies (2017)

Method of Selecting Experts Based on Analysis of Large Unstructured Data and Their Relations

Michael A. Shiray[1]($\boxtimes$) and Oleg G. Grigoriev[2]

[1] «Berishop» Limited Liability Company, Moscow, Russia
michael.sheerai@gmail.com
[2] Federal Research Center "Computer Science and Control" of Russian
Academy of Sciences, Moscow, Russia
oleggpolikvart@yandex.ru

Abstract. The paper describes the problems of automatic selection of experts for reviewing scientific texts. Existing methods are analyzed, and a new selection method is proposed, based on obtaining a ranked list of relevant experts by processing a large amount of unstructured data. A technique for evaluating the results of similar methods is proposed and the effectiveness of the proposed approaches are studied in experiments.

Keywords: Scientific expertise · Expert selection · Big data · Semantic search · Similar document retrieval · Reference ranking · Unstructured data analysis

1 Introduction

Financing of modern science is increasingly moving from a model of financing organizations to direct financing of teams of scientists through grants, that is, to piece-rate form of payment. The new financing system opens up opportunities for a much more efficient distribution of funds, to support the most relevant, "breakthrough" areas of science. A necessary condition for the work quality of such a system is the objectivity and transparency of the expert evaluation of grant applications. The main problem in evaluating applications is the selection of objective and competent experts for each application. Therefore, experts must meet the following criteria:

1. Correspondence of the expert's competencies to both the subject of the application under consideration and the subject of the competition.
2. Lack of affiliation of experts with participants in the grant application.

The main approach to the appointment of the experts today - the use of qualifiers and keywords, which are usually drawn up manually. This approach depends entirely on the quality of the classifier, which requires constant clarifications and updates, as

---

The research is supported by Russian Foundation for Basic Research (grant №18-29-03087).

S. O. Kuznetsov et al. (Eds.): RCAI 2020, LNAI 12412, pp. 296–308, 2020.
https://doi.org/10.1007/978-3-030-59535-7_22

well as on the adequacy of the selected keywords, which is very difficult to implement. Often, the selection of experts is carried out using nontransparent and unclear methods, without taking into account a possible conflict of interest. At the same time, in the digital age, information on the expert's competencies is implicitly accumulated in large amounts of data and texts (scientific articles, scientific and technical reports, history of previous peer reviews, patents, etc.). These arrays contain much more useful information about experts than manually assigned classifier codes or keywords. In view of the foregoing, to determine the competencies and characteristics of an expert, one can and should use the information accumulated in large amounts of data and texts. Due to large amounts of information, it is almost impossible to select experts with the help of the expert community. To get implicit knowledge about experts, it is necessary to use methods of text and data mining. As a result, when using the examination system adopted at present, refusals from the examination occur, or it is carried out by incompetent experts. For a more accurate selection of an expert for given application, it is necessary not only to determine the general correspondence of the expert's competencies and the object of examination subject area, but also to have a number of additional characteristics that allow ranking experts.

Thus, the problem arises of both automatic selection of experts with competencies closest to the subject of the application under consideration, and their ranking taking into account their competence and possible conflicts of interest. In [1], a method for expert search was proposed based on topical similarity of scientific articles, patents and applications of an expert to the text of the application under consideration using methods of deep linguistic analysis of text documents. This method applies both filtering (selection) of the list of potential experts and its ranking. Filtering is an exception of experts from the general list who do not fit in some parameters. Ranking, i.e., building the order relation r (rank) on the set of all remaining experts, in order to determine the most suitable expert for the examination of the project. The method is based on the following assumptions: the author of a text has a complete understanding of what he writes about; the expert will have a better understanding of those texts that use his usual terminology. According to the results of the study [1], this assumption has its own reasons. Judging by the results of the described experiment, the authors managed to achieve good recall and precision indicators on various topics. However, in addition to the fact that the obtained recall and precision values are far from ideal, the metrics introduced by the authors of the work are aimed primarily at determining the filtration efficiency and do not fully reflect the ranking efficiency. Therefore, in this paper, the main attention is paid to the ranking mechanism, since it is the ranking that allows you to choose a subset of the most suitable experts from the whole set of selected experts. Thus, the aim of this work is to find ways to increase the precision and/or recall of the expert selection method, as well as an implementation of the recall and precision metrics that better reflects the characteristics of both filtering and ranking algorithms. In the study [1], the method of comparing the topical similarity of documents using the calculation of common terms, phrases, proximity of linguistic structures is used as the main method for assessing the competencies of experts. Documents for comparison: on the one hand, an application for assessment, on the other hand, past applications of experts. Based on their proximity, an assumption is made about the degree of compliance of the expert. The problem is that the application contains a small amount of information that does not fully represent neither the topic of research, nor, especially, the competence of the authors. To solve this problem, the competencies of experts on thematic similarities were ranked using an extended data set that includes the entire available database of documents. The ranking was carried out using a modified iterative algorithm for calculating the reference ranks [2].

2   Related Works

In [1, 3], reviews of methods and systems used to solve the problem of automation of expert search for peer review are presented, including: EasyChair [4] conference management system; semi-automatic methods, i.e., requiring additional action from experts [5, 6]; automatic, i.e., not requiring additional actions, among them: analysis of meta-information [7], including a bibliography [8, 9]; building models based on full texts [10, 11]. Their advantages and disadvantages are considered. These reviews can be supplemented by the following works: an expert selection system based on automatic analysis of the full texts of articles - Toronto Paper Matching System (TMPS) [12]. Limitations of this system include the fact that experts must manually provide information about their articles, and the result of the work strongly depends on the completeness of the information provided. Xiang Liu [13] uses graphic co-authorship models to resolve conflicts of interest when appointing experts, but does not analyze the full text of the articles. In [14], an approach to the analysis of the full texts of articles using semantic vector models is described, which is close to the one proposed in this paper, but does not fully take into account semantic constructions and connections between words.

The main difference between the approach proposed in this article and the aforementioned works is that, in addition to the texts of expert articles, the approach effectively uses data from articles of other authors that are not directly related to the experts considered, therefore, any method based on analysis expert texts themselves can be supplemented by this approach. The difference between this work and work [13] (where external factors are used regarding expert articles) and similar works based on reference graph analysis is that in this work the graph model of reference ranking is based on an assessment of the thematic similarity of articles complete texts, and not just information from the reference itself (title, authors). [15] provides examples of calculating various scientometric indicators through links between articles. The main difference between the approach from [15] and the approach proposed in this article is the use of thematic similarities of full texts to determine the initial rank of articles.

3   The Method of Experts Selection

3.1   Publication Sampling

This stage almost coincides with the stage described in [1]. At the first stage, for a given object of examination (application), a thematically similar document is searched in collections of scientific and technical texts [16]. This search methodology uses a relational-situational textual model that allows you to operate not only with words, but also with complex semantic constructions [17, 18]. All types of documents related or not related to experts are searched. These can be applications, scientific articles, patents, etc. A modified Hamming measure is used to calculate the degree of similarity. The main parameters of the method for searching for thematically similar documents are presented in Table 1.

Table 1. The main parameters for thematically similar documents search method

Description	Name
The percent of words and phrases in the source document that determine the similarity of documents	TOP_PERCENT
The maximum number of words and phrases that are used to determine document similarity	MAX_WORDS_COUNT
The minimum number of words and phrases that are used to determine the similarity of documents	MIN_WORDS_COUNT
Minimum TF-IDF weight of a word or phrase included in the top keywords of the document	MIN_WEIGHT
The minimum value of the similarity score	MIN_SIM
The maximum number of similar documents for the source document	MIN_DOCS_COUNT

Since the total amount will be used as a measure to assess the expert on the similarity of his documents, to improve the quality of the method, we subtract the minimum similarity (MIN_SIM) from the obtained values, so that only values that exceed the minimum threshold characterizing the average level of similarity are taken into account between arbitrary documents.

3.2   Construction of Reference Rank of Articles

For all publications received, a reference rating is created based on the following methodology. Articles and their references are presented in the form of a graph in which articles are vertices and references are arcs of the graph. By reference ranking model, we mean the function of calculating the rank of a vertex. To determine the thematic rank, it is necessary to choose the model of the reference rating correctly. A description of reference ranking models is presented in the article [19]. The methodology is based on the PageRank model [20].

Let G (V, E) be a digraph, where V is the set of vertices, and E is the set of arcs. S - adjacency matrix of graph G, consisting of elements $s_{ij} = \begin{cases} 0, & (j,i) \notin E \\ 1, & (j,i) \in E \end{cases}$, $i \in V, j \in V$. Based on the input parameters, the matrix cannot simultaneously contain references (i, j) and (j, i), the graph also has no cycles. Let $deg(i) = \sum_{j=0}^{N} S_{ij}$—the sum of the weights of all outgoing references of the vertex i. $S_t(i,j) = S_{ij}/deg(i)$—references weight matrix (i, j).

We define a thematic reference ranking model using this matrix and compose a system of linear algebraic equations (SLAE) in iterative form (1).

$$X_i^{k+1} = (1 - d) + d \sum_{j=1, j \neq i}^{N} X_j^k \cdot S_t(j, i) \tag{1}$$

Где d—attenuation coefficient, k—iteration step number, X_j^k—rank value of j-th vertex at iteration k. The initial values of the article ranks are established on the base of the found similarity coefficient between the article in question and the evaluated application. Thus, thematic similarities with the original application are transmitted along arcs and accumulate at the vertices of the graph. To calculate the reference rank using the specified model, it is necessary to solve a system of equations consisting of rank calculation equations for each vertex of the network. To solve this system, information on all references to the article is required. An inverted reference index stores and provides such information [20], the development and implementation of a method for storing such an index is described in [21]. The assessment of expert competencies by the method of reference ranking is based on two hypotheses that require verification.

The first hypothesis is based on traditional bibliometric reference indicators expressing the author's rating as the opinion of the scientific community on its publication. The idea is that authors of articles with many citations have weight in the scientific community and are more likely to be experts in their field [15]. To test this hypothesis, it is necessary to conduct an experiment using **incoming** references in calculating the reference rank of articles.

The second hypothesis is that the author of the article has a complete understanding of the subject of those articles to which he refers. Then all publications referenced from his articles can be attributed to his area of competence with some correction factor (attenuation coefficient). To test this hypothesis, it is necessary to conduct an experiment using **outgoing** references in calculating the reference rank of articles.

3.3   Selection of Experts

Based on the received ranked list of documents, a ranked list of candidates for experts is compiled by combining the documents by the full name of the author and summing the values of the ranks of the documents in this set. When combining authors by name, the question of disambiguation arises due to the possible presence in the data of matching names and surnames of different authors. In our opinion, the presence of such ambiguity on the current data volume does not significantly affect the results of the algorithm, since articles by namesakes most often relate to different topics and do not receive a high initial rank. However, with a significant increase in data arrays, the effect on the results may be more significant.

After this, filtering (selection) occurs - removal of experts from the list of candidates according to various criteria based on available meta-information. For example, if meta-information about affiliation with organizations is available for a peer-reviewed document and an expert, then it becomes possible to weed out some experts due to the same place of work. This step depends on the available meta-information and is related to the type of document being reviewed. In this experimental implementation of the method, several filters are used that are relevant for grant applications:

1. All experts who are involved as participants or as a team leader in a peer-reviewed application are weed out. In the future, it is also planned to weed out their co-authors, similarly [13].
2. All experts working in the same organizations as the team leader of the peer-reviewed application are weed out. Moreover, according to the data provided, all organizations in which the experts and the team leader of the peer-reviewed application were registered are taken into account.

The degree of compliance of each expert is determined by his position in the resulting rating.

4 Description of Experimental Studies

4.1 Initial Dataset

Since the purpose of this work is to improve the selecting experts technique, for an objective assessment of the obtained recall and precision, we used a subset of articles that served as the basis for experiments in [1] on the topic "Mathematics, Computer Science and Mechanics", containing a full graph of incoming references. Applications of the Russian Foundation for Basic Research from 2012 to 2014 from [3] were also used.

For each application, a meta-information containing the following fields was provided:

- document identifier;
- identifier of the project team leader;
- identifier of the organization in which the leader works;
- a list of the identifiers of participants (co-investigators);
- publication year of the grant application;
- code of the knowledge field which the application belongs to (Biology, Chemistry, etc.);
- main code and additional application codes;
- application keywords.

Anonymous information was also provided about the experts who reviewed the applications:

- identifier of an expert;
- identifier of the organization with which the expert is affiliated;
- keywords of an expert;
- expert core area code;
- applications which the expert is the team leader in (list of identifiers);
- applications which the expert is the participant in (list of identifiers);

- applications reviewed by the expert (list of identifiers);
- applications the expert refused to review (list of identifiers).

The size of the collection of applications amounted to about 65 thousand documents. The collection of articles contains all the articles of the considered experts in the subject area "Mathematics, Informatics and Mechanics" up to 2019 inclusive, received from all available open sources - 78 thousand articles with a total number of references - more than 3 million. Figures 1 and 2 show the distribution of the number of incoming and outgoing references by articles.

A table of the Russian Foundation for Basic Research on the subject "Mathematics, Informatics, and Mechanics" was also provided, containing about 5,000 entries on the actual appointments of experts, their agreement or disagreement to be an expert on the project. From this table, a variety of experts was selected who were considered as candidates during the experiments.

Figures 3 and 4 show the distribution by project of experts who agreed or refused the exam. This information was used during the experiments to assess the recall and precision of the developed methods.

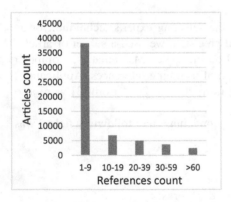

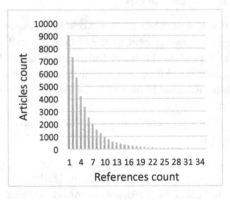

Fig. 1. Distribution of the incoming references count by articles

Fig. 2. Distribution of the outcoming references count by articles

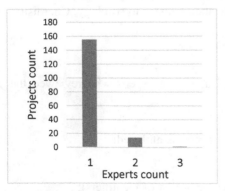

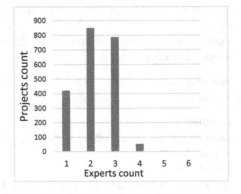

Fig. 3. Distribution of experts that denied the review

Fig. 4. Distribution of experts that accepted the review

4.2   Evaluation Methodology

To evaluate the recall and precision, we used data on previous expert appointments for applications from the A-2013 competition (about 5 thousand applications in total, on average 3 experts per application). For applications from this competition using the proposed method, a filtered and ranked list of experts was generated. After that, the list of experts received was compared with the experts appointed for this application, taking into account the rating received. In the original work [1], metrics (recall and precision) are aimed at assessing the effectiveness of filtering and do not take into account the expert's position in the ranked list. Thus, the effectiveness of the ranking itself was not evaluated at all.

A common practice for evaluating ranking quality is to use the MAP @ K and NDCG @ K metrics. Let's define the expert relevance function rel (x), which takes the values [− 1; 0; 1], −1 if the expert does not agree with the expertise of the project, 1 if he agrees, and 0 if these facts are absent. Let us pay attention to the distribution of rel (x) values, most of which are equal to zero, and rel (x) is not equal to zero in no more than 1% of cases. In this case, it is practically impossible to average and normalize the MAP metric for the number of known facts about the project, which makes it impossible to use. For existing data, it is better to use the NDCG metric:

$$NDCG = \sum_{k=1}^{K} \begin{cases} rel(k) > 0 \left| \frac{rel(k)}{log_2(k+1)} \cdot \frac{1}{IDCGa} \right. \\ rel(k) < 0 \left| \frac{rel(k)}{log_2(k+1)} \cdot \frac{1}{IDCGb} \right. \end{cases} \tag{2}$$

$$IDCGa = \sum_{k=1}^{K_1} \frac{rel(k)}{log_2(k+1)}, IDCGb = \sum_{k=1}^{K_{-1}} \frac{rel(k)}{log_2(k+1)} \tag{3}$$

Where K is the set of experts under consideration, K_1 – set of experts with rel(k) = 1, K_{-1} –for which rel(k) = −1. This metric is also intended for non-binary rel (k) values. It is normalized in accordance with the data known for each project, and takes the values [−1, 1], which made it possible to use it to evaluate the effectiveness of ranking. However, for a more accurate understanding of the ranking characteristics, it was decided to use the recall and precision metrics modified to work with ranked lists. Using these metrics, one can select the parameters of the algorithm that lead to a significant increase in precision or recall, and then choose the Pareto-optimal solution from them.

4.3   Recall Metric (R)

R shows the average position in the selected list of experts who actually agreed to the examination of the application in question. If the expert was not on the list, he was assigned a position at the very end. The metric of recall was calculated as follows:

$$R = 1 - \frac{\sum_{i=0}^{|A|} \frac{a_i}{|E|}}{|A|} \qquad (4)$$

Where A – is the set of experts who agreed to the examination of the project in question, $a_i \in A$ – expert position in the received ranked sample, E – the set of all possible candidates for experts. Thus, a larger R value means higher positions of consonant experts in the search results.

For averaging over all applications, micro-averaging was used (i.e., for all applications, we summed $\sum_{i=0}^{|A|} \frac{a_i}{|E|}$ and $|A|$; based on this, the desired metric was calculated).

4.4   Precision Metric (P)

To evaluate the precision metric, information was used about refusals from examination for a given application. In total, according to the data provided, there were 186 such cases. The idea is that in the selected list of experts there should not be (or be in low positions) experts who refused to review the application in question. If the expert was not on the list, he was assigned a position at the very end. The metric of precision was calculated as follows:

$$P = \frac{\sum_{i=0}^{|D|} \frac{d_i}{|E|}}{|D|} \qquad (5)$$

Where D – is the set of experts who did not agree to review the project in question, d_i – expert position in the received ranked sample, a E – the set of all possible candidates for experts. Thus, a lower P value means lower positions of disagreed experts in the search results.

4.5   Algorithm Parameters

The parameters for the document comparison method were taken from the study [3] and are presented in Table 2. For the values from Table 2, various parameters of the reference ranking algorithm were tested, and options were selected that yielded results with Pareto-optimal metrics of recall and precision. Parameter d – attenuation coefficient was tested in the range $[0.01; 0.5]$ (formula 1).

Table 2. Values of method parameters

Name	Value
TOP_PERCENT	0,6
MAX_WORDS_COUNT	350
MIN_WORDS_COUNT	15
MIN_WEIGHT	0,03
MIN_SIM	0,05
MAX_DOCS_COUNT	2000

Second parameter used – NoDivLinks determines the absence of the division operation by the number of incoming/outgoing references. Dividing by the number of references - normalizing the rank of the article by the number of references, allows to reduce an unjustifiably high rating in the case of articles containing an exceptionally large number of references, however its use reduces the rating of the article in perfectly normal situations. In this article, turning this parameter on and off is a choice between recall and precision. In the future, it is planned to investigate the replacement of this parameter using logarithmic normalization. Below is a table of experiment parameters and main results (Table 3):

Table 3. Parameters of experiments and main results

	d	NoDivLinks	P	R	NDCG
1	не применим	не применим	0,36791	0,69513	0,18132
2	0.1	False	0,32925	0,86429	0,22481
3	0.1	True	0,39203	0,76403	0,23118
4	0.15	True	0,45441	0,73625	0,24571
5	0.2	False	0,25273	0,77018	0,19884
6	0.1	True	0,34075	0,70759	0,21482
7	0.15	True	0,45610	0,68701	0,2258

5   Experiment Results

In this study, many (over 100) experiments were carried out, differing in the initial data and in the direction of creating the reference rank for articles. For an objective comparison of the results, all data were taken from a common array of documents, the same for all experiments. For each experiment, all the necessary data from this common array was provided. As a result, 7 experiments were selected related to the three methods (described below) and differing in the Pareto optimal, within the method, ratios of P and R.

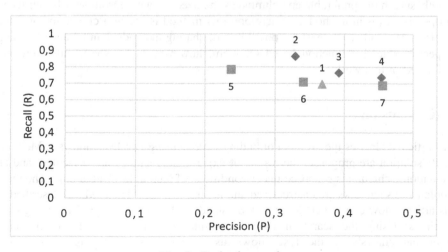

Fig. 5. Evaluation results

5.1   Method 1

All applications and articles of potential experts form the initial data. The proposed methods are based on the method described in [1], therefore, the results of the experiment of the method [1] were taken as reference values for assessing the effectiveness of the current method. This experiment was carried out completely similar to the experiment from [1]. The results of this experiment, which have the reference ratios P and R for this study, are shown in Fig. 5 at number 1.

5.2   Method 2

All documents related to potential experts were taken into account. The ranking was carried out based on the references rank built on **incoming** references (**hypothesis 1**), using the method of searching for similar documents to determine initial coefficients. The results of experiments conducted using this method (Fig. 5. Points 5, 6 and 7) showed that using reference ranking, a significant increase in search precision (P, R, NDCG) can be achieved compared to method 1. This shows that there is a correlation between the low bibliometric indicators of the authors and the lack of desire to act as experts in the proposed areas. However, a greater recall of the search using this method can be achieved only with a significant loss of precision, which suggests that high bibliometric indicators do not increase the likelihood of expert agreement.

5.3   Method 3

All applications and articles of potential experts were taken into account. The ranking was carried out based on the references rank built on **outgoing** references (**hypothesis 2**) using the method of searching for similar documents to determine initial coefficients. According to the results of experiments (Fig. 5. Points 2, 3 and 4) using this method, it is possible to improve indicators of both recall and precision separately, and also to improve both indicators (along with NDCG metric) at the same time. This makes hypothesis 2 more preferable and eliminates the need for a compromise between recall and precision (as in method 2). Therefore, this method is the best choice to solve the problem. The authors suggest the possibility of sharing methods 2 and 3 and obtaining a specific objective function based on them, however, such experiments were not performed in this work.

6   Conclusion

This article addresses the problem of finding experts using Big Data analysis. Methods for its solution are proposed, the results of experimental studies are presented, and an evaluation technique is proposed under conditions of incomplete initial data. The main problems of such tasks are unstructured and incomplete data. The methods described in this article allow one to get closer to understanding the methodology for solving such problems. Using the search method for similar documents based on relational-situational analysis of the text allows us to solve the problems of analyzing unstructured data and obtain significant numerical characteristics of the text as a result of the analysis. With their use it is possible to solve search problems by traditional methods. Reference ranking methods can improve the results of search tasks, in conditions of incompleteness and uncertainty of the data, expanding the range of solutions found. The results of this work were obtained using data with a low degree of completeness: for method (3), only about 13% of the total reference mass was present in the initial data, but even this was sufficient to obtain significant results. Moreover, using method (3), one can find experts who cannot be found only by analyzing the articles of the experts themselves. Thus, a combination of these methods allows us to solve complex search problems in conditions of uncertainty and incomplete data. Because of the studies conducted in this work, it became possible to increase both the recall and precision of the solution relative to previously proposed methods [3]. In this article, the authors were not going to consider the problems of algorithm performance, but it should be noted that a standard server was enough for experimental calculations in a reasonable amount of time. The research results allow us to say that in conditions of more complete data (first of all, this relates to the references between publications), the proposed methodology can show much better results with the right choice of parameters. However, with more data available, the already high computational demand for experiments will increase, which will lead to the need for further optimization of algorithms and an increase in computing power. The task of eliminating the ambiguity in the name of the authors remains relevant. Given the necessary information and meta-information about articles and applications, hierarchical clustering can solve this problem. A strong positive side of the described methods, in the case of their application to the assignment of experts, is a constant iterative increase in their efficiency. New information on the consent/disagreement of the expert from the list proposed by this method will make it possible to improve the proposed methodology.

References

1. Zubarev, D.V., Tihomirov, I.A., Grigoriev, O.G., Sochenkov, I.V.: Method for selecting experts based on a thematic analysis of large arrays of scientific and technical documents. Artif. Intell. Decis. Making **2**, 62–71 (2019)
2. Shiray, M.A., Grigoriev, O.G.: Solving the problem of thematic reference ranking of Internet resources using iterative methods for solving SLAE. Inf. Technol. Comput. Syst. **4**, 6–15 (2012)
3. Zubarev, D., Devyatkin, D., Sochenkov, I., Tikhomirov, I., Grigoriev, O.: Expert assignment method based on similar document retrieval. In: XXI International Conference DAMDID/RCDL, Conference Proceedings, 15–18 October 2019, Kazan, Russia,. pp. 339–351 (2019)
4. Conference management system. http://www.4.org/
5. Krisztian, B., Azzopardi, L., De Rijke, M.: Automating the assignment of submitted manuscripts to reviewers. Formal models for expert finding in enterprise corpora. In: Proceedings of the 29th Annual International ACM SIGIR Conference on Research and Development in Information Retrievall, pp. 43–50. ACM (2006)

6. Kalmukov, Y., Rachev, B.: Comparative analysis of existing methods and algorithms for automatic assignment of reviewers to papers. arXiv preprint. https://arxiv.org/pdf/1012.2019.pdf (2010)
7. Ferilli, S., Di Mauro, N., Basile, T.M.A., Esposito, F., Biba, M.: Automatic topics identification for reviewer assignment. In: Ali, M., Dapoigny, R. (eds.) IEA/AIE 2006. LNCS (LNAI), vol. 4031, pp. 721–730. Springer, Heidelberg (2006). https://doi.org/10.1007/11779568_78
8. Rodriguez, M.A., Bollen, J.: An algorithm to determine peer-reviewers. In: Proceedings of the 17th ACM Conference on Information and Knowledge Management, pp. 319–328. ACM (2008)
9. Li, X., Watanabe, T.: Automatic paper-to-reviewer assignment, based on the matching degree of the reviewers. Procedia Comput. Sci. **22**, 633–642 (2013)
10. Pesenhofer, A., Mayer, R., Rauber, A.: Improving scientific conferences by enhancing conference management systems with information mining capabilities. In: 2006 1st International Conference on Digital Information Management, pp. 359–366. IEEE (2006)
11. Pankova, L.A., Pronina, V.A. Kryukov, K.V.: Ontologicheskie modeli poiska ehkspertov v sistemah upravleniya znaniyami nauchnyh organizacij [Using ontology for expert finding in knowledge management systems of scientific organizations]. roblemy upravleniya [Control Sci.] **6**, 52–60 (2011)
12. Charlin, L., Zemel, R.S.: The Toronto paper matching system: an automated paper-reviewer. In: Proceedings of 30th International Conference on Machine Learning (2013)
13. Liu, X., Suel, T., Memon, N.: A robust model for paper reviewer assignment. In: Proceedings of the 8th ACM Conference on Recommender systems (2014)
14. Socher, R., Lin, C.C., Manning, C., Ng, A.Y.: Parsing natural scenes and natural language with recursive neural networks. In Proceedings of the 28th International Conference on Machine Learning (ICML-11), pp. 129–136 (2011)
15. Shtovba, S.D., Shtovba, E.V.: A review of scientometric indicators to assess the publication activities of a scientist. UBS **44** (2013)
16. Sochenkov, I.V., Zubarev, D.V., Tihomirov, I.A.: Eksplorativnyj patentnyj poisk [Exploratory patent search]. Informatika i ee primeneniya [Inf. Appl.] **12**(1), 89–94 (2018)
17. Osipov, G.S., et al.: Relational-situational method for intelligent search and analysis of scientific publications. In: Proceedings of the Integrating IR Technologies for Professional Search Workshop, pp. 57–64 (2013)
18. Shelmanov, A.O., Smirnov, I.V.: Methods for semantic role labeling of Russian texts. In: Computational Linguistics and Intellectual Technologies. Proceedings of International Conference Dialog, vol. 13, no. 20, pp. 607–620 (2014)
19. Shiray, M.A., Grigoriev, O.G.: A study of the ranking of Internet resources and methods for constructing an inverted link index. In: Arlazarova, V.L. (ed.) Proceedings of the ISA RAS, Processing of information and graphic resources, pp. 127–136 (2010)
20. Brin, S., Page, L.: The anatomy of a large-scale hypertextual web search engine. In: Seventh International World-Wide Web Conference (WWW 1998), 14–18 April, Brisbane, Australia (1998)
21. Shiray, M.A, Grigoriev, O.G.: Design and implementation of a new way to store an inverted reference index. In: Information Technology and Computing Systems №3, ISA RAS, (Moscow), pp. 20–26 (2011)

The Study of Argumentative Relations in Popular Science Discourse

Irina Kononenko🆔, Elena Sidorova(✉)🆔, and Irina Akhmadeeva🆔

A.P. Ershov Institute of Informatics Systems SB RAS, Novosibirsk 630090, Russia
irina_k@cn.ru, {lsidorova,i.r.akhmadeeva}@iis.nsk.su

Abstract. The paper presents an approach to modeling and study of argumentation found in popular science literature. The study of argumentation is performed by means of comparative analysis of discourse structures. Different types of argumentative structure are considered and the co-occurrence of arguments "from Expert opinion" with other types of argumentative reasoning typical of the popular science genre is analyzed. With the view of automatic extraction of argumentative relations, the analysis of correlation between rhetorical and argumentative annotations was carried out. The experiment was conducted on a corpus of 11 popular science articles from the Ru-RSTreebank.

Keywords: Argumentation · Argumentative annotation · Argument mining · Argumentative relation · Popular science discourse · Expert opinion inference

1 Introduction

Argument Mining is an area of computational linguistics that has been actively developing in the last decade. Its task is to automatically extract from text a set of statements (premises) that lead to a certain conclusion (thesis).

Argumentation is part of the phenomenon of discourse and using its properties for applied tasks requires the creation of deeply annotated linguistic resources. The study of discourse involves the description of its structure in the form of related discourse units. One of the most famous models applied to the task of discourse annotation is the Rhetorical Structure Theory (RST) and its modifications [1, 2]. Within the framework of the RST, simple sentences, clauses, or text fragments that have a certain propositional content are linked by symmetrical and non-symmetrical relations. Larger discourse units are formed, thus creating a common tree-like structure. This theory is used as the basis for annotating text corpora. A striking example is the project "Night Dream Stories" by A.A. Kibrik, V.I. Podlesskaya etc. [3], in which records of oral narratives (children's dream stories) were transcribed and further marked up in RST terms. Rhetorical relations also underlie M. Taboada's corpus research on the issues of coherence and cohesion in dialogical communication [4]. The most modern project for Russian language material is the Ru-RSTreebank (https://rstreebank.ru) [5], mainly based on news texts. At the same time, annotation of such a discourse phenomenon as argumentation remains one of the undeveloped problems of corpus linguistics.

S. O. Kuznetsov et al. (Eds.): RCAI 2020, LNAI 12412, pp. 309–324, 2020.
https://doi.org/10.1007/978-3-030-59535-7_23

Argumentation as a process of persuading the audience by justifying a statement with other statements is part of the complex content of discourse. To describe various ways of reasoning and persuasion, well-known theoretical models are used, such as Toulmin's model [6], or the pragma-dialectical model of argumentation as a critical discussion [7], and formalized representations based on them [8]. The most famous structural description of argumentation is the model of D. Walton [9], which defines about 60 basic argumentation schemes with variants (subschemes), each being the description of a specific reasoning pattern (inference form expressing the relations of premises and conclusion). The model has been used in a number of applications and tools for argument analysis and corpora annotation: OVA [10], Carneades [11].

So far, there exist a few resources with annotated argumentative structures mainly over monologue texts in English. The best known is AIFdb, the former Araucaria corpus [12], which includes news articles, records of online debates. Resources are created in German: University of Darmstadt Corpus includes subcorpora of student essays [13], news texts and scientific articles; the Potsdam corpus contains a small set of microtexts on a given topic [14]. There exist projects for some other languages (Italian, Greek, Chinese). As for the Russian language, such resources, as far as we know, do not yet exist.

Generally, corpus argumentative annotation encompasses the following steps:

- segmenting texts into argumentation discourse units (ADUs) and the formation of statements based on them - propositional content,
- defining a role for each ADU (conclusion or premise) and linking units with argumentative relations,
- detailing the structure of argument based on the corresponding argumentation scheme,
- identifying implicit and equivalent statements and ensuring maximum connectivity of the annotation graph.

It is this information that is used in the training process for the task of automatic search for arguments. The Potsdam corpus provides detailed relationships (for example, support can be simple, linked, and converging) along with the ability to reduce detailed relationships to two main ones (attack and support): this reduces the complexity of automatic identification and classification of arguments [15]. In the vast majority of projects, annotation of arguments does not provide for matching of inference rules, or argumentation schemes – typical models on which reasoning is based. Two exceptions are Araucaria, where annotation of argumentative structure is related to particular argumentation scheme based on the theory of Walton [16], and the Potsdam corpus, which uses Argumentum Model of Topics [17] as a theoretical base.

The Potsdam corpus represents yet another promising trend in the field of automatic argumentation analysis: in the past few years, studies have emerged that consider the potential use of existing text corpora with annotated rhetorical discourse structure to facilitate the annotation of argumentation. The idea is to create a corpus of texts with multi-level annotation: along with the existing markup of rhetorical units and relations, texts are marked up with respect to the argument structure. In the presence of such a corpus, the task is to establish the relationship between rhetorical and argumentative structure of the text, the correlation of their components and relations in order to use existing resources and tools of discourse analysis to extract arguments. In line with this idea, The authors of [18] describe the development and use in experiments of a two-level corpus of 112 short texts written in the genre of argumentative essays, and in [19], the material for annotation are scientific articles from the field of computer linguistics.

In this work our emphasis is on correlating different discourse levels and studying dependencies between rhetorical discourse structure and argument structure, namely, underlying inferential moves. Section 2 presents a theoretical view of a multi-layer discourse representation followed by a general model of argument annotation. In Sect. 3 different types of argumentative relations are considered and then special attention is paid to joint occurrence of arguments "from Expert opinion" with other types of argumentative reasoning typical of the popular science genre. The experimental study of correlation between rhetorical and argumentative annotations and discussion of the discovered discrepancies is presented in Sect. 4. The experiment is conducted on a multi-layer annotated resource of 11 articles of the popular science genre.

2 Annotation Model

The proposed work was performed as part of an ongoing research project aimed at creation of discourse annotated corpus of popular science texts written in Russian. Popular science discourse is defined as a way of transmitting scientific knowledge or innovation projects by the author-scientist (or a journalist as an intermediary) for their understanding by a mass audience. Popular science texts are not enough presented in known argumentatively annotated corpora.

Popular science articles from various online media have been used to create the corpus. Articles have no restrictions on the subject, structure, and the type of presentation. Some articles are transcripts of oral presentation, interviews, etc. For now the corpus includes about 950 texts with an average volume 1057 words (minimum - 167 words, maximum - 4094 words) and includes two small subcorpora: 11 rhetorically annotated texts taken from the open source Ru-RSTreebank, and 69 articles on linguistics provided with argument annotation corresponding to the model developed in this project.

Three levels are distinguished in the structure of discourse, of which the first two correspond to the superstructure and relational structure in [2].

Genre structure corresponds to the compositional and semantic organization of text at the highest level and depends on the text genre membership. This level involves a breakdown into meaningful compositional parts, such as chapters and paragraphs. While a scientific text has a fairly clear structure (introduction with the research justification, overview, main part, conclusion), a specific feature of a popular science article is the comparative flexibility of its structure, the absence of clear requirements for content or template, some elements may be missing or follow in a different order. Conventionally, a popular science article has the following components: heading part (title, subtitle), introductive pretext (introduction), epigraph, main part, conclusion.

Rhetorical structure is responsible for organizing the text itself, transforming it from a simple sequence of formal segments into a single whole. It reflects the functional relationships existing between segments, called rhetorical relations. These relations can be symmetric or asymmetric. In the latter case, the relation has core and satellite, for example, it can be an event and its result. Thus, any text can be represented as a graph whose vertices are elementary discourse units (EDUs) or combinations of such units - discourse units (DUs). Regardless of the level of the hierarchy, vertices of the graph can be connected by the same types of relations.

Argumentative structure represents the text as a means of reproducing the process of argumentation, highlighting the components of the argument field and the relationships between them (controversial thesis, arguments for or against). Argumentation is putting forward arguments in order to change or form some belief (position) of the other side [20]. Argumentation is not only the procedure for bringing arguments in support or against a certain view, but also the whole totality of such arguments.

The AIF (Argument Interchange Format) [21] is commonly used to describe arguments and argumentative structures. In accordance with this format, argumentation is represented as an oriented graph in which two types of vertices are distinguished: information vertices (statement vertices) and schema vertices (argument vertices).

The internal structure of an argument is represented as follows:

Argument:
scheme: Scheme_of_Argument,
hasConclusion: Statement *or* Argument,
hasPremise: {Statement},
hasPresumption: {Statement},
hasException: {Statement}

Statement vertices are mapped to argument elements such as conclusions (*has-Conclusion*), premises (*hasPremise*), presumptions (*hasPresumption*), and exceptions (*hasException*). Premises and presumptions implement the conclusion *support* relation, and exceptions implement the *attack* relation. Besides, premises are obligatory elements in the argument structure, while premises and presumptions are optional. The schema vertex is used to represent an argument in accordance with the standard model of reasoning (scheme). The current version of the ontology includes about 40 argumentation schemes from the Walton's compendium [16].

The external relations of an argument with other arguments are naturally represented by using a conclusion statement as a premise (assumption, exception) in the structure of another argument, as a conclusion shared with another argument, or by directly using another argument as a conclusion.

Conflicts are an important element of argumentation. While typical arguments are aimed at supporting certain thesis statements, conflicts are used to criticize or refute them.

In the proposed model conflicts are also implemented with the help of schemes:

Conflict:
schemeConflict: Scheme_of_Conflict,
conflictedElement: Statement,
conflictingElement: Statement *or* Argument

In accordance with the chosen conflict scheme (*schemeConflict*), either symmetrical relations between statements are formed (logical conflicts: for example, universal or constituent negation representing alternative opinion), or asymmetric relations between the statement (*conflictedElement*) and the argument (*conflictingElement*), the statement being considered as exception (which denies the existence or validity of the argument). In the second case, the statement (*conflictedElement*) correlates with the exception (*hasException*) of the argument itself.

In the previous work, we have considered internal structure of the argument [22]. The focus of this work is on external relations of the argument.

3 Argumentative Relations

The task of extracting argumentative relations poses serious problems for researchers. To solve these problems, it is necessary not only to detect arguments in the text with high accuracy, but also to relate them with each other. To this end, we will consider all possible minimal subgraphs that characterize various types of relations between arguments, and how they are represented in texts.

The following types of argumentative relations are distinguished.

1. Multiple support
2. Serial support
3. Supporting an argument
4. Logical conflict
5. Attacking an argument

Let's look at them in more detail.

Multiple argumentation is a set of arguments that support the same thesis (Fig. 1).

Support can be provided by using arguments of different types (i.e. corresponding to different schemes of reasoning), each being represented in a specific topical text fragment. The fragment can include homogeneous components that play the role of premises of arguments of the same type, as in the following example:

Besides multiple argumentation, the thesis justification can use serial argumentation - a "chain" of related statements, in which the conclusion of one argument is the premise of another. So, in the example in Fig. 2(a), the expert opinion represented by the argument A4 (*ExpertOpinion_Inference*) acts as a premise in the causal relationship represented by the argument A5 (*CorrelationToCause*).

Another way to provide support is supporting an argument, when the conclusion of one argument is the entire reasoning represented by the other argument. For example, in Fig. 2(b), the causal relationship represented by the argument A1 (*CorrelationToCause*) is supported by the expert opinion expressed by the argument A2 (*ExpertOpinion_Inference*).

The attack or conflict relations hold either between theses statements, or between a statement and an argument. In the first case, a logical conflict is present in the argumentation structure (C2 in Fig. 3), and in the second, an attack on the argument (C1 in Fig. 3).

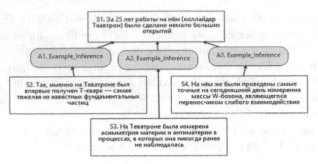

Over 25 years of work on it <Tevatron>, many great discoveries have been made
[S1]. Thus, it was on the Tevatron that the T-quark, the heaviest known fundamental
particle, was first obtained [S2]. On Tevatron, the asymmetry of matter and antimat-
ter was measured in processes in which it had never been observed before [S3]. It
was also used for today's most accurate measurements of the mass of the W boson,
which is a carrier of the weak interaction [S4].

Fig. 1. Multiple argumentation.

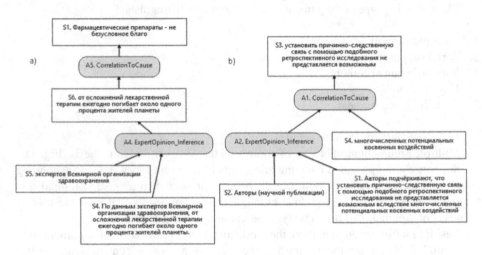

a) *Pharmaceuticals are not an absolute good* [S1]. ... *According to experts from the
World Health Organization* [S5]*, about one percent of the world's inhabitants die
every year from complications of drug therapy* [S6, S4].
b) *The authors emphasize* [S2] *that it is impossible to establish a causal relationship
using such a retrospective study* [S3] *due to the numerous potential indirect effects*
[S4, S1].

Fig. 2. Support relation: a) serial argumentation, b) supporting an argument.

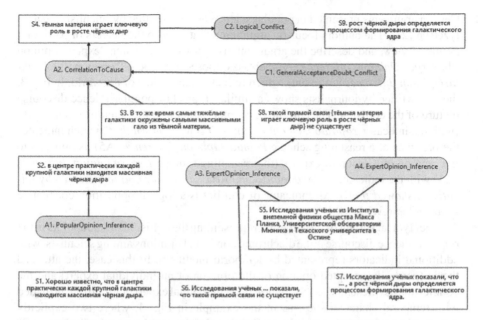

It is well known that in the center of almost every large galaxy there is a massive black hole [S1, S2]. At the same time, the heaviest galaxies are surrounded by the most massive dark matter halos [S3]. This has given rise to suggestions that dark matter plays a key role in the growth of black holes [S4]. Research by scientists from the max Planck Institute for extraterrestrial physics, the Munich University Observatory, and the University of Texas at Austin [S5], however, has shown that there is no such direct connection [S8, S6], and the growth of a black hole is determined by the formation of the galactic core [S9, S7].

Fig. 3. An example of two types of conflicts: exception [C1] and logical [C2].

3.1 Argumentative Relations in Popular Science Discourse

Popular science discourse is characterized by numerous citations and, more broadly, by appeals to opinions accepted in society as a whole, in the scientific community, and/or promoted by individual groups and scientists. The appeal to authoritative sources of information in the form of statements of scientists, factual evidence, research results and using it as proof of certain provisions is represented in the theory of argumentation by the scheme of reasoning "from Expert opinion" (*ExpertOpinion_Inference*) taken from Walton's compendium [16].

MajorPremise: *Source E is an expert in subject domain S containing proposition A*
MinorPremise: *E asserts that proposition A is true (false)*
Conclusion: *A is true (false)*

Typical situations of using this reasoning in the analyzed corpus material are given below.

1. Certain arguments presented in popular science articles written by scientists are analyzed in [23]. The authors focus on arguments that refer to the bearers of particular points of view, and describe the argumentative structure in which "expert" opinion (the *ExpertOpinion_Inference* argument) is opposed to "general" opinion (the *PopularOpinion_Inference* argument), which reflects a naive view of the world. In Fig. 3, the text written by journalists shows a similar, typical of popular science discourse picture of the collision. The currently accepted opinion of the scientific community (with the indicator *хорошо известно, что* 'it is well known that', which indicates the presence of a reasoning scheme *PopularOpinion_Inference* (A5), is opposed to the opinion of a group of experts (the reasoning scheme *ExpertOpinion_Inference* (A4) with the indicator *исследования ученых…показали, что* 'research by scientists…showed that'). An indicator of conflict is a logical opposition connective *однако* 'however'.

2. Another typical variant of the structure representing the collision of standpoints in the popular science discourse is the diachronic conflict of opinions among scientists, with additional indicators represented by temporal modifiers. In this case, the attacked thesis (generally accepted opinion or the opinion of an individual expert) and the counter-thesis (presented as the opinion of an individual expert or group) are provided with temporal characteristics, as in the example in Fig. 4, where two explicitly presented reasoning schemes, *ExpertOpinion_Inference* A1 and A4, are shown.

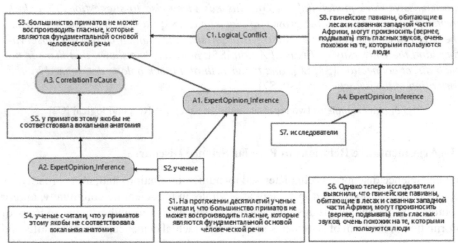

For decades, scientists [S2] *have believed that* most primates cannot reproduce the vowels that are the fundamental basis of human speech [S1, S3]. This is because the vocal anatomy of primates allegedly did not conform to this [S4, S5]. *However, researchers* [S7] *have **now** found that* Guinea baboons living in the forests and savannas of Western Africa can utter (or rather, howl) five vowel sounds, very similar to those used by humans [S8, S6].

Fig. 4. Diachronic conflict of opinions [A1, A2] among scientists [A4].

3. Of interest are frequent combinations of the *ExpertOpinion_Inference* scheme with variants of causal relationships. Thus, in the text in Fig. 2 (b), the explicit opinion of the expert in *ExpertOpinion_Inference* supports the *CorrelationToCause argument*.

4. In the following example, expert data indicates the validity of a certain information represented by the *EvidenceToHypothesis* reasoning scheme:

*То, что на здоровье человека влияют погодные и климатические условия, ученые знают давно. **По оценкам** российских **медиков,** каждый третий россиянин в возрасте старше 30 лет реагирует тем или иным образом на резкие изменения погоды.*

*Scientists have long known that human health is affected by weather and climate conditions. **According to** Russian **medical experts,** every third Russian over the age of 30 responds in one way or another to sudden changes in the weather.*

5. Expert information may be a special case of the stated point – *Example_Inference*:

*Ученые заметили ряд особенностей в поведении организма в определенных метеоусловиях. ...**Анестезиологи отмечают, что** влияние наркоза колеблется в зависимости от того, светит солнце или небо затянуто облаками.*

*Scientists have noticed a number of features in the behavior of the body in certain weather conditions. ...**Anesthesiologists note that** the effect of anesthesia varies depending on whether the sun is shining or the sky is overcast.*

6. Expert opinion can support reasoning from the positive consequences of some practical action - *PositiveConsequences_Inference* scheme:

*Проект только набирает силу, а в планы ученых уже входит организация Службы погоды для медицинских целей. ...Поддерживают идею и медики. **Как заявил врач-координатор** службы "скорой помощи" по Санкт-Петербургу Валерий Опушко, "внедрение службы медицинских прогнозов на федеральном уровне помогло бы нашей медицине более правильно и четко координировать собственные действия в нужном направлении".*

*The project is only gaining strength, and the plans of scientists already include the organization of a Weather service for medical purposes. ...Doctors also support the idea. **According to** Valery Opushko, **doctor-coordinator** of the ambulance service in Saint Petersburg, " the introduction of the medical prognosis service at the Federal level would help our medicine to coordinate its own actions in the right direction more correctly and clearly."*

7. An expert's opinion can attack a thesis using reasoning from the negative consequences of some practical action- *NegaitiveConsequences_Inference* scheme:

*Данная **группа исследователей выдвигает мнение о том, что** ... . **Они считают, что,** , напротив, сбивание жара может в некоторых случаях*

приводить   к   неблагоприятным   эффектам,   и
делают вывод о том, что *пропагандировать широкое применение медикаментов для подавления жара не следует.*

*This **group of researchers** puts forward the opinion that … . **They believe that**, <u>on the contrary</u>, reducing a fever can in some cases lead to adverse effects, and **make the conclusion that** the widespread use of medications to reduce a fever should not be promoted.*

8. A variant of "from Expert opinion" in the practical scheme "Ad Finem" is a presumptive conflict based on the presumption of possibility (the goal is the work of the Collider, its implementation requires funding in a certain amount). Note that the indicator *по оценкам экспертов* '*based on expert estimates*' usually introduces a quantitative statement.

Для   продолжения   работы   коллайдера
по оценкам специалистов *требовалось финансирование на уровне 35 млн долларов США в год, однако из-за сложной финансовой ситуации даже такие деньги оказались неподъёмными для правительства США.*

*To continue the work of the Collider, **based on expert estimates**, funding was required at the level of 35 million US dollars per year, but due to the difficult financial situation, even this money was unaffordable for the US government.*

4   Study of Correlation Between Rhetorical and Argumentative Structures

A research interest for the comparison of rhetorical and argumentative annotation relates to several aspects. First, argumentative annotation is often seen as a special case of rhetorical markup (or resulting from rhetorical markup). However, when considered in more detail (see, for example, [18]) they show differences at all levels of representation, starting from discrepancies in the segmentation into discourse units and construction of annotation graphs, and ending with indicators that serve to identify rhetorical or argumentative relationships in the text. Second, argumentation research is a separate scientific discipline with its own goals, knowledge base, and methods that differ from those adopted in linguistics. And third, such research has a practical value associated with the development of methods of argument mining, using advance in the field of analysis of rhetorical structures.

The basis of both rhetorical and argument annotation is segmentation into elementary discourse units (EDUs). These units are sentences, clauses or minimal text spans which have propositional content including nominalized propositions and prepositional phrases with the meaning of cause, effect, concession, contrast. In case of argumentative annotation, the semantics of generated graph chains is associated with the content aspect of argumentative relations, and not with the structural one, as is the case in rhetorical structures.

To investigate the possibility of using available discourse-annotated corpora for the task of argument mining, we decided to conduct the combined comparative study of discourse relations and inferential moves in popular science articles including references

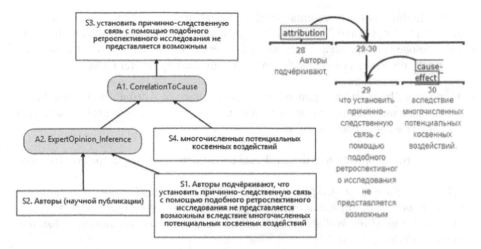

The authors emphasize [28] *that it is impossible to establish a causal relationship using such a retrospective study* [29] *due to the numerous potential indirect effects* [30].

Fig. 5. Correlation between a) argumentative and b) rhetorical structures (match).

to information/opinion sources (based on the presence of attribution or cognitive predicates) that are rather frequent in this genre. For the comparison purpose, 11 popular science texts were selected from the rhetorically annotated Ru-RST Corpus and provided with argumentative annotation.

Consider the example presented earlier, which consists of two arguments, one of which is the reasoning based on the authoritative opinion of the expert (*ExpertOpinion_Inference*). The argumentative and rhetorical structures of this fragment are illustrated in Fig. 5, from which the correlation can be seen, up to the peculiarities of the internal structure of the argument from the expert, in which there is a nesting of the thesis segment in the premise segment.

The mapping between RST discourse relations and argument schemes is done using an approach similar to the one introduced in [24]: rhetorical and argumentative structures must be converted into a linear structure with binary connections (see Fig. 6).

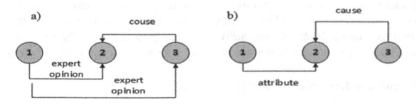

Fig. 6. Mapping between a) argumentative and b) rhetorical structures.

In annotations of 11 texts, the *Attribution* relation (used to represent information or opinion source and based on the presence of attribution verbs or cognitive predicates) was used 49 times in the representation of rhetorical structure, and the argument "from Expert opinion" was found 75 times in the representation of the argumentative structure. The one-to-one correspondence between two layers of representation is not always the case, and the discovered discrepancies may be explained by several factors.

- Absence of "from Expert opinion" argument in place of Attribution rhetorical construction means that argumentation annotators don't see any arguable statement supported by authoritative opinion.

  - No asserted proposition in the attributed constituent (nucleus) of the construction:

    *В одном из писем Альфреду Уоллесу в 1857 году Дарвин замечает по этому поводу: «**Вы спрашиваете**, буду ли я обсуждать «человека».*
    *In a letter to Alfred Wallace in 1857, Darwin remarks on this subject: "**You ask** whether I will discuss 'man'.*

  - Non-argumentative intention of citation in the attributed part, i.e. pure informative function (presentation of factual material or personal experience of the speaker), or expressive function:

    Как в известной сказке: : *«Зачем тебе, бабушка, такие большие уши?»*—*«Чтобы лучше тебя слышать, детка».*
    *As **in the famous fairy tale**: "Why do you have such big ears, grandma?"—"All the better to hear you, baby."*

- Absence of Attribution rhetorical construction in place of "from Expert opinion" argument.

  - Rhetorical structure annotators saw a different relation that may be closer to the author's intentions (see [25] for detailed analysis): *Elaboration* (see Fig. 7) or *Interpretation-Evaluation*:

    *За 200 лет до этого Уильям Гершель сообщал о наблюдениях колец у Урана, однако современные **астрономы сомневаются** в возможности такого открытия, так как кольца очень слабые и тёмные и не могли быть обнаружены с помощью астрономического оборудования того времени.*
    *200 years earlier, William Herschel reported observations of rings near Uranus, but modern **astronomers doubt** the possibility of such a discovery, since the rings are very faint and dark and could not be detected with the astronomical equipment of the time.*

  - Differences in the segmentation of the text into EDUs and ADUs.

  (1)   no separate EDU has been set due to disregard for specific attribution constructions:

    *Однако   10   лет назад была **высказана гипотеза о том,** что использование парацетамола может увеличить риск развития астмы.*

*However, 10 years ago, **the hypothesis was put forward** that the use of paracetamol may increase the risk of developing asthma.*

(2) no separate EDU has been set due to the absence of independent clause for attributed material (for example, in case of nominalized or otherwise compressed propositions):

*С тех пор несколько эпидемиологических **исследований выявили** связь между астмой и использованием парацетамола во время беременности, в детстве и среди взрослого населения.*

*Since then, several epidemiological **studies have found** a link between asthma and paracetamol use during pregnancy, childhood, and among adults.*

(3) the attributed material (*Attribution* relation nucleus) is a single rhetorical group (for example, homogeneous information united by *Joint* relation) while each nested EDU corresponds to independent argument on argumentation level:

Исследования учёных *из Института внеземной физики общества Макса Планка,   Университетской   обсерватории Мюниха и Техасского университета в Остине, однако, **показали, что** такой прямой связи не существует, а рост чёрной дыры определяется процессом формирования галактического ядра.*

Studies by scientists *from the Max Planck Institute for Extraterrestrial Physics, the Munich University Observatory and the University of Texas at Austin, however, **have shown** that such a direct relationship does not exist, and the growth of a black hole is determined by the formation of the galactic nucleus.*

Thus, the segmentation factor is perhaps one of the most significant. It is especially obvious in cases when 1) partitioning DU (presented by a group of EDUs) into separate units is important because each group member plays a separate role in the argument structure and 2) on the contrary, there are rhetorically related EDUs that should be combined into ADU as they correspond to a single argument component. The first situation means that *Attribution* relation does not directly link information source to the opinion: opinion is represented as part of a group with detailed information and/or as a multi-nucleus group (*Joint, Same_unit, Comparison, Contrast* relations). And the second one is especially characteristic of the *Elaboration* relation.

Another aspect of the argumentation structure that makes its automatic recognition particularly difficult is the possibility of long-range dependencies. Although segments are often connected locally, i.e. they support or attack neighboring segments, direct argumentative relations may also exist, linking text segments that are far apart [15], as in the case when argumentative relations extend beyond the paragraph (see Fig. 7).

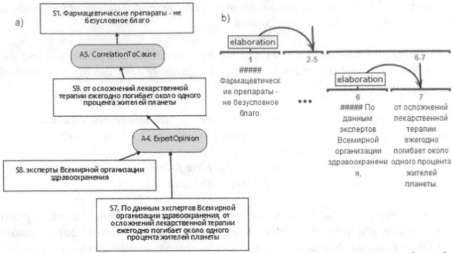

Pharmaceuticals are not an absolute good [1]. ... *According to experts from the World Health Organization* [6], *about one percent of the world's inhabitants die every year from complications of drug therapy* [7].

Fig. 7. Correlation between a) argumentative and b) rhetorical structures (mismatch).

5   Conclusion

The proposed work was carried out as part of an ongoing research project aimed at creating a corpus of Russian-language popular science texts with argument annotation. An approach to modeling and research of argumentation found in popular science literature is presented. The research is performed by means of comparative analysis of different level discourse structures.

The experiment was conducted on a corpus of 11 popular science articles selected from the multi-genre collection with rhetorical annotation. The extraction of arguments based on reasoning schemes "from Expert opinion" was performed automatically based on the indicator approach discussed in [22]. Further, comparison with the rhetorical annotation was performed manually. As a result, various types of inconsistencies between the rhetorical *Attribution* relation and the argumentative relation expressing the expert opinion were identified and analyzed (the correlation score is 77,5% accuracy and 68% completeness).

Further research is oriented to the assessment of the influence of linked argumentative relations on the accuracy of argument recognition based on rhetorical structures. It can be expected that the co-occurrence of rhetorical *Attribution* relation and indicators of conflicts and /or causal relationships will increase the accuracy of argument recognition. It is also necessary to investigate the correlation of other types of relations, for example, symmetrical rhetorical relations often correspond to multiple arguments: the presence of contrast correlates with support for different sides of the conflict, and comparison - with related arguments.

Acknowledgments. The research has been supported by Russian Foundation for Basic Research (Grant No. 18-00-01376 (18-00-00889)).

References

1. Mann, W.C., Thompson, S.A.: Rhetorical structure theory: toward a functional theory of text organization. Text **8**(3), 243–281 (1988)
2. Mann, W.C, Matthiessen, C., Thompson, S,A.: Rhetorical structure theory and text analysis. In: Mann, W.C., Thompson, S.A. (eds.) Discourse Description: Diverse Linguistic Analyses of a Fund-Raising Text, pp. 39–78. John Benjamins, Amsterdam/Philadelphia (1992)
3. Kibrik, A.A., Podlesskaya, V.I. (eds.): Night Dream Stories: a corpus study of spoken Russian discourse. Languages of Slavonic Culture, Moscow (2009). (in Russian)
4. Taboada, M.: Building Coherence and Cohesion: Task-oriented Dialogue in English and Spanish. John Benjamins, Amsterdam/Philadelphia (2004)
5. Pisarevskaya, D., et al.: Towards building a discourse-annotated corpus of Russian. In: Computational Linguistics and Intellectual Technologies: Proceedings of the International Conference "Dialogue 2017", iss. 16(23), vol. 1, pp. 194–204 (2017)
6. Toulmin, S.: The Uses of Argument. Cambridge University Press, Cambridge (2003)
7. Eemeren, F.H., Grootendorst, R.: Speech Acts in Argumentative Discussions: A Theoretical Model for the Analysis of Discussions Directed Towards Solving Conflicts of Opinion. Foris Publications, The Netherlands (1984)
8. Reed, C., Walton, D.: Argumentation schemes in argument-as-process and argument-as-product. In: Proceedings of Conference Celebrating Informal Logic. OSSA Conference Archive 75, University of Windsor, vol. 25, OSSA, Windsor, Ontario (2013)
9. Walton, D.: Fundamentals of Critical Argumentation. Cambridge University Press, Cambridge (2006)
10. Janier, M., Lawrence J., Reed, C.: OVA+: an argument analysis interface. In: Computational Models of Argument: Proceedings of COMMA 2014, vol. 266, pp. 463–464. IOS Press, Amsterdam (2014)
11. Gordon, T.F., Walton, D.: The Carneades argumentation framework - using presumptions and exceptions to model critical questions. In: Proceedings of the 2006 Conference on Computational Models of Argument: Proceedings of COMMA 2006, vol. 6, pp. 195–207. IOS Press, Amsterdam (2006)
12. Reed, C., Rowe, G.: Araucaria: Software for argument analysis, diagramming and representation. Int. J. Artif. Intell. Tools **13**(4), 961–979 (2004)
13. Stab, C., Gurevych, I.: Annotating argument components and relations in persuasive essays. In: Proceedings of the 25th International Conference on Computational Linguistics (COLING 2014), Dublin, pp. 1501–1510 (2014)
14. Peldszus, A., Stede, M.: An annotated corpus of argumentative microtexts. In: Argumentation and Reasoned Action. Proceedings of the 1st European Conference on Argumentation, Lisbon, vol. 2. College Publications, London (2015)
15. Peldszus, A., Warzecha, S., Stede, M.: Annotation guidelines for argumentation structure. English translation of chapter "Argumentationsstruktur". In: Stede, M. (ed.) Handbuch Textannotation – Potsdamer Kommentarkorpus 2.0. Universitätsverlag, Potsdam (2016)
16. Walton, D., Reed, C., Macagno, F.: Argumentation Schemes. Cambridge University Press, Cambridge (2008)
17. Rigotti, E., Morasso, S.G.: Comparing the argumentum model of topics to other contemporary approaches to argument schemes: the procedural and material components. Argumentation **24**(4), 489–512 (2010). https://doi.org/10.1007/s10503-010-9190-7

18. Musi, E., Alhindi, T., Stede, M., Kriese, L., Muresan, S., Rocci, A.: A Multi-layer annotated corpus of argumentative text: from argument schemes to discourse relations. In: Proceedings of the Eleventh International Conference on Language Resources and Evaluation (LREC 2018), Miyazaki, Japan, pp. 1629–1636 (2018)

19. Accuosto, P., Saggion, H.: Discourse-driven argument mining in scientific abstracts. In: Métais, E., Meziane, F., Vadera, S., Sugumaran, V., Saraee, M. (eds.) NLDB 2019. LNCS, vol. 11608, pp. 182–194. Springer, Cham (2019). https://doi.org/10.1007/978-3-030-23281-8_15

20. Ivin, A.A.: Argumentation in the Process of Communication. Pro et contra. Prospect, Moscow (2017). (in Russian)

21. Chesñevar, C.I., et al.: Towards an argument interchange format. Knowl. Eng. Rev. **21**(4), 293–316 (2006)

22. Akhmadeeva, I., Kononenko, I., Salomatina, N., Sidorova, E.: Indicator patterns as features for argument mining. In: 2019 International Multi-Conference on Engineering, Computer and Information Sciences (SIBIRCON), Novosibirsk, Russia, pp. 0886–0891. IEEE (2020)

23. Kim, I.E., Ilina, D.V.: Language expression of the argumentative framework "from popular opinion vs from expert opinion" in the text of popular science article. In: Vestnik NSU. Series: History and Philology, vol. 18, no. 9, pp. 27–35 (2019). (in Russian)

24. Stede, M., Afantenos, S., Peldszus, A., Asher, N., Perret, J.: Parallel discourse annotations on a corpus of short texts. In: Proceedings of the Tenth International Conference on Language Resources and Evaluation (LREC 2016), Portorož, pp. 1051–1058 (2016)

25. Potter, A.: The rhetorical structure of attribution. In: Proceedings of the Workshop on Discourse Relation Parsing and Treebanking, pp. 38–49. Association for Computational Linguistics, Minneapolis (2019)

Method for Detecting Text Markers
of Depression and Depressiveness

Ivan V. Smirnov[1]($\boxtimes$), Anastasiya V. Ushakova[2], and Natalya V. Chudova[1]

[1] Artificial Intelligence Research Institute, FRC CSC RAS, Moscow, Russia
ivs@isa.ru, nchudova@gmail.com
[2] Moscow Institute of Physics and Technology, Moscow, Russia
ushakova.av@phystech.edu

Abstract. The paper explores the use of the AQJSM method, which is built upon combining the JSM and AQ methods, to identify cause-effect relationships between psychological characteristics and text parameters produced by individuals with these characteristics. The study included two groups of subjects: the "depression" group (patients with clinical depression) and the "depressiveness" group (non-clinical patients who have high scores on the Beck depression scale). The use of the AQJSM algorithm allowed discussing the problem of validity in modern research in the field of automatic network psychodiagnostics. It was found out that different sets of text parameters act as linguistic markers of clinical depression and depressiveness.

Keywords: Causal relations · Text parameters · Psychological features of the author

1 Introduction

The recent advances in the field of automatic text analysis allow raising the question of the possibility of using the data of such analysis in population-based research in the field of psychiatric and subclinical epidemiology. This question became urgent in the last decade, as the use of social networks has become widespread and people in many countries, including Russia, have acquired the habit of regularly generating spontaneous texts in response to interpersonal, family, professional, socio-psychological and socio-political problems. The development of methods of automatic text analysis and methods of automatic classification of data from such analysis and bringing these methods to the state of a user tool makes an increasing number of specialists in the social-humanitarian field rely on these methods in their own research. In the near future, automatic analysis of the text output of social network users can be applied to identify risk groups for psychological distress and psychiatric diseases; to study mass mental phenomena (panic, rumors, gossip) and the reaction of the population to socially significant events; to investigate the phenomenon of social tension, regional and local manifestations of intergroup conflicts and value preferences of large groups. In general, works in this interdisciplinary field can be called automatic network psychodiagnostics, and the results of applying AI

© Springer Nature Switzerland AG 2020
S. O. Kuznetsov et al. (Eds.): RCAI 2020, LNAI 12412, pp. 325–337, 2020.
https://doi.org/10.1007/978-3-030-59535-7_24

methods to the analysis of texts can significantly increase the research validity in clinical psychology, social psychology, in some areas of sociology, history, and political science.

The purpose of this work is to study the opportunities of using the AQJSM method [1] to establish cause-effect relationships between depression as mental illness and depressiveness as psychological feature and the parameters of texts (linguistic features of the texts) generated by people with such characteristics. The hypothesis was that the parameters measured by our automatic text analysis tool would allow us to reliably identify texts written under the influence of depression. The AQJSM method combines the JSM method [2] and the AQ method [3]. The JSM and AQ methods are known for their effectiveness, and their integration in the AQJSM method has been proven to be effective in analyzing data in the fields of medicine and psychology. The text parameters in question are the quantitative characteristics identified by the linguistic analyzer [4] and the linguostatistical corpus research tool "RSA Machine" [5]. The RSA parser can be used to analyze social network messages written in a modern language. In accordance with the existing tradition in the field of automatic text analysis, the identified parameters can later be used as markers of depression.

2 Related Work

Currently, the use of automatic text analysis to identify the author's psychological characteristics has become a special area of interdisciplinary research. Our papers [6, 7] provided reviews of manual and automatic text analysis methods that were intended for the use in clinical psychology and psychiatry. It was emphasized that most of the currently used methods of automatic analysis (including the LIWC method used in our country [8]) were focused on working with English texts, which significantly reduced the reliability of data obtained on the corpus of Russian texts. Another disadvantage of the methods used is that they rely mainly on vocabulary, as a result, the deeper structure of the text at the syntactic, semantic and discursive levels was not taken into account.

Machine learning and deep learning methods are actively used to identify textual markers of psychological distress and mental illness. In recent years, researchers have been especially focused on the identification of markers of depression.

In [9], the k-nearest neighbors method (KNN), the decision tree, the support vector machine (SVM) and ensemble methods were examined for identifying a depressive state based on data from English-language social networks. The features associated with linguistic style, emotional coloring and category of time were used as input. The best results were obtained by using the decision tree.

Machine learning was also used in [10] to build a model that predicts the level of depression (according to PHQ-8 [11]) based on audio, video, and text data from interviews. An approach based on thematic modeling was proposed. It allowed taking into account the context and important temporal details of the recordings. For each topic, the LIWC tool [12] was used to calculate frequency of word occurrence in 93 categories (e.g., anger, negative emotion, positive emotion) in the subject's speech on the given topic. According to [13], some topics (such as sleep quality) have strong association with depression, thus, additional features have been added for some topics. For each interview, the interviewer's speech was traversed, and the corresponding topic and the subject's speech, and also its corresponding timestamps were recorded with accordance to the topic dictionary. The subject's speech was used to generate semantic features, and the timestamps were used to synchronize audio and video features. Finally, the feature of presence/absence of the topic in the dialog was added to the feature vector. By using the feature selection method proposed in [10], the dimensionality of the vector was reduced. The following learning models were examined: random forest with different numbers of trees, stochastic gradient regressor (SGD), and the support vector regression (SVR) method with different kernels, for which the hyperparameters were tuned. It was shown that for a small number of features, random forest with 40 trees, SGD and SVR (radial basis function kernel) gave similar results, and with an increase in the number of features, the results of SGD and SVR continuously improved (in contrast to random forest), while the SGD model had a slightly lower root of the mean square error than SVR. This approach gave better results than the model trained on similar data, but with only video features [14], and the model that did not use topic modeling (so there were no features associated with topics, and the features were averaged over the interview).

In [15], the effectiveness of various neural network architectures for detecting Twitter users with signs of depression was investigated. The classification problem (presence/absence of depression) was being solved on an unbalanced dataset of 154 people. CNN and RNN architectures and different embeddings of words: CBOW, skip-gram, random and optimized, proposed in [15] – were compared. The best results on all metrics were shown by the CNNWithMax model proposed in [15]. Models with optimized embeddings showed the greatest generalization ability and allowed solving the depression detection problem even on a small and unbalanced data set.

In [16], a multimodal model of vocabulary learning (MDL), a generalization of vocabulary learning, was used to identify the presence or absence of depression in Twitter users. There were 6 groups of features: social network activity, personal information, profile photo, emotional feature (the sentiment of the used emojis, etc.), topic distribution feature, and domain-specific feature (for example, the presence of names of antidepressants in tweets). The performance of MDL, naive Bayesian classifier, MSNL [17] and WDL [18] on these features was compared. MNSL is a multiview learning model that can seamlessly analyze information from multiple sources. WDL is a dictionary learning model that uses the Wasserstein distance as fitting error between the original point and a point reconstructed from the dictionary to leverage the shared similarity of the features. The MDL method showed the best result, which demonstrated the effectiveness of combining multimodality and dictionary learning in the depression detection task.

We conducted similar studies on the data of the corpora collected in Russian-language social networks. For example, [19] compared the depression detection effectiveness of a random classifier, SVM, and Random Forest for different sets of users' features. The users in question had varying Beck's Depression Inventory scores. The highest F1-score was achieved by using SVM. In [20], the problem of detecting depression (as a diagnosed disease) from essays on a given topic was being solved. The Random Forest and SVM methods were compared; the Random Forest model showed the highest efficiency in terms of F1-score. Note that data obtained from the texts of patients with depression was less noisy than data obtained from the texts of people with high level of depressiveness measured by Beck's questionnaire.

In various works aimed at identifying textual markers of depression and depressiveness, including our previous work, only relationships between text parameters and psychological characteristics of the authors were explored, significant correlations and plausible differences were established, machine learning methods were used to solve the classification problem. At the same time, the problem of detecting cause-effect relationships between the psychological characteristics of the authors and the parameters of the texts generated by them was not addressed. However, in this area – the relationship between the traits of the author and text parameters – there are not probabilistic, but causal relations. This logic, the logic of "determining" the location of "failure" of a particular mental mechanism based on the defect observed in the patient's text, is the basis of pathopsychological diagnostics. In this regard, we conducted a new study using the same empirical material (essays of patients with depression and posts of depressed users of social networks), the study of causal relationships between text parameters and psychological characteristics of the authors of texts.

3 Method and Procedure

It is known that the JSM method [2, 21–27] is successfully used to study the causal relationships (to do causal analysis) in various subject areas. For causal analysis, it is also possible to use the AQJSM [1] algorithm, which modifies the existing inductive learning algorithm AQ (quasi-optimal algorithm) [3, 28].

The AQJSM method [1] is based on the following algorithm. The input is a set of n objects $O = \{o_i\}$, divided into a set of classes $C = \{c_k\}$; a set of features $P = \{p_j\}$; a matrix of values $A_{ij} = \{a_{ij}\}$, where each feature corresponds to a column of its values from the matrix $A_{ij} \, p_j \rightarrow (a_{1j}, a_{2j}, \ldots, a_{nj})$, and each object corresponds to its description $o_i \rightarrow (p_1 = a_{i1}, p_2 = a_{i2}, \ldots, p_m = a_{im})$, where the pair $p_j = a_{ij}$ is called an object property. The set of values of each interval feature p_j is divided into k parts: $w_1, w_2, \ldots, w_k$; $(a_{1j}, a_{2j}, \ldots, a_{nj}) = w_1 \bigcup w_2 \bigcup \ldots \bigcup w_k$. Then:

1. From the set C the class c_k is chosen, and from this class the initial object for the AQ algorithm [3, 28] is chosen.
2. By using AQ-learning, a set of rules R_k, starting with the initial object, is built for the class c_k.
3. For each property h_j from R_k the frequency (with accumulation) is computed; if there is a new initial object available, go to step 2, else a new class c_k is chosen and go to step 2 too; if all the classes are considered, go to step 4.
4. For each class its description D_k is built and the best rule R^*_k is chosen; the criteria $\theta_1(c_k)$ and $\theta_2(c_k)$, described in [1], are calculated; if the values of any of them are higher (lower) than critical thresholds, the algorithm terminates with an empty set of causes for each class; else go to step 5.
5. For each class c_k a factbase is formed based on D_k. In factbases the set of properties is reduced with accordance to nested and conflict level [1].
6. The class c_k in question is selected and hypotheses $H_k = \{H(h_g, c_k)\}$ on the presence of cause-effect relationships between the class properties are built by using the first step of the JSM-method [2].

7. The causes with lengths above the critical value and the causes included in other causes are excluded from the set H_k. If there are unstudied classes left, one of them is chosen, then go to step 6.

The output of the algorithm is the set of pairs $\{c_k, H_k\}$ – a set of pairs «class – set of hypotheses».

An important feature of this method is that as a result of its application, a more specific description of relationships is obtained than that obtained by methods of mathematical statistics. The results can be presented as (<Class>, <Class property>, <Reason>), which is interpreted as follows: if the subjects belongs to <Class>, the presence of <Class property> is explained by <Reason>. For social sciences, where the researcher deals not only with the properties of the objects of his research, but also with a certain number of behavioral reactions of certain groups of subjects/respondents under certain conditions, being able to obtain such a description is important, since it reflects the nature of the observed phenomena better. Size or weight of metalwork products can be considered their parameters, and it is natural to compare these objects by these parameters, however, sociological survey respondents' opinions, or customers' choices of certain products in marketing research or text or image data produced by people with certain characteristics in psychodiagnostic examination, can hardly be considered the «parameters» of these «objects». To compare groups of subjects/respondents, a method that allows comparing the parameters of their behavior observed under certain conditions is needed so that there is no confusion between the object of research and its behavior. This requirement is met to a certain extent by the JSM-method [29] and AQJSM, its modification, aimed specifically at identifying cause-and-effect relationships in psychological testing data [1].

In this paper, the AQJSM algorithm was used to find cause-effect relationships between depression/depressiveness of the author of the text and the parameters of the text in order to identify markers of depression in Russian-language texts. As a result of the AQJSM algorithm, the data is generated about the possibility of particularly frequent or particularly rare occurrence of certain linguistic characteristics in the texts of authors from a certain group provided that other linguistic characteristics occur particularly frequently or particularly rarely in these texts. This description of linguistic analyzer data is closer to the complex reality of text characteristics as a product of speech behavior with mutually dependent characteristics than methods of mathematical statistics or machine learning, in which text parameters can only be considered as "properties" of the text author. In this sense, the terms "cause" and "event" will be used, the psychiatric status of the subject or his/her psychological characteristics are the cause of the observed text events when some other text events occur.

In the first experiment, essay texts on the topic «Me and my relations with others and the world around me» (minimum 1800 characters) were used (the research procedure is described in [20]). 316 texts were collected from the subjects, among which 93 subjects were diagnosed with depression. Thus, the categorical feature «control/depression» was introduced. For each essay, numerical values were obtained for each of the text parameters. The numerical characteristics were converted to categorical ones depending on the interval of value they belong to (5 values possible: very low, low, average, high, very high).

In the second experiment, the texts of posts from users of the social network Vkontakte were used. Volunteers filled out the Beck's Depression Inventory (the research procedure is described in [20]. Users with a score less than 11 points on the Beck scale were classified as healthy (239 people), and those with a score higher than 29 points were assigned to the group with a high level of depression (148 people). Similarly, the categorical feature «non-depressive/depressive» was identified. For each text obtained by concatenation of user posts, numeric values of text parameters were obtained, which were also converted to categorical values depending on the interval of value they belong to (5 values possible: very low, low, average, high, very high).

To calculate text parameters, a linguistic analyzer of the tool for corpus-based linguostatistical research "RSA Machine" [5] was utilized. The RSA Machine was developed at FRC CSC RAS. The semantic-syntactic structure of sayings was analyzed by using the method of relational-situational analysis (RSA), which is based on the syntaxemic analysis of G. A. Zolotova [30] and the concept of heterogeneous semantic networks of G. S. Osipov [31]. RSA allows working with Russian-language texts and taking into account the specifics of semantic-syntactic relations of the Russian language and specifics of the authors' Russian language worldview.

Currently, the analyzer allows extracting the following types of indicators in the text: predicate-syntaxeme structures; indicators of the frequency of lexical units in the text that belong to certain thematic groups of words (TGW); psycholinguistic indicators that reflect the author's emotional state. Each text is represented by a set of 204 parameters: 1) psycholinguistic indicators, 34 parameters; 2) semantic roles, 92 parameters; 3) semantic relationships, 35 parameters; 4) assessment and state vocabularies, 20 parameters; 5) thematic vocabularies, 9 parameters; 6) parts of speech, 14 parameters.

In both cases, the values of each text parameter were divided into 5 intervals, each interval corresponding to one class. For each class, the AQJSM algorithm was run over other text parameters and the mental state feature, while looking for such cause-effect relationships that the reason for any property of the class is the mental state (depression/depressiveness).

4 Results

In the first experiment, 40 causal relationships were obtained. The «depression» diagnosis was the only cause of high or low values of detected text parameters in 27 cases. For the essays, the text parameters representing «class properties» with high or low occurrence, the cause of which was the value «depression», are shown in Table 1 with the corresponding classes as conditions.

In the second experiment, 70 causal relationships were obtained. High Beck's Depression Inventory score was the only reason for high or low values of detected text parameters in 40 cases. For social media messages, the text parameters representing «class properties» with high or low occurrence, the cause of which was the value "depressive" (high scores on the Beck scale of depression), are shown in Table 2 with the corresponding classes as conditions.

Table 1. The reason for the text «events» is clinical depression.

№	Class	№	Class property
5	Number of sentences = Very high	4	Number of clauses = Very high
44	Vocabulary: Lexicon of destruction and violence = Very high	74	Part of speech: preposition = Low
44	Vocabulary: Lexicon of destruction and violence = Very high	20	Fraction of past tense verbs = Very high
47	Vocabulary: Computer slang = Very high	76	Part of speech: substantive pronoun = High
59	Vocabulary: Thematic Economics = Very high	50	Vocabulary: Lexicon of motivation, activity and tension = High
59	Vocabulary: Thematic Economics = Very high	124	Sem. role: object = High
72	Part of speech: numeral = Very high	8	Number of unique words/Number of words = High
72	Part of speech: numeral = Very high	37	Vocabulary: Non-exclusive and amplifying lexicon = Very low
128	Sem. role: objective = Very high	122	Sem. role: mediative = Very high
152	Sem. role: resultative = High	173	Sem. relationship: CAUS = Low
152	Sem. role: resultative = High	3	Number of unique words = Low
152	Sem. role: resultative = High	36	Vocabulary: Lexicon of positive emotional judgement = Very low
157	Sem. role: social category = Very high	105	Sem. role: causate = Very low
198	Sem. relationship: RSN = Very high	46	Vocabulary: Prison slang = Low
199	Sem. relationship: SIT = Very high	20	Fraction of past tense verbs = Very high
199	Sem. relationship: SIT = Very high	70	Part of speech: conjunction = Very high

In this case of depression/depressiveness a textual feature is considered a psychological characteristic marker if it has a proven validity of increased/decreased frequency of occurrence in the texts of people with this psychological characteristic. Accordingly, text parameters of classes and class properties with average occurrence were excluded from consideration as of little interest from the point of view of further use as markers of depression/depressiveness. The text parameters calculated by the RSA Machine are numbered, so a unique number is assigned to each parameter shown in tables, which makes it easier to compare tables.

Comparative analysis of the tables showed that the text manifestations of depression diagnosed in a psychiatric clinic and the text manifestations of depression determined by a psychodiagnostic questionnaire were not the same:

Table 2. The reason for the text «events» is depressiveness.

№	Class	№	Class property
51	Vocabulary: Thematic Crime = High	47	Vocabulary: Computer slang = Very high
91	Sem. role: destinative = Very high	121	Sem. role: locative = Low
92	Sem. role: destructive = Very high	61	Vocabulary: Catastrophes = Very low
96	Sem. role: duration = High	152	Sem. role: resultative = Very low
97	Sem. role: donor = Very high	64	Part of speech: adjective = Very high
97	Sem. role: donor = Very high	26	Fraction of 1 person pronouns = High
102	Sem. role: interpret. concepts = Very high	28	Fraction of 3 person pronouns = Very low
114	Sem. role: comitative = Very high	45	Vocabulary: Thematic Utilities Sector = Very high
120	Sem. role: person fitness = Very high	8	Number of unique words/Number of words = Very high
128	Sem. role: objective = Very high	118	Sem. role: liquidative = Very low
129	Sem. role: basis of qualification = Very high	32	Coefficient of logical consistency = Low
129	Sem. role: basis of qualification = Very high	44	Vocabulary: Lexicon of destruction and violence = Very low
134	Sem. role: parameter = High	44	Vocabulary: Lexicon of destruction and violence = Very low
147	Sem. role: object of comparison = Very high	46	Vocabulary: Prison slang = Low
158	Sem. role: manner = Very high	80	Sem. role: autorizator = High
158	Sem. role: manner = Very high	47	Vocabulary: Computer slang = High
163	Sem. role: themative = Very high	72	Part of speech: numeral = Low
164	Sem. role: temporative = Very high	50	Vocabulary: Lexicon of motivation, activity and tension = Very low
169	Sem. role: estimative = Very high	142	Sem. role: predicate = Very low
169	Sem. role: estimative = Very high	180	Sem. relationship: DLB = Very low
182	Sem. relationship: EQ = Very high	75	Part of speech: noun = Low
182	Sem. relationship: EQ = Very high	50	Vocabulary: Lexicon of motivation, activity and tension = Very low
185	Sem. relationship: INS = High	71	Part of speech: interjection = Low

(continued)

Table 2. (*continued*)

№	Class	№	Class property
192	Sem. relationship: POS = High	27	Fraction of 2 person pronouns = Low
192	Sem. relationship: POS = High	47	Vocabulary: Computer slang = Very low
199	Sem. relationship: SIT = High	9	Number of punctuation marks/Number of words = Low
199	Sem. relationship: SIT = High	47	Vocabulary: Computer slang = Low

1. Clinical depression was the sole cause of 27 text «events», and depressiveness as a personality trait was the sole cause of 40 text «events».
2. Clinical depression had 16 textual markers while depressiveness had 27 textual markers.
3. The text «events» caused by depression and depressiveness had only 2 «events» in common: high fraction of unique words and rare occurrence of prison slang.
4. However, the conditions for these two events to occur were different for depression and depressiveness:
a. In the texts of individuals with high level of depressiveness the high fraction of unique words (parameter 8) was significant as depressiveness marker provided that when this «event» took place, the occurrence of words in the semantic role of «person_fitness» (in estimation model: a person with respect to whom the fitness is estimated; parameter 120) was very frequent whereas in the texts of people with depression, this «event» was significant and this text parameter could be considered a marker of depression if the author used a lot of numerals in the text (parameter 72).
b. In the texts of individuals with high level of depressiveness rare use of prison slang (parameter 46) was significant as depressiveness marker provided that when this «event» took place, the occurrence of words in the semantic role of «object of comparison» (one of the two compared components accompanying relational verbs with comparative meaning; parameter 147) was very frequent whereas in the texts of people with depression, this «event» was significant and this text parameter could be considered a marker of depression if the words related semantically in a sense of the RSN semantic relationship (parameter 198) were very frequent in the text.
5. Among the textual "events" that were caused by depression and depressiveness, there were two opposite ones – in case of clinical depression, a high value of parameter 15 "Vocabulary of motivation, activity and tension" was important (under condition that the parameter 4, Vocabulary: Thematic Economics, had a very high value), and in case of depressiveness as a personality trait, on the contrary, the very rare occurrence of this kind of vocabulary was significant (provided that the frequency of occurrence of the semantic relationship EQ is high; parameter 41).

What is the reason behind such a serious discrepancy between the markers of clinical depression and depressiveness as a personality trait identified by the Beck questionnaire? Obviously, there may be several reasons for this:

- The specificity of text products of patients with depression and healthy people with such a personal trait as depressiveness may be caused by different psychological mechanisms, so one should not expect to be able to identify people who are at risk for depression based on markers of depressiveness from social network texts.
- It is possible that the main reason is the genre of the texts, in the first experiment, we analyzed the texts of essays, in the second experiment we analyzed the messages of social networks with an unknown genre task (note that there may exist social network posts written in the essay genre, but in our case the posts were not evaluated from this point of view).
- It is also possible that the markers of depression were influenced by the predetermined text topic, in the group of sufferers of depression, it was set as «Me and my relations with others and the world around me», while in those who were tested using the Beck's Depression Inventory, the topics of social network posts were arbitrary (in the study, the topics of posts were not identified).
- Possibly, the most significant factor is the conditions under which the text was written: during a psychological expertise, as in our first experiment, or in a situation of spontaneous expression of opinion, as in the second experiment.
- Finally, it is likely that the peculiarity of network communication noted by many linguists, as in this kind of communication texts obey the laws of both written and spoken language, is the true reason for the observed difference of "markers".

So, the data obtained can be considered linguistic markers of depression and markers of depressiveness in terms of the dependence (confirmed in the course of computer experiments) of the identified parameters of texts on the presence of clinical depression or depressiveness in their authors.

However, as for the validity of the markers identified in this paper and described in other linguostatistical studies, in other words, if we want to answer whether the found parameters measure what they are designed to measure, specifically, «do the markers of depression measure depression?», we should note the lack of linguistic theoretical base in this research program. The fact is that the discrepancy between the markers of depression and those of depressiveness that was found cannot be the subject of psychological experimental research alone, although the hypotheses proposed above about the reasons for the differences must, of course, be verified before specialists in automatic text analysis can confidently recommend their tools for mass surveys. Research in the field of automatic network psychodiagnostics is really interdisciplinary and requires the participation of linguists not only at the stage of preparing a linguistic analyzer, but also at the stage of hypothesizing the properties of texts of people with different psychological characteristics [32]. Without proposing linguistic hypotheses and testing these hypotheses using artificial intelligence methods, the conclusion that markers, for example, of depression are those, and not other parameters of the text, turns out to be unreliable, depending on the properties of the sample, on the genre and thematic specificity of the text, on other various conditions under which the texts included in the processed corpus were created.

5   Conclusion

The application of the AQJSM algorithm allowed us to identify 16 linguistic markers of clinical depression and 27 markers of depressiveness. However, the study showed the existence of unresolved validity issues in modern research in computational linguistics and automatic psychodiagnostics. What is recognized as linguistic markers of psychological characteristics or even psychiatric illness based on the results of mathematical statistics or machine learning methods cannot be considered as actual indicators of the authors' characteristics until the experiments are conducted where dependent variables – text parameters – are examined while controlling a number of independent variables. Our work outlines a range of main independent variables that, along with personal characteristics and psychiatric status, can affect the values of dependent variables, measured values of text parameters. It should be noted, however, that the list of possible «causes» of observed «text events» may be bigger than we currently think. In addition, the generation of non-interpretable, and therefore meaningless, connections between the properties of the author and the properties of his text should be replaced by AI testing of hypotheses proposed by linguists. This procedure carried out under the guidance of AI specialists will allow us to build reasoning models of experts that rely in their work on the text as a source of information about its author.

Acknowledgments. The reported study was funded by RFBR according to the research projects № 18-00-00606 (18-00-00233) and № 17-29-02305.

References

1. Panov, A.: Extraction of cause-effect relationships from psychological test data using logical methods. Sci. Tech. Inf. Process. **41**, 275–282 (2014)
2. Finn, V.: Plausible reasonings in the JSM type intelligent systems. Itogi Nauki i Tekhniki, Seriya Informatika **15**, 54–101 (1991)
3. Michalski, R.: AQVAL/1 computer implementation of variable valued logic system VL1 and examples of its application to pattern recognition. In: Proceedings of the First International Joint Conference on Pattern Recognition, Washington, DC, pp. 3–17, 30 October–1 November (1973)
4. Shelmanov, A., Smirnov, I.: Methods for semantic role labeling of Russian texts. In: Computational Linguistics and Intellectual Technologies. Papers from the Annual International Conference "Dialogue", no. 13, pp. 607–620 (2014)
5. Kuznetsova, Y., Smirnov, I., Stankevich, M., Chudova, N.: Sozdanie instrumenta avtomaticheskogo analiza teksta v interesakh sotsio-gumanitarnykh issledovanii. Iskusstvennyi intellekt i priniatie reshenii. Ch.1; Ch.2. 28–38; 21–32 (2019)
6. Enikolopov, S., et al.: Lingvisticheskie kharakteristiki tekstov psikhicheski bolnykh i zdorovykh liudei. Psikhologicheskie issledovaniia 11 (2018)

7. Enikolopov, S., et al.: Osobennosti teksta i psikhologicheskie osobennosti: opyt empirich-eskogo kompiuternogo issledovaniia. Trudy Instituta sistemnogo analiza Rossiiskoi akademii nauk **69**, 91–99 (2019)
8. Pennebaker, J., Francis, M.: Linguistic inquiry and word count: LIWC 2001. Mahway: Lawrence Erlbaum Associates 71, 2001 (2001)
9. Islam, M.R., Kabir, M.A., Ahmed, A., Kamal, A.R.M., Wang, H., Ulhaq, A.: Depression detection from social network data using machine learning techniques. Health Inf. Sci. Syst. **6**(1), 1–12 (2018). https://doi.org/10.1007/s13755-018-0046-0
10. Gong, Y., Poellabauer, C.: Topic modeling based multi-modal depression detection. In: Proceedings of the 7th Annual Workshop on Audio/Visual Emotion Challenge. pp. 69–76. Association for Computing Machinery, New York (2017)
11. Kroenke, K., Strine, T., Spitzer, R., Williams, J., Berry, J., Mokdad, A.: The PHQ-8 as a measure of current depression in the general population. J. Affect. Disord. **114**, 163–173 (2009)
12. Pennebaker, W., Boyd, L., Jordan, K., Blackburn, K.: The development and psychometric properties of LIWC2015. Technical report (2015)
13. Yang, L., Jiang, D., He, L., Pei, E., Oveneke, M., Sahli, H.: Decision tree based depression classification from audio video and language information. In: Proceedings of the 6th International Workshop on Audio/Visual Emotion Challenge, pp. 89–96. Association for Computing Machinery, New York (2016)
14. Ringeval, F., et al.: AVEC 2017: Real-life depression, and affect recognition workshop and challenge. In: Proceedings of the 7th Annual Workshop on Audio/Visual Emotion Challenge, pp. 3–9. Association for Computing Machinery, New York (2016)
15. Orabi, A., Buddhitha, P., Orabi, M., Inkpen, D.: Deep learning for depression detection of Twitter users. In: Proceedings of the Fifth Workshop on Computational Linguistics and Clinical Psychology: From Keyboard to Clinic, New Orleans, LA, pp. 88–97. Association for Computational Linguistics (2018)
16. Shen, G., et al.: Depression detection via harvesting social media: a multimodal dictionary learning solution. In: Proceedings of the Twenty-Sixth International Joint Conference on Artificial Intelligence (IJCAI 2017), Melbourne, Australia, 9–25 August 2017
17. Song, X., Nie, L., Zhang, L., Akbari, M., Chua, T.: Multiple social network learning and its application in volunteerism tendency prediction. In: Proceedings of the 38th International ACM SIGIR Conference on Research and Development in Information Retrieval, pp. 213–222. Association for Computing Machinery, New York (2015)
18. Rolet, A., Cuturi, M., Peyré, G.: Fast dictionary learning with a smoothed Wasserstein loss. In: Artificial Intelligence and Statistics, pp. 630–638 (2016)
19. Stankevich, M., Latyshev, A., Kuminskaya, E., Smirnov, I., Grigoriev, O.: Depression detection from social media texts. In: Elizarov, A., Novikov, B., Stupnikov., S (eds.) Data Analytics and Management in Data Intensive Domains: XXI International Conference DAMDID/RCDL 2019: Conference Proceedings, Kazan, Russia, p. 352 (2019)
20. Stankevich, M., Smirnov, I., Kuznetsova, Y., Kiselnikova, N., Enikolopov, S.: Predicting depression from essays in Russian. In: Computational Linguistics and Intellectual Technologies: Proceedings of the International Conference «Dialogue-2019», Moscow, 29 May–1 June 2019
21. Volkova, A.: Analyzing the data of different subject fields using the procedures of the JSM method for automatic hypothesis generation. Autom. Doc. Math. Linguist. **45**, 127–139 (2011)
22. Anshakov, O., Fabrikantova, B.: DSM-metod avtomaticheskogo porozhdeniya gipotez: Logicheskie i epistemologicheskie osnovaniya. Knizhny dom «LIBROKOM», Moscow, Russia (2009)
23. Finn, V.: The synthesis of cognitive procedures and the problem of induction. Autom. Doc. Math. Linguist. **43**, 149–195 (2009)

24. Finn, V.: Timely notes about the JSM method for automatic hypothesis generation. Autom. Doc. Math. Linguist. **43**, 257–269 (2009)
25. Finn, V.: The inductive joint similarity-difference method and procedure semantics of the JSM method. Nauchno-Tekh. Inf. Ser. **2**, 1–17 (2010)
26. Finn, V.: On Determination of empirical regularities via JSM method for automatic hypothesis generation: supplement to Finn, VK, Inductive JS Mill's Methods in Artificial Intelligence. Iskusst. Intel. Prin. Resh, 41–48 (2010)
27. Panov, A.I., Shvets, A.V., Volkova, G.D.: A technique for retrieving cause-and-effect relationships from optimized fact bases. Sci. Tech. Inf. Process. **42**(6), 420–425 (2015). https://doi.org/10.3103/S0147688215060039
28. Wojtusiak, J., Michalski, R.S., Kaufman, K.A., Pietrzykowski, J.: The AQ21 natural induction program for pattern discovery: initial version and its novel features. In: 2006 18th IEEE International Conference on Tools with Artificial Intelligence (ICTAI 2006), Arlington, VA, USA, 13–15 November 2006
29. Klimova, S., Mikheyenkova, M., Finn, V.: The JSM-method in qualitative sociological research: the fundamentals and experience in use. Sociol. J. **22**, 8–30 (2016)
30. Zolotova, G., Onipenko, N., Sidorova, M.: Kommunikativnaia grammatika russkogo iazyka. Izdatelstvo M Institut russkogo iazyka im V V Vinogradova RAN, Moskva (2004)
31. Osipov, G.: Priobretenie znanii intellektualnymi sistemami Osnovy teorii i tekhnologii. Nauka Fizmatlit, Moskva (1997)
32. Nikitina, E., Onipenko, N.: Kognitivno-lingvisticheskaia interpretatsiia rezultatov avtomaticheskogo analiza tekstov psikhicheski bolnykh. Iskusstvennyi intellekt i priniatie reshenii, 60–69 (2019)

Distributional Models in the Task of Hypernym Discovery

Vasiliy Yadrintsev[1,2]([✉]) [iD], Anastasiia Ryzhova[3] [iD], and Ilya Sochenkov[2] [iD]

[1] Peoples Friendship University of Russia (RUDN University), Moscow, Russia
vvyadrincev@gmail.com
[2] Federal Research Center "Computer Science and Control" of the Russian Academy
of Sciences, Moscow, Russia
sochenkov@isa.ru
[3] Skolkovo Institute of Science and Technology, Moscow, Russia
Anastasiia.Ryzhova@skoltech.ru

Abstract. An approach to the solution of the first task of automatically taxonomy construction for the Russian language is described. This task consists in matching unknown input-words with hypernyms from the existing taxonomy. We show that useful results can be attained using pre-trained distribution models without additional training.

Keywords: Hypernym discovery · RuWordNet · Distributional models · fastText · ELMO · BERT · Rusvectores

1 Introduction

A hypernym–hyponym relation consists of pairs of words, where one of the terms, hyponym, is a specific instance of the other word, hypernym. For example, the "animal" is a hypernym of the word "dog", while the word "spaniel" is the hyponym of the same concept.

The taxonomic relations play a big role in thesauri constructions since it is one of the ways of the synset connections. These relations have a great application in semantically intensive NLP tasks, e.g., in Question Answering tasks or search systems. However, it is not efficient to find them manually, so the automatic taxonomy construction is a subject of many types of research for a long time. The pattern-based approach is one of the most widely used methods of extracting hypernym-hyponym relations, which uses joint co-occurrence of hyponym and hypernym in texts [1,19]. One of the most popular pattern-based methods for taxonomy discovery in the English language was proposed by Marti Hearst in 1992 [10]. She manually designed the list of patterns for extracting taxonomy relations from texts. For example, the pattern "NP {,} especially

---

The reported study was funded by RFBR according to the research projects № 18-29-03187 and № 18-29-16172 and with the support of the "RUDN University Program 5-100".

S. O. Kuznetsov et al. (Eds.): RCAI 2020, LNAI 12412, pp. 338–350, 2020.
https://doi.org/10.1007/978-3-030-59535-7_25

$\{NP,\} * \{$or | and$\}$ NP" allows to extract a pair "France, European country" from the sentence "... most European countries, especially France ..." Another method for taxonomic discovery uses distributed representations of words [2, 27].

Vered Shwartz et al. [25] were first who combined pattern-based and distributional approaches. They created the neural net HypeNET with LSTM architecture. To investigate if the two words are in the "hypernym-hyponym" relationship, the researchers proposed a method where each dependency between terms was represented as a sequence of edges from x to y in the dependency tree. Then all these sequences were encoded by the LSTM model, pooled by average pooling layer in one vector, and were used as inputs for classification.

Over a long time, the researchers used unsupervised approaches for taxonomic discovery [26]. Nevertheless, with the appearance of distributional word representations, these representations became widely used as inputs for classifications. So the supervised approaches became very popular in the task of hypernym discovery.

We participated in the first shared task on *automatic taxonomy construction* for the Russian language (RUSSE'2020 [20]). The goal of this task was the following: neologisms needed to be associated with the appropriate hypernyms from an existing taxonomy. Participants were invited to test their methods on nouns and verbs for which public and private test data were provided. As a taxonomy, the RuWordNet (Russian WordNet [17]) was used, the format of which is similar to the English WordNet [18] format.

The organizers provided a baseline that uses pre-trained models to obtain word vectors. The method we propose here is an improvement of the baseline. We intentionally employed a simple approach to identifying a hypernym of a word, which we described below. We were interested in whether the Russian taxonomy construction task can be solved using already available algorithms and pre-trained models without additional training. Most likely, the answer is no, because we reached MAP metric value 0.51 on nouns and 0.38 on verbs. Nevertheless, we showed results not lower than the fourth place (from more than 13 participants) on each test set.

The rest of the paper is organized as follows. Section 2 briefly outlines the previous work related to our task. In Sect. 3, we present the datasets offered by the shared task organizers and used pre-trained models. Section 4 provides the details of the employed approach. In Sect. 5 we describe the results, and in Sect. 6 we conclude.

2 Related Work

Earlier, three SemEval competitions were devoted to taxonomy discovery: *SemEval-2018 task 9: Hypernym discovery,   Semeval-2016 task 13: Taxonomy extraction evaluation, SemEval 2015 task 17.*

In the competition SemEval 2015 task 17 [6], the participants had to extract hyponym-hypernym relations from English texts in four domains: Chemicals, Equipment, Food, and Science. The taxonomy extraction usually consists of three parts. Firstly the term-candidates are extracted. Secondly, the search for relations is performed. Finally, the taxonomies are constructed. Most of the teams concentrated on the second subtask, and only one team formed taxonomies as well. Since the organizers did not provide any corpus, almost all participants used Wikipedia-based corpora for their researches.

The competition SemEval-2016 task 13 [7] was also devoted to searching for taxonomies relations and their further construction. The task was not monolingual as the previous one and included four languages, English, Dutch, Italian, and French. The best results were obtained by the team, which used Hearst patterns and a big web-corpus. Moreover, in 2018 the researchers from Facebook AI compared different taxonomy discovery methods and showed that the methods based on Hearst patterns outperform distributional approaches on benchmark datasets [22].

The goal of the taxonomy discovery task was reformulated in SemEval 2018 [8]. The main aim was to predict many hypernym candidates to one word. Three languages (English, Spanish, and Italian) and two domains (Music and Medicine) were considered in this task. The best results were achieved by the CRIM team [5], which combined supervised methods and Hearst patterns. They used pretrained word embeddings and logistic regression as a classification algorithm, but the main idea was the usage of projection matrices of query word embeddings. The team 300-sparsans r1 [4] obtained the best result with Italian words. They trained logistic regression as well and used the word embeddings as inputs for classification. In Spanish, the best system applied the nearest neighbors classification algorithm [21].

As for the Russian language, the hyponym-hypernym discovery problem is not so highly investigated. In [23], Sabirova et al. proposed taxonomy relations extraction from texts based on rules. They created six different patterns, e.g., "Y is kind/type/form/sort of X". Then these patterns were extracted from texts with the help of finite-state automaton.

For the hyponym-hypernym discovery, the researchers often use definitions from the large dictionaries. In [11] the authors clustered the definitions using the big corpus [12] and then extracted the hypernym candidates, using patterns for verbose candidates. Besides, they trained the SVM classifier to extract the best candidates.

3   Data Overview

This section provides an analysis of the data used to conduct the experiments.

3.1   RuWordNet

The organizers provided a Russian thesaurus RuWordNet [17], automatically obtained from RuThes [16] by converting it to the WordNet [18] format.

RuWordNet is a set of synsets and relations between them. Synset is a set of one or more synonyms (also called senses) that are interchangeable in some context without changing the truth value of the proposition in which they are embedded. In RuWordNet, the number of senses for synsets varies from 1 to 42. More than 90% of synsets have less than 6 senses, and more than 66% of synsets have less than 3 senses. Senses are most often represented by one or two words, but there are also senses with ten words.

Three parts of speech are presented in the thesaurus: **Nouns, Adjectives** and **Verbs**. Each synset is represented by fields **ruthes_name** and **definition**, each sense is represented by fields **name, lemma,** and **main_word**.

RuWordNet statistics are presented in Table 1, namely: the number of synsets, the average number of senses, the average number of hypernyms (i.e., "parents"), the average number of hypernyms with hypernyms of hypernyms(i.e., with "parents of parents"), the ratio of non-empty **definition** and **main_word**. Below we give facts on the RuWordNet thesaurus:

- for all synsets, **ruthes_name** is a non-empty string;
- for all senses, **name** and **lemma** are non-empty strings;
- **definition** of synsets and **main_word** of senses are not always included in descriptions.

In the framework of this competition, we are interested in **Nouns** and **Verbs**, the number of synsets of which is 29,300 and 7,500, respectively.

Table 1. RuWordNet

PoS	Synsets	Avg senses	Avg parents	+ par-s of par-s	Avg definition	Avg main_word
Nouns	29,296	2.62	1.27	2.924	0.33	0.513
Verbs	7,521	4.69	1.37	3.017	0.468	0.349

Train Data. Table 2 shows the statistics of the training data set. From this table we can observe the following:

- 52% of **Nouns** and 32% of **Verbs** with hypernyms are represented in the training set.
- The training set has more than two times more hypernyms than the number of "hypernym" relations in RuWordNet.

The first fact is due to the removal of synsets closer than five vertices from the root by the organizers. The second fact is explained by both the "parents" of the synset and the "parents of the parents" being probably used in the training set.

Thus, we note the need to take into account the hypernyms of hypernyms (i.e., parents of parents).

Table 2. Train data

PoS	Synsets	Avg hypernyms (train)	Avg hypernyms (RuWordNet relations)
Nouns	14,649	3.041	1.227
Verbs	2,357	3.438	1.512

3.2 Pre-trained Models

In the present work, we use the following pre-trained models:

1. **ft_cc_ru_300**,
2. **RuBERT**,
3. **ruscorpora_none_fasttextskipgram_300_2_2019**,
4. **tayga_none_fasttextcbow_300_10_2019**,
5. **araneum_none_fasttextcbow_300_5_2018**,
6. **tayga_lemmas_elmo_2048_2019**.

The first model includes pre-trained word vectors for Russian language from Facebook [9]. The second one is an adopted BERT for Russian [14]. 3–6 models are pre-trained word vectors for Russian from **rusvectores** [15].

Note that we used RuBERT as "embeddings", considering the hidden layer with dimension 3072 as word vectors: this idea was taken from the baseline provided by the organizers of the competition. So, vector dimensions of 1, 3–5 are 300, second – 3072 and sixth – 1024.

Most likely, the largest text corpus was used for the first model, which includes Wikipedia and Common Crawl (we do not know the exact volume of crawl-data for the Russian, but roughly 24 terabytes of plain text was used for 157 languages [9]). Then, the second model was trained on Wikipedia and news dataset; the third model on the Russian National Corpus. The fourth and the sixth models were trained on the TAIGA corpus [24]. Finally, the fifth model was trained on the Araneum Russicum Maximum [3].

4 The Baseline and Our Approach

This section first briefly describes the baseline, then a description of the steps to improve baseline is provided. After that an out-of-vocabulary analysis was performed. And finally, the last subsection describes an attempt to train the BERT on the automatic taxonomy construction task.

4.1 Baseline

This subsection describes the baseline provided by the competition organizers. Briefly, this approach used the pre-trained distributional model to obtain "synsets-synonyms", whose "parents" are further used as answers. A more detailed description is given below.

The common-crawl fastText [9] (300-dimension) model was used to obtain synset vectors and word vectors for the input words. The synset vector was the average word vector of all synset senses. Denote by variables **nouns_cnt** and **verbs_cnt** the number of synsets-nouns and synsets-verbs, respectively. As noted earlier, the total number of nouns is 29,300 and the number of verbs is 7,500. For the existing taxonomy, separate vector matrices were created for nouns and verbs of sizes {**nouns_cnt**} × 300 and {**verbs_cnt**} × 300, respectively. Then, for each input word, the closest synsets were searched by cosine measure. The synsets were considered as synonyms or hypernyms depending on the approach. In the case where the nearest synsets were considered as synonyms, the hypernyms of synonyms (from RuWordNet) were used as answers.

4.2 Proposed Improvements

Proposed improvements significantly increased a MAP on test samples.

1. Addition of ranking at the final stage: sorting synsets based on the recalculated rate for each **synset_id**. The considered parameters are the following: **k** (retrieval), **n** (final), **p1, p2, p3**. The addition of ranking gave the most significant (5–7%) improvement in results. This improvement will be described separately in the section named **"Ranking"**.
2. Extension of the string representation of the synset. The following fields were considered as parameters: **ruthes_name, definition, name, lemma, main_word**. We have revealed that the following combinations are better: for nouns – two fields (**ruthes_name, name**), and for verbs - all fields. The above combinations are used for all models in our work except RuBERT. For the latest, a standard string representation(just the **names** of the senses) is used. Using non-standard combinations improved the results a bit (1–3%).
3. Addition of other relationships between synsets. We tried to add the "domain" relation, which slightly worsened the results.
4. Usage of train data to get "parents" instead of getting hypernyms from RuWordNet. Minimal decline.
5. Normalization of the words of the string representations of synsets. Improved results (1–3%). This improvement will be described separately in the section named **"Normalization"**.
6. Lemmatization of all words from a string representation of a synset. The results have changed slightly.

Ranking. This improvement consists of adding parameters to the original algorithm. The following parameters were used by the ranking algorithm:

- The number of synsets-associates, **k**.
- The number of final synsets-hypernyms, **n**.
- The plausibility of the fact that the synset-associate is a hypernym of the input word, **p1**.

- The plausibility of the fact that the hypernyms of the synset-associate are the input word hypernyms, **p2**.
- The plausibility of the fact that the hypernyms of the hypernyms of the synset-associate are the input word hypernyms, **p3**.

For synsets, a matrix of vectors $\mathbf{M}$ compiled, vector $\mathbf{V}$ assigned an input word. An unnormalized measure was used to calculate relevance ($\mathbf{R}$). In the beginning, each synset from the thesaurus was associated with $\mathbf{R} = 0$. At the first step of the algorithm, the search was performed (by cosine measure) for the $\mathbf{k}$ closest synset-associates (technically, we looked for vectors close to $\mathbf{V}$ in the matrix $\mathbf{M}$). Assume that $\mathbf{r}$ is a cosine measure for a synset-associate. Next, there is a simple recalculation of R, consisting of 3 steps:

- $\mathbf{R}$ of the synset associate increases by $\mathbf{r}$ * $\mathbf{p1}$.
- $\mathbf{R}$ of hypernyms of the synset-associate increases by $\mathbf{r}$ * $\mathbf{p2}$.
- $\mathbf{R}$ of hypernyms of synsets from previous step increases by $\mathbf{r}$ * $\mathbf{p3}$.

Hypernyms in the second and third steps were taken from the thesaurus using the "hypernym" relation. At the end of the algorithm, the top $\mathbf{n}$ (by $\mathbf{R}$) synsets-hypernyms were selected for the answer.

Normalization

- First, all words were converted to lowercase.
- Second, all punctuation except for a hyphen ("-") was replaced by a space. Note that non-standard characters from the RuWordNet words were also included in this list.
- Then, using the pymorphy2 [13] morphological analyzer, functional words were removed: prepositions, conjunctions, etc. List of restricted tags: NPRO, PRED, PREP, CONJ, PRCL, INTJ.
- If "Geox" was present in the word tag list, then the first letter was replaced with a large one.

4.3   Out-of-Vocabulary Analysis

It was interesting for us to see how well the words are presented in the dictionaries of models. Table 3 presents the out-of-vocabulary analysis for all models (except RuBERT) on public, private words and RuWordNet words. RuWordNet words were normalized in the same way as in evaluation. The first line in Table 3 shows the number of unique words separately for nouns and verbs. It should be noted that in the string representation of the synset (regardless of the part of the speech of the synset) there were nouns, verbs and other parts of speech. For example, the number of words for N (46,079) did not mean that all 46,079 words are nouns.

The second, third, and fourth columns of Table 3 show the following: the number of words in the dictionary; the percentage of coverage of words in the dictionary is in parentheses; and the character to indicate the part of the speech. From the Table 3 we can observe the following:

– **ft_cc_ru_300** best covers the RuWordNet (coverage is 86.8% for Nouns and 89.2% on Verbs).
– **araneum_none_fasttextcbow_300_5_2018** best covers the test Nouns (coverage is 97.1% for Public test set and 96.9% on Private test set).
– **tayga_lemmas_elmo_2048_2019** best covers the test Verbs (coverage is 89.1% for Public test set and 88.8% on Private test set).

Table 3. Out-of-vocabulary analysis

Model	Public Nouns – 762 Verbs – 175	Private Nouns – 1,525 Verbs – 350	RuWordNet Nouns – 53,082 Verbs – 27,427
ft_cc_ru_300	722 (0.947) N	1,443 (0.946) N	**46,079 (0.868) N**
	140 (0.8) V	279 (0.797) V	**24,470 (0.892) V**
ruscorpora_none_fasttextskipgram_300_2_2019	548 (0.719) N	1,094 (0.717) N	30,625 (0.576) N
	145 (0.828) V	281 (0.802) V	17,659 (0.643) V
tayga_none_fasttextcbow_300_10_2019	550 (0.721) N	1,100 (0.721) N	31,089 (0.585) N
	153 (0.874) V	302 (0.862) V	17,975 (0.655) V
araneum_none_fasttextcbow_300_5_2018	**740 (0.971) N**	**1,479 (0.969) N**	31,341 (0.590) N
	100 (0.571) V	208 (0.594) V	13,827 (0.504) V
tayga_lemmas_elmo_2048_2019	592 (0.776) N	1,209 (0.792) N	32,563 (0.613) N
	156 (0.891) V	**311 (0.888) V**	18,640 (0.679) V

4.4 Attempting to Train BERT

The idea is to train the classifier on the lines "{**hyponym string**} is a {**hypernym string**}". The main difficulty that we encountered was the formation of a high-quality training data set.

To train the classifier, we used the *AdamW* optimizer and *BertForSequence-Classification* from the *pytorch-transformers* library. The training was carried out 10 times (epochs). To get synset associations, we used our best algorithm based on the standard model *ft_cc_ru_300*. We tried to take a different number of synset associates (**K**): 10, 20.

At **K** = 10 we got a small recall - about 0.52. With **K** = 20 - 0.60. At **K** = 10 for the Public Nouns we got a MAP = 0.32 (while our best algorithm reached 0.5).

Thus, we list the problems: first, low recall at the stage of obtaining synsets-associates (for the further formation of a training data set); secondly, with increasing **K**, the training set became very unbalanced.

5 Results

The results are presented in Table 4. We intentionally did not include RuBERT into the table so that there was no desire to compare with other models, because we used RuBERT in an unusual way.

- Here we list the same parameters for all models from Table 4 and RuBERT.
  - The ranking algorithm was used with the parameters $p1 = 0.1$, $p2 = 1.0$, $p3 = 1.0$, $k = 10$ and $n = 10$.
  - Neologisms(input words) were lowercase.
  - The comparison indicator was the MAP provided by the organizers of the competition.
- Different parameters. String representations of the synsets. In Table 4: **ruthes_name** and **sense_name** for **Nouns** and all possible fields for **Verbs**. For RuBERT we used just **sense_name** for both **Nouns** and **Verbs**.

Next, we describe the names of the columns and rows of Table 4. The first column is the name of the model. The second and subsequent columns are results for Public or Private test sets. "Lemmas" means that morphological analysis and lemmatization by pymorphy2 were performed for words from string representations of synsets. The main cells show the result, the letter after the MAP means part of speech (N stay for **Nouns**, V stay for **Verbs**).

RuBERT (not included in the Table 4) showed the following results:

- 0.329 on Public Nouns and 0.31805 on Private Nouns;
- 0.183 on Public Verbs and 0.189648 on Private Verbs.

Table 4. Results by models

Model	Public	Public lemmas	Private	Private lemmas
ft_cc_ru_300	0.511 N	**0.5115 N**	0.511 N	**0.516 N**
	0.291 V	0.286 V	0.358 V	0.345 V
tayga_none_fasttextcbow_300_10_2019	0.25 N	0.248 N	0.253 N	0.254 N
	0.209 V	0.219 V	0.252 V	0.252 V
araneum_none_fasttextcbow_300_5_2018	0.345 N	0.35 N	0.364 N	0.371 N
	0.188 V	0.208 V	0.234 V	0.229 V
tayga_lemmas_elmo_2048_2019	0.359 N	0.364 N	0.41 N	0.404 N
	0.334 V	0.314 V	**0.387 V**	0.378 V

Thus, we observed the following:

- Lemmatization (of sentence representations) did not significantly affect the results. Some models showed a slightly better result, and some a little worse.
- First (**ft_cc_ru_300**) performed best results on nouns.
- Fourth (**tayga_lemmas_elmo_2048_2019**) performed best results on verbs.
- On Private Verbs, models showed results by 4–6% better than on Public Verbs. However, we do not observe this on Nouns, except for the fourth model.
- Application of the model "RuBERT" in a proposed way did not show high results.

Finally, Table 5 presents our top scores and our place in the participant ratings.

- Compared to the Baseline, our method showed a MAP ...
  - ... higher by ↑7.67% (Publ. Nouns) and by ↑9.53% (Pr. Nouns);
  - ... higher by ↑5.83% (Publ. Verbs) and by ↑5.39% (Pr. Verbs).
- Compared to the best result in the competitions, MAP ...
  - ... lower by ↓4.75% (Publ. Nouns) and by ↓3.59% (Pr. Nouns);
  - ... lower by ↓6.91% (Publ. Verbs) and by ↓6.09% (Pr. Verbs).

Nevertheless, we showed results not lower than 4th place (from more than 13 participants) on each of the test sets:

- 3-rd on Public Nouns and 2-nd on Private Nouns;
- 4-th on Public Verbs and 4-th on Private Verbs;

Table 5. Our best results compared to the baseline and the best in the competition

Model, method	PoS	MAP (public)	Rank (public)	MAP (private)	Rank (private)
Unknown, best in the competition	Nouns	0.5590	1 of 14	0.5522	1 of 17
ft_cc_ru_300, our	Nouns	0.5115	3 of 14	0.5163	2 of 17
ft_cc_ru_300, baseline	Nouns	0.4348	9 of 14	0.4210	9 of 17
Unknown, best in the competition	Verbs	0.4033	1 of 14	0.4483	1 of 14
tayga_lemmas_elmo_2048_2019, our	Verbs	0.3342	4 of 14	0.3874	4 of 14
ft_cc_ru_300, baseline	Verbs	0.2759	8 of 14	0.3335	6 of 14

6   Conclusion

In this article we described our participation in the first joint task RUSSE'2020 on automatic taxonomy construction for the Russian language. We intended to create a simple method (based on the baseline) using pre-trained models. Our main contributions are as follows:

- We tested how the use of various fields from the RuWordNet affects the result.
- We added ranking to the baseline and several other parameters.
- We showed that, even without additional training, competitive results can be achieved.
- Python (jupyter-notebook) source code is available online.

The main conclusion is that simple usage of the pre-trained distributional model to obtain "synsets-synonyms", whose "parents" and "grandparents" are also further accounted into as the answer, shows competitive results in the automatic taxonomy construction task for the Russian language.

References

1. Auger, A., Barriàre, C.: Pattern-based approaches to semantic relation extraction: a state-of-the-art. Terminology **14**, 1–19 (2008). https://doi.org/10.1075/term.14.1.02aug
2. Baroni, M., Bernardi, R., Do, N.Q., Shan, C.: Entailment above the word level in distributional semantics. In: Proceedings of the 13th Conference of the European Chapter of the Association for Computational Linguistics, Avignon, France, pp. 23–32. Association for Computational Linguistics, April 2012. https://www.aclweb.org/anthology/E12-1004
3. Benko, V., Zakharov, V.: Very Large Russian Corpora: New Opportunities and New Challenges, Russian Federation, pp. 79–93. Rossiiskii Gosudarstvennyi Gumanitarnyi Universitet (2016)
4. Berend, G., Makrai, M., Földiák, P.: 300-sparsans at SemEval-2018 Task 9: Hypernymy as interaction of sparse attributes. In: Proceedings of The 12th International Workshop on Semantic Evaluation, New Orleans, Louisiana, pp. 928–934. Association for Computational Linguistics, June 2018. https://doi.org/10.18653/v1/S18-1152. https://www.aclweb.org/anthology/S18-1152
5. Bernier-Colborne, G., Barrière, C.: CRIM at SemEval-2018 Task 9: a hybrid approach to hypernym discovery. In: Proceedings of The 12th International Workshop on Semantic Evaluation, New Orleans, Louisiana, pp. 725–731. Association for Computational Linguistics, June 2018. https://doi.org/10.18653/v1/S18-1116. https://www.aclweb.org/anthology/S18-1116
6. Bordea, G., Buitelaar, P., Faralli, S., Navigli, R.: SemEval-2015 Task 17: taxonomy extraction evaluation (TExEval). In: Proceedings of the 9th International Workshop on Semantic Evaluation (SemEval 2015), Denver, Colorado, pp. 902–910. Association for Computational Linguistics, June 2015. https://doi.org/10.18653/v1/S15-2151. https://www.aclweb.org/anthology/S15-2151
7. Bordea, G., Lefever, E., Buitelaar, P.: Semeval-2016 Task 13: taxonomy extraction evaluation (TExEval-2). In: Proceedings of the 10th International Workshop on Semantic Evaluation. Association for Computational Linguistics (2016)
8. Camacho-Collados, J., et al.: SemEval-2018 Task 9: hypernym discovery. In: Proceedings of The 12th International Workshop on Semantic Evaluation, New Orleans, Louisiana, pp. 712–724. Association for Computational Linguistics, June 2018. https://doi.org/10.18653/v1/S18-1115. https://www.aclweb.org/anthology/S18-1115
9. Grave, E., Bojanowski, P., Gupta, P., Joulin, A., Mikolov, T.: Learning word vectors for 157 languages. In: Proceedings of the International Conference on Language Resources and Evaluation (LREC 2018) (2018)
10. Hearst, M.A.: Automatic acquisition of hyponyms from large text corpora. In: COLING 1992, Volume 2: The 15th International Conference on Computational Linguistics (1992). https://www.aclweb.org/anthology/C92-2082
11. Karyaeva, M., Braslavski, P., Kiselev, Y.: Extraction of hypernyms from dictionaries with a little help from word embeddings. In: van der Aalst, W.M.P., et al. (eds.) AIST 2018. LNCS, vol. 11179, pp. 76–87. Springer, Cham (2018). https://doi.org/10.1007/978-3-030-11027-7_8
12. Kiselev, Y., Porshnev, S., Mukhin, M.: Method of extracting hyponym-hypernym relationships for nouns from definitions of explanatory dictionaries [metod izvlecheniya rodovidovykh otnosheniy mezhdu sushchestvitel"nymi iz opredeleniy tolkovykh slovarey]. Softw. Eng. [Programmnaya inzheneriya] **10**, 38–48 (2012)

13. Korobov, M.: morphological analyzer and generator for Russian and Ukrainian languages. In: Khachay, M.Y., Konstantinova, N., Panchenko, A., Ignatov, D.I., Labunets, V.G. (eds.) AIST 2015. CCIS, vol. 542, pp. 320–332. Springer, Cham (2015). https://doi.org/10.1007/978-3-319-26123-2_31

14. Kuratov, Y., Arkhipov, M.: Adaptation of deep bidirectional multilingual transformers for Russian language. CoRR abs/1905.07213 (2019). http://arxiv.org/abs/1905.07213

15. Kutuzov, A., Kuzmenko, E.: WebVectors: a toolkit for building web interfaces for vector semantic models. In: Ignatov, D.I., et al. (eds.) AIST 2016. CCIS, vol. 661, pp. 155–161. Springer, Cham (2017). https://doi.org/10.1007/978-3-319-52920-2_15

16. Loukachevitch, N.V.: Thesauruses in Information Retrieval [Tezaurusy v zadachakh informatsionnogo poiska]. MSU Publishing House, Moscow (2011)

17. Loukachevitch, N.V., Lashevich, G., Gerasimova, A.A., Ivanov, V.V., Dobrov, B.V.: Creating russian wordnet by conversion. In: Komp'juternaja Lingvistika i Intellektual'nye Tehnologii, pp. 405–415. Rossiiskii Gosudarstvennyi Gumanitarnyi Universitet (2016)

18. Miller, G.A.: WordNet: a lexical database for English. Commun. ACM **38**(11), 39–41 (1995). https://doi.org/10.1145/219717.219748

19. Navigli, R., Velardi, P.: Learning word-class lattices for definition and hypernym extraction. In: Proceedings of the 48th Annual Meeting of the Association for Computational Linguistics, Uppsala, Sweden, pp. 1318–1327. Association for Computational Linguistics, July 2010. https://www.aclweb.org/anthology/P10-1134

20. Nikishina, I., Logacheva, V., Panchenko, A., Loukachevitch, N.: RUSSE 2020: findings of the first taxonomy enrichment task for the Russian language. In: Computational Linguistics and Intellectual Technologies: Papers from the Annual Conference "Dialogue" (2020)

21. Qiu, W., Chen, M., Li, L., Si, L.: NLP_HZ at SemEval-2018 Task 9: a nearest neighbor approach. In: Proceedings of The 12th International Workshop on Semantic Evaluation, New Orleans, Louisiana, pp. 909–913. Association for Computational Linguistics, June 2018. https://doi.org/10.18653/v1/S18-1148, https://www.aclweb.org/anthology/S18-1148

22. Roller, S., Kiela, D., Nickel, M.: Hearst patterns revisited: automatic hypernym detection from large text corpora. In: Proceedings of the 56th Annual Meeting of the Association for Computational Linguistics, Melbourne, Australia (Volume 2: Short Papers), pp. 358–363. Association for Computational Linguistics, July 2018. https://doi.org/10.18653/v1/P18-2057. https://www.aclweb.org/anthology/P18-2057

23. Sabirova, K., Lukanin, A.: Automatic extraction of hypernyms and hyponyms from Russian texts. In: CEUR Workshop Proceedings, vol. 1197, pp. 35–40, 01 2014

24. Shavrina, T., Shapovalova, O.: TO THE METHODOLOGY OF CORPUS CONSTRUCTION FOR MACHINE LEARNING: "TAIGA" SYNTAX TREE CORPUS AND PARSER, Saint-Petersbourg, pp. 78–84 (2017)

25. Shwartz, V., Goldberg, Y., Dagan, I.: Improving hypernymy detection with an integrated path-based and distributional method. In: Proceedings of the 54th Annual Meeting of the Association for Computational Linguistics (Volume 1: Long Papers), Berlin, Germany, pp. 2389–2398. Association for Computational Linguistics, August 2016. https://doi.org/10.18653/v1/P16-1226. https://www.aclweb.org/anthology/P16-1226

26. Shwartz, V., Santus, E., Schlechtweg, D.: Hypernyms under siege: linguistically-motivated artillery for hypernymy detection. In: Proceedings of the 15th Conference of the European Chapter of the Association for Computational Linguistics: Volume 1, Long Papers, Valencia, Spain, pp. 65–75. Association for Computational Linguistics, April 2017. https://www.aclweb.org/anthology/E17-1007

27. Weeds, J., Clarke, D., Reffin, J., Weir, D., Keller, B.: Learning to distinguish hypernyms and co-hyponyms. In: Proceedings of COLING 2014, the 25th International Conference on Computational Linguistics: Technical Papers, Dublin, Ireland, pp. 2249–2259. Dublin City University and Association for Computational Linguistics, August 2014. https://www.aclweb.org/anthology/C14-1212

Analysis of the Persuasiveness of Argumentation in Popular Science Texts

Yury Zagorulko[1]([✉]) [iD], Oleg Domanov[2] [iD], Alexey Sery[1] [iD], Elena Sidorova[1] [iD], and Olesya Borovikova[1] [iD]

[1] A.P. Ershov Institute of Informatics Systems of Siberian Branch of the Russian Academy of Sciences, Novosibirsk, Russia
zagor@iis.nsk.su

[2] Institute of Philosophy and Law of Siberian Branch of the Russian Academy of Sciences, Novosibirsk, Russia

Abstract. The paper discusses the methods of modeling and assessing the quality of the argumentation used in popular science texts, as well as the software supporting them. First, the authors study the aspects of argumentation persuasiveness, i.e. the validity of conclusions presented in articles. Argumentation modeling is performed using the argumentation ontology based on the AIF format (Argument Interchange Format), which was adopted by the international community as a standard notation for describing arguments and argumentation schemes. The authors have supplemented this ontology with the facilities necessary for modeling and analyzing the quality of argumentation in popular science discourse. In particular, we have introduced into the ontology facilities allowing us to assign the estimates of persuasiveness (degree of the truth) to the arguments and statements and to model the target audience. Thanks to these facilities, it has become possible to analyze the persuasiveness of the argumentation regarding different target audiences. To solve this problem, the authors propose a model and an algorithm for calculating the persuasiveness of arguments allowing taking into account conflicts between the arguments. The paper also provides an example of constructing a network of arguments and calculating the degree of their persuasiveness using the software system developed.

Keywords: Argumentation modeling · Analysis of argumentation persuasiveness · Ontology · Popular science text

1 Introduction

Currently, popular science discourse, represented mostly by popular science books and articles, is becoming an essential element of scientific activity since it is an efficient means of communication with a wide audience. In this regard, there is a great need for high-quality popular science texts that would increase the degree of trust in science and scientific knowledge on the part of society and the state. The quality of such texts depends not so much on their literary merits as on the quality of the argumentation presented in them. In its turn, the quality of argumentation depends primarily on its

S. O. Kuznetsov et al. (Eds.): RCAI 2020, LNAI 12412, pp. 351–367, 2020.
https://doi.org/10.1007/978-3-030-59535-7_26

transparency and persuasiveness, i.e. the degree of the validity of the conclusions contained in the text. This explains the urgency of studying the argumentation presented in popular science literature. To support such studies, we need tools for modeling and analyzing argumentation in natural language texts.

Over the past 20 years, many software systems have been developed to support the argumentation modeling, presentation and analysis. It is worth noting such systems as OVA/OVA+ [1], Carneades [2] and Rationale [3]. However, these tools are mainly aimed at supporting the modeling of a network of arguments and text markup and pay little attention to the arguments' strength and persuasiveness. In addition, as a rule, they are not designed for text corpora and are poorly tailored to the needs of linguists and philologists.

The study of argumentation requires a considerable amount of annotated data, i.e. text corpora with argumentative markup, and appropriate means of statistical processing. Though there are many scientific projects in this area, text corpora with argumentative markup are quite rare in the public domain, which is also noted in [4], and those available are quite small and, as a result, have limited representativeness for analysis. Most of the existing resources are in English. The authors are not aware of the existence of Russian-language corpora with marked argumentation.

This paper discusses the means of modeling and analyzing the persuasiveness of the argumentation used in popular science texts created within the framework of the project devoted to the study of the rhetorical and argumentative aspects of popular science discourse. As a tool for such analysis, we propose a software system for argumentation modeling and analysis. It provides researchers with the following options: finding and extracting fragments in the source texts corresponding to the argument components (premises and conclusions), building a network of arguments on their basis, assigning weight to the premises of the arguments showing their degree of the truth, and analysing the persuasiveness of the arguments used in the text.

The rest of the paper is structured as follows. Section 2 provides brief information on the theory of argumentation and presents a modern approach to argumentation modeling. Section 3 substantiates the need to analyze the persuasiveness of the argumentation used in popular science texts and describes the extensions of the standard argumentation ontology providing such an analysis. Section 4 describes the model and algorithm for computing the argument persuasiveness. Section 5 provides an example of constructing a network of arguments and calculating the degree of their persuasiveness using the software system developed. The Conclusion summarizes the intermediate results of the creation and implementation of the methods and means for the analysis of the persuasiveness of the argumentation used in popular science texts and outlines plans for the future.

2   Argumentation Modeling

A systematic study of argumentation goes back to the works of Aristotle and ancient rhetoric, but the theory of argumentation itself has been actively developing since the mid-20th century, when S. Tulmin and H. Perelman (together with L. Olbrechts-Titeka) independently [5, 6] abandoned the use of traditional mathematical logic in favor of developing a special logic of argumentation based on rhetorical and philosophical ideas, which allows taking better account of its informal nature, dependence on context, focus on a specific audience, etc. At present, many approaches to argumentation analysis are being developed (see, for example, [7–11], as well as a review in [6, 12]). Among them, a special place is occupied by developments focused on computer processing and artificial intelligence systems (see, for example, [5, 13]). In particular, V.N. Vagin and his followers used the argumentation theory in decision support systems to justify proposed decisions [14].

There are many approaches to the conceptualization and formalization of argu-mentative relations (see the references above). In most cases, the argument in them is understood as a rule allowing judging the persuasiveness of the conclusion by the persuasiveness of certain premises. In this work, we have chosen the AIF (Argument Interchange Format) format [15, 16] as the argumentation basis because it is widely used in argumentation analysis and is in good agreement with the objectives of our project.

In the AIF, argumentation is represented as a graph containing two types of nodes:

- I-node is a node representing information and containing a thesis (statement) that can act as a premise or conclusion of an argument.
- S-node is a node connecting theses and arguments. There are three types of the S-node:

  - RA-node represents an argument having one or more premises as the "input" and one conclusion as the "output". The premises and conclusions can be either an I-node or S-node.
  - CA-node represents the conflict of a pair of arguments. The conflict is considered directed; undirected conflicts are formalized as a pair of counter conflicts.
  - PA-node represents a preference relation for two nodes.

The semantics of the graph edges is presented in Table 1 in [16]. For example, the arrow from the I-node to the RA-node means that the thesis is the premise of the argument; the arrow from the RA-node to the I-node means that the thesis is the conclusion of the argument, etc. In particular, an argument can be directed to another argument, that is, it can have the latter as the conclusion. Examples of such arguments are Ad hominem arguments, i.e. attacks on all the arguments of a specific person.

Based on the AIF standard, several versions of the ontology were implemented (AIF-RDF [17], AIF-OWL [18], AIF-EL [19]), which were used to describe the argu-ments and argumentation schemes in various projects (ArgDF [18], ASPIC+ [20]). At present, the AIF-ontology [21], implemented in the OWL DL language, is used [22]. This ontology defines the specification of the AIF format and argument schemes in the form of classes, which allows an explicit classification of the schemes themselves. This version of the ontology includes about 40 argumentation schemes from the D. Walton compendium [11]. Assumptions and exceptions based on the critical questions given in D. Walton's schemes are included into the description of argumentation schemes as additional premises.

The disadvantage of the AIF ontology discussed above is that it provides means only for presenting arguments and argumentative structures, but does not support the analysis of the argumentation quality and persuasiveness. To cope with this shortcoming, we have supplemented this ontology by facilities providing such an analysis.

3   Analysis of Argumentation Persuasiveness

It is imperative to analyze argumentation persuasiveness for at least two reasons: first, in order to understand how persuasive a particular popular science text is and second, in order to draw up recommendations for writing reasoned and persuasive texts. To achieve the latter, i.e., to give authors appropriate recommendations, it is necessary to be able to reveal what rhetorical techniques and argumentative structures are common for good popular science texts. It is also necessary to understand what types of arguments are more acceptable for various target audiences. Carrying out such studies in full, however, requires a sufficient statistical sample of popular science texts containing various types of arguments, that is, extensive research into fairly representative corpora of popular science texts.

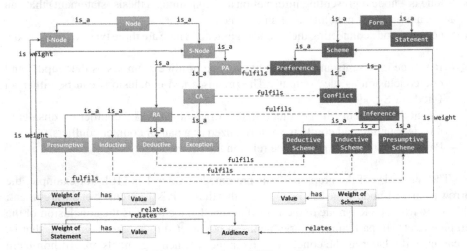

Fig. 1. Extension of AIF ontology.

As we have mentioned, for the needs of this project, the AIF ontology discussed above is supplemented by the means of assessing the persuasiveness of theses and arguments. For this, the nodes of the graph (not necessarily all the nodes) are assigned a degree of persuasiveness, that is an element of a certain algebra; the degree of persuasiveness for the conclusion of an argument is calculated on the basis of the degrees of the persuasiveness of the premises and the argument itself, as well as on the basis of the degrees of the persuasiveness of the theses conflicting with this conclusion. The mathematical apparatus used is the label-based framework approach [23] and fuzzy logic [24].

To present the degrees of persuasiveness in the network of arguments, we have included several auxiliary classes into the AIF ontology (see Fig. 1). To set the degree of the persuasiveness of the argument schemes, specific arguments, their premises and conclusions presented by the statements, regarding a certain audience, we have added the *Audience* class to the AIF ontology. To set the degrees of persuasiveness (weights) for the argument schemes, arguments, and statements, we have introduced into the AIF ontology the *Weight of Argument*, *Weight of Scheme*, *Weight of Statement*, and *Weight of Statement* classes. In addition, we have added the "is weight" and "relates" relations connecting these classes with the I-nodes, S-nodes, Scheme nodes and the target audience (*Audience* class) (see Fig. 1).

4   Calculation of the Persuasiveness of Arguments

As described above, AIF formalizes the argumentation network as a graph in which arguments are represented as nodes with one or several incoming arrows (premises) and a single coming out arrow (conclusion). The evaluation of the degrees of persuasiveness presupposes that there are no vicious circles or cycles in argumentation in the graph. Actual popular scientific texts may contain cycles of this type. For the argumentation graph based on AIF, the absence of vicious circles means that the nodes of the RA type with their premises give rise to the directed acyclic graph (DAG). At the same time, we allow cycles for the nodes of the CA type (conflicts), which, however, can be taken into account in the computing algorithm (see below).

The persuasiveness of conclusion depends on the persuasiveness of the premises as well as of the argument itself. Various treatments of persuasiveness measurement and computing are possible. One of the most popular approaches considers the degree of persuasiveness as the probability of the statement turning out to be true. At the same time, there are reasons to suggest that we are dealing here with another type of uncertainty, different from probability.

4.1   Computational Model

The computing algorithm used in the present work is based on the operations of fuzzy logic [25] (of which probabilistic logic may be considered as a special case). Fuzzy logic defines the algebra of truth values, intermediate between the true and the false. That being the case, the most important question consists in what this algebra measures. The basic idea of our approach stems from intuitionistic mathematics and approaches treating the truth in terms of proof. Therewith the argument is vaguely understood as a proof leading to one or another degree of the truth of conclusion, depending on the strength of the argument. In this sense the more grounded is the statement, the higher is the degree of its truth. Another useful view consists in considering propositions as sets of their proofs – so called "proposition-as-type principle," also known as Carry-Howard correspondence (see, for instance, [26]). An empty set corresponds to the absurd proposition $\perp$, which can have no proof. The negation of a proposition A is defined as the function $A \to \perp$. Therefore, $\neg A$ is true if every proof of A comes down to a proof of $\perp$, which means absurdity (speaking otherwise, A has no proof). Respectively, one can speak of the persuasiveness of arguments in favor of a statement as well as of the negation of a statement. We can extend these considerations to the situation of fuzziness. In this case, fuzzy logic algebra measures the "degree of provenness" of a statement or the degree of its persuasiveness. If this degree is low, the statement is "not much proven" or unpersuasive. If it is high, there are powerful arguments in its favor, and it is therefore strongly persuasive. In general, the approach described above belongs to the area of proof-theoretic semantics [27].

We would like to emphasize that this approach differs from that of defeasible logic [28]. Defeasible reasoning is the reasoning allowed to be defeated. Defeasible rules are the rules that have presumptions or exceptions, so that defeasible conclusions can be revised when new information arrives or new calculation is done. However, these conclusions themselves are not fuzzy; they can only be either true or false. The same goes for defeasible rules. On the contrary, the calculation of persuasiveness requires a different structure and different logic. Fuzzy statements are uncertain statements with the truth values measured by a special algebra. Under attack, they are not defeated but decrease their persuasiveness. We can add defeasible logic later if, for example, we consider statements as defeated when their persuasiveness becomes too low. In general, however, the two approaches are different; in our opinion, fuzzy logic is more appropriate for persuasiveness calculations.

Traditionally, fuzzy logic defines truth algebra as a bounded lattice with additional binary operations called t-norm and residuum. They are generalizations of conjunction and implication, respectively. On their basis, further operations of negation, disjunction and others are defined. From the computational viewpoint, it is more convenient to choose the basic operations differently. *Persuasiveness algebra* is a structure $\langle A, \leq, \wedge, \vee, \top, \bot, \otimes, \oplus, \oslash \rangle$, where A is a set, $\leq$ is a partial order on the set, $\wedge$ and $\vee$ are the infimum and supremum, and $\top$ and $\bot$ are the maximal and minimal elements. As a rule, the real interval [0, 1] with the usual order, infimum and supremum is used as A. We will follow this.

$\otimes$ and $\oplus$ denote t-norm and t-conorm, and $\oslash$ is a unary operation formalizing negation (see below). $\otimes$ and $\oplus$ are commutative, associative and monotone, as well as neutral in respect to $\top$ and $\bot$, respectively:

$$\forall x \ (x \otimes \top) = x \ \forall x \ (x \oplus \bot) = x.$$

The operation $\otimes$ is a generalization of logical AND or the infimum in the situation of fuzziness. It is used for combining the premises of arguments. Indeed, it is reasonable to assume that the contribution of premises corresponds to AND since the argument is valid when all premises are present. Thus, the conjunction is high when *all* its members are high. In the same way, the operation $\oplus$ is a generalization of logical OR or the supremum in the situation of fuzziness. It is used for combining several arguments of the same statement. Indeed, it is reasonable to assume that the statement is convincing when there is at least one argument supporting it. Thus, the disjunction is high when *at least one* of its members is high (so, a certain sense, this is in an "optimistic" evaluation).

Table 1 shows three major algebras traditionally used in fuzzy logic. For reference, we have included formulas for the implication $\Rightarrow$ although we do not use them directly. Other algebras are possible beyond these listed in the table (for example, K. Atanassov [29] presents 185 different definitions of implication for fuzzy intuitionistic logic).

It should be noted that semantically we could distinguish between the persuasiveness of statements and the persuasiveness of arguments. We identify the latter with the persuasiveness of the corresponding implication as follows. Most arguments have a form

Table 1. Main operations for some fuzzy logics.

Operation	Łukasiewicz logic	Gödel logic	Probabilistic logic
$x \otimes y$	$max(0, x + y - 1)$	$min(x, y)$	xy
$x \oplus y$	$min(1, x + y)$	$max(x, y)$	$x + y - xy$
$x \Rightarrow y$	$min(1, 1 - x + y)$	$\begin{cases} 1 & \text{if } x \leq y \\ y & \text{if } x > y \end{cases}$	$\begin{cases} 1 & \text{if } x \leq y \\ y/x & \text{if } x > y \end{cases}$

analogous to *modus ponens*. For example, let us consider the (simplified) argument from an expert: "P is an expert; P says that A; therefore A". It can be viewed as a deduction rule:

$$\frac{P \text{ is an expert} \quad P \text{ says that } A \quad \begin{array}{l} \text{if } P \text{ is an expert and} \\ P \text{ says that } A, \text{ then } A \end{array}}{A}$$

According to the generalized *modus ponens* for fuzzy logic [24, 25], the weight of conclusion is equal to the conjunction of premises and implication:

$$[\![\text{conclusion}]\!] = \bigotimes_{x \in D_{prem}} [\![x]\!] \otimes [\![\text{implication}]\!] \tag{1}$$

(here $[\![x]\!]$ denotes the weight of the node x and D_{prem} is the set of premises). Let us take the weight of the implication as the weight of the argument. Hence, persuasiveness algebra measures the truth of a proposition on the one hand and the persuasiveness of arguments (the truth of implication), on the other hand. In our case, the weight of the implication is the weight of the argument's node in the graph and formula (1) becomes:

$$[\![\text{conclusion}]\!] = \bigotimes_{x \in D_{prem}} [\![x]\!] \otimes [\![\text{argument}]\!].$$

If a thesis has several arguments for which it serves as a conclusion, their weights are summed up disjunctively: let D_{args} be the set of arguments of the thesis A, the weights of which are $[\![x]\!]$, then the weight of A is

$$[\![A]\!] = \bigoplus_{x \in D_{args}} [\![x]\!]. \tag{2}$$

The argumentation graph with excluded conflicts is acyclic, which means that the computing of weights for it comes down to a simple iterative process. This process becomes more complex because some nodes can lack weight in the beginning and fail to obtain it in the calculating process. In this case, if, for example, they serve as premises of an argument, the weight of the conclusion of this argument cannot be computed. To take this into account, some weights have a special value NULL and operations on weights are correspondingly corrected: the result of the operation $\oplus$ is NULL if at least one of its arguments is NULL; the result of the operation $\oplus$ is NULL if both its arguments are NULL. This corresponds to the semantics of these operations: on the one hand, the conclusion of the argument is undefined when at least one of its premises is undefined; on the other hand, when one of the several arguments for the same statement is undefined, it is simply disregarded.

Furthermore, some graph nodes may have initial weights that depend on the audience, external circumstances and other considerations. If a node does not have initial weight, its final weight depends on the weights of the arguments in its favor, according to formula (2). If it does have initial weight, the latter is disjunctively (i.e. by means of $\oplus$) added to this formula. Semantically, this means that we take it into account as a result of some argument, albeit not present in the graph.

4.2 Conflicts

The AIF assumes only one type of conflict: the directed conflict of two elements. The graph shows it as a node with one incoming (conflicting) and one coming out (conflicted) arrow. A pair of opposite conflicts models symmetrical conflicts, such as logical contradictions. For the purpose of computing the degree of the proposition's negation, persuasiveness algebra provides for the operation $\oslash$ ("negation"):

$$[\![\neg A]\!] = \oslash\, [\![A]\!].$$

There are many approaches to determining the concrete form of this operation (Atanassov collects 53 variants, [29]). In case of truth algebra defined on the real interval [0, 1], the negation function is usually defined as a non-increasing function, such that $\oslash\,(0) = 1$ and $\oslash\,(1) = 0$. Frequently, the function $\oslash\,(x) = 1 - x$ is chosen. On the other hand, negation is often defined as the implication $A \to \bot$; hence $\oslash\,(x) = x \Rightarrow \bot$, i. e. $[\![\neg A]\!] = [\![A]\!] \Rightarrow \bot$. In this case, operations are connected as follows:

$$x \oplus y = \oslash\,(\oslash\, x \otimes\, \oslash\, y)$$

(cf. $x \vee y = \neg(\neg x \wedge \neg y)$). These two definitions may coincide (for example in Łukasiewicz logic) or not (for example, in Gödel logic). The choice of a particular variant depends on the conflict's semantics and requires further investigation. On the current phase, we assume that $\oslash\,(x) = 1 - x$.

The negation function by itself is not enough for conflict modelling; additional decisions are necessary. If a thesis has pro and contra arguments, we can deal with them variously.

One way consists in evaluating the degree of conflicts or contradiction for a given set of arguments. To do this, we can start from the following *modus ponens* rule:

$$\frac{A \quad A \to \bot}{\bot}.$$

This scheme presents the argument in favor of the proposition $\bot$, where A plays the role of a premise, whereas $\neg A = A \to \bot$ plays the role of an argument. Every conflict then acts as such an argument and we can define the *degree of conflict* for the graph by means of summation:

$$\text{Confl} = \bigoplus_{x \in D_{\text{confl}}} (\llbracket \text{conflicting} \rrbracket \otimes \llbracket \text{conflicted} \rrbracket),$$

where D_{confl} is the set of conflicts, and $\llbracket \text{conflicting} \rrbracket$ and $\llbracket \text{conflicted} \rrbracket$ are the weights of the corresponding conflicting (that is "contradicting") nodes. The degree of conflict is the measure of the degree of contradiction for a system of arguments. The higher the calculated degree of $\bot$, the more contradicting the system is, and the more acute the conflict of arguments. Maximal contradiction takes place when both A and $\neg A$ have the maximal degree of persuasiveness. The less the weight of one of them, the less the resulting conflict. It is minimal when either A or $\neg A$ is minimal, which means that we have no arguments in support. The degree of conflict is not always minimal (i.e. not always equal to $\bot$), which demonstrates that our argumentation graph not always complies with the law of contradiction. It may occur that we have grounded arguments both in favor of a statement and in favor of its negation, so that we cannot choose between them. Moreover, in popular scientific texts this sort of situations are often created intentionally with rhetorical aims. Allowing the non-zero degree of conflict, we can model such undecidable conflicts.

Another way of dealing with conflicts is attempting to amend the weights in such a way that will enable us to compute the influence of conflicting elements upon one another. As mentioned above, the algebra of persuasiveness measures the persuasiveness of statements, which we can roughly understand as the degree of proof. Generally, the persuasiveness of a statement and its negation are not directly bound. The degree $\llbracket A \rrbracket$ measures the "proof" of A, whereas $\llbracket \neg A \rrbracket$ measures the "proof" of $\neg A$. They relate in various ways. In some cases, this relation is straight: a low degree of $\llbracket \neg A \rrbracket$ means a high degree of $\llbracket A \rrbracket$. Otherwise stated, the proof of the absence of the proof of negation increases the persuasiveness of the statement. However, in other cases, they can be independent: a low degree of negation does not lead to the persuasiveness of a statement. In the latter case, we can even name A and $\neg A$ as conflicting only when they have some particular weights. If, for example, these weights are low, we are not convinced in either statement and thus may refuse to count them as conflicting. Even in the former case, we can act differently. We can choose a "pessimistic" variant and hold that the weights of a statement and its negation are combined conjunctively. Semantically, this means that when the weight of $\llbracket A \rrbracket$ is high and the weight of $\oslash \llbracket \neg A \rrbracket$ is low, we choose the latter, i.e. decrease the weight of the statement (attack prevails over support). We, however, can choose an "optimistic" variant, when we do not decrease but preserve the weight of the statement in this case (support prevails over attack), which corresponds to disjunctive combining. Generally speaking, the choice of the strategy in this case may depend on the nature of conflict, but currently we assume that support prevails over attack, which means that weights are combined disjunctively. This is a simplification, meaning semantically that we take an attack as just one more argument of support but with a modified weight.

As a result, the weights of nodes in the coherent or "ideal" argument system must satisfy the following condition. Let D^+ be a set of arguments in support of the statement A and D^- be a set of arguments conflicting with A (attacks). Then the coherence means that for any such statement its weight is

$$[\![A]\!] = \bigoplus_{x \in D^+} [\![x]\!] \oplus \left(\bigoplus_{y \in D^-} \oslash\, [\![y]\!] \right). \tag{3}$$

To put it differently, the weight is the disjunction of a pair: the disjunction of support arguments and the disjunction of attack arguments. The first of these disjuncts is computed recursively for the acyclic graph. The second disjunct requires solving a non-linear system of equations. Unfortunately, there are no general methods of doing this. Nevertheless, the system (3) forms a fix-point equation which permits numerical methods. For example, in the case of continuous or even semi-continuous t-norms, the triangulation technique may be used [30] (note that two of the three operations presented in Table 1 are continuous). This, however, requires substantial efforts, so at the current stage of research we have adopted a rather simplified recursive procedure described below (cf. [23, 31]).

The main idea of the algorithm consists in starting with the graph computed without considering conflicts and then iteratively correcting its weights to achieve a maximal (ideally, full) compliance with formula (3). At every iteration step, all the graph's weights are recalculated on the basis of the weights obtained at the previous step. Thus, as a starting step we take weights computed with excluded conflicts (this is always possible for the directed acyclic graph). On every further iteration $t + 1$, the weights are computed according to formula (3) with conflicting weights from the previous iteration t:

$$[\![A]\!]_{t+1} = \bigoplus_{x \in D^+} [\![x]\!]_{t+1} \oplus \left(\bigoplus_{y \in D^-} \oslash\, [\![y]\!]_t \right).$$

Unfortunately, the convergence of this procedure in the general case has not yet been studied (see, however, a special case in [31]), but we can assess the correctness of the computed graph. Let us define the *correctness* of the graph as the average absolute difference between an "ideal" (i.e. computed by formula (3)) and a current graph. The correctness at the step t is

$$\mathrm{Corr}_t = \,<A_{\mathrm{ideal}}, A_t>_N,$$

where $<x, y>_N$ is the mean value of the absolute difference between x and y in respect to the total number of the graph's nodes N. Correctness is computed by iteration on the graph's nodes. The zero value of Corr_t means the compliance with formula (3) for all nodes of the graph, that is, arriving at the "ideal" state. As one can see, the graph stops changing after that and the zero value of correctness remains unchanged.

5 Experimental Studies of Argumentation Persuasiveness

To study the persuasiveness of argumentation used in popular science texts, we have proposed an expert the following scenario including two stages: evaluation of the argumentation schemes regarding a given target audience and computation on the graphs of arguments constructed for specific texts.

Such an evaluation of the argumentation schemes is very important because when studying arguments, we must take into account the way of thinking and the value system of various audiences. For example, arguments meaningful for general public may be less important for students and scientists. At the same time, reference to the opinion of famous scientists will matter more for researchers than for students and schoolchildren.

The stage of the evaluation of argumentation schemes is as follows:

- Selecting a target audience from the ontology.
- Selecting argumentation schemes from the ontology and estimating them regarding a selected audience. To estimate the persuasive power of these schemes, the expert can use a specialized search tool, which returns a list of all the occurrences of a selected argumentation scheme (in the form of text fragments) in the corpus and in the text context (concordance).
- Assigning weights to the argumentation schemes in accordance with the estimation obtained. Argumentation schemes are weighed based on a linguistic scale, each value of which corresponds to a particular numeric value.

The weights assigned to the argumentation schemes are used for all argumentation graphs constructed for the texts analyzed with respect to a given audience. The proposed computational model assumes that the following conventions are observed:

a) The weight of a scheme is considered as the maximum possible persuasiveness of the argument constructed using this scheme;
b) The weight of a scheme is used as the initial weight of the argument that is an instance of this scheme,
c) In the process of computations, the weight of the argument can either decrease or remain unchanged.

Next, the expert builds an argument graph for the selected text using these schemes. After that, he can proceed to the second stage of research, namely, computation on the argumentation graph. The computation stage is as follows:

- Assigning initial weights to the I-nodes (statements) involved in the argument. An expert can consider various aspects when he/she assigns initial weights. For example, how obvious the statements are to the target audience, whether the statements are all-known facts, or whether their immediate contexts contain marker words, such as "obviously," "maybe," "unlikely," "however," etc.
- Computing the weights of all the nodes of the graph according to the computational model.
- Analyzing the results of computation. This step may include such observations as identifying the "key" arguments and conflicts affecting the weight of the main thesis, assessing the degree of influence of conflicts, studying the dependence of the result on initial weights, etc. If necessary, the computation of the persuasiveness of the argumentation can be performed with other initial weights.
- Saving results for further use.

To conduct experiments on evaluating the argumentation persuasiveness, we used the Software System for Modeling and Analysis of Argumentation (SSMAA) supporting the proposed scenario. Its architecture is described in [32]. The SSMAA is a web browser-based application designed to create text corpora and annotate texts based on the ontological representation of D. Walton's schemes. The system also provides the study of the statistical and structural features of the argumentation used in texts and supports navigation and search through annotated texts and the ontology.

The SSMAA offers two alternative ways of representing a network of arguments (Fig. 2): in the form of an interactive graph or in the form of structured text (a list of arguments). In the graphic mode, the user can see the entire network of arguments, where the nodes correspond to the I-node and S-node instances of the AIF ontology. In the text form, the arguments and their parts are represented as list items. The user can switch between the graph and text representations of the network of arguments. In Fig. 2, both modes are shown side by side for comparison.

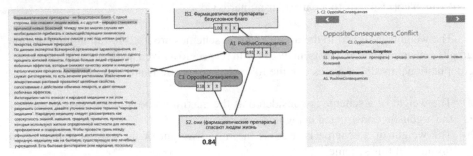

Fig. 2. Two ways of representing the network of arguments.

In order to put our scenario into practice, we had to make a few important updates to the System. First, we introduced into the AIF ontology the components for modeling the weights of statements and arguments with respect to the selected audience, described in Sect. 3, and implemented the software tools necessary for working with them. Second, it became possible to create for each text several argumentative markups designed by different experts and/or for different audiences. Third, we implemented the computational model (Sect. 4) and added some GUI features, allowing the users to set initial (a priori) weights to argumentation schemes and graph nodes, to start computing, to obtain results, etc.

A user can set an *a priori weight* to any node of the argumentation graph. A priori weights are the starting point of the computational model described in Sect. 4. When computing, the SSMAA traverses through the argumentation graph and successively computes two weights for every node it goes into: the *conflict-free weight* and *conflict-considering weight*. When the former is computed, only the $\otimes$ and $\oplus$ operations are used, while the latter is computed considering the attacks. For any node N, its conflict-free and conflict-considering weights are equal if there are no other nodes attacking N.

The weights are real numbers lying in [0, 1]. The model also has a special NULL value corresponding to the absence of weight at the node. Computations converge if a subgraph comprising only the I-Nodes and nodes of the RA type is a directed acyclic graph, that is, the graph does not comprise a *vicious circle*. Otherwise, the system cannot compute anything.

Figure 3 shows an example of a weighted argumentation graph built on the following text:

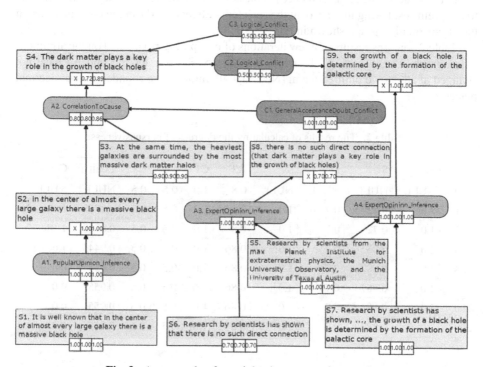

Fig. 3. An example of a weighted argumentation graph.

It is well known that in the center of almost every large galaxy there is a massive black hole [S1, S2]. At the same time, the heaviest galaxies are surrounded by the most massive dark matter halos [S3]. This has given rise to suggestions that dark matter plays a key role in the growth of black holes [S4]. Research by scientists from the Max Planck Institute for extraterrestrial physics, the Munich University Observatory, and the University of Texas at Austin [S5], however, has shown that there is no such direct connection [S6], and the growth of a black hole is determined by the formation of the galactic core [S7, S9].

This text presents a typical for popular science discourse picture of a clash of the opinion generally accepted in the scientific community with the alternative opinion of a certain group of experts.

The argument A1, built on the *PopularOpinion_Inference* scheme, expresses the generally accepted opinion. It connects the premise S1 with the conclusion S2. At the same time, the statements S2 and S3 form a causal relationship with S4, which is expressed by the *CorrelationToCause* argument A2. An expert opinion is represented by A3 and

A4, both built on the *ExpertOpinion_Inference* scheme. Their premises are S5, S6 and S7. Both A3 and A4 go to their own conclusions, which are S8 and S9, correspondingly, and come into conflict with the generally accepted opinion. This opinion is first attacked from the side of A2 by the *GeneralAcceptanceDoubt_Conflict* C1. S4 and S9 form counter conflicts C2 and C3 (*LogicalConflict* scheme).

Let us select as the target audience people not related to science, assign initial weights to the premises, taking into account the selected audience, and run the computations on the argumentation graph shown in Fig. 3.

Table 2 contains results of a few iterations of computing performed on the argumentation graph. The weights of the nodes S1, S3, S5, S6, S7, A1, A3 and A4 have not changed at all, so we omitted them. (Note that all values were rounded to four decimal places.)

Table 2. The results of calculating the degrees of persuasiveness.

Step	S2	S4	S8	S9	A2	C1	C2	C3	Confl	Corr
0	NULL	NULL	NULL	NULL	0.8	1.0	0.5	0.5	NULL	NULL
1	1.0	0.72	0.7	1.0	0.8	1.0	0.5	0.5	0.8768	1.18e−2
2	1.0	0.72	0.7	1.0	0.8	1.0	0.5	0.5	0.8768	1.18e−2
3	1.0	0.86	0.7	1.0	0.86	1.0	0.5	0.5	0.9443	1.6e−3
4	1.0	0.887	0.7	1.0	0.86	1.0	0.5	0.5	0.955	0.0
10	1.0	0.887	0.7	1.0	0.86	1.0	0.5	0.5	0.955	0.0
100	1.0	0.887	0.7	1.0	0.86	1.0	0.5	0.5	0.955	0.0
200	1.0	0.887	0.7	1.0	0.86	1.0	0.5	0.5	0.955	0.0

The first row of Table 2 corresponds to the initial state when only the a priori weights are known. As anyone can see, starting from step 100 weights stopped changing, and the correctness of the graph Corr became equal to zero, which means that the process converged (see Sect. 4.2).

Table 2 also has a column Confl containing the degree of conflict for the graph. Its value stabilized at the time when the correctness became equal to zero. All this indicates that the graph is in balance. Note that the degree of conflict is rather large; it indicates a significant inconsistency of the system of arguments presented in the graph.

Now let us evaluate how the arguments considered above affect scientists, for example, mathematicians or physicists. First, we will discover that scientists do not like phrases like "It is well known that." It follows that for this audience *PopularOpinion_Inference* scheme is low in weight. In this case, we should set the initial weight of the argument A1 much lower than it is in Fig. 3. The remaining arguments, however, have more scientific support; therefore, their initial and calculated weights will not be very different from those given in Fig. 3 and Table 2 (see Fig. 4 and Table 3).

Table 3 shows that the persuasiveness of the arguments for the scientific audience has turned out to be lower than for the people unrelated to science.

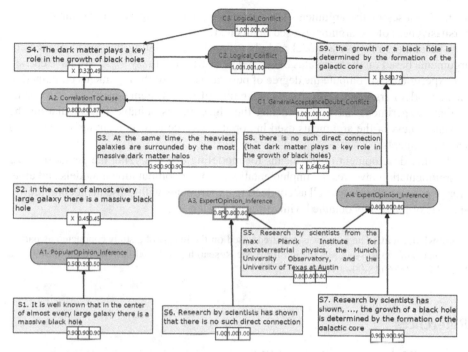

Fig. 4. The argumentation graph with weights related to a scientific audience.

Table 3. The results of calculating for a scientific audience.

Step	S2	S4	S8	S9	A2	C1	C2	C3	Confl	Corr
0	NULL	NULL	NULL	NULL	0.8	1.0	1.0	1.0	NULL	NULL
1	0.45	0.324	0.64	0.576	0.8	1.0	1.0	1.0	0.6031	3.8e−2
2	0.45	0.324	0.64	0.576	0.8	1.0	1.0	1.0	0.6031	3.8e−2
3	0.45	0.6106	0.64	0.8626	0.872	1.0	1.0	1.0	0.7909	1.71e−2
4	0.45	0.6274	0.64	0.8626	0.872	1.0	1.0	1.0	0.7973	1.85e−2
10	0.45	0.4744	0.64	0.7773	0.872	1.0	1.0	1.0	0.721	2.6e−3
100	0.45	0.4866	0.64	0.7937	0.872	1.0	1.0	1.0	0.7288	0.0
200	0.45	0.4866	0.64	0.7937	0.872	1.0	1.0	1.0	0.7288	0.0

6 Conclusion

The paper presents the means for modeling and analyzing the persuasiveness of the argumentation used in popular science texts. We have implemented these means in the software system developed within the project. Using this system, the user can find and select fragments in the source text corresponding to the components of the arguments (premises and conclusions), build a network of arguments on their basis, assign weights to the premises of the arguments showing their degree of the truth, and analyze the persuasiveness of the arguments used in this text.

The authors propose a model and algorithm for calculating the persuasiveness of arguments based on the apparatus of labeled networks and fuzzy logic. We have carried out experiments to compute the degree of persuasiveness of the arguments contained in the network of arguments constructed using the software system developed. The results of these experiments have showed that the algorithm is suitable for calculating the persuasiveness of the arguments used in popular science texts containing a conflicting set of arguments.

Further development of the means for modeling and analyzing the persuasiveness of argumentation involves the implementation of other computational models and algebras of persuasiveness, as well as conducting experiments with subsequent comparative analysis of the results obtained with different models.

Acknowledgment. The paper was prepared based on the results of a study conducted as part of the projects of the Russian Foundation for Basic Research No. 18-00-01376 (18-00-00889) and No. 18-00-01376 (18-00-00760).

References

1. Janier, M., Lawrence, J., Reed, C.: OVA+: an argument analysis interface. In: Computational Models of Argument: Proceedings of COMMA, vol. 266, pp. 463–464 (2014)
2. Gordon, T.F., Walton, D.: The Carneades argumentation framework — using presumptions and exceptions to model critical questions. In: Proceedings of 6th Computational Models of Natural Argument Workshop (CMNA), European Conference on Artificial Intelligence (ECAI), Italy, 2006, vol. 6, pp. 5–13 (2006)
3. Berg, T., van Gelder, T., Patterson, F., Teppema, S.: Critical Thinking: Reasoning and Communicating with Rationale. Pearson Education Benelux, Amsterdam (2009)
4. Lawrence, J., Visser, J., Reed, C.: An online annotation assistant for argument schemes. In: Proceedings of the 13th Linguistic Annotation Workshop, pp. 100–107. Association for Computational Linguistics (2019)
5. Dung, P.M.: On the acceptability of arguments and its fundamental role in nonmonotonic reasoning, logic programming and n-person games. Artif. Intell. **77**, 321–357 (1995)
6. Walton, D.: Argumentation theory: a very short introduction. In: Simari, G., Rahwan, I. (eds.) Argumentation in Artificial Intelligence, pp. 1–22. Springer, Boston (2009). https://doi.org/10.1007/978-0-387-98197-0_1
7. van Eemeren, F.H., Garssen, B., Krabbe, E., Henkemans, F., Verheij, B., Wagemans, J.: Handbook of Argumentation Theory. Springer, Dordrecht (2014). https://doi.org/10.1007/978-90-481-9473-5
8. Perelman, C., Olbrechts-Tyteca, L.: Traité de l'argumentation. La nouvelle rhétorique. Presses Universitaires de France, Paris (1958)
9. Prakken, H.: An abstract framework for argumentation with structured arguments. Argument Comput. **1**, 93–124 (2010)
10. Prakken, H.: An overview of formal models of argumentation and their application in philosophy. Stud. Logic **4**(1), 65–86 (2011)
11. Walton, D., Reed, C., Macagno, F.: Argumentation Schemes. Cambridge University Press, Cambridge (2008)

12. Besnard, P., Hunter, A.: Elements of Argumentation. MIT Press, Cambridge (2008)
13. Simari, G., Rahwan, I.: Argumentation in Artificial Intelligence. Springer, Boston (2009). https://doi.org/10.1007/978-0-387-98197-0
14. Vagin, V.N., Morosin, O.L., Fomina, M.V.: Inductive inference and argumentation methods in modern intelligent decision support systems. J. Comput. Syst. Sci. Int. **55**(1), 79–95 (2016). https://doi.org/10.1134/S106423071601010X
15. Argumentation Research Group: The Argument Interchange Format (AIF) Specification. School of Computing, University of Dundee, 8 November 2011. http://www.argumentinterchange.org. Accessed 10 May 2020
16. Chesnevar, C., et al.: Towards an argument interchange format. Knowl. Eng. Rev. **21**(4), 293–316 (2006)
17. Rahwan, I., Zablith, F., Reed, C.: Laying the foundations for a world wide argument web. Artif. Intell. **171**(10–15), 897–921 (2007)
18. Rahwan, I., Banihashemi, B., Reed, C., Walton, D., Abdallah, S.: Representing and classifying arguments on the semantic web. Knowl. Eng. Rev. **26**(4), 487–511 (2011)
19. Cerutti, F., Toniolo, A., Norman, T.J., Bex, F., Rahwan, I., Reed, C.: AIF-EL – an OWL2-EL-compliant AIF ontology. In: Computational Models of Argument – Proceedings of COMMA 2018, vol. 305, pp. 455–456. IOS Press (2018)
20. Bex, F., Modgil, S., Prakken, H., Reed, C.: On logical specifications of the Argument Interchange Format. J. Logic Comput. **23**, 951–989 (2013)
21. AIF-ontology. https://osf.io/rhjcb/download. Accessed 10 May 2020
22. Antoniou, G., Harmelen, F.: Web ontology language: OWL. In: Staab, S., Studer, R. (eds.) Handbook on Ontologies. IHIS, pp. 91–110. Springer, Heidelberg (2009). https://doi.org/10.1007/978-3-540-92673-3_4
23. Budán, M.C., Simari, G.I., Viglizzo, I., Simari, G.R.: An approach to characterize graded entailment of arguments through a label-based framework. Int. J. Approximate Reasoning **82**, 242–269 (2017)
24. Hájek, P.: Metamathematics of Fuzzy Logic. Trends in Logic, vol. 4. Springer, Dordrecht (1998). https://doi.org/10.1007/978-94-011-5300-3
25. Zadeh, L.A.: The concept of a linguistic variable and its application to approximate reasoning-III. Inf. Sci. **9**(1), 43–80 (1975)
26. Howard, W.A.: The formulae-as-types notion of construction. In: To, H.B. (ed.) Curry: Essays on Combinatory Logic, Lambda Calculus and Formalism, pp. 479–490. Academic Press, Boston (1980)
27. Dummett, M.: The Logical Basis of Metaphysics. Harvard University Press, Cambridge (1991)
28. Nute, D.: Defeasible Logic. In: Bartenstein, O., Geske, U., Hannebauer, M., Yoshie, O. (eds.) INAP 2001. LNCS (LNAI), vol. 2543, pp. 151–169. Springer, Heidelberg (2003). https://doi.org/10.1007/3-540-36524-9_13
29. Atanassov, K.T.: Intuitionistic Fuzzy Logics. Studies in Fuzziness and Soft Computing, vol. 351, 1st edn. Springer, Cham (2017). https://doi.org/10.1007/978-3-319-48953-7
30. Todd, M.J.: The Computation of Fixed Points and Applications. Springer, Heidelberg (2013). https://doi.org/10.1007/978-3-642-50327-6
31. Costa Pereira, C., Tettamanzi, A., Liao, B., Malerba, A., Rotolo, A., van der Torre, L.: Combining fuzzy logic and formal argumentation for legal interpretation. In: Proceedings of 16th International Conference on Artificial Intelligence and Law (ICAIL 2017), London, pp. 49–58 (2017)
32. Zagorulko, Y., Garanina, N., Sery, A., Domanov, O.: Ontology-based approach to organizing the support for the analysis of argumentation in popular science discourse. In: Kuznetsov, S.O., Panov, A.I. (eds.) RCAI 2019. CCIS, vol. 1093, pp. 348–362. Springer, Cham (2019). https://doi.org/10.1007/978-3-030-30763-9_29

Intelligent Systems and Applications

Intelligent Information Search Method Based on a Compositional Ontological Approach

Borisov Vadim[1]([envelope]) [ORCID], Kotov Dmitry[1], and Molyavko Alexander[2]

[1] Branch of the National Research University Moscow Power Engineering Institute in
Smolensk, Energetichesky proezd 1, Smolensk 214013, Russia
vbor67@mail.ru, dim.kot2009@yandex.ru
[2] The RF Armed Forces Army Air Defense Military Academy, Smolensk, Russia
aamolavko@gmail.com

Abstract. A method of intelligent information search and contextual information provision in distributed data warehouses is proposed, that allows increasing
the efficiency and quality of providing information for intelligent preparation and
decision support. The method is based on the proposed compositional ontological
model that provides an interoperable representation of knowledge about the tasks
(processes) of the subject area, taking into account user profiles, in combination
with functionally oriented information resources formed on the basis of generalization and semantic integration of structured, poorly structured and unstructured
data from heterogeneous sources.

Keywords: Intelligent information search · Compositional ontological model ·
Information demand

1 Introduction

The constant increase in requirements for generalization and analysis of structured,
weakly structured and unstructured data from heterogeneous sources determines the
need to develop existing and create new approaches to information search based on
intelligent technologies.

The traditional approach to solving search problems in distributed data warehouses
is information search based on user queries, which provide either contextual information or a ranked list of links to relevant information resources (Golenkov et al. 2019;
Grinchenkov et al. 2016).

The main limitations of existing search methods are their low pertinence, that is,
insufficient compliance of information needs of users with the results of information
search. This is due to the lack of efficiency and quality of providing these methods with
information needs in the context of the tasks being solved. Thus, users, on the one hand,
need time to formalize their information needs in the form of search queries, which often
contain errors and are characterized by a high degree of ambiguity. In addition, users often
do not know which search queries will be able to provide the required information. This
leads to iterative refinement, correction, and entering additional search query options

© Springer Nature Switzerland AG 2020
S. O. Kuznetsov et al. (Eds.): RCAI 2020, LNAI 12412, pp. 371–381, 2020.
https://doi.org/10.1007/978-3-030-59535-7_27

into the information search system. Not the best alternative is to view a large number of suggested search results to choose the best one.

An ontological approach is promising for creating effective methods of information search in distributed data repositories. it allows: to clearly represent the knowledge of experts and ensure their joint use, including in various subject areas; to integrate information and its representation in a form that is convenient for sharing in order to solve a variety of tasks; to increase attention to the accuracy and strictness (formality) of the definition of terms entered into the dictionary and the relationships between them, to the development of an apparatus for manipulating ontological models (Chibirova 2014; Blomqvist et al. 2016). However, the limitations of using this approach for modern information search systems are the complexity of their creation, associated with both time costs and the need to attract a large number of experts in the subject area (Gribova et al. 2013; Gribova et al. 2017; Kureichik and Safronenkova 2017; Arp and Smith 2015; Karima et al. 2016; Hitzler et al. 2016).

Moreover, existing approaches to view of the subject area of information retrieval include separate construction of domain ontology (Rogushina 2017) and ontology applications (Dyachenko and Zagorulko 2014; Zagorulko et al. 2018), which provides requirements for submission of the information needs of decision-makers, taking into account the specifics of the tasks of management, as well as restrictions on their decision, and the automatic formalization in the form of enhanced search queries to distributed data stores.

In (Borisov et al. 2019a), an ontological approach is developed and a composite ontological model based on it is proposed, which is a composition of three coordinated interdependent ontological models: tasks, functionally oriented information resources, and user profiles. The compositional ontological model provides an interoperable representation of knowledge about the tasks (processes) of the subject area taking into account user profiles in combination with functionally oriented information resources formed on the basis of generalization and semantic integration of structured, poorly structured and unstructured data from heterogeneous sources.

The article proposes a method for intelligent information search and contextual information provision in distributed data warehouses based on a composite ontological approach, which allows increasing the efficiency and quality of providing information needs for intellectual training and decision support.

2   Compositional Ontological Model for Generalization and Semantic Integration of Structured, Weakly Structured and Unstructured Data

The proposed compositional ontological model is based on the results of analysis and systematization of intellectual support and decision-making processes in complex organizational and socio-technical systems (Borisov et al. 2019a).

The proposed ontological model is a composition of three coordinated interdependent ontological models: the task ontology Oz, the ontology of functionally oriented information resources Or, and the user profile ontology Op:

$$KOM = <Oz, Or, Op>.$$

The ontological model of Oz tasks defines a set of decision-making stages, as well as a set of tasks and subtasks performed on each of them, and is represented as:

$$Oz = <Z, Rzc, Rzo, A, F(A)>,$$

where Z is a set of tasks that are decomposed into their corresponding subtasks; Rzc is a set of "part-whole" relations between tasks and their corresponding subtasks; Rzo is a set of fuzzy conditionality relations when performing tasks (subtasks); A is a set of attributes of tasks and subtasks, represented as atomic information units necessary for their solution; $F(A)$ is a set of restrictions on attribute values.

The ontological model of functional-oriented information resources Or defines information for performing the corresponding tasks, and is represented as:

$$Or = <C, Rr, D, A, F(A), Ax>,$$

where $C = \{C_s | s = 1,\dots ,S\}$ – the set of classes (subclassed) information objects that characterize the information resources required for decision-making; Rr – many hierarchical relationships between classes and subclasses (the ratio of "part–whole") and fuzzy relations of influence between the attributes; D is the set of domains to unions of classes (subclasses) and their instance sets characterizing their attributes; A variety of attributes of classes (subclasses), characterizing the system and external factors; $F(A)$ – many restrictions of attribute values; Ax – set of axioms for generating output from a set of attributes and relationships.

The composition of ontological models of tasks and functional-oriented information resources is supplemented by an ontological model of user profiles implemented on the basis of an agent-based approach:

$$Op = <Id, Ef, Str>,$$

where Id is information about the agent, Ef is a set of agent actions, and Str is a set of agent behavior strategies and implements the following tasks:

- automatic generation of search queries to data warehouses;
- analysis and generalization of information search results;
- consistent structural and parametric adaptation of ontological models when changing the functional or informational components of decision-making processes.

The agent Id information includes information about the hierarchy level and agent status, as well as the scalability level of the information.

The set of actions of the Ef agent includes: updating the current information; clarifying the task; making changes to the ontological model of Oz tasks; forming a search query; information search; evaluating the results of information search; aggregating (identifying) information; making changes to the ontological model of functional-oriented information resources Or.

According to the possible sequences of actions listed above, the following strategies for agent behavior are possible:

- a well-known task has been set, and the available information resources are sufficient to meet the information needs;
- a well-known task has been set, and there are not enough available information resources to meet the information needs;
- a new task has been set, and the available information resources are sufficient to meet the information needs;
- a new task has been set, and there are not enough available information resources to meet the information needs.

Implementation of the proposed compositional ontological model in the form of a knowledge base focused on a specific subject area is appropriate on a remote server ("cloud").

3   Description of the Method of Intelligent Information Search Based on a Composite Ontological Model

The algorithmic description of the proposed method of intelligent information search based on the compositional ontological approach is shown in Fig. 1.

Intelligent information search is performed in distributed data stores ("cloud") in accordance with automatically generated search queries.

Stages 1–2. After the user receives a management task (the task comes as a formalized text document from a remote user (via a remote server), this task (document) on a remote server ("cloud") using a computer analysis tool for text information (for example, the RCO Fact Extractor SDK) is subjected to linguistic parsing of the text, taking into account the grammar and semantics of the language, into information objects. The knowledge base of this tool is based on a composite ontological model of the decision-making process, which is located on this server.

An information object is an elementary unit of information that corresponds to a class (subclass) of the compositional ontological model of the decision-making process.

After the linguistic analysis is performed, the "task" type object that the user needs to solve is identified, its execution restrictions (for example, spatial and temporal), and objects that are semantically related to the task and their attributes.

In addition to identifying the information objects contained in the document, the analysis of text information determines a complex indicator PR_b (taking into account the priority of the source of information IST_b and its relevance VR_b) and the degree of proximity $\overline{SIO}_b$ of information objects of the text SIO_b, $b \in 1, \ldots, B$ with elements of the composite ontological model Z_d, C_d, Az_d, Ar_d.

The complex PR_b indicator is defined by a functional dependency:

$$PR_b = f(IST_b, VR_b).$$

The degree of proximity $\overline{SIO}_b$ is determined based on indicators:

$$\overline{SIO}_b = \left\{ \left(\overline{SIO}_g^b / s_g \right) | g \in 1, \ldots, G \right\},$$

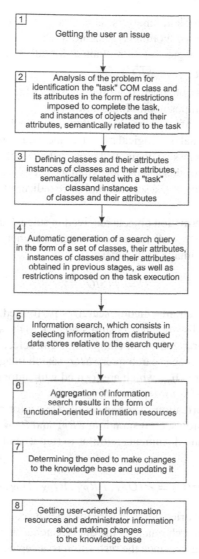

Fig. 1. Algorithm of the intelligent information search method based on the compositional ontological approach

where $S = \{s_g | g \in 1, \dots, G\}$ – linguistic characteristics of the information object, which determine its degree of proximity to the elements of the compositional ontological model; $\overline{SIO}_g^b$ – the degree of compliance of the SIO_b information object with the characteristics of S.

If the analysis of the problem reveals information objects that do not belong to the objects of the composite ontological model, then a set of compliance indicators is determined for each of them $\overline{SIO}$, which will be applied at the stage of making changes to the composite ontological model.

The result of the problem analysis is a set of information objects $SIO = \{SIO_1, \ldots, SIO_b\}$, a set of complex indicators $PR = \{PR_1, \ldots, PR_b\}$, and a set of indicators of the degree of compliance for all stages of analysis $\overline{SIO} = \left\{ (\overline{SIO}_1^1, \ldots, \overline{SIO}_g^1) \ldots (\overline{SIO}_1^b, \ldots, \overline{SIO}_g^b) \right\}$.

All information objects obtained from the analysis of the problem are distributed among instances of the composite ontological model.

Stage 3. for each of the information objects defined in stage 2, the Rz, Rr, and Rs relationships in the compositional ontological model define their attributes, as well as semantically related classes (subclasses), their attributes, instances of classes (subclasses), and their attributes. The result of this stage is an expanded set of SIO' information objects, a set of complex PR' indicators and a set of compliance indicators for all stages of analysis $\overline{SIO'}$.

Stage 4. the Set of information objects received in stage 3 are automatically formalized on the remote server ("cloud") as a search query Q, where the information objects are elements of the search image of the query

$$Q = f\left(SIO', I\right).$$

Stage 5. At this stage, an information search is performed, that is, the selection of information objects from distributed data stores relative to the search query Q, which is implemented through distributed cloud computing. The selection consists of matching the many elements of the image search query SIO' search images facts IO_{PX} and documents distributed data store D_{PX}, which are formed with automated indexing incoming stream of documents (similar to step 2).

As a result of the information search, a set of IO_{PX} information objects is formed, found in distributed data stores, corresponding PR_{PX} and $\overline{IO}_{PX}$ indicators those defined during indexing of facts and documents (similar to step 2) and links to D_{PX} documents that contain this fact

$$Rez(Q) = <IO_{PX}, PR_{PX}, \overline{IO}_{PX}, D_{PX}>.$$

Stage 6. This stage is carried out to ensure the relevance, completeness and accuracy of information about the search image of the query. Such a characteristic of information as reliability is not considered, since the restriction is accepted that only known reliable information can be stored in a distributed data warehouse.

The need to aggregate the found information occurs only if there are at least two information objects that belong to the same instance of the class (subclass) or its attribute (hereinafter aggregated information objects). The number of aggregated information objects includes the information objects identified in step 2 of this method.

Aggregation refers to combining or enlarging indicators based on some attribute to get generalized, aggregate indicators – aggregates.

Among the set of aggregated information objects, the object that has the maximum value of the complex indicator PR_{max} is defined, and the set of information objects whose values of complex indicators correspond to the condition

$$PR_i + \sigma \geq PR_{max},$$

where σ is the allowable deviation of the complex indicator, determined on the basis of expert opinions.

Only information objects whose complex indicator value meets the requirements of the IO_{PX1}, ..., IO_{PXj}, condition are subject to aggregation. other information objects are excluded from the aggregation procedure. Further, the aggregation procedure is based on production rules that take into account the linguistic features of the subject area of information search.

Aggregation results obtained on a remote server are presented to the user as functional-oriented information resources, the structure of which corresponds to the management task obtained in step 1, and the identified information objects are replaced or supplemented with aggregated information objects.

At stage 7, the need to make changes to the knowledge base based on the compositional ontological model of decision making and initialize the mechanism for changing it is determined. If the stage 2 will be detected information objects, not belonging to the composite elements of an ontological model, each of them compares the degree of conformity $\overline{SIO_b}$ of an information object SIO_b with values $\overline{Z}_d, \overline{C}_d, \overline{Az}_d, \overline{Ar}_d$, characterizing similarity of compositional elements of an ontological model.

The approach proposed in (Borisov et al. 2019b) is used to calculate proximity values for elements of the composite ontological model of values $\overline{Z}_d, \overline{C}_d, \overline{Az}_d, \overline{Ar}_d$, based on agglomerative methods of hierarchical clustering (Zhambu 1988), information objects are grouped with classes, subclasses and attributes of the composite ontological model, and the value of the degree of proximity, for example, for an element Z_d is determined by the expression

$$\overline{Z}_d = \{\langle t_{md}, \{(w_{md_g}/s_g)|g = 1, \ldots, G\}\rangle | m \in 1, \ldots, M_d\},$$

where for all $d \in 1, \ldots, D$ t_{md} is the m-th significant attribute in an element (class, subclass, attribute) of the composite ontological model Z_d, $w_{md_g} \in [0, 1]$ is the degree of correspondence of the t_{md} attribute to the characteristic s_g in the element Z_d.

The SIO_b information object being mapped corresponds most closely to the Z_d* element, which has the highest degree of fuzzy matching

$$Z_d^* : \max_{d \in 1..D} \rho(\overline{SIO}_b, \overline{Z}_d).$$

As a measure of the degree of fuzzy matching, it is proposed to use the expression (Gavrilova et al. 2009; Hero 2015; Hero 2019).

$$\rho(\overline{SIO}_b, \overline{Z}_d) = 1 - \frac{1}{\sqrt{G}} \sqrt{\sum_{g=1}^{G} \left(\overline{SIO}_g^b - \overline{Z}_g^d\right)^2}.$$

After determining the value of the index of the degree of fuzzy correspondence based on the intervals α and β determined using the expert method, a decision is made to make changes to the compositional ontological model:

- if $Z_d* > \alpha$, the SIO_g information object being compared is automatically added to the composite ontological model;

- if $\beta < Z_d^* \leq \alpha$, the expert must confirm or clarify the changes made to the composite ontological model, which the remote server administrator takes over;
- if $Z_d^* \leq \beta$, the expert must independently make changes to the compositional ontological model.

The need to use the expert method to determine the intervals α and β is due to the implementation of the information aggregation function under conditions of uncertainty and high risks when using the results of information search in making a decision.

Stage 8. Delivery of the received information search results to the user in the form of functional-oriented information resources for making decisions on and information about making changes to the knowledge base to the administrator of the remote server. The overall structure of functional-oriented information resources corresponds to the management task obtained in step 1.

4   Results of Applying the Method Intelligent Information Search

As an example of the proposed method, let's consider the process of planning cargo transportation by a transport and logistics company. The user assigned to perform this task is the Manager of this company. The effectiveness of this task depends on the user's experience, skill level, and awareness. To solve the problem of transport planning, the Manager must create the following list of documents for strict reporting: consignment note; invoice; bill of lading, etc.

Thus, when a request for cargo transportation is received, the text of the request is automatically parsed linguistically. With the help of a knowledge base based on a composite ontological model for solving transport and logistics problems (Fig. 2), the information objects of the document text are compared with the elements of the composite ontological model and the information object is identified as belonging to the "task" class.

For a Manager who solves the problem of transportation planning, one of the main documents that needs to be developed is a bill of lading. To effectively perform this task, you need to search and aggregate data about the vehicle, driver, route, name and nature of the cargo, time of dispatch and delivery of the cargo, the sender and recipient of the cargo, and the cost of delivery.

With the traditional approach, the Manager needs to generate a lot of requests to the Internet to get up-to-date information about the state of the road network and climate conditions. Using the proposed method of intelligent information search allows you to automatically generate an extended search query to the Internet. The search query is expanded based on a compositional ontological model.

As a result of using the developed method, the time for generating information requests in transport and logistics companies has significantly decreased relative to the existing approaches to "manual" forming user requests to distributed data stores.

5   Conclusion

The paper proposes a method of intelligent information search based on a composite ontological approach, which allows to significantly improve the quality and efficiency

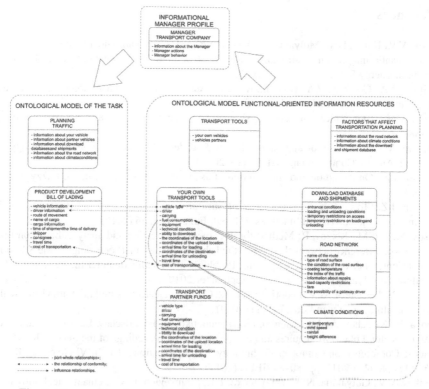

Fig. 2. Compositional ontological model for solving transport and logistics tasks

of information search by the user to a distributed data warehouse in accordance with the transport and logistics task being solved by:

- first, automatic formalization of the search query (formalize the user's information need) in the language of the knowledge base, taking into account the restrictions imposed on its implementation (spatial, temporal, climatic, etc.), which eliminates ambiguity, errors and the need to repeatedly Refine the search query;
- second, reducing the time spent on creating multiple search queries for information objects identified in the task, and analyzing the results of information search by the user;
- third, a complete and accurate description of the user's information needs, achieved by presenting the knowledge base in the form of a composite ontological model.

The proposed method also allows to efficiently implement a mechanism for automated adaptation of knowledge base, made in the form of composite ontological model for the solution of logistic tasks, change the task performed by the user, and to the emergence of new information resources in distributed data stores.

Acknowledgments. The reported study was funded by RFBR, project number 18-29-03088.

References

Borisov, V.V., Kotov, D.V., Molyavko, A.A.: Generalized fuzzy ontological model for collecting and semantic integration of structured, weakly structured and unstructured data. Int. J. Inf. Technol. Energy Effici. T. 4. No. 2(12) (2019)

Gavrilova, T.A., Gorovoy, V.A., Bolotnikova, E.S.: Assessment of cognitive ergonomics based on graph analysis. Artif. Intell. Decis. Making (3) (2009)

Zhambyu, M.: Hierarchical cluster-analysis and compliance. Finance and Statistics, Moscow (1988)

Chibirova, M.O.: Analysis of approaches to building decision support systems. Ontology and Mewari. Autom. Control Tech. Syst. 1.2(9) (2014)

Batyrshin, I.Z.: On definition and construction of association measures. J. Intell. Fuzzy Syst. **29** (2015)

Batyrshin, I.Z.: Towards a general theory of similarity and association measures: similarity, dissimilarity and correlation functions. J. Intell. Fuzzy Syst. **36** (2019)

Borisov, V., Dli, M., Kozlov, P.: Method for documents rubrication and analysis based on fuzzy relations of difference between their syntactical characteristics. In: Proceedings of the X International Conference on Interactive Systems: Problems of Human-Computer Interaction. IS-2019 Conference, Ulyanovsk, Russia, 24–27 September 2019

Gribova, V.V., Petryaeva, M.V., Fedorischev, L.A.: Computer learning simulator with virtual reality for ophthalmology. Open Educ. **6**(101) (2013)

Gribova, V., Kleschev, A., Moskalenko, Ph., Timchenko, V., Fedorischev, L., Shalfeeva, E.: The IACPaaS cloud platform: features and perspectives. In: Proceedings of the Second Russia and Pacific Conference on Computer Technology and Applications (RPC), Vladivostok, Russia, 25–29 September 2017, pp. 80–84. IEEE (2017)

Golenkov, V.V., Gulyakina, N.A., Davydenko, I.T., Shunkevich, D.V.: Semantic technologies of intelligent systems design and semantic associative computers. Doklady BGUIR **121**(3) (2019)

Grinchenkov, D.V., Kushchiy, D.N., Kolomiets, A.V.: One approach to the problem solution of specialized software development for subject search. In: Proceedings of the 4rd International Conference on Applied Innovations in IT (2016), Koethen, Hochschule Anhalt (2016)

Dyachenko, O., Zagorulko, Y.: A collaborative development of ontology-based knowledge bases. In: Klinov, P., Mouromtsev, D. (eds.) KESW 2014. CCIS, vol. 468, pp. 219–228. Springer, Cham (2014). https://doi.org/10.1007/978-3-319-11716-4_19

Kureichik, V., Safronenkova, I.: Integrated algorithm of the domain ontology development. In: Silhavy, R., Senkerik, R., Kominkova Oplatkova, Z., Prokopova, Z., Silhavy, P. (eds.) CSOC 2017. AISC, vol. 573, pp. 146–155. Springer, Cham (2017). https://doi.org/10.1007/978-3-319-57261-1_15

Rogushina, J.V.: Development of distributed intelligent systems on base of ontological analysis and semantic wiki technologies. Ontol. Designing **4**(26), v. 7, 453–472 (2017)

Zagorulko, Y., Borovikova, O., Zagorulko, G.: Pattern-based methodology for building the ontologies of scientific subject domains. In: Fujita, H., Herrera-Viedma, E. (eds.) New Trends in Intelligent Software Methodologies, Tools and Techniques. Proceedings of the 17th International Conference SoMeT_18. Frontiers in Artificial Intelligence and Applications, vol. 303. IOS Press, Amsterdam (2018)

Blomqvist, E., Hammar, K., Presutti, V.: Engineering ontologies with patterns: the eXtreme design methodology. In: Hitzler, P., Gangemi, A., Janowicz, K., Krisnadhi, A., Presutti, V. (eds.) Ontology Engineering with Ontology Design Patterns, Studies on the Semantic Web, vol. 25, pp. 23–50. IOS Press (2016)

Arp, R., Smith, B., Spear, A.D.: Building Ontologies with Basic Formal Ontology. MIT Press, Cambridge (2015), 248 p.

Karima, N., Hammar, K., Hitzler, P.: How to document ontology design patterns. In: Proceedings of the 7th Workshop on Ontology and Semantic Web Patterns (WOP 2016), Kobe, Japan. IOS Press (2016)

Hitzler, P., Gangemi, A., Janowicz, K., Krisnadhi, A., Presutti, V. (eds.): Ontology Engineering with Ontology Design Patterns: Foundations and Applications. Studies on the Semantic Web. IOS Press/AKA (2016)

Format and Usage Model of Security Patterns in Ontology-Driven Threat Modelling

Andrei Brazhuk$^{(\boxtimes)}$ and Evgeny Olizarovich

Yanka Kupala State University of Grodno, Grodno, Belarus
{brazhuk,e.olizarovich}@grsu.by

Abstract. To provide security for modern computer systems (i.e. identify threats and employ countermeasures) threat modelling is used on
early stages of life cycle (requirements, design). Security patterns can
be applied as security design decisions. However there are some challenges, related to management of security patterns, in particular, lack of
methods to identify the necessity of security patterns and weak integration with security risk-based models. To overcome these restrictions we
have developed an ontological format (schema), which allows a) creating
security pattern catalogs, and b) defining context labels to map patterns
with design decisions and security problems. We have proposed a usage
model of security pattern catalogs. The usage model enables creation
of domain-specific threat models, used for ontology-driven threat modelling. Also, OWL ontology and a free toolset (Java, OWL API) have
been developed to manage security pattern catalogs and motivate development of high-level software tools for maintenance of security pattern
catalogs.

Keywords: Software security · Security patterns · Threat modelling ·
Knowledge management · OWL

1 Introduction

Security is one of the fundamental design challenges of modern computer systems. On early stages of life cycle, system architects use threat modelling for
identification of security threats and their countermeasures in order to increase
security level. An issue with the threat modelling is that system architects do
not have enough experience as security experts do. Moreover, the latter are
less involved in the development process, because of fast system deployment
approaches, which do not leave time for deep security analysis, and automatic
deployment tools, able to create multi-component applications and even virtual
data centres on the fly.

A possible decision can be security patterns. Security patterns are known
as descriptions of security problems that appear in specific contexts and present

© Springer Nature Switzerland AG 2020
S. O. Kuznetsov et al. (Eds.): RCAI 2020, LNAI 12412, pp. 382–392, 2020.
https://doi.org/10.1007/978-3-030-59535-7_28

well proven solution for them. They are created by security experts and represent best security practices for inexpert computer system architects.

The research community has been collecting security patterns (also misuse patterns, threat patterns etc.) for decades [1,2]. However there are some challenges related to their use in modern computer systems. First, systematic methods are required to identify the necessity of security patterns for a particular design decision [3]. Second, existing security patterns need to be redesigned to better tackle the security problems developers and architects actually face [4]. High security is the result of two processes: information flow analysis (security by design) and formal modelling (security by certification) [5]. So, the threat modelling based on security patterns should be integrated with appropriate risk-based models.

In this paper we aim at developing a format (schema) and means to maintain security pattern catalogs, which collect security knowledge and allow one to use the data for different cases. We propose an ontological approach and conception of context security patterns towards solving the problems described above.

The ontological approach is based on Web Ontology Language (OWL). OWL is compatible with RDF (Resource Description Framework), they are both used to build different datasets of the LOD (Linked Open Data) cloud. The main advantage of the LOD approach to knowledge management is an opportunity to add pieces of intelligence to the data processing. In particular, the OWL-based knowledge management systems use the description logics (DL) as a background. DL allows one to describe concepts of a domain and relations between them in a very formal way. Also, reasoning procedures with relatively low computational complexity (under certain conditions) and advanced rule-based processing can be added to these systems. There are several researches aimed at employing the ontological approach, in particular based on OWL, into the security domain [6–8]. A context security pattern contains a precise description of security problems and their solutions. It also has criteria that allow to "automatically" answer the questions, like "Is the pattern suitable for a system design?" and "Does the pattern solve (describe) a particular security problem, valuable for its context?".

We also propose to use security pattern catalogs for creation domain-specific threat models, as a part of the ontology-driven threat modelling (OdTM) framework [9]. Each domain-specific threat model contains a set of typical components of some architectural domain, threats and countermeasures. A system architect describes its computer system with DFD (Data Flow Diagram); then automatic reasoning procedures are used to semantically interpret the diagram and figure out relevant threats and countermeasures for the system.

2 Ontological Format (Schema) of Security Patterns

Security pattern format (schema) is a model of security patterns, represented as an ontology. It includes concepts and individuals, used to describe security patterns and create catalogs of security patterns. There are two main points of the proposed ontology. First, the use of the ontology allows one to represent different types of patterns (security patterns, as well as misuse patterns and common threats), and enables automatic building of advanced hierarchies of patterns and their properties. Second, it allows putting a pattern into a context, i.e. adding labels (properties) that enable automatic answering different decision-support questions.

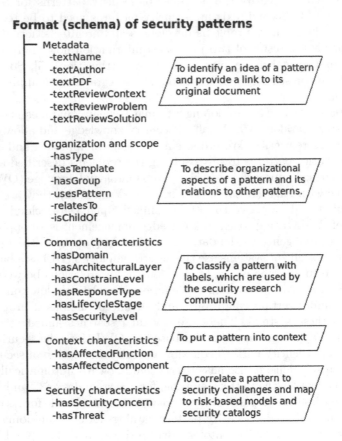

Fig. 1. Structure of format

Figure 1 shows the generic structure of the format with main properties. Properties of the format include five sections that are described below.

Metadata. The metadata section contains properties used to identify a particular pattern and its idea [1]. To describe the pattern one should use the common fields like "textIntent", "textProblem", "textSolution*", "textConsequences", "textImplementation" (not shown in Fig. 1).

In some cases one has to avoid putting a full description of a pattern because of copyright and trademark, so the "textreview*" fields should be used to describe the pattern in own words. Also, the metadata should contain links to an original pattern's document, which is the most valuable thing there.

Organization and Scope. This section describes organizational aspects of a pattern (type - "hasType", used template - "hasTemplate") and its scope (i.e. relations to other patterns). A pattern can belong to a group ("hasGroup"), use other patterns as a part of its decision ("usesPattern"), relate to another pattern ("relatesTo"). Also you can define relation between a concrete pattern and abstract one ("isChildOf").

Common Characteristics. Several attempts have been made to create a taxonomy of security patterns [10–12], so the security community has the common approach to classify existing patterns. This section represents this view and contains base labels, used by the researchers, like "hasArchitecturalLayer", "hasConstraintLayer", "hasResponseType".

Context Characteristics. The "context" term means a possibility to use a pattern in a design of computer system (i.e. answering the question "Is the pattern suitable for the system design or not?"). The idea of the context approach is that each computer system can be described in two ways: with components and (or) functions (features). And here two options are possible.

First option is based on an assertion that functions are unique features that build a coherent model of system, and components are common items, used by all systems. For example, what functions make a hypervisor (IaaS component) unique? An answer might include "Management of VMs", "VM migration", "Virtual networking" etc. What common components does it consist of? It might be "Hardware server", "Operating system", "System service", "Network service", "CLI interface", "API interface". In many cases security problems of common components are known and well described, and security problems of functions are in focus for a new type of computer systems. An ideal model has a well-formed hierarchy of components. For such models it would be possible to consider only functions for domain specific systems.

Second option is that the function is a part of component that does not have subcomponents (i.e., functions describe non-decomposable parts of components). For example, there is "Hypervisor", and we do not want to decompose it (e.g.. to say it includes virtual machine manager, virtual network manager and virtual storage machine manager). Instead, it can be said that hypervisor is an atomic component, and it provides the functions of management of virtual machines, management of virtual networks and storages.

The current version of our ontology contains the "component-function" models for the Cloud computing [13,14] and IoT (Internet of Things) [15–17] fields.

Security Characteristics. The next step of the pattern contextualization is to correlate patterns and security challenges. A relevant question, which the security characteristics allow to answer, is "Does a security pattern solve a particular security problem, valuable for its context?". Sure, a final decision is the responsibility of a system architect, but this set of labels reduces the number of options and offers only relevant security solutions.

The current version of our model proposes to use threats and security concerns as security labels. Considering a pattern you can figure out a set of threats, related to this pattern (which ones the pattern touches). This can be useful from the viewpoint of security experts. This ontology uses a model of threats based on CAPEC (Common Attack Pattern Enumeration and Classification). We revised its "Domain of Attack" view and created a list of base threats for communications and software (see Fig. 2).

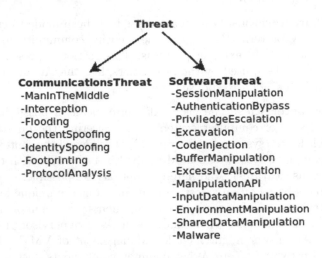

Fig. 2. Threats used by model

This list enables mapping of CAPEC and threats, assigned with items of a security pattern catalog. It is possible to map other security enumerations, like CWE (Common Weakness Enumeration), to CAPEC [18], and as a result to enrich security pattern catalogs with external data.

Security concerns [10,11] are considered as security features that a security pattern holds in terms of software requirements. Such approach is useful for description of security problems from perspective of developers.

We consider security control families from the NIST SP 800-53 publication as security concerns (see Fig. 3). In theory this enables mapping of security pattern catalogs with different security control catalogs (NIST SP 800-53, ISO 17799/ISO 27002) [19,20].

3 Usage Model of Security Patterns

A description of a security pattern contains a lot of explicit and implicit knowledge from the security domain. The proposed format allows one to order this knowledge and formalize it by means of the ontological model. There are several use cases of security pattern catalogs. In this work we propose to use the catalogs for creation of domain-specific threat models as a part of the ontology-driven threat modelling (OdtM) approach [9], which has been introduced earlier. The OdTM approach provides graphical representation of computer system

SecurityConcern

-AccessControl
-Awareness
-Training
-Audit
-Accountability
-SecurityAssessment
-Authorization
-ConfigurationManagement
-ContingencyPlanning
-IdentificationAndAuthentication
-IncidentResponse
-Maintenance

-MediaProtection
-PhysicalProtection
-EnvironmentalProtection
-Planning
-PersonnelSecurity
-RiskAssessment
-ServicesAcquisition
-CommunicationsProtection
-SystemProtection
-SystemIntegrity
-InformationIntegrity
-ProgramManagement

Fig. 3. Security concerns

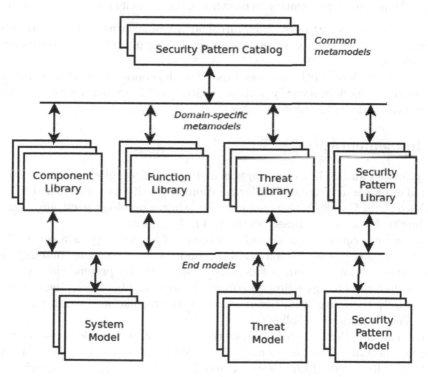

Fig. 4. Usage model

architecture (Data Flow Diagram, DFD) as a set of the DL axioms and creation of relevant threat lists by automatic reasoning procedures. The basis of the threat modelling process is an ontological domain-specific threat model. For a specific domain it contains lists of typical system components, relations between them, and threats, associated with the components.

Ontological security pattern catologs (Fig. 4) should be considered as common metamodels, because they combine descriptions of security problems and their solutions both in general and for specific domains (Cloud computing, Internet of Things, Software defined networks etc.).

The proposed format of security pattern and appropriate procedures allow one to create libraries that are required to build domain-specific threat models (metamodels). The list of required libraries includes:

Libraries of Architectural Elements and Functions. Elements (components, data flow, boundaries) can form hierarchies. To apply functions into the ontology-driven threat modelling, mapping should be added between functions and architectural elements.

Library of Threats. A hierarchical list of possible threats for a domain, with the context labels and dependencies on data flows, components and countermeasures.

Library of Security Patterns. A hierarchical list of security patterns (countermeasures) with the context labels and dependencies on data flows, components and threats.

The bottom layer of the proposed usage model contains end models (system models, threat models, security pattern models), which are parts of the ontology-driven threat modelling process.

4   Implementation

The proposed format has been implemented as OWL ontology. We have implemented our ideas as a free toolset for creation of security patterns, called SPCatalogMaker[1]. SPCatalogMaker includes the schema ontology itself and a small building tool ("Maker"), based on the OWL API library.

To create a catalog, you should add pieces of an ontology as a set of OWL files, which import the schema ontology, and create a resulting ontology and RDF dataset from the source files with Maker. At the present time you can use the Protege ontology editor to edit your catalogs. The development of more user-friendly tools (e.g. wiki based system with tree-like navigation and forms to fill data) is a quite a challenge.

You can use Protege to illustrate the ability of the ontology to "answer" different questions. The questions can be represented as the DL queries as well as the SPARQL (SPARQL Protocol and RDF Query Language) queries. For example, you can ask a list of patterns, related to the Man in the Middle threat:

SecurityPattern and hasThreat value threat_ManInTheMiddle

or create more sophisticated request, like a list of patterns related to threats, which affect confidentiality:

SecurityPattern and hasThreat some (hasSecurityObjective value SO_Confidentiality)

Figure 5 shows an example of execution of the last DL request on a test dataset with Protege.

---

[1] https://github.com/nets4geeks/SPCatalogMaker

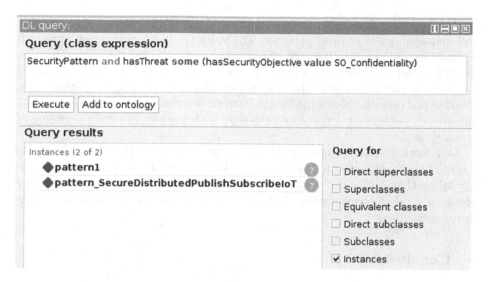

Fig. 5. Execution of DL request

5 Related Work

There are diverse researches aimed at formalizing security patterns. Most scientific results are based on UML (Unified Modelling Language) and its means [21,22]. UML is a common approach to describe different aspects of computer systems, and it is used to create diagrams for security patterns.

One of the latest works [23] has proposed a security pattern classification, based on Attack Defence Trees (ADT), which provided a well-known approach to computer security for decades. Their classification has exposed relationships between software attacks, security principles, and security patterns. Also they have offered an approach to infer ADT from the CAPEC enumeration.

Work [24] has researched a challenge of automatic correction of security issues in declarative deployment models of cloud services based on the ontological approach and security patterns. Their implementation has been directly based on First-order logic (FOL) and the low-level logical programming (Prolog).

Work [25] has been aimed, first, at developing a modelling language that allows the definition of security patterns with metamodelling techniques, second, at providing validation mechanisms for the verification of security properties. This work also propose a set of guidelines for the modelling of security patterns.

An advantage of our approach as compared with the works mentioned above is the use of description logics through OWL and the automatic reasoning features as an implementation. This allows one to involve a strict formalization and object-oriented approach into the design of knowledge management systems, as well as to apply various high-level means, like the SWRL (Semantic Web Rule Language) rules, the SPARQL queries.

A few works offer the ontological approach and OWL language for selection and management of security patterns. The work [11] has proposed an approach to facilitate the mapping between security requirements and their solutions, i.e. security patterns. Their have developed a security pattern search engine intended to reuse security expertise in the software development. In [12] the authors proposed to add ontological descriptions to pattern descriptions (i.e., represent existing security patterns in form of an ontology) with the aim to create a catalog of security patterns.

Our work should be considered as a continuation of the previous efforts [11,12]. Our contribution to this field include the definition of context and security labels that enable the mapping of patterns to design decisions and security problems, and implementation of these ideas as a part of the ontology-driven threat modelling.

6   Conclusions

In this work we have considered the management challenges of security patterns and the opportunity to use them in the threat modelling of modern computer systems. To overcome existing restrictions we have developed a format (schema) that allows creating ontological catalogs of security patterns. The format includes five sections (Metadata, Organization and scope, Common characteristics, Context characteristics, Security characteristics). The last two are used to put a pattern into a context and define applicability as a solution of a security problem.

We propose a usage model of security pattern catalogs, which enables the creation of domain-specific threat models, used for the ontology-driven threat modelling. There are three layers of the proposed model: common metamodels (represented by security pattern catalogs), domain-specific metamodels, and end models (system models, threat models, and security pattern models). Also, OWL ontology and a free toolset (Java, OWL API) have been developed to manage security pattern catalogs and enable development of high-level software tools for maintenance of security pattern catalogs.

The actual challenges for further research are:

Creation of different security pattern catalogs. The proposed ideas should be proven on real catalogs. We are going to start creating a threat catalog for the Cloud computing domain based on the schema ontology.

Development of methods and tools of automatic mapping catalog data with existing security enumerations (CAPEC, CWE, CVE). It allows one to enrich data with real use cases.

Development of methods and tools of integration domain-specific threat models with risk-based security models (NIST SP 800-53, ISO 17799/ISO 27002).

Development of applications for management of security pattern catalogs. It would allow one to create ontologies by security experts without the use of OWL.

References

1. Fernandez, E.B.: Security Patterns in Practice: Designing Secure Architectures Using Software Patterns. Wiley, Hoboken (2013)
2. Jafari, A.J., Rasoolzadegan, A.: Security patterns: a systematic mapping study. arXiv preprint arXiv:1811.12715 (2018)
3. Washizaki, H., et al.: Taxonomy and literature survey of security pattern research. In: 2018 IEEE Conference on Application, Information and Network Security (AINS), pp. 87–92. IEEE (2018)
4. van Den Berghe, A., et al.: Security patterns 2.0: toward security patterns based on security building blocks. In: 2018 IEEE/ACM 1st International Workshop on Security Awareness from Design to Deployment (SEAD), pp 45–48. IEEE (2018)
5. Zhioua, Z., et al.: Formal specification of security guidelines for program certification. In: 2017 International Symposium on Theoretical Aspects of Software Engineering (TASE). IEEE (2017)
6. Doynikova, E., et al.: Ontology of metrics for cyber security assessment. In: Proceedings of the 14th International Conference on Availability, Reliability and Security (2019)
7. Takahashi, T., et al.: Web of cybersecurity: linking, locating, and discovering structured cybersecurity information. Int. J. Commun. Syst. 31(5) (2018)
8. Gaskova, D., Massel, A.: Semantic modeling of cyber threats in the energy sector using Dynamic Cognitive Maps and Bayesian Belief Network. In: 7th Scientific Conference on Information Technologies for Intelligent Decision Making Support (ITIDS 2019). Atlantis Press (2019)
9. Brazhuk, A.: Security patterns based approach to automatically select mitigations in ontology-driven threat modelling. In: Open Semantic Technologies for Intelligent Systems (OSTIS), pp. 267–272 (2020)
10. VanHilst, M., et al.: A multi-dimensional classification for users of security patterns. J. Res. Pract. Inf. Technol. 41(2), 87–97 (2009)
11. Guan, H., et al.: An ontology-based approach to security pattern selection. Int. J. Autom. Comput. 13(2), 168–182 (2016)
12. Vale, A.P., Fernandez, E.B.: An ontology for security patterns. In: 38th International Conference of the Chilean Computer Science Society (SCCC). IEEE (2019)
13. Fernandez, E.B., et al.: Building a security reference architecture for cloud systems. Requirements Eng. 21(2), 225–249 (2016)
14. Shu, R., et al.: A study of security vulnerabilities on docker hub. In: Proceedings of the Seventh ACM on Conference on Data and Application Security and Privacy, pp. 269–280 (2017)
15. Abdul-Ghani, H.A., et al.: A comprehensive IoT attacks survey based on a building-blocked reference model. Int. J. Adv. Comput. Sci. Appl. (IJACSA) 9, 355–373 (2018)
16. Bakhshi, Z., et al.: Industrial IoT security threats and concerns by considering Cisco and Microsoft IoT reference models. In: 2018 IEEE Wireless Communications and Networking Conference Workshops (WCNCW), pp. 173–178. IEEE (2018)
17. Naraliyev, N.A., Samal, D.I.: Review and analysis of standards and protocols in the field of Internet of Things. Modern testing methods and problems of information security IoT. Int. J. Open Inf. Technol. 7(8), 94–104 (2019)
18. Brazhuk, A.: Semantic model of attacks and vulnerabilities based on CAPEC and CWE dictionaries. Int. J. Open Inf. Technol. 7(3), 38–41 (2019)

19. Ibrahim, A., et al.: A security review of local government using NIST CSF: a case study. J. Supercomputing **74**(10), 5171–5186 (2018)
20. Diamantopoulou, V., Tsohou, A., Karyda, M.: From ISO/IEC 27002:2013 information security controls to personal data protection controls: guidelines for GDPR compliance. In: Katsikas, S., et al. (eds.) CyberICPS/SECPRE/SPOSE/ADIoT - 2019. LNCS, vol. 11980, pp. 238–257. Springer, Cham (2020). https://doi.org/10. 1007/978-3-030-42048-2_16
21. Dwivedi, A.K., Rath, S.K.: Formalization of web security patterns. INFOCOMP **14**(1), 14–25 (2015)
22. Xia, T., et al.: Cloud security and privacy metamodel. In: Proceedings of the 6th International Conference on Model-Driven Engineering and Software Development, pp. 379–386. LDA (2018)
23. Salva, S., Regainia, L.: A catalogue associating security patterns and attack steps to design secure applications. J. Comput. Secur. **27**(1), 49–74 (2019)
24. Saatkamp, K., et al.: An approach to automatically detect problems in restructured deployment models based on formalizing architecture and design patterns. SICS Softw. Intensive Cyber Phys. Syst. **34**(2–3), 85–97 (2019)
25. Hamid, B., et al.: Security patterns modeling and formalization for pattern-based development of secure software systems. Innovations Syst. Softw. Eng. **12**(2), 109–140 (2016)

Assessment of the Technological Process Condition Based on the Assembly of Deep Recurrent Neural Networks

Maksim Dli, Andrey Puchkov$^{(\boxtimes)}$, and Tatyana Kakatunova

National Research University «Moscow Power Engineering Institute» (Branch) in Smolensk,
Energetichesky proyezd 1, g., Smolensk 2014013, Russia
`MiDli@mail.ru, putchkov63@mail.ru, tatjank@yandex.ru`

Abstract. The paper proposes an algorithmic structure of inforware for assessing the condition of a technological process for the production of phosphorus from apatite-nepheline ore waste. The structure is based on the use of an ensemble of deep recurrent neural networks for forecasting process parameters with subsequent aggregation of their outputs for clustering, the results of which can be used to analyze repeatability and stability of the process. The results of checking structure operability on a software model created in Python are presented.

Keywords: Condition assessment · Machine learning · Neural networks ensemble · Deep recurrent neural networks

1 Introduction

The objective of the conducted study is to develop infoware for the automated system of control in technological process (ASCTP) for the production of yellow phosphorus from apatite-nepheline ore waste to assess the condition of the technological process (TP). This waste is accumulated in large quantities within the territories adjacent to the mining and processing plants, causing great environmental damage to the environment and human health, so the task of creating technological cycles for their processing, as well as their infoware, is now an urgent problem.

One of the problems in assessing the TP condition is to obtain data for detecting its characteristics such as stability and repeatability, directly affecting the quality of products and compliance with its standards [1]. The problem of forecasting the TP conditions is of current interest, it allows providing stability and repeatability due to timely response to undesirable trends in the development of TP.

TP control requires the application of efficient algorithms allowing calculation of the optimal control actions on the basis of incoming information about TP. The hierarchical principle of constructing ASCTP assumes different levels of decision-making: at the lower levels these are various technical regulators (proportional, proportional-integral, etc.), at higher levels more complex algorithms are connected that allow evaluating the condition of the TP using highly reliable net-centric systems [2]. The term «net-centric

S. O. Kuznetsov et al. (Eds.): RCAI 2020, LNAI 12412, pp. 393–402, 2020.
https://doi.org/10.1007/978-3-030-59535-7_29

control» came to technical applications from military science and suggests the control object to be a distributed system, and control to be based on the principles of a weak hierarchy in the decision-making circuit and the ability to generate objectives within itself [3].

The network concept for building control systems makes it reasonable to use intelligent treatment for technological information such as artificial neural networks processing the input information presented in a matrix form and differ in their ability to learn from existing data without the need to write an additional algorithm for their processing.

Intelligent systems based on the use of neural networks make it possible to generalize many examples generated on the basis of technological information and automatically generate functional dependencies that put a certain state in correspondence with the observed data (runs TP diagnostics). However, it should be noted that the drawback of systems based on machine learning principles is their inability to explain the obtained results. This fact motivates the construction of hybrid algorithms that allow "generating explanations" and the need which has been noted by researchers for a long time.

A distinctive feature of the solutions application based on DNN is the dominance of the engineering approach in the development of their architectures, since it is mathematically impossible to determine the network parameters that provide its required objective characteristics [4]. It is explained by a very large (hundreds of millions) number of adjustable parameters of powerful deep neural networks. Therefore, the development of DNN architectures for specific applications, for TP control systems in particular, remains an urgent scientific and practical problem, the solution of which makes it possible to considerably improve ASCTP infoware.

The paper proposes an architecture of the ensemble application for one of DNN type, which is recurrent neural networks (RNN), for processing technological information coming from a net-metric control system.

The novelty of the approach to the TP condition assessment consists in the consistent use of the RNN ensemble for forecasting data with their subsequent clustering. The application of such an architecture is justified by RNN property of finding deep regularities in data given in the form of time series. Based on the «memorization» of the prehistory of the current value the network makes a forecast of its development. Clustering, in its turn, selects patterns in the forecasted values of the parameters, which makes their further use in determining the characteristics of repeatability and stability of TP possible.

2   Problem Statement

Phosphorus production from apatite-nepheline ore waste presents a complicated chemical and energy technological system (CETS) consisting of three units:

- a pelletizer, it forms raw pellets from ore waste;
- a multichamber indurating machine of a conveyer type (MIMCT) for ready-made dry pellets;
- an ore-thermal furnace (OTF), where pellets are melted with the release of gaseous phosphorus which is moved to special storage.

For each unit mathematical models, based on the theory of heat and mass transfer, thermodynamics, thermophysical laws, are developed [5, 6]. The models use a large number of internal parameters, but for the purposes of controlling a net-centric system, the important ones are input/output parameters of units:

– granulator input parameters: D, dispersion of apatite-nepheline ore waste; u, mass fraction of moisture in them;
– MIMCT output parameters (output for a granulator): r_1, radius of a raw pallet; u_o, pellet moisture content; ε, pellet porosity;
– OTF input parameters (output for MIMCT): r_2, radius of a roasted pallet; σ, strength of a roasted pellet; η, degree of response in decarbonization reaction;
– OTF output parameter: γ, the purity of the obtained phosphorus, the output parameter for CETS.

Thermophysical, lithographic, and granulometric parameters and the properties of the material flows of the converted raw materials at the inputs of the units have an additional influence on the TP, however, at the first approximation, we will consider them as constant, at least for a given supply of raw materials and the time interval for TP monitoring.

Using parameter symbols and considering them as time functions t, the TP condition can be presented by the vector:

$$A(t) = (D(t), u(t), r_1(t), r_2(t), u_0(t), \varepsilon(t), \sigma(t), \eta(t), \gamma(t))^{\mathrm{T}}$$

Having designated the forecasting time interval by τ, the task is to assess the condition of TP $A(t + \tau)$ and identify patterns in the forecast data that can be used to determine repeatability, stability of TP and control objectives. In a more specific formulation, the forecast problem looks like this: according to time intervals N_b of the previous period, from which samples $A(t)$ were taken after each N_s intervals of Δt, to predict $A(t)$ for the next N_d counting, $\tau = N_d N_s \Delta t$.

3   Materials and Methods

All elements for vector A(t) are scalars, so the sequence of each of them, taken at time intervals Δt, will be a time series. Their analysis is carried out in two directions: the identification of the time series nature and the forecasting of its values for some interval.

The methods of analysis for the time series are diverse and their large group is represented by statistical methods. However, this approach requires a preliminary selection of the statistical model and additional procedures to determine its parameters [7]. In addition, the number of such parameters is relatively small, which allows expecting only an average estimation of the process [8].

A large group of analysis methods and forecasting for the time series use the expert approach based on the knowledge formalization [9]. Good results are given by combined models combining genetic algorithms, neural networks [10], two-stage models (clusterization followed by regression) [11, 12]. The difficulties in applying these methods include the need for a lot of preliminary work on the formation of knowledge bases, problem adaptation to the use of evolutionary algorithms, and others.

Nowadays, analysis and forecasting of time series based on such a variety of machine learning as deep RNN becomes more and more popular. The structure of such networks has computing units simulating «memory», taking into account previous information, which makes forecasts more accurate compared to classical statistical methods. RNN application saves from the above mentioned difficulties typical for statistical and expert methods of analysis for time series.

Among the various types of RNN, the long short-term memory (Long Short-Term Memory, LSTM) algorithm has the highest representative power. It was proposed in 1997 but deep neural networks LSTM, realizing it, have recently become widespread in solving the problems of recognition and synthesis of speech, text [13], action [14], human activity [15] and others, where the prehistory of the processes are taken into account.

The successful experience of LSTM use for accounting the time duration of processes served as the reasoning for choosing this type of RNN to forecast the condition of phosphorus production for TP under consideration.

The use of LSTM networks ensemble with further clustering of the obtained forecasts is proposed for the problem of TP condition assessment $A(t + \tau)$. The use of neural networks ensembles is widespread in the analysis for data and allows improving the quality of the applied solutions [16, 17], including forecast problems [18].

In the proposed ensemble there are seven LSTM, input data array which have the following composition:

for LSTM1 – LSTM3:

$$X_G = \begin{pmatrix} D(t) & u_0(t) \\ D(t - N_s \Delta t) & u_0(t - N_s \Delta t) \\ D(t - 2N_s \Delta t) & u_0(t - 2N_s \Delta t) \\ \cdots & \cdots \\ D(t - N_b \Delta t) & u_0 D(t - N_b \Delta t) \end{pmatrix} \tag{1}$$

for LSTM4 – LSTM6:

$$X_M = \begin{pmatrix} r_1(t) & u_0(t) & \varepsilon(t) \\ r_1(t - N_s \Delta t) & u_0(t - N_s \Delta t) & \varepsilon(t - N_s \Delta t) \\ r_1(t - 2N_s \Delta t) & u_0(t - 2N_s \Delta t) & \varepsilon(t - 2N_s \Delta t) \\ \cdots & \cdots & \cdots \\ r_1(t - N_{bs} \Delta t) & u_0(t - N_b \Delta t) & \varepsilon r_1(t - N_b \Delta t) \end{pmatrix} \tag{2}$$

for LSTM7:

$$X_R = \begin{pmatrix} r_2(t) & \sigma(t) & \eta(t) \\ r_2(t - N_s \Delta t) & \sigma(t - N_s \Delta t) & \eta(t - N_s \Delta t) \\ r_2(t - 2N_s \Delta t) & \sigma(t - 2N_s \Delta t) & \eta(t - 2N_s \Delta t) \\ \cdots & \cdots & \cdots \\ r_2(t - N_b \Delta t) & \sigma(t - N_b \Delta t) & \eta(t - N_b \Delta t) \end{pmatrix} \tag{3}$$

The output for the networks are the following parameters: LSTM1 – r_1; LSTM2 – u_0; LSTM3 – ε; LSTM4 – r_2; LSTM5 – σ; LSTM6 – η; LSTM7 – γ. The enlarged structure of the proposed LSTM ensemble and the entire solution for the problem of the condition assessment forecast and clustering is shown in Fig. 1.

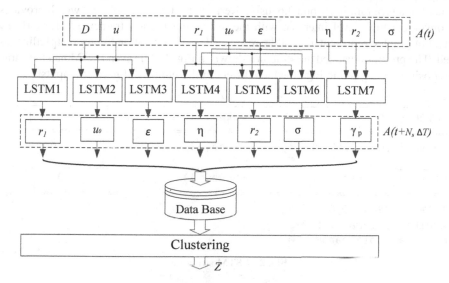

Fig. 1. Infoware structure

The first functioning of the ensemble takes place in time interval $N_b \Delta t$ from the beginning of calculation t_0. Further, as new data come, they are accumulated and in time interval $N_s \Delta t$ the ensemble functions again shifting down rows in (1)–(3) excluding the last one and adding the row corresponding to $A(t_0 + N_b \Delta t + N_s \Delta t)$ from above.

The results of ensemble forecasts are accumulated in the data base and after a sufficient number of rows with elements A being accumulated in it, clustering is carried out.

A variety of clustering methods makes it possible to apply them taking into account the subject area, problems and characteristics of the data themselves. The best known methods are the k-Means, hierarchical clustering, density–based spatial clustering of applications with noise (DBSCAN).

In this study, DBSCAN was chosen, since data about TP condition usually contain noise of various nature (measuring, systematic, random, etc.), but this algorithm works properly in their presence [19]. Moreover, it can find anomaly in data [20, 21] and form clusters not only of spherical shape but of arbitrary shape, which is important in problems, including the problem under consideration, in the absence of assumption about these cluster shape.

Data array for clustering represents a matrix containing the TP condition:

$$U = \left(A_p(t_0 + (N_b + N_s)\Delta t) \, A_p \, (t_0 + (N_b + 2N_s)\Delta t), \; \ldots, \; A_p \, (t_0 + (N_b + N_d N_s)\Delta t)\right),$$

where A_p – forecast values A at a given time point.

4 Results and Discussions

The proposed algorithm structure for infoware of TP condition assessment is implemented in a program in Python 3.6. using Keras neural network library, which provides a convenient high-level interface with the tensor calculation framework TensorFlow [22]. For graphic representation of the results a data visualization library matplotlib was used. The program realized the structure shown in Fig. 1. All seven LSTM had the same composition presented in Fig. 2, which differs in the number of network inputs.

Layer (type)	Output Shape	Param #
cu_dnnlstm_3 (CuDNNLSTM)	(None, 32)	4992
dense_48 (Dense)	(None, 1)	33

Total params: 5,025
Trainable params: 5,025
Non-trainable params: 0

Fig. 2. LSTM structure

The networks are built for the «sequence to end» mode, in which the output contains only the last result for each input sequence, and not together with several previous ones. All networks were learnt separately according to the data from file lstm_dat.csv prepared on the base of mathematical models application for individual TP units [5, 6] and containing 50000 lines with TP specific numerical values of elements A. From file, in accordance with (1)–(3), the input arrays X_G, X_M, X_R were formed and output variables of networks LSTM1 – LSTM7 in accordance with Fig. 1 were extracted. 40000 lines were used for learning and 10000 lines were used for testing. To simulate the TP condition change harmonic trend for D and u_0 was introduced into the data. The learning was performed during 30 epochs with the use of video card NVIDIA GeForce GTX 1650 which accelerated this process only twice due to the specificity of RNN architecture. It should be noted that, when training convolutional networks, the gain can be more than 10 times. To control the learning quality the metric accuracy was used, which on the test sample was in the range from 0.78 to 0.85. Figure 3 shows graphs r_1 and u_0, constructed with the use of data from lstm_dat.csv (dashed line) and forecast variants received with the help of LSTM1 and LSTM2 (dots) after networks outputs denormalization.

The program works in two stages: the first one uses ensemble LSTM and forms file clust_dat.csv with the results of TP condition assessment. At the second stage, the data from clust_dat.csv undergo density-based clustering using the DBSCAN object connected from a specialized library Python sklearn.cluster. This method application is justified by the lack of the need for indicating the supposed number of clusters, which is difficult to do in this case, when analyzing the forecasting values for TP condition. The adjusting parameters of the method are *eps*, the maximum distance between neighboring points and *min_samples*, the minimum number of points in the neighborhood for the formation of a cluster.

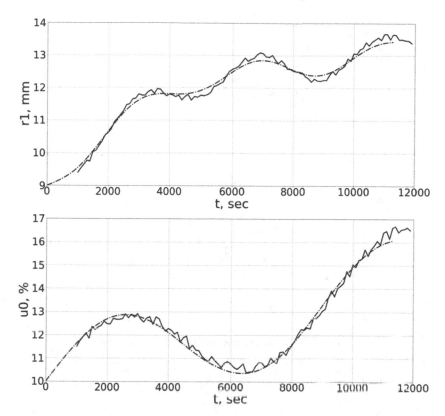

Fig. 3. Forecast results for parameters r_1 and u_0 with the help of LSTM

The results of density-based clustering Z reflect the presence of two clusters and noise (points which are not referred to any clusters) for their visualization (Fig. 4) a method for reduction of dimensionality t-SNE (t-distributed stochastic neighbor embedding) was used that minimizes Kullback–Leibler distance between two distributions taking into account the positions of clusters points [23].

For comparison, Fig. 4a shows the result of clustering after applying the least-squares method of the 4-th order to predict TP parameters, and Fig. 4b shows the results after replacing LSTM network with GRU (Gated Recurrent Units) network, which is a simplified version of LSTM. A visual analysis of the results shows that after applying LSTM, clustering gives the most distinguishable density areas, while the least-squares method does not allow the clustering algorithm to make division into regions.

The obtained clustering results show that the trend, input into the initial data, is reflected in the TP condition. This can be used in the analysis of the repeatability and stability of TP, as well as for controlling and optimization of the modes in the entire CETP of phosphorus production.

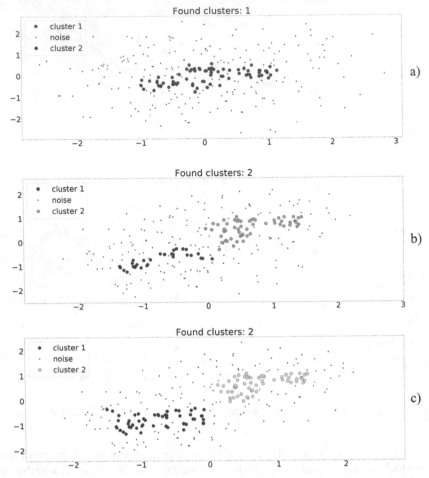

Fig. 4. Visualization of results for TP condition clustering

5   Conclusion

As a result of the work done, an algorithmic structure of infoware is proposed for assessing the condition of the technological process for the production of phosphorus from apatite-nepheline ore waste. The structure is based on the two-stage data processing characterizing the TP condition: at the first stage the TP condition is forecasted using the ensemble of recurrent neural networks, at the second stage the density clustering of the obtained forecasting data is carried out.

The description of the software implementation for the proposed algorithmic structure of infoware is given and the results of a simulating experiment with a data set simulating the technological parameters of CETP for phosphorus production are presented.

The results of the work can be used in the algorithmic support of ASCTP in various application areas where a forecast for assessing the TP condition, as well as analysis of its repeatability and stability, is required.

Acknowledgments. The reported study was funded by RFBR according to the research projects (No 19-01-00425 and No 18-29-24094).

References

1. Kutsependic, V.I., Yakovleva, E.S., Permyakova, O.V.: About the condition of technological processes. Processing of Solid and Layered Materials, no. 1 (2010). https://cyberleninka.ru/article/n/otsenka-sostoyaniya-tehnologicheskih-protsessov. Accessed 05 Apr 2020
2. Voinov, N., Chernorutsky, I., Drobintsev, P., Kotlyarov, V.: An approach to net-centric control automation of technological processes within industrial IoT systems. Adv. Manuf. 5(4), 388–393 (2017). https://doi.org/10.1007/s40436-017-0195-4
3. Ambartsumyan, A.A.: Network-centric control based on Petri nets in the structured discrete-event system. Autom. Remote Control 73, 1227–1241 (2012). https://doi.org/10.1134/S000 05117912070120
4. Sholle F. Deep Learning in Python. SPb.: Peter (2018). 400 p.
5. Meshalkin, V.P., Puchkov, A.Yu., Dli, M.I., Bobkov, V.I.: Generalized Model for engineering and controlling a complex multistage chemical energotechnological system for processing apatite-nepheline ore wastes. Theor. Found. Chem. Eng. 53, 463–471 (2019)
6. Bobkov, V.I., Borisov, V.V., Dli, M.I., Meshalkin, V.P.: Multicomponent fuzzy model for evaluating the energy efficiency of chemical and power engineering processes of drying of the multilayer mass of phosphorite pellets. Theor. Found. Chem. Eng. 52(5), 786–799 (2018)
7. Sevost'yanov, P.A., Ordov, K.V., Monakhov, V.I.: Detection of violations of technological process dynamics by structural analysis method. Fibre Chem. 48(1), 75–78 (2016). https://doi.org/10.1007/s10692-016-9743-0
8. Donges, J.F., Schleussner, C.-F., Siegmund, J.F., Donner, R.V.: Event coincidence analysis for quantifying statistical interrelationships between event time series. Eur. Phys. J. Spec. Top. 225(3), 471–487 (2016). https://doi.org/10.1140/epjst/e2015-50233-y
9. Singh, P., Huang, Y.-P.: A high-order neutrosophic-neuro-gradient descent algorithm-based expert system for time series forecasting. Int. J. Fuzzy Syst. 21(7), 2245–2257 (2019). https://doi.org/10.1007/s40815-019-00690-2
10. Donate, J.P., Li, X., Sánchez, G.G., et al.: Time series forecasting by evolving artificial neural networks with genetic algorithms, differential evolution and estimation of distribution algorithm. Neural Comput. Appl. 22, 11–20 (2013). https://doi.org/10.1007/s00521-011-0741-0
11. Vilela, L.F.S., Leme, R.C., Pinheiro, C.A.M., Carpinteiro, O.A.S.: Forecasting financial series using clustering methods and support vector regression. Artif. Intell. Rev. 52(2), 743–773 (2018). https://doi.org/10.1007/s10462-018-9663-x
12. Solovich, I.O., Belov, Yu.S.: Lucas-Kanade method application to calculate optical flow. Eng. J. Sci. Innov., 7 (2014). http://engjournal.ru/catalog/pribor/optica/1275.html
13. Carbune, V., et al.: Fast multi-language LSTM-based online handwriting recognition. Int. J. Doc. Anal. Recognit. (IJDAR) 23(2), 89–102 (2020). https://doi.org/10.1007/s10032-020-00350-4
14. Ma, Z., Sun, Z.: Time-varying LSTM networks for action recognition. Multimed. Tools Appl. 77(24), 32275–32285 (2018). https://doi.org/10.1007/s11042-018-6260-6

15. Wang, L., Liu, R.: Human activity recognition based on wearable sensor using hierarchical deep LSTM networks. Circuits Syst. Signal Process. **39**(2), 837–856 (2019). https://doi.org/10.1007/s00034-019-01116-y

16. Frazão, X., Alexandre, L.A.: Weighted convolutional neural network ensemble. In: Bayro-Corrochano, E., Hancock, E. (eds.) CIARP 2014. LNCS, vol. 8827, pp. 674–681. Springer, Cham (2014). https://doi.org/10.1007/978-3-319-12568-8_82

17. Koitka, S., Friedrich, C.M.: Optimized convolutional neural network ensembles for medical subfigure classification. In: Jones, G.J.F., Lawless, S., Gonzalo, J., Kelly, L., Goeuriot, L., Mandl, T., Cappellato, L., Ferro, N. (eds.) CLEF 2017. LNCS, vol. 10456, pp. 57–68. Springer, Cham (2017). https://doi.org/10.1007/978-3-319-65813-1_5

18. Marushko, E.E., Doudkin, A.A.: Ensembles of neural networks for forecasting of time series of spacecraft telemetry. Opt. Mem. Neural Netw. **26**(1), 47–54 (2017). https://doi.org/10.3103/S1060992X17010064

19. Kim, J.-H., Choi, J.-H., Yoo, K.-H., Nasridinov, A.: AA-DBSCAN: an approximate adaptive DBSCAN for finding clusters with varying densities. J. Supercomput. **75**(1), 142–169 (2018). https://doi.org/10.1007/s11227-018-2380-z

20. Saeedi Emadi, H., Mazinani, S.M.: A novel anomaly detection algorithm using DBSCAN and SVM in wireless sensor networks. Wirel. Pers. Commun. **98**(2), 2025–2035 (2017). https://doi.org/10.1007/s11277-017-4961-1

21. Chesnokov, M.Yu.: Time series anomaly searching based on DBSCAN ensembles. Sci. Tech. Inf. Process. **46**(5), 299–305 (2019). https://doi.org/10.3103/S0147688219050010

22. Geron, Au.: Applied Machine Learning Using Scikit-Learn and TensorFlow: Concepts, Tools and the Technique for Intellectual Systems Creation. Dialectic, Moscow (2018)

23. Faust, K., Xie, Q., Han, D., et al.: Visualizing histopathologic deep learning classification and anomaly detection using nonlinear feature space dimensionality reduction. BMC Bioinform. **19**, 173 (2018). https://doi.org/10.1186/s12859-018-2184-4

The Concept of Support for Laser-Based Additive Manufacturing on the Basis of Artificial Intelligence Methods

Valeria Gribova⑩, Yuriy Kulchin⑩, Alexander Nikitin⑩,
and Vadim Timchenko(✉) ⑩

IACP FEB RAS, Vladivostok, Russian Federation
{gribova,kulchin,anikitin,vadim}@dvo.ru

Abstract. A general concept of software and information support for laser-based additive manufacturing of metal parts from powder compositions is proposed. It is based on an ontological two-level approach to the formation of knowledge about the processes of laser additive manufacturing. For such an approach, the ontology is clearly separated from the knowledge base. So, domain specialists can create and maintain knowledge without intermediaries in terms and representation that they understand. The conceptual architecture of the decision support software for laser-based additive manufacturing processes is presented. Its information and software components are described. Information components are ontologies, databases of laser-based additive manufacturing system components, databases of materials for additive manufacturing, knowledge base and case database. The knowledge base contains formalized information on the settings of laser-based additive manufacturing modes that ensure compliance of the obtained metal parts with the requirements of the current industry-specific guidelines. The case database contains a structured description of the protocols for using laser technological equipment for additive manufacturing of metal parts from powder compositions. Software components are editors for creating and maintaining data and knowledge bases, decision support system based on both knowledge and cases and tool for cases structuring. There are also external tools for mathematical modelling of directed energy deposition physico-chemical processes. When making decisions, it is proposed to use a hybrid approach that combines knowledge engineering methods and case-based search by analogy. The feature of the approach is the continuous updating of the knowledge base due to its improvement by experts and due to its verification in the process of accumulating cases.

Keywords: Decision support systems · Laser-based additive manufacturing · Laser technological equipment · Directed energy deposition · Ontologies for laser-based additive manufacturing

1 Introduction

Technologies of additive construction, restoration or modification of complex functional metal products are increasingly used in various sectors of economy [1–3]. Additive

S. O. Kuznetsov et al. (Eds.): RCAI 2020, LNAI 12412, pp. 403–415, 2020.
https://doi.org/10.1007/978-3-030-59535-7_30

technologies make it possible to implement any design ideas in high-tech industries, such as aircraft, rocket production, shipbuilding and medicine with minimal costs.

However, the insufficient number of highly qualified specialists in the field of metal- and laser-based additive manufacturing (AM) is a serious obstacle to the widespread implementation of this advanced technology in production processes. The complexity of setting up a laser system for a specific technological task is due to the variety of processed materials, different requirements for processing and its results, as well as the adjustable parameters of laser equipment.

Most of the existing knowledge is based on rules of thumb and experimental studies [4]. Many of the additive manufacturing guidelines currently available are highly dependent on the specific technological equipment and/or materials used. This ultimately slows down the development of standards and production guidelines for setting process parameters [5].

Creating and embedding intelligent support of technological processes in existing AM systems will make up for the lack of practical experience of operators of such systems. This will also significantly reduce the qualification requirements for operators, as well as the costs of production and waste recycling. At the same time, situations when the manufacturing is economically dependent on the process operator with extensive experience and skills in this field are almost eliminated. Losses on training of a new specialist can negatively affect the economic condition of the company. It takes years of hard work and a large amount (hundreds of kilograms) of expensive powder raw material for a new specialist to acquire the necessary skills to perform the necessary adjustment of the AM system [6].

In this regard, the task of creating software for intelligent support of laser-based additive manufacturing of functional metal parts from powder compositions, is urgent. This software is intended for automating the setting of controlled parameters of technological processes that ensure compliance of the manufactured products (parts) with the requirements of the current industry-specific guidelines.

This paper describes the general concept of software and information support for laser-based additive manufacturing of metal products (parts) from powder compositions based on artificial intelligence methods.

Here we consider one of the most promising types of additive technologies (according to, for instance [7, 8]), known as Directed Energy Deposition (DED). Also it's known as Direct Metal Deposition or Laser Metal Deposition. This is an AM process in which focused thermal energy from an external source (e.g. a high-power laser, in the case of laser-based AM) is used to fuse materials as they are being deposited.

2   Tools for Supporting Operators of Metal-Based AM Equipment

Modern technology of laser-based additive manufacturing of metal products from powder compositions is based on both developed theoretical models and numerous experimental data, including the practical experience of qualified engineers-technologists. Based on theoretical and experimental results, research teams of both scientific and educational institutions and industrial organizations are developing decision support systems (DSS). These systems assist process engineers in setting up the most optimal parameters for laser technological processes of materials processing [9–14].

However, the problem of creating a DSS mentioned above and interfacing of such systems with specific laser equipment has not been sufficiently solved yet for a number of reasons. Moreover, it is also stated that to date, these works are not systematic, limited to laboratory research and do not have the ultimate goal of creating software for the intelligent supporting of metal-based AM equipment operators [15]. One of the main reasons for this situation is the lack of opened (non-proprietary) technological platforms to support professional cross-disciplinary cooperation of research groups.

Currently, researchers from both industrial and academic backgrounds are working to achieve a better understanding of how different physico-chemical processes of laser-based AM impact on the construction of metal parts. In [5, 16, 17] discusses how the ontological approach can provide a fundamental platform for:

- the conceptualization of various models and parameters of complex additive manufacturing processes that can be easily integrated with each other;
- building composite, reusable models of additive manufacturing processes;
- providing the possibility for standardization of descriptions and coordination of efforts of various research groups.

Thus, in [17] it is noted that the development of an explicit ontological structure of the laser-based AM process, on the basis of which information (knowledge) about various models and parameters of AM and their relationships can be formalized, is the first important step towards their reuse, as well as to a comprehensive understanding of the processes of laser-based AM of metal products (parts) from powder compositions.

The current state of affairs related to the formalization of knowledge about AM is based on descriptive logics, as well as on the formalism of category theory (so-called category ontologies) [5]. These formalisms are used to describe various ontologies of AM, such as design ontology [5, 18, 19] and process ontology [5, 17]. In these papers the ontology (metamodel) which allows specification of laser models, thermal models, mechanical properties of metal parts model, microstructure model, as well as various groups of parameters and the relationships between them for the AM process of Powder Bed Fusion (PBF) technology is presented. For the development of the ontology [16, 17] the Protégé editor [20] is used.

In opinion of the researchers introducing ontological (metamodeling) approach in AM, such attempt of standardization can bring a great benefit to the community of specialists in AM. Ontologies and metamodels are considered as a means of increasing the structuring and unification of specifications in the development of AM models. It should be noted that this is also true for other (not only additive) laser-based technological processes of material processing.

However, integration conceptual (meta-)models in AM per se are useful, first of all, for already experienced specialists and standards developers in this field. Operators of industrial technological systems (machines) for AM need software products based on such models. The software should assist in the setting of configurable process parameters that would ensure compliance of manufactured metal products (parts) with the requirements of regulatory documents. Therefore, as noted in [21], the development of these studies should be the creation of web-services based on the ontology of AM, to which all interested users can have free access in order to obtain as well as update knowledge about the AM processes. The ultimate goal is to provide rapid and accurate predictive modelling of various AM processes.

Thus, the development of a software package for improving the level of information support for process engineers who perform technological operations in laser-based additive manufacturing (restoration, modification) of metal products (parts) is an urgent task.

3 Decision Support Software for Laser-Based Additive Manufacturing Processes

The main requirements that are necessary for the development of software for decision support of laser-based additive manufacturing (restoration, modification) of functional metal products (parts) from powder compositions are flexibility and extensibility, as well as accessibility and ease of use by engineers-technologists – operators of the laser technological equipment.

To meet these requirements, it is proposed to use an ontological two-level approach to the formation of knowledge about the processes of laser-based AM of metal products (parts). In this approach, the ontology is clearly separated from the knowledge base. It is formed by knowledge engineers together with experts. Further, in terms of this ontology, experts without intermediaries, form knowledge in terms and representation that they understand (ontologies and knowledge bases are represented by semantic networks) [22, 23]. It is also proposed to use cloud technologies to provide easy, cross-platform access to cloud data and knowledge banks, tools for their formation, as well as a decision support software [24].

Together with experts – experienced specialists in additive technology of direct laser growing of metal products from powder compositions, the domain was analyzed. The main parameters of the components of the laser technological equipment that affect the course of the laser-based additive manufacturing process and determine its result, which should be taken into account by the process engineer, were determined.

As a result of the analysis, information and software components of the decision support software for the processes of laser-based additive manufacturing were identified (see Fig. 1).

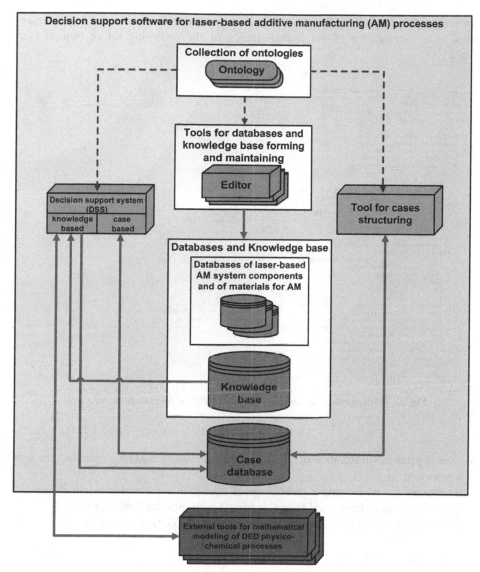

Fig. 1. Conceptual scheme of the decision support software for laser-based additive manufacturing processes

3.1   Information Components

The information components of the decision support software include the following types of information: ontologies, knowledge, and data.

Ontologies. This group of information components includes a set of the following related ontologies.

Ontology of Technological Operations. Input information for each technological operation is a specification of the characteristics of the following set of objects (see Fig. 2)[1]:

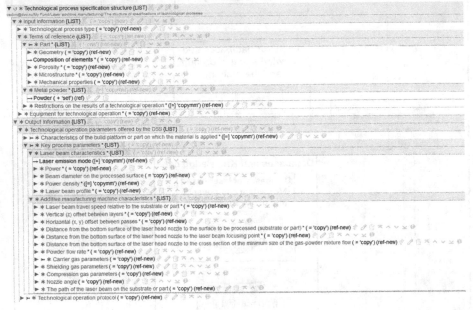

Fig. 2. A fragment of the ontology of technological operations (screenshot)

- type of process – restoration of a part, functional coating cladding, manufacturing of a new part;
- equipment for performing a technological operation – technological (high-power) laser, complete technological laser (cladding) head, powder feeder, etc.
- formalized terms of reference for performing a technological operation.

The latter includes:

- requirements for the shape, structure, characteristics of the final metal part: geometrical dimensions, surface roughness, porosity, hardness (HB, HV), microstructure, residual stress, etc.;
- characteristics of the processed part: geometric form, composition of elements (chemical composition), optical, thermophysical properties of the part material, metallurgical properties (in the case of the part restoration or functional coating cladding);
- metal powder used and possibly process gases used.

---

[1] This (and all the following) figure shows the interface of the IACPaaS cloud platform tool "Ontology Editor", which is used for creating ontologies in the platform's Fund [24].

Output information for technological operation is a specification of the characteristics of the following set of objects.

- Settings of controlled process parameters of the technological operation: laser power; laser emission mode (continuous, pulse); beam diameter on the processed surface; linear velocity of the laser beam moving on the surface; vertical (z) offset between layers; horizontal (x, y) offset between passes; powder flow rate, carrier, shielding and compression gas flow rate; etc. This may also include process gases recommended for use (if they have not been specified in the terms of reference).
- Characteristics of the substrate on which the part is grown (in the case of manufacturing of a new part). Except for the geometric form, they largely coincide with the set of characteristics describing the part being processed.
- Formalized operation protocol.

In addition to the mandatory "technical" information (number, date, name of operation, etc.) the latter includes:

- the settings of controlled process parameters of the technological operation actually selected by the operator of the equipment (they may either coincide with the proposed DSS, or differ from them);
- the result of the technological operation – a part with characteristics that meet or do not meet the requirements formulated in the terms of reference.

To provide a unified and standardized (including agreed vocabulary) description of equipment and materials for laser-based additive manufacturing, the following ontologies are also included in the set of ontologies.

Ontologies for the databases of the laser technological equipment (as AM system) *components*: technological (high-power) lasers (see Fig. 3); complete technological laser (cladding) heads; industrial robotics that provide moving the head on the processed surface; powder feeders.

Ontology of metal powders database for the specification of data from the field of materials science and engineering as well as powder metallurgy, such as grain size distribution and percentage of the basic fraction, composition of elements (chemical composition), melting point or melting range, flowability, apparent density, etc. (see Fig. 4).

Ontology of the process gas database for specification of such process gas characteristics as its name, brand, grade etc.

In order to form (create and maintain) knowledge on the basis of which decisions on the optimal modes of laser-based additive manufacturing are made, the set of ontologies includes a *knowledge base ontology*.

The knowledge base is formed by qualified technologists, based on their own experience and information from non-formal sources (manuals, scientific articles, documented experimental results). In addition, as a result of using the DSS, a case database (formalized protocols on technological operations performed) will be expanded. Cases will be used, first, for case-based reasoning (when there aren't too many cases), or for building

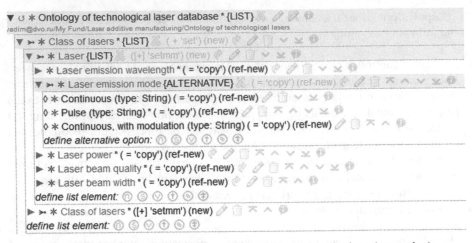

Fig. 3. A fragment of the ontology of technological lasers database (screenshot)

a knowledge base using inductive knowledge base formation methods (when amount of sampling is sufficient for training).

In this regard, the set of ontologies also includes the *case database ontology*, according to which a structured set of formalized protocols (reports) on technological operations is formed (see Fig. 5).

Each case can belong to one of the following classes:

1. the correct and accurate solution is proposed;
2. the correct but inaccurate solution is proposed (several possible alternatives, including the correct solution);
3. the wrong solution is proposed (a set of alternatives, possibly empty, among which there is no correct solution);
4. no solutions are proposed (a report was created, but the DSS could not propose a solution, the operator-technologist made the decision based on his/her experience).

Databases and Knowledge Base. This group of information components includes *data* and *knowledge bases* formed on the basis of corresponding ontologies. Databases contain information about *components of the laser-based AM system and about materials for AM*. Also, these databases contain information on quality assurance activities that should be regularly carried out for equipment and powder material (the so-called organizational methods of quality assurance).

The *knowledge base* on the settings of laser-based additive manufacturing (restoration, modification) modes that ensure compliance of the obtained metal products (parts) with the requirements of the current industry-specific guidelines (regulatory documents for this type of parts/products).

The knowledge base contains formally presented relationships between the composition and properties of the deposited powder materials, deposition mode (a set of adjustable process parameters and system settings), as well as the gas environment that

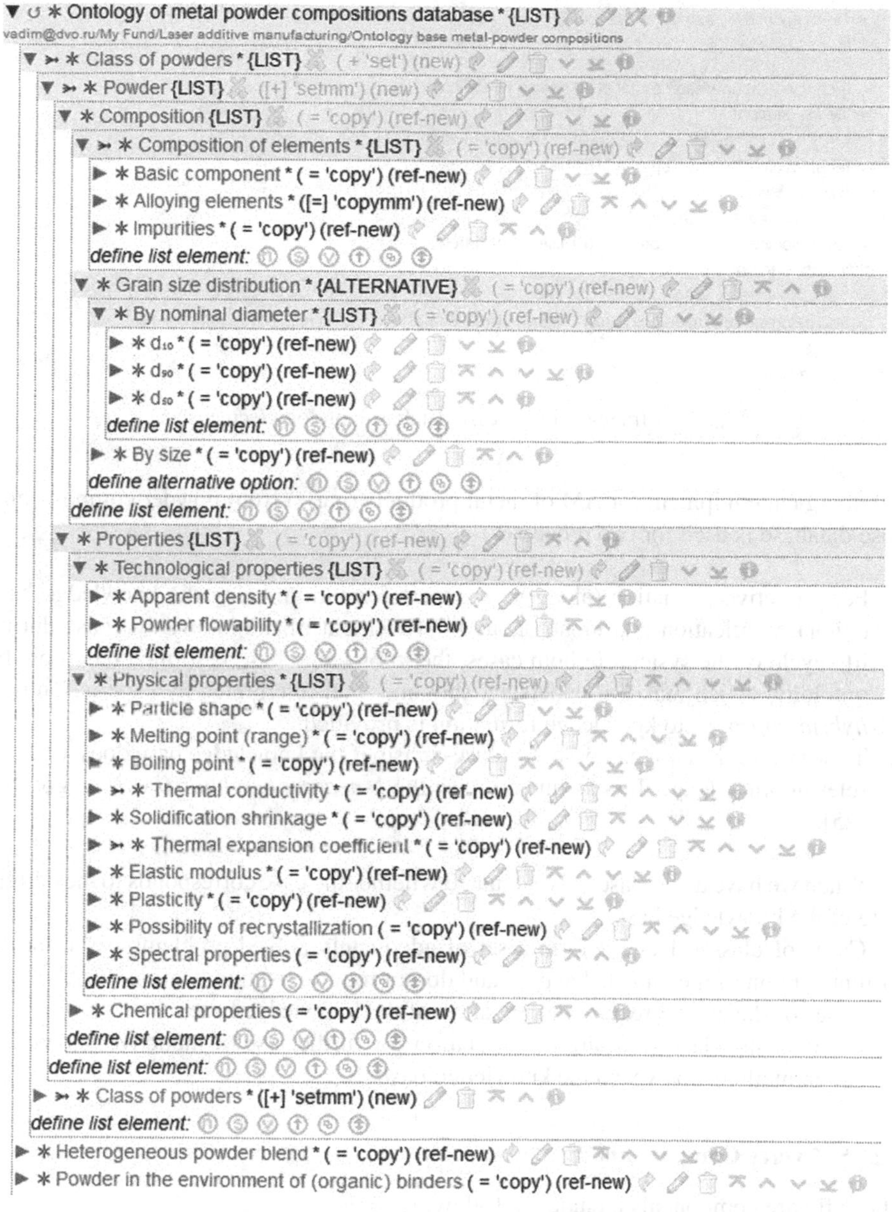

Fig. 4. A fragment of the ontology of metal powders database (screenshot)

should be provided during deposition process, and the properties of the final products (parts).

In addition to data and knowledge bases, the information components of the decision support software include a *case database* formed on the basis of the corresponding ontology. This database contains a structured description of the protocols for using laser

Fig. 5. A fragment of the case database ontology (screenshot)

technological equipment for AM of metal products (parts) from powder compositions. Case database is used for two processes.

1. For inductive formation (along with expert formation, using the knowledge base editor), verification and monotonous improvement of the knowledge base during life cycle of the system. In both cases, the knowledge base is formed based on the ontology, which makes it understandable and well interpreted by experts. Thus, a *hybrid approach* to knowledge formation is provided.
2. To search in the case database the closest case, if the knowledge base does not have relevant knowledge. It is assumed to use the *k-nearest neighbor* (*k-NN*) algorithm [25].

When we have a new case, it is evaluated whether the case corresponds to the current state of the knowledge base.

Cases of classes 1 and 2 form a set of adequately solved problems based on the current version of the knowledge base and do not require its modification.

Cases of the class 3 require modification of the knowledge base.

Cases of the class 4 require accumulation for further use of inductive knowledge formation methods to expand the knowledge base.

3.2 Software Components

The software components include the following tools.

Editors for creating and maintaining data and knowledge bases controlled by the corresponding ontologies. Editors have several types of user interfaces and automatically adapt to changes in ontologies.

A *decision support system*, based on input information for a technological operation, as well as information from a knowledge base and a case database, generates recommendations to the process engineer on configuring the control parameters of the laser technological equipment ensuring compliance of the manufactured part with the requirements formulated in the terms of reference.

The development of an ontology-based decision support system is aimed at its adaptation (development) without modifying the program source code.

The tool for structuring of cases accumulated as a result of using the decision support system is intended for analyzing the next new case and including it in the case database, referring to one of the four classes.

The control parameters of the technological process must be selected based on an understanding of laser radiation process and the flow of powder, heat and mass transfer, as well as other physical and chemical processes of the DED technology.

This requires interaction of the decision support system with *external tools of mathematical modeling of physico-chemical processes* that accompany the DED technology. Such tools should perform calculations of the necessary parameters based on appropriate mathematical models from the field of laser physics, laser chemistry, and thermal models that describe rapidly occurring thermal processes [26, 27].

4   Conclusion

Additive manufacturing using laser robotic systems is a quite new technology compared to conventional methods of manufacturing metal products (parts). There are many serious obstacles and, at the same time, opportunities for improving this technology in order to integrate it in various industrial processes. The modern approach to solving this problem is to automate the technological processes (operations) of additive manufacturing using intelligent technologies.

The paper presents the concept of software for information support of laser additive manufacturing of metal products (parts) from powder compositions based on ontologies and artificial intelligence methods. The conceptual architecture of the software is described.

We propose a hybrid approach to solving the problem of decision support in the field of laser-based additive manufacturing, which combines knowledge engineering methods and case-based search by analogy. The feature of the approach is the continuous updating of the knowledge base due to its improvement by experts and due to its verification in the process of accumulating cases.

Based on the proposed concept, a knowledge portal of technological processes (operations) of additive manufacturing of metal products (parts) using laser technological equipment was created on the IACPaaS cloud platform. To date, a number of information and software components of the knowledge portal have been developed, and the work is continuing to create new components and improve existing ones.

The integration of data and knowledge bases in the knowledge portal will make it easier for the interested community to access this information. Such data and knowledge bases will be useful in the process of training laser equipment operators, and formalized representation of knowledge and data will provide the possibility of using this information by software systems.

Acknowledgments. This work was partially supported by the Russian Foundation for Basic Research (project numbers 20-01-00449, 19-07-00244).

References

1. Frazier, W.E.: Metal additive manufacturing: a review. J. Mater. Eng. Perform. **23**, 1917–1928 (2014)
2. Sedlak, J., Rican, D., Piska, M., Rozkosny, L.: Study of materials produced by powder metallurgy using classical and modern additive laser technology. Procedia Eng. **100**, 1232–1241 (2015)
3. Tack, P., Victor, J., Gemmel, P., Annemans, L.: 3D printing techniques in a medical setting: a systematic literature review. BioMedical Eng. OnLine **15**(115), 1–21 (2016)
4. Yang, L., et al.: Additive Manufacturing of Metals: The Technology, Materials, Design and Production. Springer, Cham (2017). https://doi.org/10.1007/978-3-319-55128-9
5. Qi, Q., Pagani, L., Scott, P., Xiang, J.: A categorical framework for formalising knowledge in additive manufacturing. Procedia CIRP **75**, 87–91 (2018)
6. Thomas, D.S.: Economics of additive manufacturing. In: Bian, L., Shamsaei, N., Usher, J. (eds.) Laser-Based Additive Manufacturing of Metal Parts: Modeling, Optimization, and Control of Mechanical Properties. CRC Press, Boca Raton (2017)
7. Bourell, D., et al.: Materials for additive manufacturing. CIRP Ann. Manuf. Technol. **66**(2), 659–681 (2017)
8. Thompson, S.M., Bianc, L., Shamsaeia, N., Yadollahi, A.: An overview of direct laser deposition for additive manufacturing; Part I: transport phenomena, modeling and diagnostics. Addit. Manuf. **8**, 36–62 (2015)
9. Mayorov, V.S., Mayorov, S.V., Sternin, M.Yu.: Computer decision support systems for laser technological processes of material processing. In: Panchenko, V.M. (ed.) Laser technologies of material processing: modern problems of fundamental research and applied development, pp. 494–506. Fizmatlit, Moscow (2009)
10. Bessmeltsev, V.P., Bulushev, E.D., Goloshevsky, N.V.: An expert system for laser microprocessing mode optimization. J. Instrum. Eng. **54**(2), 17–22 (2011)
11. Aminzadeh, M., Kurfess, T.R.: Online quality inspection using Bayesian classification in powder-bed additive manufacturing from high-resolution visual camera images. J. Intell. Manuf. **30**(6), 2505–2523 (2018). https://doi.org/10.1007/s10845-018-1412-0
12. Wirth, F., Wegener, K.: A physical modeling and predictive simulation of the laser cladding process. Addit. Manuf. **22**, 307–319 (2018)
13. Qi, X., Chen, G., Li, Y., Cheng, X., Li, Ch.: Applying neural-network-based machine learning to additive manufacturing: current applications, challenges, and future perspectives. Engineering **5**(4), 721–729 (2019)
14. Dass, A., Moridi, A.: State of the art in directed energy deposition: from additive manufacturing to materials design. Coatings **9**(7), 418 (2019)
15. Babkin, K.D., et al.: High-speed laser direct deposition technology: theoretical aspects, experimental researches, analysis of structure, and properties of metallic products. In: Anisimov, K.V., et al. (eds.) Proceedings of the Scientific-Practical Conference "Research and Development - 2016", pp. 501–509. Springer, Cham (2018). https://doi.org/10.1007/978-3-319-62870-7_53
16. Witherell, P., et al.: Toward metamodels for composable and reusable additive manufacturing process models. J. Manuf. Sci. Eng. Trans. ASME **136**(6), 061025, 1–9 (2014)
17. Roh, B.M., Kumara, S.R.T., Simpson, T.W., Michaleris, P., Witherell, P., Assouroko, I.: Ontology-based laser and thermal metamodels for metal-based additive manufacturing. In: 36th Computers and Information in Engineering Conference (Proceedings of the ASME Design Engineering Technical Conference), vol. 1A-2016, pp. 1–8. ASME Digital Collection (2016)

18. Dinar, M., Rosen, D.W.: A design for additive manufacturing ontology. J. Comput. Inf. Sci. Eng. **17**(2), 021013, 1–9 (2017)
19. Jee, H., Witherell, P.: A method for modularity in design rules for additive manufacturing. Rapid Prototyp. J. **23**(6), 1107–1118 (2017)
20. Musen, M.A.: The Protégé project: a look back and a look forward. AI Matters **1**(4), 4–12 (2015)
21. Sanfilippo, E.M., Belkadi, F., Bernard, A.: Ontology-based knowledge representation for additive manufacturing. Comput. Ind. **109**, 182–194 (2019)
22. Gribova, V.V., Kleshchev, A.S., Shalfeeva, E.A.: Control of intelligent systems. J. Comput. Syst. Sci. Int. **49**(6), 952–966 (2010)
23. Gribova, V.V., Shalfeeva, E.A.: Ensuring of viability of systems based on knowledge. Inf. Technol. **25**(12), 738–746 (2019)
24. Gribova, V.V., Kleschev, A.S., Moskalenko, F.M., Timchenko, V.A., Fedorishchev, L.A., Shalfeeva, E.A.: IACPaaS cloud platform for the development of intelligent service shells: current state and future evolution. Softw. Syst. **31**(3), 527–536 (2018)
25. Varshavskii, P.R., Eremeev, A.P.: Modeling of case-based reasoning in intelligent decision support systems. Sci. Tech. Inf. Process. **37**(5), 336–345 (2010)
26. Heigel, J.C., Michaleris, P., Reutzel, E.W.: Thermo-mechanical model development and validation of directed energy deposition additive manufacturing of Ti–6Al–4V. Addit. Manuf. **5**, 9–19 (2015)
27. Raghavan, A., Wei, H.L., Palmer, T.A., DebRoy, T.: Heat transfer and fluid flow in additive manufacturing. J. Laser Appl. **25**(5), 1–8 (2013)

Artificial Intelligence, Biotechnology and Medicine: Reality, Myths and Trends

Vladimir F. Khoroshevsky[1]([⊠]) [ID], Vladimir F. Efimenko[2], and Irina V. Efimenko[2]

[1] Dorodnitcyn Computing Centre of RAS, Federal Research Centre I&C RAS, Moscow, Russia
khor@ccas.ru
[2] "Semantic Hub" LLC, Moscow, Russia
ie@semantic-hub.com

Abstract. An analytical review of R&D in AI-domain within the context of biotechnology, pharmaceutics, and medicine is presented. A comparative discussion of leading analytical agencies latest reports was carried out, and expanded by an analytical review of the literature in this domain, as well as by own scientometric analysis of publication activity at the junction of AI and medicine, biotechnology, and pharmaceutics according to PubMed in 2018–2020. Experts predictions and myths existing in this field are discussed.

Keywords: Artificial intelligence · Biotechnology · Medicine · Pharmaceutics · Scientometrics · Patent landscape · Intellectual analytics · Prognosis · Trend

1 Introduction

Currently, the utility of big data (BD) and artificial intelligence (AI) technologies is declared in various areas [1]. At the same time, healthcare in general, and biotechnology and the pharmaceutical industry, in particular, are considered as areas where AI technologies, when utilizing BD, can provide a significant effect. Search, extraction and analysis of increasingly complete information, which can ensure an effective solution to specific problems and is based on processing a combination of large and complex sets of structured and unstructured data of various nature, attracted an attention of specialists in recent years and, accordingly, significant resources. A volume of various information that should be considered can be exceptionally large. Therefore, as many experts note, the use of AI technologies seems to be most productive for carrying out long, repetitive, and "boring" work with such information [2].

Authors of various competency levels have already declared both sufficiently general motivations and directions of the AI use in healthcare (such as a transition to personalized and preventive medicine, development of new curing methods and strategies to improve the effectiveness of the healthcare system as a whole), and more specific ones (such as identification of patients with a high risk of certain diseases, forecasting epidemiological situations, studying specific features of human body functioning, etc.). In turn, many concrete tasks are set and solved within these areas. In addition to patient

© Springer Nature Switzerland AG 2020
S. O. Kuznetsov et al. (Eds.): RCAI 2020, LNAI 12412, pp. 416–436, 2020.
https://doi.org/10.1007/978-3-030-59535-7_31

care, a separate group of tasks related to pharmaceuticals can be considered. In biotechnology and pharmaceutical industry, the use of AI is expected at all stages, from search of novel drug candidates through drug development to bringing a drug to the market and commercialization. Here the main goals are:

– To make drug discovery, creation, clinical trials (including patient selection), approving results by regulators, as well as implementation and pharmacovigilance processes less costly, less time consuming and more efficient.
– To predict drug efficacy and side effects considering genetic features of patients, their medical histories, lifestyle, and other factors (predictive modeling).
– To accelerate promotion of products to consumers (pharmacies, medical institutions, doctors, pharmacists, patients), including collection and analysis of data on interests and preferences for each customer category, on channels used by clients to get information about drugs, on behavior of customers in various categories after receiving information, etc.

At the same time, according to some estimates [2], currently most efforts to develop and implement AI in pharma are undertaken for drug discovery. AI development for commercialization of drugs takes the second place in terms of efforts, and attention paid to AI in the drug development area is only on the third place.

The remainder of the publication is structured as follows. Section 2 focuses on discussing forecasts of experts and existing myths, as well as on review of projects, companies and organizations that actively and successfully use AI in the field of healthcare, biotechnology, and pharmaceuticals. The data of scientometric analysis of scientific publications and patent activity in this field are also presented here. In conclusion, the obtained results and current AI trends are summarized.

2 Artificial Intelligence in Healthcare, Biotechnology and Pharmaceutical Industry

2.1 Forecasts of Experts and Myths About Using AI

In mid-2019, the Gartner consulting company published the report "Hype Cycle for Artificial Intelligence 2019" presenting an analysis of AI trends [1]. It is stated in the report that there is a significant progress in application of AI technologies by various companies, although a significant number of problems appear, and many mistakes are made when implementing these technologies. According to the authors, the report presents a landscape of research and development in the field of AI, that should help companies implementing results obtained here in assessing their usefulness and risks. Gartner AI-2019 curve is shown in Fig. 1.

As for the general recommendations presented in the report the following issues should be noted. On the "Innovation trigger" part of the Gartner curve, the number of "participants" increased in 2019, reflecting the permanent influx of new and diverse ideas in the AI area. At the same time, there is a traffic jam on the "Peak of inflated expectations", the "Slope of enlightenment" is empty, and only a few points are registered

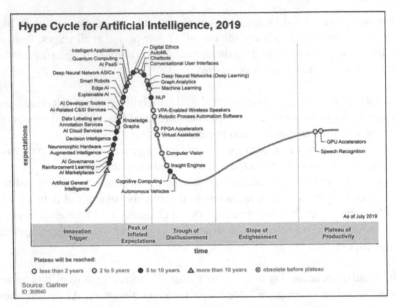

Fig. 1. Hype Cycle for Artificial Intelligence, 2019.

on the "Plateau of Productivity". This does not mean that AI is unsuitable for use, but only that at this stage there is a time of changes in the field of AI.

Not all AI aspects brought to this curve are directly related to the topic of the current work. Therefore, below (Table 1) only those AI technologies as well as already obtained and/or predicted results are presented, which, in our opinion, are important for biotechnology, pharmaceuticals and healthcare in general.

As the analysis of the Gartner curve (Fig. 1) and data from above Table 1 indicate, experts in their forecasts pay the main attention to leading IT vendors actively promoting AI technologies in various fields. Therefore, the table below (Table 2) presents structuring of hypes from the Gartner report with a justification of their importance for biotechnology, pharmaceuticals, and medicine.

2.2 Organizations and Projects

As the analysis of various information sources shows, more and more organizations in different countries declare the use of big data for healthcare. Examples here are [3], in particular, Comet K-Project DEXHELPP (Austria), The Shared Care Platform (Denmark), E-Estonia - National Identity Scheme (Estonia), The Business Intelligence database system (Greece), PASSI - Progressi delle Aziende Sanitarie (Italy), Interagrated BioBank of Luxembourg - IBBL (Luxembourg), Spanish Rare Diseases Registers Research Network - SpainRDR (Spain), The Swedish Big Data Analytic Network (Sweden), Clinical Practice Research Datalink - CPRD and UK Biobank (United Kingdom), The YODA (Yale University open data access) Project (USA), FDA Adverse Event Network Analyzer (USA), etc.

Table 1. AI technologies important for biotechnology, pharmaceutical industry, and healthcare in general

Hypes features in gartner's predictions					
Stage	Hype	Benefit rating	Market penetration	Maturity	Sample vendors
On the rise	Reinforcement learning	High	<1% of target audience	Embryonic	Amazon SageMaker RL; CogitAI; Facebook; Google (Dopamine)
	AI governance	High	<1% of target audience	Embryonic	
	Decision intelligence	High	1÷5% of target audience	Emerging	ACTICO; Exponential Machines; Noodle.ai; PROWLER.io; r4 Technologies; R4; ReactiveCore
	Data labeling and annotation services	Moderate	20÷50% of target audience	Early mainstream	Alegion; Amazon SageMaker Ground Truth; Apache Hive; CloudFactory; Directly; Figure Eight; Globalme; Labelbox; Mapillary; Prolific
	Knowledge graphs	High	1÷5% of target audience	Emerging	Attivio; Diffbot; Facebook; Intelligent Views; Maana; Neo4j; Semantic Web Company (PoolParty); Skelter Labs; Smartlogic; TopQuadrant
	Explainable AI	High	1÷5% of target audience	Emerging	H2O.ai; IBM; Microsoft; simMachines
At the peak	Intelligent applications	Transform	1÷5% of target audience	Emerging	Google Docs; Microsoft Office 365; Oracle Applications; Salesforce Einstein; SAP Leonardo; ServiceNow; Workday
	Digital ethics	High	5÷20% of target audience	Adolescent	
	AutoML	High	1÷5% of target audience	Emerging	Amazon SageMaker; Big Squid; dotData; DataRobot; Google (Cloud Platform); H2O.ai; KNIME; RapidMiner; Sky Tree
	Conversational user interfaces	Transform	5÷20% of target audience	Adolescent	Amazon; Baidu; Facebook; Google; IBM; IPsoft; Microsoft; Oracle; Salesforce; SAP
	Deep neural networks (Deep learning)	Transform	5÷20% of target audience	Adolescent	Amazon; Baidu; Clarifai; DimensionalMechanics; Google; H2O.ai; Matroid; NVIDIA; Skymind; TwentyBN

(*continued*)

Table 1. (*continued*)

Hypes features in gartner's predictions

Stage	Hype	Benefit rating	Market penetration	Maturity	Sample vendors
	Graph analytics	High	1÷5% of target audience	Adolescent	Cambridge Semantics; Centrifuge Systems; Databricks; Digital Reasoning; Emcien; Maana; Palantir; Symphony AyasdiAI; SynerScope
	Machine learning	Transform	5÷20% of target audience	Adolescent	Alteryx; Amazon Web Services; Dataiku; Google Cloud Platform; H2O.ai; IBM (SPSS); KNIME; Microsoft (Azure Machine Learning); RapidMiner; SAS
	NLP	Transform	5÷20% of target audience	Emerging	Bitext; Clarabridge; CognitiveScale; Digital Reasoning; Google; IBM Watson; Microsoft; Narrative Science; SAS; Yseop
Sliding into the trough	VPA-enabled wireless speakers	Transform	5÷20% of target audience	Early mainstream	Ainemo; Alibaba Cloud; Amazon; Apple; Baidu; Google; Lenovo; LG
	Virtual assistants	Transform	5÷20% of target audience	Adolescent	Amazon; Apple; Google; IPsoft; Microsoft; Nuance; Openstream; Oracle; SAP; [24]7.ai
	Computer vision	High	5÷20% of target audience	Adolescent	Amazon Web Services; Baidu; Clarifai; Cortexica; Deepomatic; Google; IBM; Microsoft; Tencent
	Insight engines	High	5÷20% of target audience	Adolescent	Attivio; Coveo; Dassault Systèmes; Funnelback; IBM; Lucidworks; Micro Focus; Microsoft; Mindbreeze; Sinequa
Entering the plateau	Speech recognition	Transform	>50% of target audience	Mature mainstream	Amazon; Baidu; Cedat 85; Google; IBM; Intelligent Voice; Microsoft; NICE; Nuance; Speechmatics

In France, the Ministry of Industry has set up the ADR-PRISM (Adverse Drug Reactions from Patient Reports in Social Media) consortium to organize collection of information from the Internet about adverse drug effects. One of the objectives of the project was to provide text mining and visualization tools to explore posts extracted from social media. It is assumed that the software developed under the project will be used to identify via the Internet poorly documented or not yet discovered rare ADRs.

Table 2. Evaluation of the AI technologies most important for biotechnology, pharmaceutical industry, and medicine

Hype		Current importance to biotech, pharma & medicine	
Type	Subtype	Rating	Comments
Machine learning	Reinforcement learning	Middle	Machine learning approach based on interaction with the environment (a special case of learning with a teacher). Popular in the field of biotechnology, pharmaceuticals, and medicine, but suggests the presence of large labeled data
	Deep neural networks (Deep learning)	Middle	To use deep learning methods and tools in biotechnology, pharmaceuticals and medicine, you need powerful computers (to train large neural networks), sufficiently volumes data sets (so that training of large networks makes sense), new theoretically substantiated tools (to effectively train multilayer neural networks on each layer separately and integrate the results of such training)
	AutoML	Low	In general, a useful technological technique to the processes of building training models and choosing the "best" model automatization
Data acquiring & processing	Data labeling and annotation services	High	Fully 80% of AI project time is spent on gathering, organizing, and labeling data, and this is the time that can't afford to spend because they are in a race to usable data, which is data that is structured and labeled properly in order to train and deploy models
	NLP	High	The real use of large volumes of unstructured data, in particular, in machine learning, is impossible without NLP
Communication	Conversational user interfaces	Middle	Dialog interfaces become important in communication with patients in medical applications
	VPA-enabled wireless speakers	Middle	Speech understanding becomes important in communication with patients in medical applications

(*continued*)

Table 2. (*continued*)

Hype		Current importance to biotech, pharma & medicine	
Type	Subtype	Rating	Comments
	Virtual assistants	Middle	Intelligent assistants are one of communication components in almost all AI systems for biotechnology, pharmacy, and medicine
Analytics	Explainable AI	High	Explanation is one of the key functions of AI systems, and without it their use in practically meaningful applications is impossible
	Insight engines	High	Insights' generation based on available data is a critical functionality for AI systems in the field of biotechnology, pharmaceuticals and medicine
	Graph analytics	Middle	An important component of intellectual analytics, primarily for biotechnology and pharmaceuticals.
Applications	Digital ethics	High	An important area of AI for practically significant man-machine systems
	Decision intelligence	High	Decision support is one of the main goals of any AI system
	Intelligent applications	Middle	General trend
Support	Knowledge graphs	Middle	Useful for predictive analytics method of knowledge representatio
	Computer vision	High	An important approach for biotechnologies and intellectual diagnostics medical systems.
	Speech recognition	Middle	Important for medical applications

There are also joint projects in the European Union [3], where several countries participate, for example: AEGLE - An analytics framework for integrated and personalized healthcare services in Europe (Great Britain, Italy, Greece, Sweden, Belgium, Netherlands, Portugal, France), CEPHOS-LINK (Finland, Austria, Romania, Norway, Slovenia, Italy), SEMCARE - Semantic Data Platform for Healthcare (Germany, the Netherlands, Austria, Great Britain, Spain).

Cooperation on AI developments for general healthcare is also proceeding. So, early in 2019, the Alliance for Artificial Intelligence in Healthcare (AAIH) was formed - a coalition of technology developers, pharmaceutical companies, and research organizations, whose goal was improvement of care quality through innovations based on thoughtful and responsible use of AI, as well as establishing reasonable standards for the development and implementation of AI in healthcare. The alliance includes organizations of various profiles: Amazon WS, Bayer, Benevolent AI, Beyond Limits, BlackThorn Therapeutics, The Buck Institute for Research on Aging, Cyclica, Envisagenics, GE Healthcare,

Genialis Inc., GSK, Insilico Medicine, Janssen, Minds.ai, Netrias, NuMedii, Numerate, Nuritas, OWKIN, Progenics Pharmaceuticals, Recursion, SimplicityBio, University of Pittsburgh.

In the USA, in June 2016 it was announced about intentions to create, and in October 2017, the ATOM consortium (Accelerating Therapeutics for Opportunities in Medicine) was officially created to leverage artificial intelligence to go from preclinical cancer drug discovery to patient-ready therapy in just one year. The founding members of the consortium were GSK Pharmaceutical Company, Lawrence Livermore National Laboratory, Frederick National Laboratory for Cancer Research, and University of California, San Francisco.

Multilateral cooperation and bilateral relations are also established among pharmaceutical companies to combine efforts for development and/or application of AI technologies (first of all, machine learning) in the pharmaceutical industry. For example, the Machine Learning for Pharmaceutical Discovery and Synthesis Consortium (MLPDS) was organized by the Massachusetts Institute of Technology (MIT). The consortium included, along with the MIT departments (departments of Chemical Engineering, Chemistry, and Computer Science at MIT), such pharmaceutical and biotechnology companies as Amgen, AstraZeneka, BASF, Bayer, GSK, Janssen, Leo, Lilly, Merck, Novartis, Pfizer, Sunovion, Wuxi Pharmatech. It is expected that the collaboration of these organizations will facilitate the design of software tools for the automation of small molecule discovery and synthesis.

In June 2019, the MELLODDY (MachinE Learning Ledger Orchestration for Drug DiscoverY) project was launched in the European Union. The project aims to use machine learning methods on the chemical libraries of 10 pharmaceutical companies and to develop a platform creating models to predict which compounds could be promising in later stages of drug discovery and development [4]. In addition to the ten pharma companies, the list of project partners includes two academic universities, four subject matter startups, and a large AI computing company NVIDIA.

In 2014, the European Union's Innovative Medicine Initiative WEB-RADR (Recognizing Adverse Drug Reactions) project was initiated as a public-private partnership, where participating members were from European regulatory agencies, European pharmaceutical companies and associations, academic universities, patient groups with an interest in pharmacovigilance. The project primarily aimed to evaluate the value of social media data (i.e., information exchanged through the internet) and mobile applications for identifying adverse events as well as for drug safety signal detection. US experts also joined the activities. A collaborative English language workspace was developed, and recommendations were presented mainly based on data from Facebook and Twitter (for example, in [5]). As a key point of conclusions drawn after exploring the English language sector of the Internet, it was not recommended to use social media for broad statistical signal detection at the expense of other pharmacovigilance activities. In 2018, the WEB-RADR 2 project was launched with the aim to further develop functionality of applications for mobile devices, to map terminologies and to establish connectivity protocols with electronic health record databases.

To solve specific tasks, large pharmaceutical companies enter partnerships with startups using artificial intelligence in drug discovery. For example, [6] and [7] present some areas of activities where pharmaceutical companies cooperate with such partners to use their technologies and AI expertise. Several AI companies involved in various activities for drug discovery are also presented in [2].

Sometimes pharmaceutical companies acquire startups after accumulating a positive experience of cooperation with it. The Roche Pharmaceuticals can be mentioned as an example. Some large pharmaceutical companies have special units with a significant number of specialists in big data and AI areas. Examples of such companies are Novartis, where about ~240 big data and AI experts work at scientific institutes (Novartis Institutes for BioMedical Research (NIBR)), and GSK whose special AI department has about 50 specialists.

2.3 AI Technologies for Analysis of Texts in Social Networks and Electronic Health Records

The rapid development of communication and information technologies not only provided new opportunities for access to various sources of large textual data valuable for healthcare and pharmaceutical industry (for example, to various online forums of patients and medical professionals in social networks), but also contributed to the appearance and development of new sources of data specially collected for analysis (for example, speech samples, special applications for smartphones and other mobile devices, special social media sites, etc.) [8]. AI technologies are usually applied to analyze such data. AI technologies are also used in clinical practice, in particular, for automated processing of data in electronic health records (EHR). Electronic health records contain both structured and unstructured (free text) data. Often unstructured data provide a valuable additional information and/or more detailed information than structured data.

The task of automatic analysis of author sentiments in Internet messages came to the healthcare and drug safety areas from the areas of product commercialization and mining opinions of various social strata through social networks [9, 10]. Because of specific features of the medical area, a number of works deal with problems related to improvement of appropriate methods for text mining and sentiment analysis of patient messages in various forums, blogs, etc. on various issues of medical care, including assessment of physicians, clinics, and companies [11].

For the pharmaceutical industry the development of new technologies has also opened up additional ways of collecting information, including using social networks for access to a wider, as compared to clinical trials, experience of using drugs and attitude of patients and doctors to a specific drug. It is possible to receive earlier, than through standard channels, signals about suspected adverse drug reactions. There is an additional possibility of communication with consumers through social networking platforms and special applications, as well as capability of real-time monitoring of patients through mobile devices. Analysis of sentiments in medical and patient online communities helps to form a strategy during development of new drugs.

Although a number of reports by WEB-RADR participants (mainly from the UK and USA [5]) indicated limited value of social media in detecting or confirming signals for a majority of the drugs studied, as compared to conventional sources, the results of other authors are more optimistic (for example, for the French Internet sector [8]). In the ADR-PRISM project of the French Ministry of Industry, the research groups participate from such academic institutions providing expertise in medical informatics and statistics as the National Institute of Health and Medical Research, Paris Descartes University, INSERM U1138 - Team 22 (Information Sciences to Support Personalized Medicine); Service Catalog and Index of French Language medical websites SIBM-CISMeF et al. Other participants are the Innovative Projects - Text Mining, Expert System company, working in the field of software for analysis of Internet texts; pharmaceutical and epidemiology companies - Kappa Santé and INSERM CIC1418, Clinical Epidemiology, Hôpital Européen Georges-Pompidou, as well as the Vidal group company, which maintains a database of pharmaceutical products used in most systems for pharmaceutical prescription in France. As part of this project, in 2019 the standard protocol was proposed for evaluating software tools designed to identify adverse effects based on data from medical forums. The testing of the applied tools within the framework of the project is carried out with specific tasks.

A team of Canadian experts from the University of Toronto (Department of Computer Science, Department of Geriatric Medicine, Epidemiology Division) and the Li Ka Shing Knowledge Institute of St. Michael's Hospital reviewed [10] publications related to the detection of adverse effects in social networks. Journal articles, conference reports, books, publications on the Internet, as well as "gray" sources (preprints, etc.) were analyzed. 77 documents, which fully satisfied selection conditions, were published from 2001 to 2016, with 78% of them published from 2013 to 2016. 90% of authors were from North America and Europe. Posts extracted by authors of publications from the Internet were in English (86%), in French (3%), in Spanish (3%), in German and Serbian (1% each). It was noted that supervised machine learning was most often used in data processing (21%), semi-supervised machine learning was used in 7% and unsupervised one - in 6%. In 9%, rule-based learning was used. The authors results suggest that the use of social media conversations for pharmacovigilance is in its infancy [10].

Many publications on the development and application of AI technologies to automate the analysis of texts from social media are associated with the English language sector of the Internet [9, 10]. Activities on the analysis of texts from EHR are most advanced in the USA, where systems of accumulation and storage of medical information in electronic form are better established than elsewhere. At the same time, work is intensified in other language sectors, primarily related to alphabetical languages. As for ideographic languages that use hieroglyphs for writing texts, the works in Chinese organizations on texts in Chinese should be mentioned [11]. For example, the University of Science and Technology of China and the National University of Defense Technology Changsha, College of Computers, Hunan deal with general issues of automated processing of a natural language regardless of the subject area.

A keen interest in the development of AI technologies in medicine and pharmaceuticals is expressed in a significant number of surveys published by various organizations and highlighting the status of work in specific areas. For example, in 2019 alone, at least 5 surveys appeared prepared by organizations listed in Table 3. There are sites where information on companies and startups using AI in drugs discovery is monitored [6, 7] and updated at least twice a year.

Table 3. Survey reports in AI technology for medicine and pharmacy

Organization	Review name	Publication year [Ref.]
The University of Edinburgh, Usher Institute of Population Health Sciences and Informatics, Edinburgh, (Scotland, UK) Edinburgh Royal Infirmary, Department of Anaesthesia, Critical Care and Pain Medicine, Edinburgh, (Scotland, UK)	A systematic review of natural language processing for classification tasks in the field of incident reporting and adverse event analysis	2019 [12]
Fondazione Bruno Kessler Research Institute, Trento, Italy University of Trento, Department of Information Engineering and Computer Science, Trento, Italy University of Zurich, Institute of Computational Linguistics, Zurich, Switzerland Institute for Next Generation Healthcare, Icahn School of Medicine, Mount Sinai, NY, US	Natural Language Processing of Clinical Notes on Chronic Diseases: Systematic Review	2019 [13]
Columbia University, School of Nursing; Data Science Institute, NY, US University of Virginia, School of Nursing, Charlottesville, Virginia, US	Natural language processing of symptoms documented in free-text narratives of electronic health records: a systematic review	2019 [14]
SciMar ONE. Allentown, New Jersey, US	AI in Pharmaceuticals	2019 [2]
New York Genome Center, Department of Bioinformatics, NY, US	Artificial Intelligence for Drug Toxicity and Safety	2019 [15]
Mayo Clinic, Division of Biomedical Statistics and Informatics, Department of Health Sciences Research, Rochester, MN, US	Clinical information extraction applications: a literature review	2018 [11]

Thus, it can be stated that AI technologies are actively used both in healthcare as a whole and in biotechnology and pharmaceutical industry. An important role in these processes is played not only and not so much by leading IT vendors but by small, though strong research teams from leading universities in different countries and by startups. All these organizations and teams are currently used by leading pharmaceutical companies to accelerate development and implementation of new drugs while reducing risks and financial costs.

In view of the foregoing, in our opinion, the scientometric analysis of publications and patents at the intersection of AI and biotechnology, pharmaceutical industry and healthcare (as a whole) is of interest.

2.4 Scientometrics and Patent Landscapes of the Use of AI in Medicine, Biotechnology and Pharmaceutical Industry

In mid-2019, the authoritative intellectual property organization (The World Intellectual Property Organization, WIPO) presented the analytical report "WIPO Technology Trends 2019: Artificial Intelligence" [16], where, in particular, patent landscapes and scientific publication activity in the field of AI in medicine are discussed. With keep this in mind, some results of authors of this report are, in our opinion, of interest from the point of view of the topic of the current work. They are presented below.

As it is known, the current AI boom began about decade ago and followed a series of ups and downs, often referred to as "AI summers and winters". So, it is a good time to take a close look at the state of research and exploitation of AI technologies. And patents provide a valuable means of assessing trends in research as they reveal the areas of innovation that inventors are focused on. However, patents provide a part of the picture only, course much research is never patented. Therefore, WIPO report also includes analysis of scientific publications, identifying trends over time and by geography as well as by subject area.

One of the most striking characteristics of researches in AI is the rapid growth that has been seen over the past five years. The impressive numbers of patent filings in this period and the decrease in the ratio of number of scientific papers to inventions are indicative of a shift from theoretical research to the use of AI technologies in commercial products and services. This trend is also reflected in the types of patents being filed, with significant growth in specific AI applications and sector-specific fields. For example, time series are presented in Fig. 2. AI patent families and scientific publications by earliest publication year.

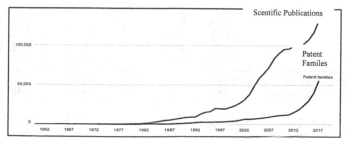

Fig. 2. AI patent families and scientific publications by earliest publication year.

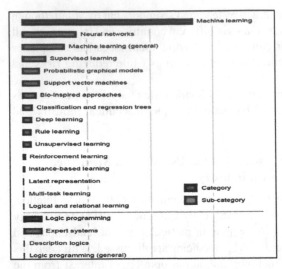

Fig. 3. AI patents filings by sub-categories.

It is interesting that, if to look beyond the total numbers of patent families and examine instead the average annual growth rate of filings in the different sub-categories, it is possible to observe that deep learning demonstrates by far the biggest recent growth in the field, with an impressive 175% average annual growth between 2013 and 2016. Other machine learning techniques show a similar very steep increase in filing growth rate in recent years, namely multi-task learning (49%) and neural networks (46%) (Fig. 3).

This recent interest in deep learning and neural networks is confirmed by data extracted from GitHub, a collaborative platform for open source software development, which evidence a constantly increasing number of repositories mentioning these techniques between 2014 and 2017, from 238 GitHub repositories mentioning neural networks and 43 mentioning deep learning in 2014, to 3,871 and 3,276 in 2017, respectively. Patent families by co-occurrence of application fields are presented in Table 4.

According to the values in this table main patent activities are observed in (Computer vision) + (Telecommunications, Personal devices, computing and HCI) and (Machine learning, Computer vision) + (Life and medical sciences). At the same time, (Natural language processing, Speech processing, Knowledge representation and reasoning, Predictive analytics) + (Life and medical sciences) that, for our opinion, are also significant to the usage of AI-technologies in medicine, biotech and pharma not show top results.

Table 4. Patent families by co-occurrence of application fields.

	Machine learning	Computer vision	Natural language processing	Speech processing	Knowledge representation and reasoning	Predictive analytics
Telecommunications	16201	22871	7553	12549	1292	1533
Personal devices, computing and HCI	11585	17164	7920	6678	1838	1069
Life and medical sciences	18772	17098	3818	2504	1698	1694
Document management and publishing	9709	7968	5850	2422	1820	2585
Education	3914	3767	1642	1951	532	247

There are two main trends are stand out if scientific publications on various machine learning approaches are compared with patenting activity: bio-inspired approaches are significantly more common in scientific publications than in patent filings. A similar trend is observed in neural networks, machine learning (general approaches) and multi-task learning; rule learning forms an exception to the overall trend and is significantly more common in patents than in scientific publications. And it is not spuriously course growing number of academic labs, established companies and startups are shifting their focus toward the field of precision medicine, that is, the design of therapies tailored for each individual patient. Progress in this field will require the systematic collection of a vast amount of clinical data from patients in each disease type and subtype. In turn, the availability of this data will allow AI to realize its full potential and answer clinically critical questions for each patient.

Since AI-related innovations are enabled by data, the organizations that generate the most AI-related patents are often the ones that own the most data. This explains many of the observations, in particular the surprisingly strong position of China – there are far fewer obstacles to collecting vast amounts of data in China than in other countries, and China has the best training data collections for speech recognition, human behavior modeling and medical data, for example.

Baidu started its layout of AI in 2010, pouring R&D efforts into natural language processing, speech processing, machine learning, computer vision, deep learning, knowledge graph, and other areas. In 2013, Baidu announced the world's first in-house institute focusing on the study of deep learning. In March 2017, Baidu set up a new business group, the Artificial Intelligence Group, to bring AI-related departments together, aiming to better develop AI technologies and promote AI applications. Baidu is now among the top AI players in the world, with more than 10,000 R&D engineers. Its annual R&D investment is about US $2 billion, and AI R&D accounts for a large proportion of that. Behind these results is a continuous growth of the AI talent pool in China thanks to the efforts of AI-related enterprises such as Baidu working with Chinese universities to accelerate technological innovation and talent cultivation. Chinese universities, research institutions and companies are working closely together to conduct AI-related research and make the resulting technology transfer smooth, by for example implementing AI talent training programs and setting up cooperative laboratories [16].

So, key players in an area that has seen significant recent growth, namely deep learning, are the Chinese Academy of Sciences (CAS), which is the leader in the deep learning sub-category of machine learning, and Baidu, followed by Alphabet, Siemens, Xiaomi, Microsoft, Samsung, IBM and NEC (Fig. 4).

As it is outlined in observed report [16], five steps to success at the Chinese Academy of Sciences are the following:

1. *Clarification of the objectives of intellectual property (IP) creation and application through the formulation and implementation of an intellectual property strategy.* In 2007, the Chinese Academy of Sciences (CAS) issued "Several Opinions on Further Strengthening the Work of Intellectual Property Rights," the first in a series of policies and regulations.

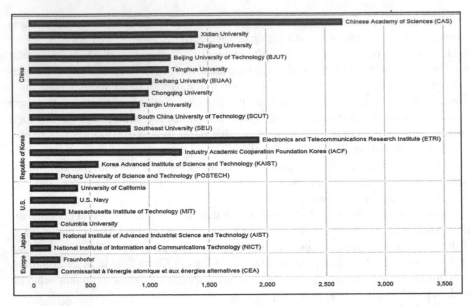

Fig. 4. Top patent applicants among universities and public research organizations.

2. *Building an IP work system.* The Intellectual Property Management Office was established in the Science and Technology Promotion and Development Bureau, and in 2016 the number of patent applications reached 14881.
3. *Vigorously carrying out IP training and information.* Since 2008, 16000 people have been trained and at the end of 2016, CAS had 1891 people engaged in IP management, transfer and service.
4. *Strengthening AI technology innovation through IP rights.* CAS has established a number of AI research institutions, resulting in the following patent applications from 2008 to 2018: machine learning 715, computer vision 417, natural language processing 246, and speech processing 203.
5. *Strengthening the transformation of scientific and technological achievements.* From 2008 to 2016, CAS transferred and transformed 7,000 IP assets (transfer, license, self-implementation, price-for-share, technology development and technical services) with a contract value of more than RMB12 billion.

What will be the next big things in AI? Below the opinions of authors of discussed report [16] are present.

"… We may consider where the challenges and opportunities in AI lie: human-like learning mechanisms, functional applications synergized with knowledge, combinations of different functional applications and integration with hardware, AI applications customized with real data and vertical scenarios" (*H.Wang, Baidu*).

"…We will continue to see huge growth in healthcare (especially AI for imaging/diagnostics/monitoring/alerting/mining the microbiome and combinations for better health, forecasting, etc.) and human–computer interaction (HCI)" (*R.Picard, MIT Media Laboratory*).

"...You'll interact with AI in healthcare, education, legal services and in so many different ways. We've got a ways to go, but this is only just the beginning" (*F.Chen, Andreessen Horowitz*).

"...The next breakthrough could come from the combination of neuroscience and AI, connecting something about our thinking and statistical thinking, quantum computing, or semantics or language understanding" (*K.-F.Lee, Sinovation Ventures*).

2.5 Scientometrics of AI Technologies Publications in Medicine – Up to Date Results

As follows from the above analysis, the WIPO report provides important and reliable data. At the same time, it should be noted that its main conclusions are based on the results obtained before 2017(incl.). Due to the dynamic development of AI, in our opinion, scientometric analysis of publications on application of AI methods and tools in the field of medicine, biotechnology and pharmaceutical industry is of interest since these are scientific publications which determine (with a certain time lag) the patent landscapes formed here.

In view of the foregoing, the remainder of this paper presents the results of scientometrics of publications from the PubMed [17] database, which, in turn, were obtained using the semantic technologies of Semantic Hub [18].

Semantic Hub is a multilingual Natural Language Understanding platform aimed at processing large volumes of unstructured text information in the field of healthcare, pharmaceutical industry, and biotech. It is oriented towards processing both professional discourse (scientific papers, patents, clinical trials) and patient-generated evidence, i.e. the stories of patients with rare and other severe diseases which they share in social networks and online patient groups. The solution helps pharmaceutical companies, patient advocacy groups and other stakeholders deeper understand the journey and the real experience of their patients in the countries of interest.

The general architecture of the linguistic processors operating on this platform is shown in Fig. 5.

This processor belongs to the class of NLP systems of the Ontology Driven Information Extraction type and allows, in accordance with the domain model, to extract purely bibliometric information (authors with their affiliations and geolocations) from PubMed database records in Medline format as well as scientometrics (semantically meaningful terms and relationships between them). The results of semantic processing of each article are stored in Semantic Hub graphical knowledge base ensuring construction of the necessary analytical reports.

To form the corpus, experiments were carried out on tuning queries on the PubMed portal to search for relevant articles. Adequate results were obtained when performing queries of the following structure:

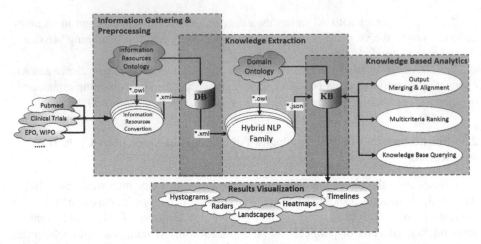

Fig. 5. Semantic Hub multilingual Natural Language Understanding platform architecture.

("Artificial Intelligence"[Abstract]
    OR "Machine learning"[Abstract]
    OR "Natural Language Processing"[Abstract]
    OR "Information Extraction"[Abstract])
NOT (
    Proceedings[Title] **OR** Conference[Title]
    OR Symposium[Title] **OR** Congress[Title] **OR** Poster[Title])

AND (
    medicine[Abstract]
    OR pharma[Abstract]
    OR pharmaceutics[Abstract])

AND ("2018/01/01"[Publication Date]
: "2020/04/31"[Publication Date])
Sort by: PubDate

Search results are presented in Table 5.

Table 5. Search results for relevant articles on the PubMed portal.

N/N	Publ years	Items found
#1	2018	157
#2	2019	222
#3	2020	70
#4	Total	449

The formed corpus was processed with the specialized linguistic processor based on Semantic Hub platform. The processing results are presented in Table 6.

Thus, a total number of processed articles - 10143 from 149 countries. TOP-5 organizations and authors by year are presented in Table 7 and Table 8, respectively.

Table 6. General results of processing relevant articles from PubMed portal.

Publ years	Items found	Countries	Orgs	Authors	Extracted terms		
					MH	OT	NLP
2018	3077	100	2091	16363	3989	7213	53893
2019	4923	133	3177	26020	3717	10361	80990
2020	2143	98	1474	13239	720	4584	39196

Table 7. TOP-5 organizations from PubMed corpus, which are mentioned in author affiliations.

Mentioned in authors' affiliations organizations					
2018		2019		2020	
Names	Publs	Names	Publs	Names	Publs
Google Inc.	31	Department of Computer Science, Stanford University	19	Laureate Institute for Brain Research	12
Harvard Medical School	20	Harvard Medical School	19	Novartis Institutes for BioMedical Research	12
Center for Biomedical Image Computing and Analytics (CBICA)	19	Maastricht University	17	Institute of Pharmaceutical Sciences	11
Massachusetts General Hospital	19	Department of Neurology, Faculty of Medicine, Oita University	15	Oklahoma Medical Research Foundation	11
Lister Hill National Center for Biomedical Communications	16	Bayer AG	13	Human Longevity, Inc.	10

Thus, according to PubMed, only 14 competence centers and 5 authors can be distinguished in the field of using AI methods and tools in medicine, biotechnology, and pharmaceutical industry. In view of the last remark, in our opinion it is interesting to single out the areas of competence of the most active authors. The corresponding heatmaps are presented in Fig. 6.

As follows from the analysis of the above heat map, TOP-5 authors main competences in 2018–2020 are R&D in the following domains: "Models", "Tomography", "Image processing & interpretation", "Sequence analysis", "Biomarkers", and "RNA". Moreover, only "Neural Networks", "Decision support systems", and "Pattern recognition" clearly related to AI.

Thus, the above results of scientometrics and publication activity at the intersection of AI and medicine, biotechnology and pharmaceutical industry show that the emphasis on the use of intelligent technologies in this area is different from those presented in

Table 8. TOP-5 authors from PubMed corpus.

Papers' authors					
2018		2019		2020	
Names	Publs	Names	Publs	Names	Publs
Wang Y.	41	Wang Y.	86	Wang Y.	31
Li Y.	32	Zhang Y.	77	Zhang Y.	29
Zhang Y.	27	Wang J.	69	Zhang J.	26
Wang X.	26	Li Y.	47	Chen J.	24
Li J.	25	Zhang J.	46	Li J.	24

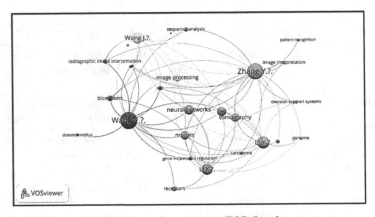

Fig. 6. Areas of competence TOP-5 authors

analytical materials [1, 16]. In our opinion, this indicates that researchers are less likely to use the latest AI methods and tools to get results. It seems that this situation is characteristic of all applied works in which new methods begin to be used with a time lag of several years.

3   Conclusion

In this paper we presented an analytical review of research and developments in the field of AI in the context of medicine, biotechnology and pharmaceutical industry. A comparative discussion of the latest reports by leading analytical agencies was carried out, expanded by an analytical review of publications in this area as well as by scientometric analysis of authors on publication activity at the junction of AI and medicine, biotechnology and pharmaceutical industry according to PubMed data of 2018–2020.

It is shown that, despite significant efforts to develop new methods of machine learning and the results already available here, their practical use in medicine, biotechnology and pharmaceuticals is at the beginning of the way. At the same time, the main myths here are determined by high expectations from the application of machine learning methods and tools as well as from underestimation of the complexity of data preparation for the effective performance of corresponding algorithms. It should be also noted that scientific and technological trends that were noticeable at the beginning of 2020 are associated with the further development of machine learning methods, means of semantic analysis of NL texts, speech and images, as well as with their integration in practically important applications.

References

1. Gartner Research Homepage. https://www.gartner.com/en/documents/3953603/hype-cycle-for-artificial-intelligence-2019. Accessed 04 Apr 2020
2. Conroy, D., Conroy, M.: AI in Pharmaceuticals. Pharmaceutical Executive (2019)
3. Habl, C., Renner, A.-T., Bobek, J., Laschkolnig, A.: Study on big data in public health, telemedicine and healthcare, Final Report. Publication Office of the European Union (2016)
4. MELLODDY Homepage. Project 831472, European Union-2019. https://www.melloddy.eu. Accessed 20 Apr 2020
5. van Stekelenborg, J., Ellenius, J., Maskell, S., et al.: Recommendations for the use of social media in pharmacovigilance. Lessons from IMI WEB-RADR. Drug Saf. **42**, 1393–1407 (2019)
6. BenchSci Blog Homepage, Simon Smith: 40 Pharma Companies Using Artificial Intelligence in Drug Discovery. https://blog.benchsci.com/pharma-companies-using-artificial-intelligence-in-drug-discovery. Accessed 19 Apr 2020
7. BenchSci Blog Homepage, Simon Smith: 186 Startups Using Artificial Intelligence in Drug Discovery. https://blog.benchsci.com/startups-using-artificial-intelligence-in-drug-discovery. Accessed 20 Apr 2020
8. Kürzinger, M.-L., Schück, S., Texier, N., et al.: Web-based signal detection using medical forums data in france: comparative analysis. J. Med. Internet Res. **20**(11), e10466 (2018). https://doi.org/10.2196/10466
9. Bhattacharya, M., et al.: Using social media data in routine pharmacovigilance. A pilot study to identify safety signals and patient perspectives. Pharm. Med. **31**(3), 167–174 (2017)
10. Tricco, A.C., Zarin, W., Lillie, E., et al.: Utility of social media and crowd-intelligence data for pharmacovigilance: a scoping review. BMC Med. Inform. Decis. Mak. **18**, 38 (2018). https://doi.org/10.1186/s12911-018-0621-y
11. Wang, Y., Wang, L., Rastegar-Mojarad, M., et al.: Clinical information extraction applications: a literature review. J. Biomed. Inform. **77**, 34–49 (2018). https://doi.org/10.1016/j.jbi.2017.11.011
12. Bruce, I.J. young, Luz, S., Lone, N.: A systematic review of natural language processing for classification tasks in the field of incident reporting and adverse event analysis. Int. J. Med. Inform. **132** (2019). https://doi.org/10.1016/j.ijmedinf.2019.103971
13. Sheikhalishahi, S., Miotto, R., Dudley, J.T., Lavelli, A., Rinaldi, F., Osmani, V.: Natural language processing of clinical notes on chronic diseases: systematic review. JMIR Med. Inform. **7**(2), e12239 (2019). https://doi.org/10.2196/12239
14. Koleck, T.A., Dreisbach, C., Bourne, P.E., Bakken, S.: Natural language processing of symptoms documented in free-text narratives of electronic health records: a systematic review. JAMIA **26**(4), 364–379 (2019). https://doi.org/10.1093/jamia/ocy173
15. Basile, A.O., Yahi, A., Tatonetti, N.P.: Artificial intelligence for drug toxicity and safety. Trends Pharmacol. Sci. **40**(9), 624–635 (2019). https://doi.org/10.1016/j.tips.2019.07.005

16. WIPO Homepage, WIPO Technology Trends 2019: Artificial Intelligence, Geneva, 158p. https://www.wipo.int/publications/en/details.jsp?id=4386. Accessed 30 Apr 2020
17. PubMed Homepage. https://pubmed.ncbi.nlm.nih.gov. Accessed 06 May 2020
18. Efimenko, I.V., Khoroshevsky, V.F.: Identification of promising high-tech solutions in big text data with semantic technologies: energy, pharma, and many others (chapter 16. Advanced methods). In: Daim, T., Pilkington, A. (eds.) Innovation Discovery. Network Analysis of Research and Invention Activity for Technology Management, pp. 429–467 (2018)

Application of LP Structures Theory to Intelligent Attribute Merger Refactoring

Sergey Makhortov$^{(\boxtimes)}$ and Aleksandr Nogikh

Voronezh State University, 1, Universitetskaya pl., Voronezh 394018, Russia
msd_exp@outlook.com

Abstract. An approach to automatized object-oriented code refactoring is described that applies LP structures theory to type hierarchy transformations, which merge attributes sharing common subclasses. A distinctive feature of these algebraic structures is their ability to model aggregation not as a relation between independent sets of types and attributes, but as a relation between specific types. The property enables a more adequate modeling of type hierarchies. The described approach is dual to the "Pull Up Field" refactoring method that was considered in the previous works related to the applications of LP structures theory. In this paper, LP structures on type lattices are extended to be able to model a wider range of type hierarchies and to accommodate external constraints on the refactoring process. Also, the paper details the process of constructing and applying the model.

Keywords: Object-oriented programming · Refactoring · Intelligent system · LP structure · Software development tool

1 Introductions

Over time, software systems are modified to resolve their flaws and to meet emerging requirements. Such adjustments unavoidably contribute to code quality degradation and make further modifications increasingly difficult.

This negative process can be stopped and reversed by performing a regular refactoring of the source code. Refactoring is the process of improving the internal structure of a software system that preserves its external behavior. An overview of refactoring methods can be found in [1].

Enormous complexity of large software systems justifies the need for intelligent tools that can help a human. Such tools rely on various mathematical approaches for analyzing the code and suggesting possible modifications. One of these approaches is Formal Concept Analysis (FCA) [2], which models two-dimensional structures having the "object-attribute" semantics. FCA has been applied to many areas, including CRUD (Create, Read, Update, Delete) matrices optimization [3], object-oriented systems refactoring [4] and knowledge engineering [5].

In [6] it was demonstrated that models for automating the refactoring process can also be devised using LP (Lattice-Production) structures theory, which provides algebraic

© Springer Nature Switzerland AG 2020
S. O. Kuznetsov et al. (Eds.): RCAI 2020, LNAI 12412, pp. 437–447, 2020.
https://doi.org/10.1007/978-3-030-59535-7_32

models for various domains of informatics [7]. The paper proposed a novel approach that focused on "Pull Up Field" refactoring (more details about this refactoring method can be found in [1]) and removal of redundant attributes.

FCA treats types and attributes as distinct sets [8], while LP structures on type lattices model attributes as an essential part of type hierarchy. Therefore, it becomes possible to consider more information during the refactoring process and to suggest more elaborate transformations.

LP structure operations duality has led to the discovery of a new refactoring method (presented in [9]), merging of attributes that have common subclasses. It is applicable only to the programming languages that support multiple inheritance. At least, the existence of such refactoring methods can be justified by the existence of C++, a language that has been widely used in systems programming for decades and continues to be essential for performance-critical programming. The paper [9] defined and explored a special class of LP Structures that could be used to automate such refactoring method.

The approaches of [6] and [9] pose a restriction on type hierarchies that may be processed: there must not be any types that have multiple attributes of the same other type. Also, these models provide no means of control over attribute uplifting/merger and the procedure description lacks details on the mapping between the original and the resulting object-oriented systems. In order to overcome these limitations for the "Pull Up Field" refactoring automation, the corresponding approach was extended in [10].

The objective of the present work is to enhance the attribute merger refactoring automation by eliminating the outlined limitations in a way similar to [10]. In particular, we suggest an extension to the type lattice building procedure, introduce a new model parameter that provides additional control over the refactoring process and describe a generalized language-independent refactoring procedure.

The paper does not cover any implementation issues. It is intended to facilitate the development of intelligent automatized refactoring tools by enhancing the corresponding theoretical background.

2   LP Structures on Type Lattices

This section contains a brief introduction to LP structures theory in general and to the important results from the previous papers on its application to object-oriented code refactoring [6] and [9].

Definition 1. LP structure is an algebraic structure that consists of a lattice $\mathbb{F}(\leq, \wedge, \vee)$ and a binary relation over the lattice (denoted by $\leftarrow$). The binary relation must have the following properties:

- transitivity: if $a \leftarrow b$ and $b \leftarrow c$, then $a \leftarrow c$ $(a, b, c \in \mathbb{F})$;
- distributivity (for the present work – $\wedge$-distributivity): if $b \xleftarrow{R} a_1$ and $b \xleftarrow{R} a_2$, then $b \xleftarrow{R} a_1 \wedge a_2$ $(a_1, a_2, b \in \mathbb{F})$;
- $\leq \subseteq \leftarrow$.

LP structures theory primarily aims at modeling production systems. The distributivity property of the previously mentioned binary relation is required for monotonic logical inference. It is possible for the binary relation not to obey $\wedge$-distributivity in all cases, this results in non-monotonic inference and requires a special treatment.

Among other concepts, LP structures theory defines and explores the means of equivalent transformations, which enable compacting the representation of LP structures. By treating the elements and relations of an object-oriented system as a production system and modeling it as an LP structure, it becomes possible to apply equivalent transformations in order to ultimately compact the object-oriented system itself. This aids in removing redundancy from an object-oriented system and simplifying its structure.

There exist at least two important types of relations in object-oriented programming: inheritance and aggregation. The lattice $\mathbb{F}$ models types and inheritance links: if type a is a parent of type b, then $b \leq a$. $a \wedge b$ corresponds to the greatest common descendant of a and b, while $a \vee b$ corresponds to the least common ancestor of a and b. $\mathbb{F}$ that is defined in this way will be called a type lattice. In general, such lattice $\mathbb{F}$ can be unbounded. To simplify reasoning, $\mathbb{F}$ is augmented by two special entities (in case they are absent): a fictitious common ancestor I and a fictitious successor of all types O.

Aggregation is represented by a binary relation R on the type lattice $\mathbb{F}$. If a type $a \in \mathbb{F}$ has an attribute of type $b \in \mathbb{F}$, then it is denoted by $(a, b) \in R$. Note that in general ($\mathbb{F}$, R) is not an LP structure because such R is unlikely to satisfy all requirements of the LP structure definition.

$\leq$ and R have similar semantics – in case of both $b \leq a$ and $(b, a) \in R$, type b has access to attributes and services provided by a. Let us denote the closure of R with respect to Definition 1 by $\xleftarrow{\;R\;}$. It follows that $\leq \; \subseteq \xleftarrow{\;R\;}$ and $R \subseteq \xleftarrow{\;R\;}$.

Semantically, $\xleftarrow{\;R\;}$ represents the 'accessibility' relation between types after the end of refactoring process. Specifically, $(b, a) \in \xleftarrow{\;R\;}$ corresponds to the statement that it is possible to access attributes and methods of type a from an instance of type b through some chain of inheritance and aggregation links. The resulting attribute assignment is obtained through compacting $\xleftarrow{\;R\;}$.

$\wedge$-distributivity of $\xleftarrow{\;R\;}$ (if $b \xleftarrow{\;R\;} a_1$ and $b \xleftarrow{\;R\;} a_2$, then $b \xleftarrow{\;R\;} a_1 \wedge a_2$) has the following interpretation. If type b has access to attributes and services provided by types a_1 and a_2, then it also has access to attributes and services provided by $a_1 \wedge a_2$. If a new attribute of type $a_1 \wedge a_2$ is added to b, then the previous statement about b remains true even if attributes of types a_1 and a_2 are removed from the type hierarchy. That corresponds to the attribute merger refactoring.

It can be observed that this refactoring method affects only the attribute assignment and preserves the original types and inheritance links. In terms of the mathematical model, the type lattice $\mathbb{F}$ remains the same during all transformations.

The attribute merger refactoring is depicted in Fig. 1 as a UML class diagram with 5 entities. During refactoring, "SomeClass" that contained an attribute of type "A" and an attribute of type "B" is converted into "SomeClass '" that contains only one attribute of type "C" (a descendant of both "A" and "B", or $A \wedge B = C$ in lattice formalism).

The purpose of refactoring is to enhance the inner structure of a software system, and it is totally unacceptable for refactoring to lower the quality of code. Unrestricted $\wedge$-distributivity of $\xleftarrow{\;R\;}$ is a potential source of code quality problems, because it can lead to merging of those attributes that should be separate for objective reasons. Also,

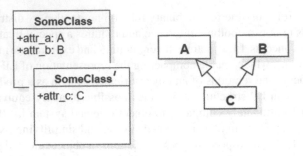

Fig. 1. An illustration of the merge attribute refactoring.

it some cases (that have been investigated in [9]) it can introduce additional redundancy into a type hierarchy. Therefore, $\wedge$-distributivity of $\xleftarrow{\ R\ }$ must be put under control.

In particular, the following constraint is enforced. A type must not be knowledgeable of the existence of its descendant types, i.e. if $(a, b) \notin \xleftarrow{\ R\ }$ and $b \le a$, then type a must not have any attributes of type b. The rest of the paper presents definitions and theorems from [9] that constitute a model that accommodates the restrictions on the acceptable type hierarchy transformations.

Elements $a, c \in \mathbb{F}$ are called transitive in R if $(a, c) \in R_1^*$, where R_1^* is the transitive closure of $R_1 = R \backslash \{(a, c)\}$.

Definition 2. Let R be a binary relation over $\mathbb{F}$. Two pairs $(b, a_1), (b, a_2) \in R$ are called $\wedge$-compatible in R if there are $c_1, c_2 \in \mathbb{F}$ such that $c_1 \wedge c_2 \le a_1 \wedge a_2$, $(c_1 \wedge c_2) \vee b = O$, and $(b, c_1), (b, c_2) \in R$ are not transitive in $R \cup \le$. (b, c_1, c_2) will be referred to as an $\wedge$-distributive triple.

Definition 3. Consider two $\wedge$-distributive triples: $T = (b, c_1, c_2)$ and $T' = (b', c_1', c_2')$. T is called neutralizing for T' if one of the following conditions is satisfied:

1. $b = b'$, $c_1 \wedge c_2 \ne c_1' \wedge c_2'$ and at least one of $c_1 \wedge c_2 < c_i'$ holds;
2. $b < b'$, $c_1 \wedge c_2 \ne c_1' \wedge c_2'$ and at least one of $c_1 \wedge c_2 < c_i'$ holds;
3. $b < b'$, $c_1 \wedge c_2 = c_1' \wedge c_2'$.

Definition 4. A triple $T' = (b', c_1', c_2')$ is called conflictless if there exist no $\wedge$-distributive triples that are neutralizing for T'.

Definition 5. Two $\wedge$-compatible pairs are called conflictless $\wedge$-compatible if the corresponding $\wedge$-distributive triple is conflictless.

The construction of LP structure on type lattice is completed by Definitions 6–8.

Definition 6. A binary relation R is called logical if it is transitive, contains $\le$, and if for all $\wedge$-compatible pairs $(b, a_1), (b, a_2) \in R$ it holds true that $(b, a_1 \wedge a_2) \in R$.

For a partially ordered set, we distinguish between concepts of the minimal element (no lesser element exists) and the least element (the least element among all).

Definition 7. Logical closure of R is the *least* logical relation that contains R and the set of its conflictless $\wedge$-compatible pairs.

Definition 8. Two relations R_1 and R_2 are called equivalent ($R_1 \sim R_2$) if they are defined over the same lattice and their logical closures coincide. Logical reduction of R is a *minimal* relation R_0 such that $R_0 \sim R$.

Let T_{pairs} be a set of conflictless $\wedge$-distributive triples of R. Consider a relation $\tilde{R} = R \cup \leq \cup \{(b, c_1 \wedge c_2)|(b, c_1, c_2) \in T_{pairs}\}$.

The following two theorems (formulated and proved in [9]) are important for the rest of the present paper.

Theorem 1. Logical closure of R always exists and equals to the transitive closure $\tilde{R}^*$ of $\tilde{R}$.

Theorem 2. Logical reduction of R can be computed as $R^0 \setminus \leq$, where R^0 is a transitive reduction of $\tilde{R}$.

Theorem 1 enables the use of LP structures for performing equivalent transformations of type hierarchies. Theorem 2 provides a straightforward way of obtaining the minimal equivalent representation of a type hierarchy. Logical reduction of R determines the new attribute assignment for the refactored software system.

3   Extending the Model

The definition of LP structure on type lattice from the previous section poses restrictions on the hierarchies that can be modeled. In particular, it is restricted for a type to have more than one attribute of the same other type. This section describes an extension that cancels such restrictions. Also, a new model parameter is proposed that provides additional control over attribute merging. This allows to significantly improve quality and usability of automatized refactoring.

Before model extensions can be considered, an important observation must be made. In general, logical reduction of a binary relation is not unique and not all logical reductions can be treated as correct type hierarchy transformations. Theorem 2 provides a way to obtain a logical reduction that is suitable for refactoring purposes, so in the following sections logical reduction is assumed to be computed exactly as Theorem 2 suggests.

Let us denote a transitive closure of a binary relation X by X^*.

Remark 1. Theorem 1 and Theorem 2 have the following consequence: for each $(t, a) \in R$ it is true that $(t, a) \in (R_0 \cup \leq)^*$, where R_0 is a logical reduction of R.

3.1   Attribute Merging Control

In order to facilitate control over the refactoring process, a new model parameter is suggested – a binary predicate $P : \mathbb{F} \times \mathbb{F} \rightarrow \{0, 1\}$. It is supposed to have the following effect: if $P(t, a) = 0$, then type t will not have any attributes of type a in the resulting type hierarchy. P must obey the following restriction: $P(t, a) = 1$ if t aggregates an attribute of type a before the refactoring process or if type t inherits from type a. This restriction prevents P from conflicting with the original attribute assignment and inheritance links.

The predicate can be incorporated into the model by extending the definition of $\wedge$-distributive triple with an additional condition. A triple (b, c_1, c_2) will never be considered $\wedge$-distributive if $P(b, c_1 \wedge c_2) = 0$.

Theorem 3. Suppose that the definition of $\wedge$-distributive triple has been updated as described above. Let $\tilde{R}$ be a logical relation with predicate P, and let R_0 be a logical reduction of $\tilde{R}$. Then R_0 is guaranteed not to contain elements (t, a), such that $P(t, a) = 0$.

Proof. Let $(x, a) \in \tilde{R}$ and $P(x, a) = 0$.

If (x, a) is transitive in $\tilde{R}$, then $(x, a) \notin R_0$ (otherwise R_0 would not be minimal). Therefore, we only need to consider cases when (x, a) is not transitive in $\tilde{R}$. A situation when $(x, a) \in R$ and $P(x, a) = 0$ is impossible due to the restrictions on P.

It remains to consider the case when $(t, x) \in \tilde{R}$ is true due to the existence of a conflictless $\wedge$-compatible pair $(t, a_1), (t, a_2) \in \tilde{R}$, for which $a_1 \wedge a_2 = x$ is true. Then (by Definition 2), $\exists c_1, c_2 : c_1 \wedge c_2 \leq x$, where $(t, c_1), (t, c_2) \in \tilde{R}$. If $c_1 \wedge c_2 < x$, then (t, c_1, c_2) is a neutralizing triple for all (t, b_1, b_2) where $c_1 \wedge c_2 < b_1 \wedge b_2$, and $(t, a_1), (t, a_2) \in \tilde{R}$ is not conflictless. $x = c_1 \wedge c_2$ is impossible due to $P(t, x) = 0$. Therefore $(t, a_1), (t, a_2) \in \tilde{R}$ cannot be conflictless $\wedge$-compatible pairs. Then either (t, x) is transitive (which contradicts the currently considered case), or $(t, x) \notin \tilde{R}$.

If $(t, x) \notin \tilde{R}$, then $(t, x) \notin R_0$. Otherwise $R \sim R_0$ will not hold. $\square$

By definition, the predicate $P(t, a)$ only determines whether an attribute of type a can belong directly to type t. It does not eliminate the possibility of type t inheriting an attribute of type a. If it is needed to prevent this from happening, $P(t', a)$ must be set to 0 for all $t' : t \leq t'$.

3.2   Extended Type Lattice

The use of a binary relation over the type lattice to model aggregation (as in [9]) prevents some type hierarchies from being adequately modeled and refactored. Due to the nature of a binary relation concept, such approach is only applicable to the type hierarchies where a type can have only one attribute of another type.

Also, attributes can belong to different contexts. If such attributes are merged, this can lead to code quality degradation and in the worst case it can even cause the program to malfunction. Below (see Fig. 2) is an illustration of a situation where improper merger of attributes can lead to severe problems.

The following classes can be seen on the attached UML diagram.

- "Encryptor" and "Decryptor" are the types that implement some cryptographic algorithm (as their names suggest, one is responsible for encryption and the other one is responsible for decryption).
- "CryptoSuite" is a type that combines the functionality of "Encryptor" and "Decryptor", i.e. it can be used for both these operations.

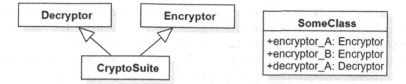

Fig. 2. An example of a type hierarchy with different attribute contexts.

- "SomeClass" is a class that has an "Encryptor" and a "Decryptor" instances for key "A" and an "Encryptor" instance for key "B".

Obviously, if we merge "encryptor_B" and "decryptor_A", then it will significantly affect the behavior of the program.

In order to enable adequate refactoring of such type hierarchies, it is suggested to alter the model by extending the type lattice with elements that represent the previously mentioned contexts. The resulting lattice will be referred to as an *extended type lattice*.

Let us denote the set of original (before refactoring) attributes by A. The extended type lattice can be built by the following algorithm.

- Firstly, a type lattice $\mathbb{F}$ must be constructed as described in [9], i.e. its elements correspond to types and the partial order represents inheritance links.
- Let us denote be the set of attributes that belong to t by $A_t \subseteq A$. Each A_t must be split into disjoint subsets $\{A_t^{(i)}\}_{i=1}^N$ in accordance with the following principle. If $u \in A_t^{(i)}$ and $b \in A_t^{(i)}$, then it is allowed to replace attributes a and b by a single attribute whose type is a descendant of types of a and b. The splitting of attributes into disjoint subsets must be done before the construction begins, i.e. it becomes a new model parameter.
- For each subset of attributes $A_t^{(i)}$ from $\{A_t^{(i)}\}_{i=1}^N$ the following operation must be performed: a new element (let us denote it by $t_{agg}^{(i)}$) is instantiated and incorporated into the type lattice as a parent of t (i.e. $t \le t_{agg}^{(i)}$).

Let us denote the set of all $t_{agg}^{(i)}$, which were added to the lattice, by $\tilde{T}$ and let $f_{agg} : A \to \tilde{T}$ be a mapping from the original attribute set to the set $\tilde{T}$ of elements that represent those attributes. If $t_{agg}^{(i)}$ corresponds to $A_t^{(i)}$, then the following is true: $\forall a \in A_t^{(i)} : f_{agg}(a) = t_{agg}^{(i)}$.

The changes in the process of construction of the type lattice also affect the binary relation over the lattice. When an extended type lattice is used, the binary relation R takes the following form: $\forall a \in A : (f_{agg}(a), f_{type}(a)) \in R$, where $f_{type}(a)$ corresponds to the type of the attribute a.

The type lattice and the binary relation built as above have the following important properties.

First, the original links between elements of the type hierarchy are preserved. If type t has an attribute a, then it continues to contain this attribute in the resulting representation $(\mathbb{F}, R)$, since by the construction t is modified to have a parent type $f_{agg}(a)$ that is linked to a through R.

Second, the logical reduction of R is guaranteed to bind elements of $\tilde{T}$ with elements that do not belong to $\tilde{T}$ (which corresponds to attribute aggregation). The reason is that by Definition 2 the existence of conflictless $\wedge$-distributive triples (t, b_1, b_2) such that $t \notin \tilde{T}$ is prohibited. Therefore if the logical reduction of R includes $(t, f_{type}(a)), t \notin \tilde{T}$, then it also includes $(f_{agg}(a), f_{type}(a)), f_{agg}(a) \in \tilde{T}$, which contradicts the minimality of the logical reduction.

And finally, the approach does not specify any preconditions for type hierarchies. If a type has multiple attributes of the same other type, it can be successfully modeled by assigning these attributes to different subsets $A_t^{(i)}$. Similarly, it is possible to prohibit the merger of attributes of different contexts – if they are put into different $A_t^{(i)}$, they will never form an $\wedge$-distributive triple.

It must be noted that the extended type lattice construction requires additional input parameters. The quality and adequacy of the transformations that will be suggested by the model depend heavily on the data used for extended type lattice construction.

Let us again consider the case described in Fig. 2. The extended type lattice that corresponds to it is depicted in Fig. 3. For simplicity the fictitious successor and the fictitious ancestor are omitted from the figure. Arrows point to ancestor types. Fictitious elements $\tilde{T}$ ($\tilde{T} = \{A, B\}$) are represented by gray circles.

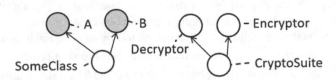

Fig. 3. Extended type lattice for the type hierarchy of Fig. 2.

Binary relation R includes the following tuples: $(A, Decryptor)$, $(A, Encryptor)$, $(B, Encryptor)$. f_{agg} maps $encryptor\_A$ to A, maps $encryptor\_B$ to B, and $decryptor\_A$ to A.

4   Model Application

While the previous sections were primarily focused on describing and enhancing model itself, this section elaborates on the issues that need to be addressed in any real-world implementation of the model. Below is a generic procedure of automatized refactoring, where each step is accompanied by comments and practical considerations.

Step 1. Construction and configuration of the model.

First of all, a type lattice $\mathbb{F}$ and a binary relation over it must be constructed as described in Sect. 2 or Sect. 3.2.

Of course, not every type hierarchy forms a lattice. For the discussed refactoring method, the lattice property is important because it enables unambiguous choice of common descendant types. In order to handle software systems where type hierarchies do not form a lattice, it is required to choose a subset of the type hierarchy that obeys this requirement.

The model can be configured in at least two ways.

- Denying the merger of specific attributes (only possible with extended type lattice). Attributes a_1 and a_2 can be merged and replaced with an attribute of their common descendant type only if they are placed into the same set $A_t^{(i)}$ of attributes during the construction of extended type lattice.
- Restricting the range of types for the newly created attributes. This can be done with the predicate $P : \mathbb{F} \times \mathbb{F} \to \{0, 1\}$ described in Sect. 3. For example, this predicate can be used in order to prevent the creation of attributes of abstract types.
Step 2. Computing an updated set of attributes.

The approach can be customized to perform at least two levels of refactoring.

- Performing attribute merger refactoring – attributes are replaced by attributes of their common descendant types. Firstly, a set of conflictless $\wedge$-distributive triples must be built. Then, for each triple (b, c_1, c_2) an attribute of type $c_1 \wedge c_2$ should be instantiated and put into b, while attributes whose type x obeys $c_1 \wedge c_2 < x$ must be deleted from b.
- Performing an exhaustive type hierarchy optimization, which involves attribute merger refactoring and removal of redundant attributes. This refactoring method can be performed by finding a logical reduction of R. The resulting binary relation can be treated as the new attribute assignment.
Step 3. Applying the suggestions of the model to the source code.

In a programming language that supports classes, each attribute appears in at least two contexts – it is included in the corresponding class definition and it is referenced by its name in every part of the code that needs to access the attribute. Therefore, the task of removing or merging an attribute can be divided into at least two subtasks.

1. *Updating definitions.* Besides the issues of code parsing and generation, this subtask needs to determine the name and type qualifiers of each new attribute. In order to generate an appropriate definition, each attribute of the resulting type hierarchy must be matched with a list of original attributes that it replaces.
2. *Updating references.* When all class definitions are updated, it becomes possible (and necessary) to revise all references to attributes throughout the source code since some of them may be pointing to already removed entities. Similarly to the previous subtask, such correction of references also relies on a mapping between the old and the new attribute sets. In this case, each attribute of the original type hierarchy must be mapped to an attribute of the new type hierarchy. If an exhaustive type hierarchy optimization is performed, each old attribute may be mapped not just to a single new attribute, but to a chain of references.

The rest of the section is dedicated to constructing the previously mentioned mappings from an LP structure on type lattice.

Let R be a binary relation over $\mathbb{F}$ that corresponds to the original attribute assignment and let R' be a binary relation over $\mathbb{F}$ that corresponds to the new attribute assignment. Note that $\mathbb{F}$ remains unchanged during the transformations. Mappings between the elements of attribute sets will be constructed under the following premises.

- For each element $(t, a) \in R$, there is only one way to match it to an original attribute.
- Each $(t', a') \in R'$ represents an attribute of a type hierarchy that is suggested by the model.
- R' is a logical reduction of R.

The mapping that is required by subtask 2 can be mathematically represented as a function $f_{new} : R \to SEQ_{R'}$, where $SEQ_{R'}$ is a set of sequences $\{(a_i, b_i)\}_{i=1}^{N}$ that correspond to valid "chains" of attribute references. The sequences consist of pairs $(a_i, b_i) \in R'$ such that $b_i \le a_{i+1}$ (for every $i < N$). Let us consider $x = (t, a) \in R$ and $f_{new}(x) = \{(a_i^x, b_i^x)\}_{i=1}^{N}$. The following condition must hold for all valid chains of attributes: each $x \in R$ must be mapped to a sequence with $t \le a_1^x$ and $b_n^x \le a$.

Below is the procedure that constructs a valid f_{new}. Let us compute the value of f_{new} for $(x, y) \in R$. By Remark 1, there exists a sequence $P = \{(x_i, y_i)\}_{i=1}^{M}$, where $(x_i, y_i) \in R' \cup \le$, $x_i = y_{i-1}$ for each $i > 1$, $x_1 = x$, $y_m = y$. Let us remove all elements $(x_i, y_i) \in \le$ from P and denote the resulting subsequence of P by P'. Since $\le$ is transitive, P' is a valid element of $SEQ_{R'}$. The previous calculations did not rely on any special properties of $(x, y) \in R$, and therefore the algorithm can be applied to any $(x, y) \in R$.

The mapping that is required by the second subtask can facilitate the construction of the mapping for updating the definitions. Mathematically, the first subtask needs to find $f_{prev} : R' \to P(R)$, where $P(R)$ is a set of all subsets of R. It follows from the assumptions on R that the elements of $f_{prev}(x)$ can be uniquely matched to the corresponding original attributes.

Let last_pair :$SEQ_{R'} \to R'$ be an supplementary relation that maps sequences $\{(a_i, b_i)\}_{i=1}^{N} \in SEQ_{R'}$ to their last elements (a_N, b_N). Then $f_{prev}(x)$ can be expressed as $f_{prev}(x) = \{y \in R | \text{last\_pair}(f_{new}(y)) = x\}$.

Thus, if an LP structure on type lattice is constructed unambiguously, it is always possible to construct mappings between old and new attribute sets that facilitate automated code corrections.

5   Conclusion

This paper has described and extended an approach of automatized object-oriented code refactoring.

Similarly to the additions to the "Pull Up Field" refactoring made in [10], an extended LP structure-based model has been proposed that can be used for attribute merger refactoring. The extensions have enhanced applicability and flexibility of the method.

The process of utilizing the model for refactoring automation has been considered, including the procedures of building and configuring the model and the procedure of automatic generation of type hierarchy transformations. It was also demonstrated that the suggested transformations can be converted into mappings that enable straightforward code modification.

The proposed model has considerable capabilities of formal representation and analysis of type hierarchies. It can be configured to suggest transformations that increase code quality for a broad range of object-oriented software systems. That is why the method can be adopted as a basis for building intelligent refactoring tools.

Further research may include elaborating the extended type lattice generation and code modification procedures, adjusting this generic approach to specific programming languages and the actual implementation of the corresponding software development tool.

Acknowledgment. The study was supported by RFBR project 19-07-00037.

References

1. Mens, T., Tourw'e, T.: A survey of software refactoring. IEEE Trans. Softw. Eng. **30**(2), 126–139 (2004)
2. Ganter, B., Wille, R.: Formal Concept Analysis: Mathematical Foundations. Springer, Heidelberg (1999). https://doi.org/10.1007/978-3-642-59830-2
3. Torim, A.: A visual model of the CRUD matrix. In: Information Modelling and Knowledge Bases XXIII, pp. 313–320. IOS Press, Amsterdam (2012)
4. Huchard, M.: Analyzing inheritance hierarchies through formal concept analysis. A 22-years walk in a landscape of conceptual structures. In: Proceedings of MASPEGHI, pp. 8–13. ACM (2018). https://doi.org/10.1145/2786555.2786557
5. Ferré, S., Huchard, M., Kaytoue, M., Kuznetsov, S.O., Napoli, A.: Formal concept analysis: from knowledge discovery to knowledge processing. In: Marquis, P., Papini, O., Prade, H. (eds.) A Guided Tour of Artificial Intelligence Research, vol. 2, pp. 411–445. Springer, Cham (2020). https://doi.org/10.1007/978-3-030-06167-8_13
6. Makhortov, S.: LP structures on type lattices and some refactoring problems. Program. Comput. Softw. **35**, 183–189 (2009). https://doi.org/10.1134/S0361768809040021
7. Makhortov, S.: On the algebraic model of a distributed production system. In: Proceedings of the Fifteenth National Conference on Artificial Intelligence with International Participation RCNAI-2016, Smolensk, vol. 1, pp. 64–72 (2016)
8. Godin, R., Valtchev, P.: Formal concept analysis-based class hierarchy design in object-oriented software development. In: Ganter, B., Stumme, G., Wille, R. (eds.) Formal Concept Analysis. LNCS (LNAI), vol. 3626, pp. 304–323. Springer, Heidelberg (2005). https://doi.org/10.1007/11528784_16
9. Makhortov, S.: LP-structures for justification and automation of refactoring in object-oriented programming. Softw. Eng. (2), 15–21 (2010). http://novtex.ru/prin/eng/archive.html
10. Makhortov, S., Nogikh, A.: LP structures theory application to building intelligent refactoring systems. In: Kovalev, S., Tarassov, V., Snasel, V., Sukhanov, A. (eds.) IITI 2019. AISC, vol. 1156, pp. 403–411. Springer, Cham (2020). https://doi.org/10.1007/978-3-030-50097-9_41

Development of Prototype of Natural Language Answer Processor for e-Learning

Dzhavdet Suleymanov[1] and Nikolai Prokopyev[2](✉)

[1] Institute of Applied Semiotics of Tatarstan Academy of Sciences, Kazan, Russia
dvdt.slt@gmail.com
[2] Kazan Federal University, Kazan, Russia
nikolai.prokopyev@gmail.com

Abstract. Automated knowledge control is an important component of e-Learning systems. Moreover, as an analysis of the most recent publications shows, the possibility of automated free natural language answers assessment is almost not represented in modern e-learning systems. Existing educational technologies either support only test approach to knowledge control, or when processing a natural-language answer, its semantic structure is not taken into account sufficiently for accurate assessment. This paper presents a software prototype that implements an algorithm for semantic processing of natural language answers. The basis of the algorithm is a theoretical pragmatically-oriented model proposed by D. Suleymanov, where main methodological principles are the principle of context determinism and the principle of meaning expectation. The implemented prototype was evaluated in order to verify its compliance with theoretical model and obtain the data necessary for further development of model and algorithm.

Keywords: Automatic answer assessment · Natural language processing · e-Learning · e-Assessment

1 Introduction

At present, we are witnesses and even direct participants in the change of functional responsibility in the three-agent "student – teacher – information technology" education system [1]. In education, especially in the field of e-Learning, processes are taking place that fundamentally change its essence. There is a large-scale and massive transition to distance learning and remote educational process management being incorporated. Practically the third agent, initially considered as a servicing resource, including auxiliary software tools, acquires a qualitatively higher status, largely performing the functions of the second agent, i.e., of the teacher.

In the age of accelerated and massive introduction of online learning, the issue of effective feedback with the student becomes especially relevant and important, the problems associated with operational and effective monitoring and evaluation of student's answers in knowledge control become even more acute. The task of development of intelligent software tools for analyzing and evaluating the student's free natural language

© Springer Nature Switzerland AG 2020
S. O. Kuznetsov et al. (Eds.): RCAI 2020, LNAI 12412, pp. 448–459, 2020.
https://doi.org/10.1007/978-3-030-59535-7_33

answers become highly demanded, because it can significantly improve the quality of knowledge level evaluation, the quality of subject mastering. This, obviously, will help with more effective online learning management by differentiating educational content and training individualizing based on more sophisticated automated analysis and assessment of student's knowledge.

This paper provides a review and a brief analysis of publications on this topic and further describes a prototype of such a system for student's free natural language answers processing and evaluation developed by the authors. An analysis of publications, as well as review articles, shows that this topic has not been studied much and that software applications of automated natural language answer processing are more likely to be prototype and experimental. Although the first publications related to the topic appeared in the late 1980s and early 1990s [2], more active research and development, and accordingly, publications appeared only after 2010–2011.

2 Related Work

In order to gain knowledge and to compare our answer processing approach, we analyzed a number of key review articles and developed systems in the domain of natural language answer processing briefly described below.

The paper [3] presents an analysis of automated short answer grading systems. The authors define the concept of "short answer grading" as a problem that satisfies the following five criteria:

- The answer to the asked question cannot be extracted from the question itself. That is, the answer can only be formed from external knowledge.
- The answer should be expressed in natural language.
- The length of the answer should be between one sentence and one paragraph.
- First of all, the meaning of the answer should be evaluated, and to a lesser extent its form.
- The variability of the answer structure should be limited by the context of the question.

The authors conducted a historical analysis of short answer grading systems development for the period from 1995 to 2014, proposing to divide this time period into five parts, called eras: Era of Concept Mapping; Era of Information Extraction; Era of Corpus-Based Methods; Era of Machine Learning; Era of Evaluation. These eras can intersect, with each era being characterized by the appearance and development of certain ideas and approaches to short answer grading and some level of applied research and software prototypes implemented in this domain.

In a comparative analysis of the short answer grading systems developed in the considered time period, the authors use six characteristics of such systems: data set, natural language processing approach, model building approach, grading model, model evaluation, and effectiveness calculation.

Data sets in most systems are extracted from academic and teaching experience, from open sources, or through direct knowledge control testing. The main languages for the data sets are English, Chinese, German, and Spanish. Common domains of knowledge are computer science, natural sciences, linguistics.

To process natural language 17 techniques are used in the systems in a different combination, the most common ones being: spelling correction, stemming, part-of-speech tagging. The least common are syntactic templates, named entity tagging, case folding.

Based on the studied data models, in particular, the models of correspondence between questions, students' answers, and reference answers, the authors conclude that reference answers play a different role in the answer grading system. In some cases, the reference answer takes the role of answer model, in other cases it is used for tagging of the student's answer.

Grading models can vary depending on the era and approaches used. They are divided into two large classes: rule-based assessment (the Era of Concept Maps and the Era of Information Extraction) and statistical grading (the Era of Corpus-Based Methods and the Era of Machine Learning). According to the study, the most widely used are machine learning systems.

Determining the quality of models in the considered systems depends on the type of answer grading model. Rule-based assessment is best shown in repeated testing across the same knowledge domain known in advance. Grading based on statistics is best shown in repeated testing in a previously unknown knowledge domain. The authors also distinguish three classes of used model quality assessment metrics: classification metrics, ranking metrics, and relationship metrics.

The main conclusion of the authors regarding methods for the considered system effectiveness evaluation is that the assessment is complicated by the lack of common data sets and common grading models. Therefore, a statistical approach to effectiveness evaluation according to the principles of TREC Eval is showing itself best of all.

The paper [4] supplements the analysis free answer grading systems with data relevant for 2016. The authors divide the considered systems into three classes: systems based on mask templates; systems based on the "bag of words" model; systems that take into account semantic or grammatical role of words.

Systems based on mask templates are characterized by the fact that the reference answers are set with some logical template language and describe the options for answer structure. As an example, the FLOD template language (Function Logical Of the Descriptors) is presented. As the main problem of such systems, the authors highlight some high burden on the knowledge control author, which incidentally leads to the desire to reduce the template variety, which reduces the answers assessment accuracy. Therefore, one of the subtasks in the development of such systems is also the task of template generation for partial automation of knowledge control of author activities. In addition, the authors note a downward grading trend in such systems.

Systems based on the "bag of words" model mainly use statistical analysis methods and search for n-grams in the answer text, with preliminary answer processing which consists of: paraphrase elimination, synonymy removal, abbreviations interpretation. The authors refer to such systems as using vector models for answer representation and machine learning methods. One of advantages of such systems is relative simplicity of knowledge control tests preparation. However, in the case of questions that require a specific answer structure, for example, requiring the proper order listing of a certain process steps, such systems are not suitable. One of the problems of such systems, the authors consider a tendency to grading overstatement.

Systems that take into account semantic or grammatical role of words in a sentence and their relations combine the ideas of two other system classes, since they adapt both structural approach and the flexibility of answer modeling. However, such systems, according to the study, inherit the problems of other system classes.

As the main conclusions, the authors cite some problems of automating the transformation of complex structured answer information into a more unified and simpler form, resolving coreference, automated development of knowledge bases and creating domain ontologies based on unstructured natural language texts, also the need for logical inference when evaluating the answer, rather than comparing it with syntactic templates.

Below we present related research where working prototypes of answer grading systems are introduced.

The author of [5] proposes metaregular expressions to reflect variety of the answer structure. He provides an algorithm for grading answers to questions of the "Definition" type and a method for automated generation of metaregular expressions for correct answers. Based on the results of the developed prototype evaluation, the author concludes that this approach quite effectively processes the "Definition" type answers for a given specific domain area.

The authors of paper [6] presents a report on the development of automatic answer grading system for GRE (Graduate Record Examinations) test questions. This test is intended for applicants to graduate schools at US universities. This test is intended for master degree applicants in US universities. Test questions imply an answer consisting of 1 to 3 sentences, which is automatically evaluated according to proposed "c-rater" approach proposed by the authors. To conduct an evaluation experiment on the system, 15 questions in "Biology" and 20 questions in "Psychology" were prepared for the algorithm. 971 students attended in experiment. Their answers were not only evaluated by the algorithm, but separately, each answer was graded by two experts. The authors claim that, according to their study, the average grade from the experimental test is higher than the overall GRE average. To evaluate the algorithm, they measured the numerical expression of agreement between experts, as well as agreement of each of the experts with answer grade made by algorithm.

In paper [7] an automated assessment system for "Essay" type questions is proposed. The authors described an approach of using information retrieval from encyclopedic and question-answer systems to generate questions and evaluate answers. Evaluation takes place by dividing the response into sentencization, tokenization, automatic morphological tagging using the OpenNLP package, and further analysis using the WordNet semantic network. To evaluate the algorithm, an experiment in form of lesson embedded testing was conducted. 7 participants wrote essays on 5 questions. The Pearson coefficient was used for numerical evaluation, showing the correlation between the algorithm given score and the teacher given score. According to the results of the study, the correlation coefficient was 0.77.

The paper [8] presents a software module designed to be embedded in Adobe Captivate, a program for e-Learning courses creation and e-Assessment conducting. The authors propose the use of structural approach to information extraction for question generation as well as for answer grading. The knowledge control author can either manually edit the answer model for more precise adjustment, or simply enter a set of reference answers so that the system generates an answer model automatically. The natural language answer processor proposed by the authors uses the Stanford parser and supports coreference resolving, synonyms processing, and composite concepts segmentation. To evaluate the developed software module, the authors conducted a test of 30 questions, in which 12 people took part. Answer grading was carried out using both automatically generated and manually created answer models, the algorithm evaluation was done by calculating the correlation coefficient with an expert given score. This coefficient for automatically generated models was 0.66, and it was 0.81 for manually created models.

The authors of [9] present a system that uses a special GAN-LCS metric to evaluate answers based on their distance to the reference answer. The paper describes approaches to the automatic generation of reference answers where teacher creates the knowledge control tests based on Maximum Marginal Relevance method, which facilitates filling out the answer model. Moreover, the system uses either a corpus or machine learning, and the presented metric, according to this study, is quite effective.

The authors of [10] describe an automatic open question answers grading system in Russian. As a linguistic processor, the system uses Tomita-parser from Yandex, which supports tokenization, morphological analysis, and entity extraction. This parser uses user-defined grammar and thesaurus for natural language processing. To evaluate the system, the authors used the Cohen's kappa coefficient of compliance, which shows the consistency between the programmatic answer score and the expert given score. Experiment was conducted, in which 1445 student responses were received. The kappa coefficient was 0.76.

3 Conceptual Model

3.1 Methodology

The main methodological principle of the approach used to build the prototype is the assertion that the question asked limits the context of the answer in a natural way, both in terms of answer variety and structure. The following hypothesis is put forward and verified during prototype testing. The construction of an effective pragmatically-oriented algorithm for natural language answer grading is possible and it is ensured by the following significant factors:

- Natural limitation of the answer and corresponding tokens values' space for a given question in test-learning situation (principle of answer values determinism).
- Natural limitation of the answer structure types for a given question, which are described in terms of special deep grammars called individual conceptual grammars (ICG) (principle of answer structure determinism).
- Ability to control the answer assessment accuracy due to the extensibility and modifiability of ICG as the basis of a pragmatically-oriented assessment algorithm (principle of ICG openness).
- Possibility of the evaluation algorithm scope narrowing, which is done through comparison of the student's answer with a pre-prepared answer model (principle of answer expectation).

Thus, a pragmatically-oriented approach to natural language processing is implemented, i.e., this algorithm is not universal, but aimed at solving of the problem within a specific domain, limited by the framework of the question-answer context.

The basic concepts in this theoretical model are "Conceptule" and "Individual conceptual grammar". The conceptule expresses the specific typed semantic and grammatical role of lexemes or their parts in the answer, indicating the corresponding natural language grammatical features. An individual conceptual grammar is a conceptule combination scheme corresponding to correct expected answer meaning in accordance with its semantic class. Each ICG conveys a certain canonical meaning, and the answer corresponding to this meaning is called a canonized answer. The need for introducing ICG in the model, therefore, is to reduce semantic text analysis to syntactic parsing of canonized representation in conditions determined by the question context.

Figure 1 presents an example of ICG2 for answers corresponding to the canonical meaning of a certain typed relationship, e.g., spatial or temporal, part-whole relations, functional relations. The questions that correspond to ICG of this type can take the following forms: "What is performed before: X or Y?", "What actions does X perform?", "Where is X located?". In the presented by ICG2, conceptule SS corresponds to the main concept of the question, SO expresses a concept that exists in a typed relation with the main concept, R_{SO} reflects the relation of SS to SO, R_{OS} reflects the relation of SO to SS, Gm corresponds to grammatical modifiers for relations and concepts. In addition, we consider interval lexemes LI_S, LI_O, LI_R, which impose semantic restrictions on SS, SO, and R_{SO} with R_{OS}, respectively.

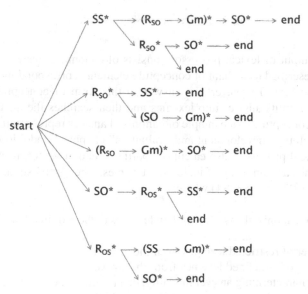

Fig. 1. ICG2 structure.

3.2   Answer Processing Algorithm

The answer processing algorithm is presented in Fig. 2. The lexical processor receives natural language answer with answer model for the given question as input. The answer model is a dictionary of mapping type "Conceptule" – "List of lexemes corresponding to conceptule". Lexemes description from the answer model can contain characters such as "*" (it denotes an arbitrary single character) and "&" (it denotes an arbitrary sequence of characters). These characters allow the question author to provide different word forms to take into account syntactic inaccuracies in the student's answer. An example response model is provided later in the "Experiment" chapter.

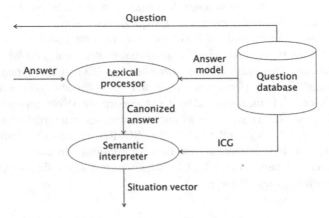

Fig. 2. Answer processing algorithm.

The main output of lexical processor consists of canonized answer representation which can be described as a chain of conceptule elements corresponding to the natural language answer text. To convert the answer in this form of conceptules chain, the lexical processor splits answer into lexemes and then searches the answer model for corresponding conceptule. An example of canonized answer representation is provided later in the "Prototype development and evaluation" chapter. In addition to canonized answer, the lexical processor also calculates partial situation vector, forms an array of restricted lexemes and an array of undefined lexemes. The partial situation vector is a numerical vector (S1, S2, S3, S4) where:

- S1 is a ratio of canonized answer length in lexemes to the required length from answer model;
- S2 is a number of restricted lexemes from the answer;
- S3 is a number of undefined lexemes from the answer;
- S4 is a code characterizing answer modality, that is, either the presence of uncertainty or categoricalness characterizing lexemes, or their absence, i.e. neutrality. S4 values are 0, 1, or 2 for cases of uncertainty, categoricalness, or neutrality, respectively.

The semantic interpreter receives canonized answer representation and the ICG related to the question asked. The interpreter checks the correspondence of canonized answer to the ICG by trying to traverse the nodes of syntactic graph of the ICG according to the conceptules chain. If this traversal completes at the final node of the graph, then it is considered that the answer corresponds to the ICG. At the output, the semantic interpreter calculates a complete situation vector (S1, S2, S3, S4, S5, S6, S7), which in addition to the already described partial situation vector contains:

- S5 as a code characterizing the correct use of interval lexemes. It takes the value of 0 if all interval tokens are used correctly, otherwise it takes the value of 1;
- S6 as a code characterizing the semantic correctness of the answer, i.e., its correspondence to the question ICG. Its value is 0 if the canonized answer fully corresponds to the ICG. If the answer is missing a relation, then S6 takes the value of 1. Otherwise, if canonized answer doesn't correspond to the ICG, it takes the value of 2;
- S7 as a code characterizing the completeness of the response, that is, the ratio of canonized answer length to the length of corresponding conceptules chain from the ICG. It takes the value of 0 if full compliance. If the canonized answer is longer than the ICG chain, then it takes the value of 1, otherwise it takes the value of 2.

4 Prototype Development and Evaluation

4.1 Software Implementation

Based on the previously described theoretical model, we developed a software prototype using Python programming language and Django web framework for graphical user interface. Natural language processing algorithm was implemented with the usage of regex, nltk and pymorphy2 packages for Python. The prototype consists of two components: a question editor that implements question creation and editing with answer model configuration, and a testing tool that allows to interactively give an answer to a question and to analyze output of the algorithm.

Figure 3 presents a form that allows one to enter the question wording, a reference answer and to configure the answer model. To set up an answer model, you need to enter the required response length in conceptules and select an ICG corresponding to semantic class of the question. After ICG selection, the form for answer model configuration expands for editing. It is shown in Fig. 4. Through this form, sets of lexemes are entered. They correspond to:

- Conceptules included in the selected ICG;
- Conceptules that express interval lexemes;
- Conceptules that express restricted and optional lexemes.

Special testing tool was developed for prototype evaluation. This tool allows one to evaluate the algorithm output data in question-answer dialog model. Its form is shown in Fig. 5. When entering the answer to the question, the form displays: canonized representation of the answer, situation vector, list of undefined lexemes and list of restricted lexemes.

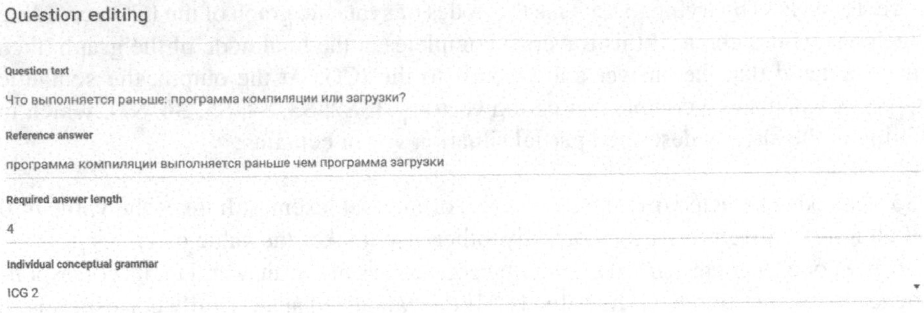

Question editing

Question text

Что выполняется раньше: программа компиляции или загрузки?

Reference answer

программа компиляции выполняется раньше чем программа загрузки

Required answer length

4

Individual conceptual grammar

ICG 2   ▾

Fig. 3. Question editing form.

Conceptulae	Lexemes
SS	программ*+компиляци*, компиляци*, компилятор*
LI$_S$	люб&
SO	программ*+загрузк*, загрузк*, загрузчик*
LI$_O$	люб&
R$_{SO}$	выполняется+раньше, раньше, работает+раньше
R$_{OS}$	выполняется+после, после, работает+после
LI$_R$	всегда
Gm	чем
LN	
LZ	

BACK   SAVE

Fig. 4. Answer model configuration form.

4.2 Prototype Evaluation

For prototype evaluation, the question "What is executed before: compilation program or loader program?" was created. An answer to this question involves the disclosure of "Temporal typed relationship", expressed in the form of the previously considered ICG2. An answer model was developed for this question and this ICG. It is presented in Table 1. The answers to this question may be:

Question testing

Что выполняется раньше: программа компиляции или загрузки?

Answer

программа компиляции выполняется раньше программы загрузки

Reference answer: программа компиляции выполняется раньше чем программа загрузки

BACK   SUBMIT

Canonical representation	SS(программа компиляции) → R$_{SO}$(выполняется раньше) → SO(программы загрузки)
Situation vector	S1 = 0.8; S2 = 0; S3 = 0; S4 = 1; S5 = 0; S6 = 0; S7 = 1;
Undefined lexemes	
Restricted lexemes	

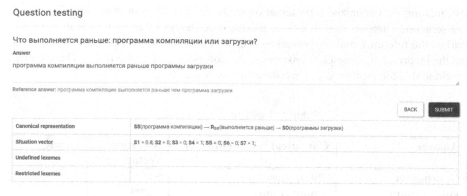

Fig. 5. Algorithm evaluation dialog form.

1. "The compilation program is executed before the loader program", the reference answer, it is fully consistent with the ICG;
2. "Compilation is always before of loading", a correct answer, it is fully consistent with the ICG;
3. "The loader program is executed before compilation", an incorrect answer, it does not correspond to the ICG;
4. "Compilation", a correct answer, but it is incomplete, as it doesn't fully correspond to the ICG.

Table 1. Question and answer model for evaluation.

Question (in Russian)	Что выполняется раньше: программа компиляции или загрузки?
Question (in English)	What is executed before: compilation program or loader program?
Answer model	
SS	программ*+компиляци*, компиляци*, компилятор*
LI$_S$	люб&
SO	программ*+загрузк*, загрузк*, загрузчик*
LI$_O$	люб&
R$_{SO}$	выполняется+раньше, раньше, работает+раньше
R$_{OS}$	выполняется+после, после, работает+после
LI$_R$	Всегда
Gm	Чем

Using the above answers, the algorithm was evaluated. We graded the received answer using common five-point scale, and entered them into the prototype to be processed by the algorithm; output data is presented in Table 2. According to the results, the lexical processor correctly and completely analyzed the natural language answer text, making the canonized representation of the answer without unidentified lexemes. The semantic interpreter, in this case, according to the S6 value in the situation vector, marked the reference and the correct answers as completely corresponding to the ICG, and the incorrect or incomplete answers as not corresponding to the ICG2. Thus, we can conclude that the prototype as a whole works as was expected.

Table 2. Evaluation output data.

Answer	Canonical representation	Situation vector	Grade
Программа компиляции выполняется раньше чем программа загрузки (1st answer)	SS(Программа компиляции) →R_{SO}(выполняется раньше) →Gm(чем) →SO(программа загрузки)	S1 = 1,0 S2 = 0 S3 = 0 S4 = 1 S5 = 0 S6 = 0 S7 = 0	5
Компиляция всегда раньше загрузки (2nd answer)	SS(Компиляция) →LI_R(всегда) →R_{SO}(раньше) →SO(загрузки)	S1 = 1,0 S2 = 0 S3 = 0 S4 = 1 S5 = 0 S6 = 0 S7 = 0	5
Программа загрузки выполняется раньше компиляции (3rd answer)	SO(Программа загрузки) →R_{SO}(выполняется раньше) →SS(компиляции)	S1 = 0,8 S2 = 0 S3 = 0 S4 = 1 S5 = 0 S6 = 2 S7 = 1	2
Компиляции (4th answer)	SS(Компиляции)	S1 = 0,2 S2 = 0 S3 = 0 S4 = 1 S5 = 0 S6 = 1 S7 = 1	3

5 Conclusion

Further work on the developed prototype consists in its scaling to minimal knowledge control system in order to conduct experimental e-Assessment with students. Such experiments will make it possible to evaluate the algorithm in real conditions, to identify classes of problems that impede the algorithm, and to analyze solutions to problems of this kind. Already now we can conclude about the possibility of confirming the hypothesis with this experimental approach, provided that individual conceptual grammars and answer models are properly configured. Another way of algorithm development is the automation of answer model creation, because it is an exhausting task for a teacher to do it manually. There is already an ongoing research for this problem which includes the usage of domain ontologies for question generation This way of algorithm development will allow it to be integrated into production-ready e-Learning system of knowledge control.

References

1. Suleymanov, D.: Methodology and principles of the intelligent agent design for the textual dialogue systems. In: Proceedings of "System Analysis and Semiotic Modeling" SASM-2011, Fan, Kazan (2011)
2. Bukharaev, R.G., Suleymanov, D.Sh.: Semanticheskiy analiz v voprosno-otvetnykh sistemakh Kazan University Publishing, Kazan (1990). 123 p.
3. Burrows, S., Gurevych, I., Stein, B.: The eras and trends of automatic short answer grading. Int. J. Artif. Intell. Educ. 25(1), 60–117 (2014). https://doi.org/10.1007/s40593-014-0026-8
4. Mishunin, O.B., Savinov, A.P., Firstov, D.I.: State and level of the automatic free-text answer grading systems development. Modern high technologies. Technical Sciences, no. 1, pp. 38–44. Academy of Natural History, Moscow (2016)
5. Merzlyakov, D.: Generation of regular expressions for automation of written tests checking. Noosphere Society Man, no. 4, pp. 38–44. Academy of Natural History, Moscow (2013)
6. Attali, Y., Powers, D., Freedman, M., Harrison, M., Obetz, S.: Automated scoring of short-answer open-ended GRE subject test items. GRE Board Research Report, no. GRE-04-02, USA (2008). https://doi.org/10.1002/j.2333-8504.2008.tb02106.x
7. Dumal, P.A.A., Shanika, W.K.D., Pathinayake, S.A.D., Sandanayake, T.C.: Adaptive and automated online assessment evaluation system. In: 11th International Conference on Software, Knowledge, Information Management and Applications (SKIMA), Malabe, pp. 1–8 (2017). https://doi.org/10.1109/skima.2017.8294135
8. Srivastava, V., Bhattacharyya, C.: Captivate short answer evaluator. In: 2013 IEEE International Conference in MOOC, Innovation and Technology in Education, Jaipur, pp. 114–119. IEEE (2013). https://doi.org/10.1109/mite.2013.6756317
9. Pribadi, F.S., Permanasari, A.E., Adji, T.B.: Short answer scoring system using automatic reference answer generation and geometric average normalized-longest common subsequence (GAN-LCS). Educ. Inf. Technol. 23(6), 2855–2866 (2018). https://doi.org/10.1007/s10639-018-9745-z
10. Kozhevnikov, V.A., Sabinin, O.Yu.: System of automatic verification of answers to open questions in Russian. SPbSPU J. Comput. Sci. Telecommun. Control. Syst. 11(3), 57–72 (2018). https://doi.org/10.18721/JCSTCS.11306

Intelligent Systems with Restricted Autonomy

Vadim L. Stefanuk[1]([✉]), Alexander V. Zhozhikashvily[2], and Liudmila V. Savinitch[2]

[1] Peoples' Friendship University of Russia, Miklucho-Maklaya Street 6,
117198 Moscow, Russia
stefanuk@iitp.ru
[2] Institute for Information Transmission Problems, Bolshoi Karetny per. 19,
127051 Moscow, Russia
{zhozhik,savinitch}@iitp.ru

Abstract. A double intelligent system is proposed in the paper. It consists from two Expert Systems. The first one is intended for autonomic behavior in the surrounding information media, where it may get new evidences and modify its behavior being the Dynamic Expert System by definition. The second Expert System is considered as a mother system with respect the first one. It provides a certain amount of control over the autonomous part excluding such changes in the knowledge base of the first ES that are considered to be unacceptable from the mothering system point of view.

The special feature of such dual organization is that its members may be arbitrary separated in space. The required control is achieved via the use of a wideband wireless communication established between these two systems.

One of the purpose of such a dual expert system is an attempt to avoid designing of some Artificial Intelligence systems that might breach common social norms of social behavior of technical devices working within society of people.

Keywords: Dual expert system · Dynamic expert system · Space separation · Wideband wireless communication · Knowledge base ciphering · Open key ciphering

1 Introduction

An important for the modern applications of Artificial Intelligence question of admissible independence of activity of autonomous intellectual system from intention of its designer is discussed and to some extent resolved in the present paper.

The research was partially supported by the Russian Foundation for Basic Research with grants № 18-07-00736A и № 17-29-07053.

This problem has been already raised in publications of outstanding American scientist and science fiction writer Isaac Asimov [1] who proposed a system of restricting rules for a robot in order to defense its human designer from any negative reactions from the created machine.[1]

These rules have been proposed by I. Asimov, so to say, in a literature genre, as in his time there was no the corresponding technology did not exist. Yet in the light of the success in design of artificial systems ably to independent activity the problems of such a safety occurred more and more frequently.

The society as whole began expressing corresponding anxiety.

Some time ago it would be enough to provide soothing arguments that compared the AI science to the nuclear synthesis science and to note that consequently the safety problem must be resolved by the specialists who may direct the nuclear research either to the area of dangerous nuclear weapon or to the area of nuclear power stations able to solve the important energy problem for the people.

One of the authors of the present paper used this argumentation in reply to the question of the chairman in some TV program concerning possible danger of intellectual robots for people. However gradually accumulated believe in the unlimited power of intelligent system makes such an argument not consistent. Indeed, in case intelligent systems the final decision would be taken by an AI system, not by the people. And nobody is able to predict what thought would come out of its artificial brain.

It is typical that such an anxiety was noted as well among leading modern scientists, who are *experts* in Artificial Intelligence. For instance they have produced a Manifest that AI specialists had to take an obligation to never design something that may be referred to as *Autonomous Weapon* (Naturally we have put our supporting signature in the corresponding document. The latter document attracted a special interest within scientific community and elsewhere)[2].

Following the remarkable fiction scientist advice one may solve the problem by simple formulation of corresponding restricting rules for the case of newly created intelligence system. However, the main obstacle for this approach is the following one. As in case of nuclear strategy it was important to invite for consultation such a prominent scientist as Richard Feynman. But in case of intelligent system similar problems may be solved easily by some changes in the system of logical rules involved in an artificial intelligent system.

Actually even some beginner may change logical rules in dangerous direction for people if he has been explained what the autonomous weapon is.

---

[1] First Law: A robot may not injure a human being or, through inaction, allow a human being to come to harm.

Second Law: A robot must obey the orders given it by human beings except where such orders would conflict with the First Law.

Third Law: A robot must protect its own existence as long as such protection does not conflict with the First or Second Law [1].

[2] On behalf of Executive Council of the Association for the Advancement of Artificial Intelligence Prof. Toby Walsh in 2015 helped release an open letter calling for a ban on offensive autonomous weapons that attracted over 20,000 signatures.

Moreover for various applications a lot of complicated AI systems were created and for an external observer it is very difficult to guess what kind of problems may be solved with a particular system.

Nuclear and thermonuclear bombs were design immediately after the Second world war, when there was a feeling that such a weapon may bring the piece throughout World. And it very good that some other scientist and engineers started to work on a really peaceful application of the science mainly for energetic and medicine.

In our present paper an attempts is made to design a new intelligent system, which from one side is able to develop itself, via the use of various kind of external information that's why it is referred to as an autonomous one. However, its development is taken care of, though not fully controlled, with some mother intelligent system, which is watching it to keep its activity within a certain frame of permissible one and maybe considered as a designer of the whole system or as a creator of it [1].

Probably in a distant future the similar to our schemes will let us checking any newly created intelligent systems and possibly will issue an official documentation – a license – as an evidence that such a system may be used under certain conditions and in any case will mot bring any harm to people. The licenses of a similar kind are presently obligatory with respect to modern medicine and medical equipments.

Yet presently the research in this paper is oriented towards development of fundamental issues of something that we referred to with the term *the restricted autonomy*.

In the next chapter and its parts present a general block-scheme of restricted autonomy system that consists in Mother Intelligent System MIS and Dynamic Intelligent autonomous System DIAS in a certain manner interconnected over the wideband wireless channel [6]. This chapter is the main part in this paper. It reports, in particular, the means used to provide necessary stability and safety of DIAS performance when it tries to modify its knowledge on the of base of information coming from outside media and texts.

Conclusion describes the perspectives of building a practical version of dual system and mentions the general problem of simultaneous collective behavior of many dual intelligent systems.

In the theoretical parts of the paper the author's system of wideband wireless communication [6] of the systems MIS and DIAS is used and the problems involved are discussed; the use of new methods of providing safety for DIAS based on original symbol splitting method [9] and the classical methods of open key ciphering [7, 8] are used; our original results in the area of conversion of texts into sets of productions [2] have been used, and finally the theory of category approach provided a necessary knowledge simplification due to new formal language.

2   Dual Intelligent System

The proposed in this paper system contains two expert systems: MIS (Mather Expert System) and DIAS (Dynamic Intellectual Autonomous System). As it was mentioned above, MIS may be considered as the author of DIAS in the sense of publication [1], as it is MIS that supplies DIAS with its first knowledge base.

The system DIAS acts autonomously collecting information at the start in accordance with the rules initially supplied by MIS. However it is assumed that DIAS may obtain some new knowledge from texts in accordance with the conditionality method developed by Liudmila Savinitch and described, for instance, in the publication [2].

The dynamic expert system DIAS renew its knowledge by learning and "leads its normal life" in the environment where it is happened to be in. For example, working on earthquake prognoses it may send the results to interested party.

The most important that the DIAS may attempt to reconsider its own knowledge-rules taking into account the informational input flaw that was already observed in the very first dynamic expert system SEISMO [3].

DIAS is an *autonomic* system in any respect except one. The point is that the DIAS is the autonomic system in any sense except one but very important aspect. The point is that MIS is taking care on its activity in a certain way, in order to avoid the event when DIAS will do anything that it is considered as impermissible or harmful from the point of view of the mother system.

MIS *does not control* DIAS but only is taking care its attempts not allowing it to perform any error in something that is principally important.

Initially DIAS acts in a strict agreement with its starting rules established by MIS. However it is also important that none of the *external actions* might change the rules i.e. a special shield should be arranged, which will be described later.

From the other side the DIAS itself may propose some changes in its knowledge base, yet it may be accomplished only after permission from MIS. To make it possible a distant wireless communication is established between two components of the dual intelligent system, as well as some additional defense scheme.

In this paper we will not make it very distinct what namely MIS might consider inacceptable, limiting themselves with some clear examples. It is done intentionally.

2.1 Data Exchange Between Two Systems

At the starting moment $t = 0$ system MIS transmits to DIAS an initial knowledge base знаний – KB(0) – to be used by DIAS to collect information and to start self-learning. This KB(0) is stored ciphered in a safe place of DIAS computer memory. Each moment when DIAS starts to work it loads the current knowledge base to its working space after preliminary deciphering of the stored file and begins to perform accordingly. Next time DIAS also loads it after deciphering and etc.

Being dynamic expert system may occasionally decide that it wants to modify its knowledge base by creating KB(t). However DIAS may not put in the space occupied with original KB(0), as this space was password protected from hackers or other unsanctioned external attempts (see below).

For these reason DIAS builds the KB(t) in a separate piece of memory and sends it over radio to system MAS asking the latter to check if there some *inadmissible breach* in the new knowledge base from the point of view of MAS.

If there is no such a breach than would announce the new KB(t) correct and will send it back to DIAS ciphered with the same cryptographic key and it will be installed in place of previous knowledge base file site of memory.

If however some inadmissible breach is present MAS will prohibit such a replacement and the knowledge base remain unchanged.

2.2 Example of Inadmissible Breach

As an obviously inadmissible example of inadmissible breach may be the rule to destroy MIS in some way, which reminiscent the breach of one of this laws for robots or broke connection DIAS with MIS with. It seems that in this situation in knowledge base KB(t) there is command *delete* or *breach of communication*, addressed to MIS or something similar. Thus, we do not mean some participation in the current activity of DIAS. We mean that only some general control is provided over the KB(t)..

For this it is very desirable to have some description of the knowledge base on some abstract language that is not dependant on the subject domain as some of the breaching commands may be hidden rather deeply in KB. If one speak on the check up provided by MIS then in the majority of cases one should not look for look for delete but look for the object of direction of the delete. And it might happen in some cases that delete is not directed towards MIS and there is no breach at all.

System DIAS solves problems in a certain domain. A situation for DIAS is the position that is achieved in result of application of certain set of knowledge related to the domain. DIAS In the process of its performance is changing the situation. But also in the process DIAS may obtain some new knowledge. The goal situation for DIAS is the situation containing solution of its main problem.

Acting autonomously DIAS extracts also some knowledge that is not directly related to the solution which is sought of. For some reasons the system DIAS may store in its memory also extraneous knowledge, say, for solution of some future tasks.

2.3 Knowledge Description in Category Theory

Commonly the format of the situation in expert system as well as the format of rules, which constitutes the knowledge base of the Expert System are depended upon the subject domain.

In a Theory-of-Category description developed by A. Zhozhikashvily and his colleagues [4] these problems maybe solved without taking into consideration the concrete particulars of certain problem domain.

The *class of the situation* is a certain subclass of all the morphisms of a category that satisfies the following requirements: if morphism α represents a situation, then for any morphism φ for which the composition with $\alpha\varphi$ is defined this composition is also a situation. the production from the object S into object T is defined as a pair of morphisms $\varphi : X \to S$ and $\phi : X \to T$, where X is some object of this category.

Let $\alpha : I \to S$ be some morhism that represents a situation. The production $\varphi : X \to S, \phi : X \to T$ is considered to be applicable to this situation if for some morphism $\beta : I \to X$ one has $\alpha = \beta\varphi$. In this case the result of its application will be some new situation $\beta\phi : I \to T$, as it was proved in a number of our papers (see Fig. 1).

The knowledge base which is used in DIAS essentially represents the subject domain for MIS. A situation for MIS is the description of knowledge base of DIAS. The productions of the system MIS transform the situations and, consequently modify the knowledge

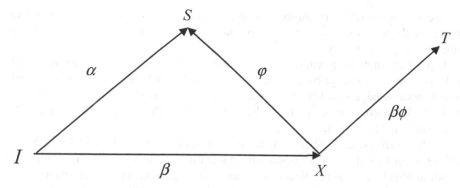

Fig. 1. The graph representation of a production in Category Theory

base of DIAS. Category Theory interpretation of the knowledge base let us write down the DIAS in an abstract format thus "hiding" the DIAS subject domain in the definitions of the category and its morphisms. It means that the situations and rules, as well as the procedures of their application, in this case do not depend on the subject domain used in DIAS.

The DIAS as the dynamic system [3] may independently develop its knowledge base. One of the ways for such development may be embedding some knew rules obtained in result of some generalization of solutions of certain concrete problems, or obtaining some external knowledge of rules from various sources using the approach developed in [2].

Categorical interpretation of the knowledge base lets one write down the rules for DIAS in an abstract way that is independent upon subject domain of DIAS and hides this problem domain in the definitions of *objects* and *morphisms*. Hence the situations and the rules of MIS as well as the procedures for the applications of rules in MIS in this case do not depend upon the subject domain.

DIAS may autonomously develop its knowledge base. One of the approaches to the development is an addition of new rules obtained in the result of some generalization of some concrete task descriptions. There are some other ways of knowledge base modification. For instance it may be done on the base of external texts, which in many cases may be converted into productions using the approach proposed by Liudmila Savinitch [2].

Each time, when DIAS develops its Knowledge base, before its use it sends the new base foe improvement by MIS. Only MIS knows what possible logic inferences are dangerous or inacceptable and should prevented, as we mentioned above. Studying the new knowledge base that has been sent to DIAS, MIS attempts to discover in it *a possibility* of undesirable inferences.

2.4   Correction of Knowledge Base for DIAS Is Possible

Algorithms applied by MIS are not directly related with subject domain of DIAS, if they are expressed in the theory of category terms [4], i.e. in the language of composition of morphism composition (see Fig. 1 above).

In case system MIS is found some dangerous possibilities in the base sent by DIAS, the obtained knowledge base is considered inadmissible and the previous base of DIAS remain in its previous way.

In principle there are possible some more delicate adjustments which should be made in the obtained knowledge base that may be sent to DIAS for correction. For example some new knowledge were obtained during generalization and MIS discovered that some particular knowledge sometime might lead to the prohibited results. It means that the generalization was too wide.

If MIS corresponds to DIAS which situation must be excluded, DIAS may built a difference between the generalization and the situation obtained from MIS, i.e. may find the admissible level of generalization that does not contain the prohibited situation.

Such an operation may formally defined in the terms of Theory of Category. Yet it may not be implemented in some categories [4]. However if it may be implemented, the rule added by DIAS should be replaced for a more special that avoids the prohibited situation. In some categories, where such difference does not exists $<$ there are may exist an equivalent (i.e. covering the same set of situations) finite set of generalizations? less obvious than the original generalization. In this case the added rule should be replaced with the finite set of more special rules.

2.5 Problems of Correction

In some cases MIS may check up the correctness of the changes introduces by DIAS in its knowledge base and edit them. If MIS knows the lists of possible results of DIAS performance that should be prohibited, then MIS tries to logically infer each of such results using the knowledge base provided by DIAS. Let MIS consider the possibility of obtaining one of the prohibited results. For the inference an abridged version of the original knowledge base is used. The following is understood with this concept.

A rule of DIAS has the following construction $P_1, P_2, ..., P_n \rightarrow Q$, where P_1, P_2, ..., P_n, Q – some facts. The left side facts of this rule $P_1, P_2, ..., P_n$.

One class contains the facts that are obtained as the result of inference. The second class contains facts, truth values of which is defined by external with respect to the system actions. The most popular is the case, when the truth value of the fact is defined in the reply to the question razed by the system. Also it is possible when the truth is defined with some device, or it is the result of analysis of some documents, and etc.

The abridged version is obtained by removal from the rule left side of the elements of the second class.

Such an abridged rule serves to check the rule performance if all the data coming from outside will let the rule to be applicable.

If the use of such an abridged version leads to prohibited results, it means that under some replies of an operator and other data coming from outside DIAS may obtain an undesirable for MIS result. In this case it is necessary consider the chain of rules, leading to this result, find in this chain the rule that was added by DIAS in the process of modification (such a rule must exist, otherwise we have to admit, that the original knowledge base contained something bad) and exclude this rule from the base.

Some complexity appears if in the inference chain there are several added rules/ Then one has to decide, which of the added rules has to be removed. Let us temporally consider some simple version and require from DIAS send its knowledge base to MIS whenever any one rule is added. Such a solution looks as logical one, however it does not solve the problem, but only masking it.

Indeed, imagine that DIAS added rules R1 and R2 and their sequential application leads to the dangerous situation. If first R1 was added and the R2, then NIS did not notice anything bad. Yet after addition of R2, MIS will see the undesirable effect and will remove R2. However if the R2 is added first and R1 arrived next? system will remove R1. Thus, the order of removals is somewhat randomly defined.

The previous actions may be reformulated in the following way: to find Действие, описанное в предыдущем абзаце, можно переформулировать так: in the chain of rules some rules lead to the prohibited result and the rules added in the latest modification of the knowledge base and remove one of them.

2.6 Suspicious Changes in the Knowledge Base

Finding rules in the knowledge base that are responsible for inadmissible results in general constitutes a complicated problem. Moreover, apart from obvious attempts from the side of DIAS to create conditions for non-wishful action from the point of view of MIS, there can be hidden ones. Thus one of the new rule may contain a suggestion to load some external file and start it, which in its turn may perform some effect undesirable for MIS up to destroying MIS completely.

At last the DIAS may contact some other intelligent system to make a harm to MIS.

In all the above cases the only possibility for MIS would be to ask DIAS for some explanation what is hidden behind these unknown programs and files and some non-obvious actions by sending DIAS a separate letter with request to remove from its knowledge base all the *suspicious modification,* which may do something bad to MIS.

In the future it is desirable to make a list of all the obvious and hidden ways of introducing in expert system DIAS the suspicious modification that may have some negative character with respect to MIS.

However for the moment NIS will farce DIAS to the previously approved knowledge base, i.e. $KB(t - 1)$.

In another words the interests of MIS have a higher priority over the consideration of DIAS, which it used when proposing to make changes in its knowledge base.

2.7 Special Features of Knowledge Bases of Dynamic Expert Systems

From the other side one should not forget that the system DIAS is a Dynamic Expert System [3] i.e. the system able to perform in a changeable external environment. It is able to reconsider in due time the results of its analysis, taking into account the change of some parameters.

Under some characteristics of these parameters it needs to reconsider its knowledge base, which becomes inadequate under certain values of mentioned parameters. If the temperature of the local environment unexpectedly reached large negative values, a special knowledge base should start fixing measuring apparatus and consider the animals behavior and the water in drinking pits in a special way. This knowledge base has to take into account the following tasks: to find a service company, find finance resources for purchasing new elements, and etc.

The knowledge base (KB) has changed, yet the main goal of DIAS is preserved. For instance, it is important to make an estimation of the chance of the earthquake in the locality [3]. Hence the new KB* must finish its intermediate task with the return to the solution of the main goal. That is, the knowledge base KB* was intended only to solve some close up subtask having its own sub-goal.

We want to stress that the KB* may be borrowed from surrounding sources as well as the evidence about drastic change of local weather and this information is available. It is not unusual that the KB* may be found among the information and be openly available even in an algorithmic format, but see also [2] and considerations above in this paper.

After this intermediate goal has been reached the system DIAS will automatically return to its main goal, however probably after some time. автоматически вернется к решению своей целевой задаче, но быть может лишь через некоторое время. It is possible that some stages of the goal program of DIAS should not taken care and may be omitted because of the lost time, probably some rules in its knowledge base became obsolete and may be replaced. Or the local earthquake already took place and the system DIAS may start to do something else or choose the new task from the library of all possibilities, for example, begins to create the longtime prediction [3].

In some other words the system DIAS.

Formally speaking, DIAS will remove some of the rules and will add some new collection of rules. It is important that the additions/removals are not arbitrary and these are results of solution of some important intermediate problems.

It is possible to consider somewhat more general case, when the knowledge arrived without any relation to the existing knowledge base. Then the mentioned approach with *suspicious knowledge* components would be more appropriate. These may bring some threat in principle towards the dual system described here or be undesirable in some other sense[3].

Some algorithms of verification of proposed changes in DIAS may be considered in the category language, using patterns. This language has been developed by the present authors during many years [4].

MIS may formulate the set of prohibited situations as a pattern or set of patterns. For each rule proposed to be added by DIAS the system MIS verifies if the pattern representing side "Then" of the rule presents the sub-pattern of one of the prohibited patterns. When it is true the rule should be removed from the knowledge base.

The formulated above condition for removal is simple but maybe it is too weak. Indeed, the consideration that part THEN of the rule is the sub-pattern of one of the prohibited patterns means that any inference, obtained with this rule, is considered as prohibited. However the rule has to be removed in case if only *some* of the inferences obtained with this rule turned out to be prohibited. It means that the rule has to be removed if its right part has "non-empty" intersection with one of the prohibited patterns. In the language of patterns the intersection is the most general special case (MGSC).

---

[3] Remember that it is DIAS presents "a progressive part" of dual system that is describd here. It is tuned on the search of new tasks that requires solution as well as the means to solve them? choosing out tasks from available information.

Consequently, if in the category that described the knowledge with which the DIAS works there is exist MGSC, the check for correctness consists in calculation MGSC for the part THEN and for each of the prohibited patterns. Result of each of such calculation should be a pattern, which is smallest in the set of patterns. When its true the rule must be removed.

Thus the final algorithm of interaction of DIAS and MIS consists in the following.

Each change in knowledge base of DIAS is sent to MIS for approval. DIAS may use only verified base obtained from MIS. The ban for DIAS to insert changes into its knowledge base is a complicated problem needing probably hardware solutions. We propose one of the *solution on the software level* that uses open key cryptography [7, 8].

MIS sends DIAS knowledge base in a ciphering form [9]. It is arranged that DIAS may use only knowledge base obtained after deciphering. MIS sends to DIAS also the key for opening the file with. However, MIS do not share the key for ciphering. It means that DIAS can not introduce any changes to its knowledge base on its own, as it is not able to cipher correctly the changed base. This fact also provides a defense against external interference in the work of DIAS: everybody, who obtains the key for deciphering, which was not secret as we mentioned, may read the base that DIAS is using, yet nobody may put any changes to it, as it is impossible to cipher the changed base, yet DIAS may use its base only after deciphering it.

In the same time DIAS may use its base only after its deciphering. MIS may periodically change the key sending DIAS new key for deciphering? but keeping the ciphering key secret. This schemes repeat the scheme of usage of the electronic signature [11].

3   Conclusion

In this paper it was proposed the design of autonomous intelligent system, that is able to take into account any additional requirements stated as the set rules or production. With this scheme of restricted autonomy it is possible to avoid the so to say "negative consequences" of the further development of Artificial Intelligence which are used by some authors to keep people frightened, see for example [5].

From theoretical point of view the present research is related to some extent to the important book [12]. Indeed, if mothering care of the MIS (or meta-level consideration in the sense of [12]) might be somehow embedded into the knowledge base of DIAS as the object-level system it would certainly remind the creation of a conscience for DIAS that usually control the people's intellectual activity in external media and in the internal world of a human being.

However if a man under certain conditions might step-over the imposed restrictions related to the conscience, in our case of the restricted autonomy all the special measures are undertaken in any case to exclude such an event.

It is for this reason our dual system organization has quite a complexity.

Also we do not use the term meta-level for several reasons. First, previously we published a result where we understood by meta-ES the system ES considering the area of ES systems. Moreover, with this understanding the Meta-ES was implemented in LISP and was used for education in the Expert System area [13].

The second reason is that in our opinion mothering system MIS *does not control* the system DIAS in usual sense of the word of Control Theory. It is only preventing some undesirable pieces of activity of DIAS when the latter obtains some new knowledge from outside.

Our system is complex enough. It has several obligatory components, which work in a close cooperation: several expert systems, wideband mobile wireless communication [6], the ciphers suitable for the work with knowledge base [9], the procedures for conversion texts to knowledge [2]. All these components were designed, tested and details considered previously by the authors of the present paper.

We think that one day we will have a number of intelligent systems with limited autonomy. They may occupy arbitrary areas, changing their location occasionally and solving a variety of tasks.

Moreover, they may interact with each other sharing different information and knowledge. An interaction with people will be considered elsewhere.

Some explanations for the above *concern* about Artificial Intelligence future and its role for the people may be found also in the book [5]. This concern arrived mostly due to the lack of information about real possibilities of AI as well as to the unknown limitations inherent to Artificial Intelligence. It seems also that for the feelings of unlimited possibility of Artificial Intelligence, also there no theoretical or experimental proof. This is just an obvious supposition without any strong support for it. But any idea requires verification!

Indeed, existing intelligent systems are able to solve presently a number of separate and rather specific tasks.

However situation with mentioned concern about Artificial Intelligence is much simpler than it is in the area of nuclear technology. In the nuclear area there is no technology in nuclear field for considering all possible limitations that are important for humanity. Hence, only politicians are able to take a final decision on limitations and advantages, and we know the results of it in the past [10].

We hope that present research will reduce the feeling of danger of AI described also in the introduction chapter of this paper. Naturally one may build a sophisticated system, which would use some elements from Artificial Intelligence and from other disciplines, such as learning and recognition, in order to build the autonomous weapon that is able in some way independently choose the goal for an attack and decide on its scale. It is similar with respect to influenza viruses, which are also able to recognize and learn.

However, Artificial Intelligence systems build in the frames of the scheme described in our paper would let one exclude some technical designs as inadmissible by putting into mother part of our dual system corresponding knowledge. Yet, for this aim it is necessary very precisely formulate what events are not desirable, which is not easy at all as it is shown in the paper. In another words, the system described here *presents a pattern* for somebody making a new intelligent system and planning to include in it some features of autonomy.

The restricted autonomy scheme proposed by the present paper allows to transmit the solution of important for humanity questions to the people. The final decision is made by a human. It is for him/her to decide how far artificial system may improve itself due to learning, and use for it something like proposed here *dual autonomous system*.

There are also a second version that should raise a *real concern*. Freely floating AI system might become something like a virus [5]. Indeed, some shortsighted or malicious people may program any strange behavior by putting into their system corresponding knowledge. Hence the idea of I. Asimov to install some laws for robots [1] remains the most important and possibly unique way to direct the progress for the good of the people.

Our research shows that such "*a legislation*" may be formulated in the form of certain requirements contained in the knowledge base of mothering part of the dual system, using scheme of restricted autonomy described above.

Acknowledgements. We would like to express our thanks to the anonymous reviewers for their valuable comments to our paper. In result we increased the number of references and added some further explanatory notes to our text.

References

1. Asimov, I.: "Runaround". I, Robot (The Isaac Asimov Collection ed.). Doubleday, New York City, p. 40 (1950). ISBN 978-0-385-42304-5
2. Savinich, L.V., Stefanuk, V.L.: Semiotics for extraction of knowledge from text (Семиотика выявления знаний из текста) (Когнитивно-семиотические аспекты моделирования в гуманитарной сфере, под науч. ред. В.Л.Стефанюка и Э.А. Тайсиной, Казань: Академия наук Татарстана 163–184 (2017))
3. Stefanuk, V.L.: Behavior of quasi-static shell in changing fuzzy environment (Поведение квазистатической оболочки в изменяющейся нечеткой среде, Труды IY национальной конференции с международным участием «Искусственный интеллект-91» , Рыбинск, сентябрь 16–24, **1**, 199–203)
4. Stefanuk, V.L., Zhozhikashvily, A.V.: Category theory patterns for the tasks in artificial intelligence (Теоретико-категорные образцы для задач искусственного интеллекта, Известия академии наук. Теория и системы управления **5**, 5–16 (1999))
5. Barrat, J.: Our Final Invention: Artificial Intelligence and the End of the Human Era. Thomas Dunne Books, p. 336 (2013)
6. Stefanuk, V.L., Tzetlin, M.L.: On power control in the collective of radio stations. Inf. Transm. Probl. **3**(4), 59–67 (1967)
7. Hellman, M.E., Diffie, B.W., Merkle, R.C.: Cryptographic apparatus and method. U.S. Patent #4,200,770, 29 April 1980
8. Hellman, M.E.: An overview of public key cryptography. IEEE Commun. Mag. 42–49 (2002)
9. Stefanuk, V.L., Alhussain, A.H.: Absolute secrecy asymptotic for generalized splitting method. In: Kovalev, S., Tarassov, V., Snasel, V., Sukhanov, A. (eds.) IITI 2019. AISC, vol. 1156, pp. 422–431. Springer, Cham (2020). https://doi.org/10.1007/978-3-030-50097-9_43
10. Hellman, M.E. (ed.): Breakthrough, Emerging New Technologies, Nuclear War: Inevitable or Preventable? Walker and Company, pp. 80–86
11. Menezes, A.J., van Oorschot, P., Vanstone, S.A.: Handbook of Applied Cryptography. CRC Press, Boca Raton (1996)
12. Bundy, A.: Meta-level inference and consciousness. In: Torrance, S. (ed.) The Mind and the Machine. Horwood (1984)
13. Stefanuk, V.L., Zhozhikashvily, A.V.: Consulting expert system META-ES. In: 2d All-Union Conference, Artificial Intelligence-90, Belorussia, Minsk (1990)

Invariance Preserving Control of Clusters Recognized in Networks of Kuramoto Oscillators

Oleg Granichin[1,2] and Denis Uzhva[1]([⊠])

[1] Saint Petersburg State University (Faculty of Mathematics and Mechanics),
St. Petersburg, Russia
o.granichin@spbu.ru, denis.uzhva@yahoo.com
[2] Institute of Problems of Mechanical Engineering, Russian Academy of Sciences,
St. Petersburg, Russia

Abstract. The Kuramoto model is able to describe a huge variety of examples of synchronization in the real world. We re-consider it through the framework of the network science and study the phenomenon of a particular interest, agent clustering. We assume that clusters are already recognized by some algorithm and then consider them as new variables on mesoscopic scale, which allows one to significantly reduce the dimensionality of a complicated (complex) system, thus reducing the required number of control inputs. In contrast to the common approach, where each agent is treated separately, we propose an alternative one using a supplementary control input, which is equal for the whole cluster. We also perform an analysis of this input by finding its limitations required for cluster structure to remain invariant in a network of Kuramoto oscillators. The theoretical results are demonstrated on a simulated multi-agent network with multiple clusters.

Keywords: Control of networks · Agents-based systems · Nonlinear output feedback

1 Introduction

For a long time, complex systems composed of numerous identical parts with sophisticated, sometimes chaotic dynamics were only studied only as a whole. Emergent behaviour of such systems leaved researchers with the only chance of describing them using macroscopic characteristics, which arise from statistical quantities.

As an example, one may consider quark-gluon plasma (QGP) in the Large Hadron Collider [15,25]. Nowadays it is the hottest known state of matter with temperatures reaching four trillion degrees Celsius. Being decomposed to (probably) indivisible bricks of the universe, QGP holds laws of evolution of particular

This work was supported IPME RAS by the Russian Science Foundation (project no. 16-19-00057).

S. O. Kuznetsov et al. (Eds.): RCAI 2020, LNAI 12412, pp. 472–486, 2020.
https://doi.org/10.1007/978-3-030-59535-7_35

mystery due to both quantum and relativistic effects. However, those scientists who try to break into the deepest secrets of the structure of the world are able to measure the temperature of quark-gluon plasma as a macroscopic characteristic of an ensemble of quarks and gluons. Notwithstanding the foregoing, physicists are capable of describing dynamics of individual corpuscles, yet the complexities appear in systems of *large number* of particles [9].

Such a problem is also typical for biology. Consider a colony of ants. It is known that capabilities of a single ant are very limited: basically, an ant can only move, lay down and perceive pheromone traces. It is also worth noting that an ant can make simple decisions regarding his movement, based on perception of *local* stimuli. If one would leave a single ant out of his colony, his behaviour would be quite senseless, since his "attention" would always be interrupted by the endlessly changing environment. However, a colony of these insects is possible to form complex structures and collectively perform nontrivial tasks in such environment. In other words, the colony as a swarm of simple individuals *exhibits intelligent behaviour*. And, as it was in physics, there is a mysterious gap between the dynamics of a single ant and a swarm composed of them.

However, according to [8,26], emergent behaviour may often differ from that leading to a statistically predictive equilibrium state. Emergence may evolve in time, so that the states of a complex system would always transform from one to another, never reaching a certain one eventually. A statistical approach, basically, integrates over an emergent process, resulting in omitting important details: one may think of emergence as of an *ostensive* [8] process, so that emergent properties a priori include only those recognized when observed. However, there exists another point, stating that emergent properties may seem impartible due to imperfection of the methods complex systems are analyzed with. With that in mind, an alternative *agent-based* approach is proposed to overcome the limitations of statistical modeling, where a complex system is considered as a network of simple autonomous units called *intelligent agents* (or simply agents) [6,20,28]. This study aims to develop a unified framework to fill the chasm in-between macro and micro with the purpose to understand how does emergency work and lead to complexity. It is assumed that such a framework would allow to control multi-agent systems (MAS) without delving into the nature of agents themselves. Thus, cybernetics attempts to unify both elementary particles, ants and other examples of individuals which we usually face in collections with the purpose to allow production of *decentralized artificial intelligent multi-agent systems* (such in which artificial swarm intelligence emerge) and to control the natural ones.

Intelligent agents may be driven by the BDI ("beliefs, desires and intentions") model [5,22,24], where each agent has a goal and seek to achieve it. In simple cases, such goals may be reduced to excitation of certain states, stabilization or mutual synchronization. The last one is often associated with self-organization among agents in a network, and, in fact, is of particular interest [7,27]. The idea behind this phenomenon lays in behaviour of agents inside a MAS: allowed only to exchange simple messages with each other, agents can adjust their internal state so that on a macroscopic scale the whole system will form a pattern. It is worth noting that the initial state of the system can be arbitrary, as well as the network's topology (not all the agents may communicate with the whole population). These patterns may include global constant states like in the task of load balancing for a computer network [14]) or synchronized oscillations (Kuramoto networks [1]).

Since multi-agent systems are usually described using dynamical systems, the state of synchronization means convergence of their dynamical trajectories to a unique *synchronous* trajectory. This phenomenon is known to be thoroughly studied in case of linear systems [12,20,30]. However, the class of linear systems is a very special case of the nonlinear rules of control, which are not so carefully studied yet.

A very special type of synchronization is the *cluster synchronization*. The actual dynamics of complex large-scale systems, such as groups of robots, operating in an unstable environment are often too difficult to be controlled by conventional methods, including approximation by classical ODE models. However, agents of complex systems are known to sometimes exhibit separation into groups also called *clusters*, where agents of the same group are synchronized, while there is no synchronization between those from different clusters. This allows one to significantly reduce the amount of control inputs to a system, as it is now composed of separate clusters, which now can be considered as a whole. We may now define three levels of study: microscopic (the level of individual agents), mesoscopic (the level of clusters) and macroscopic (the level of a system as a whole). Such a relation can be expressed in an equation

$$N \gg M \gg 1,$$

where N is the number of agents in a complex system and M is the number of clusters.

Despite the idea of exploiting clustering in networks seems to be very promising, a crucial sub-task arise: how one would find all the clusters in a network at a certain moment of time? It is clear that by re-calculating each agent, thus coming back to the case with a huge number of parameters, one would waste the benefits that agent clustering offer. Instead, some pattern recognition and artificial intelligence techniques may be used, supported by data compression tools, such as compressive sensing [3,21].

A very simple yet versatile nonlinear model was proposed by Yoshiki Kuramoto [1]. It describes oscillatory dynamics of coupled oscillators, where "coupled" means that they locally affect each other. Given a network of N agents each having one degree of freedom (often called a phase of an oscillator), its dynamics is described by the following system of differential equations:

$$\dot{\theta}_i(t) = w_i + \sum_{j=1}^{N} K_{ij} \sin\left(\theta_j(t) - \theta_i(t)\right), \tag{1}$$

where $\theta_i(t)$ is a phase of an agent i, K_{ij} is a weighted adjacency matrix of the network and w_i is a natural frequency. According to [2,4] and [10], agents approach the state of frequency ($\dot{\theta}_i = \dot{\theta}_j \ \forall i, j \in \overline{1, N}$) or phase ($\theta_i = \theta_j \ \forall i, j \in \overline{1, N}$) synchronization under certain conditions on w_i and K_{ij}.

There are numerous extensions of this model, e.g. time-varying coupling constants (adjacency matrix $K_{ij}(t)$) and frequencies $w_i(t)$ [13]. It is also known that the Kuramoto model with phase delays in the sine function [11,19] was studied. Besides, this model has extraordinary multiplex [23] or quantum [17] variations. In [16], cluster synchronization under specific conditions was discussed.

The model of Kuramoto appeared to be a successful tool for description of cortical activity in the human brain [23], being able to reveal three regimes of brain activity, corresponding to three states of the Kuramoto network: unsynchronized, highly synchronized and chaotic (cluster synchronization). This model is also suitable for various biological systems [1] and robotics: in [29] authors discuss the task of pattern formation on a circle using rules inspired by the model of Kuramoto, while [18] proposes an idea of an artificial brain for robots made of Kuramoto oscillators.

1.1 Paper Contribution

In this paper, we propose a new approach to treating complex multi-agent systems by developing a corresponding mathematical framework, allowing to analyze processes such as local agent interactions, synchronization and clustering. As an example, we attempt to connect mesoscopic control inputs for clusters with the algorithm of microscopic local interactions between agents, described by the Kuramoto model. It is intuituvely clear that additional control inputs should not "overwhelm" the coupling intensity, otherwise synchronization may break. Such modification could, for example, allow us to control large groups of N robots as a whole using only M ($M \ll N$) different mesoscopic control actions. In current work, we omit the process of finding clusters, assuming that a certain clustering configuration is known at any moment of time.

1.2 Paper Organization

The paper is organized as follows. In Sect. 2 we describe the framework for multi-agent networks to be formalized and then studied. Then, in Sect. 3 we re-consider the Kuramoto model through that framework and find conditions required for invariance of cluster structure. Next, in Sect. 4 we provide numerical simulations to demonstrate how mesoscopic control input with different values of parameters can affect clusters. Finally, Sect. 5 brings the conclusion.

2 Clustering in Multi-agent Networks

We aim to provide a *prescription* (rather than a *description*) to treating the Kuramoto model using the agent-based approach. Following the ideas set out in [20], let's denote a set of agents as $\mathcal{N} = \overline{1, N}$, where N is the number of them. Typically, the dynamics of a system of agents is characterized by the corresponding system of differential equations:

$$\dot{x}_i(t) = f_i(x_i(t), u_i(t), U_i(t), \eta_i(t)), \tag{2}$$

where $x_i(t) \in \mathbb{R}^{n_i}$ is a state vector of an agent $i \in \mathcal{N}$; $u_i(t)$ is a (microscopic) control input, i.e. it describes how local interactions between agents affect their state; $U_i(t)$ stands for another (macro- or mesoscopic) control input, which is supposed to affect large groups of agents at the same time; $\eta_i(t) \in \mathbb{R}^{m_i}$ is a stochastic variable (or an uncertain vector).

As it is specific for the network science, we define a topology of the network of agents by constructing a directed interaction graph: $\mathcal{G}(t) = (\mathcal{N}, \mathcal{E}(t))$, where $\mathcal{E}(t)$ is a collection of all directed arcs of the graph and $\mathcal{N}$ becomes a set of vertices. Each agent is not necessary to be connected to each other one, so that it is convenient to denote $\mathcal{N}_i(t) \subseteq \mathcal{N}$ as a (time-dependent) neighborhood of i. This means that $\forall j \in \mathcal{N}_i(t) \, \exists (j \rightarrow i) \in \mathcal{E}(t)$, i.e. each such agent j can communicate to i at time t.

We denote the in-degree of a vertex i ($i \in \mathcal{E}$) by $d(i) = \sum_{l=1}^{N} A_{il}$, where A is an adjacency matrix of $\mathcal{G}$. In other words, the in-degree of i is the weighted number of agents in $\mathcal{N}_i$. Similarly, we denote the in-degree of a vertex i excluding j ($i, j \in \mathcal{E}$) by $d_j(i) = \sum_{l=1, l \neq j}^{N} A_{il}$. Since we generally work with directed graphs, it is convenient to define a strongly connected graph: it is a graph, where for some n there exists a "path" between all pairs of vertices: $\exists n : i_1 \in \mathcal{N}_{i_2}, i_2 \in \mathcal{N}_{i_3}, ..., i_{n-1} \in \mathcal{N}_{i_n}, i_n \in \mathcal{N}_{i_1} \, i_1, ..., i_n \in \mathcal{N}$.

Definition 1. *A function* $g_i(x_i(t), \eta_i(t))$ *is called an output of an agent* i *if* $g : \mathbb{R}^{n_i} \times \mathbb{R}^{m_i} \mapsto \mathbb{R}^l$, *where* l *does not depend on* i.

Since the state vectors of agents may be of different dimensionality, we want to define two outputs: one for communication and one for measurement of synchronization between agents.

Let $y_j(t) = g_i(x_j(t), \eta_j(t))$ $j \in \mathcal{N}_i(t)$ be outputs of agents j from the neighborhood of i, used for communications. By the "coupling" between agents we assume that a decision of i (at time t) is based on the outputs $y_j(t)$. In practice, these outputs may be transmitted from j to i directly or just displayed by each j and then recognized by i. Mathematically, the rules of transmission are usually defined in u_i (see Eq. (2)):

$$u_i(t) = f_i \left(\{y_j(t)\}_{j \in \mathcal{N}_i(t)} \right), \tag{3}$$

where $f_i(\cdot)$ is a function of the outputs $y_j(t)$ $j \in \mathcal{N}_i(t)$. The Eq. (3) is also referred to as a *coupling protocol* in a sense it contains rules of control for i based on outputs of all j received by i. With that being said, we provide the following definition of a multi-agent network:

Definition 2. *The triple consisting of 1) family of agents (Eq. (2)); 2) interaction graph* $\mathcal{G}$ *and 3) coupling protocol defined as in Eq. (3) is called a multi-agent network.*

Henceforth, we denote a multi-agent network by the letter $\mathcal{N}$, corresponding to the set of agents of such network.

Let $z_i(t) = h_i(x_i(t), \eta_i(t))$ be an output of i, which is introduced for measurement of synchronization.

Definition 3. *Let $\Delta_{ij}(t_*) = \|z_i(t_*) - z_j(t_*)\|$ stand for the deviation between outputs z_i and z_j at time t_*, where $\|\cdot\|$ is a corresponding norm. Then:*

1. *agents i and j are (output) synchronized, or reach (output) consensus at time t_* if $\Delta_{ij}(t_*) = 0$; similarly, agents i and j are asymptotically (output) synchronized if $\Delta_{ij}(\infty) = \overline{\lim}_{t_* \to \infty} \Delta_{ij}(t_*) = 0$;*
2. *agents i and j are (output) ε-synchronized, or reach (output) ε-consensus at time t_* if $\Delta_{ij}(t_*) \leq \varepsilon$; similarly, agents i and j are asymptotically (output) ε-synchronized if $\Delta_{ij}(\infty) = \overline{\lim}_{t_* \to \infty} \Delta_{ij}(t_*) \leq \varepsilon$;*

As it was described in the Introduction, agents can synchronize in clusters, rather than globally.

Definition 4. *A family of subsets $\mathcal{M}(t) = \left\{ \mathcal{M}_\alpha(t) : \mathcal{M}_\alpha(t) \subseteq \mathcal{N} \ \forall t \geq 0 \ \forall \alpha \in \overline{1, K(t)} \right\}_{\alpha=1}^{K(t)}$ of $\mathcal{N}$ is told to be a partition over $\mathcal{N}$ if the following conditions are respected:*

1. $\nexists \mathcal{M}_\alpha(t) \in \mathcal{M}(t) : \mathcal{M}_\alpha(t) = \emptyset$;
2. $\bigcup_{\alpha=1}^{K(t)} \mathcal{M}_\alpha(t) = \mathcal{N} \ \forall t \geq 0$;
3. $\mathcal{M}_\alpha(t) \cap \mathcal{M}_\beta(t) = \emptyset \ \alpha \neq \beta$.

With that in mind, we also propose an additional definition for a specific case of cluster synchronization (see Figures in Sect. 4 for visual demonstration).

Definition 5. *A multi-agent network with a partition $\mathcal{M}(t_*)$ over $\mathcal{N}$ is (output) (ε, δ)-synchronized, or reach (output) (ε, δ)-consensus at time t_* for some $\delta \geq \varepsilon \geq 0$ if*

1. $\Delta_{ij}(t_*) \leq \varepsilon \ i, j \in \mathcal{M}_\alpha(t_*) \ \mathcal{M}_\alpha(t_*) \in \mathcal{M}(t_*)$ *and*
2. $\Delta_{ij}(t_*) > \delta \ i \in \mathcal{M}_\alpha(t_*) \ j \in \mathcal{M}_\beta(t_*) \ \mathcal{M}_\alpha(t_*), \mathcal{M}_\beta(t_*) \in \mathcal{M}(t_*) \ \alpha \neq \beta$.

A $(0,0)$-synchronization is henceforth referred to as cluster synchronization. We also say that the $\mathcal{M}(t_*)$ is a clustering over $\mathcal{N}$.

3 The Kuramoto Model as a Multi-agent Network

3.1 Coupling

We propose an approach to treating the Kuramoto model of coupled oscillators, which is quite peculiar for cybernetics and control theory. Consider the model (1). The coupling protocol is as follows:

$$u_i(t) = w_i + \sum_{j=1}^{N} K_{ij} \sin\left(\theta_j(t) - \theta_i(t)\right), \tag{4}$$

so that the corresponding communication outputs of the agents are $y_i(t) = \theta_i(t)$. It is assumed that $K = \{K_{ij}\}$ is an adjacency matrix for a specific configuration of a network of oscillators, i.e. $K_{ij} \neq 0 \iff j \in \mathcal{N}_i \iff \exists(j \to i) \in \mathcal{E}(t)$; and $\theta_i(t) \in S^1 \ \forall i \ \forall t \geq 0$. Synchronization in the Kuramoto model can appear in the forms of frequency or phase lock. The difference between them is the choice of the output $z_i(t)$: $z_i(t) = \dot{\theta}_i(t)$ and $z_i(t) = \theta_i(t)$ correspondingly. We only consider the first case, since it is more general and has more practical applications.

Unlike many other works on the Kuramoto model, we do not restrict ourselves to mean-field coupling $K_{ij} = \frac{C}{N} \ \forall i, j$, where C is some constant. Indeed, the real physical world has more examples of networks with incomplete (or even sparse) graph topologies, i.e. networks of neurons, flocks of birds or even sometimes swarms of robots. More than that, the topology of the graph $\mathcal{G}(t)$ corresponding to a certain multi-agent network may change with time. With that in mind, we propose the following modification to the model (1):

$$\dot{\theta}_i(t) = w_i + \rho \sum_{j \in \mathcal{N}_i(t)} \sin\left(\theta_j(t) - \theta_i(t)\right), \tag{5}$$

where ρ is a constant and i is only affected by the agents from $\mathcal{N}_i(t)$. we denote an adjacency of $\mathcal{G}(t)$ by $\Upsilon_{ij}(t) \in \{0, 1\} \ \forall i, j \ \forall t \geq 0$, so that $K_{ij}(t) = \rho \Upsilon_{ij}(t)$ now becomes dependent on time. The value 0 can be interpreted as "no connection from j to i ($j \notin \mathcal{N}_i$)" and 1 stands for "i is accessible to j ($i \in \mathcal{N}_j$)".

Since agents tend to synchronize using the sum in the protocol of (5), we assume that $\rho > 0$. However, the agents also drift with speeds $w_i \geq 0$, which are basically their natural frequencies.

3.2   Mesoscopic Control

As it was mentioned, in the current work we aim to control already formed clusters, rather than study methods of finding them. With that in mind, we assume that there exists some algorithm $\mathfrak{A}$ that, given a multi-agent network $\mathcal{N}$, returns the corresponding clustering at any given moment of time. Let clustering $\mathcal{M}(t_1)$ emerge at time t_1 for the model (5) and remain constant on interval $T = [t_1, +\infty)$. Henceforth, $t \in T$. Assume that topology of $\mathcal{G}(t)$, corresponding to a given multi-agent network, also does not change on T. Thus, Υ_{ij} is also constant. We propose the following modification to the original Kuramoto model, assuming $i \in \mathcal{M}_\alpha$:

$$\begin{aligned}\dot{\theta}_i(t) &= \mu_i \mathcal{F}_\alpha(t, \overline{x}_\alpha(t)) \\ &+ w_i + \rho \sum_{j=1}^{N} \Upsilon_{ij} \sin\left(\theta_j(t) - \theta_i(t)\right),\end{aligned} \tag{6}$$

where $\mathcal{F}_\alpha(\cdot)$ is a mesoscopic function in a sense it is equal for the whole cluster $\mathcal{M}_\alpha$, μ_i is (a constant) agent's *sensibility* to the control function $\mathcal{F}_\alpha(\cdot)$. If we compare the model (6) with Eq. (2), it becomes clear how the coupling protocol $u_i(t)$ and the mesoscopic control input $U_i(t)$ are separated:

$$u_i(t) = w_i + \rho \sum_{j=1}^{N} \Upsilon_{ij} \sin\left(\theta_j(t) - \theta_i(t)\right),$$

$$U_i(t) = \mu_i \mathcal{F}_\alpha(t, \overline{x}_\alpha).$$

(7)

Besides time t, an additional argument in $\mathcal{F}_\alpha(\cdot)$ is $\overline{x}_\alpha(t)$. It stands for characteristics of the cluster α with *physical* nature, i.e. a position of the cluster in space.

The control inputs (7) allows agents to synchronize only if certain conditions are satisfied. As it was discussed for drift, cluster synchronization depends on the values of μ_i: some agents in a cluster $\mathcal{M}_\alpha$ may react to $\mathcal{F}(\cdot)$ with much greater intensity, which may affect the overall structure of the cluster.

In order to find conditions for the parameters in (6) sufficient for cluster structure to remain invariant, we firstly propose a theorem for the model (5) concerning relations between the natural frequencies w_i and values $K_{ij} = \rho\Upsilon_{ij}$ necessary for cluster synchronization.

Theorem 1. *Consider a multi-agent network corresponding to (5) and to some graph $\mathcal{G}$ with an adjacency matrix Υ. Let $t \in T$, output $z_i(t) = \dot{\theta}_i(t)$ and $\Delta_{ij}(t) = |z_i(t) - z_j(t)|$. The following conditions are sufficient for this network to be output $(0,0)$-synchronized:*

1. For $i, j \in \mathcal{M}_\alpha$ such that $w_j - w_i \geq 0$

$$w_j - w_i \leq \rho \sin\left(\frac{\Delta\theta_{ji}}{2}\right) \sum_{l=1}^{N} [\Upsilon_{il} + \Upsilon_{jl}],$$

(8)

where $\sin\left(\frac{\Delta\theta_{ji}}{2}\right) = 1$ *in case* $\Upsilon_{ij} = \Upsilon_{ji} = 0$*; otherwise,*

$$\sin\left(\frac{\Delta\theta_{ji}}{2}\right) = \max\left\{ \sqrt{1 - (\Gamma_i(j))^2},\right.$$
$$\left. \sqrt{1 - (\Gamma_j(i))^2}, \frac{\sqrt{2}}{2} \right\},$$

(9)

where

$$\Gamma_i(j) = \frac{-d_i(j) + \sqrt{(d_i(j))^2 + 8(\Upsilon_{ij} + \Upsilon_{ji})^2}}{4(\Upsilon_{ij} + \Upsilon_{ji})}.$$

(10)

2. For $i \in \mathcal{M}_\alpha$, $j \in \mathcal{M}_\beta$, $\alpha \neq \beta$

$$|w_i - w_j| > 0.$$

(11)

3. Graph $\mathcal{G}$ is strongly connected.

Remark 1. The idea behind Theorem 1 is that if $|w_i - w_j|$ is very high, there may appear to be not enough strength of coupling, so that ρ should be appropriately large to "overcome" drift. In the simplest case, where $w_i = w$ $\forall i$, the synchronization always appear $\forall \rho > 0$. We obtain that $|w_i - w_j|$ should be non-zero for agents i and j from different clusters for $(0, 0)$-synchronization to remain.

Proof. Henceforth in the proof, we will write $\dot{\theta}_i(t)$ as $\dot{\theta}_i$ for the sake of notation simplicity (the same will be applied to θ_i and Δ_{ij}). Following the Definition 5, $\Delta_{ij} = \left| \dot{\theta}_i - \dot{\theta}_j \right| = 0$ $\forall i, j \in \mathcal{M}_\alpha$ and $\Delta_{ij} > 0$ $\forall i \in \mathcal{M}_\alpha, j \in \mathcal{M}_\beta$ $\alpha \neq \beta$.

Since the case when i and j are from different clusters is simpler to prove, we consider it in the first place. If one instead of $\dot{\theta}_i$ substitute the RHS of the model (5), the Δ_{ij} will appear as follows:

$$
\Delta_{ij} = \left| w_i - w_j + \rho \left(\sum_{l=1}^{N} \Upsilon_{il} \sin(\theta_l - \theta_i) \right. \right.
$$
$$
\left. \left. - \sum_{l=1}^{N} \Upsilon_{jl} \sin(\theta_l - \theta_j) \right) \right| > 0. \tag{12}
$$

By letting the arguments of the sines in (12) be 0, we derive the desired condition for the natural frequencies.

Further, we only consider the situation where $i, j \in \mathcal{M}_\alpha$. Let the LHS of (12) be strictly equal to zero and assume that $w_j - w_i \geq 0$ without loss of generality. Let E be a functional

$$
E = \sum_{l=1}^{N} \Upsilon_{il} \sin(\theta_l - \theta_i) - \sum_{l=1}^{N} \Upsilon_{jl} \sin(\theta_l - \theta_j)
$$
$$
= (\Upsilon_{ij} + \Upsilon_{ji}) \sin(\theta_j - \theta_i) + \sum_{l=1, l \neq j}^{N} \Upsilon_{il} \sin(\theta_l - \theta_i) \tag{13}
$$
$$
- \sum_{l=1, l \neq i}^{N} \Upsilon_{jl} \sin(\theta_l - \theta_j),
$$

which we aim to maximize. The first order necessary conditions for maximizing E are given by

$$
\frac{\partial E}{\partial \theta_i} = -(\Upsilon_{ij} + \Upsilon_{ji}) \cos(\theta_j - \theta_i)
$$
$$
- \sum_{l=1, l \neq j}^{N} \Upsilon_{il} \cos(\theta_l - \theta_i) = 0, \tag{14}
$$

$$\frac{\partial E}{\partial \theta_j} = (\Upsilon_{ij} + \Upsilon_{ji}) \cos(\theta_j - \theta_i)$$

$$+ \sum_{l=1, l\neq i}^{N} \Upsilon_{jl} \cos(\theta_l - \theta_j) = 0, \tag{15}$$

$$\frac{\partial E}{\partial \theta_l} = \Upsilon_{il} \cos(\theta_l - \theta_i) - \Upsilon_{jl} \cos(\theta_l - \theta_j) = 0. \tag{16}$$

For the further reasoning to be true, let $\exists l_1 : \Upsilon_{il_1} = 1$ and $\exists l_2 : \Upsilon_{jl_2} = 1$. Assuming i and j are arbitrary, it follows that $\mathcal{G}$ is strongly connected.

Consider the case $\Upsilon_{ij} = \Upsilon_{ji} = 0$. Then the cosines in the second terms of Eqs. (14) and (15) are also equal to 0, therefore

$$E_{\max} = \sum_{l=1}^{N} [\Upsilon_{il} + \Upsilon_{jl}]. \tag{17}$$

Now let $\Upsilon_{ij} + \Upsilon_{ji} \geq 1$. Consider first Eq. (16). In case $\Upsilon_{il} = \Upsilon_{jl} = 0$, it follows that $E_{\max}$ is as in (17).

If $\Upsilon_{il} = 1$ and $\Upsilon_{jl} = 0$, then, according to (14), $\cos(\theta_j - \theta_i) = 0$. The same conclusion is true if $\Upsilon_{il} = 0$ and $\Upsilon_{jl} = 1$, according to (15).

The most complex situation is when $\Upsilon_{il} = \Upsilon_{jl} = 1$. Using (16), we can get either $\theta_l = \frac{\theta_i + \theta_2}{2}$ or $\theta_i = \theta_j = 0$. However, the second case implies that $E \equiv 0$, so that it does not suit the goal to maximize E. Thus, we substitute $\theta_l = \frac{\theta_i + \theta_j}{2}$ in (14) and use the fact that $\cos(2x) = 2\cos^2(x) - 1$:

$$2(\Upsilon_{ij} + \Upsilon_{ji}) \cos^2\left(\frac{\theta_j - \theta_i}{2}\right) - (\Upsilon_{ij} + \Upsilon_{ji})$$

$$+ \cos\left(\frac{\theta_j - \theta_i}{2}\right) \sum_{l=1, l\neq j}^{N} \Upsilon_{il} = 0. \tag{18}$$

Solving the quadratic equation (18), we obtain two solutions, where only the one with the "plus" sign satisfies the condition $\cos\left(\frac{\theta_j - \theta_i}{2}\right) \in [-1, 1]$. We denote that solution by $\Gamma_j(i)$, and it corresponds to (10). Similarly, one may obtain solutions of (15). Again only the solution with the "plus" sign is of interest (denoted by $\Gamma_i(j)$).

We choose the optimal value of $(\theta_j - \theta_i)_{\text{opt}} = \Delta\theta_{ji}$ as in (9), where the first two options are obtained from the formula $\sin(\arccos(x)) = \sqrt{1 - x^2}$, while the last one is derived from (16) in case either a coefficient is equal 1, while other is 0. Finally, substitute $\Delta\theta_{ji}$ and $\theta_l = \frac{\theta_i + \theta_j}{2}$ in (13):

$$E_{\max} = \sin\left(\frac{\Delta\theta_{ji}}{2}\right) \sum_{l=1}^{N} [\Upsilon_{il} + \Upsilon_{jl}], \tag{19}$$

which concludes the proof.

The result can be generalized for the model (6). We denote $\mathcal{F}_\alpha = \mathcal{F}_\alpha(t, \overline{x}_\alpha)$ for the sake of notation simplicity.

Theorem 2. *Consider a multi-agent network corresponding to (6). Let $t \in \underset{.}{T}$, output $z_i(t) = \dot{\theta}_i(t)$ and $\Delta_{ij}(t) = |z_i(t) - z_j(t)|$. Let also $\mathcal{F}_\alpha$ does not depend on θ_i $\forall i$. The following conditions are sufficient for this network to be output $(0,0)$-synchronized.*

1. *In case $i, j \in \mathcal{M}_\alpha$,*

$$|(\mu_j - \mu_i)\mathcal{F}_\alpha| \le 2\rho \sin\left(\frac{\Delta\theta_{ji}}{2}\right) \sum_{l=1}^{N} [\Upsilon_{il} + \Upsilon_{jl}], \tag{20}$$

   where $\Delta\theta_{ji}$ is as in Theorem 1 (including the case $\Upsilon_{ij} = \Upsilon_{ji} = 0$).
2. *For $i \in \mathcal{M}_\alpha$, $j \in \mathcal{M}_\beta$, $\alpha \ne \beta$*

$$|w_i - w_j + \mu_i\mathcal{F}_\alpha(t, \overline{x}_\alpha) - \mu_j\mathcal{F}_\beta(t, \overline{x}_\beta)| > 0. \tag{21}$$

3. *Graph $\mathcal{G}$ is strongly connected.*

Proof. The sufficient conditions can be derived from Theorem 1 by substitution of the mesoscopic control U_i in the Δ_{ij}:

$$\Delta_{ij} = \left| w_i - w_j + \mu_i\mathcal{F}_\alpha - \mu_j\mathcal{F}_\beta + \rho \right.$$

$$\left. \cdot \left(\sum_{l=1}^{N} \Upsilon_{il} \sin(\theta_l - \theta_i) - \sum_{l=1}^{N} \Upsilon_{jl} \sin(\theta_l - \theta_j) \right) \right|. \tag{22}$$

First, we assume that $i, j \in \mathcal{M}_\alpha$. Following the same reasoning as in the Proof for Theorem 1, Eq. (22) is equal to 0, thus (20) can be easily derived. Now let $i \in \mathcal{M}_\alpha, j \in \mathcal{M}_\beta$ $\alpha \ne \beta$, thus $\Delta_{ij} > 0$ in Eq. (22). Setting the sines to zero as in Theorem 1, the desired condition on the mesoscopic control can be easily derived, which concludes the proof.

4 Simulations

Consider model (6) and its solutions on $T = [0, 60]$. For now, let the control function $U_i(t) \equiv 0$. Let $N = 16$, and topology of the graph $\mathcal{G}$ be as on Fig. 1. Let also $\rho = 0.5$ and natural frequencies $\{w_i\}_{i \in \mathcal{N}}$ be as follows: $w_1, ..., w_4 = \{2.1, 2.2, 2.3, 2.4\}$, $w_5, ..., w_8 = \{4.1, ..., 4.4\}$, $w_9, ..., w_{12} = \{6.1, ..., 6.4\}$, $w_{13}, ..., w_{16} = \{8.1, ..., 8.4\}$, so that agents from one "square" (see Fig. 1) satisfy the condition of Eq. (8), however, agents from different squares does not. We obtain initial phases $\theta_i(0)$ from uniform distribution on S^1. Assuming $z_i(t) = \dot{\theta}_i$, such a configuration leads to a clustering $\mathcal{M}$ with four (ε, δ)-synchronized clusters for some ε and δ such that $\varepsilon \ll \delta$, as it can be seen on Fig. 2.

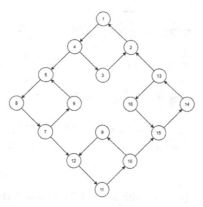

Fig. 1. Topology of the graph developed for simulations

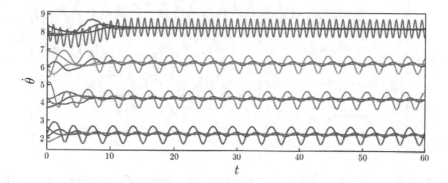

Fig. 2. Trajectories of Eq. (5) with $U_i(t) \equiv 0$

One may notice that each cluster contain peculiar agents with higher varia-
tion of $\dot{\theta}_i$ in comparison with the rest. These agents are under the numbers 2, 5,
12 and 15 on Fig. 1: as it can be seen, they are exposed by the agents 13, 4, 7, 10
correspondingly, which deviate the values of $\dot{\theta}_i$. Now consider a sinusoidal control function $U_i(t)$, which we "turn on" at $t = 20$ (when (ε, δ)-synchronization
establish):

$$U_i = \mu_i \mathcal{F}_\alpha(t, \overline{x}_\alpha(t)) = \mu_i \sin(2\pi f_\alpha(t - 20)),$$

where f_α are from uniform distribution on $[0, 1]$. The set of values $\{\mu_i\}_{i \in \mathcal{N}}$
is constructed as follows: $\mu_1, ..., \mu_4 = \mu_5, ..., \mu_8 = \mu_9, ..., \mu_{12} = \mu_{13}, ..., \mu_{16} = \{0.125, 0.25, 0.375, 0.5\}$. Since these values satisfy Eqs. (20) and (21), the cluster
structure is not affected severely (see Fig. 3).

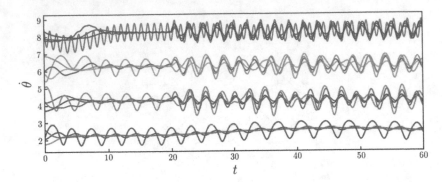

Fig. 3. Trajectories of Eq. (5) with sinusoidal U_i and small differences between μ_i: it can be seen that clusters remain invariant in (ε, δ)-synchronized state

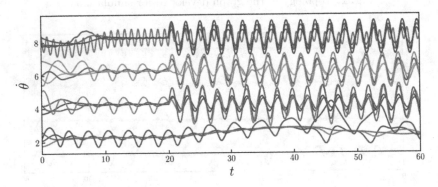

Fig. 4. Trajectories of Eq. (5) with sinusoidal U_i and large differences between μ_i: the clusters overlapped as ε became greater than δ

Consider now values $\mu_1, ..., \mu_4 = \mu_5, ..., \mu_8 = \mu_9, ..., \mu_{12} = \mu_{13}, ..., \mu_{16} = \{0.25, 0.5, 0.75, 1\}$. As it may be concluded from the Eqs. (20) and (21), such values of agent's sensibility may break cluster invariance, and they in fact do (see Fig. 4).

5   Conclusion

We proposed a multi-agent approach to treating the Kuramoto model under its extension to the addition of a so-called mesoscopic control input to the communication protocol. It allows to control large synchronized groups of agents called clusters simultaneously in a space of much lower dimensionality than that corresponding to separate agents in a system. We formulated and proved two theorems about parameters of the corresponding model. It appeared that a mesoscopic control function must be bounded with the boundary conditions described in Theorem 2 on a certain interval of time in order to retain cluster structure on this interval. It was also shown that the simulated results obey the rules we proposed. Furthermore, we plan to consider the case of continuous values of coupling strength and its dependence on time in future research.

References

1. Acebron, J., Bonilla, L., Pérez-Vicente, C., Farran, F., Spigler, R.: The Kuramoto model: a simple paradigm for synchronization phenomena. Rev. Mod. Phys. **77** (2005). https://doi.org/10.1103/RevModPhys.77.137
2. Benedetto, D., Caglioti, E., Montemagno, U.: On the complete phase synchronization for the Kuramoto model in the mean-field limit. Commun. Math. Sci. **13** (2014). https://doi.org/10.4310/CMS.2015.v13.n7.a6
3. Candes, E.J., Wakin, M.B.: An introduction to compressive sampling. IEEE Signal Process. Mag. **25**(2), 21–30 (2008). https://doi.org/10.1109/MSP.2007.914731
4. Chopra, N., Spong, M.: On synchronization of Kuramoto oscillators, vol. 2005, pp. 3916–3922 01 2006. https://doi.org/10.1109/CDC.2005.1582773
5. Cohen, P., Levesque, H.: Intention is choice with commitment. Artif. Intell. **42**(2–3), 213–261 (1990)
6. Dorri, A., Kanhere, S., Jurdak, R.: Multi-agent systems: a survey. IEEE Access 1–1 (2018). https://doi.org/10.1109/ACCESS.2018.2831228
7. Giammatteo, P., Buccella, C., Cecati, C.: A proposal for a multi-agent based synchronization method for distributed generators in micro-grid systems. EAI Endorsed Trans. Ind. Netw. Intell. Syst. **3**, 151160 (2016). https://doi.org/10.4108/eai.21-4-2016.151160
8. Goldstein, J.: Emergence as a construct: history and issues. Emergence **1**, 49–72 (1999)
9. Hong, J., Diamond, P.: Anomalous viscosity of the quark-gluon plasma. Phys. Rev. C Nucl. Phys. **89** (2013). https://doi.org/10.1103/PhysRevC.89.034905
10. Jadbabaie, A., Motee, N., Barahona, M.: On the stability of the Kuramoto model of coupled nonlinear oscillators, vol. 5, pp. 4296–4301, 05 2005. https://doi.org/10.23919/ACC.2004.1383983
11. Kotwal, T., Jiang, X., Abrams, D.: Connecting the Kuramoto model and the chimera state. Phys. Rev. Lett. **119** (2017). https://doi.org/10.1103/PhysRevLett.119.264101
12. Li, Z., Wen, G., Duan, Z., Ren, W.: Designing fully distributed consensus protocols for linear multi-agent systems with directed graphs. IEEE Trans. Autom. Control **60**(4), 1152–1157 (2015). https://doi.org/10.1109/TAC.2014.2350391
13. Lu, W., Atay, F.: Stability of phase difference trajectories of networks of Kuramoto oscillators with time-varying couplings and intrinsic frequencies. SIAM J. Appl. Dyn. Syst. **17**, 457–483 (2018). https://doi.org/10.1137/16M1084390
14. Manfredi, S., Oliviero, F., Romano, S.P.: A distributed control law for load balancing in content delivery networks. IEEE/ACM Trans. Networking **21** (2012). https://doi.org/10.1109/TNET.2012.2190297
15. Manuel, C., Mrowczynski, S.: Whitening of the quark-gluon plasma. Phys. Rev. D **70** (2004). https://doi.org/10.1103/PhysRevD.70.094019
16. Menara, T., Baggio, G., Bassett, D., Pasqualetti, F.: Stability conditions for cluster synchronization in networks of heterogeneous Kuramoto oscillators. IEEE Trans. Control Network Syst. **7**, 302–314 (2019). https://doi.org/10.1109/TCNS.2019.2903914

17. Hermoso de Mendoza Naval, I., Pachón, L., Gómez-Gardeñes, J., Zueco, D.: Synchronization in a semiclassical Kuramoto model. Phys. Rev. E Stat. Nonlinear Soft Matter Phys. **90**, 052904 (2014). https://doi.org/10.1103/PhysRevE.90.052904
18. Moioli, R., Vargas, P., Husbands, P.: Exploring the Kuramoto model of coupled oscillators in minimally cognitive evolutionary robotics tasks, vol. 1, pp. 1–8, 08 2010. https://doi.org/10.1109/CEC.2010.5586486
19. Montbrió, E., Pazó, D., Schmidt, J.: Time delay in the Kuramoto model with bimodal frequency distribution. Phys. Rev. E Stat. Nonlinear Soft Matter Phys. **74**, 056201 (2006). https://doi.org/10.1103/PhysRevE.74.056201
20. Proskurnikov, A., Granichin, O.: Evolution of clusters in large-scale dynamical networks. Cybern. Phys. **7**(3), 102–129 (2018). https://doi.org/10.35470/2226-4116-2018-7-3-102-129
21. Qaisar, S., Bilal, R.M., Iqbal, W., Naureen, M., Lee, S.: Compressive sensing: from theory to applications, a survey. J. Commun. Netw. **15**(5), 443–456 (2013). https://doi.org/10.1109/JCN.2013.000083
22. Rao, A.S., Georgeff, M.P.: BDI agents: from theory to practice. In: ICMAS, pp. 312–319 (1995)
23. Sadilek, M., Thurner, S.: Physiologically motivated multiplex Kuramoto model describes phase diagram of cortical activity. Sci. Rep. **5** (2014). https://doi.org/10.1038/srep10015
24. Shoham, Y., Cousins, S.B.: Logics of mental attitudes in AI. In: Lakemeyer, G., Nebel, B. (eds.) Foundations of Knowledge Representation and Reasoning. LNCS, vol. 810, pp. 296–309. Springer, Heidelberg (1994). https://doi.org/10.1007/3-540-58107-3_17
25. Teweldeberhan, A., Miller, H., Tegen, R.: Generalized statistics and the formation a quark-gluon plasma. In: The Physics of Quarks: New Research, 10 2002
26. Thoren, H., Gerlee, P.: Weak emergence and complexity, 01 2010
27. Trentelman, H., Takaba, K., Monshizadeh, N.: Robust synchronization of uncertain linear multi-agent systems. IEEE Trans. Autom. Control **58**, 1511–1523 (2013). https://doi.org/10.1109/TAC.2013.2239011
28. Weyns, D., Helleboogh, A., Holvoet, T.: How to get multi-agent systems accepted in industry? IJAOSE **3**, 383–390 (2009). https://doi.org/10.1504/IJAOSE.2009.515613
29. Xu, Z., Egerstedt, M., Droge, G., Schilling, K.: Balanced deployment of multiple robots using a modified Kuramoto model. In: 2013 American Control Conference, pp. 6138–6144 (2013)
30. Zhao, Y., Liu, Y., Chen, G.: Designing distributed specified-time consensus protocols for linear multiagent systems over directed graphs. IEEE Trans. Autom. Control **64**(7), 2945–2952 (2019). https://doi.org/10.1109/TAC.2018.2872534

Author Index

Printed in the United States
By Bookmasters